LEGAL HANDBOOK FOR EDUCATORS

SIXTH EDITION

ANTHONY F. BROWN, LL.B., LL.M., M.ED.

CARSWELL®

A cataloguing record for this publication is available from Library and Archives Canada.

ISBN: 978-0-7798-2150-1

THOMSON REUTERS

CARSWELL, A DIVISION OF THOMSON REUTERS CANADA LIMITED

One Corporate Plaza
2075 Kennedy Road
Toronto, Ontario
M1T 3V4

Customer Relations
Toronto 1-416-609-3800
Elsewhere in Canada/U.S. 1-800-387-5164
Fax 1-416-298-5082
www.carswell.com
E-mail www.carswell.com/email

For Catherine, Sebastian and Lisa

Table of Contents

List of Statutes and Regulations

Statutes

Canadian Charter of Rights and Freedoms (being Part I of the Constitution Act, 1982
[en. by the Canada Act, 1982 (U.K.), c. 11, Sched. B])
Education Act, R.S.O. 1990, c. E.2, ss. 264, 265, 286
Teaching Profession Act, R.S.O. 1990, c. T.2
Trespass to Property Act, R.S.O. 1990, c. T.21

Regulations

Collection of Personal Information, O. Reg. 521/01
Continuing Education, R.R.O. 1990, Reg. 285
Electronic Meetings, O. Reg. 463/97
General, O. Reg. 72/97
Honoraria for Board Members, O. Reg. 357/06
Identification and Placement of Exceptional Pupils, O. Reg. 181/98
Opening or Closing Exercises, O. Reg. 435/00
Operation of Schools — General, R.R.O. 1990, Reg. 298
Principals and Vice-Principals — Redundancy and Reassignment, O. Reg. 90/98
Professional Misconduct, O. Reg. 437/97
Regulation made under the Teaching Profession Act
School Councils, O. Reg. 612/00
School Year Calendar, R.R.O. 1990, Reg. 304
Student Trustees, O. Reg. 7/07
Supervisory Officers, R.R.O. 1990, Reg. 309
Suspension and Expulsion of Pupils, O. Reg. 472/07
Teacher Performance Appraisal, O. Reg. 99/02
Teachers Qualifications, O. Reg. 184/97

INTRODUCTION TO THE SIXTH EDITION

The primary purpose of the *Legal Handbook for Educators* is to provide a guide to those areas of education law that are most relevant to school administrators, educators and parents. It is intended to be a handy resource that summarizes pertinent legislation, and that provides easy access to the statutory and regulatory provisions most important to an understanding of the legal environment of schools and school boards. Of course, no book is a substitute for advice from a lawyer about a particular issue that you may encounter.

This Edition has been reorganized to focus more on the school administrator's legal environment. It addresses, and comments upon, significant changes to the law with respect to "safe schools", particularly suspensions and expulsions, and it expands the chapter on negligence and liability. Almost every topic has been updated and expanded. The preface contains an explanation of what is meant by "education law", although it does not pretend to be the final word on that topic.

School administrators are busy people. They deal with numerous crises throughout the day, whether the event is a lockdown, injured student, upset parent or missing child. They do not necessarily share a lawyer's fascination with legal argument. They want answers. The *Legal Handbook* endeavours to provide the "straight goods", to the extent that this is possible given all of the exceptions and conditions found in our statutes.

I wish to express my thanks to the many readers who have used the *Legal Handbook* over the years. I hope that you will continue to find it a useful resource and a good starting point for your legal research. My sincere thanks go to Lisa Gordon, Product Development Manager, and to all of the editorial and production staff at Carswell for their patience and assistance throughout the process of revising the *Handbook*. Finally, I wish to express my profound gratitude to my spouse Catherine, for her constant support that has permitted me the time and energy to write this new edition.

New Legislation

Bill 177, the *Student Achievement and School Board Governance Act, 2009*, amends the *Education Act*. If passed in its current form, the major amendments to the *Education Act* will be as set out below. Legislation and regulations are constantly being amended, and this Bill, if passed, will add to or change certain information in the *Handbook*, particularly in respect of the "roles" of trustees and school board officials. The role of a board chair is outlined and there are new duties imposed on a director of education and on individual board members. Of particular interest are the provisions concerning an enforceable "code of conduct" for trustees. In addition, the ability to charge a fee to a secondary school pupil after seven years of attendance will be repealed.

1. Purpose

The Act will now have a "purpose section" (s. 0.1). This provides that:

- A strong public education system is the foundation of a prosperous, caring and cohesive society.
- The purpose of education is to provide students with the opportunity to realize their potential and develop into highly skilled, knowledgeable, caring citizens who contribute to their society.
- All partners in the education sector have a role to play in enhancing student achievement and well-being, closing gaps in student achievement and maintaining confidence in the province's publicly funded education system.

Comment: Although "purpose" sections in statutes do not prescribe duties or establish rights, they can be used by courts when interpreting other sections of the Act.

2. Unilateral Expansion of Powers and Duties

The Act will provide that:

> The Lieutenant Governor in Council may make regulations governing the roles, responsibilities, powers and duties of boards, directors of education and board members, including chairs of boards.

Comment: Among other things, this gives the government the power to reshape and expand what a school board "is", without having to go the Legislature. Unlike "public interest regulations" in section 11.1, there are no safeguards about consulting school boards before regulations are made under this section.

3. New Board Duty re Achievement

There are new "duties" for boards which are intended to ensure that boards are in sync with provincial priorities.

169.1 (1) Every board shall,

(a) promote student outcomes specified in regulations made under section 11.1 ["provincial interest regulations"];

(b) ensure effective stewardship of the board's resources;

(c) deliver effective and appropriate education programs to its pupils;

(d) develop and maintain policies and organizational structures that,

(i) promote the goals referred to in clauses (a) to (c),

(ii) promote the well-being of the board's pupils, and

(iii) encourage pupils to pursue their educational goals;

(e) develop multi-year plans aimed at achieving the goals referred to in clauses (a) to (c); [A board will have to report to its employees and supporters about its plans and progress.]

(f) monitor the performance of the board's director of education, or the supervisory officer acting as the board's director of education, in meeting his or her obligations under the plans referred to in clause (e); and

(g) annually review the plans referred to in clause (e) with the board's director of education or the supervisory officer acting as the board's director of education.

Comment:

- this may open up a board to litigation on the ground that it has failed to provide "effective and appropriate education" to pupils. Thus far, educational malpractice has not been recognized as a tort in Canada. Does this legislation provide an alternative route to be able to attack school boards who fail to meet a parent's expectations?
- what is the scope of the duty to promote the "well-being of the board's pupils" — does this extend to emotional, health, mental and physical well-being of pupils outside school hours? If so, why is the provision of social workers and psychologists still optional for boards?

4. Stewardship

Every board shall,

(a) effectively use the resources entrusted to it;

(b) use the resources entrusted to it for the purposes of delivering effective and appropriate education; and

(c) manage the resources entrusted to it in a manner that upholds public confidence.

Comment: Although virtually meaningless in a legal sense, this section harks back to the traditional role of a trustee as guardian of the assets of a board on behalf of school supporters. The section does provide an indication that a board's resources are to be used for the "purposes of delivering effective and appropriate *education*".

Expansion into other areas outside education would arguably contravene the section.

5. Parent Involvement Committees

> The Lieutenant Governor in Council may make regulations requiring boards to establish parent involvement committees and providing for the composition, mandate and functions of the committees.

The details of these committees will be fleshed out in a regulation. They clearly do not replace school councils (which include persons who are not parents).

6. Audit Committee

Every district school board will be required to have an Audit Committee, which may include members who are *not* trustees. It will have the powers of an auditor under the Act. A regulation will provide more details about the requirements for Audit Committees.

7. Number of Trustees

The number of trustees on a district school board will be set at the *2006* election level. This eliminates the need for the existing regulation establishing the number for each board. Boards can apply to the Minister to increase the number of members. An increase can be granted if the Minister is of the opinion that "the increase is justified by a demographic change in the board's geographical area of jurisdiction or by a change in the size of the board's geographical area of jurisdiction". The provisions in the Act for *reducing* the number of members are not changing.

8. Duties of Board Members

This new section speaks to the individual responsibility of board members, as opposed to their collective responsibility as a "board".

> 218.1 A member of a board shall,
>
> (a) attend and participate in meetings of the board, including meetings of board committees of which he or she is a member;
>
> (b) consult with parents, students and supporters of the board on the board's multi-year plans under clause 169.1(1)(e);
>
> (c) bring concerns of parents, students and supporters of the board to the attention of the board;
>
> (d) support the implementation of any board resolution after it is passed by the board;
>
> (e) refrain from interfering in the day-to-day management of the board by its officers and staff;
>
> (f) maintain focus on student achievement and well-being; and
>
> (g) comply with the board's code of conduct.

Comment:

- Arguably, the only really significant change is that dealing with the obligation to comply with a code of conduct.

- The obligation not to interfere in "day-to-day management" simply clarifies the existing conceptual framework of the *Education Act*: trustees govern; the director and staff organize, manage and administrate.
- Trustees have a duty to bring the concerns of parents, etc. to the board. It is not clear how this advocacy role is to be reconciled with the obligation not to interfere with day-to-day management. Does it mean that concerns can only be raised at the board, but not raised with the school or the director? That hardly seems practical.

9. Code of Conduct

The Minister will be able to regulate a code of conduct for board members. A board will also be able to adopt additional rules as part of its code of conduct.

A board member may bring breaches of the code of conduct to the attention of the board, which shall then "make inquiries" into the matter and determine if there has been a breach. A board may impose one or more of the following sanctions:

1. Censure of the member.
2. Reduction of the honorarium payable to the member under section 191.
3. Barring the member from attending all or part of a meeting of the board or a meeting of a committee of the board.
4. Barring the member from sitting on one or more committees of the board, for the period of time specified by the board.

Board meetings are not to be closed to the public only because a sanction may be imposed on a member at the meeting.

10. Duties of Board Chair

The role of the board chair is clarified, particularly in the important areas of setting the agenda, acting as the board's "sole spokesperson" to the public (unless otherwise determined), and acting as the intermediary between the board and the director of education.

In addition to any other duties under the Act, the chair of a board shall,

(a) preside over meetings of the board;

(b) conduct the meetings in accordance with the board's procedures and practices for the conduct of board meetings;

(c) establish agendas for board meetings, in consultation with the board's director of education or the supervisory officer acting as the board's director of education;

(d) ensure that members of the board have the information needed for informed discussion of the agenda items;

(e) act as spokesperson to the public on behalf of the board, unless otherwise determined by the board;

(f) convey the views and decisions of the board to the board's director of education or the supervisory officer acting as the board's director of education;

(g) provide leadership to the board in maintaining the board's focus on the multi-year plans established under section 169.1; and

(h) assume such other responsibilities as may be specified by the board.

11. Additional Duties of Director of Education

A new section, s. 283.1(1), will provide that, in addition to his or her other duties under this Act, the director of education shall,

(a) annually review with the board the plans developed under clause 169.1(1)(e);

(b) ensure plans developed under clause 169.1(1)(e) establish the board's priorities and identify specific measures and resources that will be applied in achieving those priorities and in carrying out its duties under this Act, in particular, its responsibility for student achievement as set out in section 169.1;

(c) implement and monitor the implementation of the plans developed under clause 169.1(1)(e);

(d) report periodically to the board on the implementation of the plans developed under clause 169.1(1)(e);

(e) act as secretary to the board;

(f) immediately upon discovery bring to the attention of the board any act or omission by the board that in the opinion of the director of education may result in or has resulted in a contravention of this Act or any policy, guideline or regulation made under this Act; and

(g) if a board does not respond in a satisfactory manner to an act or omission brought to its attention under clause (f), advise the Minister of the act or omission.

Comment: This section clearly gives the director a shared responsibility to ensure that the board's annual plan complies with provincial mandates. Further, it requires that every director shall be the board's secretary. Thirdly, it requires the director to inform the board when it is considered not to be in compliance with the Act or provincial regulations, policies or guidelines, and to inform the Minister if the board does not respond in a satisfactory manner. Although this reinforces the accountability of boards to the Minister by ensuring that the CEO can report these matters to the Minister, there is no specific sanction against a director who fails to make a report to the Minister — nor does it say what the Minister is to do upon receiving this information. The Act has always contained a requirement for boards to comply with the law.

12. Debentures

School boards will no longer have the power to borrow for permanent improvements by means of a debenture or other debt instrument. Existing debentures are not affected. The government may delegate "specified duties related to the borrowing of money and the incurring of debt by the board for permanent improvements" to the Minister or other body.

13. Declaration and Oath Taken By Members

There are minor changes to the *declaration* required of board members upon taking office. More significantly, the Oath of Allegiance to the Queen will be *optional.*

14. Housekeeping

- the director will automatically be the secretary of a district school board
- references in the Act to "co-instructional activities" have been removed.
- references to "old boards" are removed. This was relevant at the time that district school boards were created by merger in 1998.
- references to the Education Improvement Commission are deleted. The Commission assisted with the implementation of district school boards.
- the Minister will have the power to make policies and guidelines about professional activity days
- the right to charge fees to students after seven years of secondary school is deleted
- provisions about School Board Advisory Committees are repealed
- there are 90 days to fill a board vacancy by appointment, instead of 60 days
- transitional safe schools provisions are repealed.

1

THE PRINCIPAL'S LEGAL ENVIRONMENT

1.1 Introduction

When this *Handbook* was first published in 1989, principals did not have ready access to legal information. Now, of course, all legislation is available on-line through the internet and school boards have binders full of policies on everything from anaphylaxis to lockdowns. Any topic can be researched through the internet. An internet search on, for example, cyber-bullying will fetch you well over one million hits. The Ontario Ministry of Education website offers excellent guidelines on such topics as special education and school councils. So, the challenge is no longer the unavailability of information. It is understanding the information and being able to focus on what is particularly relevant.

This chapter is therefore about the legal environment that most directly affects principals and vice-principals. It is about the school law that matters most, and covers the statutory duties of principals, community relations, dealing with difficult parents, student discipline, school safety, the confidentiality of students' personal information, reporting child abuse, and the *Youth Criminal Justice Act*. These areas of law give rise to most of the day-to-day questions and concerns of principals. This is where I hope you find out what you need to know to swim and stay afloat in the legal currents surrounding your school.

1.2 The Statutory Framework for Principals

1.2.1 A Principal's Duties

The *Education Act* and regulations prescribe many legal requirements for school principals. Some of the duties of principals have existed on the statute books for a very long time, but others are relatively new. Some seem antiquated and paternalistic, while other, more recent provisions impose cumbersome and arguably unrealistic duties that do not reflect the busy workload of today's principals.

According to the *Education Act* and Regulation 298, a principal's primary duties are to:

- organize and manage the school
- be in charge of, and supervise, the instruction of pupils
- maintain proper order and discipline of pupils.

Everything else that a principal is required to do flows from these three components. This includes the suspension of pupils, granting credits, promoting and admitting pupils, arranging home instruction, assisting and evaluating teachers, inspecting the school, and ensuring the safety, health and comfort of pupils.

The following list contains more examples of a principal's legal powers and duties:

- recommend to the Minister that diplomas be granted to pupils
- retain on file all courses of study used in the school
- timetable the school
- initiate the IPRC process
- suspend pupils or recommend expulsion
- ensure appropriate "condition and appearance" of the school and the care of all teaching materials and other school property
- hold fire and emergency/lockdown drills
- assign suitable quarters to pupils to eat lunch
- record pupil attendance in the register
- receive pupil absence notes from parents or guardians
- deal with trespassers and anyone who disrupts the pupils
- ensure occasional teachers are in place if regular teachers are absent
- ensure school announcements and advertisements comply with board policy
- ensure that the board approves any canvassing or fundraising activity involving pupils
- inspect school premises weekly
- report lack of attention on the part of school maintenance staff
- report on necessary repairs to the school
- instruct pupils in the care of school premises
- refuse admission to the school of any person suspected of being infected with or exposed to a communicable disease
- report to the board and Medical Officer of Health if he or she suspects the existence of a communicable disease in the school
- promote and maintain co-operation of the school with others in the community
- serve on the school council and provide information to it as required by the Minister
- ensure parent/guardian consents are obtained for field trips, athletics and extracurricular activities
- ensure the proper handling of each pupil's Ontario Student Record (OSR)
- ensure compliance within the school with respect to privacy and freedom of information, *Youth Criminal Justice Act* confidentiality, and *Education Act* confidentiality provisions pertaining to pupils and/or staff
- ensure compliance with the policies of the board and the Ministry respecting the administration of medication to pupils
- maintain a visitor's book
- fulfill other duties assigned by the board.

The work of a principal includes such additional matters as:

- attend meetings with supervisors, parents, trustees, union representatives, police, children's aid, lawyers, insurance adjusters, teachers, support staff, school nurses, volunteers, other principals, and pupils
- interview candidates for job vacancies
- be a curriculum or instructional leader
- take professional development courses
- coach sports
- be a role model for staff, pupils and the community
- serve on committees and organize staff meetings
- manage school funds
- help organize school assemblies, school fairs, school trips, concerts, professional activity days, parent interview days, student photographs, etc.
- document accidents on the premises affecting pupils, staff and visitors
- deal with vandalism at the school.

A principal may choose to delegate duties to a vice-principal. While each school must have a principal, there is no requirement to appoint a vice-principal. The principal has the power to assign duties to the vice-principal and the vice-principal has the duty to perform those duties. In the absence of the principal, the vice-principal is in charge of the school and shall perform the duties of the principal (Reg. 298, ss. 11 and 12). A principal or vice-principal may perform the duties of a teacher, despite any provision in a collective agreement (s. 287.1(1)).

Some of a principal's duties have complementary duties imposed on teachers. For example, a principal has a duty to develop co-operation and coordination of effort among staff in the school, and teachers have a duty to assist the principal in this respect. Whereas teachers must prepare and submit teaching plans and outlines as required, the principal must retain on file outlines of all courses of study taught in the school. The principal has a duty to prepare a timetable, conduct the school according to the timetable, and make the timetable accessible to pupils, teachers, and supervisory officers. A teacher must conduct his or her class in accordance with a timetable (see generally ss. 264 and 265 of the Act and ss. 11 and 20 of Reg. 298).

However, a school is truly about students, their teachers and their parents. The principal's job, or one of them, is to hold it all together using the skills of a diplomat, the firmness of a leader and the integrity of a community role model. Survival as a principal comes from working successfully with the community.

1.2.2 Working with the School Community

As any principal knows, considerable time and effort must be spent by a principal on fostering good community relations. The school is, after all, a part of the community. Indeed, it may be the central hub of the community. A principal has a duty to promote and maintain close co-operation with the residents, industry, business and other groups and agencies in the community, and teachers have a duty to assist in this respect (Reg. 298, ss. 11 and 20). The principal must also serve on the school council (Ministry Guideline for School Councils; O. Reg. 612/00).

The "community" is not always welcoming to a school administrator. In some areas, principals must surmount cultural or other barriers and mistrust, and bring students and parents to a realization that the school is there to help. They may have to mediate between conflicting groups of parents within the school. They cannot do any of this without the help and respect of the student body, teachers, support staff, local trustee, and community leaders. This ability to "translate" a school, and everything it stands for, beyond its borders distinguishes a merely competent principal from a really successful one. This leadership prepares a principal to become a superintendent of schools. It is also vitally important to foster a healthy and mutually-respectful working (not *reporting*) relationship with the local school trustee.

1.2.3 Dealing with Difficult Parents

Principals are teachers, and as teachers, they are "comfortable" with students. They "know" them. However, when a classroom teacher becomes principal or vice-principal, the focus frequently changes. All of a sudden, there are a lot of balls in the air, and most of them have to do with parents. Parents who are worried. Parents who are separated or divorced and engaged in a custody dispute. Parents who face the challenges of raising a child with special needs.

Parents have many legitimate concerns, and they have different ways of expressing their dissatisfaction with their child's school or classroom teacher. Merely being loud or obnoxious does not mean that a parent is necessarily guilty of harassment. Parents who are affected by other sources of stress such as divorce, poverty, linguistic and cultural barriers, or the challenges of raising children are not "problem" parents.[1]

However, the behaviour of some parents goes well beyond being merely difficult or demanding. These are persons who do not respond to negotiations or concessions unless it means that the school has totally capitulated. They are quite capable of driving teachers and administrators out of the workplace, on stress leave. I recall one parent who wrote rude comments about his child's teacher in the child's student planner. I suggested that the comments be physically deleted and that the planner should no longer be sent home if the parent was going to be so abusive. There are other ways of letting a parent know what his child is doing in school. The principal was so concerned about this parent that a security guard had to be present when the parent came in for an interview to discuss his child.

The Alberta Teachers' Association defines "parental harassment" in the school context "as persistent parental or community criticism of or interference with school programs, teacher performance or interaction with students that is unwarranted and/or unsubstantiated."[2]

---

[1]Readers may find the following book to be particularly helpful in listing strategies for dealing with difficult parents: R.L. Curwin et al., *Discipline with Dignity*, 3d ed. (Alexandria, Virginia: Association for Supervision and Curriculum Development, 2008) pp. 196–214.

[2]The Alberta Teachers' Association, *Beyond the Norm: Dealing with Parental Harassment* (August 2006), http://www.teachers.ab.ca/Quick%20Links/Publications/Other%20Publications/Teaching%20Students%20with%20Learning%20Disabilities/Teachers%20Guides/Pages/Beyond%20the%20Norm.aspx.

The problem is very real. The Elementary Teachers' Federation of Ontario participated in a survey entitled *Bullying in the Workplace*, conducted by James Matsui and Lang Research and commissioned by the Elementary Teachers' Federation of Ontario, the Ontario English Catholic Teachers' Federation of Ontario, and the Ontario Secondary Teachers' Federation of Ontario. Among other things, the survey found that over one-half of Ontario's elementary and secondary teachers have been personally bullied during their professional careers and that bullying by parents is the second most prevalent form of bullying, with 36% of teachers working in elementary schools and 22% of teachers working in secondary schools being bullied.

The parent who is guilty of harassment has one or more of the following characteristics:

- makes unreasonable demands of the school administration and classroom teacher
- cannot accept "no" for answer
- sends countless (and often lengthy) emails and leaves countless voice messages
- often copies numerous other parties to emails, such as the Ministry, the Premier, fellow parents, board members, etc.
- barges into the classroom
- oblivious to the needs of other students and parents
- indoctrinates own children to oppose school authority
- cannot accept that child may have done something inappropriate
- demands answers to questions in writing
- threatens litigation; mentions that a family member is a lawyer
- threatens to go the media
- disrupts school council meetings
- spreads rumours and innuendo about staff, sometimes on the internet.

There are two things that must be kept in mind in dealing with this kind of parent:

1. After you have made an honest attempt to respond to the person's concerns, *stop bending over backward.* You are simply feeding the person's needs, and the unreasonable demands will keep coming. Shut it down. And focus on serving the child.
2. Seek help from your supervisor, and do it early. It is vitally important that the school administrator be supported by the supervisory officer and board executive. Principals are weakened when they do not feel supported.

Survival Tips:

1. Do not feel you need to respond to every email and voice message. There is no legal requirement to respond to every list of questions from a parent. Be extremely cautious about what kind of email "trail" you are building — it could end up in court or in the newspaper.
2. Be careful — your phone conversations might be recorded. Always assume that a recording is being made.

3. You can have the parent's emails to the school blocked by the IT Department.
4. Parents can be directed to communicate only through one person — e.g. through the superintendent and not the principal or teacher.
5. Parents can be "trespassed" or "denied access" to the school.
6. Websites such as Facebook can be informed of inaccurate or offensive content and asked to remove it.
7. You must respect the privacy of staff and students. Therefore, you often cannot respond to a parent's demands for information, even if you want to.
8. You can ask your superintendent to request the board's legal counsel to write to the parent to remind him/her of parental obligations under the Provincial Code of Conduct.
9. You can sue a parent for defamation.
10. Any threats should be reported to the police.

1.3 Keeping the School Safe

1.3.1 Introduction

School safety is a concept that involves much more than enforcing good behaviour. It also involves protection against a long list of real or potential dangers such as contagious disease, asbestos, poor drinking water, slippery sidewalks, etc. Moreover, even though a student's behaviour may pose a safety risk to staff or students in the school, there may not be cause for disciplinary consequences if the student does not understand that the behaviour is wrong or cannot control his or her behaviour. Conversely, a student may be disciplined for activities (e.g. swearing) that do not pose a safety risk to others. However, in most cases, the rationale for imposing a suspension or expulsion is that the student has done something that contributes to making the school unsafe (e.g. assault, extortion, dealing drugs, etc.).

It is very difficult to know precisely how safe our schools really are. The majority of students say that they feel relatively safe at school, even though many have witnessed incidents involving bullying, fighting and weapons. Indeed, insidious forms of hurtfulness, such as cyber-bullying, are probably a bigger problem in most schools than more "traditional" or obvious methods of inflicting harm. Many schools in Ontario rarely need to impose suspensions and never have occasion to recommend students for expulsion. A tiny minority of schools have a high proportion of serious discipline, i.e. expulsion and suspension, relative to their total enrolment. Is this a reflection of the community around the school, or of the school's culture, or of the competence of school officials? Can we blame school violence on, perhaps, the "internet" or "video games" or the absence of a responsible father-figure in the family? In some quarters, people are convinced that suspensions and expulsions are the result of systemic discrimination against students from racialized backgrounds or with special needs. Others are in favour of a "zero tolerance" approach, despite its many failings.

There are two central facts about school safety:

> Although students and education employees have been victims of violence on or near school grounds, schools are not any less safe than other similarly populated communities.
>
> School violence transcends the school and is a societal problem, with its roots in community and family dysfunctions — and exacerbated by issues such as racism, sexism, and high unemployment.

These conclusions would appear to be incontrovertible and are supported by "Road to Health", the findings of the School Community Safety Advisory Panel commissioned by the Toronto District School Board,[3] and by the "Roots of Youth Violence" report by former Chief Justice Roy McMurtry and the Honourable Alvin Curling, former Speaker and Member of the Ontario Legislature.[4]

1.3.2 The Duty to Maintain Order

The power and duty of principals and teachers to maintain discipline in their school and classroom is firmly entrenched in the *Education Act* and its regulations:

> The principal has the duty to maintain proper order and discipline in the school. (s. 265(1)(a)), and is "in charge of" discipline in the school (Reg. 298, s. 11(1)).
>
> The principal must report any neglect of duty or infraction of the school rules by a pupil to the pupil's parent (Reg. 298, s. 11(3)(n)).
>
> A teacher has the duty to cooperate with the principal and other teachers to establish and maintain consistent disciplinary practices in the school (Reg. 298, s. 20(h)).
>
> A teacher must maintain, under the direction of the principal, proper order and discipline in the classroom and while on duty in the school and on the school grounds (s. 264(1)(e)).
>
> The principal must provide information to the appropriate supervisory officer and the Minister respecting discipline in the school (s. 265(1)(i)).
>
> A pupil has a duty to exercise self-discipline and to accept such discipline as would be exercised by a kind, firm and judicious parent (Reg. 298, s. 23).
>
> A pupil is responsible to the principal for his or her conduct at the school, on school activities and on the school bus (Reg. 298, s. 23).

It is important that educators and the school community be aware of the Policy Program Memoranda of the Ministry of Education pertaining to safe schools. These are:

- PPM 141, "School Board Programs for Students on Long-Term Suspension"
- PPM 142, "School Board Programs for Expelled Students"
- PPM 144, "Bullying Prevention and Intervention"
- PPM 145, "Progressive Discipline and Promoting Positive Student Behaviour"

In addition, Ontario's "Safe Schools Action Team" has released a recent series of recommendations for government action to make schools healthier places.

---

[3]http://www.tdsb.on.ca

[4]http://www.rootsofyouthviolence.on.ca/english/index.asp

1.3.3 School Discipline — Suspensions and Expulsions

1.3.3.1 New Legislation on an Old Problem

Legislation on suspending and expelling students has evolved since 2000 from a few short sections in the *Education Act* to a regime of mandatory discipline and, now, to a new scheme that promotes progressive discipline and mitigation. On February 1, 2008, the *Education Amendment Act (Progressive Discipline and School Safety Act), 2007* came into force, amending Part XIII of the *Education Act*, or what I refer to as the "safe schools provisions" of the Act. The amending statute is sometimes referred to as "Bill 212". The emphasis is now on discouraging schools from suspending or expelling students at all. However, the pendulum seems to have swung in the direction of tying the hands of principals to make it more difficult to protect the general student body against the violence of a few. Nowhere is this better reflected than in misguided changes that now prohibit principals from denying dangerous students access to school on *safety* grounds under Ontario Regulation 474/00, the Denial of Access Regulation.

The details pertaining to suspension and expulsions are discussed later in this chapter. However, at the outset I discuss the significant changes underlying the new safe school provisions.

(a) School Climate

The legislation now expressly permits the discipline of students for an "activity" at school, while they are engaged in school-related activity and "in other circumstances where engaging in the activity will have an impact on the school climate". We can usually determine if an activity occurred at school or on a school-related activity such as a fieldtrip or school athletic competition. The concept of "school climate" is more difficult. The reference to "school climate" simply codifies, in a vague sort of way, what has always been the law, namely that students can be disciplined for infractions that are off-site but that have a sufficient nexus to the school. "School climate" is an extraordinarily nebulous term to be found in legislation, and we are no closer to a clear definition of what the "nexus" should look like.

The concept of school climate is particularly relevant in the context of "cyber-bullying", which has no physical boundaries but is frequently aimed at students by other students. However, school climate also pertains to other activities such as fights between students that may have occurred off-site but which affect the school. The principal should determine if the following considerations apply to an off-site incident:

- Did the incident create fear for safety among the students of the school? (In one incident I recall, students from one school travelled to a second school during the lunch hour and initiated a fight in which knives and guns were involved. The principal of the first school, where the culprits were enrolled, recalled the fear generated in the school when the students discovered that their classmates had been toting around guns and knives in their backpack. The students were expelled after their release from prison.)
- Did the incident begin in the school and resume/continue off the premises?
- Did the incident begin off-site and resume/continue at the school?
- When did the incident occur — after hours, during lunch, on the weekend?

- How far away from the school did the incident occur? An incident across the street from the school usually has a stronger connection to the school than one several kilometres away.
- Did the behaviour (such as cyber-bullying) threaten students or affect the school climate by encouraging or promoting racist, sexist or homophobic behaviour at the school?

You are likely to find disagreement about what "off-site" incidents should lead to school discipline. If two students get into a fight on the weekend, should the principal discipline them? What about a fight in the evening during the week, or after school? In my view, it is not enough that the incident merely involved students. That is, the board and its schools are not there to police the community by responding to all kinds of inappropriate behaviour just because it happens to involve one or more students of the board.

Principals should think twice (and seek legal advice) before they discipline students for off-site conduct. The prohibited activity must have a tangible connection to the school and the principal should be able to identify clearly how the "climate" of the school was detrimentally affected. Consider whether there was (1) a nexus between the physical proximity and timing of the conduct and the school day or the school-sponsored activity, or (2) whether the conduct materially or substantially disrupted the educational environment, or (3) whether the conduct poses a direct threat or danger to safety in the school. Such a connection may exist, for example, where a fight starts in school and then continues at the local mall during lunch or on the sidewalk immediately after school is dismissed. It may also be found when a student distributes inappropriate information about, or photographs of, another student (or staff) over the internet.

Not all objectionable internet content posted by students can lead to school discipline. Students have the freedom to express themselves outside school (and to a lesser extent inside school). They have the freedom to post obnoxious, upsetting and even insulting comments, but they do not have the freedom to defame or threaten another person on the internet, or to post comments that are disrespectful or hurtful towards staff or students. Todd DeMitchell, a Professor of Education at the University of New Hampshire suggests:[5]

- Ascertain if the cyber-bullying took place at school. If yes, treat the behavior as you would any other act of bullying at school and act accordingly.
- Take action if the cyber-bullying took place away from school and did not involve the school's computers or software but it caused a material and substantial disruption or such disruption can be reasonably forecast.
- If the cyber-bullying that took place away from school did not cause a material and substantial disruption, consider it a key for persuasion to discuss with the student how such actions are harmful and inappropriate. Don't underestimate

[5]"As school year begins, cyber-bullying presents a complex legal landscape", *Shrink Rap: Tri-City Psychology Services reports on the latest psychology research, news and gossip* (August 25, 2008), http://www.tricitypsychology.com/blog/?p=1628, citing University of New Hampshire *Newswise*.

the power of an educator talking frankly with a student. The administrator may not be able to take action because the private speech of the student may be protected.

- Respond to all "true threats" of harm.

In "Learning & Leading with Technology", March 2007, published by the International Society for Technology in Education, educational experts Nancy Willard and Lynn Wietecha debate what it is reasonable to expect schools to do about off-site cyber-bullying. Both agree that schools must include education about the dangers of cyber-bullying in their curriculum, and must follow up with parents when it is determined that a student has used the internet inappropriately. But Wietecha argues that although schools should intervene when a student posts a threat on the internet, "cyber patrol" should not be a school responsibility and that it is "unreasonable to hold schools accountable for things that are simply beyond their control." On the other hand, Willard emphasizes how harmful cyber-bullying can be (even leading to suicide):

> As much as school officials might want to think it is not our business, the harmful effects are real and they are directly affecting the school climate and emotional well-being of students — and affecting their learning.[6]

(b) Expulsions

The legislative amendments in Bill 212 eliminated the power of principals to expel students, and the power of teachers to suspend students for one day.

Only the school board (sitting as a whole or a committee of at least three trustees) can expel a student.

All expulsions are subject to appeal to the Child and Family Services Review Board.

The concepts of "limited" and "full" expulsion are gone. A board can no longer expel a person from all schools in the province. Instead, it must decide whether to expel the student from his or her school or from all of the board's schools. Students will not be prevented from enrolling at another school board, subject to some requirements in the legislation.

As legislation about school discipline has evolved in Ontario, we have arguably reached the point at which the traditional concept of "expulsion" has effectively disappeared. Expulsion used to mean that students were banned from school, rarely to return. No programs were in place to assist them towards readmission. Now, thankfully, expelled students must be offered alternative programs in which they can continue to learn, and from which they can often successfully go back to regular programs. The difficulty is that some students need, but do not receive, "treatment" to end their anti-social behaviour before they should ever be readmitted to school. Moreover, after spending time (e.g. a 20-day suspension) in an alternative program, it is not always practical or sensible to return the young person to his or her regular school setting, having missed so much of the term. Designing programs, and transitions to and from programs, is the great challenge of Bill 212.

---

[6]http://www.iste.org/Content/NavigationMenu/Publications/LL/L_L.htm

(c) Detailed Procedural Requirements

The legislation prescribes the paperwork that must be completed by a school principal in respect of suspensions or recommendations for expulsion. These procedural requirements are intended to achieve a consistent and fair process, but they impose a considerable administrative burden in some schools. Boards should provide principals with the advice and support they need to ensure that the process is followed correctly.

(d) Other "Factors"

The legislation expanded the list of "factors" that must be considered before imposing a suspension or expulsion. These "other" factors result from the settlement of a human rights complaint between the Ontario Human Rights Commission and the Ministry of Education.

(e) More Discretion

The former safe schools provisions in the Act were often incorrectly described as requiring "zero tolerance" in that, subject to three mitigating factors, certain infractions required a suspension or an expulsion. The legislation now requires a principal to "consider" a suspension if he or she believes the student has engaged in certain kinds of "activities" (s. 306). The legislation also lists a number of prohibited activities which require a principal to suspend a student believed to have engaged in the activity, while the matter is being investigated pending a possible recommendation for expulsion (s. 310).

(f) Alternative Programs

Students who have been suspended (over five days) or expelled are entitled to attend alternative programs established in accordance with Ministry of Education policy.

1.3.3.2 Suspensions and Expulsions — General Considerations

(a) Role of School Trustees

School Trustees:

- establish policies and procedures required by the Act
- conduct expulsion hearings
- hear and determine suspension appeals.

Trustees may sit as the whole board or may establish a committee to deal with suspension appeals and expulsions. The decision of the committee is deemed to be the decision of the Board. The legislation does not envisage a further appeal to the whole board from the decision of such a committee.

(b) Role of the Principal

The Principal:

- may impose a suspension for up to 20 school days
- shall impose a "suspension pending possible expulsion" for up to 20 school days

- may recommend to the Board that a student should be expelled
- must investigate what happened, in order to form a belief that a student has engaged in a prohibited activity
- will attend the suspension appeal or expulsion hearing to state how he or she formed a belief that the student engaged in a prohibited activity
- will also be able to state that he or she considered the mitigating factors and other factors (including progressive discipline) before considering more serious discipline.

(c) Progressive Discipline

The logic behind progressive discipline is so obvious (especially to an educator) that one must wonder whether we really needed a Ministry of Education policy telling us all about it. Serious infractions (i.e. serious violations of the school rules; engaging in prohibited activities) obviously require a significant and proportionate disciplinary response. However, a student who repeatedly gets into trouble at school should normally be dealt with through a series of progressively more severe disciplinary measures. Simply put, suspensions and expulsions are measures of last resort and should only be used if the facts reveal:

(i) a record of prior progressive discipline, or

(ii) an infraction of such magnitude that serious consequences are the only appropriate response in the circumstances.

Ministry of Education Policy/Program Memorandum No. 145 explains progressive discipline as follows:

> **Progressive Discipline**
>
> Progressive discipline is a whole-school approach that utilizes a continuum of interventions, supports, and consequences to address inappropriate student behaviour and to build upon strategies that promote positive behaviours described above. When inappropriate behaviour occurs, disciplinary measures should be applied within a framework that shifts the focus from one that is solely punitive to one that is both corrective and supportive. Schools should utilize a range of interventions, supports, and consequences that include learning opportunities for reinforcing positive behaviour while helping students to make good choices.
>
> In some circumstances, short-term suspension may be a useful tool. In the case of a serious incident, long-term suspension or expulsion, which is further along the continuum of progressive discipline, may be the response that is required.
>
> For students with special education needs, interventions, supports, and consequences must be consistent with the student's strengths, needs, goals, and expectations contained in his or her Individual Education Plan (IEP).
>
> Schools are expected to actively engage parents in the progressive discipline approach.
>
> A progressive discipline approach includes the use of early and ongoing intervention strategies and strategies to address inappropriate behaviour, which are described below. [The Memorandum continues with more information.]

(d) Mitigating and Other Factors

"Mitigating factors" are considerations that are used to reduce (or negate) the disciplinary consequences of a student's actions. "Other" factors shall be taken into account if they "would mitigate the seriousness of the activity" (O. Reg. 427/07, s. 2, 3).

Prior to imposing any suspension or recommending any expulsion, the Principal must consider whether one or more mitigating factors apply. Failure to do so will jeopardize the legal validity of the suspension or the recommendation for expulsion, and could result in an expulsion being overturned by the Child and Family Services Review Board if it is appealed.

According to Ontario Regulation 472/07, the mitigating factors are as follows:

> 2. For the purposes of subsections 306 (2), 306 (4), 310 (3), 311.1 (4) and clauses 311.3 (7) (b) and 311.4 (2) (b) of the [Education] Act, the following mitigating factors shall be taken into account:
>
> > 1. The pupil does not have the ability to control his or her behaviour.
> >
> > 2. The pupil does not have the ability to understand the foreseeable consequences of his or her behaviour.
> >
> > 3. The pupil's continuing presence in the school does not create an unacceptable risk to the safety of any person.
>
> 3. For the purposes of subsections 306 (2), 306 (4), 310 (3), 311.1 (4) and clauses 311.3 (7) (b) and 311.4 (2) (b) of the [Education] Act, the following other factors shall be taken into account if they would mitigate the seriousness of the activity for which the pupil may be or is being suspended or expelled:
>
> > 1. The pupil's history.
> >
> > 2. Whether a progressive discipline approach has been used with the pupil.
> >
> > 3. Whether the activity for which the pupil may be or is being suspended or expelled was related to any harassment of the pupil because of his or her race, ethnic origin, religion, disability, gender or sexual orientation or to any other harassment.
> >
> > 4. How the suspension or expulsion would affect the pupil's ongoing education.
> >
> > 5. The age of the pupil.
> >
> > 6. In the case of a pupil for whom an individual education plan has been developed,
> >
> > > i. whether the behaviour was a manifestation of a disability identified in the pupil's individual education plan,
> > >
> > > ii. whether appropriate individualized accommodation has been provided, and
> > >
> > > iii. whether the suspension or expulsion is likely to result in an aggravation or worsening of the pupil's behaviour or conduct.

Mitigating and other factors are not concerned with whether the student committed the prohibited activity. They pertain to what if any disciplinary consequences will be imposed. They are nothing more than a requirement to consider the "whole picture" of the student, instead of a lock-step, automatic, arbitrary imposition of disciplinary consequences free of any genuine use of discretion or other hallmarks of judicious or educationally-sound decision-making.

1.3.3.3 Suspensions — the Details

(a) Power to Suspend

Section 306 of the *Education Act* gives a principal the power to suspend a pupil.

> 306. A principal shall consider whether to suspend a pupil if he or she believes that the pupil has engaged in any of the following activities while at school, at a school-related activity or in other circumstances where engaging in the activity will have an impact on the school climate:
>
> 1. Uttering a threat to inflict serious bodily harm on another person.
> 2. Possessing alcohol or illegal drugs.
> 3. Being under the influence of alcohol.
> 4. Swearing at a teacher or at another person in a position of authority.
> 5. Committing an act of vandalism that causes extensive damage to school property at the pupil's school or to property located on the premises of the pupil's school.
> 6. Bullying.
> 7. Any other activity that is an activity for which a principal may suspend a pupil under a policy of the board.

After *considering* whether to suspend, the principal may then *decide* whether to suspend.

Things to Note:

- Suspensions under section 306 are discretionary.
- A board can add to the list of "activities" that are prohibited. Although students will presumably be aware that certain activities such as fighting and trafficking are prohibited, they may not know all of the school rules. Students must be told (often) about prohibited activities, including the prohibited activities that have been added by board policy or the local code of conduct.
- The suspension cannot exceed 20 school days.
- "Mitigating" and "other" factors in Ontario Regulation 472/07 must be considered (1) in deciding whether to suspend a pupil for engaging in the activity and (2) in considering the duration of the suspension.
- A pupil cannot be suspended more than once for the same occurrence.
- A suspended pupil is entitled to attend an alternative program in accordance with Ministry of Education policy. See Policy Program Memoranda 141 and 142.

(b) Notice of Suspension

Section 308 prescribes the notice provisions for a suspension. A board should provide principals with a template to be used when giving notice.

> 308. (1) A principal who suspends a pupil under section 306 shall,
>
> (a) inform the pupil's teacher of the suspension; and

(b) make all reasonable efforts to inform the pupil's parent or guardian of the suspension within 24 hours of the suspension being imposed, unless,

(i) the pupil is at least 18 years old, or

(ii) the pupil is 16 or 17 years old and has withdrawn from parental control.

(2) A principal who suspends a pupil under section 306 shall ensure that written notice of the suspension is given promptly to the following persons:

1. The pupil.

2. The pupil's parent or guardian, unless,

i. the pupil is at least 18 years old, or

ii. the pupil is 16 or 17 years old and has withdrawn from parental control.

3. Such other persons as may be specified by board policy.

(3) The notice under subsection (2) must include the following:

1. The reason for the suspension.

2. The duration of the suspension.

3. Information about any program for suspended pupils to which the pupil is assigned.

4. Information about the right to appeal the suspension under section 309, including,

i. a copy of the board policies and guidelines governing the appeal established by the board under subsection 302 (6), and

ii. the name and contact information of the supervisory officer to whom notice of the appeal must be given under subsection 309 (2).

(c) Suspension Appeals

A suspension can be appealed under section 309 of the Act.

309. (1) The following persons may appeal, to the board, a principal's decision to suspend a pupil under section 306:

1. The pupil's parent or guardian, unless,

i. the pupil is at least 18 years old, or

ii. the pupil is 16 or 17 years old and has withdrawn from parental control.

2. The pupil, if,

i. the pupil is at least 18 years old, or

ii. the pupil is 16 or 17 years old and has withdrawn from parental control.

3. Such other persons as may be specified by board policy.

Section 309(8) states who is a party to the appeal, thereby having a right to attend and participate.

309. (8) The parties to the appeal are:

1. The principal who suspended the pupil.

2. The pupil, if,

i. the pupil is at least 18 years old, or

ii. the pupil is 16 or 17 years old and has withdrawn from parental control.

3. The pupil's parent or guardian, if the pupil's parent or guardian appealed the decision to suspend the pupil.

4. The person who appealed the decision to suspend the pupil, if the decision was appealed by a person other than the pupil or the pupil's parent or guardian.

5. Such other persons as may be specified by board policy.

Section 309(10) states what a board may do on the appeal.

309. (10) The board shall,

(a) confirm the suspension and the duration of the suspension;

(b) confirm the suspension, but shorten its duration, even if the suspension that is under appeal has already been served, and order that the record of the suspension be amended accordingly; or

(c) quash the suspension and order that the record of the suspension be expunged, even if the suspension that is under appeal has already been served.

Things to Note:

- a pupil may be present at the suspension appeal even if he or she is not a party, and may make a statement.
- the board must "hear and determine" the appeal within 15 school days of receiving the notice of appeal. The parties may agree to extend this deadline. The legislation does not address what happens if the 15-day deadline is missed. In many cases, the suspension will have been served before the board hears the matter.
- the person appealing must give a written notice of appeal to the board's designated supervisory officer; and the person also has a right to discuss the appeal with the supervisory officer.
- the notice of appeal must be delivered within 10 school days of the commencement of the suspension.
- the appeal is conducted according to the requirements in board policy.
- there is no express requirement to hold a "hearing" of a suspension appeal. A board is entitled to devise its own procedures. A formal hearing is not required and, although an option, would be cumbersome and unnecessary in many instances. However, even if there is no formal hearing, the parties are entitled to "procedural fairness". This requires that the trustees hearing the matter not be biased, arbitrary or discriminatory; that they determine the matter on the basis of relevant information before them; that the student and parent know the allegations against the student and have a reasonable opportunity to respond; and that the parent and student have disclosure of all relevant information. As always, mitigating and other factors in Ontario Regulation 472/07 must be considered.

1.3.3.4 Suspension Pending Possible Expulsion — the Details

(a) Power to Suspend "Pending"

A suspension pending possible expulsion is one that is imposed under certain parameters and which may lead to a recommendation for an expulsion. When the principal believes that a student has engaged in a prohibited activity mentioned in section 310 (which may include an activity added by the board), then section 310 "kicks in".

> 310. (1) A principal shall suspend a pupil if he or she believes that the pupil has engaged in any of the following activities while at school, at a school-related activity or in other circumstances where engaging in the activity will have an impact on the school climate:
>
> 1. Possessing a weapon, including possessing a firearm.
> 2. Using a weapon to cause or to threaten bodily harm to another person.
> 3. Committing physical assault on another person that causes bodily harm requiring treatment by a medical practitioner.
> 4. Committing sexual assault.
> 5. Trafficking in weapons or in illegal drugs.
> 6. Committing robbery.
> 7. Giving alcohol to a minor.
> 8. Any other activity that, under a policy of a board, is an activity for which a principal must suspend a pupil and, therefore in accordance with this Part, conduct an investigation to determine whether to recommend to the board that the pupil be expelled.
>
> 311. (1) A principal who suspends a pupil under section 310 shall,
>
> (a) inform the pupil's teacher of the suspension; and
>
> (b) make all reasonable efforts to inform the pupil's parent or guardian of the suspension within 24 hours of the suspension being imposed, unless,
>
> (i) the pupil is at least 18 years old, or
>
> (ii) the pupil is 16 or 17 years old and has withdrawn from parental control.
>
> (2) A principal who suspends a pupil under section 310 shall ensure that written notice of the suspension is given promptly to the following persons:
>
> 1. The pupil.
> 2. The pupil's parent or guardian, unless,
>
>   i. the pupil is at least 18 years old, or
>
>   ii. the pupil is 16 or 17 years old and has withdrawn from parental control.
> 3. Such other persons as may be specified by board policy.
>
> (3) The notice under subsection (2) must include the following:
>
> 1. The reason for the suspension.
> 2. The duration of the suspension.
> 3. Information about any program for suspended pupils to which the pupil is assigned.

4. Information about the investigation the principal will conduct under section 311.1 to determine whether to recommend that the pupil be expelled.

5. A statement indicating that,

i. there is no immediate right to appeal the suspension,

ii. if the principal does not recommend to the board that the pupil be expelled following the investigation under section 311.1, the suspension will become subject to appeal under section 311.2, and

iii. if there is an expulsion hearing because the principal recommends to the board that the pupil be expelled, the suspension may be addressed by parties at the hearing.

A section 310 suspension is limited to a duration of not more than 20 school days. The principal must act fast once the student is issued a notice under section 310. This is not always possible if the police are investigating the same incident and do not want the principal interfering with witnesses. In some instances, where an investigation cannot be commenced, it may be appropriate to exclude the student from school, if there are safety concerns, under section 265(1)(m) in order to buy time before triggering a section 310 timeline.

After conducting an investigation, and considering mitigating and other factors, the principal has three options:

(i) recommend expulsion

(ii) do not recommend expulsion and instead confirm or shorten the suspension

(iii) withdraw the suspension and expunge the record

311.1 (5) **If expulsion not recommended** — If, on concluding the investigation, the principal decides not to recommend to the board that the pupil be expelled, the principal shall,

(a) confirm the suspension and the duration of the suspension;

(b) confirm the suspension but shorten its duration, even if the suspension has already been served, and amend the record of the suspension accordingly; or

(c) withdraw the suspension and expunge the record of the suspension, even if the suspension has already been served.

(6) **Same: notice** — If the principal does not recommend to the board that the pupil be expelled, the principal shall ensure that written notice containing the following information is given promptly to every person to whom he or she was required to give notice of the suspension under section 311:

1. A statement that the pupil will not be subject to an expulsion hearing for the activity that resulted in the suspension.

2. A statement indicating whether the principal has, under subsection (5), confirmed the suspension and its duration, confirmed the suspension but reduced its duration or withdrawn the suspension.

3. Unless the suspension was withdrawn, information about the right to appeal the suspension under section 311.2, including,

i. a copy of the board policies and guidelines governing the appeal established by the board under subsection 302(6), and

ii. the name and contact information of the supervisory officer to whom notice of the appeal must be given under section 311.2.

(7) **If expulsion recommended: report** — If, on concluding the investigation, the principal decides to recommend to the board that the pupil be expelled, he or she shall prepare a report that contains the following:

1. A summary of the principal's findings.

2. The principal's recommendation as to whether the pupil should be expelled from his or her school only or from all schools of the board.

3. The principal's recommendation as to,

i. the type of school that might benefit the pupil, if the pupil is expelled from his or her school only, or

ii. the type of program for expelled pupils that might benefit the pupil, if the pupil is expelled from all schools of the board.

Things to Note:

- a board policy may add to the list under section 310. Pupils should be informed of the kinds or classes of activities for which they may be subject to suspension or expulsion.
- there is no immediate right to appeal a section 310 suspension, because its purpose is to allow the principal time to investigate.
- following the suspension, the principal must investigate "promptly" (s. 311.1(2)). The investigation shall be conducted in accordance with the Act and board policy.
- "All reasonable efforts" must be made to speak with the pupil, the parents/guardians (when applicable), and with any other person who may have relevant information (s. 311.1(2)).
- if the principal decides to impose a suspension, (and thus *not* to recommend an expulsion) this suspension is in effect the suspension that he or she imposed under section 310, although the principal may shorten the duration. Once the student is informed of the suspension, there is a right to appeal. The notice provisions are set out in section 311.1(6).
- if the principal decides to recommend an expulsion, he or she must comply with the reporting provision in section 311.1(7), including whether the recommendation is for expulsion from the pupil's school or all schools. The persons receiving the report may respond to it in writing; this response will be considered by the trustees hearing the expulsion.
- the prevalent view is that a principal may withdraw a recommendation for expulsion prior to the expulsion hearing, without any need to have the board or committee agree to the withdrawal. Until the hearing commences, the board or committee are not seized of the matter.

1.3.3.5 Expulsion — the Details

The board (or a committee of at least three trustees) must hold a hearing to determine whether the pupil should be expelled. This is true even if there are Minutes of Settlement, which must be presented to the trustees so that they can confirm (or reject) them.

The board cannot expel a student without receiving a recommendation from a school principal following a section 310 suspension.

The board "shall not expel a pupil if more than 20 school days have expired since the pupil was suspended under section 310, unless the parties to the expulsion hearing agree on a later deadline." (s. 311.3(8)) This provision deprives the board of the authority to hold an expulsion hearing after 20 school days. After the 20-day period (assuming no agreed extension by the parties), the board is without jurisdiction. What happens, then, if the board cannot impose an expulsion? It presumably cannot impose a suspension as an alternative, because its jurisdiction to suspend flows from having the power to consider suspension as an alternative to a possible expulsion. The legislation has left a gap. It must be kept in mind that the student's status is that he or she is out of regular school while under a section 310 suspension, and he or she has had no opportunity to appeal anything at this point. The Legislature cannot have intended that the student not be disciplined merely because the 20-day deadline has passed. Also, it cannot have intended that the student not be able to appeal.

Once the board has lost jurisdiction, the logical solution is for the *principal* to consider whether to impose a suspension. If a suspension is supported by the facts, such a suspension would essentially convert the already-served section 310 "pending" suspension into a "normal" suspension (although the principal could amend the student's record to reduce the length of the suspension). The principal would then issue a notice of the suspension to the parent in the usual manner, and should specify a period for filing an appeal. This process would accord the student the right to appeal the fact that he or she had been placed under suspension. Otherwise, there is a complete denial of that right.

Subject to the Act, the board may establish its own "powers and duties" in respect of holding the expulsion hearing. The Act has specific requirements in section 311.3, below.

Although the Act expressly gives the right of a party to make "submissions", there may be cases where submissions are inadequate for the purposes of making a determination. Parties should be provided with a reasonable opportunity to present evidence, including witnesses, where the evidence is relevant to the outstanding issues. Often the salient facts as to the student's role in the incident are not in dispute, and the real dispute is about the severity of the discipline. However, in some cases, the trustees will have to make a determination of credibility, and may have to hear from witnesses who have conflicting recollections of the events. There is discretion to admit hearsay evidence, including written witness statements and the trustees will have to determine the weight that should be given to such evidence. A tribunal has the discretion to impose reasonable limits on the time each party has to present its case.

Section 311.3 specifies that the parties to the hearing are:

1. The principal.
2. The pupil, if,
    i. the pupil is at least 18 years old, or
    ii. the pupil is 16 or 17 years old and has withdrawn from parental control.

3. The pupil's parent or guardian, unless,
   i. the pupil is at least 18 years old, or
   ii. the pupil is 16 or 17 years old and has withdrawn from parental control.
4. Such other persons as may be specified by board policy.

Even when not a party, the pupil has the right to be present at the hearing and to make a statement.

The board's mandate is to decide whether to expel or to suspend, or do neither:

i. If there is to be no expulsion, then the Board must decide whether to confirm the suspension, to confirm the suspension but shorten its duration, or to withdraw and expunge the suspension. There is no appeal from a Board-imposed suspension.

ii. If there is to be an expulsion, the Board must decide whether to expel the student from his or her school or all schools of the board. A decision to expel can be appealed to the Child and Family Services Review Board. A principal cannot appeal a decision of the trustees.

The Act contains requirements for notifying the pupil of the board's decision, of the school or alternative program to which the pupil is assigned, and of any applicable right of appeal (ss. 311.6 to 314).

In addition to the submissions, the evidence, and the response to the principal's report under section 311.1(7), the board must consider the mitigating and other factors in Ontario Regulation 472/07. It must therefore be provided with sufficient information about the pupil in order to do so.

The parties to an appeal to the Child and Family Services Review Board are:

1. The board.
2. The pupil, if
   i. the pupil is at least 18 years old, or
   ii. the pupil is 16 or 17 years old and has withdrawn from parental control.
3. The pupil's parent or guardian, if the parent or guardian appealed the decision.
4. The person who appealed the decision to expel the pupil, if the decision was appealed by a person other than the pupil or the pupil's parent or guardian.

The principal will only be permitted to be a party if the Child and Family Services Review Board gives him or her intervenor status.

The legislation does not address a situation in which the student is incarcerated either as a result of the act for which he or she is being disciplined or for something else. A student in detention is going to have difficulty attending his or her expulsion hearing, to say the least. The legislation provides a right to a quick determination of the disciplinary matter, but does not provide for situations in which the student cannot attend within the statutory timelines and does not wish to extend them. This forces the board to proceed in absentia where the student is an adult. This result is hardly satisfactory. Where the student is a minor, his or her parent or guardian is the "party" and will attend the proceeding, but the student is denied the right to be present and to participate.

One possible answer is to exclude the student on safety grounds under section 265(1)(m) and then impose the discipline when he or she is released from prison, at which time the statutory timelines will start running. However, this runs contrary to the need for the matter to be investigated and decided promptly. Moreover, the availability and reliability of witnesses could be jeopardized by any significant delay in the hearing.

1.3.3.6 Discipline of Pupils with Special Needs

As seen above, Ontario Regulation 472/07 makes it clear that a factor to be considered in imposing a suspension or expulsion is whether or not the pupil has an IEP. Consideration must take into account, "in the case of a pupil for whom an individual education plan has been developed,

i. whether the behaviour was a manifestation of a disability identified in the pupil's individual education plan,

ii. whether appropriate individualized accommodation has been provided, and

iii. whether the suspension or expulsion is likely to result in an aggravation or worsening of the pupil's behaviour or conduct."

These factors must be considered along with all the other applicable mitigating and other factors. The first two mitigating factors in Ontario Regulation 472/07 are primarily directed toward pupils with disabilities:

1. The pupil does not have the ability to control his or her behaviour.
2. The pupil does not have the ability to understand the foreseeable consequences of his or her behaviour.

The principal cannot possibly take into account these factors unless he or she is intimately familiar with the child's educational background. This requires a careful study of the IEP and IPRC decision (if any). (All pupils who have been "IPRC'd" will have an IEP, but not all pupils with an IEP will have undergone an IPRC identification and placement.) However, that is only the starting point. After becoming familiar with the educational background, the principal must determine if the behaviour was a manifestation of the child's disability. Did the behaviour arise as a direct result of the disability or was it substantially related or connected to the disability? This requires a certain degree of expertise, and the principal would be well-advised to consult with special education professionals. Along with considering the question of "manifestation", the principal must determine whether there has been "individualized accommodation" provided to the pupil and whether the suspension or expulsion is likely to result in an aggravation or worsening of the pupil's behaviour or conduct. All of these factors must be considered.

The need for individualized accommodation connects with the pupil's human rights. In short, every pupil has a right not to be discriminated against, and pupils with disabilities must be accommodated under the *Human Rights Code* with respect to the provision of educational services. The Ontario Human Rights Commission states:[7]

> Once a disability-related need has been identified, or where a *prima facie* case of discrimination has been established, education providers have a duty to accommodate the needs of students with disabilities in order to allow them to access educational services equally, unless to do so would cause undue hardship.
>
> There is no set formula for accommodation. Each student's needs are unique and must be considered afresh when an accommodation request is made. At all times, the emphasis must be on the individual student and not on the category of disability. Blanket approaches to accommodation that rely solely on categories, labels and generalizations are not acceptable.
>
> Although many accommodations will benefit large numbers of students with similar needs, it must be kept in mind that an accommodation solution that meets one student's requirements may not meet the needs of another. Two students with the same disability may have very different needs; for example, while some students with visual impairments read Braille, many do not. Different effects of a disability and different learning styles may call for different approaches.

It should be noted that, apart from the regulations, the *Education Act* allows a board to establish different policies for different circumstances, locations and classes of pupils. This enables boards to ensure that policies are sensitive to the requirements of exceptional pupils or others who for educational reasons should not be subject to a policy of general application.

Do all of these requirements mean that a pupil who has a disability or an IEP should never be disciplined? Not at all. However, they do call for cautious and careful analysis. If the purpose of discipline is to encourage pupils to become responsible members of society by teaching them that their behaviour is unacceptable, then it does not make sense to discipline a pupil upon whom that message will be lost by reason of the pupil's inability to control behaviour or understand its consequences. However, some pupils who have an IEP do understand that their behaviour is unacceptable. They know exactly what they are doing, and they are capable of making choices.

What happens if a pupil with special needs cannot be suspended or recommended for expulsion? How can the safety of the school be ensured? In appropriate circumstances, the pupil can be excluded by the principal under section 265(1)(m) of the Act. An exclusion of a pupil under section 265(1)(m) must be temporary. Its purpose is not only to ensure the safety and well being of other pupils in the school, but also to give the school and special education department time to develop a safety plan, to get proper staffing in place, to arrange transportation, or to explore programming options for the pupil.

In *Bonnah (Litigation Guardian of) v. Ottawa-Carleton District School Board* (2003), 170 O.A.C. 248, 64 O.R. (3d) 454, [2003] O.J. No. 1156, 2003 CarswellOnt 1210 (Ont. C.A.), the Ontario Court of Appeal held that, although a school board does not have the right to "administratively transfer" a pupil on the ground of

---

[7]The Commission provides a full analysis of the duty of accommodation on its website: "Principles of Accommodation", http://www.ohrc.on.ca/en/resources/Guides/AccessibleEducation?page=AccessibleEducation-PRINCIPL.html

safety issues pending the decision on appeal of an Identification Placement Review Committee decision about the student's placement, it may exclude an exceptional pupil from school for legitimate safety reasons. In this case, the pupil was an 11-year-old boy with learning disabilities. The principal of the pupil's school requested a review of the pupil's placement based, in part, on safety concerns, stemming from the student's disruptions in class, kicking and hitting the educational assistant, and increased physical aggression towards others including his teacher and his fellow students.

The pupil's parents disagreed with the placement that resulted from the IPRC review. The Court held that the board did not have the authority to transfer the pupil while the appeal of the placement decision was outstanding. Ontario Regulation 181/98, on Special Education, specifically provides for the existing placement to be stayed when a parent appeals. In keeping with this provision, the Court stated that the right to remain in the placement cannot be overridden by any implied power to transfer for safety reasons. The question then arose as to whether the board had the authority to *exclude* the pupil from school for safety reasons. The board argued that the principal's authority to exclude a pupil from the school is found in section 265 of the *Education Act* which outlines the duties of a principal, and in a regulation passed under section 305 of the Act which allows the Minister to make regulations governing access to school premises. Note that the relevant provisions of Ontario Regulation 474/00 have been repealed, so that pupils can no longer be "denied access" to school. They can still be excluded under section 265(1)(m).

The Court of Appeal confirmed that the purpose of section 265(1)(m) of the Act and [then] section 3(1) of Ontario Regulation 474/00 is to preserve school safety. These provisions are not concerned with the placement of students according to their educational needs. The Court held that, read together, section 265(1)(m) and section 3(1) of Ontario Regulation 474/00 authorized principals to refuse to allow persons into a school where the principal has determined that the presence of that person in the school would be detrimental to the safety of others in the school. The provisions allow principals to act quickly where the conduct of a person puts the safety of those under the charge of the principal at risk. A principal can properly exercise powers where the safety concerns are genuine and the principal's response to those concerns is reasonable in all of the circumstances.

1.3.3.7 Investigating Incidents at Schools

Principals are educators, not detectives. One of the most challenging aspects of school discipline is the "investigation". From a legal perspective, this is the area where the principal is most likely to make a mistake that could result either in an unfair conclusion or in an inability to substantiate one's conclusion even if it is correct.

The principal has a duty to investigate any serious infraction of the school rules. Not every minor infraction has to be investigated and not every investigation will result in a reliable finding. Principals make "judgment calls" about student behaviour every day, and in doing so, they assess how to respond. Many minor infractions can be handled without formal discipline. Principals develop a sense of what disciplinary measure is appropriate for a particular student under the circumstances.

There are, moreover, some situations in which the principal will simply be unable to determine what happened, who is guilty, or who is telling the truth. Competing versions of events from two students, where neither can produce a witness or corroborating evidence, leaves the principal on tenuous ground in trying to form a belief as to who may be the guilty party. Principals should not jump to conclusions under pressure to resolve a case. If a competent investigation fails to lead anywhere, then the principal cannot simply "guess". The police face the same problem, and they have far more tools and training than school administrators.

(a) Who Should Do the Investigation?

The principal is ultimately responsible for the investigation. The investigation should be conducted by the principal or the vice-principal (if any). The principal or vice-principal will appear at a suspension appeal or expulsion hearing, and should therefore be able to provide information about how the facts were ascertained. However, to a limited extent, it is possible to delegate certain parts of the investigation. For instance, a caretaker could be asked to take photographs of the schoolyard. A guidance counsellor or social worker could be asked to speak with a witness on behalf of the principal where the witness only feels comfortable speaking with that particular staff person.

If the principal is personally involved in the incident (e.g. was assaulted by a student) then the school superintendent should conduct the investigation (or delegate it to a vice-principal) and should make the decisions flowing from the investigation.

(b) Characteristics of a Competent Investigation

- pursue each credible lead
- take detailed notes of all contacts with witnesses, police, staff, etc.
- gather and secure physical evidence (unless police take possession). Do not store guns or drugs.
- use photographs and diagrams (e.g. photographs of the premises or of a student's injuries)
- interview the victim and the alleged perpetrator(s)
- interview witnesses and anyone else who could have relevant information (students, parents, staff, visitors). Witnesses must be interviewed separately and in a space that provides privacy. If a person refuses to speak with you or did not respond to your reasonable attempts to contact them, this should be noted.
- ask each witness for a signed and dated statement, or write down what that witness had to say and have the witness confirm through a signature or initials that you have recorded the information correctly.

(c) Characteristics of a Competent Interview

- the interviewer is impartial, objective, non-judgmental
- provide appropriate resources, supports or an interpreter for a student being interviewed, depending on whether the student has a behavioural, physical or learning disability

- avoid leading questions — ones that suggest the answer you are seeking
- clarify whether the witness is speaking from first-hand knowledge or from something he or she was told by someone else (hearsay)
- Ask questions about:
  - name, address, phone number, age, school, grade, place of employment of the person, as appropriate
  - date, time and location of incident(s)
  - what did you see or hear? — what "happened"?
  - names and contact information or description of other persons directly involved
  - names and contact information or description of possible witnesses
  - whether the witness previously informed school staff or anyone else about the incident, including who, when, where, and the response, if any
- when interviewing a student who may have engaged in a prohibited activity, the principal should inform the student about the allegations and provide the student with an opportunity to respond. In some cases, the student will have been charged by police, and may not wish to be interviewed or may wish to bring a lawyer to the interview.

Note: A principal cannot promise a witness that the information provided to the administrator will be kept confidential under any and all circumstances. If the principal is called to testify about the investigation, he or she can be required to disclose the source of the information.

(d) Writing a Report

After the investigation, the principal should write down a summary of the findings.

The report should commence by describing why the report was being written — lay the groundwork.

- Set out the events in chronological order.
- Be objective; stick to the facts.
- Summarize the information provided by witnesses.
- If evidence is conflicting, state which evidence is considered to be more reliable, and why.

First-hand evidence is usually more reliable than hearsay evidence but this does not mean that hearsay evidence is automatically irrelevant. The trustees may hear and even rely on hearsay evidence if they consider it to have sufficient weight.

Sample Report

> On November 3, 2010, a student was attacked with a knife after school assembly, and required medical treatment. This report is about my investigation into the incident.
>
> The victim, J. Griswald, is a 15-year-old male, Grade 10 student at Wilberforce High.
>
> At approximately 3:00 p.m., just prior to the scheduled all-school assembly, J. Griswald got into a verbal altercation with another student, S. Brown.

Brown is 16 years old, female, in Grade 11 at Wilberforce High.

At 4:00 p.m. the assembly ended and the students were dismissed.

At about 4:15 p.m., Griswald and Brown got into a shouting match on the front steps of the school.

About 15 other students were present. Three witnesses were directly proximate to the incident, and they were interviewed separately from each other.

The three witnesses all report seeing Brown pull a knife from her backpack and stab Griswald in the right arm.

First aid was administered by Ms. Jones, the office administrator.

An ambulance and police responded to the scene, and parents were notified.

The injured student was also interviewed. His version is consistent with that of the three witnesses.

S. Brown refused to make a statement on the advice of her lawyer.

The evidence of the three witnesses was reasonably consistent. As indicated in the attached witness statements, one witness (A. B.) was unclear whether Griswald may have made threatening motions toward Brown prior to the stabbing. The other two witnesses did not report any physically threatening or provocative actions on the part of Griswald, although Griswald and Brown were yelling at each other. None of the three witnesses reported any close friendship or personal ties with Brown or Griswald that might have influenced what they recounted. They all had a good view of the incident, which took place in daylight.

My conclusion is that although the two students were yelling at each other, there was no provocation by Griswald leading up to the incident. Griswald did admit that there was "no love lost" between Brown and him. He had dated Brown for about a year, but they had broken up a few days prior to the incident. I draw no inference from Brown's refusal to provide a statement. However, I must make conclusions based on the relevant information gathered in my investigation. On a balance of probabilities, I conclude that Brown was in possession of a knife in her backpack and she used that knife to stab Griswald on school premises shortly after dismissal from school assembly. A photograph of the knife is attached, along with a photograph of Griswald's bandaged arm.

Both students do well in school; there is no IEP or IPRC for either.

Neither student has a record of prior discipline.

There is no evidence to suggest that race or other factors under Regulation 427/07 played any part in the incident.

Griswald was released from hospital with 15 stitches to his right upper arm.

(e) Police Involvement

An incident that may lead to a suspension or expulsion is often sufficiently serious that it will also involve the police. Sometimes the principal will call the police, but it may also be the victim, a parent or someone else who makes the call even before the school can do so.

The principal must contact the police if:

- required by Police/Board Protocol,
- required by Board or Ministry of Education policy, or
- requested by student or parent.

All activity by students at school or on a school-related activity should be reported to police if it may involve criminal conduct, including assault, sexual assault, robbery, extortion, gang-related activities, illicit drugs, use or possession of weapons, etc. Police may also be called where there are instances of vandalism, theft, trespass, or to assist victims of crime. When in doubt, make the call.

Whether or not charges are laid by the police, the principal is still responsible for conducting an investigation independent of the police and taking appropriate disciplinary action under the Act.

When the police have been contacted, the principal should stop his or her own investigation of the incident until either the police investigation is complete or the principal's investigation will not interfere with the police investigation.

As mentioned below, while the police investigation is ongoing, it may be necessary to exclude the student who is suspected of the prohibited activity, on safety grounds, under section 265(1)(m) of the Act.

The principal will normally speak with the officer who was called to the scene of the incident in order to find out what the officer has discovered or concluded.

However, the criminal process is separate from the suspension/expulsion process under the Act. The principal or vice-principal must conduct an independent investigation, and should not rely solely on the conclusions drawn by the police, or the fact that the police have charged a student with a criminal offence.

The Police/Board Protocol, which is required by the provincial government, will normally require the police to make every effort to minimize disruption to school routines and to conduct the interviews of students and staff in an appropriate and private setting.

The principal should be prepared, upon request, to provide a copy of all notes to the police. The *Municipal Freedom of Information and Protection of Privacy Act* expressly permits a school board to disclose confidential information to the police to aid in an investigation undertaken with a view to a law enforcement proceeding or from which a law enforcement proceeding is likely to result.

In general, the principal may also provide the police with other information about a student including contact information and yearbook photographs. Information which is only found in the Ontario Student Record should not be provided to the police without a warrant or without the required consent from the parent or adult pupil.

Unless instructed otherwise by the police, the parent, guardian or adult contact person should be called as soon as the police indicate that they wish to interview a student. Indeed, the Police/Board Protocol will likely outline circumstances in which the parent should be called after an incident even before the police are notified.

1.3.4 School Safety — Other Aspects

As noted above, it is not uncommon to find the expression "safe schools" used to refer to student discipline. However, student discipline is only a small part of keeping schools safe. School safety is about many things, including hall and yard supervision, fire drills, worker safety, lockdowns, community relations, anti-bullying programs, safety hotlines, police protocols, and intercepting intruders. Some of these topics are covered below.

1.3.4.1 Visitors

Schools are private property. The *Education Act* gives certain persons the right to "visit" schools. In other words, there is recognition that these persons have some legitimate "business" being in the school. These persons have no right to disrupt or interrupt the classrooms or the school administration or to wander through halls. They are visitors.

According to the *Education Act*, a parent or guardian may visit the school that his or her child is attending and a member of the board may attend a school that is operated by the board. A member of the Assembly (i.e. Ontario Legislature) may visit a school in the member's constituency. A member of the clergy may visit a public school in the area where the member has pastoral charge. A member of the clergy of the Roman Catholic Church may visit a Roman Catholic school in the area where the member has pastoral charge. These provisions are in section 50 (public) and section 53 (Roman Catholic) of the Act.

1.3.4.2 Trespassers and Troublemakers

There are three options for dealing with people who should not be on the school premises, depending on the circumstances. This assumes that they will not voluntarily leave or stay away from the premises. Depending on the circumstances, they may be:

- excluded under section 265(1)(m) of the *Education Act*
- denied access under the *Education Act*
- "trespassed" under the *Trespass to Property Act*.

(a) Exclusion From a Classroom or School

Subject to an appeal to the school board, a principal has the duty to refuse to admit to the school or classroom a person whose presence in the school or classroom would in the principal's judgment be detrimental to the physical or mental well-being of the pupils (*Education Act*, s. 265(1)(m)). It is an offence to willfully interrupt or disquiet the proceedings of a school or class. There is a maximum fine of $200 upon conviction (s. 212(1)).

A "refusal to admit" under section 265 is commonly referred to as an "exclusion". There is no restriction on who can be excluded. It could apply to a parent or a complete stranger. An exclusion can also be applied against a student of the school. An exclusion is based on a judgment that the person's presence is a detriment to the safety or well-being of *pupils*. An exclusion is not a disciplinary measure. It is a temporary measure used to ensure the safety and well-being of pupils, not to discipline or punish a student.

In appropriate circumstances, exclusions can be used to exclude a student of the school while the police are investigating an incident and before the principal has had an opportunity to investigate. A student who is a danger to other students can be excluded pending completion of a safety plan for the student. The Act does not require an exclusion to be in writing. However, a student of the school, who would otherwise have the right to attend classes, should always be informed in writing if he or she is being excluded under the Act; a verbal exclusion must be immediately followed up by a letter. However, even when you are excluding a complete stranger, you should endeavour to follow up a verbal exclusion ("I am ordering you out of the school") with a letter informing the person (if name and address are known) that he or she is excluded and briefly explaining why and for how long. If a stranger is ordered off the property under section 265, his or her name and address may not be obtainable. Any letter of exclusion should mention the right to appeal the exclusion.

An excluded person may appeal the exclusion to the board. Unlike suspension appeals and expulsions, there is no power of the board to delegate its consideration of the appeal to a committee for a final decision.

(b) Denial of Access

The *Education Act* provides another tool for keeping unwanted persons out of schools or for restricting the purposes for which they are permitted to enter or remain on the premises. Section 305 permits the Minister of Education to make regulations governing access to school premises, specifying classes of persons who are permitted to be on school premises, and specifying the days and times at which different classes of persons are prohibited from being on school premises.

Subsection 305(2) prescribes a blanket prohibition against any person entering or remaining on school premises unless authorized to be there under the regulation. Moreover, a board may, by policy, prohibit any person from entering or remaining on school premises:

> 305. (2) No person shall enter or remain on school premises unless he or she is authorized by regulation to be there on that day or at that time.
>
> (3) A person shall not enter or remain on school premises if he or she is prohibited under a board policy from being there on that day or at that time.
>
> (4) The principal of a school may direct a person to leave the school premises if he or she believes that the person is prohibited by regulation or under a board policy from being there.

It is an offence to contravene a prohibition in the regulation.

As mentioned above, school property is private property. The starting point in section 305 is that persons may not be on school premises and must find something in the regulation that lets them enter or remain there. The law then permits a school board to prohibit persons from being on school premises.

According to Ontario Regulation 474/00, the following persons are permitted to be on school premises on any day and at any time:

- a person enrolled as a pupil in the school
- a parent or guardian of such a pupil
- a person employed or retained by the board
- a person who is otherwise on the premises for a lawful purpose.

The first three of the above items are logical. The fourth item permits persons on the school premises if they are there for a lawful purpose. "Lawful purpose" is not defined.

The school board can devise a policy to place limits on the access that will be permitted to any of the four classes of persons listed above. The prohibition can be a blanket prohibition covering all days and times, or it may define the day and time during which it applies. It could, for example, permit members of the general public to have access to the schoolyard during the evenings and weekends, but prohibit access during school hours.

Ontario Regulation 474/00 also states that a person is not permitted to remain on school premises if his or her presence is detrimental to the safety or well-being of a person on the premises, in the judgment of the principal, a vice-principal, or another person authorized by the board to make such a determination (s. 3(1)). Ontario Regulation 474/00 is broader than the section 265(1)(m) exclusion clause, in that it refers to protecting the safety or well-being of *persons*, not exclusively pupils. It gives the principal, vice-principal, and other authorized person the power to exclude others from the school, whereas section 265(1)(m) is a "duty" of a principal. In addition, there is no right of appeal to the school board under the regulation, whereas there is under section 265(1)(m).

Section 3 of Ontario Regulation 474/00 states:

> 3. (1) A person is not permitted to remain on school premises if his or her presence is detrimental to the safety or well-being of a person on the premises, in the judgment of the principal, a vice-principal or another person authorized by the board to make such a determination.
>
> (2) A person is not permitted to remain on school premises if a policy of the board requires the person to report his or her presence on the premises in a specified manner and the person fails to do so.
>
> (3) Subsections (1) and (2) do not apply to a pupil enrolled in the school or to a pupil attending a program for suspended or expelled pupils that is located on the school premises.

As seen from section 3 above, a person is not permitted to remain on school premises if a policy of the board requires the person to report his or her presence on the premises in a specified manner and the person fails to do so. Therefore, for example, if a person fails to report to the school office upon entering the school, where there is a policy that requires reporting by visitors, the principal has the authority to ask the person to leave.

(c) Trespass to Property

The *Trespass to Property Act* says that a school board has the rights and duties of an occupier in respect of its school sites. A "school site" means "land or premises or an interest in land or premises required by a board for a school, school playground, school garden, teacher's residence, caretaker's residence, gymnasium, offices, parking areas or for any other school purpose" (*Education Act*, s. 1).

Under the *Trespass to Property Act* the offence of trespassing consists of any of the following, where the person is not acting under a right or authority conferred by law:

(a) Entering premises when entry is prohibited. Entry may be prohibited by means of notice to that effect. The Act also presumes that entry is prohibited in some circumstances without notice (e.g. property enclosed in a manner that indicates the occupier's intention to keep persons off the premises).

(b) Engaging in an activity on premises when the activity is prohibited. An occupier may give notice as to the restricted or prohibited activities on the premises (e.g. no hardball; no skateboarding; no swimming).

(c) Failing to leave the premises immediately after being directed to do so by the occupier of the premises or a person authorized by the occupier.

Notice under the *Trespass to Property Act* may be given orally, in writing, by means of signs, or by means of a marking system.

A police officer, or the occupier, or a person authorized by the occupier, may arrest without warrant any person he or she believes on reasonable and probable grounds to be trespassing in contravention of the Act. If the person making the arrest is not a police officer, he or she must promptly call for a police officer and deliver the person arrested to the police officer. If the suspected trespasser is off the premises, only a police officer may make an arrest under the Act. A person placed under arrest has certain rights under the *Canadian Charter of Rights and Freedoms*, including the right not to be arbitrarily arrested or imprisoned, the right to retain and instruct counsel, and the right to be informed of the reason for arrest. Infringement of these rights may result in the arrested person being acquitted at trial.

The *Trespass to Property Act* gives an occupier the right to obtain a judgment for up to $1,000 in damages against a convicted trespasser. Where granted, such a judgment extinguishes the right to seek damages in a civil lawsuit arising out of the same facts.

It should be kept in mind that the *Trespass to Property Act* gives rights to occupiers of lands or premises to keep people off their property. Unlike the "denial of access" provisions, the trespass provisions are not specifically designed for school boards, but "trespass" can be used to deny entry to strangers, students enrolled at *other* schools, former students, and even parents, whose presence on the school is considered undesirable. Even skateboarding can be cause for trespass, whereas it would not fall within the denial of access provisions because it does not affect the safety or well-being of persons in the school. A person may be trespassed from all or some of the board's premises — such a blanket trespass should be issued by an executive officer, not a school principal. It is important to keep in mind that a *student* who is enrolled in a school must not be trespassed from it during school hours or school activities, unless the trespass prohibition only applies to a period during which the student is suspended or expelled from the school and therefore has no business being there.

It is common practice to issue "trespass letters" rather than relying on oral notice to the trespasser. If a person is provided with a trespass letter, the police are more likely to be satisfied that there are grounds to step in and help the school. A letter makes it more difficult for the recipient to argue that he or she did not know of the trespass notice. Trespass letters should be copied to the local police force. The trespass letter should state the reasons for the trespass notice. It should invite the recipient (particularly if a parent) to contact the principal if he or she wishes to resolve the matter.

Issue a warning first: if possible, it is advisable (especially in respect of a disruptive parent) to warn the person in writing that they could be trespassed under the *Trespass to Property Act* or denied access under the *Education Act*, or both. A warning often suffices.

(d) Searching Lockers and Personal Belongings

The *Canadian Charter of Rights and Freedoms* (s. 8) states that "Everyone has the right to be secure against unreasonable search or seizure".

The Ontario Court of Appeal, in *R. v. G. (J.M.)* (1986), 25 C.R.R. 366, 33 D.L.R. (4th) 277, 29 C.C.C. (3d) 455, 54 C.R. (3d) 380, 56 O.R. (2d) 705, 1986 CarswellOnt 138, 17 O.A.C. 107 (Ont. C.A.); leave to appeal refused (1987), 21 O.A.C. 239n, 59 O.R. (2d) 286n, 76 N.R. 78n, 28 C.R.R. 206n, 33 D.L.R. (4th) 277n, 29 C.C.C. (3d) 455n, 54 C.R. (3d) 380n (S.C.C.), stated that a principal may search a student in carrying out the duty to maintain order and discipline in the school.

In this case, after receiving a report that a student was seen with drugs, and after inviting him to the office, the school principal removed some tinfoil from the student's pant cuff; it was later discovered to contain marijuana. A search must not be conducted for arbitrary reasons: there must be reasonable grounds. The Court will ask whether the search was reasonably justified at its inception, and whether the scope of the search was reasonable in view of the objectives of the search. Was the search excessively intrusive in light of the age and sex of the student and the nature of the infraction?

The Court of Appeal in *G. (J.M.)* spoke strongly in support of the power and duty of the school principal to maintain discipline. It noted that the principal in fact has a duty to carry out his or her own investigation until he or she knows the nature and extent of the suspected offence: "It is often neither feasible nor desirable that the principal should require prior authority before searching his or her student and seizing contraband." When it becomes apparent that an offence may have been committed, the police should be notified. The requirement that a search must be conducted on reasonable grounds also applies to students' purses and knapsacks.

In *R. v. M. (M.R.)*, 129 C.C.C. (3d) 361, 20 C.R. (5th) 197, 166 D.L.R. (4th) 261, 233 N.R. 1, [1998] S.C.J. No. 83, 5 B.H.R.C. 474, 57 C.R.R. (2d) 189, 1998 CarswellNS 347, [1998] 3 S.C.R. 393, 519 A.P.R. 125, 171 N.S.R. (2d) 125, 1998 CarswellNS 346 (S.C.C.), on appeal from the Court of Appeal for Nova Scotia, the Supreme Court of Canada dealt with the issue of searching students, again involving drugs. In this case, the accused junior high school student was suspected of drug dealing. He was searched by the vice-principal. A bag of marijuana was found in one of the student's socks. A plain-clothed RCMP officer was present during the search but said and did nothing during the search. The trial judge had found that the vice-principal had been acting as an agent of the police, that the search violated the student's rights under the Charter, and that the evidence should therefore be excluded at trial. The Court of Appeal allowed the Crown's appeal and the student took the issue to the Supreme Court of Canada.

The Supreme Court of Canada (Major J. dissenting) found that there was no violation of the accused's rights. The Court said:

> A student's reasonable expectation of privacy is diminished at school because the student knows that teachers and school authorities are responsible for providing a

> safe school environment and maintaining order and discipline in the school. Students know that this responsibility may require searches of students and their personal effects, and the seizure of prohibited items. To require a search warrant would be impractical and unworkable in a school environment. Teachers and principals must be able to react quickly. They must have the power to search students.

A search may be conducted if there are reasonable grounds to believe that a school rule has been or is being violated and that evidence will be found in the location or on the person of the student searched. All the circumstances surrounding a search must be taken into account in determining if the search was reasonable. Reasonable grounds for a search can be based on information received from a credible student, information from more than one student, the teacher's own observations, or any combination of these, all taken in the context of the circumstances existing at the school. The permissible extent of the search depends on the gravity of the suspected infraction. The search itself must be carried out in a sensitive and minimally intrusive manner. On the facts of this case, the vice-principal was not acting as an agent of the police. The officer was at all times completely passive (until the evidence was handed over to him and an arrest was made).

The Court also found that the student has not been "detained" (in the school's office) within the meaning of section 10(b) of the *Charter*. It also clarified that its ruling only applies to elementary and secondary school pupils, and that no consideration was given to searches made in a post-secondary setting.

It is sometimes necessary to search a student's locker. When this need arises, an issue can arise as to who "owns" the property that is to be searched. It is recommended that students be informed that their lockers are school property and could be searched by school staff at any time. The school should have a record of each student's locker and the combination for each student's lock. If feasible, the student should be present at the locker during the search, along with a staff member as a witness. This will help to avoid allegations that school staff planted something in the locker, and will help establish in court the "continuity of possession" of the locker contents. It should be noted that, once the police are involved, they are governed by all the rules and laws that govern search and seizure by police. They are not clothed by the principal's statutory authority in respect of student discipline.

In *R. v. D. (R.M.)*, [2008] N.S.J. No. 374, 2008 CarswellNS 473, 2008 NSPC 52 (N.S. Prov. Ct.), the Nova Scotia Youth Justice Court applied the law in *R. v. M. (M.R.).* when, after reviewing the circumstances of a principal's search of a student's belongings, it found:

> 31. I am satisfied, on the whole of the evidence before me on the *voir dire*, that the Principal of the school based her decision to search the Applicant upon the following factors:
>
> > (a) Within two minutes of the end of an assembly in the school gym, the Principal received complaints from between three and five senior students (students whom she trusted and whom had exhibited leadership qualities in the past). Those students reported that some of their property was missing.
> >
> > (b) The same students reported that the accused had been seen in the area of their backpacks, located immediately outside the gym in which the assembly was being conducted, shortly prior to their discoveries of missing items.

(c) As the Principal exited the gym, a teacher confirmed that the Applicant had been in the area of the backpacks while the assembly was being conducted. The same teacher mentioned that the Applicant had not been in attendance at school that day.

(d) School was ending for the day and whatever action the Principal might decide to take concerning the possible theft of students' property was time sensitive and needed to be taken before the student population would disperse.

I am also satisfied that the search, when conducted, resulted in the Principal locating a drug pipe in the coat of and marijuana in the backpack of the Applicant.

34. It is entirely clear from the evidence before this court that the Principal was not acting on mere suspicion; rather, she had information from multiple sources she considered credible and trustworthy, including eyewitness evidence of the accused being in the vicinity from which the items had gone missing during the very narrow time frame in which the assembly was in session, and on that basis, she formulated reasonable grounds that the accused could be in possession of stolen property. I am satisfied on the evidence before me that the Principal acted swiftly and decisively, but not carelessly or recklessly, and made a decision which was time sensitive, to avoid having any potential culprits disperse from the school. It is to be emphasized that the Principal did not ultimately have to be correct or accurate about her reasonable grounds; it is the formation of her grounds that is subject to the scrutiny of this court, and not the outcome or results emanating from their formation.

35. It strikes this Court as impractical for the Applicant to suggest that a reasonable alternative to the decision to search the accused would, under the existing circumstances, have been for the Principal to "lock down" the entire building and prevent the egress of any student until the entire school could be searched with a view to locating the missing property of the complainants. Given Principal M.'s evidence that the school serves approximately 400 students, it would, in my view, be most impractical for the Principal to have reached such a decision to try to prevent the exit of 400 students from the building, particularly given that the assembly had been an emotionally charged event related to its purpose in marking the tragic death of seven high school basketball players from New Brunswick. Surely the cumulative effect of all of the information the Principal had before her, which needed to be acted on swiftly, could easily eliminate the practicality of a decision to detain the entire student body. Were the situation such that there was nothing more or less to connect the Applicant to the area where the items went missing any more than any other student, then such a decision to detain everyone, while still highly impractical, might have been the only one able to be logically reached. However, the Principal was possessed of very specific information from more than one source, which she considered reliable, all of which reasonably pointed to the real potential that the Applicant and his companion were involved.

36. There is no doubt, as asserted by the Applicant, that the decision to search him was ultimately based upon a series of "circumstantial observations" of other students and teachers, as opposed to any direct observation of him by the Principal or, in the alternative, any direct observation by anyone that the Applicant had been going through students' belongings. However, it is to be remembered that the circumstances of that day were not that there were many students in the hallway area in the vicinity of the book bags from which the items were discovered missing within a short time following the end of the assembly; rather, the evidence was that all of the school population was inside the gym in an assembly and certain students and a teacher had noted only the Applicant and another male student outside the gym in the area of students' book bags during that time. In my view, there was nothing

> random about the Principal's identification of R.M.D. as possibly being involved in the fact that there were items missing.
>
> 39. The evidence clearly establishes that Ms. M. approached the Applicant in the hall and asked him to accompany her to her office. The evidence further establishes that once at the office, the Applicant was separated from the other party and placed in an office by himself. Both the Applicant and the Principal are at one in their evidence that the reason for the Applicant's presence in the office, the concern of the Principal, and the indication that the Applicant would be searched were all clearly explained to him. The evidence of the Applicant makes it clear that he believed he had no choice but to submit to such a search, although the whole of the evidence of both the Applicant and the Principal supports that the search was conducted in a dignified fashion, in private, and no physical contact was ever made by the Principal or the Vice Principal with the Applicant. There is nothing about the evidence that suggests the search was conducted in anything but a professional, calm and measured manner by the school authorities, and likewise that the Applicant responded in a calm fashion.

In *R. v. M. (A.)*, [2008] S.C.J. No. 19, 2008 CarswellOnt 2257, 2008 CarswellOnt 2258, 55 C.R. (6th) 314, 236 O.A.C. 267, 293 D.L.R. (4th) 187, 2008 SCC 19, 230 C.C.C. (3d) 377, 92 O.R. (3d) 398 (note), 373 N.R. 198, [2008] 1 S.C.R. 569 (S.C.C.), the Supreme Court of Canada deals with the use of "sniffer dogs" in schools. The principal of St. Patrick's High School, in Sarnia, had issued a standing invitation to the Sarnia police to bring sniffer dogs to the school whenever convenient to the police. The accused young person argued that sniffer dogs may only be used where the police have reasonable grounds to believe a drug offence has been committed by the individual who is the subject of the search and that a search will lead to discovery of evidence or, perhaps, to the apprehension of the perpetrator. A central issue was whether or not the use of sniffer dogs constitutes a "search" under section 8 of the *Canadian Charter of Rights*. The trial court held that neither the police nor the school authorities had anything more than a "hunch" to suspect the presence of drugs in the school at the relevant time of the search and thus excluded evidence from the dog sniff and the subsequent search by the police of the student's backpack.

The members of the Supreme Court of Canada did not take a uniform approach but the majority found that the search of the backpack violated the student's *Charter* rights. The key points in the Court's analysis are summarized from the decision in abbreviated form below:

- While the dog sniff constituted a search, it is a search of a minimally intrusive and tightly targeted type that did not require prior judicial authorization (via a search warrant).
- In the context of a routine criminal investigation, the police are entitled to use sniffer dogs based on a "reasonable suspicion". If there are no grounds of reasonable suspicion, the use of the sniffer dogs will violate the reasonableness standard required by section 8.
- Where there are grounds of reasonable suspicion, the police should not obtain prior judicial authorization to use the dogs in an area where the police are already lawfully present. All "searches" do not have the same invasive and disruptive quality.

- If the sniff is conducted on the basis of reasonable suspicion and discloses the presence of illegal drugs on the person or in a backpack or other place of concealment, the police may confirm the accuracy of that information with a physical search. All such searches by the dogs or the police are subject to after-the-fact judicial review if it is alleged that no grounds of reasonable suspicion existed, or that the search was otherwise carried out in an unreasonable manner.
- This case involved a random speculative search. The *Charter* weighs other values, including privacy, against police efficiency. A hunch is not enough to warrant a search of citizens or their belongings by police dogs.
- Students are no less deserving of constitutional protection than adults, although their age, vulnerability and presence in a school environment, all factor into the "totality of the circumstances".
- If the police had been called to investigate the potential presence of guns or explosives at the school using dogs trained for that purpose, the public interest in dealing quickly and efficiently with such a threat to public safety, even if speculative, would have been greater and more urgent than routine crime prevention. Generally speaking, the legal balance would have come down on the side of the use of sniffer dogs to get to the bottom of a possible threat to the lives or immediate safety and well-being of the students and staff.
- The Court must consider the significance of the information obtained as a result of the police intervention.
- In *R. v. M. (M.R.)*, 129 C.C.C. (3d) 361, 20 C.R. (5th) 197, 166 D.L.R. (4th) 261, 233 N.R. 1, [1998] S.C.J. No. 83, 5 B.H.R.C. 474, 57 C.R.R. (2d) 189, 1998 CarswellNS 347, [1998] 3 S.C.R. 393, 519 A.P.R. 125, 171 N.S.R. (2d) 125, 1998 CarswellNS 346 (S.C.C.), the issue was the constitutionality of the body search of a student for drugs at a school dance by the vice-principal. The Court specifically held that if the *body search* had been conducted by the police, or the school authorities acting as agents of the police, reasonable and probable grounds of belief would have been required. However, reasonable suspicion was sufficient for school authorities. The teaching of *M. (M.R.)* is that in matters of school discipline, a broad measure of discretion and flexibility (para. 49) will be afforded the school authorities, but when police are conducting a body search, even on school premises, the ordinary standard of justification applicable to police will be required.
- Significantly greater latitude must be given to school authorities in the discharge of their responsibilities than to the police. If evidence sufficient to ground a prosecution should come to light in the course of a school investigation, the evidence no doubt will be passed on to the regular prosecutorial authorities if the school authorities think it appropriate to do so.
- Canadian courts have accepted that section 8 protects "people, not places". People do not shed their reasonable expectations of privacy in their person or in the concealed possessions they carry when they leave home, although those expectations may have to be modified depending on where they go, and what "place" they find themselves in.

- The backpacks from which the odour emanated here belonged to various members of the student body including the accused. As with briefcases, purses and suitcases, backpacks are the repository of much that is personal, particularly for people who lead itinerant lifestyles during the day as in the case of students and travellers. No doubt ordinary businessmen and businesswomen riding along on public transit or going up and down on elevators in office towers would be outraged at any suggestion that the contents of their briefcases could randomly be inspected by the police without "reasonable suspicion" of illegality. Because of their role in the lives of students, backpacks *objectively* command a measure of privacy.
- While teenagers may have little expectation of privacy from the searching eyes and fingers of their parents, ... they expect the contents of their backpacks not to be open to the random and speculative scrutiny of the police.

1.4 Reporting Child Abuse

1.4.1 The Duty to Report Child Abuse

The legal responsibility to report child abuse is found in the *Child and Family Services Act* (*CFSA*).

The duty applies to "a person", that is, to everyone. However, only certain persons are subject to prosecution under the *CFSA* for failing to report. Teachers, principals and other school professionals such as social workers are among those professionals who may be found guilty of an offence if:

(1) they fail to report a suspicion, and

(2) the information upon which the suspicion was based was obtained in the course of their professional or official duties.

For the purposes of reporting abuse under the *CFSA*, a "child" does not include a child who is actually or apparently 16 years of age or older (unless the child is already the subject of an order under Part III of the Act). (Violence against children 16 or older should be reported to the police.)

The duty to report child abuse is provided in section 72 of the *CFSA*, reproduced below. The duty arises if a person "has reasonable grounds to suspect" anything described in paragraphs 1 to 13 of subsection 72(1).

A report of abuse must be made directly to a "Society", i.e. Children's Aid Society or Catholic Children's Aid Society, Jewish Child and Family Services or Native Child and Family Services.

The duty to report is upon the person who has the suspicion of abuse. The legislation specifically states that the person cannot rely upon any other person to make the report on his or her behalf (s. 72(3)). Reporting abuse to a school administrator is not good enough.

The duty to report is ongoing. If the Society does not respond, or if there are reasonable grounds to suspect that the abuse is continuing, then the person must continue to report his or her suspicion.

Having reasonable grounds to "suspect" is a low threshold. A suspicion can be based on third-party reports, hearsay or overheard conversations.[8] It does not require having a reasonable "belief". It is important that school personnel must not engage in an investigation of possible abuse. Such an investigation must be left to the police or a children's aid society. You do not have to satisfy yourself that what you have heard or seen might be "abuse". Simply report your suspicion. Any effort on your part to investigate may jeopardize the successful prosecution of persons who may be guilty of child abuse.

It is important to note that no action for making a report can be instituted against a person who acts under section 72 unless the person acts maliciously or without reasonable grounds for the suspicion.

The duty to report child abuse does not apply to student-on-student assault, such as fights in the schoolyard. Most of the "abuse" provisions pertain to the conduct or neglect of the person "having charge of the child". However, section 72(1)3 and 4 are drafted more broadly.

> 72. (1)
>
> 3. The child has been sexually molested or sexually exploited, *by the person* having charge of the child or by *another person* where the person having charge of the child knows or should know of the possibility of sexual molestation or sexual exploitation and fails to protect the child. (emphasis added)
>
> 4. There is a risk that the child is likely to be sexually molested or sexually exploited as described in paragraph 3.

This paragraph says that you have to report suspected sexual molestation or sexual exploitation by the person having charge of the child (e.g. parent, guardian, teacher, camp counsellor) and also where you suspect that the person having charge of the child, although not the abusive party, is permitting the sexual molestation or exploitation to occur (e.g. by a sibling, friend or classmate of the victim). This does not mean that every instance of sexual molestation or exploitation between students at school must be reported to a children's aid society. However, if for example, a teacher suspects that a student is being sexually molested or sexually exploited by another student and that the person in charge of the allegedly abusive student (e.g. a classroom teacher) is permitting the abuse to occur or continue, then section 72(1)3 arguably gives rise to a duty to report. The lack of clarity about the exact scope of this provision means that, "when in doubt" it is safer to make a report to a children's aid society than to face the possible legal consequences of failing to do so. Board policy should impose a completely separate and distinct duty to report the sexual molestation or exploitation to the police.

Student-on-student violence should never be covered up or ignored. This is recognized in the Ministry of Education's "Safe Schools Action Team" report on Gender-based Violence, Homophobia, Sexual Harassment and Inappropriate Sexual

---

[8]G. Bowers et al., *Sexual Misconduct in Education: Prevention, Reporting and Discipline*, 2d ed. (Markham: Butterworths, 2006), p. 87.

Behaviour in Schools"[9] released December 11, 2008, some of which will find its way into legislative change. (See Bill 57, *Education Amendment Act*, (Keeping Our Kids Safe at School), 2009, which requires a principal to report to parents/guardians when their child is harmed at school as a result of a prohibited activity.) Among the recommendations:

General

- School staff must continue to respond to a child who is or may be in need of protection as required by the *Child and Family Services Act* (CFSA).
- Principals must report serious incidents that occur in school or at school-related activities to police as outlined in Policy/Program Memorandum 120 and in the Provincial Model for a Local Police/School Board Protocol (see Appendix D). The details of reporting serious incidents involving children under twelve are found in Policy/Program Memorandum 120.
- All school staff must report to the principal:
  - any incident that should be considered for suspension; and
  - any incident that the principal is required to report to the police, including those for which expulsion must be considered.
- Schools must inform the parents of victims as well as the parents of the aggressors/perpetrators about serious student-on-student incidents involving their child or children. This is particularly important for the parents of students with special education needs.
- Schools must provide parents of victims with information regarding discipline/management of the aggressors/perpetrators, when asked, and with information about the steps being taken to protect the victim from future victimization.
- If a school must separate students after an alleged incident, it is preferable that the alleged aggressor/perpetrator rather than the alleged victim be moved. Supports must be provided to the student who is required to change schools.
- The Ministry of Education should request that the Ontario College of Teachers amend the Standards of Practice for the Teaching Profession to include fostering and maintaining a safe and caring school environment.

Sexual Assault

- School staff must report to the principal any allegations/suspicions of sexual assault of a student by another student *on school premises or during school activities*, and the principal must report this incident to the police.
- In cases where students disclose/report allegations or suspicions of student-to-student sexual assaults *off school premises* to school staff, staff must:
  - for secondary students, ask them whether or not to contact their parents or police, and offer them information about professional supports such as sexual assault services; and

---

[9]*Shaping A Culture of Respect in Our Schools: Promoting Safe and Healthy Relationships, Safe Schools Action Team Report on Gender-based Violence, Homophobia, Sexual Harassment and Inappropriate Sexual Behaviour in Schools*, http://www.edu.gov.on.ca/eng/teachers/RespectCulture.pdf.

- for elementary students, call the parents and offer to put the parents in touch with police and professional supports for the student.

The reporting requirement under the *Child and Family Services Act* applies even though the information reported may be confidential or privileged. The confidentiality of the Ontario Student Record is therefore not an obstacle to making a report under section 72 of the *CFSA*.

Members of the Ontario College of Teachers should note that the Professional Misconduct regulation (O. Reg. 437/97) under the *Ontario College of Teachers Act, 1996*, states that professional misconduct includes "failing to comply with the member's duties under the *Child and Family Services Act*."

Section 72 of the *CFSA* states as follows:

> 72. (1) **Duty to report child in need of protection** — Despite the provisions of any other Act, if a person, including a person who performs professional or official duties with respect to children, has reasonable grounds to suspect one of the following, the person shall forthwith report the suspicion and the information on which it is based to a society:
>
> 1. The child has suffered physical harm, inflicted by the person having charge of the child or caused by or resulting from that person's,
>
> i. failure to adequately care for, provide for, supervise or protect the child, or
>
> ii. pattern of neglect in caring for, providing for, supervising or protecting the child.
>
> 2. There is a risk that the child is likely to suffer physical harm inflicted by the person having charge of the child or caused by or resulting from that person's,
>
> i. failure to adequately care for, provide for, supervise or protect the child, or
>
> ii. pattern of neglect in caring for, providing for, supervising or protecting the child.
>
> 3. The child has been sexually molested or sexually exploited, by the person having charge of the child or by another person where the person having charge of the child knows or should know of the possibility of sexual molestation or sexual exploitation and fails to protect the child.
>
> 4. There is a risk that the child is likely to be sexually molested or sexually exploited as described in paragraph 3.
>
> 5. The child requires medical treatment to cure, prevent or alleviate physical harm or suffering and the child's parent or the person having charge of the child does not provide, or refuses or is unavailable or unable to consent to, the treatment.
>
> 6. The child has suffered emotional harm, demonstrated by serious,
>
> i. anxiety,
>
> ii. depression,
>
> iii. withdrawal,
>
> iv. self-destructive or aggressive behaviour, or
>
> v. delayed development,

and there are reasonable grounds to believe that the emotional harm suffered by the child results from the actions, failure to act or pattern of neglect on the part of the child's parent or the person having charge of the child.

7. The child has suffered emotional harm of the kind described in subparagraph i, ii, iii, iv or v of paragraph 6 and the child's parent or the person having charge of the child does not provide, or refuses or is unavailable or unable to consent to, services or treatment to remedy or alleviate the harm.

8. There is a risk that the child is likely to suffer emotional harm of the kind described in subparagraph i, ii, iii, iv or v of paragraph 6 resulting from the actions, failure to act or pattern of neglect on the part of the child's parent or the person having charge of the child.

9. There is a risk that the child is likely to suffer emotional harm of the kind described in subparagraph i, ii, iii, iv or v of paragraph 6 and that the child's parent or the person having charge of the child does not provide, or refuses or is unavailable or unable to consent to, services or treatment to prevent the harm.

10. The child suffers from a mental, emotional or developmental condition that, if not remedied, could seriously impair the child's development and the child's parent or the person having charge of the child does not provide, or refuses or is unavailable or unable to consent to, treatment to remedy or alleviate the condition.

11. The child has been abandoned, the child's parent has died or is unavailable to exercise his or her custodial rights over the child and has not made adequate provision for the child's care and custody, or the child is in a residential placement and the parent refuses or is unable or unwilling to resume the child's care and custody.

12. The child is less than 12 years old and has killed or seriously injured another person or caused serious damage to another person's property, services or treatment are necessary to prevent a recurrence and the child's parent or the person having charge of the child does not provide, or refuses or is unavailable or unable to consent to, those services or treatment.

13. The child is less than 12 years old and has on more than one occasion injured another person or caused loss or damage to another person's property, with the encouragement of the person having charge of the child or because of that person's failure or inability to supervise the child adequately.

(2) **Ongoing duty to report** — A person who has additional reasonable grounds to suspect one of the matters set out in subsection (1) shall make a further report under subsection (1) even if he or she has made previous reports with respect to the same child.

(3) **Person must report directly** — A person who has a duty to report a matter under subsection (1) or (2) shall make the report directly to the society and shall not rely on any other person to report on his or her behalf.

(4) **Offence** — A person referred to in subsection (5) is guilty of an offence if,

(a) he or she contravenes subsection (1) or (2) by not reporting a suspicion; and

(b) the information on which it was based was obtained in the course of his or her professional or official duties.

(5) **Same** — Subsection (4) applies to every person who performs professional or official duties with respect to children including,

(a) a health care professional, including a physician, nurse, dentist, pharmacist and psychologist;

(b) a teacher, school principal, social worker, family counsellor, operator or employee of a day nursery and youth and recreation worker;

(b.1) a religious official, including a priest, a rabbi and a member of the clergy;

(b.2) a mediator and an arbitrator;

(c) a peace officer and a coroner;

(d) a solicitor; and

(e) a service provider and an employee of a service provider.

(6) **Same** — In clause (5)(b),

"youth and recreation worker" does not include a volunteer.

(6.1) **Same** — A director, officer or employee of a corporation who authorizes, permits or concurs in a contravention of an offence under subsection (4) by an employee of the corporation is guilty of an offence.

(6.2) **Same** — A person convicted of an offence under subsection (4) or (6.1) is liable to a fine of not more than $1,000.

(7) **Section overrides privilege** — This section applies although the information reported may be confidential or privileged, and no action for making the report shall be instituted against a person who acts in accordance with this section unless the person acts maliciously or without reasonable grounds for the suspicion.

(8) **Exception: solicitor client privilege** — Nothing in this section abrogates any privilege that may exist between a solicitor and his or her client.

(9) **Conflict** — This section prevails despite anything in the *Personal Health Information Protection Act, 2004*.

1.5 Youth Criminal Justice Act

1.5.1 Guiding Principles of the Act

The *Youth Criminal Justice Act* (*YCJA*) was proclaimed in force effective April 1, 2003, and replaced the *Young Offenders Act*. The *YCJA* applies to young persons.

"Young person" is defined in the Act as:

> a person who is or, in the absence of evidence to the contrary, appears to be twelve years old or older, but less than eighteen years old and, if the context requires, includes any person who is charged under this Act with having committed an offence while he or she was a young person or who is found guilty of an offence under this Act.

Section 3 of *YCJA* sets out a comprehensive set of "principles" that are to govern youth criminal justice:

3. (1) The following principles apply in this Act:

(a) the youth criminal justice system is intended to

(i) prevent crime by addressing the circumstances underlying a young person's offending behaviour,

(ii) rehabilitate young persons who commit offences and reintegrate them into society, and

(iii) ensure that a young person is subject to meaningful consequences for his or her offence in order to promote the long-term protection of the public;

(b) the criminal justice system for young persons must be separate from that of adults and emphasize the following:

(i) rehabilitation and reintegration,

(ii) fair and proportionate accountability that is consistent with the greater dependency of young persons and their reduced level of maturity,

(iii) enhanced procedural protection to ensure that young persons are treated fairly and that their rights, including their right to privacy, are protected,

(iv) timely intervention that reinforces the link between the offending behaviour and its consequences, and

(v) the promptness and speed with which persons responsible for enforcing this Act must act, given young persons' perception of time;

(c) within the limits of fair and proportionate accountability, the measures taken against young persons who commit offences should

(i) reinforce respect for societal values,

(ii) encourage the repair of harm done to victims and the community,

(iii) be meaningful for the individual young person given his or her needs and level of development and, where appropriate, involve the parents, the extended family, the community and social or other agencies in the young person's rehabilitation and reintegration, and

(iv) respect gender, ethnic, cultural and linguistic differences and respond to the needs of aboriginal young persons and of young persons with special requirements; and

(d) special considerations apply in respect of proceedings against young persons and, in particular,

(i) young persons have rights and freedoms in their own right, such as a right to be heard in the course of and to participate in the processes, other than the decision to prosecute, that lead to decisions that affect them, and young persons have special guarantees of their rights and freedoms,

(ii) victims should be treated with courtesy, compassion and respect for their dignity and privacy and should suffer the minimum degree of inconvenience as a result of their involvement with the youth criminal justice system,

(iii) victims should be provided with information about the proceedings and given an opportunity to participate and be heard, and

(iv) parents should be informed of measures or proceedings involving their children and encouraged to support them in addressing their offending behaviour.

The process for transferring certain young persons to "adult court" has been eliminated. Instead, if the youth court has determined whether or not the young person is guilty of the offence, it may impose an adult sentence under certain circumstances as set out in sections 61 to 81 of the *YCJA*. The young person must have been found guilty of an offence for which an adult could receive a sentence of more than two years and he or she must have been at least 14 years old at the time the offence was committed. With respect to certain very serious offences (e.g. murder) or for repeat serious violent offenders, there is a presumption that an adult sentence will follow a finding of guilt. In any situation where no presumption applies, the Crown must apply to the Court if it wishes an adult sentence to be considered.

1.5.2 Restrictions on Publication of Identity

The *YCJA* protects from publication (1) the identity of young persons who are in trouble with the law (i.e. being "dealt with under the Act" — under investigation, arrested, charged, convicted, discharged, etc.) or (2) any information that would identify the young person.

The Act also prohibits the publication of the identity of children or young persons who are *victims* of, or *witnesses* in connection with, an offence committed or alleged to have been committed by a young person.

Section 110(1) and 111(1) of the *YCJA* state:

> 110. (1) Subject to this section, no person shall publish the name of a young person, or any other information related to a young person, if it would identify the young person as a young person dealt with under this Act.
>
> 111. (1) Subject to this section, no person shall publish the name of a child or young person, or any other information related to a child or a young person, if it would identify the child or young person as having been a victim of, or as having appeared as a witness in connection with, an offence committed or alleged to have been committed by a young person.

The non-publication is intended to maximize the chances of rehabilitation for young persons.

There are exceptions to the general rule against publication. The first exception permits publication of the names of young persons who have received an adult sentence. Another exception applies where the young person is convicted of a "presumptive" offence and received a youth sentence although an adult sentence was sought. Here the youth court judge must exercise his or her discretion to allow publication. A third exception occurs where publication is made in "the course of the administration of justice" and where the purpose of the disclosure is not to make the information known in the community. An *ex parte* court order must be obtained to allow disclosure where the police are pursuing a young person who is a suspect (s. 110(2)(c)). A fourth exception allows authorities to seek public assistance in apprehending a suspect or a young person who is unlawfully at large, if the young person is dangerous. A fifth exception applies where the young person wants his or her name publicized and the court agrees. In addition, young persons who have attained the age of 18 may publicize identifying information about themselves if they are not in custody.

Section 111 of the Act contains exceptions to the general prohibition against publication of the identity of a victim or witness. A victim or witness may choose to be identified upon attaining the age of 18, or earlier with parental consent, or where the victim or witness is deceased, upon parental request. A court may also permit disclosure where it is satisfied that it would not be contrary to the young person's interest or the public interest. It should be noted that disclosure of a victim or witness does not mean that the identity of the "young person" can be disclosed.

1.5.3 Sharing Information with Schools

The *YCJA* sets out stringent provisions about who may *keep* records on young persons and who has a right of access to *any* such record (ss. 114 to 119). Disclosure to any person is permitted under section 119(1)(s) if deemed by a youth court to have a valid interest in the record provided disclosure is desirable in the interest of the proper administration of justice.

Section 125 allows the authorities to disclose information in a record to a school engaged in the supervision or care of a young person. Section 125 states:

> 125. (1) A peace officer may disclose to any person any information in a record kept under section 114 (court records) or 115 (police records) that it is necessary to disclose in the conduct of the investigation of an offence.
>
> . . . . .
>
> (6) The provincial director, a youth worker, the Attorney General, a peace officer or any other person engaged in the provision of services to young persons may disclose to any professional or other person engaged in the supervision or care of a young person — including a representative of any school board or school or any other educational or training institution — any information contained in a record kept under sections 114 to 116 if the disclosure is necessary
>
> (a) to ensure compliance by the young person with an authorization under section 91 or an order of the youth justice court;
>
> (b) to ensure the safety of staff, students or other persons; or
>
> (c) to facilitate the rehabilitation of the young person.
>
> (7) A person to whom information is disclosed under subsection (6) shall
>
> (a) keep the information separate from any other record of the young person to whom the information relates;
>
> (b) ensure that no other person has access to the information except if authorized under this Act, or if necessary for the purposes of subsection (6); and
>
> (c) destroy their copy of the record when the information is no longer required for the purpose for which it was disclosed.

1.5.4 The Right to Legal Counsel

A young person has the right to have a lawyer without delay at any stage of the proceedings, including arrest or detention, before the person makes a voluntary statement, during consideration of extrajudicial sanctions, and at a hearing. A young person is guaranteed access to counsel under the Act, regardless of whether he or she is qualified for legal aid (although provinces may determine rules for recovery of the costs of counsel). A "hearing" includes pre-trial detention, trial, sentencing, and various other hearings and reviews held under the Act (*YCJA*, s. 25(3)). The right to counsel belongs to the young person, not a parent or guardian, and the right may be waived.

1.5.5 Making a Voluntary Statement

There are strict requirements for taking voluntary statements from a young person by "a peace officer or other person who is, in law, a person in authority." To begin with, section 146 of the Act requires that a person taking the statement must caution the young person that he or she has the right to consult counsel and a parent (or if the parent is absent, an adult relative or if the parent or relative is absent, another appropriate adult). Indeed, any statement must be made in the presence of counsel, a parent, or other appropriate adult unless the young person declines this right.

In order for a statement to be admissible in court, the person taking a statement from a young person must, before the statement is taken, clearly inform the young person that he or she is under no obligation to make a statement, that any statement made may be used as evidence against the young person, that the young person has the right and reasonable opportunity to consult counsel and a parent, and that any statement is to be made in the presence of counsel, a parent, or other adult unless the young person desires otherwise (s. 146(2)(b)).

The requirement to explain the above rights to the young person does not apply to oral statements if they are made spontaneously by the young person to a peace officer or other person in authority before the person has had a reasonable opportunity to make the explanation to the young person.

The courts have generally taken a narrow approach as to who is, in law, a "person in authority". Although parents and teachers may be regarded by a young person as having a position of authority, they would not normally be a person in authority under the Act. The test is whether there is a realistic expectation that they are associated with the investigation. The question depends on the extent to which the young person believed the person could influence or control the proceedings against him or her. "A parent, doctor, teacher or employer all may be found to be a person in authority if the circumstances warrant, but their status, or the mere fact that they may wield some personal authority over the accused, is not sufficient to establish them as persons in authority for the purposes of the confessions rule." (per Cory J. in *R. v. Hodgson*, 1998 CarswellOnt 3417, 1998 CarswellOnt 3418, [1998] S.C.J. No. 66, (sub nom. *R. v. M.C.H.)* 230 N.R. 1, 127 C.C.C. (3d) 449, 163 D.L.R. (4th) 577, 18 C.R. (5th) 135, (sub nom. *R. v. M.C.H.)* 113 O.A.C. 97, [1998] 2 S.C.R. 449 (S.C.C.) at para. 35.)

Because statements to peace officers and persons in authority are inadmissible in evidence unless the above-noted statutory precautions are taken, it is important that teachers and principals be aware of the requirements. A principal or teacher can be a person in authority for the purposes of section 56.

In *R. v. H.* (1985), [1985] A.J. No. 567, 1985 CarswellAlta 291, 43 Alta. L.R. (2d) 250 (Alta. Prov. Ct.), the Court stated:

> The test is whether the accused believed that the person he dealt with had some degree of power over him and whether he thought that person could either make good his promise or carry out his threats. It is reasonable to presume that a 13-year-old boy would believe that his teacher would exercise power over him and could make good her promises.

In this case, as a result of statements to the teacher, the young person and his accomplices were interrogated by the school principal and further implicated themselves. They were not informed of their rights. On the facts of this particular case, the Court said the principal "became inextricably involved in the administration of justice by doing the work of the police themselves. The evidence he provided the police became the evidence in this case; there was no need for the police to attempt to obtain the statement from the accused; the principal had done their work for them."

In *R. v. R. (F.)* (November 10, 1988), [1988] M.J. No. 523, Garfinkel Prov. J. (Man. Prov. Ct.), the Court ruled that a teacher was a person in authority:

> She ought not to have embarked upon an investigation. This was not a situation of maintaining school discipline. This was an investigation of a crime. When a crime is being investigated Charter rights, principles of fundamental justice, principles of Y.O.A. and legal procedures come into play. The police could have been called upon discovery of the theft. The actions of the young person should have been described to them and they should have conducted the investigation.

The test of whether or not a person is a "person in authority" is a subjective one: how would the young person view the teacher or principal? The courts do not question the legality, or desirability, of letting principals and teachers exercise their disciplinary role over young persons. There is a point, however, at which school discipline turns into investigation of a crime. At that point, the police should be called in.

1.5.6 Extrajudicial Measures

The *Youth Criminal Justice Act* is guided by the fundamental principle that extrajudicial measures are often the most appropriate and effective way to address youth crime. The idea is to keep young persons out of court altogether. There is a presumption that a first-time, non-violent offender will be dealt with outside the court process, although the measures are not limited to those who have not previously committed an offence. Section 6 of the Act requires a police officer, before charging a young person, to consider whether it would be sufficient to:

- take no further action
- warn the young person
- give the young person a formal caution (where a province has established such a program)
- with the consent of the young person, refer him or her to a community program or agency that may assist him or her not to commit offences.

The Act also allows the Crown attorney to use certain extrajudicial measures, namely a caution (where such a program is implemented by the province) or refer the young person to an extrajudicial sanctions (formally alternative measures) program (if one exists). Section 10 imposes restrictions on the use of extrajudicial sanctions (as opposed to "measures"), including a requirement for the consent of the young person. The Crown may decide not to proceed with the charge. The Crown may also refer the young person to a community program or agency.

The police, Crown, a youth court judge, a justice of the peace, or a youth worker may convene or cause to be convened a "conference" under section 19 of the Act to obtain advice on appropriate extrajudicial measures. A conference is "a group of persons who are convened to give information in accordance with section 19". That group may include, for example, the young person, the parents of the young person, the victim, a police officer, a teacher, a guidance counsellor, a social worker, a coach, a youth worker and others who are familiar with the young person, community agencies, and professionals with relevant expertise. A conference may be a professional case conference, but it may also be a restorative justice mechanism that provides advice on ways to repair the harm done to the victim. A conference can be called to assist with any decision that has to be made under the *YCJA*.

1.5.7 Parental Involvement

A key emphasis in the *YCJA* is the need for parental involvement. Parents are required to be kept informed at every stage of the involvement of their child in proceedings, including at arrest and detention, upon issuance of a summons or appearance notice, upon release on an undertaking or recognizance, or upon issuance of a ticket. If a parent is not available, an appropriate adult relative may be given notice (s. 26(4), (5)). If a parent does not attend court with the young person, the court may order the parent's attendance if it is of the opinion that it is necessary or in the best interests of the young person (*YCJA*, s. 27).

1.5.8 Sentencing

The *YCJA* contains a broad range of sentencing options, including some that did not exist in the *Young Offenders Act*. Sentences are either custodial or non-custodial. Non-custodial options are:

- reprimand — a formal rebuke or scolding by the judge in court
- absolute discharge
- conditional discharge
- fine up to $1,000
- compensation to another person for loss, damage or injury
- restitution of property to the person who owned it at the time of the offence
- reimbursement of an innocent purchaser of property
- compensation by way of personal service (up to 240 hours and completed within 12 months) for a loss, damage or injury, or alternatively, compensation in kind
- community service (up to 240 hours and completed within 12 months)
- order of prohibition, seizure or forfeiture that is authorized under federal legislation (e.g. prohibition against owning a firearm)
- probation with conditions, for up to two years; the range of mandatory and optional conditions is found in section 55 of the *YCJA* — the conditions may include attending school intensive support and supervision program order (where the program is implemented by the province)
- attendance order, requiring the young person to attend a program at specified times (up to 240 hours within a six-month period) where the program has been implemented by the province
- deferred custody and supervision order — the sentence is served in the community but, if conditions are breached, this may result in the young person serving the remainder of the sentence in custody and supervision
- custody and supervision order — all custody orders must include a period of supervision in the community under conditions; supervision conditions may include a requirement to attend school. The length of custody and supervision depends on the offence. Over the course of the custody portion of a sentence, a

young person may seek a reintegration leave for the purpose of rehabilitation and preparation for eventual reintegration back into the community. The purpose of the leave can include, for example, attending school, and

- intensive rehabilitative custody and supervision order, intended for serious violent offenders, under the criteria set out in section 42(7) of the Act.

APPENDIX

Signs of Child Abuse

(a) Ministry of Children and Youth Services[10]

Child abuse happens when a child's parent or other person in charge harms or neglects a child.

What are the types of child abuse?

In general, there are four major types of child abuse:

- physical abuse
- sexual abuse
- emotional abuse
- neglect

What is physical child abuse?

Physical abuse could result from a parent or person in charge causing physical injury to a child, or failing to adequately supervise a child or from a pattern of neglect of the child. Here are some examples of physical abuse:

- beating
- slapping
- hitting
- pushing
- throwing
- shaking
- burning

A child who is physically abused may:

- have burns, bite marks, cuts, bruises, or welts in the shape of an object
- not want to go home
- be afraid of adults

What is sexual abuse?

Sexual abuse happens when a parent or other person in charge sexually molests or uses a child for sexual purposes or knowingly fails to protect a child from sexual abuse. Here are some examples of sexual abuse:

- any sexual act between an adult and a child, including intercourse
- fondling

[10]© Queen's Printer for Ontario, 2007. Reproduced with permission.

- exposing a child to adult sexual activity
- sexual exploitation through child prostitution or child pornography

A child who is sexually abused may:

- have an inappropriate knowledge of sexual acts
- be very compliant or extremely aggressive
- be afraid of a certain person or a family member
- have difficulty walking or sitting

What is emotional abuse?

Emotional abuse occurs when a parent or other person in charge causes emotional harm or fails to protect a child from emotional harm that results from verbal abuse, mental abuse and psychological abuse.

Here are some examples of emotional abuse:

- yelling at, screaming at, threatening, frightening, or bullying a child
- humiliating the child, name-calling, making negative comparisons to others, or saying things like: "You're no good. You're worthless. You're bad. Having you was a mistake."
- showing little to no physical affection (such as hugs) or words of affection (praise or saying "I love you.")
- saying that everything is the child's fault.
- withdrawing attention, giving the child the "cold shoulder"
- confining a child in a closet or a dark room, or tying the child to a chair for long periods of time
- allowing the child to be present during violent behavior of others, including the physical abuse of others

A child who is emotionally abused may:

- show signs of serious anxiety, depression or withdrawal
- show self-destructive or aggressive behaviour
- show delays physical, emotional or mental development

What is neglect?

Neglect happens when a child's parent or other person in charge does not provide for a child's physical, developmental, emotional or psychological needs.

Here are some examples of neglect:

- failing to provide:
    - proper food
    - clothing suitable for the weather
    - supervision
    - a home that is clean and safe
    - medical care, as needed
- failing to provide emotional support, love and affection

A child who is neglected may:

- not wear clothing that's suitable for the weather
- be dirty or unbathed

- be very hungry
- not be properly supervised

(b) The Royal Canadian Mounted Police[11]

Types of Child Abuse

Neglect: Failure to give due attention or care to a child resulting in serous emotional or physical harm.

Behavioural Indicators

- pale, listless, unkept
- frequent absence from school
- inappropriate clothing for the weather
- dirty clothes
- inappropriate acts or delinquent behaviour
- abuse of alcohol/drugs
- begging /stealing food
- frequently tired
- seeks inappropriate affection
- mature for their age
- reports their [sic] is no caretaker

Physical Indicators

- poor hygiene
- unattended physical or medical needs
- consistent lack of supervision
- underweight, poor growth, failure to thrive
- constant hunger
- under nourished

Emotional Abuse: Verbal attacks or demeaning actions that impact on a childs self esteem and self worth.

Behavioural Indicators

- depression
- withdrawal or aggressive behaviour
- overly compliant
- too neat and clean
- habit disorders (sucking, biting, rocking, etc.)
- learning disorders
- sleep disorders
- unusual fearfulness
- obsessive compulsive behaviour

---

[11]©(2008) HER MAJESTY THE QUEEN IN RIGHT OF CANADA as represented by the Royal Canadian Mounted Police (RCMP). Reproduced with the permission of the RCMP.

- phobias
- extreme behaviour
- suicide attempts
- developmental delays

Physical Indicators

- bed-wetting
- headaches
- nausea
- speech disorders
- lags in physical development
- disruptive behaviour

Physical Abuse: the intentional use of force against a child resulting in injury or causing bodily harm.

Behavioural Indicators

- inconsistent explanation for injuries or cannot remember
- wary of adults
- flinch if touched unexpectedly
- extremely aggressive or extremely withdrawn
- feels deserving of punishment
- apprehensive when others cry
- frightened of parents
- afraid to go home

Physical Indicators

- injuries not consistent with explanation
- numerous injuries in varying stages of recovery or healing
- presence of injuries over an extended period of time
- facial injuries
- injuries inconsistent with the child's age and developmental phase

Sexual Abuse: any form of sexual conduct (touching, exploitation, intercourse) directed at a child.

Behavioural Indicators

- sexual knowledge or play inappropriate to age
- sophisticated or unusual sexual knowledge
- prostitution
- poor peer relationships
- delinquent or runaway
- reports sexual assault by caretaker
- change in performance in school
- sleeping disorders
- aggressive behaviour
- self-abusive behaviours

- self mutilation

Physical Indicators

- unusual or excessive itching in the genital or anal area
- stained or bloody underwear
- pregnancy
- injuries to the vaginal or anal areas
- venereal disease
- difficult in walking or sitting
- pain when urinating
- vaginal/penile discharge
- excessive masturbation
- urinary tract infections

Facts about child abuse

- Child abuse usually reflects patterns of behaviour rather than an isolated incident.
- The vast majority of child abusers are parents, relatives, or trusted adults, not strangers.
- Children rarely lie about abuse. They are more likely to deny abuse and take back truthful statements than to make false reports.
- Child abuse knows no class boundaries.

What should you do if a child discloses abuse?

Believe in the child

- lack of belief will discourage the abused from disclosing

Listen openly and calmly

- give the child your full attention
- put the child first and put your feelings (anger, frustration or pain) aside

Reassure the child

- be supportive
- tell the child what has happened is not his/her fault
- never make promises

Write down the facts

- record all the facts the child has disclosed to you
- avoid interpreting what the child has said, use the child's exact words
- contact your local police or your local child welfare agency

2

GOING TO SCHOOL

This chapter discusses the provisions of the *Education Act* that govern who has a right to go to school and who *must* go to school. This is an important distinction; just because a person has a right to attend school does not mean he or she must attend. The Act only *requires* children who are of "compulsory school age" to attend school unless they are legally excused from attending. Logically, the right to attend is different for elementary and secondary schools. For example, the age limit to attend elementary school is 21 years; there is no age limit to attend secondary school (although some pupils may be directed to continuing education courses, and pupils may be required to pay a fee after seven years in secondary school). There are minimum age limits only in respect of when a board *must* admit a pupil to school. This chapter also discusses certain questions that may arise when parents are separated or divorced, when a parent has designated a person as a "guardian", or where a child has withdrawn from parental control. The final section of this chapter covers the school year and the school year calendar.

2.1 The Right to Attend School

(a) Where Do I Have a Right to Attend School?

The *Education Act* uses many words to say that you can attend school where you and your parent or guardian live. Actually, it isn't quite that simple, as this chapter explains. Here's the legal labyrinth:

(b) Elementary School Attendance

You have a right to attend elementary school if you are "qualified to be a resident pupil" of a board. The following steps will help you determine if you are "qualified":

Step One — How Old Are You?

IF ENTERING GRADE ONE	IF ENTERING KINDERGARTEN	IF ENTERING JUNIOR KINDERGARTEN
If you attain 6 years of age during the year you can enter school in September of that year. You can stay in school until the last school day in June in the year in which you attain 21 years of age (s. 33).	If you attain 5 years of age during the year you can enter school in September of that year. You can stay in school until the last school day in June in the year in which you attain 21 years of age (s. 34).	If you attain 4 years of age during the year you can enter school in September of that year (if JK is offered). You can stay in school until the last school day in June in the year in which you attain 21 years of age (s. 34).

Step Two — Where Do You Live?

The person must reside in the board's jurisdiction and a parent or guardian of the person must reside in the board's jurisdiction (s. 33).

Step Three — Additional Requirements

French-language public DSB	English-language public DSB or public school authority	French-language separate	English-language separate (or Roman Catholic school authority)
1. Must be a French-speaking person (see definition below). 2. Parent or guardian is either not a tax supporter or, if entitled to be a tax supporter, directs support to the French-language public board.	1. Parent or guardian must *not* be a separate school supporter or French-language board supporter.	1. Must be a French-speaking person. 2. Parent or guardian must be Roman Catholic. 3. Parent or guardian must direct tax to the French-language separate board.	1. Parent or guardian must be Roman Catholic. 2. Parent or guardian must direct tax support to the English-language separate board.

Step Four — Enrolment

To be a "pupil", you have to enrol in a school operated by the board (or in another board's school under an arrangement between the two boards) (s. 33(6)). It is the responsibility of the parent or guardian to submit evidence that the child has a right to attend an elementary school, including proof of age (s. 33(5)). It is the responsibility of the person or the person's parent or guardian to submit evidence that the person has a right to attend a secondary school (s. 36(8)).

(c) Secondary School Attendance

You have a right to attend secondary school if you are "qualified to be a resident pupil" of a board in respect of secondary school. The following steps will help you determine if you are "qualified". There is no specified age requirement for attending secondary school.

French-language public DSB	**English-language public DSB**	**French-language separate DSB**	**English-language separate DSB**
(A) Person and parent/guardian reside in the board's jurisdiction *and* the parent or guardian is either not a tax supporter or, if entitled to be a tax supporter, directs support to the French-language public board	(A) Person and parent/guardian reside in the board's jurisdiction *and* the parent/guardian is not a separate school supporter or a French-language DSB supporter	(A) Person and parent/guardian reside in the board's jurisdiction *and* the parent/guardian is a French-language separate district school board supporter (Must be Roman Catholic and a French-speaking person)	(A) Person and parent/guardian reside in the board's jurisdiction *and* the parent/guardian is a separate school supporter (Must be Roman Catholic to direct support to a separate board)
or	or	or	or
(B) Person is a tax supporter of a French-language public board, resides in the board's jurisdiction, *and* is the owner or tenant of separately assessed residential property in the board's jurisdiction	(B) Person is a tax supporter of an English-language public board, resides in the board's jurisdiction *and* is the owner or tenant of separately assessed residential property in the board's jurisdiction	(B) Person is a French-language separate district school board supporter (therefore Roman Catholic), resides in the board's jurisdiction *and* is the owner or tenant of separately assessed residential property in the board's jurisdiction	(B) Person is a separate school supporter (therefore Roman Catholic), resides in the board's jurisdiction *and* is the owner or tenant of separately assessed residential property in the board's jurisdiction
or	or	or	or

French-language public DSB	English-language public DSB	French-language separate DSB	English-language separate DSB
(C) Person is a French-speaking person, at least 18 years of age and resides in the board's jurisdiction, and is not a tax supporter of any board	(C) Person is at least 18 years of age, resides in the board's jurisdiction, and is not a tax supporter of any board	(C) Person is at least 18 years of age, is a French-speaking person and a Roman Catholic, resides in the board's jurisdiction, and is not a tax supporter of any board	(C) Person is Roman Catholic, at least 18 years of age, resides in the board's jurisdiction, and is not a tax supporter of any board
or	or	or	or
(D) Person is a French-speaking person, resides in board's jurisdiction and is 16 or 17 years of age and has withdrawn from parental control.	(D) Person resides in board's jurisdiction and is 16 or 17 years of age and has withdrawn from parental control.	(D) Person is a French-speaking person, is a Roman Catholic, resides in the board's jurisdiction and is 16 or 17 years of age and has withdrawn from parental control.	(D) Person is Roman Catholic, resides in the board's jurisdiction and is 16 or 17 years of age and has withdrawn from parental control.
Person must be a French-speaking person.		Person must be a French-speaking person. Parent/guardian must be Roman Catholic under (A). Person must be Roman Catholic under (B), (C), and (D).	Parent/guardian must be Roman Catholic under (A). Person must be Roman Catholic under (B), (C), and (D).

Enrolment and Admission — Secondary School

To be a "pupil", you have to enrol in a secondary school operated by the board (or in another board's school under an arrangement between the two boards) (s. 36(5)).

A pupil will be admitted to secondary school if the pupil has been promoted from "elementary school" (a defined term) (s. 41(1)).

A person who has not been promoted from elementary school shall be admitted if the principal of the secondary school is satisfied that the applicant "is competent to undertake the work of the school" (s. 41(2)).

If you are refused admission to secondary school by the principal, you may appeal the principal's decision to the school board (s. 41(3)).

Definitions

"French-speaking person" means a child of a person who has the right under subsection 23(1) or (2), without regard to subsection 23(3), of the *Canadian Charter of Rights and Freedoms* to have his or her children receive their primary and secondary school instruction in the French language in Ontario.

Note that the "person" being defined is the child, but the child's rights depend upon whether his or her parents have section 23 *Charter* rights. Section 23 of the *Charter* states:

> 23. (1) **Language of instruction** — Citizens of Canada
>
> (a) whose first language learned and still understood is that of the English or French linguistic minority population of the province in which they reside, or
>
> (b) who have received their primary school instruction in Canada in English or French and reside in a province where the language in which they received that instruction is the language of the English or French linguistic minority population of the province,
>
> have the right to have their children receive primary and secondary school instruction in that language in that province.
>
> (2) **Continuity of language instruction** — Citizens of Canada of whom any child has received or is receiving primary or secondary school instruction in English or French in Canada, have the right to have all their children receive primary and secondary school instruction in the same language.
>
> (3) **Application where numbers warrant** — The right of citizens of Canada under subsections (1) and (2) to have their children receive primary and secondary school instruction in the language of the English or French linguistic minority population of a province
>
> (a) applies wherever in the province the number of children of citizens who have such a right is sufficient to warrant the provision to them out of public funds of minority language instruction; and
>
> (b) includes, where the number of those children so warrants, the right to have them receive that instruction in minority language educational facilities provided out of public funds.

Education Act, section 1:

> "guardian" means a person who has lawful custody of a child, other than the parent of the child;
>
> [. . .]
>
> "separate school supporter" means an English-language Roman Catholic board supporter or a French-language separate district school board supporter;
>
> [. . .]
>
> "English-language Roman Catholic board supporter" means a Roman Catholic,
>
> (a) who is shown as an English-language Roman Catholic board supporter on the school support list as prepared or revised by the assessment commissioner under section 16 of the *Assessment Act*, or
>
> (b) who is declared to be an English-language Roman Catholic board supporter as a result of a final decision rendered in proceedings commenced under the *Assessment Act*,
>
> and includes his or her Roman Catholic spouse;

[. . .]

"English-language public board supporter" means a person who is an owner or tenant of residential property in the area of jurisdiction of a board and who is not.

(a) a separate school supporter,

(b) a French-language public district school board supporter, or

(c) a Protestant separate school board supporter;

[. . .]

"French-language separate district school board supporter" means a Roman Catholic French-language rights holder,

(a) who is shown as a French-language separate district school board supporter on the school support list as prepared or revised by the assessment commissioner under section 16 of the *Assessment Act*, or

(b) who is declared to be a French-language separate district school board supporter as a result of a final decision rendered in proceedings commenced under the *Assessment Act*,

and includes his or her Roman Catholic spouse if the spouse is a French-language rights holder;

[. . .]

"French-language public district school board supporter" means a French-language rights holder,

(a) who is shown as a French-language public district school board supporter on the school support list as prepared or revised by the assessment commissioner under section 16 of the *Assessment Act*, or

(b) who is declared to be a French-language public district school board supporter as a result of a final decision rendered in proceedings commenced under the *Assessment Act*,

and includes his or her spouse if the spouse is a French-language rights holder;

Is there a Right to Attend Continuing Education Courses?

A board is not required to offer continuing education courses or classes. (International languages at the elementary level offered in accordance with Regulation 285 are an exception.) If continuing education is offered, a person is entitled to enrol in a credit course or class if the principal is satisfied that the person is competent to undertake the work of the course or class (s. 41(6)).

(d) Special Attendance Rules

Switching from a School Authority to a District School Board for Secondary Education

If you are qualified to be a resident pupil in a school authority that only provides elementary education and is *not* a *public* school authority, you have a right to attend secondary school provided by a public district school board that shares geographic jurisdiction with the school authority. This is designed to protect the secondary school attendance rights of pupils who are attending an elementary school operated by a rural separate school board, combined separate school board, or Protestant separate school board. (However, attendance under this section at a French-language public district school board is still conditional upon the person being a French-speaking person.) (Subsections 36(6), (7).)

Non-Resident Secondary School Pupils Switching Boards

If

(i) you are 18 years of age or older,

(ii) you have been promoted or transferred to secondary school,

(iii) you would qualify as a resident pupil of a board except for the fact that you do not reside in the board's jurisdiction,

(iv) you reside in the jurisdiction of another school board,

then:

> the other board (i.e. where you reside) must admit you, without fee, to a secondary school of the same type (English-language public, French-language public, English-language Roman Catholic, French-language Roman Catholic), if its supervisory officer certifies that it can accommodate you in a secondary school (s. 37).

Going to a More Accessible Elementary School

If you are a resident pupil for elementary school, you may attend an elementary school of the same type (English-language public, French-language public, English-language Roman Catholic, French-language Roman Catholic) at another board that is nearer to your residence than the school you are required to attend in your "home" board. For this to apply, your home board's school must be at least 3.2 kilometres from your residence, and more than 0.8 kilometres from the point from which transportation is provided, and nearer by the shortest distance by road to another school of the same type that is in another section or zone (i.e. board) than to the school that the pupil is required to attend (s. 35).

Going to a More Accessible Secondary School

If you are qualified as a resident pupil to attend secondary school, you may attend a secondary school of the same type (English-language public, French-language public, English-language Roman Catholic, French-language Roman Catholic) at another board if it is more accessible than any secondary school at your "home" board. This attendance right is conditional upon a supervisory officer certifying that the receiving board can accommodate you (s. 39(1)(a)).

You may also use this provision to go to a secondary school at another board in order to take secondary courses that you need to get your diploma, to enter university or college or to enter a trade, profession or calling, presumably because your "home" board does not offer the courses (s. 39(1)(b)). However, this does not apply if your home board has made an agreement with another board to provide the relevant subjects (s. 39(4)).

Living on Tax-Exempt Land

A person who resides on tax-exempt land is not treated as a true "resident" of a board. The person shall be admitted by the board to an accessible school (if otherwise qualified) if the board has space for the person "for the current year". This person can be charged fees in accordance with the annual "Calculation of Fees" regulation. (See s. 46.)

However, if the person or his/her parent or guardian is assessed for education taxes for the board, then he or she can qualify as a resident pupil (and therefore must be admitted in the usual manner). For example, if you live on Crown land but your parent owns or rents a property in the board's jurisdiction on which education taxes are assessed, then you are eligible to qualify as a resident pupil.

There are special attendance rights for people who reside on Defence property owned by Canada (s. 46.1) to enable them to attend school without payment of a fee in the municipality where the defence establishment is located.

Sole Support Parent

If a person is supported by only one parent and the parent

(1) resides in Ontario in a residence that is not assessed for school purposes, and

(2) boards the person in a residence that is not a children's residence under Part IX of the *Child and Family Services Act*,

then the person (if otherwise qualified as a resident pupil) is deemed to be qualified to be a resident pupil in the area where the residence is located, and in accordance with the tax support of the residence (s. 45).

Ward of Children's Aid Society or Training School

If a child is under the care or supervision of a children's aid society, receives child protection services from a children's aid society or resides in a children's residence or foster home, he or she can attend school in the jurisdiction where he or she resides. The child must be otherwise qualified to be admitted to elementary or secondary school (s. 47).

Child in Custody of a Corporation or Society

A child who is in the custody of a "corporation" or "society" and who does not have a right to attend the school where the corporation or society has sent him or her, shall be admitted to the school if there is sufficient accommodation for the current year (assuming that the child is otherwise qualified to be admitted). The regulations may prescribe fees to be paid by the corporation or society to the board (s. 48).

What is the "Seven Year" Rule for Charging Fees?

Where a pupil has completed elementary school and has attended one or more secondary schools for a total of seven or more years, the board may charge the pupil a fee under the regulations (s. 38). This section is often misunderstood to mean that you have a right to attend secondary school for only seven years. In fact the limitation is only as to whether a fee may be charged. In some jurisdictions, this resulted in adults attending school for reasons that had nothing to do with obtaining a diploma or qualifying for post-secondary school entry. In 1996, the Legislature enacted provisions that would make it easier for a board to redirect an adult pupil into continuing education courses. These provisions are found in section 49.2. They include protection for exceptional pupils who have been placed in a day school program, and for pupils who need courses not offered in the continuing education program for the purpose of obtaining a secondary school diploma, to qualify for admission to a university or college of applied arts and technology, or to enter a trade, profession or calling.

Can a Child Attend School Even if His or Her Parent is Unlawfully in Canada?

Yes, a person who is otherwise entitled to be admitted to school and who is less than 18 years of age cannot be refused admission because the child's parent or guardian is unlawfully in Canada (s. 49.1).

(e) Movement of Secondary School Pupils between Public and Separate Boards

When separate school boards were given the right to have public funding in order to "extend" their secondary school to offer all secondary grade levels, the *Education Act* provided that there would be "open access" at the secondary school level for public school pupils and separate school pupils. This basic concept was preserved in the amendments found in the *Education Quality Improvement Act, 1997*, and are now found in section 42 of the *Education Act*. To make sense of them, it is important to refer to the definitions of the different kinds of "boards" in the *Education Act*. Some terms include "school authorities" and some do not.

Open access occurs where the boards are coterminous, i.e. share part or all of their (geographic) areas of jurisdiction. It only applies to secondary education.

RESIDENT PUPIL OF:	MAY ATTEND:
English-language public board	English-language Roman Catholic board
French-language public DSB	French-language separate DSB
English-language Roman Catholic board	English-language public board
French-language separate DSB	French-language public DSB
French-language separate DSB	English-language public board
French-speaking person — pupil of English-language public board	French-language separate DSB
French-language public DSB	English-language separate DSB
French-speaking person — pupil of English-language separate DSB	French-language public DSB

(f) Movement between French-Language and English-Language Boards

The *Education Act* provides for movement between French-language district school boards and English-language district school boards that are coterminous. However, a qualified resident pupil of an English-language board who is not a French-speaking person has no right to transfer to a French-language district school board. Movement under section 43 is permitted at the elementary and secondary level. Section 43 covers only public-to-public and separate-to-separate transfers.

RESIDENT PUPIL OF:	MAY ATTEND:
French-speaking person — pupil of English-language public board	French-language public DSB
French-language public DSB French-speaking person — pupil of English-language Roman Catholic board	English-language public board French-language separate DSB
French-language separate DSB	English-language Roman Catholic board

What Happens if a Person has Moved into a Residence but has not had Time to Change Tax Support?

If you move into a residence that is assessed for the "wrong" type of tax support for the school that you want to attend, you can still attend the school if you file a notice of change of support for the following year. For example, if you move into a residence that is assessed for public school purposes and you are past the deadline to change your tax support to the separate school board, you can still attend a separate school if you file the notice for next year (s. 44).

Can a Board Admit a Person Even if He or She Does Not Have the Right to Attend One of its Schools?

As can be seen from the above references, the *Education Act* covers many situations in which a board either "shall" or "may" admit a person to school. What happens if the Act does not specifically cover a situation? A board has considerable discretion to admit a person to its schools where there is no provision in the Act that specifically covers the circumstances.

For example, section 32(2) states:

> Despite the other provisions of this Part, but subject to subsection 49(6), where it appears to a board that a person who resides in the area of jurisdiction of the board is denied the right to attend school without the payment of a fee, the board, at its discretion, may admit the person from year to year without the payment of a fee.

Note, this covers persons who are resident in the board's jurisdiction.

Section 49(5) states:

> A board may admit to a school that it operates a person whose admission with or without the payment of a fee is not otherwise provided for in this Act but who, except as to residence, is qualified to attend such school, and may, at its discretion,

require the payment by or on behalf of the person of the fee, if any, payable for the purpose under the regulations.

Note, this covers persons who are not resident in the board's jurisdiction, and permits discretion as to whether or not a fee will be charged. The fee is calculated in accordance with the applicable regulation.

A French-language district school board may admit persons who are not French-speaking persons (s. 293). A school authority that operates a French-language instructional unit also has this discretionary power.

Must a Board Charge a Fee to a Non-Resident?

There are several instances where a board has the discretion as to whether or not to charge a fee to a non-resident pupil. However, if a board admits a person who is a temporary resident within the meaning of the *Immigration and Refugee Protection Act* (Canada) or a person who is in possession of a study permit under that Act, the board must charge the person the maximum fee calculated under the regulations (s. 49(6)), subject to specific exceptions for diplomats, refugees and others set out in section 49(7).

2.2 Compulsory School Attendance

(a) Does a Child Have to Go to School?

Thus far, this chapter has discussed whether a person has a right to go to school. But does anyone have a right to make you go to school? Yes. Every child of compulsory school age must attend school unless legally excused from attendance.

(a) If a person turns six on or before the first school day in September, he or she must start attending school commencing with the first school day in September of that school year. The person must attend school until he or she turns 18. There is no obligation to finish out the school year once the person turns 18.

(b) If a person turns six after the first school day in September, he or she must start attending school from the first school day in September of the *next succeeding* school year. The person must attend school until the *last school day in June* in the year in which he or she turns 18. The person finishes the school year, but has no obligation to start the next September even though his or her 18th birthday lies somewhere between September and December.

(b) What are the "Legal Excuses" for Not Attending School?

Children have devised many excuses for not showing up for school, but the *Education Act* has the "official" list (s. 21(2)(a)-(h)):

(a) the person is receiving satisfactory instruction at home or elsewhere;

The Act does not define "satisfactory instruction". It is a duty of a board, through its local school attendance counsellor, to ensure that all persons of compulsory school age in the board's jurisdiction attend school unless legally excused.

A board has a duty to find out if absent children are being educated. Because parents, in the absence of a legal excuse, have the obligation to send their children to school (s. 21(5)), they should take reasonable steps to satisfy board officials that their child is legally excused. The obligation to ensure attendance does not apply if the child is 16 or 17 years of age and has withdrawn from parental control.

The Supreme Court of Canada has confirmed the need for parents to comply with compulsory education laws. *R. v. Jones*, 25 C.R.R. 63, 28 C.C.C. (3d) 513, 73 A.R. 133, 47 Alta. L.R. (2d) 97, [1986] 6 W.W.R. 577, 31 D.L.R. (4th) 569, [1986] 2 S.C.R. 284, [1986] S.C.J. No. 56, 69 N.R. 241, EYB 1986-66948, 1986 Carswell-Alta 716, 1986 CarswellAlta 181 (S.C.C.). However, a board official does not have a right to enter any premises without the occupier's consent to discover if satisfactory instruction is being delivered.

Being educated "elsewhere" usually means that the child is enrolled in a private (independent) school.

> (b) the person is unable to attend school by reason of sickness or other unavoidable cause;

Note: if medical reasons require that a child be educated at home, the principal can arrange "home instruction" to be provided by a board teacher (Reg. 298, s. 11(11)). This should not be confused with "home schooling". Home instruction is provided by the board. The Ministry of Education requirements for home schooling are set out in Policy Program Memorandum 131. (See Appendix E.)

> (c) transportation is not provided by a board for the person and there is no school that he or she has a right to attend situated,
>
> > (i) within 1.6 kilometres from the person's residence measured by the nearest road if he or she has not attained the age of seven years on or before the first school day in September in the year in question, or
> >
> > (ii) within 3.2 kilometres from the person's residence measured by the nearest road if he or she has attained the age of seven years but not the age of 10 years on or before the first school day in September in the year in question, or
> >
> > (iii) within 4.8 kilometres from the person's residence measured by the nearest road if he or she has attained the age of 10 years on or before the first school day in September in the year in question;
>
> (d) the person has obtained a secondary school graduation diploma or has completed a course that gives equivalent standing;
>
> (e) the person is absent from school for the purpose of receiving instruction in music and the period of absence does not exceed one-half day in any week;
>
> (f) the person is suspended, expelled or excluded from attendance at school under any Act or under the regulations;
>
> (g) the person is absent on a day regarded as a holy day by the church or religious denomination to which he or she belongs; or
>
> (h) the person is absent or excused as authorized under this Act and the regulations.

For example, parents may temporarily withdraw a child from school with the permission of the principal (Reg. 298, s. 23(3)).

If a person *under* compulsory school age enrols in an elementary school (e.g. in junior kindergarten), then the obligation to attend school (unless legally excused) applies during the period for which he or she is enrolled as if the person were of compulsory school age (s. 21(4)).

(c) Can a Pupil be Excluded from School if He or She is Not Immunized?

Yes. The *Immunization of School Pupils Act* (s. 3) says that the medical officer of health can order a person who operates a school (i.e. a board or a private school operator) to suspend a pupil until the pupil has completed the "prescribed program of immunization" in respect of diseases designated under the Act, or until the parent of the pupil has filed:

- a current statement of medical exemption or
- a statement of conscientious belief or
- a statement of religious belief.

The suspension is for 20 days, and may be repeated until the statutory conditions are satisfied (immunization or valid exemption).

If there is an outbreak, or risk of outbreak, of a designated disease in a school, the medical officer of health can order that a pupil be excluded from attendance at school if the pupil has not been immunized or granted an exemption under the Act. The order lasts until it is rescinded (s. 12).

If the medical officer of health makes a suspension or exclusion order, the parent and pupil (if 16 or 17 years old) must be advised of their entitlement to a hearing before the Health Services Appeal and Review Board. No hearing is required *before* an order is made by the medical officer of health.

Regulation 645 prescribes the contents of the record of immunization, and the required immunization schedule for designated diseases. It also contains the forms for obtaining an exemption, and for transferring records between schools if the pupil moves.

Under the *Education Act* (s. 265), a principal must report cases of suspected communicable disease in the school to the board and the local medical officer of health. A principal must refuse to admit to school a person whom he or she believes is infected with or exposed to a communicable disease, until the person has been medically "cleared".

(d) Who is the School Attendance Counsellor?

Every board must have one or more school attendance counsellors. Boards may share a school attendance counsellor. The counsellor has jurisdiction and is responsible for the enforcement of compulsory school attendance of every child who is required to attend school and who is qualified to be a resident pupil of the board, or is or has been enrolled during the current school year in a school operated by the board (other than a pupil under the jurisdiction of a person appointed under s. 119 of the *Indian Act*). The counsellor must inquire into every case of failure to attend school within his or her knowledge, or when requested to do so by the appropriate supervisory officer, the principal of a school or a ratepayer. The counsellor is responsible for instituting the prosecution of habitually absent persons under section 30(5) of the *Education Act*. The parent or guardian of a person of compulsory school age can also be prosecuted for not sending the person to school under section 30(1).

2.3 Custody, Guardianship and Withdrawal from Parent Control

Normally, both parents of a child have custody of the child. If the parents separate or divorce, they may have "joint custody". More typically, one parent has custody and the other parent has "access". (In some cases, a parent may be deprived of any right to access to his or her child.) Subject to the terms of a separation agreement or court order, the parent with custody will normally be the educational decision-maker responsible for the child. The parent with access is still entitled to education information about his or her child.

Where neither parent has custody, the child will have a "guardian", which is defined in section 1 of the *Education Act* as a "person who has lawful custody of a child, other than the parent of the child." Educational decision-making for the child rests with the guardian, who stands in the shoes of the parent for the purposes of the *Education Act*.

In many cases, guardianship results from a court order, for example, where the parents are deceased or no longer able to care for their child. Traditionally, school boards insisted that a court order be obtained to transfer custody from a parent to a guardian. Courts have recognized, however, that an agreement to transfer custody to a guardian can, under the right circumstances, be legally valid. Therefore, more recently, schools are being presented with "agreements" or "declarations" purporting to transfer custody of a child from a parent to a "guardian". Although these documents can be legitimate, they should be viewed by principals with some caution, and legal advice should be sought where appropriate. It is a huge decision to give away custody — a child is not simply a chattel who can be transferred with a scrap of paper. Some questions for principals to ask are:

- is there a legitimate intent to transfer custody, or is this simply an attempt to circumvent the board's attendance area policy and get the child into a "better" school. What are the circumstances motivating the transfer? I recall one situation where the mother was trapped at the Canada/U.S.A. border with immigration problems and couldn't re-enter Canada. Dad was not on the scene. Mother transferred custody of her children to their aunt, as she had no idea when she would be permitted back into the country. However, in another case, a father from another Ontario city simply deposited his son with the son's older brother (an adult) in another board's jurisdiction, and then told the school that the older brother was the child's guardian; my advice was that the "guardianship" was not valid under the circumstances, as the father clearly intended to remain as the ultimate decision-maker for his younger son. In another situation, the mother purported to transfer guardianship of a child to a relative, but continued to play an active role in her child's education at the school — she clearly had no real intention of giving up her decision-making authority.
- what does the guardianship document actually say? Does it state clearly that the purported guardian is to have complete decision-making over the child's education? Once custody is transferred, the parent is no longer in the picture as far as the school is concerned. School communication will be with the guardian, as will access to the OSR.
- is the document signed by both parents? If not, why?
- does the "guardian" also agree in writing to accept the custody of the child?

It is preferable for the transfer of custody to be stated by the parent in a legal declaration, sworn before a Commissioner of Oaths. Law firms and legal clinics are able to assist in this regard.

As a result of amendments to the *Education Act* in 2006 changing the compulsory school age to 18 years, the Act now recognizes that some children withdraw from parental control at age 16 or 17. It should be noted that in dealing with a person who has withdrawn from parental control, the school no longer needs to deal with the person's parent or guardian. Essentially, the school is dealing with the child as if he or she were 18 years of age. It is not always easy to determine if a person has withdrawn from parental control. The person should be able to present documentary proof that he or she is not dependent financially on a parent or guardian, lives at a separate address from a parent or guardian, and is in charge of his or her own day-to-day affairs. In some cases, the young person will be receiving social assistance. Simply moving in with a relative after a fight with one's parent is not necessarily withdrawing from parental control, especially if the young person is dependent on the relative for food and lodging.

2.4 The School Year and the School Calendar

Regulation 304 under the *Education Act* contains the legal parameters within which school boards establish their school calendars. A school year must have at least 194 school days and shall commence on or after September 1st and end on or before June 30th. A board may obtain the Minister's permission to have a school calendar or calendars that modify the usual requirements.

A school year is made up of school holidays, instructional days and professional activity days. A "school day" is a day that is within the "school year" and that is not a "school holiday". Therefore, a school day is either an instructional day or a professional activity day.

An instructional day is a day on which the pupils are required to be in attendance at school. Examination days are also instructional days. Section 1 of Regulation 304 states that "instructional day" means "a school day that is designated as an instructional day on a school calendar and upon which day an instructional program that may include examinations is provided for each pupil whose program is governed by such calendar".

An instructional day is thus a school day that is not a professional activity day. A school day may be split, with half as an instructional day and the remainder as a professional activity day.

No more than 10 examination days in any school year may be scheduled on a school calendar (s. 11(7.1) of the Act).

A professional activity day is a school day on which pupils do not attend school and which is scheduled for teachers to engage in professional activities. Regulation 304 states that:

> "professional activity" includes evaluation of the progress of pupils, consultation with parents, the counselling of pupils, curriculum and program evaluation and development, professional development of teachers and attendance at educational conferences, but does not include preparation by teachers for classes or instruction.

A school year calendar must have at least two professional activity days, and a board may designate two additional professional activity days (Reg. 304, s. 2(3.1)). Sections 4 and 4.1 of Regulation 304 prescribe requirements pertaining to how boards must use the two mandatory professional activity days and publicize certain information about them. The Schedule to Regulation 304 contains a list of possible topics for the mandatory professional activity days.

The minimum length of the instructional program of each school day for pupils of compulsory school age is five hours (300 minutes), excluding recesses and scheduled intervals between classes (Reg. 298, s. 3).

The length of the instructional program may be reduced for pupils in special education programs (Reg. 298, s. 3(3)).

The instructional program cannot be scheduled to start earlier than 8:00 a.m. or end later than 5:00 p.m. The Minister may permit exceptions to these start and end times (Reg. 298, s. 3(2)).

A board may establish the length of the instructional program on each school day for pupils in junior kindergarten and kindergarten (Reg. 298, s. 3(4)).

Lunch Break

The lunch break for pupils and teachers is a minimum of 40 consecutive minutes. The lunch break is a scheduled interval between classes — it is part of the school day. Accordingly, religious indoctrination and religious instruction cannot occur during the lunch break.

A pupil's scheduled lunch break need not coincide with the lunch break for any other pupil or any teacher. Similarly, a teacher's scheduled lunch break need not coincide with the lunch break of any other teacher or any pupil (Reg. 298, ss. 3(5), (5.1), (5.2)).

Recess

In the primary and junior division, there must be a morning and afternoon recess of not less than 10 minutes and not more than 15 minutes.

In the intermediate and senior divisions, the principal may, with the board's approval, provide for recesses or for intervals between periods.

Open Hours

The board may determine when its school buildings and playgrounds will be open to its pupils. However, the buildings and playgrounds must be open to pupils during the period beginning 15 minutes before classes begin for the day and ending 15 minutes after classes end for the day (Reg. 298, s. 3(7)).

"Modified" School Calendars

A modified school calendar for a school or schools is one that does not adhere to the regular calendar requirements. For instance, it might have a start date earlier than September 1st or it might end later than June 30th. It could have less than 194 school days, or more. It could involve "year-round schooling".

If a board wants to have a modified calendar, it must submit it by March 1st for approval by the Minister of Education, for the following school year. If the Minister has not approved the requested calendar, or a revised request, by April 15th, the board must resubmit a calendar (by May 1st) that is not modified (i.e. complies with the "usual" requirements).

Changing a School Calendar

A board may change the date of a professional activity day or an examination day. It must notify the parents and the Minister of the change (Reg. 304, ss. 6(1) and (2)). Any other changes must be approved by the Minister (Reg. 304, s. 6(3)).

The school calendar or calendars for the board's schools must be published each year. The board must ensure that copies are available at the beginning of the school year for parents and pupils. The information must also indicate "in a general manner" the nature of the professional activities to be conducted on professional activity days.

Remembrance Day

Remembrance Day is not a school holiday. However, Remembrance services must be held by the school on Remembrance Day, at the school or in conjunction with a community service (Reg. 304, s. 9).

School Holidays

According to subsection 2(4) of Regulation 304, school holidays are:

- Every Saturday and Sunday
- Canada Day (if school is open in July)
- Labour Day
- Thanksgiving Day (or a day appointed by the Governor General or Lieutenant Governor as a public holiday)
- Christmas Vacation — two weeks (14 consecutive days commencing on the Monday next following the Friday preceding the 21st day of December, but when the 21st day of December is a Thursday or a Friday, commencing on the Monday next following)
- Family Day — the third Monday in February
- March Break — one week (five consecutive days commencing on the Monday next following the Friday preceding the 14th day of March)
- Good Friday
- Easter Monday
- Victoria Day.

These holidays can be changed in a modified school year calendar, with Ministerial approval.

Religious Holy Days

As noted earlier in this chapter, the *Education Act* prescribes the circumstances under which a pupil may be excused from attendance at school (s. 21(2)). For example, a pupil may be absent on a religious holy day. Boards often try to avoid scheduling key school events that coincide with high holidays of the major religions of persons within their jurisdiction. Alternative arrangements for examinations should be provided to any pupil who cannot write an examination on the normal date for religious reasons.

3

THE STATUTORY FRAMEWORK OF ONTARIO EDUCATION

3.1 Introduction

The *Education Act* (the Act) and its many regulations provide the statutory basis for publicly-funded education in Ontario. While perhaps not the most complex legislation, the Act does present its own challenges. Aside from its tremendous length, the Act contains provisions that are deeply rooted in the history and evolution of education (e.g. the list of teachers' duties in s. 264). Moreover, various bits and pieces have been added in a mostly *ad hoc* manner by successive governments, all of which have shied away from an overhaul of the whole Act since the Act was originally passed in 1974. (Prior to 1974, there were several different education statutes in Ontario.) The complexity is increased because, in some cases, it is necessary for the Act to have separate sections dealing with a single topic in respect of the four types of district school board. For example, the attendance rights of persons entitled to attend a board's schools will differ according to the type of board.

The Act does not make much sense unless one is familiar with the definitions in section 1, and yet this is a section that readers often overlook. Definitions are critically important. For example, a "teacher" is someone who is a member of the Ontario College of Teachers, whereas a "temporary teacher" is not a "teacher" at all, but rather a person who is allowed to teach under a Letter of Permission. A "teacher" for collective bargaining purposes is defined more narrowly than a "teacher" for other purposes in the Act. A "supervisory officer" is someone who not only has a supervisory officer's certificate but is also employed as a supervisory officer.

It also cannot be overemphasized that the regulations and policies made under the Act are critically important to our understanding of the law. Indeed, more and more "law" is now made through regulations, policies and guidelines, all of which must be authorized by statute.

This chapter provides a general overview of the Act and some of its regulations, and explains many of the key provisions that relate to the operation of boards and their schools. I have not dealt in detail with certain narrow, highly specialized areas such as education development charges because these would be of limited interest to most readers. If you are researching a specific issue, it is important to refer to the wording of the relevant provisions in the legislation because there could be exceptions to the usual rules that cannot be covered here. Some of the provisions of the Act are reproduced within the text. Unless otherwise noted, all section references are to the *Education Act*. The term "trustee" is interchangeable with the term "member of a board" (Act, s. 1(12)).

3.2 Governance Through Elected Representatives

Under the Canadian Constitution, the provinces have exclusive jurisdiction over education. Local school boards exercise powers delegated to them by the province. A school board is a "corporation". A board exists separate and apart from the people elected locally as trustees, who are responsible for governance. A board is a form of "local government". The legal structure for education governance in Ontario reflects the Constitutional rights of Roman Catholics to have separate schools, and the education rights of the linguistic minority protected by section 23 of the *Canadian Charter of Rights and Freedoms*. In Ontario, the linguistic minority is comprised of French-speaking persons as defined in section 23 of the *Charter*.

The *Education Act* refers to two distinct kinds of "boards": District School Boards and School Authorities.

3.2.1 District School Boards

Prior to 1998, there were no district school boards. All district school boards became newly-created legal entities on January 1, 1998. On January, 1, 1998, 129 "old" school boards were "merged" into 72 district school boards. This merger was accomplished by means of Ontario Regulation 460/97. The process is often incorrectly referred to as an "amalgamation".

There are four types of District School Board:

- English-language public
- English-language separate
- French-language public
- French-language separate.

There is no longer an entity called a "board of education".

The geographic areas of jurisdiction for district school boards are set out in Ontario Regulation 486/01, which also sets out their names. The election, number and distribution of trustees to district school boards are determined by Ontario Regulation 412/00. A district school board may not have more than 22 or fewer than five members (s. 58.1(10)).

3.2.2 School Authorities

On January 1, 1998, a "school authority" became the term that describes any of the following types of board:

- a board of a district school area
- a board of rural separate school
- a board of a combined separate school zone
- a board of a secondary school district (i.e. James Bay Lowlands Secondary School District)
- a board established under section 68 of the Act
- a board of a Protestant separate school.

Unlike district school boards, the boards listed above were not created as new legal entities by the *Education Quality Improvement Act, 1997*. Also, unlike a district school board, a school authority is responsible for provision of education to the linguistic minority within its jurisdiction. It should also be noted that members of "section 68 boards" are appointed by the Minister of Education; they are not elected.

3.3 The Role and Conduct of Board Members

School boards exist in order to operate schools within their jurisdiction. The *Education Act* states what a board *shall* do and what it *may* do. A board has the powers that are either set out expressly in legislation or regulation, or that are necessarily incidental to the exercise of the legislated powers. The Act therefore does not say what a board *cannot* do, because a board can only do things that are delegated to it by the province. No delegation — no power. Other statutes, such as the Ontario *Corporations Act* and the *Municipal Freedom of Information and Protection of Privacy Act*, also determine the powers of school boards.

Elected trustees govern the board. Collectively, they are its "mind". The Director of Education executes the will of the board. The Director is the chief executive officer and the chief education officer and under section 283(2) "shall, within policies established by the board, develop and maintain an effective organization and the programs required to implement such policies".

The Act therefore envisualizes a division of responsibilities, making the Director responsible for the day-to-day management of the school system. In addition, supervisory officers, principals, teachers and school attendance counsellors all have prescribed duties and powers, discussed elsewhere in this book. Supervisory officers (and all other staff) report to the board through the Director of Education (s. 286(3)).

A trustee may vote and act as a member of the board but has no individual decision-making authority.

Obviously, a trustee performs many functions in addition to those that occur during board meetings, including visiting schools, talking to parents, staff, pupils and others, and voicing his or her opinions on education issues. This is quite a different matter from purporting to act on behalf of the board as a whole or assuming the role of teachers and administrators. Individual trustees should not issue orders or directions to staff.

Some trustees view their role as being an "advocate", and indeed trustees are advocates for parents who have problems with their local school, for school communities that need school nutrition programs or repairs to school property, for marginalized students who need extra support, etc. Sometimes it is difficult to balance the role of local advocate, who urges change, with the role of "governor" who must respect the will of the majority of board members. Nevertheless, our school system would be very much the poorer without some form of local decision-making as a counter-balance to the perspective of the provincial government.

3.3.1 Code of Ethics for Trustees

A board may establish its own code of conduct or ethics, to guide members in their relations with fellow board members, staff and the public. The Ontario Public School Boards' Association suggests the following "Code of Ethics" for trustees:[1]

As a school board member, I will:

1. Be motivated by an earnest desire to serve my school board to the best of my ability to meet the educational needs of all students.

2. Recognize that the expenditure of school funds is a public trust, and I will endeavour to see that the funds are expended efficiently, in the best interests of the student.

3. Not use my position for personal advantage or to the advantage of any other individual apart from the total interest of the school board, and I will resist outside pressure to so use my position.

4. Act with integrity, and do everything possible to maintain the dignity of the office of a school board member.

5. Carry out my duties objectively, and consider all information and opinions presented to the board in making my decisions, without bias.

6. Work with other board members in a spirit of respect, openness, courtesy, co-operation and proper decorum, in spite of differences of opinion that arise during debate.

7. Accept that authority rests with the board and that I have no individual authority outside the board, and I will abide by the majority decisions of the board once they are made, but I shall be free to repeat the opinion that I upheld when the decision was made.

8. Express any contrary opinion respectfully and honestly, and without making disparaging remarks, in or outside board meetings, about other board members or their opinions.

9. Accept the right of every board member to hold and express their individual opinions.

10. Communicate and conduct my relationship with staff, the community or other school boards and the media in a manner that focuses on all of the facts about their schools, and to that end provide the finest possible school program, school staff and school facilities.

11. Not divulge confidential information, which I obtain in my capacity as a board member, and I will not discuss those matters outside the meetings of the board or the board's committees.

12. Endeavour to participate in trustee development opportunities to enhance my ability to fulfil my obligations as a school board member.

13. Not conduct myself in a manner which is intended to be to the detriment of my own board or any other board.

---

[1] "OPSBA on Good Governance" (2003), http://www.opsba.org/Policy_Program/goodgovernance _FINAL.pdf.

The Ontario Catholic School Trustees' Association also issues expectations for trustees in fulfilling their role within the Catholic school system.[2]

3.3.2 Oversight and Accountability

The vast majority of school trustees are dedicated, hard-working and committed individuals, who are prepared to put in countless hours for the public good, for very little remuneration. But what laws govern the conduct of our school trustees? What happens if a trustee is guilty of unethical behaviour or if a board as a whole violates the law? Are there ways of holding trustees to account for their individual or collective conduct?

There are several accountability mechanisms:

- the power of the electorate at elections held every four years to express its pleasure or displeasure with an incumbent member
- stringent campaign-related provisions in the *Municipal Elections Act*
- obligations to provide reports to the Minister of Education
- statutory limits on borrowing and investments
- obligation to have an independent auditor
- oversight by the courts — judicial review
- criminal law sanctions against breach of trust
- "supervision" by the Minister of Education (discussed below)
- offences relating to conflict of interest (discussed below)
- internal sanctions imposed by the board upon a member
- laws that prohibit disclosure of personal information of pupils
- specific "offence" provisions in the *Education Act* (e.g. failure to take security from the Board Treasurer)
- civil liability for torts or breach of fiduciary duty, including personal liability
- responsibilities toward school councils and the Special Education Advisory Council.

3.3.2.1 Conflict of Interest

(a) General

The *Municipal Conflict of Interest Act* is the statute that governs conflict of interest for trustees. In a strictly legal sense, "conflict of interest" for a school trustee is confined to direct, indirect and deemed *pecuniary* interest.

The onus is on the trustee to declare if he or she has a conflict of interest in a matter under consideration by the board, or by a committee of which the trustee is a member. The declaration must be recorded in the minutes. Having made such a declaration, the trustee must not vote on the matter, attempt to influence the vote, or participate in the discussion of the matter. If the meeting is in closed session, the

---

[2] http://www.ocsta.on.ca/resources/1/Resources/Publications/OCSTA137_roleTrustee_press-ready.pdf.

trustee must leave the meeting during consideration of the matter, and have this fact recorded in the minutes.

If a trustee is absent from a meeting that dealt with a matter in respect of which the trustee has a conflict of interest, the trustee must disclose the interest at the next meeting of the board or committee that the trustee attends, and must not vote on, influence, or discuss the matter.

(b) Indirect Interest

A member of the board has an *indirect interest* in a matter if,

(a) the member or his or her nominee

(i) is a shareholder in, or a director or senior officer of, a corporation that does not offer its securities to the public;

(ii) has a controlling interest in, or is a director or senior officer of, a corporation that offers its securities to the public; or

(iii) is a member of a body

that has a pecuniary interest in the matter; or

(b) the member is a partner of a person or is in the employment of a person or body that has a pecuniary interest in the matter.

(c) Deemed Interest

The direct or indirect pecuniary interest of a parent or the spouse or any child of the trustee is *deemed* to be the pecuniary interest of the trustee, if known to the trustee.

(d) Exceptions

The *Municipal Conflict of Interest Act* has a list of "exceptions" that do not constitute a pecuniary interest. For example, a pecuniary interest "in common with electors generally", or that is "so remote or insignificant in its nature that it cannot reasonably be regarded as likely to influence the member" does not have to be declared under the Act.

(e) Failure to Declare

What happens if a trustee fails to declare a conflict of interest at a meeting? The trustee cannot be forced to declare an interest or to leave the meeting during discussion of a matter. After the fact, the only remedy is an expensive, cumbersome and risky one. An "elector" may apply (within six weeks after the fact comes to his or her knowledge, but never more than six years after the date of alleged contravention) to a judge for a determination of the question of whether the Act has been complied with. If a contravention of the Act is found to have occurred, the trustee's seat can be declared vacant, the person can be prohibited from serving as trustee for seven years and, where appropriate, an order for restitution can be made. If the Court finds that the Act was contravened through "inadvertence or error of judgment", the trustee is not subject to having his or her seat declared vacant or to being disqualified from running again. The decision of the judge may be appealed to the Divisional Court.

The failure of a member to declare an interest in a matter does not invalidate the board's proceedings in respect of the matter, but the matter is voidable at the instance of the board unless this would adversely affect the rights of any person who acquired rights as a result of the proceedings and who was acting in good faith and without actual notice of the member's contravention (s. 12).

(f) Loss of Quorum

Where declarations of interest result in a loss of quorum, section 7 deems the remaining number of members to constitute a quorum, provided such number is not less than two. Where it is reduced to less than two, the board may apply to a judge for a declaration that section 5 (duty to declare) does not apply in respect of the matter under consideration. The judge may permit the members to proceed as if there were no conflict, subject to such conditions and directions as the judge may consider appropriate (s. 7(3)). This section has practical significance in the case of very small school boards, which may be comprised of only three trustees.

3.3.2.2 Accountability Safeguards in the Education Act

(a) Duty to Comply with Act

A board has the duty to ensure that every school under its charge is conducted in accordance with the *Education Act* and regulations (s. 170(1)(10)). A board is also required to do anything that it is required to do under the *Education Act* or any other Act (s. 170(1)(18)). The Act contains only limited means by which a board can be forced to comply with its statutory obligations. However, the provincial government, a ratepayer, or other person with legal standing, can bring an application for judicial review in Ontario Superior Court seeking a declaration that a board has not complied with its legal obligations and an order instructing the board as to what it must do (or cease doing) to remedy the situation.

The Minister may withhold grants from a board that is not in compliance with the *Education Act* and regulations or any other Act that is assigned to the Minister. This power is found in the annual regulations prescribing the grants for school boards (see, e.g. s. 9 of O. Reg. 85/08).

(b) Financial Reporting and Audit Requirements

Every year, the treasurer of the board must prepare the financial statements of the board (s. 252(1)). Two copies of the statements, along with the auditor's report, are sent to the Minister. These statements and the auditor's report must be made public (s. 252(2)).

Every board must appoint one or more auditors (s. 253(1)). Auditors are appointed for up to five years. Their duties may be prescribed by the Minister of Education and by the school board. An auditor has a right of access to all records of the board and can require any information and explanation that in the auditor's opinion may be necessary to enable the auditor to carry out his or her duties. It is an offence for a trustee or board officer not to co-operate with the auditor by withholding information and access to records (s. 253(6)). An auditor has a right to attend any meeting of the board or a committee of the board, and can even compel a person to give evidence under oath or affirmation.

(c) Reporting to the Minister

The Minister has extensive powers to obtain information from a board. Under section 8(1)(27.1), the Minister may require a board,

(a) to prepare any report that the Minister may require,

(b) to submit, in the form directed by the Minister, a copy of the report to the Ministry and to such other persons as the Minister may direct,

(c) to attach a copy of the report to the financial statements of the board referred to in section 252.

The Minister may also designate a provincial supervisory officer or other person to have access to any school and to the books and records of a board or a school (s. 286(5)).

When the Minister provides grants to a board for a specific program such as "student success", there are stringent requirements for reporting on how the money was spent. The Act also has provisions requiring boards to submit various local policies (such as a policy on ethno-cultural equity) to the Minister for approval. Many board policies must adhere to guidelines issued by the Province.

(d) Investment and Borrowing Restrictions

There are many financial safeguards in the *Education Act* that govern the use of public money by a board. For instance, the Act prescribes, through regulation, the kinds of securities in which a board may invest. The Act sets out a board's investment powers, including how it may borrow its capital and reserve funds to finance current needs. The government may, by regulation, provide for "debt, financial obligation and liability limits for boards or classes of boards" (s. 242). "Current borrowing" by boards, to meet their day-to-day financial needs and debt charges, is permitted by section 243, but a board may not borrow more money than it expects to receive in the year, according to its estimates. School boards may issue debentures. In the case of a Roman Catholic school board, this includes a "mortgage" (ss. 244 and 245). Public boards do not have the power to mortgage their real estate. Boards may also borrow money or incur debt for permanent improvements — see the regulations made under section 247 of the Act. There are also stringent requirements about how a board may dispose of a school or school site, including a provision that requires that surplus property must be offered to other public entities (at fair market value) before being offered to the public. (See s. 194 of the Act and O. Reg. 444/98.)

(e) Placing Boards Under "Supervision"

The Act contains two distinct circumstances under which the provincial government may essentially take over the control and administration of all or part of a board's operations.

These methods of ensuring compliance are colloquially known as "supervision", although that term is not used in the Act. One form of supervision occurs under section 257.30 of the Act when there are "financial" concerns about a board. The other type of supervision occurs under Part VIII of the Act to ensure compliance by the board with certain statutory obligations. (The procedures for imposing supervision under Part VIII and section 257.30 are similar but not identical.)

(i) Non-Financial Supervision

Part VIII (ss. 230 to 230.19) of the Act allows the Minister of Education to intervene in situations where the Minister has concerns that the board may have done something or omitted to do something where the act or omission contravenes specific sections of the Act that impose obligations on the board in respect of:

- prescribed courses of study (s. 8(1)2)
- prescribed curriculum guidelines or areas of study (s. 8(1)3)
- "equivalent learning" requirements (s. 8(1)3.0.1.)
- "provincial interest" regulations under section 11.1, prescribing, respecting and governing the duties of boards so as to further and promote the provincial interest in education
- class size regulations (s. 170.1(1))
- trustee honoraria and expenses
- application or intended application of funds contrary to the grant regulations.

If the report of an investigator appointed by the Minister discloses evidence of non-compliance or that the board will likely be in non-compliance, the Minister may issue directions to the board to address the matter. If the board fails to comply with the direction, the Minister may seek a vesting order from the Ontario Cabinet, giving the Ministry charge and control over the administration of the affairs of the board and the Act gives the Minister extensive powers in this regard (ss. 230.5 to 230.17), including dismissing any officer or employee of the board who fails to obey an order, direction or decision of the Minister.

(ii) Financial "Supervision"

The Minister of Education can direct an investigation of the financial affairs of a board if:

- the financial statements or auditor's report indicate that the board had a deficit
- the board fails to make a debenture or interest payment on time
- the board fails to meet any other debt or liability on time
- the Minister has concerns about the board's ability to meet its financial obligations (s. 257.30(1)).

On receiving the investigator's report, the Minister may give directions to the board to address its financial affairs. If it fails to comply with the Minister's directions, or if the investigator's report recommends assumption of control, the Lieutenant Governor in Council may make an order vesting in the Ministry control and charge over the administration of the affairs of the board (s. 257.31(2), (3)).

The Act sets out very extensive supervision powers of the Minister (ss. 257.30 to 257.52). However, a supervision order does not authorize the Minister to interfere with or control the denominational aspects of a Roman Catholic board or Protestant separate school board, or the linguistic or cultural aspects of a French-language district school board. It does give the Minister control over staffing, budgeting, accounting/auditing systems, borrowing, and disposition of assets. The order is revoked when the board is no longer in debt or when otherwise specified by the Lieutenant Governor in Council.

The power to supervise a board is not new. Provisions respecting supervision of municipalities and school boards were found in the *Municipal Affairs Act*, (Part III), since the 1930s.

3.3.2.3 Personal Liability of Board Members

Although it is very rare, a school trustee may be held personally liable if he or she acts in bad faith or willfully acts outside the scope of his or her statutory authority.

The Ontario Divisional Court (Desmarais J.) held in *Deschamps v. Prescott-Russell (Conseil des écoles séparées catholiques de langue française)* that school trustees were not personally liable where a superintendent was declared redundant and transferred to a lesser position. The Court adopted the principle as stated under "Education" in 10 C.E.D. (Ont. 3rd), Title 52, para. 133:

> Where school trustees are constituted as a corporation with capacity to sue and be sued, in carrying out their statutory duties, acting in their public corporate capacity and within the scope of their authority, it is only in that character that they are liable and not in their private individual capacity. Hence no action will lie against trustees individually for acts done in their corporate capacity.[3]

Desmarais J. noted that trustees can be held individually liable where it can be shown they acted in bad faith. In the case before him, he found insufficient evidence to conclude that the individual trustee defendants had acted in bad faith.

However, under the supervision sections of the Act, (ss. 230.12(3) and 257.45(3)), if a board that is subject to an order under section 230.3(2)(3) or section 257.31(2)(3) (i.e. an order by the Lieutenant Governor in Council to vest in the Ministry of Education control and charge over the administration of the affairs of the board), applies any of its funds otherwise than as ordered or authorized by the Minister, the members of the board who voted for the application are jointly and severally liable for the amount so applied. The school board is not permitted to indemnify the board members for any such liability.

---

[3](1993), 1993 CarswellOnt 1092, [1993] O.J. No. 2850, 16 O.R. (3d) 278 (Ont. Gen. Div.); reversed (1997), 1997 CarswellOnt 111, [1997] O.J. No. 125 (Ont. C.A.); leave to appeal allowed (1997), 108 O.A.C. 159 (note), 224 N.R. 317 (note) (S.C.C.); leave to appeal allowed (1997), (sub nom. *Abouchar v. Conseil scolaire de langue française d'Ottawa-Carleton)* 225 N.R. 159 (note), (sub nom. *Abouchar v. Conseil scolaire de langue française d'Ottawa-Carleton)* 109 O.A.C. 200 (note) (S.C.C.); reversed 1999 CarswellOnt 2758, 1999 CarswellOnt 2759, [1999] S.C.J. No. 53, 125 O.A.C. 279, 47 C.C.E.L. (2d) 1, [1999] 3 S.C.R. 281, 15 Admin. L.R. (3d) 175, 177 D.L.R. (4th) 23, 245 N.R. 201, 39 C.P.C. (4th) 1 (S.C.C.); reversed 1999 CarswellOnt 2756, 1999 CarswellOnt 2757, 47 C.C.E.L. (2d) 91, (sub nom. *Abouchar v. Board of Education (French Language) of Ottawa-Carleton)* 125 O.A.C. 82, (sub nom. *Abouchar v. Ottawa-Carleton French Language School Board — Public Sector)* [1999] 3 S.C.R. 343, 15 Admin. L.R. (3d) 221, (sub nom. *Abouchar v. Board of Education (French Language) of Ottawa-Carleton)* 244 N.R. 391, (sub nom. *Abouchar v. Ottawa-Carleton French Language School Board — Public Sector)* 177 D.L.R. (4th) 68, 39 C.P.C. (4th) 91 (S.C.C.). See also *Anderson v. Vansittart* (1849), 5 U.C.Q.B. 335, 1849 CarswellOnt 23 (U.C. Q.B.).

In addition, section 198(4) provides that a board member may be held personally liable for losses if the board refuses or neglects to take proper security from its treasurer or other person to whom it entrusts money.

3.3.2.4 Listening to School Councils

All provinces in Canada have recognized the need to give parents a strong voice at the school level, and have formalized the role of school councils, parent councils or planning councils in providing input into decisions by elected trustees. Parents, school staff and community representatives thus have a forum to discuss issues and make recommendations to the school administration and the board.

The *Education Act* requires a school board to establish a school council for each school operated by the board in accordance with the regulations (s. 170(1)(17.1)). Ontario Reguation 612/00 defines the roles and responsibilities of school councils.

Regulation 612/00 states that the purpose of a school council is "through the active participation of parents, to improve pupil achievement and to enhance the accountability of the education system to parents" (s. 1(1)). The regulation also states that a council's "primary means of achieving its purpose is by making recommendations in accordance with this Regulation to the principal of the school and the board that established the council" (s. 2(2)).

The principal, a teacher, a non-teaching staff representative and a community member are required members for the council, but the majority of positions are given to parents of children in the school.

Subsections 9(1) and (2) state that the Ministry may "for the purpose of consulting and communicating directly with members of school councils, collect the names, mailing addresses, telephone numbers and email addresses of the chair or co-chairs of a school council and of other members of the council". As well, "the Ministry may disclose information collected under subsection (1) to the Ontario Parent Council, which may use the information for the purpose of consulting and communicating directly with members of school councils". These provisions address concerns that disclosure of this personal information would otherwise violate privacy legislation.

The regulation outlines the areas that school boards are required to solicit views of school councils. These include: conduct of persons in schools, a dress code for students, school improvement plans responding to provincial pupil testing, the process and criteria for the selection of principals and vice-principals, policies regarding board funding of school councils, fundraising activities of school councils, conflict resolution procedures for school councils and policies regarding reimbursement of expenses incurred by school council members and officers (s. 19). Subsection 19(2) "does not limit the matters on which a board may solicit the views of school councils". Section 20 states that "a school council may make recommendations to the principal of the school or to the board that established the council on any matter." Section 21 of the regulation requires the board to respond to "each recommendation made to the Board by the council" and "advise the council of the action taken in response to the recommendation".

Clearly, therefore, although schools councils are advisory in nature, the legislation is intended to ensure that their advice is at least listened to, if not accepted.

3.4 Becoming a School Trustee

3.4.1 Who Can Be Elected as a Trustee of a District School Board?

The *Education Act* specifically provides that a board member may also be referred to as a "trustee" and these terms are often used interchangeably (s. 1(12)).

A board member is a person elected by "electors" to serve on a school board. You will find the definition of "public school elector" and "separate school elector" in the *Municipal Elections Act, 1996* because most school board elections are held in accordance with the provisions of that Act as well as the provisions of the *Education Act.*

District school board members are elected in the same manner as the election of members of a council of a municipality (ss. 58.6, 58.7, 58.8).

In order to be elected as a trustee you must be qualified to *vote* for members of the board and you must be *resident* anywhere in the board's jurisdiction. A trustee must remain a "resident" of the board's jurisdiction in order to remain qualified as a trustee. Under subsection 1(10) of the *Education Act*, in order to vote, on voting day you must be at least 18 years of age, a Canadian citizen and not prohibited from voting under the *Municipal Elections Act, 1996*. Section 17(2)(d) of the *Municipal Elections Act, 1996* prohibits the following from voting:

- a person who is serving a sentence of imprisonment in penal or correctional institution
- a corporation
- a person acting as an executor, trustee or other representative capacity except as a voting proxy under section 44 of the *Municipal Elections Act, 1996*
- a person who was convicted of a corrupt practice described in subsection 90(3) of the *Municipal Elections Act*, 1996 if the voting day is less than five years after voting day in the election in respect of which he or she was convicted.

Under section 219 of the *Education Act*, you are not qualified to be *elected* (which means you cannot run for election) or to *act* as a member of the board if:

- you are employed by a school board in Ontario (unless on unpaid leave)
- you are the clerk, treasurer, deputy clerk or deputy treasurer of a municipality or upper-tier municipality, all or part of which is included in the area of jurisdiction of the district school board or the school authority (unless on unpaid leave)
- you are an Ontario MPP, Federal MP or Senator
- you are otherwise ineligible or disqualified under the *Education Act* or any other Act. (E.g. under the *Municipal Conflict of Interest Act.)*

It is an offence to sit or vote at a meeting of the board after becoming disqualified from sitting (s. 213(1)).

The number of members to be elected to a district school board is determined by Ontario Regulation 412/00. The *Education Act* says that a district school board cannot have fewer than five members or more than 22 members (excluding native representatives under s. 188) (s. 58.1(10)(11)). A board may vote to reduce the number of members that it has, subject to the minimum level of five members (s. 58.1(10.1)).

The members of an English-language public district school board are to be elected by persons entitled to vote, and who are not separate school supporters (or on the preliminary list) and are not qualified to be electors for a French-language district school board under section 58.8.

The members of an English-language separate school board are to be elected by persons who are entitled to vote, and who are separate school supporters (or on the preliminary list) and are not qualified to be electors for a French-language district school board under section 58.8.

The members of a French-language public district school board are to be elected by persons who entitled to vote, and are not separate school supporters (or on the preliminary list) and are qualified to be electors for a French-language district school board.

The members of a French-language separate school board are to be elected by persons who are entitled to vote, and are separate school supporters (or on the preliminary list) and are qualified to be electors for a French-language district school board. (See s. 54 with respect to a resident Roman Catholic person who is not a supporter of any board but who wishes to be entered on a "preliminary list" of electors to be able to vote for members of a Roman Catholic board.)

A person may only run for one seat on the board (s. 219(10)).

3.4.2 Resignation of Trustee

A board (being a corporation) does not cease to exist by reason only of a lack of members (s. 220(2)).

A trustee can resign with the consent of a majority of the other board members, unless it would reduce the board to below quorum (s. 220). After the resignation, the remaining board members must decide whether to fill the vacancy by appointing a person to the board or by holding a by-election.

3.4.3 Vacancy on the Board

Section 219(11) of the Act states that the seat of a member who is not qualified or entitled to act as a member of the board is vacated.

Section 228 provides that a member of a board vacates his or her seat on the board if he or she:

- is convicted of an indictable offence — the vacancy cannot be filled until the time for taking any appeal has elapsed or until the final determination of any appeal; if the conviction is quashed, then the seat is deemed not to have been vacated
- absents himself or herself from three consecutive regular meetings of the board, without being authorized by board resolution. (There is no definition of "regular" meeting, and it is unclear whether a regular meeting includes the "organizational" meeting of the board that is required every December.)
- ceases to hold the qualifications required to act as a member

- becomes disqualified under section 219(4); i.e. becomes an employee of the board, becomes a clerk, treasurer, deputy clerk or deputy treasurer of a municipality or upper-tier municipality sharing jurisdiction with the board, becomes a member of the Legislative Assembly, or the Senate or the House of Commons, or becomes otherwise ineligible or disqualified under any Act
- fails to be physically present in the board's meeting room for at least three regular board meetings in a 12-month period.

3.4.4 Filling a Vacancy

Section 221 provides how the board is to fill a vacancy.

The members may appoint a person within 60 days of the vacancy, if a majority of members remains in office in order to make the appointment. Alternatively, the board may by resolution require that an election be held to replace the trustee if the vacancy occurs:

(a) in a year in which there is no regular election

(b) before April 1 in the year of a regular election, or

(c) after the new board is organized in the year of a regular election (s. 221(2)).

If no majority remains to make an appointment or to choose an optional by-election, the Act provides that a by-election must be held (s. 221(b)).

A member appointed or elected to fill a vacancy does so for the remainder of the term of the member who vacated the office.

3.4.5 Trustee Honoraria

Section 191 authorizes the *Minister* to make regulations about trustee honoraria. Ontario Regulation 357/06 prescribes the maximum honorarium payable to a board member. The amount varies for each board according to a formula set out in the regulation. An additional honorarium may be paid to the chair and vice-chair. Boards are required to make a policy regarding trustee honoraria, after establishing a Citizens' Advisory Committee, as set out in the regulation.

Section 191.2 states that trustees may be reimbursed for travel expenses to attend meetings. Under section 191.2(3), a board may establish a policy for reimbursement of out-of-pocket expenses "reasonably incurred in connection with carrying out the responsibilities of a board member."

A board may not provide insured benefits to its members. Board members, by definition, are not "employees" of the board, and are not entitled to employment-related benefits such as severance.

3.4.6 Board Meetings Open to the Public

Meetings of a board and its committees are open to the public (s. 207). The location of a board meeting is determined by the board (ss. 208(2) and (6)). The public *may* be excluded when a *committee* of the board (including committee of the whole) is considering an item that is one of the following:

- the security of the property of the board

- disclosure of intimate, personal or financial information about a board or committee member, an employee, a prospective employee of the board, a pupil or a pupil's parent or guardian
- acquisition or disposal of a school site
- decisions about negotiations with employees
- litigation affecting the board.

Trustees and board employees must also comply with the *Municipal Freedom of Information and Protection of Privacy Act*. Disclosure of certain confidential items outside the confines of a closed meeting could result in an offence being committed under that Act. All trustees (and employees) should be provided with information about their obligations under the legislation. They should also be aware that the *Education Act* requires that student records must be kept secret (s. 266).

A person who is guilty of "improper conduct" at a board meeting may be expelled from it by the presiding officer (s. 207(3)). It is an offence to disrupt a meeting from which one has been expelled (s. 212(2)).

A board is entitled to determine its own procedures for meetings. These procedures are set out in the board's by-laws. For example, a board will determine the order and content of its agenda, and the rules about making various kinds of motions. The board may determine whether it will hear delegations and can establish the rules and time limits for presentations by delegates. If the board is conducting a "hearing" (e.g. expulsion hearing) it must adhere to the applicable provisions of the *Education Act* and the *Statutory Powers Procedure Act*.

3.4.7 Electronic Meetings

District school boards have the authority to hold electronic meetings. Ontario Regulation 463/97, made under the authority of section 208.1 of the Act, states that every district school board shall develop a policy providing for the use of electronic means for holding meetings of the board and its committees. The policy must be consistent with any policies or guidelines issued by the Minister about electronic meetings (Act, s. 8(1)(3.6)). The board's policy must provide that a board member or a pupil representative shall be provided with the means of participating in meetings by electronic means and must be able to hear and be heard by all the other participants (s. 3 of O. Reg. 463/97).

Subject to Ministry policies and guidelines, the board shall determine whether the *public* is to be able to participate by electronic means, and if so, the extent and manner of participation. In all cases, it is vital that precautions be taken so that persons who are not eligible to attend closed meetings do not have access to them through electronic means.

Section 229 of the Act requires members to be physically present at a meeting of the board at least three times during each twelve-month period commencing December 1st (although a higher number can be provided for under s. 208.1(5). The board chair (or designate), at least one other member and the director of education (or designate) must be physically present in the meeting room of the board. At *committee* meetings the chair of the committee (or designate) and the director (or designate) must be physically present at the meeting (Reg. 463/97, s. 5, O.).

Except where a meeting is closed in accordance with the *Education Act*, the meeting room of the board or a committee must be open to those who wish to attend.

3.5 Student Trustees

Pupils are entitled to be represented on the school board where they are enrolled. Subsections 55(1)–(8) of the *Education Act* provide as follows:

> 55. (1) The Minister may make regulations providing for elected student trustees to represent, on district school boards and on boards established under section 67, the interests of pupils in the last two years of the intermediate division and in the senior division.
>
> (2) A student trustee is not a member of the board and is not entitled to exercise a binding vote on any matter before the board or any of its committees.
>
> (3) A student trustee is entitled to require that a matter before the board or one of its committees on which the student trustee sits be put to a recorded vote, and in that case there shall be,
>
> (a) a recorded non-binding vote that includes the student trustee's vote; and
>
> (b) a recorded binding vote that does not include the student trustee's vote.
>
> (4) A student trustee is not entitled to move a motion, but is entitled to suggest a motion on any matter at a meeting of the board or of one of its committees on which the student trustee sits, and if no member of the board or committee, as the case may be, moves the suggested motion, the record shall show the suggested motion.
>
> (5) A student trustee is not entitled to be present at a meeting that is closed to the public under clause 207(2)(b).
>
> (6) Subject to subsections (2) to (5), a student trustee shall have the same opportunities for participation at meetings of the board and of its committees as a member has.
>
> (7) A student trustee has the same status as a board member with respect to access to board resources and opportunities for training.
>
> (8) A student trustee is entitled to receive an honorarium from the board in accordance with the regulations, if the specified conditions are satisfied.

Ontario Regulation 7/07 is the regulation about Student Trustees. It provides as follows:

> 1. This Regulation applies to every district school board and every secondary school board established under section 67 of the Act.
>
> 2. (1) The board shall develop and implement a policy providing for matters relating to student trustees and to the payment of honoraria for student trustees.
>
> (2) The policy shall be in accordance with this Regulation and with any policies and guidelines established by the Minister under paragraph 3.5 of subsection 8(1) of the Act.
>
> 3. The board shall have at least one but not more than three student trustees.
>
> 4. (1) Student trustees shall be elected in one of the following ways:
>
> 1. Directly, by students of the board.
>
> 2. Indirectly, by student representative bodies such as student councils.
>
> (2) An election shall be held not later than April 30 in each year.

5. (1) A person is qualified to act as a student trustee if he or she is a full-time pupil of the board in the senior division.

(2) Despite subsection (1), a person is not qualified to be elected or to act as a student trustee if he or she is serving a sentence of imprisonment in a penal or correctional institution.

(3) A person who ceases to be qualified to act as a student trustee shall resign from the position.

(4) In this section,

"full-time pupil" has the same meaning as in the most recent regulations made under section 234 of the Act. [Section 234 deals with grants for student needs.]

6. A student trustee's term of office starts on August 1 of the year in which he or she is elected and ends on July 31 of the following year.

7. If the board determines that a vacancy shall be filled, it shall be filled by a by-election.

8. If the board has established a policy under subsection 191.2 (3) of the Act, the board shall reimburse student trustees for out-of-pocket expenses as if they were members of the board.

9. The amount of the honorarium referred to in subsection 55 (8) of the Act is,

(a) $2,500, if the student trustee holds office for a complete term of office;

(b) $2,500 prorated according to the proportion of a term for which the student trustee holds office, if the student trustee holds office for less than a complete term of office.

10. The board shall provide the Ministry with the names of the student trustees elected, not later than 30 days after the date of the election or by-election.

4

Handling Students' Personal Information

4.1 Introduction

One of the most common legal questions asked by school administrators is about when it is permissible to release personal information about a student. Schools routinely receive requests for information about students from all kinds of sources: law firms, insurance adjusters, estranged spouses, relatives, children's aid societies, the police, etc.

The Basic Rule: personal information about a student is confidential. Unless you are sure you have the right to discuss a student or to reveal a student's documentation, don't.

Confidentiality of student information is mandated by the *Education Act* (s. 266) and the *Municipal Freedom of Information and Protection of Privacy Act* (*MFIPPA*). Health-related information is also protected by the *Personal Health Information Protection Act, 2004*. In addition, confidentiality is mandated by ethical codes governing teachers, social workers and psychologists. Information about young persons involved with the law is protected by the *Youth Criminal Justice Act*.

4.2 Confidentiality of the "Ontario Student Record"

Section 266 protects the confidentiality of a pupil's Ontario Student Record (OSR).

The Act says that a pupil's Ontario Student Record is "privileged" for the information and use of the supervisory officers, the principal and teachers of the school for the improvement of the instruction of the pupil.

The information contained in a record is not available to any other person except:

(a) the pupil

(b) the pupil's parent or guardian if the pupil is a minor

(c) the local medical officer of health

(d) a Ministry-appointed person who is hearing a dispute about the contents of a record under subsection 266(5).

The Ontario Student Record can be made available to another person if you have the written permission of the parent or guardian (of a pupil who is a minor), or of the pupil (if the pupil is an adult). Having an informed, written consent to release or even *discuss* the contents of an OSR is critically important. In section 266, a "guardian" includes a person, society or corporation who or that has custody of a pupil (s. 266(11)).

Unfortunately, section 266 ignores the fact that many other board employees are required to have access to a pupil's OSR in the regular course of business. School secretaries, special education assistants, centrally-assigned special education consultants, board psychologists and therapists, and other staff may all need to see the OSR or at least know the relevant portions of its content, and yet the Act does not, if read narrowly, allow them access without permission. However, the Act allows a local attendance counsellor to require a principal to provide information about a pupil for the purpose of enforcing compulsory attendance (s. 28(1)(b)).

Ideally, when a child is being registered at school, a parent should be asked to sign a consent that would allow other specified board personnel to have access to the OSR, but as a practical matter this may be difficult to administer. Boards that allow staff to access *electronic* student records must be very vigilant about which staff have on-line access to a pupil's record and about what the staff do with those records.

Not all information about a pupil is contained in the OSR, although certain information must be kept there. The requirements about OSR contents are contained in the Ontario Student Record Guideline which is issued by the Minister under the authority of paragraph 8(1)27 of the *Education Act*.

A pupil has one official OSR, and if the pupil transfers from one school to another school within Ontario, the OSR is sent to the receiving school. The OSR is not transferred out of Ontario (see s. 6 of the OSR Guideline).

The local medical officer of health may request limited information about pupils:

- the pupil's name, address, telephone number
- the pupil's birthdate
- the name, address and telephone number of the pupil's parent or guardian.

The school principal may divulge information from the OSR if he or she is making a report that is required under the *Education Act* or regulations. Section 266 does not prevent the principal from compiling and delivering information that is required by the Minister of Education or the board (s. 266(7)).

The school principal may also divulge information from the OSR if he or she is making a report (1) for an educational institution, a pupil or a former pupil in respect of an application for further education, or (2) for a pupil or former pupil in respect of an application for employment, if a written request for the report is made by the former pupil, the adult pupil or the parent/guardian of the pupil who is a minor.

The principal of the pupil's school and the school board may use the OSR for the purpose of a disciplinary proceeding against the pupil instituted by the principal.

OSR Contents are Secret

Except as permitted in section 266, every person must "preserve secrecy in respect of the content of a record that comes to the person's knowledge in the course of his or her duties or employment" (s. 266(10)). The information within the person's knowledge cannot be communicated to any other person except:

- as may be required in the performance of his or her duties, or
- with the written consent of the parent or guardian of the pupil where the pupil is a minor, or
- with the written consent of the pupil where the pupil is an adult.

No person can be required in any trial or other proceeding to give evidence in respect of the content of a record except where the record has been introduced as evidence as provided in section 266. Unless the written permission of the parent/guardian or adult pupil is obtained, the record is not admissible in evidence for any purpose in any trial, inquest, inquiry, examination, hearing or other proceeding, except to prove the establishment, transfer, maintenance, retention or transfer of the record (s. 266(2)). The exception to this is a hearing held under subsection 266(5) by a Ministry-appointed person. Despite these restrictions against admissibility, courts and tribunals do order school boards to produce the OSR in criminal and civil proceedings if the contents may be relevant.

Removal of Information from the OSR

Much of the information in a pupil's OSR is included because the OSR Guideline gives the principal no choice about the matter. However, disputes do arise about some information that a school has included in the OSR. An adult pupil, or the parent or guardian of a pupil who is a minor, may request the removal of information in a record if he or she is of the opinion that the information is inaccurately recorded or is not conducive to the improvement of instruction of the pupil. A request must be in writing and must ask the principal to correct the alleged inaccuracy or to remove the impugned information from the record. If the principal refuses to comply with the request, the person making the request may, in writing, require the principal to refer the request to the appropriate supervisory officer. The supervisory officer must:

(1) require the principal to comply with the request, or

(2) submit the record and the request to a person designated by the Minister.

The person designated by the Minister, usually an experienced education officer, must hold a hearing. The principal and the person making the request are the parties at the hearing. The designated person decides the matter and his or her decision is final and binding upon the parties.

According to the OSR Guideline, if material is removed, it must either be destroyed or handed to the parent. It is not uncommon for a principal to remove information about a suspension or expulsion from the OSR with the agreement of a parent. This normally occurs after the pupil has shown that he or she is back on track, educationally and behaviourally. As part of an agreement with the parent about the removal, the parent can be asked to agree that this disciplinary information will be kept under seal at a confidential location outside the OSR in case it is needed in future litigation with the parent or in other defined circumstances.

4.3 Municipal Freedom of Information and Protection of Privacy Act (MFIPPA)

The *Municipal Freedom of Information and Protection of Privacy Act* governs the use, collection and storage of information, including personal information, by municipalities, school boards and many other institutions. It is based upon two fundamental principles. The first is that the public has the right to have access to records held by these institutions. The second is that personal information should be protected to ensure privacy.

A school board cannot *collect* personal information, directly or indirectly, unless it has the legal authority to do so, and unless the individual affected has been informed that the information will be collected and there is authority for doing so. Boards must be prepared to show that the purpose of the collection is consistent with an educational rationale. For example, a parent survey that has little or no research value in an educational context, and which enables the board to know the identity of the person responding to the survey, could violate *MFIPPA*. When in doubt, boards are well-advised to consult with their legal counsel and the Ontario Information and Privacy Commissioner about the collection of personal information.

The Act is also intended to ensure that personal information is only disclosed to a third party if there is lawful authority to do so, either under a particular provision of the Act or by obtaining an informed consent from the individual affected. Consent under *MFIPPA* does not have to be in writing, although written consent is preferable in case the individual subsequently disputes that consent was provided.

Almost all information you have about a student is "personal". The privacy of a student's personal information is protected by *MFIPPA*. Personal information includes class lists, addresses, email addresses, phone numbers, and even the fact that the student is registered at the school. A tape or disc from a surveillance video camera showing a student is also personal information about that student.

According to section 2 of *MFIPPA*, "personal information" means recorded information about an identifiable individual, including:

(a) information relating to the race, national or ethnic origin, colour, religion, age, sex, sexual orientation or marital or family status of the individual

(b) information relating to the education or the medical, psychiatric, psychological, criminal or employment history of the individual or information relating to financial transactions in which the individual has been involved

(c) any identifying number, symbol, or other particular assigned to the individual

(d) the address, telephone number, fingerprints or blood type of the individual

(e) the personal opinions or views of the individual except if they relate to another individual

(f) correspondence sent to an institution by the individual that is implicitly or explicitly of a private or confidential nature, and replies to that correspondence that would reveal the contents of the original correspondence

(g) the views or opinions of another individual about the individual

(h) the individual's name if it appears with other personal information relating to the individual or where the disclosure of the name would reveal other personal information about the individual.

Section 31 of *MFIPPA* states:

> 31. An institution shall not use personal information in its custody or under its control except,
>
> (a) if the person to whom the information relates has identified that information in particular and consented to its use;
>
> (b) for the purpose for which it was obtained or compiled or for a consistent purpose; or
>
> (c) for a purpose for which the information may be disclosed to the institution under section 32 or under section 42 of the *Freedom of Information and Protection of Privacy Act*.

Section 32 provides some exceptions that permit the disclosure of personal information:

> 32. An institution shall not disclose personal information in its custody or under its control except,
>
> (a) in accordance with Part I;
>
> (b) if the person to whom the information relates has identified that information in particular and consented to its disclosure;
>
> (c) for the purpose for which it was obtained or compiled or for a consistent purpose;
>
> (d) if the disclosure is made to an officer, employee, consultant or agent of the institution who needs the record in the performance of their duties and if the disclosure is necessary and proper in the discharge of the institution's functions;
>
> (e) for the purpose of complying with an Act of the Legislature or an Act of Parliament, an agreement or arrangement under such an Act or a treaty;
>
> (f) if disclosure is by a law enforcement institution,
>
> (i) to a law enforcement agency in a foreign country under an arrangement, a written agreement or treaty or legislative authority, or
>
> (ii) to another law enforcement agency in Canada;
>
> (g) if disclosure is to an institution or a law enforcement agency in Canada to aid an investigation undertaken with a view to a law enforcement proceeding or from which a law enforcement proceeding is likely to result;
>
> (h) in compelling circumstances affecting the health or safety of an individual if upon disclosure notification is mailed to the last known address of the individual to whom the information relates;
>
> (i) in compassionate circumstances, to facilitate contact with the spouse, a close relative or a friend of an individual who is injured, ill or deceased;
>
> (j) to the Minister;
>
> (k) to the Information and Privacy Commissioner;
>
> (l) to the Government of Canada or the Government of Ontario in order to facilitate the auditing of shared cost programs.

33. The purpose of a use or disclosure of personal information that has been collected directly from the individual to whom the information relates is a consistent purpose under clauses 31(b) and 32(c) only if the individual might reasonably have expected such a use or disclosure.

Right of Access

The right of a third party to have *access* to a record held by a school board is subject to a number of specific *exemptions* listed in Part I of the Act that permit a board to refuse disclosure. These include:

- records of meetings that are authorized by law to be held in private
- advice or recommendations to the board
- law enforcement records
- information received in confidence from another government
- information from a third party containing trade secrets or scientific, technical, commercial, financial or labour relations information
- information which might prejudice the economic, financial, competitive, or negotiating interests of an institution
- information covered by solicitor-client privilege
- information which if made public, may seriously threaten the safety or health of an individual
- personal information.

Note that the personal information can be disclosed in compelling circumstances affecting the health or safety of an individual (*MFIPPA*, s. 14(1)(b)). If, for example, you are concerned that a student may harm himself or herself, or is intending to harm others, you should disclose the student's relevant personal information to other persons, and indeed may be negligent if you fail to do so. Moreover, a board may *refuse* to disclose any record whose disclosure could reasonably be expected to seriously threaten the safety or health of an individual (*MFIPPA*, s. 13). However, an exemption under sections 7, 9, 10, 11, 13, or 14 of the Act does not apply if a compelling public interest in disclosure clearly outweighs the purpose of the exemption (*MFIPPA*, s. 16).

Under *MFIPPA*, a "record" means any record of information however recorded, whether in printed form, on film, by electronic means or otherwise, and includes:

(a) correspondence, a memorandum, a book, a plan, a map, a drawing, a diagram, a pictorial or graphic work, a photograph, a film, a microfilm, a sound recording, videotape, a machine readable record, any other documentary material, regardless of physical form or characteristics, and any copy thereof and

(b) subject to the regulations, any record that is capable of being produced from a machine readable record under the control of an institution by means of computer hardware and software or any other information storage equipment and technical expertise normally used by the institution.

Records include information that is stored electronically, and an institution must therefore be able to retrieve its electronic records in a manner that will enable it to respond to requests for information under *MFIPPA*.

Oral communications are not records because they are not recorded or retrievable in physical form. (However, in sections 28 and 29 (collection and retention of personal information) a record can include personal information that is not recorded.)

The provisions in the *Education Act* and OSR Guideline with respect to the confidentiality, retention and storage of a pupil's student record apply in conjunction with provisions of the *Municipal Freedom of Information and Protection of Privacy Act*. Boards must comply with both statutes, although in case of conflict, the privacy legislation prevails (s. 53, *MFIPPA*). Under the *Municipal Freedom of Information and Protection of Privacy Act*, a consent for the release of personal information may be obtained from an individual who is 16 years of age or older. If the individual is under 16 years of age, consent must be obtained from a person having lawful custody of the individual. The fact that 16 and 17 year olds can consent to disclosure of personal information under *MFIPPA* does not operate to deprive parents of those pupils from having access to their child's student record, or from giving consent to allow a third party access to the OSR.

4.4 Personal Health Information

The *Personal Health Information Protection Act, 2004* (*PHIPA*) governs the collection, use, and disclosure of personal health information. The Ministry of Health and Long-Term Care website states:

> Personal health information is identifiable information relating to your health and health care history. This includes information that may be contained in your medical files such as diagnostic, treatment and care information, your OHIP number, and genetic information if it is part of your health record. Personal health information also includes any other identifying information included in a record of personal health information.[1]

The legislation covers "health information custodians", a term that includes doctors, other health care practitioners, hospitals, and long-term care facilities. It also includes health care clinics, laboratories, pharmacies, the Ministry of Health and Long-Term Care, and other health-related organizations. However, the legislation also applies to individuals and organizations that receive personal health information from the health care system, such as school boards and schools. Schools and boards are not health care custodians. However, a nurse employed by a school board to provide health care is a "custodian employed by a non-custodian" and as such has specific duties under *PHIPA* with respect to the collection, use and safeguarding of health information that comes into his or her possession.

A health information custodian, such as a doctor or hospital, cannot disclose personal health information to a non-custodian, including the non-custodian for whom the custodian is working, unless:

- the individual whose personal health information is at issue has given express consent;
- the disclosure is permitted or required by *PHIPA*; or

---

[1]"Health Information Custodians Working for Non-Health Information Custodians", *Fact Sheet* (Information and Privacy Commissioner of Ontario) 11 (February 2006), http://www.ipc.on.ca/images/ Resources/up-2fact_11_e.pdf.

- the disclosure is permitted or required by another law.

School records may contain information about the health of a pupil. Because schools may have to deal with medical emergencies involving pupils, they routinely request the pupil's OHIP (health card) number. Parents cannot be required to disclose the OHIP number, but this can diminish the school's ability to deal expeditiously with medical agencies in an emergency. The Information and Privacy Commissioner provides the following information with respect to health cards and schools:

> Generally, *third parties* are forbidden from collecting, using or disclosing your health number except for purposes related to the provision of provincially funded health resources to you. For the purposes of health numbers and health cards, *third parties* are individuals and institutions not directly involved in the delivery of provincially funded health care services. To be clear, *third parties* may *ask* you for your health number, but only for purposes directly related to the provision of provincially funded health resources to you.
>
> This prohibition applies to most individuals or institutions in Ontario including municipal and provincial government agencies, private employers, insurance companies, retailers, health clubs, and private individuals.
>
> For example, a school, daycare, or camp may invite you to volunteer your child's health number so that they have it on record to disclose it to hospital staff in the event of an urgent medical development requiring the immediate hospitalization of your child. In some circumstances, employers may also invite their employees to volunteer their health numbers. For example, an employer may invite its employees to volunteer their health numbers where employees are performing work that routinely exposes them to a significant risk of injury.
>
> Similarly, in the event that you were injured and unconscious, it might be appropriate for a friend, colleague or Good Samaritan to take note of your health number and disclose it to the staff at the emergency ward of a hospital.

4.5 Responding to Subpoena or Summons

What happens when you are subpoenaed or summoned?

A subpoena or summons is a document that commands you to appear before a court or tribunal. The document frequently requires you to bring with you certain documents, such as student records. The subpoena or summons will typically be issued at the request of a party to civil litigation or to criminal proceedings. For example, you could be summoned by a party to a child custody dispute in court, or by a party to an arbitration, Labour Board hearing, or human rights hearing.

The subpoena or summons is not a licence to talk to anyone. That is, if you are properly served with a subpoena or a summons requiring you to appear before a court or tribunal with student records, this does not give you permission to disclose information about the student or to hand over the records to the person who caused you to be subpoenaed or summoned (unless there is consent to disclosure given by the student's parent or guardian).

If a principal receives a summons in a civil proceeding (i.e. not in criminal court) to produce a student record, and there is no written consent for the release of the record, he or she should (subject to advice from the board solicitor) respond to the summons by attending court, and should explain (directly or through counsel) to the court that the *Education Act* prohibits the release of the record. The court may nevertheless order that the OSR be produced either to the court itself or to the requesting party who may then seek to adduce the record as evidence.

In proceedings under federal legislation, such as the *Criminal Code* (Canada), the rules are different. If a subpoena or summons is issued under federal legislation, it takes precedence over the non-disclosure provisions in section 266 of the *Education Act*. A subpoena does not give you the authority to talk to a police officer, defence counsel or Crown attorney about a student's personal information. Principals must obey a search warrant, and they must obey a subpoena or summons to attend a court with documents. The judge may be asked by a party to make a determination of the relevance of the documents before admitting them as evidence. The principal is normally summoned to testify to identify the student records as being authentic and accurate. The principal should, through counsel, seek permission of the court to leave a copy of the OSR with the court, rather than the original. Always take a copy of the documents to hand over — one that you can verify is complete and accurate.

Personal information other than the contents of an OSR can be disclosed to the police who are involved in a law enforcement investigation, because disclosure is permitted "if disclosure is to an institution or a law enforcement agency in Canada to aid an investigation undertaken with a view to a law enforcement proceeding or from which a law enforcement proceeding is likely to result" (*MFIPPA*, s. 32(g)). Other situations where a principal may be permitted to disclose personal information include an emergency affecting the life or safety of the person, or in compassionate circumstances if the information is needed to facilitate contact with a next of kin or friend of a person who is injured, ill, or deceased (ss. 32(h) and (i)).

The section 32(g) exemption would permit disclosure of a student's personal information (other than the OSR) to a children's aid society if it is conducting an investigation under the *Child and Family Services Act*. A further ground for disclosure would apply to the children's aid society under section 32(e) — for the purpose of allowing the society to comply with legislation.

Pursuant to the *Child and Family Services Act*, a court may order the principal of a school to produce the OSR for inspection and copying by a children's aid society if the court is satisfied that the record contains information that may be relevant to whether the child is suffering abuse or is likely to suffer abuse and the person in control of the record has refused to permit a society director to inspect it. The OSR should not be released to a children's aid society without an appropriate court order (assuming no written permission has been given by a parent or guardian). If a child is under the protection of a society or under its care and supervision, then the society is entitled to the child's educational information.

As noted above, personal information can be disclosed in compelling circumstances affecting the health or safety of an individual (*MFIPPA*, s. 14(1)(b)). To repeat, if you are concerned that a student may harm himself or herself, or is intending to harm others, you should disclose the student's relevant personal information to other persons as needed. Secondly, you may *refuse* to disclose any record whose disclosure could reasonably be expected to seriously threaten the safety or health of an individual. Thirdly, an exemption permitting you not to disclose, under sections

7, 9, 10, 11, 13, or 14 of the Act does not apply if a compelling public interest in disclosure clearly outweighs the purpose of the exemption (*MFIPPA*, s. 16).

Teachers have an ethical duty to maintain the confidentiality of personal information about students. However, other school or board staff, including social workers, psychologists and guidance counsellors, all receive information in confidence from students. When can that information be disclosed to other persons? Members of regulated health professions are guided by the ethical and professional standards of their profession. They will maintain the confidentiality of personal information unless they are ordered by a court or tribunal to disclose it, or unless there is a consent to disclosure or a need for disclosure to protect the health and safety of the individual or other individuals. A guidance counsellor, although not a health professional, will maintain the confidential information provided by a student under similar constraints (i.e. court order, public safety). In the course of litigation, a court or tribunal may be asked to determine whether the qualified privilege attached to the confidential information is subordinate to some other interest (such as the right to a fair trial or hearing) that compels disclosure. If a court is asked to order disclosure, it will consider factors such as whether there was an expectation that it would be kept confidential, the effect on the student, the probative value of the information, and the public interest.[2]

It is important to remember that a teacher or health professional cannot give a student an absolute promise that confidential information will never be disclosed. If a student divulges information that really should be disclosed (e.g. for the student's own good), the first step is to speak with the student about the need to come forth with the information to the appropriate authorities. A student may know information about a crime. A student may be pregnant and may not want to tell her parents. The teacher, counsellor or other professional should try to work with the student to create the conditions under which the student will divulge the information.

4.6 Don't Talk to Lawyers

Lawyers do not have any special status when they call a school seeking personal information about a pupil. Do not discuss a student with a lawyer or legal clinic unless you have the consent of the parent or adult pupil. If the OSR is involved, the consent must be in writing.

If you are contacted in your capacity as a board employee by a lawyer who acts for the school board and who seeks information to enable him or her to represent the board, you may discuss a student's personal information with that lawyer. The lawyer is ethically bound to respect the confidentiality of the information. Similarly, you should co-operate with an insurance adjuster who represents the board's insurer and who is investigating an incident about which you have information.

So, for example, if a child had an accident in the school gym, a lawyer from the board's insurance company may call you to find out more about the accident. In some labour arbitration cases and in some civil court cases, arbitrators and courts have ordered board representatives to disclose personal information about students

---

[2]See also E. Roher and S. Wormwall, *The Role of the Principal*, 2d ed. (Aurora: Canada Law Book, 2008) pp. 124–130.

to the opposing side where the information is arguably relevant to the case being heard. The opposing side is under strict ethical rules about how they use a student's personal information obtained in this manner.

If you have any doubts about disclosing information to someone purporting to be a board lawyer, check with your supervisor.

4.7 Do Talk to the Office of the Children's Lawyer

Schools get letters from the Office of the Children's Lawyer requesting information about students and often requesting an interview with the student and teachers at the school.

These letters invariably have parental consents attached. Information may therefore be disclosed to the Office of the Children's Lawyer. Moreover, the lawyer is appointed to represent the student and is assisting a court in determining the child's best interests in a custody dispute. By co-operating, you are not "taking sides" between spouses; you are helping the child.

4.8 Separated or Divorced Parents

In my law practice as in-house counsel, I find that an extraordinary number of calls from schools are about getting caught in the middle of disputes between separated or divorced spouses.

In the event of a formal separation or divorce, the parents will have a separation agreement or a court order establishing their custodial rights over the children of the marriage. A parent may have "joint custody", "sole custody", "access", or may be prohibited from having anything to do with the child.

If there is a separation agreement or court order determining the parental rights of custody and access, get a copy of it. It is not your job to enforce it, but if you are in the middle of a dispute, it helps to know some of the rules. Ask the parent whether it is the most recent court order or agreement.

The usual situation sees one parent with custody and the other with "access" to the child. Court orders and separation agreements make all kinds of different provisions about sharing parental duties and decision-making. However, the custodial parent is normally authorized to make the decisions about the child's education, and is responsible for signing school forms, consents, releases, etc.

However, a parent who "only" has access is still a parent, and the *Children's Law Reform Act* gives an access parent the right to have "educational information" about the child. This means you must share information with the "access" parent about how his or her child is doing in school, including the OSR, report cards, attendance records, etc. Where feasible, the parents should be given separate parent-teacher interviews unless the parents wish to attend together.

It is important that schools not be manipulated by one spouse against another. Do not accept "instructions" from a custodial parent who tells you to deny educational information to the other parent. If a parent wants to impose these restrictions, they have to be backed up with a court order.

There may be occasions when you are concerned that disclosure of information to an access parent may be detrimental to the health or well-being of your student.

Let's say, for example, that you are aware of a history of violence or abuse in the family. The mother and children left home for their own safety, and they may wish to keep their address secret. Although Dad has "access" according to the most recent court order, he has not been seen for two years, and unexpectedly shows up at the school looking for information about his child. This could be quite innocent or unremarkable. Or, it may set off all kinds of warning bells for the school administrator. In these circumstances, the principal should err on the side of safety and should not reveal any information about the family until he or she has checked with the mother and advised her that her former spouse has appeared. At that point, the mother will indicate her position on the matter and if she wants to prohibit the father from accessing the educational information, she can seek a court order. In the meantime, although it may be feasible to provide the father with some information, nothing should be disclosed (such as an address) that would endanger the student or his/her family. The above scenario is based on situations that I see with surprising frequency, and, of course, the roles are sometimes reversed as between the mother and father.

A parent who has no custody or access in respect of his or her child has no right to see the child's educational information without the consent of the person who has custody.

4.9 Guardians

A guardian is someone, other than a parent, who has lawful custody of a child. In most cases, a court will appoint someone to act as guardian. Parents are also able to sign documents clearly signifying their intention that another adult shall have custody of their child. The document must state that the guardian is to have the power to make decisions in respect of the child's education. (This documentation is discussed in more detail in the chapter on Going to School.)

4.10 Photographs of Students

Taking photographs of students is a collection of their personal information. This collection is not expressly authorized by the *Education Act*, nor is it necessary to the proper administration of a lawfully authorized activity. Therefore the consent of the parent or guardian should be obtained for the taking of the photographs and their use and collection. This is true even with respect to the annual "photo day". Ontario's Information and Privacy Commissioner advises that:[3]

> Before the photo day, the parent/guardian should receive notice that school photographs will be taken and afforded the opportunity to provide consent.

If a request is received from any party seeking to photograph, film, or otherwise record students, a consent must be obtained from the parent or guardian if the students are under 18 years of age. This includes photographers from the local media or working from the board office or a trustee's office.

---

[3]"F.A.Q.: Access and Privacy in the School System" (joint project of the Toronto District School Board and the Information and Privacy Commissioner of Ontario, February 2001) http://www.ipc. on.ca/images/Resources/up-faq_e.pdf.

The Information and Privacy Commissioner advises:

> Where personal information is collected in the form of photographs taken by board employees, there should be clear notice of collection, including the authority and the consent of the individual to whom the information relates.
>
> A school should develop a workable policy regarding the taking of photographs of its students on school property or at school events by non-board employees. Such a policy should be developed in consultation with parents/guardians and communicated to them.
>
> Remember, these considerations should apply to all images, including photographs, digital images, postings to the Internet, films, and video recordings. Ideally, this policy should be based on the consent of the photographed subject, or, if it is a student who is under age, that of the parent or guardian.
>
> If parents or students are concerned about the use of photographs within the school community or by the media, they should speak to the principal. It is not unreasonable for a parent to request that photographs of his or her child not be taken or used without particular consent.
>
> [I]t is useful to note that these same considerations apply to interviews with students as well. A person's opinions or views, except if they relate to another individual, are defined as personal information as described in section 2(1) of *MFIPPA*.

4.11 Student Yearbooks

Student yearbooks clearly contain personal information. However, putting photographs of students and staff in a yearbook, such as class and team photographs, would in most instances be consistent with the purpose of taking the photographs and individual consents for inclusion from the individuals in the photographs are therefore not required. This is particularly true of photographs taken on "photo day", or by a school photographer — people expect these photographs to show up in the yearbook. However, this expectation does not apply to all photographs of students, and careful consideration must be given as to what material is appropriate for inclusion. Who took the photograph, where and when was it taken, and what use would the student or staff member expect to be made of it? When in doubt, individual consents should be obtained.

4.12 Graduation Lists

Schools publish lists of students who are graduating, typically as part of the program of a commencement or graduation ceremony. They also provide these lists to trustees and to local MPPs and MPs in order for the publicly-elected official to be able to send congratulations to the students. Although the practice of providing these lists to MPPs and MPs is not without controversy (from a privacy perspective), there is a reasonable argument that the distribution is a "consistent purpose" under *MFIPPA* that would allow the information to be appropriately distributed without a consent having been obtained. In addition, as mentioned, the lists are usually printed and distributed at the graduation, and any person attending would presumably have access to a copy. Persons working in the office of the MPP or MP should respect the privacy of the information and destroy any such student lists after congratulatory letters or certificates have been sent to the students.

4.13 Providing Information to the Ontario College of Teachers

Section 47(1) of the *Ontario College of Teachers Act* states:

> For the purpose of carrying out its objects, the College may require the Provincial Schools Authority, a school board or any other person or body designated by the regulations to provide the College with information, including personal information within the meaning of section 38 of the *Freedom of Information and Protection of Privacy Act* or section 28 of the *Municipal Freedom of Information and Protection of Privacy Act*, in respect of members of the College.

The College has extensive powers to investigate the conduct of its members and may even obtain a search warrant from a Justice of the Peace. Because the College may require information "in respect of *members* of the College" it is not entirely clear whether section 47(1) allows an investigator (who has *not* been appointed under section 36) to have access to a student's personal information without the consent of the parent or adult student. However, the term "in respect of" is usually interpreted broadly. Therefore, an investigator who is essentially acting for the College's Investigation Committee with respect to an actual or possible law enforcement proceeding by the College against a member, arguably does come within the exemption found in section 32(g) of *MFIPPA*. Because *MFIPPA* prevails over the confidentiality provisions in the *Education Act*, section 32(g) would permit a board to give a College investigator a student's personal information if it is required in the course of a College investigation.

5

Statutory Roles and Responsibilities in the School System

5.1 Introduction

This chapter explains the statutory roles and responsibilities of pupils, parents, teachers, directors of education, supervisory officers, the Ontario Teachers' Federation, the Education Quality and Accountability Office, the Ministry of Education, and the Ontario College of Teachers. The roles of the various "players" in education can only be properly carried out if there is co-operation among them. Education is rarely a topic upon which there is universal agreement, but somehow the Ministry, boards, unions, parents and ratepayers have sustained a system which, despite its flaws, still serves society and children well. It has done this through partnership, albeit at times a grudging one. Sometimes it is important to remind ourselves of the obvious: no one player can function in the absence of respect for the role of the other partners.

5.2 School Boards

School boards are discussed in detail in Chapter Three. The powers and duties of school boards are numerous, and they include such matters as negotiating collective agreements; being the "employer" of teachers and of many other persons who dedicate themselves to education; setting local budget priorities; ensuring that their huge budgets are spent wisely; and ensuring the construction, maintenance and repair of schools. Much of the *Education Act* is about telling boards how to exercise their powers, and although many sections of the Act deal with the duties and powers of school boards, two sections are particularly important: section 170 prescribes what a board *shall* do and section 171 prescribes what a board *may* do. For example, a board *must* hire a principal and an adequate number of teachers for each school, and must provide textbooks, instruction, and special education. It *may* provide continuing education, pupil transportation, child care, etc. A board must ensure that every school under its charge is conducted in accordance with the *Education Act* and the regulations, and it must do anything that a board is required to do under any provision of the *Education Act* or any other Act (ss. 170(1)10 and 18).

There are, of course, many other statutes that affect school boards, including, for example, the *Occupational Health and Safety Act*, *Day Nurseries Act*, *Human Rights Code*, *Labour Relations Act*, and *Employment Standards Act*. Indeed, you will find references to school boards in over 30 Ontario and Federal statutes.

5.3 Pupils

Pupils are governed or affected by specific provisions in the *Education Act*, Regulation 298, the Provincial Code of Conduct, the *Education Quality and Accountability Office Act*, the *Smoke-Free Ontario Act*, and the *Alcohol and Gaming Regulation and Public Protection Act, 1996*. These are discussed in this chapter. A person's right to attend school is discussed in Chapter Two — Going to School. Indeed, the most fundamental *right* in the *Education Act* is the right to attend school, and the most fundamental *duty* is to attend school unless legally excused.

5.3.1 Pupils' Duties

Most pupils will be aware of the school rules established by their own school. They and their parents may not be aware of section 23 of Regulation 298 which outlines in rather quaint, even archaic language, the duties of a pupil. Section 23(1) states that a pupil shall,

(a) be diligent in attempting to master such studies as are part of the program in which the pupil is enrolled;

(b) exercise self-discipline;

(c) accept such discipline as would be exercised by a kind, firm and judicious parent;

(d) attend classes punctually and regularly;

(e) be courteous to fellow pupils and obedient and courteous to teachers;

(f) be clean in person and habits;

(g) take such tests and examinations as are required by or under the Act or as may be directed by the Minister; and

(h) show respect for school property.

The importance of attending school is reinforced in subsection 23(2) which puts the onus on the parent or adult pupil to explain the pupil's absence from school:

> 23. (2) When a pupil returns to school after an absence, a parent of the pupil, or the pupil where the pupil is an adult, shall give the reason for the absence orally or in writing as the principal requires.

Subsection 23(3) allows a pupil may be temporarily absent from school if excused by the principal:

> 23. (3) A pupil may be excused by the principal from attendance at school temporarily at any time at the written request of a parent of the pupil or the pupil where the pupil is an adult.

Subsection 23(4) makes it clear that a pupil must behave both in and outside the classroom:

> 23. (4) Every pupil is responsible for his or her conduct to the principal of the school that the pupil attends,
>
> (a) on the school premises;
>
> (b) on out-of-school activities that are part of the school program; and
>
> (c) while travelling on a school bus that is owned by a board or on a bus or school bus that is under contract to a board.

It is interesting that the *Education Act* permits a student to be suspended or expelled who is engaged in certain activities "while at school, at a school-related activity or in other circumstances where engaging in the activity will have an impact on the school climate." (See ss. 306 and 310.) This broadens the responsibility of pupils to the school for their behaviour, beyond that contemplated by section 23 of Regulation 298. See Chapter One for a discussion of school discipline and school climate.

I had an unusual inquiry from a school principal who was dealing with an argumentative parent. Students and parents of this "middle" school had been asked by their teachers to sign a "contract" in which the student and parent would signify their intent to obey a basic and common list of school and class rules. Remarkably, the parent wrote to his local trustee demanding to know if the "contract" was legally binding and then proceeded to nitpick at various other minor perceived failings of various staff. It is, of course, essential that schools respond to inquiries from parents, but there comes a point at which some parental inquiries are simply silly or completely unreasonable. Clearly, the "contract" was a means of making the student and parent aware of the expectations of the school and classroom teacher. It was not a contract in a legal sense, and the student could not be barred from class for failure to sign it. But the student still had to obey the same rules as everyone else.

5.3.2 Provincial Testing

Pupils are required under the *Education Quality and Accountability Office Act, 1996*, section 4(6), to take a test administered under that Act, unless exempted in accordance with directives issued by the Education Quality and Accountability Office (EQAO). (Students in "section 23" programs provided in settings such as psychiatric institutions, detention centres, and hospitals, are exempt from the requirement to take the Grade 3, 6 and 9 assessments.) Private schools are not required to administer EQAO tests to their pupils, but may do so through an agreement with the EQAO.

5.3.3 A Voice on the Board

Pupils of a board have a right to elect or appoint persons to sit on the board as "student trustees". More information can be found in Chapter Three.

5.3.4 Canvassing and Fundraising

Pupils are not permitted to do canvassing or fundraising on school property without the board's consent (Reg. 298, s. 25) and principals cannot authorize pupils to participate in canvassing or fundraising without the board's prior approval. This section was enacted in response to safety concerns for pupils, and in response to parental and community concerns about the amount of fundraising in which students were becoming involved. (See below for more details.)

5.3.5 Pupil Involvement in Games of Chance

It should be noted that under the *Alcohol and Gaming Regulation and Public Protection Act, 1996*, persons under the age of 18 are not permitted to buy tickets for games of chance such as raffles, bingos, or lotteries. Moreover, if a school wishes to hold a game of chance it must obtain a licence to do so, either from the local municipality or the provincial agency depending on the circumstances.

Section 206 of the *Criminal Code* (Canada) provides that it is an indictable offence to participate in a lottery scheme. However, the *Code* provides an exemption from the general prohibition against gambling and allows provincial governments to conduct and manage lottery schemes. Furthermore, the *Code* allows eligible charitable and religious organizations to conduct lottery schemes under the authority of a licence. The charitable organizations must use the lottery proceeds for a "charitable object". The *Code* allows the Ontario Cabinet (Lieutenant Governor in Council) to delegate licensing authority. This is done by means of an Order-in-Council which gives municipal councils the authority to issue licences for most lottery events conducted in their communities, including:

- bingo events with prize boards of up to $5,500;
- raffles with prizes of up to $50,000;
- Break Open Ticket events that are not conducted in conjunction with another event, and where the tickets are sold within the municipality;
- Bazaar gaming events; and
- Media Bingo.

The legal requirement that schools must obtain a licence to operate a game of chance is not commonly known, and the rules and regulations that must be complied with are onerous. It is no wonder, then, that schools rarely bother to comply with the law. Given that schools are not, in themselves, legal entities, it would seem reasonable to allow school boards to obtain a blanket licence from the local municipality covering all of their schools. This would ensure that the legal protections are in place and that the municipality does not lose revenue. In my experience, the province and/or municipalities are not receptive to such an idea.

5.3.6 Smoking in Schools

Under the *Smoke-Free Ontario Act*, it is an offence to supply or sell tobacco to a person under the age of 19 (s. 3). The Act also provides that:

> 9. (2) No person shall smoke or hold lighted tobacco in the following places or areas:
>
> 1. A school as defined in the *Education Act*.
>
> 2. A building or the grounds surrounding the building of a private school, where the private school is the only occupant of the premises, or the grounds annexed to a private school, where the private school is not the only occupant of the premises.

5.3.7 Provincial Code of Conduct

The Provincial Code of Conduct, set out in Policy/Program Memorandum 128 of the Ministry of Education, specifies expectations for the school community, principals, parents, students, community partners and police. In respect of students, the Code states:

> Students are to be treated with respect and dignity. In return, they must demonstrate respect for themselves, for others, and for the responsibilities of citizenship through acceptable behaviour. Respect and responsibility are demonstrated when a student:
>
> - comes to school prepared, on time, and ready to learn
> - shows respect for themselves, for others, and for those in authority
> - refrains from bringing anything to school that may compromise the safety of others
> - follows the established rules and takes responsibility for his or her own action.

5.4 Parents

Ontario law says very little about the rights of parents in respect of their child's education. They have a right to send their child to school, to participate fully in "special education" matters, and to receive educational information about their child. They have a right to see the Ontario Student Record and to request corrections to inaccurate information in the OSR, and may ask to have information removed which is "not conducive to the improvement of instruction" of their child (s. 266(4)). If their child is suspended by a principal, they have the right to appeal the suspension to the school board. If their child is recommended for expulsion, there must be an expulsion hearing, and parents are a "party" at such a hearing. They can appeal an expulsion to the Child and Family Services Review Board.

Parents must ensure that their child (of compulsory school age) goes to school unless the child is legally excused. Parents are not responsible for ensuring that their child goes to school if the child is at least 18 years of age, or is 16 or 17 years of age and has withdrawn from parental control. More information on school attendance is found in Chapter Two.

5.4.1 Duty to Provide Enrolment Information

It is the responsibility of the parent or guardian to submit evidence that the child has a right to attend an elementary school, including proof of age (s. 33(5)). It is the responsibility of the person or the person's parent or guardian to submit evidence that the person has a right to attend a secondary school (s. 36(8)).

A school is not required to register a child whose parent or guardian cannot produce evidence that the child is qualified to register in the board's jurisdiction. Moreover, a board has a right to enforce its attendance boundaries. A school has a right to question documentation produced to show that a family has an address in an attendance area if the school has reason to believe that the parent and child do not actually reside at the alleged address. It is not unheard of for schools to be provided with manufactured documents and false affidavits where parents are trying to get their child into certain favoured schools.

5.4.2 Parental Responsibilities under the Provincial Code of Conduct

The Provincial Code of Conduct reinforces the responsibilities of parents in their dealings with the school. Parents deserve respect and they must also show respect to school staff. The Code is a useful means of reminding some parents about how they must conduct themselves within their child's school. The Code states:

> Parents play an important role in educating their children and have a responsibility to support the efforts of school staff in maintaining a safe and respectful learning environment for all students. Parents fulfill their role when they:
>
> - show an active interest in their child's school work and progress
> - communicate regularly with the school
> - help their child be neat, appropriately dressed, and prepared for school
> - ensure that their child attends school regularly and on time
> - promptly report to the school their child's absence or late arrival
> - become familiar with the provincial Code of Conduct, the board's code of conduct and school rules
> - encourage and assist their child in following the rules of behaviour
> - assist school staff in dealing with disciplinary issues involving their child.

If a parent wishes to remove a pupil from school temporarily, the parent must make a request in writing to the school principal (Reg. 298, s. 23).

Parents have a key role in providing input into the identification and placement of their child as an "exceptional" pupil under the *Education Act* and Ontario Regulation 181/98. (Please see chapter on Special Education.)

Once a pupil reaches the age of 18 years, the legal rights and responsibilities of a parent or guardian are vested in the pupil. Section 1(2) of the Act states:

> (2) **When authority or obligation of parent vests in pupil** — Where by or under this Act any authority or right is vested in, or any obligation is imposed upon, or any reimbursement may be made to, a parent or guardian of a pupil, such authority, right, obligation or reimbursement shall be vested in or imposed upon or made, as the case may be,
>
> (a) to the pupil, if he or she is 18 years old or older; and
>
> (b) with respect to a pupil who is at least 16 years old but under 18 years old, to the pupil in such circumstances or for such purposes as may be prescribed by the regulations.

5.4.3 School Councils

School councils are an important vehicle for parents to express their views. Section 170(1)17.1 of the Act requires a school board to establish a school council for each school that it operates, in accordance with the regulations. Section 170(3) permits the government to make regulations respecting school councils. Section 265(3) requires a school principal to consult the school council at least once in each school year respecting the school plan for co-instructional activities that the principal is required to implement under section 265(2).

Ontario Regulation 612/00 governs school councils. It states that the purpose of a school council is, "through active participation of parents, to improve pupil achievement and to enhance the accountability of the education system to parents" (s. 2(1)). A council's primary means of achieving its purpose is by making recommendations in accordance with the regulation to the principal of the school and to the board (s. 2(2)).

A board must solicit the views of school councils with respect to establishing or amending board policies and guidelines that relate to pupil achievement or to the accountability of the education system to parents. This includes fundraising, codes of conduct, dress codes, funding of councils by the board, reimbursement of members' expenses, and conflict resolution processes to be used by the council.

Boards must also consult councils about the development and implementation plans for new education initiatives that relate to pupil achievement or accountability, about board action plans for improvement based on reports from the Education Quality and Accountability Office, and about the process and criteria applicable to the selection and placement of principals and vice-principals (s. 19). A board must consider and respond to recommendations from a school council (s. 21).

The council must meet at least four times during the school year. Its meetings are open to the public and must be held in a location that is accessible to the public (s. 12). It is entitled to meet at the school. A school council may not be incorporated (s. 17). The council may engage in fundraising activities in accordance with board policy (s. 22). The council must consult with parents about matters under consideration by the council (s. 23). It must also file an annual report on its activities to the principal and the board, copies of which must be provided by the principal to parents of pupils in the school (s. 24).

Under section 3 of the regulation, a school council must be composed of the following persons:

- Parents who have a child enrolled in the school. The number of parent representatives is to be determined in accordance with the school council by-law, or if there is no by-law, then in accordance with board policy. Parent representatives must form a majority of the council. Section 4 sets out requirements concerning the election of parent representatives, which must be held within the first 30 days of each school year. Election is by secret ballot. The principal must give written notice of the election to parents at least 14 days before the election.
- The principal of the school. The principal is not entitled to vote at council meetings. Everyone else gets a single vote (s. 14). The principal may delegate his or her duties as a council member to a vice-principal of the school (s. 18(1)).
- One teacher employed at the school, other than the principal or vice-principal, elected by other teachers at the school within the first 30 days of the school year.
- One other person employed at the school, other than the principal, vice-principal or any other teacher, elected by persons employed at the school other than a principal, vice-principal or any teacher, within the first 30 days of the school year.
- In a school with one or more secondary grades, a pupil enrolled in the school who is appointed by the student council or, if there is no student council, elected by pupils enrolled in the school within the first 30 days of the school year.

- If a school does not have secondary grades, the school council may include a pupil appointed by the principal if the principal determines after consulting with the members of the council that it should include a pupil.
- A community representative appointed by members of the school council. The council's by-law may specify that two or more community representatives can be appointed, provided that parents remain a majority on the council. A community representative cannot be employed at the school, but may be employed elsewhere by the board provided this is revealed to the council before the person's appointment.
- One person appointed by an association that is a member of the Ontario Federation of Home and School Associations, the Ontario Association of Parents in Catholic Education, or *Parent Partenaires en Education*, if the association that is a member of the Ontario Federation of Home and School Associations, the Ontario Association of Parents in Catholic Education, or *Parent Partenaires en Education* is established in respect of the school.

Pupil representatives are not required to be appointed or elected in a school established primarily for adults. Members of the board cannot serve on a school council (s. 3(7)).

A council member holds office until the first meeting of the school council in the next school year, and he or she may be re-elected or reappointed if still qualified. The school council shall have a chair, or if permitted by its by-laws, it may have co-chairs (s. 8). The chair or a co-chair must be a parent representative. A person on the council who is employed by the board cannot be a chair or co-chair. The by-laws may determine whether the council shall have other officers. A council member shall not receive remuneration for serving as a member, but may be reimbursed for expenses (s. 11).

The Ontario Ministry of Education publishes an extensive Guideline to assist school councils, and it is available on the Ministry's website.

5.4.4 The Ontario Parent Council

Section 17.1 of the Act establishes the Ontario Parent Council, which is comprised of not more than 20 members (parents or guardians of pupils in elementary or secondary education) appointed by the Minister of Education. The purpose of the Council is to advise the Minister on:

> (a) issues related to elementary and secondary school education; and
>
> (b) methods of increasing parental involvement in elementary and secondary school education.

5.4.5 Canvassing and Fundraising

A school's connection to the community requires that it should give careful consideration to the amount and type of canvassing and fundraising that it will undertake. Many schools now conduct "spring fairs" or arrange to sell items such as Christmas Wrap directly to parents, instead of asking students to sell door-to-door. Indeed, by law, no principal, vice-principal or teacher, without the approval of the board, shall authorize any canvassing or fundraising activity that involves the participation of one or more pupils attending the school. Moreover, a pupil must ensure that any canvassing or fundraising activity on school property by the pupil is carried on only with the consent of the board (Reg. 298, s. 25).

It should be noted that Ontario Regulation 612/00 permits school councils to engage in fundraising:

> 22. (1) Subject to subsection (2), a school council may engage in fundraising activities.
>
> (2) A school council shall not engage in fundraising activities unless,
>
> > (a) the activities are conducted in accordance with any applicable policies established by the board; and
> >
> > (b) the activities are to raise funds for a purpose approved by the board or authorized by any applicable polices established by the board.
>
> (3) A school council shall ensure that the funds raised by it are used in accordance with any applicable policies established by the board.

The Ministry of Education Guideline for School Councils has this important reminder:[1]

> School councils should be aware that, because the school board is a corporate entity and the school is not, any funds raised by the school council (and any assets purchased with those funds) belong, legally, to the board. The board may have policies specifying that the money raised by the council (and any assets purchased by the council) will remain with the school. However, such policies are not legally binding in the event that the school is closed. All fund-raising activities conducted by the school council must be included in the annual report prepared by the school council.

5.4.6 Duty to Provide Medical Information

Common sense dictates that parents should provide sufficient information about their children to enable school staff to respond to medical emergencies, medication requirements, allergic reactions, etc. If this information is not supplied, the school can hardly be held liable for not responding appropriately in situations where the information would have made a difference. For example, peanut allergies and bee sting allergies may require instantaneous response should an allergic reaction occur. This requires full disclosure of information about the child's allergy and the steps to be taken should an emergency occur during school activities.

5.4.7 Administration of Medication

Ministry of Education Policy/Program Memorandum No. 81 outlines the responsibilities of various government Ministries and of school boards in respect of the administration of medication to pupils. The following is an excerpt from PPM No. 81:

> The Home Care Program of the Ministry of Health, at the request of a school board, will be responsible for assessing pupil needs, and for providing such services as injection of medication, catheterization, manual expression of the bladder, stoma care, postural drainage, suctioning and tube feeding. The Ministry of Health will also be responsible for intensive physio-occupational and speech therapy, and for

[1]School Councils, A Guide for Members (Ontario Ministry of Education: 2002) http://www.edu. gov.on.ca/eng/general/elemsec/council/council02.pdf., p. 3.4.

> assisting school boards in the training and direction of school board staff performing certain other support services.
>
> The Ministry of Community and Social Services will continue to be responsible for ensuring the provision of health support services in children's residential care and treatment facilities.
>
> The school boards will be responsible for the administration of oral medication where such medication has been prescribed for use during school hours. For physically disabled pupils, the school boards will provide such services as lifting and positioning, assistance with mobility, feeding and toiletting, and general maintenance exercises. Boards will also continue to be responsible for necessary speech remediation, correction and habilitation programs.
>
> School boards should establish or update their policies for the provision of these support services. Such policies should define administrative procedures, personnel roles, and routine safeguards. The local boards of health, local Home Care Program administrators, and local medical societies can provide valuable assistance in the development of such policies. The procedures for the administering of oral medication, in particular, should provide:
>
>> That such procedures be applied only to those services, requested by the parent and prescribed by a physician or other health care professional, which must be provided during school hours.
>>
>> That a request for the service and the authorization to provide such service be made in writing by the parent and the physician, specifying the medication, the dosage, the frequency and method of administration, the dates for which the authorization applies, and the possible side effects, if any.
>>
>> That the storage and safekeeping requirements for any labelled medication be stated.
>>
>> That a record of administration be maintained which includes the pupil's name, date, time of provision, dosage given, name of person administering, etc.
>>
>> That the telephone numbers of the parent and physician be readily accessible in the school.
>>
>> That the medication be administered in a manner which allows for sensitivity and privacy and which encourages the pupil to take an appropriate level of responsibility for his or her medication.

The "model" that accompanies PPM No. 81 indicates that oral medication is to be administered to pupils by the pupil, the parent or "aide or other personnel" of the school board. Aides or other personnel of a board are also responsible for lifting and positioning, assistance with mobility, feeding, and toiletting. Many of these duties fall naturally into the role of a special needs or special education assistant. These are trained individuals who work with children having a variety of disabilities. Less clear is the question of who should administer oral medication. It is left to a school board, and often the school administrator, to "find" someone to administer the medication. Unless there is a restriction in a collective agreement, there is no legal barrier to assigning this task to a teacher. The list of teacher's duties in the *Education Act* and Regulation 298 is not exhaustive, and boards have a right to assign other duties where such an assignment is reasonable. Administering oral medication is consistent with the notion of serving the interests of students. It is not incompatible with the role of a teacher. Principals can ask other employees, such as educational assistants, to help out, as well. Most staff will not object unless they feel that they are not adequately trained or the task is usually complex. For example, some students require frequent blood tests through "finger pricks". It is acceptable for school staff to perform this task, with proper training, but some staff, such a special needs assistant, may feel more comfortable doing it.

All school boards have developed policies and procedures on the Administration of Medication and they contain safeguards with respect to the handling and storage of medication, obtaining authorization forms, storage of medication, recording dosages, availability of epipens, etc.[2]

Board policies should also give attention to medication issues that might arise on a school bus. What training and equipment does the bus driver have? Is the driver aware of which children may encounter allergic reactions?[3]

5.4.8 Anaphylaxis

In 2005, the Province enacted *Sabrina's Law* (S.0. 2005, c. 7) to require boards to establish an anaphylactic policy. *Sabrina's Law* provides as follows:

> 1. (1) In this Act,
>
> "anaphylaxis" means a severe systemic allergic reaction which can be fatal, resulting in circulatory collapse or shock, and "anaphylactic" has a corresponding meaning;
>
> "board" means a district school board or a school authority;
>
> "consent" means consent given by an individual with the capacity to provide consent to treatment for the purposes of the *Health Care Consent Act, 1996*;
>
> "employee" means an employee of a board who regularly works at the school, in the case of a school operated by the board.
>
> (2) Expressions in this Act related to education have the same meaning as in the Education Act, unless the context requires otherwise.
>
> 2. (1) Every board shall establish and maintain an anaphylactic policy in accordance with this section.
>
> (2) The anaphylactic policy shall include the following:
>
> > 1. Strategies that reduce the risk of exposure to anaphylactic causative agents in classrooms and common school areas.
> >
> > 2. A communication plan for the dissemination of information on life-threatening allergies to parents, pupils and employees.
> >
> > 3. Regular training on dealing with life-threatening allergies for all employees and others who are in direct contact with pupils on a regular basis.

---

[2]For example, the Hamilton-Wentworth DSB has a complete and comprehensible policy: "Policy No. 7.15 — Administration of Oral Prescription Medication" (Hamilton-Wentworth District School Board: June, 2003) http://www.hwdsb.on.ca/aboutus/policies/pdfs/administration_of_oral_medication.pdf.

[3]See for example the policy of the Superior-Greenstone District School Board's Manitouwadge Public School: "Oral Medication Policy & Procedure", http://we.sgdsb.on.ca/OralMedication.pdf.

4. A requirement that every school principal develop an individual plan for each pupil who has an anaphylactic allergy.

5. A requirement that every school principal ensure that, upon registration, parents, guardians and pupils shall be asked to supply information on life-threatening allergies.

6. A requirement that every school principal maintain a file for each anaphylactic pupil of current treatment and other information, including a copy of any prescriptions and instructions from the pupil's physician or nurse and a current emergency contact list.

(3) An individual plan for a pupil with an anaphylactic allergy shall be consistent with the board's policy and shall include:

1. Details informing employees and others who are in direct contact with the pupil on a regular basis of the type of allergy, monitoring and avoidance strategies and appropriate treatment.

2. A readily accessible emergency procedure for the pupil, including emergency contact information.

3. Storage for epinephrine auto-injectors, where necessary.

3. (1) Employees may be preauthorized to administer medication or supervise a pupil while he or she takes medication in response to an anaphylactic reaction, if the school has up-to-date treatment information and the consent of the parent, guardian or pupil, as applicable.

(2) It is the obligation of the pupil's parent or guardian and the pupil to ensure that the information in the pupil's file is kept up-to-date with the medication that the pupil is taking.

(3) If an employee has reason to believe that a pupil is experiencing an anaphylactic reaction, the employee may administer an epinephrine auto-injector or other medication prescribed to the pupil for the treatment of an anaphylactic reaction, even if there is no preauthorization to do so under subsection (1).

(4) No action for damages shall be instituted respecting any act done in good faith or for any neglect or default in good faith in response to an anaphylactic reaction in accordance with this Act, unless the damages are the result of an employee's gross negligence.

(5) This section does not affect or in any way interfere with the duties any person may have under common law.

5.4.9 Duty to Provide Proof of Immunization

A pupil is required to be immunized against certain designated diseases, in accordance with the *Immunization of School Pupils Act*. Parents must ensure that their children are immunized in order for them to be admitted to school, unless the child is exempt for medical reasons or as a matter of religious or conscientious belief. (Please see the chapter on Going to School.)

5.5 Role of Board Administration

As discussed in Chapter Three, the duty of the members of a school board is to "govern" by establishing policy. It is the duty of a board's administration to implement board policy.

5.5.1 Director of Education

A district school board *must* employ a supervisory officer as a Director of Education. Two or more school *authorities* may agree to appoint a Director of Education with the approval of the Minister, and they cannot abolish the Director's position without the approval of the Minister.

The Director is the chief executive officer and the chief education officer of the board, and must be a supervisory officer who qualified as such as a teacher, in other words, has an academic supervisory officer's certificate.

The *Education Act* states that the Director shall, within policies established by the board, develop and maintain an effective organization and the programs required to implement the board's policies (s. 283(2)).

He or she is required to make an annual report to the board, with a copy to the Minister (s. 283(3)). The Minister may establish policies and guidelines respecting the roles and responsibilities of Directors of Education and supervisory officers (s. 8(1)3.4).

5.5.2 Supervisory Officer

A district school board may employ "such other supervisory officers as it considers necessary to supervise all aspects of the programs under its jurisdiction" (s. 279). A board is not required to obtain the Minister's approval to hire a Director of Education or any other supervisory officer. It must, however, confirm with the Minister that a person it wants to appoint as a supervisory officer in fact holds the qualifications of a supervisory officer, namely the "supervisory officer's certificate". This certificate is issued by the Ministry. In the case of "academic" supervisory officers, it is issued if the Ontario College of Teachers confirms that the person has completed the supervisory officer's qualification program. The Ministry of Education takes the position that it can waive the requirement that a Director shall hold an academic supervisory officer's certificate, if, for example, a board wished to hire a person without the qualification. Under section 8(1)14 of the Act, the Minister can accept qualifications in lieu of those that are prescribed. This is very rare.

The term "supervisory officer" is defined in the *Education Act* as:

> . . . a person who is qualified in accordance with the regulations governing supervisory officers and who is employed,
>
> (a) by a board and designated by the board, or
>
> (b) in the Ministry and designated by the Minister
>
> to perform such supervisory and administrative duties as are required of supervisory officers by [the *Education Act*] and the regulations . . .

The definition therefore has three components: the person must be qualified (hold a certificate), must be employed by a board or the Ministry, and must be designated to perform supervisory officers' duties. The board must designate the "title and area of responsibility" of each supervisory officer and can assign the person duties in addition to those prescribed in the Act and regulations (s. 285(1)).

School *authorities* must appoint one or more supervisory officers. They are permitted to share the services of a supervisory officer with another board, or to agree to use the services of a Ministry supervisory officer (s. 284).

The statutory duties of a supervisory officer are prescribed in section 286 of the *Education Act*:

> 286. (1) Subject to the policies and guidelines established under paragraph 3.4 of subsection 8 (1) and subject to the regulations, a board or the Minister shall assign the following duties to its or the Minister's supervisory officer or officers,
>
> (a) to bring about improvement in the quality of education by assisting teachers in their practice;
>
> (b) to assist and co-operate with boards to the end that the schools may best serve the needs of the pupils;
>
> (c) to visit schools and classrooms as the Minister may direct and, where the supervisory officer has been appointed by a board, as the board may direct;
>
> (d) to prepare a report of a visit to a school or classroom when required by the Minister and, where the supervisory officer has been appointed by a board, when required by the board and to give to a teacher referred to in any such report a copy of the portion of the report that refers to the teacher;
>
> (e) to ensure that the schools under his or her jurisdiction are conducted in accordance with this Act and the regulations;
>
> (f) to make a general annual report as to the performance of his or her duties and the condition of the schools in his or her area of jurisdiction when required by the Minister and, where the supervisory officer has been appointed by a board, when required by the board;
>
> (g) to report to the appropriate medical officer of health any case in which the school buildings or premises are found to be in an unsanitary condition;
>
> (h) to furnish the Minister with information respecting any school in his or her area of jurisdiction whenever required to do so;
>
> (i) to supervise the business functions of the board;
>
> (j) to supervise the use and maintenance of the buildings and property of the board; and
>
> (k) to exercise such other powers and perform such other duties as may be prescribed by a regulation made, or a policy established, under Part XIII (Behaviour, Discipline and Safety).

The *Education Act* also has many references to actions or decisions being made by the "appropriate supervisory officer". For example, he or she must decide whether to support a school principal if there is a dispute with a parent about the removal or correction of information in a pupil's Ontario Student Record (s. 266(5)). A supervisory officer's job is full time, and the Minister must consent before he or she takes on any other job or office while employed as a supervisory officer (s. 286(4)). A supervisory officer appointed by a board (as opposed to the Ministry) is responsible to the board "through the chief executive officer" (s. 286(3)). Staff are *employed* by the board but they report through the CEO, i.e. the Director of Education.

A supervisory officer can only be suspended or dismissed by a board for "neglect of duty, misconduct or inefficiency" (s. 287(1)).

Regulation 309 (s. 8) says that a board shall not suspend or dismiss a supervisory officer without first giving the supervisory officer reasonable information about the reasons for the suspension or dismissal and an opportunity to make submissions to the board. Submissions can be made orally or in writing.

The suspension and dismissal requirements in Regulation 309 reflect the common law right to be "heard". The duty of fairness obliges a board to give a supervisory officer reasonable advance notice that a suspension or dismissal is being considered, along with complete information about the allegations against the supervisory officer. The supervisory officer must have an opportunity to respond to the allegations and to provide all relevant information to the board before it considers the matter.

An employment contract between a board and a supervisory officer may deal expressly with the rights and obligations of the parties if the employment relationship is to be terminated for any reason. Because Regulation 309 prescribes a minimum standard of fairness, the contract could contain other conditions, such as notice periods and severance payments that do not derogate from the rights contained in the regulation.

The *Education Act* requires a board to notify a supervisory officer of its decision to suspend or dismiss, with reasons.

If a supervisory officer's position is declared redundant by a board, he or she has some protection under Regulation 309. The supervisory officer must be given at least three month's notice of the redundancy. He or she must be transferred to another position for which he or she is qualified with supervisory and administrative responsibilities as similar as possible to those of his or her previous position. He or she must be paid for at least a year after the transfer with no reduction of salary (Reg. 309, s. 7(2)).

5.6 Education Quality and Accountability Office

The Education Quality and Accountability Office is a corporation without share capital established by the *Education Quality and Accountability Office Act, 1996* as a Crown Agency, to do the following:

- evaluate the quality and effectiveness of elementary and secondary school education
- develop tests and require or undertake the administering and marking of tests of pupils in elementary and secondary schools
- develop systems for evaluating the quality and effectiveness of elementary and secondary school education
- research and collect information on assessing academic achievement
- evaluate the public accountability of boards and collect information on strategies for improving that accountability
- report to the public and to the Minister of Education on the results of tests and generally on the quality and effectiveness of elementary and secondary school education and on the public accountability of boards
- make recommendations on any matter related to the quality and effectiveness of elementary and secondary school education or to the public accountability of boards.

The Minister may delegate powers and duties to the Office that it needs for the "carrying out of its objects". The Minister may also issue directives and policies that the Office is obliged to follow. The objects of the Office can be added to by regulation.

The Office is covered by the *Freedom of Information and Protection of Privacy Act*. It has a board of directors (seven to nine persons) and a chief executive officer appointed by the Lieutenant Governor in Council.

The Office may require school boards to administer tests to pupils, to mark them, and to report the results. It can require boards to provide information, including personal information. Pupils are required to take any test administered by a board on behalf of the Office. Parents of children enrolled in publicly-funded schools do not have the legal right to choose not to have their child take a test administered on behalf of the Office. As mentioned above, pupils can be exempted from a test administered by the Education Quality and Accountability Office in accordance with directives issued by the Office. (Pupils in "section 23" programs provided in settings such as psychiatric institutions, detention centres, and hospitals, are exempt from the requirement to take the Grade 3, 6 and 9 assessments.)

It is a duty of a teacher to "co-operate and assist in the administration of tests under the *Education Quality and Accountability Office Act, 1996*" (Reg. 298, s. 20(j)).

5.7 Ontario Teachers' Federation

The Ontario Teachers' Federation (OTF) was formally established in 1944 by the *Teaching Profession Act*. Its objects are:

- to promote and advance the cause of education
- to raise the status of the teaching profession
- to promote and advance the interests of teachers and to secure conditions that will make possible the best professional service
- to arouse and increase public interest in educational affairs
- to co-operate with other teachers' organizations throughout the world having the same or like objectives
- to represent all members of the pension plan established under the *Teachers' Pension Act* in the administration of the plan and the management of the pension fund.

The OTF is governed by a board of governors representing its affiliated bodies: Elementary Teachers' Federation of Ontario, the Ontario Secondary School Teachers' Federation, the Ontario English Catholic Teachers' Association and l'Association des enseignantes et des enseignants franco-ontariens.

All teachers and occasional teachers employed to teach by a school board, other than principals and vice-principals, are required to be OTF members.

The pension representation function performed by OTF requires that it represent all members of the teachers' pension plan. This includes supervisory officers, principals, vice-principals, some private school teachers, and others. The representation function is actually carried out by the OTF executive under section 9 of the *Teaching Profession Act*. The executive may appoint persons to the pension board, enter into agreements under the *Teachers' Pension Act*; and agree to changes to the Schedule to that Act.

5.8 Ministry of Education

In respect of elementary and secondary education, the Minister of Education is responsible for administering various statutes, including the *Education Act, Education Quality and Accountability Office Act, 1996*, and the *Ontario College of Teachers Act, 1996*. There are very few things that the Minister is *required* to do under these statutes, but there are many things that the Minister *may* do and does do. The primary functions are:

- student success — improving graduation rates
- prescribing curriculum, courses of study, diploma requirements, and approved textbooks
- issuing grants to school boards in accordance with the regulations
- policy development and education reform.

Some other key policy areas within the Ministry are:

- special education
- safe schools
- French-language education
- Native education
- schools for the blind, deaf and deaf-blind, and demonstration schools for the learning disabled
- adult education
- religious education
- school board governance and compliance
- finance policy.

The Minister of Finance is responsible for establishing education property tax rates for residential and business property. The Minister of Labour and the Minister of Education have a shared role in respect of teachers' collective bargaining issues, because of the linkage between the *Education Act* and the *Labour Relations Act, 1995*. The Ministry plays a key role in resolving salary and benefit-related issues, and some workload issues, at provincial collective bargaining tables by working toward framework agreements which must then be ratified by local boards and by unions.

The Minister does not have the power to intervene in local employment issues (e.g. hiring and firing), human rights complaints, school bus transportation disputes, or other local matters. The Minister is not "vicariously" liable for the conduct or negligence of board employees because the Minister does not employ, hire, supervise, evaluate or discipline them. However, the *Education Act* is highly prescriptive about teacher performance appraisal and new teacher induction.

5.9 Teachers

The job of a teacher is to teach. The term "teach" is not defined in the *Education Act*. However, a glance at the dictionary shows that "teach" can have different interpretations, including "direct", "instruct", "train", "guide", "discipline", "school", "tutor", "coach", "show how", and "cause to know". Teaching can occur by precept, example or experience. Unless the context of a particular statutory or regulatory provision requires otherwise, "teach" means exactly what we commonly understand it to mean in schools, and we should therefore use its ordinary dictionary meaning interpreted in the overall context of education legislation and the realities of how schools operate. Broadly viewed, "teach" can include what any person imparts to any other person, by whatever means. In the school setting, however, the definition needs some parameters. I view teaching as the systematic or regular imparting of knowledge, skills or values to one or more pupils, following a course of study and curriculum, usually followed by an evaluation of the pupil's academic progress.

In the context of Ontario education law, our understanding of what a teacher does is enhanced if we look at how the *Education Act* and regulations describe the *duties* of a teacher. Although these prescribed duties tell a teacher what his or her legal obligations are, they paint a mere sketch of what a teacher actually does during the day. The picture is partly completed by the teacher's collective agreement and local employment policies of the board.

5.9.1 Teachers' Duties

(a) General

"Teachers' duties" are prescribed in the *Education Act* (primarily s. 264) and section 20 of Regulation 298, with respect to teachers employed by school boards. (Regulation 298 is included in the Appendices.) A teacher may be assigned these statutory and regulatory duties by a board and can also be assigned other duties. A collective agreement may impose duties on a teacher and may limit the duties that a teacher must perform. For example, a collective agreement could state that a teacher must fill in for absent teachers ("on-call" time), but may limit the time spent supervising pupils outside the classroom. The agreement may limit the average number of pupils that a teacher can be required to teach in one day ("pupil-teacher contact"), or impose other "workload" restrictions and requirements. In addition, a school board will have various policies that must be obeyed by its employees, including policies dealing with workplace harassment, use of the internet, avoidance of conflict of interest, prohibition against alcohol on board premises, etc. In addition, Canadian courts are clear that teachers can be held to a high standard of conduct in the community at large. That is, they are a role model in the community.[4]

(b) Preparation for Class

It is a duty of a teacher, unless otherwise assigned by the principal, to be present in the classroom or teaching area and to ensure that the classroom or teaching area is ready for the reception of pupils at least fifteen minutes before the commencement of classes in the school in the morning and, where applicable, five minutes before the commencement of classes in the school in the afternoon (Reg. 298, s. 20).

---

[4] A. Brown and M. Zuker, *Education Law*, 4th ed. (Toronto: Thomson Carswell, 2007), c. 6.

(c) Returning Property to the Board

A teacher has a duty to deliver the register, the school key and other school property in his or her possession on demand, or when his or her agreement with the board has expired, or when his or her employment has ceased for any reason. By refusing to deliver school property to the board on demand, the teacher forfeits any claim against the board (Act, s. 264).

(d) Keeping an Accurate Register

It is an offence for a teacher to keep a false register. The maximum fine is $200 (Act, s. 213). The principal has a duty to register pupils and to ensure that the attendance of pupils at the school is recorded (Act, s. 265).

(e) Reporting Child Abuse

It is a teacher's professional duty to report suspected child abuse. The *Child and Family Services Act* says that a person who has reasonable grounds to suspect that a child has suffered or is at risk of suffering the kinds of harm or other situations described in section 72(1) of the *CFSA* (e.g. physical, sexual, emotional) shall immediately report the suspicion and the information to a Society. A teacher or principal who fails to report a suspicion commits an offence under section 72(4) of the Act. More details on this duty are found in Chapter One.

5.9.2 Duties as a Member of the Profession

Further duties are prescribed in the *Teaching Profession Act* regulation and in the *Ontario College of Teachers Act, 1996*. These apply to teachers, not as employees, but by virtue of their membership in the Ontario Teachers' Federation and the College.

The Ontario College of Teachers has both a Professional Misconduct Regulation and an Ethics By-law that regulate the standard of conduct of teachers: The Professional Misconduct Regulations states as follows:

> **Ontario Regulation 437/97 Professional Misconduct**
>
> 1. The following acts are defined as professional misconduct for the purposes of subsection 30 (2) of the Act:
>
> 1. Providing false information or documents to the College or any other person with respect to the member's professional qualifications.
> 2. Inappropriately using a term, title or designation indicating a specialization in the profession which is not specified on the member's certificate of qualification and registration.
> 3. Permitting, counselling or assisting any person who is not a member to represent himself or herself as a member of the College.
> 4. Using a name other than the member's name, as set out in the register, in the course of his or her professional duties.
> 5. Failing to maintain the standards of the profession.
> 6. Releasing or disclosing information about a student to a person other than the student or, if the student is a minor, the student's parent or guardian.

The release or disclosure of information is not an act of professional misconduct if,

i. the student (or if the student is a minor, the student's parent or guardian) consents to the release or disclosure, or

ii. if the release or disclosure is required or allowed by law.

7. Abusing a student verbally.

7.1 Abusing a student physically.

7.2 Abusing a student psychologically or emotionally.

7.3 Abusing a student sexually.

8. Practising or purporting to practise the profession while under the influence of any substance or while adversely affected by any dysfunction,

i. which the member knows or ought to know impairs the member's ability to practise, and

ii. in respect of which treatment has previously been recommended, ordered or prescribed but the member has failed to follow the treatment.

9. Contravening a term, condition or limitation imposed on the member's certificate of qualification and registration.

10. Failing to keep records as required by his or her professional duties.

11. Failing to supervise adequately a person who is under the professional supervision of the member.

12. Signing or issuing, in the member's professional capacity, a document that the member knows or ought to know contains a false, improper or misleading statement.

13. Falsifying a record relating to the member's professional responsibilities.

14. Failing to comply with the Act or the regulations or the by-laws.

15. Failing to comply with the *Education Act* or the regulations made under that Act, if the member is subject to that Act.

16. Contravening a law if the contravention is relevant to the member's suitability to hold a certificate of qualification and registration.

17. Contravening a law if the contravention has caused or may cause a student who is under the member's professional supervision to be put at or to remain at risk.

18. An act or omission that, having regard to all the circumstances, would reasonably be regarded by members as disgraceful, dishonourable or unprofessional.

19. Conduct unbecoming a member.

20. Failing to appear before a panel of the Investigation Committee to be cautioned or admonished, if the Investigation Committee has required the member to appear under clause 26 (5) (c) of the Act.

21. Failing to comply with an order of a panel of the Discipline Committee or an order of a panel of the Fitness to Practise Committee.

22. Failing to co-operate in a College investigation.

23. Failing to take reasonable steps to ensure that the requested information is provided in a complete and accurate manner if the member is required to provide information to the College under the Act and the regulations.

24. Failing to abide by a written undertaking given by the member to the College or by an agreement entered into by the member with the College.
25. Failing to respond adequately or within a reasonable time to a written inquiry from the College.
26. Practising the profession while the member is in a conflict of interest.
27. Failing to comply with the member's duties under the *Child and Family Services Act*.

O. Reg. 437/97, s. 1; O. Reg. 134/08, s. 1

2. A finding of incompetence, professional misconduct or a similar finding against a member by a governing authority of the teaching profession in a jurisdiction other than Ontario that is based on facts that would, in the opinion of the Discipline Committee, constitute professional misconduct as defined in section 1, is defined as professional misconduct for the purposes of subsection 30 (2) of the Act.

O. Reg. 437/97, s. 2

In addition to avoiding being found guilty of professional misconduct, teachers must adhere to the College's ethical requirements, as listed in section 32 of the College By-laws:

Section 32 Professional and Ethical Standards

32.01 The following are hereby prescribed as standards of practice for the teaching profession:

Commitment to Students and Student Learning

Members are dedicated in their care and commitment to students. They treat students equitably and with respect and are sensitive to factors that influence individual student learning. Members facilitate the development of students as contributing citizens of Canadian society.

Professional Knowledge

Members strive to be current in their professional knowledge and recognize its relationship to practice. They understand and reflect on student development, learning theory, pedagogy, curriculum, ethics, educational research and related policies and legislation to inform professional judgment in practice.

Professional Practice

Members apply professional knowledge and experience to promote student learning. They use appropriate pedagogy, assessment and evaluation, resources and technology in planning for and responding to the needs of individual students and learning communities. Members refine their professional practice through ongoing inquiry, dialogue and reflection.

Leadership in Learning Communities

Members promote and participate in the creation of collaborative, safe and supportive learning communities. They recognize their shared responsibilities and their leadership roles in order to facilitate student success. Members maintain and uphold the principles of the ethical standards in these learning communities.

Ongoing Professional Learning

Members recognize that a commitment to ongoing professional learning is integral to effective practice and to student learning. Professional practice and self-directed learning are informed by experience, research, collaboration and knowledge.

> *32.02.* The following are hereby prescribed as the ethical standards for the teaching profession:
>
> ***Care***
>
> The ethical standard of Care includes compassion, acceptance, interest and insight for developing students' potential. Members express their commitment to students' well being and learning through positive influence, professional judgment and empathy in practice.
>
> ***Respect***
>
> Intrinsic to the ethical standard of Respect are trust and fair-mindedness. Members honour human dignity, emotional wellness and cognitive development. In their professional practice, they model respect for spiritual and cultural values, social justice, confidentiality, freedom, democracy and the environment.
>
> ***Trust***
>
> The ethical standard of Trust embodies fairness, openness and honesty. Members' professional relationships with students, colleagues, parents, guardians and the public are based on trust.
>
> ***Integrity***
>
> Honesty, reliability and moral action are embodied in the ethical standard of Integrity. Continual reflection assists members in exercising integrity in their professional commitments and responsibilities.

5.9.3 Duties under the Teaching Profession Act

A teacher also has duties as a member of the Ontario Teachers' Federation. The regulation made under the *Teaching Profession Act* prescribes a member's duties to his or her pupils, to educational authorities, to the public, to the Federation, and to fellow members. A member is required to "strive at all times to achieve and maintain the highest degree of professional competence and to uphold the honour, dignity, and ethical standards of the teaching profession" (*TPA*, Reg. s. 13). Other ethical requirements are prescribed in sections 14 to 18 of the regulation under the *Teaching Profession Act.*

Ontario *Teaching Profession Act*, ss. 13–18 state as follows:

> 13. **General Duties of Members** — A member shall strive at all times to achieve and maintain the highest degree of professional competence and to uphold the honour, dignity, and ethical standards of the teaching profession.
>
> 14. **Duties of a Member to His or Her Pupils** — A member shall,
>
> (a) regard as his first duty the effective education of his pupils and the maintenance of a high degree of professional competence in his teaching;
>
> (b) endeavour to develop in his pupils an appreciation of standards of excellence;
>
> (c) endeavour to inculcate in his pupils an appreciation of the principles of democracy;
>
> (d) show consistent justice and consideration in all his relations with pupils;
>
> (e) refuse to divulge beyond his proper duty confidential information about a pupil; and
>
> (f) concern himself with the welfare of his pupils while they are under his care.

15. **Duties of a Member to Educational Authorities** — (1) A member shall,

(a) comply with the Acts and regulations administered by the Minister;

(b) co-operate with his educational authorities to improve public education;

(c) respect the legal authority of the board of trustees in the management of the school and in the employment of teachers;

(d) make in the proper manner such reports concerning teachers under his authority as may be required by the board of trustees; and

(e) present in the proper manner to the proper authorities the consequences to be expected from policies or practices which in his professional opinion are seriously detrimental to the interests of pupils.

(2) A member shall not,

(a) break a contract of employment with a board of trustees;

(b) violate a written or oral agreement to enter into a contract of employment with a board of trustees; or

(c) while holding a contract of employment with a board of trustees, make application for another position the acceptance of which would necessitate his seeking the termination of his contract by mutual consent of the teacher and the board of trustees, unless and until he has arranged with his board of trustees for such termination of contract if he obtains the other position.

16. **Duties of a Member to the Public** — A member shall,

(a) endeavour at all times to extend the public knowledge of his profession and discourage untrue, unfair or exaggerated statements with respect to teaching; and

(b) recognize a responsibility to promote respect for human rights.

17. **Duties of a Member to the Federation** — A member shall co-operate with the Federation to promote the welfare of the profession.

18. **Duties of a Member to Fellow Members** — (1) A member shall,

(a) avoid interfering in an unwarranted manner between other teachers and pupils;

(b) on making an adverse report on another member, furnish him with a written statement of the report at the earliest possible time and not later than three days after making the report;

(c) notwithstanding section 18 (1) (b), a member who makes an adverse report about another member respecting suspected sexual abuse of a student by that other member need not provide him or her with a copy of the report or with any information about the report. (WB02)

(d) refuse to accept employment with a board of trustees whose relations with the Federation are unsatisfactory; and

(e) where he is in an administrative or supervisory position, make an honest and determined effort to help and counsel a teacher before subscribing to the dismissal of that teacher.

(2) Under clause (c) of subsection (1), the onus shall be on the member to ascertain personally from the Federation whether an unsatisfactory relationship exists.

(3) A member shall not attempt to gain an advantage over other members by knowingly underbidding another member, or knowingly applying for a position not prop-

> erly declared vacant, or by negotiating for salary independently of his local group of fellow-members.

5.9.4 Section 43 — Criminal Code — Defence Against Criminal Charges of Assault

If a teacher is charged with assaulting a student, section 43 of the *Criminal Code* (Canada) provides a defence if the teacher's action was "by way of correction" and did not exceed what is reasonable in the circumstances. Section 43 states:

> Every school teacher, parent or person standing in the place of a parent is justified in using force by way of correction toward a pupil or child, as the case may be, if the force does not exceed what is reasonable in the circumstances.

The constitutionality of this provision was unsuccessfully challenged in court. The Ontario Court of Appeal, as well as the Court below, found that section 43 does not contravene the *Charter*. In *Canadian Foundation for Children, Youth & the Law v. Canada (Attorney General)* (2002), 2002 CarswellOnt 32, [2002] O.J. No. 61, 207 D.L.R. (4th) 632, 23 R.F.L. (5th) 101, 161 C.C.C. (3d) 178, 57 O.R. (3d) 511, 48 C.R. (5th) 218, 154 O.A.C. 144, 90 C.R.R. (2d) 223 (Ont. C.A.); leave to appeal allowed (2002), [2002] S.C.C.A. No. 113, 2002 CarswellOnt 3410, 2002 CarswellOnt 3411, 172 O.A.C. 400 (note), 96 C.R.R. (2d) 376 (note), 302 N.R. 199 (note) (S.C.C.); affirmed 2004 CarswellOnt 252, 2004 CarswellOnt 253, [2004] S.C.J. No. 6, REJB 2004-53164, 2004 SCC 4, 315 N.R. 201, 183 O.A.C. 1, 70 O.R. (3d) 94 (note), [2004] 1 S.C.R. 76, 115 C.R.R. (2d) 88, 16 C.R. (6th) 203, 46 R.F.L. (5th) 1, 234 D.L.R. (4th) 257, 180 C.C.C. (3d) 353 (S.C.C.), Goudge J.A., in the appellate court, observed at paragraph 49:

> The force [applied by the parent, surrogate parent or teacher] must be reasonable in the circumstances which will inevitably include consideration of the age and character of the child, the circumstances of the punishment, its gravity, the misconduct of the child giving rise to it, the likely effect of the punishment on the child and whether the child suffered any injuries. Finally, the person applying the force must intend it for "correction" and the child being "corrected" must be capable of learning from the correction. Hence s. 43 infringes the child's security of the person only to the extent of decriminalizing the limited application of force to the child in circumstances where the risk of physical harm is modest.

An appeal to the Supreme Court of Canada was dismissed (*Canadian Foundation for Children, Youth & the Law v. Canada (Attorney General)*, 2004 CarswellOnt 252, 2004 CarswellOnt 253, [2004] S.C.J. No. 6, REJB 2004-53164, 2004 SCC 4, 315 N.R. 201, 183 O.A.C. 1, 70 O.R. (3d) 94 (note), [2004] 1 S.C.R. 76, 115 C.R.R. (2d) 88, 16 C.R. (6th) 203, 46 R.F.L. (5th) 1, 234 D.L.R. (4th) 257, 180 C.C.C. (3d) 353 (S.C.C.)). The issue before the Court was the constitutionality of allowing children's parents and teachers to use minor corrective force in some circumstances without facing criminal sanction. The *Criminal Code* (R.S.C. 1985, c. C46, s. 265) prohibits intentional, non-consensual application of force to another person. However, section 43 of the Code excludes from this crime reasonable physical correction of children by their parents and teachers.

The majority of the Court rejected the position of the applicant Foundation that section 43 violates the *Charter*. The Foundation's position was that the section: (1) violates section 7 of the *Canadian Charter of Rights and Freedoms* because it fails to give procedural protections to children, does not further the best interests of the child, and is both overbroad and vague; (2) violates section 12 of the *Charter* because it constitutes cruel and unusual punishment or treatment; and (3) violates section 15(1) of the *Charter* because it denies children the legal protection against assaults that is accorded to adults.

The Court held that section 43 does not exempt from criminal sanction conduct that causes harm or raises a reasonable prospect of harm. The section can be invoked only in cases of non-consensual application of force that results neither in harm nor in the prospect of bodily harm. This limits its operation to the mildest forms of assault. The Court stated that: "People must know that if their conduct raises an apprehension of bodily harm they cannot rely on s. 43. Similarly, police officers and judges must know that the defence cannot be raised in such circumstances."

The court decision (per McLachlin C.J.) contains the following summary at paragraphs 38 and 40:

> Contemporary social consensus is that, while teachers may sometimes use corrective force to remove children from classrooms or secure compliance with instructions, the use of corporal punishment by teachers is not acceptable. Many school boards forbid the use of corporal punishment, and some provinces and territories have legislatively prohibited its use by teachers: see, e.g., *Schools Act, 1997*, S.N.L. 1997, c. S-12.2, s. 42; *School Act*, R.S.B.C. 1996, c. 412, s. 76(3); *Education Act*, S.N.B. 1997, c. E-1.12, s. 23; *School Act*, R.S.P.E.I. 1988, c. S-2.1, s. 73; *Education Act*, S.N.W.T. 1995, c. 28, s. 34(3); *Education Act*, S.Y. 1989-90, c. 25, s. 36. . ..
>
> . . .Generally, s. 43 exempts from criminal sanction only minor corrective force of a transitory and trifling nature. On the basis of current expert consensus, it does not apply to corporal punishment of children under two or teenagers. Degrading, inhuman or harmful conduct is not protected. Discipline by the use of objects or blows or slaps to the head is unreasonable. Teachers may reasonably apply force to remove a child from a classroom or secure compliance with instructions, but not merely as corporal punishment. Coupled with the requirement that the conduct be corrective, which rules out conduct stemming from the caregiver's frustration, loss of temper or abusive personality, a consistent picture emerges of the area covered by s. 43. It is wrong for law enforcement officers or judges to apply their own subjective views of what is "reasonable under the circumstances"; the test is objective. The question must be considered in context and in light of all the circumstances of the case. The gravity of the precipitating event is not relevant.

It should be noted that a school board is expressly authorized in the *Education Act* (s. 171(1)18) "to pay [part or all of the legal costs of a] teacher, officer or other employee in successfully defending any legal proceeding brought against him or her [. . .] for assault in respect of disciplinary action taken in the course of duty".

5.10 Ontario College of Teachers

The teaching profession is controlled and influenced in different ways by several organizations, chiefly the Ontario College of Teachers, the Ontario Teachers' Federation, the teachers' unions, and the Ministry of Education. Among these, it is the College that is charged with the mandate of governing the teaching profession and protecting the public interest with respect to the profession.

5.10.1 Role of the College

The mandate of the College is set out in a series of "objects" in section 3 of the *Ontario College of Teachers Act, 1996*: The College has the following objects:

> 3. (1) To regulate the profession of teaching and to govern its members.
>
> (2) To develop, establish and maintain qualifications for membership in the College.
>
> (3) To accredit professional teacher education programs offered by post-secondary educational institutions.
>
> (4) To accredit ongoing education programs for teachers offered by post-secondary educational institutions and other bodies.
>
> (5) To issue, renew, amend, suspend, cancel, revoke and reinstate certificates of qualification and registration.
>
> (6) To provide for the ongoing education of members of the College, including professional learning required to maintain certificates of qualification and registration.
>
> (7) To establish and enforce professional standards and ethical standards applicable to members of the College.
>
> (8) To receive and investigate complaints against members of the College and to deal with discipline and fitness to practise issues.
>
> (9) To develop, provide and accredit educational programs leading to certificates of qualification additional to the certificate required for membership, including but not limited to certificates of qualification as a supervisory officer, and to issue, renew, amend, suspend, cancel, revoke and reinstate such additional certificates.
>
> (10) To communicate with the public on behalf of the members of the College.
>
> (11) To perform such additional functions as are prescribed by the regulations.

The College is a body corporate without share capital, with all the powers of a natural person. The *Corporations Act* and *Corporations Information Act* do not apply to the College except as specified in the Act or regulations.

5.10.2 Governing Council

The College is governed by a Council composed of 23 persons who are members of the College and who are elected by the members of the College and 14 persons who are appointed by the Lieutenant Governor in Council. (See section 4 of the *OCTA*, O. Reg. 292/00 and O. Reg. 345/96.)

The term for Council members cannot exceed three years, except if permitted by regulation (s. 5, Act). Elections are held every three years. Appointments by the government are of different lengths, so that some members are appointed for one year, two years or three years. No person can be a Council member for more than ten consecutive years.

The College has several committees, one of which is the Executive Committee (Act, s. 15). This Committee can be delegated powers and duties by the Council, but it cannot make, amend or revoke a by-law or regulation (Act, s. 16). The Council must meet at least four times a year. The College must hold an annual meeting of the membership (s. 13).

The Chief Executive Officer of the College is the "Registrar".

5.10.3 Membership Fees

The members of the College establish their fees through by-laws approved by their Council.

Aside from the annual membership fee, there are also fees for:

- registration
- evaluation of qualifications obtained outside Ontario or outside Canada
- penalty for late payment of annual fee
- reinstatement of suspended membership
- reinstatement of revoked membership
- registration appeal
- duplicate certificate
- duplicate tax receipt
- statement of good standing.

5.10.4 The "Register"

The Register is a list of all members of the College. Any person may inspect the Register and, for a fee, may obtain a copy of any part of it. A College by-law deals with how a member can change his or her name on the Register. Before hiring a teacher, a board should contact the College to confirm that the person is on the Register as a member in good standing with the appropriate basic and additional qualifications.

The Register contains information about each member's teaching qualifications. It also reveals if a member's certificate has been suspended, revoked or cancelled. The by-laws also permit the removal of certain information from the Register. For example, if conditions had been placed upon the member's certificate and were subsequently removed, then the Register would be amended to remove any reference to the condition. Persons wishing to register must provide a report of a Criminal Reference Check.

5.10.5 College Regulations

It is not always the government that makes regulations. Self-governing bodies are often given this power. The College's regulation-making powers are listed in section 40 of the Act. Note that the Minister of Education has the opportunity to *review* any College regulation before it is made, and the regulation must be *approved* by the Lieutenant Governor in Council. For this reason, College regulations are presented to the Ontario Cabinet for approval. They are then signed by the Lieutenant Governor. The regulations made by the College are gazetted in the Ontario Gazette.

The major regulations are:

Ontario Regulation 345/96 — Appointments to Council

Ontario Regulation 184/97 — on teachers' qualifications

Ontario Regulation 437/97 — which defines "professional misconduct"

Ontario Regulation 72/97 — a general regulation setting out various administrative and organizational matters for the College

Ontario Regulation 293/00 — election of council members

Ontario Regulation 347/02 — Teacher Education Programs, Accreditation

5.10.6 College By-laws

The College has the power to make by-laws to govern its administration and operations. These include the following:

- establishing the fees for membership and services
- the calling of regular and special Council meetings
- meeting procedures, including the taking of minutes
- naming officers of the College (Chair, Vice-Chair, Registrar and other officers as determined from time to time)
- electing the Chair and Vice-Chair of the Council, and filling vacancies of these positions
- responsibilities of the Registrar
- dealing with vacancies on Committees. This by-law outlines how an elected member of the Council can be suspended or disqualified from serving on the Council or its committees. It states how and when a vacancy must be filled. Vacancies are filled by appointment by the Executive Committee, and its decision is placed before the Council for confirmation at its next regular meeting. Note that Ontario Regulation 72/97 has specific provisions dealing with disqualification and vacancies on Council and statutory committees. Persons appointed by the Lieutenant Governor in Council are not "elected" Council members, and their removal and replacement is not within the scope of the by-law.
- committee reports
- appointing signing officers for College documents
- banking and finance, including investments and borrowing
- audit
- indemnifying Council members and College employees for acts done in the execution of their duties
- purchasing liability insurance and property insurance
- conducting the annual meeting
- delegating to the Executive Committee all the powers and duties of the Council (note, this cannot include the power to make or change by-laws or regulations).

Conflict of Interest

The Conflict of Interest By-law requires all members of Council and officers of the College to disclose any conflict of interest that they may have in any matter coming before the Council or a committee. They shall not participate in the discussion or vote on a matter where they have a conflict of interest. A member or officer has a conflict when he or she makes a decision or is present when a decision is made or participates in making a decision in the carrying out of his or her role that may directly or indirectly confer a benefit on the member or officer or any person with whom the member or officer does not deal at arm's length, and at the same time knows that in making the decision there is the opportunity to further his or her private interest or the private interest of a party with whom the member or officer does not deal at arm's length. There is no conflict of interest when approving resolutions relating to remuneration of Council, indemnification of Council members, or the acquisition of insurance relating to indemnification of Council members.

Code of Ethics By-law for Council Members

Council members must:

- comply with the *Ontario College of Teachers Act*, the regulations and the College by-laws
- familiarize themselves with the Act, regulations, by-laws and any other records and documents that may be necessary for the performance of the duties of their office
- take part in the committee work of the College and serve actively during their term of office on any committees to which they have been appointed
- ensure that confidential matters coming to their attention as members of the Council are not disclosed by them except as required for the performance of their duties or as directed by the Council or the Chair
- recognize the distinction between their corporate and individual authority as council members and conduct themselves accordingly with College staff, members of the College and the public
- exercise care, diligence, skill and prudence in carrying out the business of the College
- conscientiously perform duties on behalf of the officers of the College, as requested
- seek to enhance the public perception of the College and the profession of teaching.

5.10.7 Complaints and Discipline

A complaint about a member of the College is sent to the Registrar. Under section 26 of the Act, a person may make a complaint regarding the conduct or actions of a member if the person is:

- a member of the public
- a member of the College
- the Registrar
- the Minister of Education.

(a) Complaint Process

The usual situation involves a person who has called the College to find out whether a complaint should be filed and, if so, how. College staff work with the person to find out if it is a matter that is within the jurisdiction of the College, i.e. involves professional misconduct, incompetence or fitness to practise. In many instances, the issue can and should be resolved at the local level of the school board. If the person still wishes to file a complaint, College staff will provide information on how to do so.

The College provides the following steps to be taken when a person is considering filing a complaint:

- Talk to the Teacher or Principal First

  When a member of the public expresses a concern about a member of the College, he or she is encouraged to talk to the teacher, principal of the school or a board official, if appropriate.

- Talk to the College

  When certain concerns are not resolved at the local school or board level, College staff may be able to assist you in finding a local solution. Contact the Investigations and Hearings Department at 416-961-8800.

- Submit a Complaint in Writing

  You may wish to file a formal complaint with the College. College staff will investigate the matter if it relates to professional misconduct, incompetence or incapacity and all pertinent material will be submitted to the Investigation Committee for its consideration. A complaint must be in writing and sent to the Registrar of the College, 121 Bloor Street East, Toronto, Ontario M4W 3M5. You must provide your name, address and telephone number as well as the nature of the complaint, the name of the member and any other pertinent information. Anonymous complaints are not investigated by the College. This standard procedure ensures that all parties concerned have access to the same complete information.

- Informing the College Member

  If the Investigation Committee determines the complaint falls within the College's jurisdiction, the member is informed of the complaint and is given an opportunity to respond in writing within 35 days. The response is then shared with the complainant.

- Dispute Resolution

  Most complaints are first considered for their suitability under the Dispute Resolution Program, which is voluntary and consented to by both parties. The College uses dispute resolution to facilitate the resolution of complaints without a full investigation or full hearing. All parties must agree to participate in dispute resolution, the result must be in the public interest and the outcome must be similar to what a hearing would have produced.

- Investigating the Complaint

  If the matter is not resolved via the Dispute Resolution Program, the College will then conduct an investigation, which could include interviewing individuals the complainant and the member feel can provide relevant information.

A complaint must be filed with the Registrar in the format prescribed in the by-laws. It must be in writing, and must provide the name of the member who is the subject of the complaint, along with a description of the conduct or actions of the member.

Bylaw Section 28 — Complaints

28.01 A complaint filed pursuant to section 26 of the *Ontario College of Teachers Act, 1996* shall:

- be in writing,
- contain the name of the member who is the subject of the complaint,
- in the case of a complaint under paragraph 26(1) (a) or (b) of the Act, contain the full name, address and telephone number of the person making the complaint,

include a description of the conduct or actions of the member about which the complaint is being made, and contain a "Request to Initiate Investigation" form as provided for in the bylaws and signed by the complainant.

The matter is referred to the "Investigation Committee" (see ss. 25 and 26). The Committee can refuse to consider and investigate a complaint if, in its opinion,

(a) the complaint does not relate to professional misconduct, incompetence or fitness to practise, or

(b) the complaint is frivolous, vexatious or an abuse of process.

The College notifies the member about the complaint and the member has 35 days to respond in writing to the Investigation Committee. The member's response is shared with the complainant. A College investigator attempts to gather pertinent information and documents for consideration by the Investigation Committee.

(b) Investigation Committee

The Investigation Committee reviews the complaint, the member's response and relevant information gathered by the Investigator. The Council must appoint at least seven of its members to the Investigation Committee, at least two of whom must have been appointed by the Lieutenant Governor in Council.

The Investigation Committee "need not" hold a hearing or even afford an opportunity to make oral or written submissions. It must give its decision in writing to the member and the complainant, with reasons for the decision. It must use its best efforts to make a decision within 120 days of the filing of the complaint with the Registrar.

The Committee may:

- refer the matter to the Discipline Committee
- choose not to refer the matter to the Discipline Committee
- caution or admonish the member against whom the complaint is filed
- take such action as it considers appropriate in the circumstances (consistent with the Act, regulations and by-laws).

(c) Discipline Committee

The Council must appoint at least 11 members to the Discipline Committee, at least four of whom must have been appointed by the Lieutenant Governor in Council.

While most matters before the Discipline Committee will have been referred there by the Investigation Committee, it is possible for the Council or the Executive Committee to refer matters directly to the Discipline Committee for a hearing. When such a direct referral is made, the Council or Executive Committee may also order the Registrar to suspend the member or impose terms, conditions or limitations on the member's certificate, if it is of the opinion that the actions or conduct of the member exposes or is likely to expose students to harm or injury (s. 29(3)). No hearing need be held before a direct referral is made. However, a member is to be given notice of the direct referral and 14 days to make written submissions about it, before the referral is made. The 14-day period does not apply if the Council or Executive Committee is of the opinion that the delay would be inappropriate in view of the risk of harm or injury to students. Any matter that has been referred directly by the Council or the Executive Committee must be dealt with expeditiously by the Discipline Committee.

When a matter is referred to the Discipline Committee, it must hear and determine the matter.

After a hearing, it can:

(1) find a member guilty of professional misconduct as defined in the regulations, or

(2) find a member to be incompetent if, in its opinion, the member has displayed in his or her professional responsibilities a lack of knowledge, skill or judgment, or disregard for the welfare of a student of a nature or extent that demonstrates that the member is unfit to continue to carry out his or her professional responsibilities, or that a certificate held by the member under the *Ontario College of Teachers Act* should be made subject to terms, conditions or limitations (s. 30).

Upon finding a member incompetent or guilty of professional misconduct, the Discipline Committee can make an order:

- directing the Registrar to revoke any certificate of the member
- directing the Registrar to suspend any certificate of the member for a stated period not to exceed 24 months
- directing the Registrar to impose specified terms, conditions or limitations on any certificate of the member
- directing that the imposition of a penalty be postponed for a specified period and not be imposed if specified terms are met within that period.

If the finding is one of professional misconduct (i.e. not incompetence), there are additional measures that can be taken by the Discipline Committee. It may make an order:

- requiring that the member be reprimanded, admonished or counselled
- imposing a fine on the member (up to $5,000 payable to the Minister of Finance)
- directing publication of its order against the member
- fixing costs to be paid by the member.

The parties before the Discipline Committee are the College and the member whose conduct or actions are being investigated (s. 32(2)). Hearings are conducted in public unless the Committee orders that the public be excluded for any of the reasons listed in subsection 32(7), e.g. a civil or criminal proceeding could be prejudiced. The Act sets out various procedural requirements in section 32, including the right of a party to see all documents, before the hearing, that will be used at the hearing. Where the Act does not deal specifically with a procedural item, the *Statutory Powers Procedure Act* will apply (e.g. right to cross-examine witnesses and to be represented).

Under Part VI of the Act, the Discipline Committee also has the duty to hear applications for reinstatement of membership, or for variation of its previous orders. These hearings are closed to the public. The parties are the College and the applicant. The Council or Executive Committee may, without a hearing, make an order removing a suspension or reinstating a member (s. 34). A decision of the Discipline Committee may be appealed to Divisional Court (s. 35).

(d) Fitness to Practise Committee

A complaint about a member usually infers that the member has deliberately done something wrong. However, the member's alleged failings as a professional may not be a matter of "fault". The Fitness to Practise Committee has the duty to hear matters referred to it by the Investigation Committee, or directly by Council or the Executive Committee, or on an application for reinstatement or variation. It may, after a hearing, find a member to be incapacitated if, in its opinion, the member is suffering from a physical or mental condition or disorder such that the member is unfit to continue to carry out his or her professional responsibilities or that a certificate held by the member should be made subject to terms, conditions or limitations. Upon finding a member to be incapacitated, it may make an order:

- directing the Registrar to revoke any certificate of the member
- directing the Registrar to suspend any certificate of the member for a stated period not to exceed 24 months
- directing the Registrar to impose specified terms, conditions or limitations on any certificate of the member
- directing that the imposition of a penalty be postponed for a specified period and not be imposed if specified terms are met within that period.

The Fitness to Practise Committee will follow many of the same procedures as the Discipline Committee in ensuring that the member receives a full and fair hearing. However, due to the nature of the matters being considered, its hearings are closed to the public. The member can request that the hearing be open. The Committee can refuse this request if it is satisfied that it should be closed for any of the reasons specified in subsection 32(9), e.g. safety of a person may be jeopardized, ongoing civil or criminal proceedings, etc. Pursuant to subsection 33(14), the Fitness to Practise Committee also has the duty to hear applications for variation of its orders or for reinstatement of a revoked or suspended certification. The procedures outlined in section 33 apply.

(e) Public Interest Committee

Section 17.1 of the Act establishes the Public Interest Committee, whose purpose is to "advise the Council with respect to the duty of the College and the members of the Council to serve and protect the public interest in carrying out the College's objects" and such other duties as may be prescribed by regulation. The Minister of Education must designate no fewer than three and no more than five persons to serve on the Committee and they shall not be members of the College. They serve for terms of up to three years and no person may serve more than six consecutive years on the Committee.

The remuneration of persons on the Public Interest Committee is prescribed by Ontario Regulation 370/07. Section 25.1 of Ontario Regulation 72/97 prescribes the requirements for holding meetings of the Public Interest Committee, along with a requirement for the Committee to have a work plan and to make an annual report to the Council containing information about its activities during the previous year, along with a copy of any reports requested by the Council.

5.10.8 General Regulation

Ontario Regulation 72/97, made pursuant to the *Ontario College of Teachers Act, 1996*, covers a number of different operational and administrative matters.

(a) Annual Membership Fees

Section 2 requires a board, private school and the Ministry of Education (for members employed by the Provincial Schools Authority) to submit the annual membership fee to the College on behalf of members in their employ, and authorizes them to deduct the fee from the member's salary. The fee must be submitted no later than 35 days after the due date specified for the year in the College by-laws. The employer's deadline can be delayed by the College if the employer is facing extraordinary circumstances that warrant an extension. The employer may be required to pay interest on dues in arrears. Members whose employers do not submit fees on their behalf must pay the annual fee directly. The College can and will suspend a member who has not paid his or her dues.

(b) Quorum at Council Meetings

Council quorum is 19 members of Council, at least five of whom are appointees of the Lieutenant Governor in Council (s. 5).

(c) Disqualification of Council Members

Elected Council members can be disqualified:

- if found to be guilty of professional misconduct, incompetent, or unfit to practise
- for failure without cause to attend:
    - three consecutive meetings of Council
    - three consecutive meetings of a committee on which he or she serves, or
    - at least half the meetings of Council in a 12-month period

- for failure to attend a hearing of a panel of a committee on which he or she serves
- if he or she fails or ceases to meet the criteria under which he or she was elected to the Council (see criteria in O. Reg. 293/00).

(d) Vacancies on Council

A vacancy occurs when a member dies, resigns or is disqualified from sitting on Council (s. 7). If the vacancy occurs within six months of the end of the elected member's term of office, the Council may leave the seat vacant or fill the seat by appointment. If the vacancy is more than six months from the end of the term, the seat must be filled by appointment. There are provisions about how the appointments are to be made (ss. 8 to 10). If vacancies bring the Council below quorum, then an election to fill the vacancies must be held (s. 11). The newly-appointed or elected person fills the seat until the end of the former member's term.

(e) Statutory Committees

The *Ontario College of Teachers Act, 1996* (s. 15), prescribes the College's "statutory committees":

- Executive Committee
- Investigation Committee
- Discipline Committee
- Registration Appeals Committee
- Fitness to Practise Committee.

Ontario Regulation 72/97 provides for the appointment of a chair of each committee by Council. A vice-chair is elected by the committee members. The College Council determines the number of members of each committee provided that this does not conflict with conditions set out in subsections 25(1), 27(1) and 28(1) of the Act (s. 14).

The quorum of the Investigation Committee, Discipline Committee and Fitness to Practise Committee is a majority; the quorum of the Executive Committees is four; the quorum of the Registration Appeals Committee is three; and in all cases, at least one member present must be a government-appointed Council member (s. 15). There are procedures for filling vacancies on the statutory committees (s. 16), and for the calling of meetings (s. 17).

(f) Executive Committee

The Executive Committee comprises the chairs of:

- Fitness to Practise Committee
- Discipline Committee
- Registration Appeals Committee
- Investigation Committee
- Standards of Practice and Education Committee
- Finance Committee

- Accreditation Committee.

The chair and vice-chair of Council must be on the Executive Committee, and the chair of the Council is the chair of Executive Committee. There are also provisions, in section 19, that ensure that the Executive Committee has both elected and government-appointed members.

(g) Investigation Committee

In considering a complaint under the Act, the Investigation Committee will work in "panels" of at least three members selected by the Committee chair (s. 21).

(h) Discipline Committee

In performing its duties under the Act, the Discipline Committee will work in "panels" of at least three members selected by the Committee chair (s. 22).

(i) Registration Appeals Committee

The Registration Appeals Committee is composed of five members, at least two of whom are elected and at least two of whom are government-appointed. In performing its duties under the Act, the Committee will work in "panels" of at least three members selected by the Committee chair (s. 24).

(j) Fitness to Practise Committee

In performing its duties under the Act, the Fitness to Practise Committee will work in "panels" of at least three members selected by the Committee chair (s. 25).

(k) Collection of Information

Section 26 of the Regulation lists organizations for the purposes of section 47(1) of the Act, from which the College may require information, including personal information. These are:

- private schools
- colleges of applied arts and technology
- universities
- Ontario Teachers' Pension Plan Board
- Ontario Teachers' Federation
- Affiliates of the Ontario Teachers' Federation.

5.11 Role of the Minister in Governing the Teaching Profession

5.11.1 Teachers' Qualifications

The government no longer has a *direct* role in deciding what is necessary in order for a person to become a teacher or to obtain additional teaching qualifications. The College has jurisdiction to determine *how* a person may obtain basic and additional teaching qualifications. The *Education Act* states that (except as otherwise provided in or under the *Education Act*) a person must be a member of the College in order to be employed or act as a teacher in an elementary or secondary school. The Minister, with the approval of the Lieutenant Governor in Council, may make regulations prescribing the qualifications of teachers. (A "teacher" is defined as a member of the College.) For example, Regulation 298 requires that a principal must have "principal's qualifications", and a special education teacher must have additional qualifications to teach special education.

5.11.2 Review

The Minister has the power to review the activities of the Council of the College and require the Council to provide reports and information. The Minister may require the Council to do anything that, in the opinion of the Minister, is necessary or advisable to carry out the intent of the *Ontario College of Teachers Act, 1996*. The Minister may also require the College to make, amend or revoke a regulation (s. 12). This power reflects the fact that, although the government has delegated some of its control over "education" to the College, education remains fundamentally a responsibility of the provincial government in accordance with the Canadian Constitution. However, an attempt to use this power to interfere with the day-to-day operations of the College would be contrary to the policy behind establishing the College in the first place, namely that teachers should govern themselves.

5.11.3 Members' Duties

In the *Education Act* and Regulation 298, the government prescribes duties of teachers and principals. However, the College, not the Minister, may discipline a teacher for professional misconduct or incompetence. (Of course, the teacher's employer will likely be involved as well.) The College, not the Minister, may prescribe a code of ethics for members. It should be kept in mind that not all members work for school boards. Some members work for private schools, the provincial government, the teachers' unions, and the faculties of education. Some members are not employed.

5.11.4 Suspension

The College may suspend a person's membership. A person may not teach for a school board while under suspension. The government may prescribe, by regulation, the consequences of having one's membership suspended, or of having terms, conditions or limitations placed upon a certificate of qualification (*Education Act*, s. 11(1)26.1 and Reg. 298, s. 22).

5.11.5 University Faculties of Education

The government provides funding to faculties of education, but the College "accredits" the faculties' programs of professional education for teaching candidates.

5.11.6 Supervisory Officers

The government issues the "Supervisory Officer's Certificate". However, under Regulation 309, to obtain a certificate as an "academic" (as opposed to "business") supervisory officer, a person must show the Ministry that he or she has "additional qualifications" as a supervisory officer issued by the College. The College does not issue the Supervisory Officer's Certificate; it issues "additional qualifications" to members who have completed the prescribed qualifications in Part V of Ontario

Regulation 184/97. Regulation 309 also prescribes the requirements to obtain a Business Supervisory Officer's Certificate.

5.12 Teachers' Qualifications

5.12.1 General

Section 262 of the *Education Act* states:

> Except as otherwise provided in or under this Act, no person shall be employed in an elementary or secondary school to teach or to perform any duty for which membership in the College is required under this Act unless the person is a member of the Ontario College of Teachers.

Clause 170(1)12 of the Act states that a board shall

> appoint for each school that it operates a principal and an adequate number of teachers, all of whom shall be members of the Ontario College of Teachers.

Therefore, once it is determined that a person is being hired to "teach", that person must be a "teacher" as defined in the *Education Act*, i.e. a member of the Ontario College of Teachers. An exception to this rule occurs when a board obtains the Minister's permission to hire a "temporary teacher" (i.e. a person who is not a College member) on a "Letter of Permission". Regulation 298 specifies whether any additional qualifications are required for a teacher to teach in a specific position or subject.

5.12.2 Role of the Minister Respecting Qualifications

The Minister has jurisdiction over:

- whether a given position or subject requires additional teaching qualifications beyond the basic certificate (e.g. principal, special education, French-language education)
- granting supervisory officer certificates (academic and business). In the case of academic supervisory officers, the person must produce the necessary evidence of completion of the College's program leading to an additional qualification as a supervisory officer
- granting letters of permission to boards to hire unqualified persons to teach on a temporary basis up to one year (s. 8(1)10)
- excluding individuals on a case-by-case basis from the need to meet some or all of the qualification requirements by accepting equivalent qualifications (see s. 8(1)14). This power is rarely exercised.

Ontario Regulation 142/08 prescribes the requirements for issuance of a Letter of Permission: It states:

> 1. (1) The Minister may grant to a board a letter of permission for a period specified in the letter if,
>
> > (a) the director of education or secretary of the board or, in the case of a school authority, the appropriate supervisory officer, submits to the Ministry an application in the form required by the Minister, which shall include the declaration of the person submitting the application that,
> >
> > > (i) the board has publicly advertised, at least once, a position for which a teacher is required under the regulations,

(ii) the advertisement,

(A) was published in a daily newspaper having provincial circulation in Ontario for at least three days, and at least one of those days was within the five days before the closing date of the competition for the position, or

(B) was published on a publicly accessible website approved by the Minister for at least ten days and was not removed before the closing date of the competition for the position,

(iii) every day that the advertisement appeared was within the 30 days before the closing date of the competition for the position,

(iv) no teacher has applied for the position or no teacher who has applied for the position has accepted it,

(v) the individual that the board proposes to employ under the authority of a letter of permission is 18 years of age or older and holds an Ontario secondary school diploma, a secondary school graduation diploma or a secondary school honour graduation diploma, or an equivalent to any of them,

(vi) the individual is not and has never been a member of the Ontario College of Teachers;

(vii) the individual has provided to the board a written statement that any teaching certificate or licence granted to him or her by another jurisdiction is not cancelled, revoked or suspended for any reason other than for failure to pay fees or levies to the governing body,

(viii) the board has collected a personal criminal history, as defined in Ontario Regulation 521/01 (Collection of Personal Information) made under the Act, of the individual, and

(ix) the board has conducted a reference check of the individual and is satisfied with the results;

(b) the person submitting the application attaches to the application such evidence as the Minister may require of the facts set out in the declaration under clause (a);

(c) the application and evidence are submitted no earlier than seven days after the closing date of the competition for the position; and

(d) the anticipated start date of the position for which the board proposes to employ the individual is no later than 30 days after the closing date of the competition for the position.

(2) If a letter of permission is granted, it shall be effective as of the start date of the position.

5.12.3 Role of the College Respecting Qualifications

The Ontario College of Teachers has jurisdiction over:

- how a person obtains a certificate of qualification as a teacher
- how to obtain additional teaching qualifications, including principals' qualifications and academic supervisory officers' qualifications
- accreditation of university faculty of education programs as leading to the granting of a College certificate

- suspension, revocation and cancellation of certificates
- imposing terms, conditions and limitations on certificates
- granting temporary letters of approval to boards. These authorize a board to assign or appoint a teacher to a position or subject for which the teacher does not hold the qualifications required by the regulations made under the *Education Act* for teaching the subject or holding the position. (See section 50 of Ontario Regulation 184/97.)

Regulation 297 (now revoked) formerly prescribed the forms for the "Ontario Teacher's Certificate" and other teaching qualifications. Ontario Regulation 184/97 does not prescribe the forms of the College's certificates. Instead, these forms are prescribed by by-law. This makes it easier to change the form should the need arise. Like Regulation 297, Ontario Regulation 184/97 prescribes how a teacher may obtain "additional basic" qualifications and "additional" qualifications. It also contains several schedules setting out what qualifications can be obtained in the pre-service (faculty) program of professional education and those that can be obtained as additional qualifications.

A "certificate of qualification and registration" is a certificate granted by the College that has two components:

- a certificate of registration as a member of the College
- a certificate of qualification showing the holder's basic and additional teaching qualifications.

The "Ontario Teacher's Certificate" and a "Ontario Teacher's Qualifications Record Card" are things of the past. The permanent letter of standing, provisional letter of standing and temporary letter of standing are also relegated to history.

Teachers who held valid Ministry certificates on May 20, 1997 were automatically entitled to be granted an equivalent certificate of qualification and registration by the College. Persons enrolled in a faculty of education during 1997–98 were similarly protected upon successful completion of their program.

6

NEGLIGENCE, LIABILITY AND RISK MANAGEMENT

6.1 Introduction

When a child gets hurt in your school, your priority is making sure he or she is properly cared for and that the parents are notified. No one wants accidents or injuries to happen. However, they do happen. Educators can reduce harm and loss by "managing risk". Most school boards in Ontario are members of the Ontario School Boards Insurance Exchange (OSBIE). OSBIE has an excellent website containing a number of suggestions on how to avoid or minimize risk in your school.

Children are hurt at school as a result of accidents and intentional actions such as bullying, taunting, extortion, and assault. After an accident or other incident, parents must be informed by the school about any actual or suspected injury to their child as soon as possible.

Regardless of how an accident or incident occurred, or who may be at fault, sympathetic communication of clear information to parents by the appropriate school or board official will be appreciated by any concerned parent. Lack of communication may lead to hostility and a greater chance of being sued.

However, it is important to be aware that statements by board representatives can be used by a plaintiff in a lawsuit against the board. Therefore, there are limits to what should be said. The board's insurer is responsible for investigating incidents in accordance with the board's insurance policy. Board staff must be careful not to jeopardize the proper handling of an insurance investigation, or indeed, of a police investigation (e.g. of suspected assault).

Principals and teachers:

- should not admit liability to any parent or parent-representative for an accident or other incident that occurs on school property
- should not give oral or written statements to parents or opposing lawyers
- should co-operate with the insurance adjuster and lawyer who act for the school board or its insurer
- should keep detailed notes on any incident resulting in suspected or actual personal injury or loss of property
- should not share any insurance reports or personal notes with parents unless permitted to do so by the board's insurer
- should immediately inform senior administration and the board's insurer about the accident or other incident, using the board-approved forms and procedures.

(Note: injuries to employees at the workplace must be reported by the employer as required by the *Workplace Safety and Insurance Act, 1997.*)

Educating hundreds of young people in a school is an inherently risky activity. It is not surprising, therefore, that educators are always conscious of the need to enforce safe practices and that many are fearful of being sued if something goes wrong. An unreasonable or unfounded fear not only creates individual stress, but also results in limitations upon the programs that boards are willing to allow in our schools. However, court decisions show that if a teacher has taken reasonable safety precautions in the instruction and supervision of students, the court is not likely to make a finding of negligence in a lawsuit resulting from an accident at school. The onus of proof is on the plaintiff to prove his or her case upon a "balance of probabilities", rather than the standard used in criminal law of "beyond a reasonable doubt".

There is no duty upon teachers to foresee every conceivable accident or to supervise their students every minute of the school day. However, teachers do have a duty to act as a careful parent would act and to foresee the risks that a careful parent would foresee. Teachers are under a duty to ensure that adequate safety precautions are taken, that safety equipment is used and that pupils are fully aware of the dangers involved in a given activity. This is particularly important in the science laboratory, the technical shop and in physical and outdoor education. If it can be shown that pupils were properly instructed, warned of possible dangers, and adequately supervised (given their skill, age and experience), then the teacher and board will reduce the possibility of being found liable.

Although written in 1856, the following definition still conveys a general idea of what we understand to be negligence: "Negligence is the omission to do something which a reasonable man, guided upon those considerations which ordinarily regulate the conduct of human affairs, would do, or doing something which a prudent and reasonable man would not do. The defendants might have been liable for negligence, if, unintentionally, they omitted to do that which a reasonable person would have done, or did that which a person taking reasonable precautions would not have done." (*Blyth v. Birmingham Water Works Co.* (1856), [1843-60] All E.R. Rep. 478, 156 E.R. 1047, 11 Exch. 781 (Eng. Exch.) at 784 [Exch.].) In more modern terms, negligence may be described as the failure to use reasonable care. That is, it is the doing of something that a reasonably prudent person would not do, or the failure to do something that a reasonably prudent person would do under like circumstances.

6.2 Establishing Proof of Negligence

As a general rule, a defendant will not be found liable for negligence unless the plaintiff is able to prove four essential elements:

(1) There must be a duty of care owed by the defendant to the plaintiff.

(2) There must be a breach of the duty of care by the defendant. That is, did the defendant's conduct meet the required standard of care?

(3) There must be actual damages — i.e. an injury or loss sustained by the plaintiff.

(4) There must be a sufficient causal connection between the loss or injury sustained by the plaintiff and the defendant's act or omission. If the con-

nection is not present or is too remote, the defendant will not be held liable.

The court will also determine whether the plaintiff contributed to his or her own loss or injury.

6.3 Duty of Care

In negligence cases, the court must first determine if the defendant owed a duty of care toward the plaintiff. In circumstances where there is no statutory or common law duty to ensure the safety or well-being of another person, there cannot be a finding of liability in negligence if the person is injured. However, it is well-established in both common law and statutory law that there is a duty upon boards and their staff to ensure the safety and well-being of students. Therefore, most reported cases on school negligence focus, not on arguments as to whether a duty of care exists, but on the nature of the duty in a given fact situation, whether the defendant has failed to discharge that duty, and whether the injury or loss was reasonably foreseeable.

In *Hanke v. Resurfice Corp.*, [2007] 1 S.C.R. 333, 357 N.R. 175, [2007] R.R.A. 1, 278 D.L.R. (4th) 643, 45 C.C.L.T. (3d) 1, [2007] 4 W.W.R. 1, 2007 SCC 7, 2007 CarswellAlta 131, 2007 CarswellAlta 130, 394 W.A.C. 333, 404 A.R. 333, 69 Alta. L.R. (4th) 1, [2007] S.C.J. No. 7 (S.C.C.) the Supreme Court of Canada stated:

> Liability for negligence requires breach of a duty of care arising from a reasonably foreseeable risk of harm to one person, created by the act or omission of another: *Jordan House Ltd. v. Menow*, [1974] S.C.R. 239 at p. 247, *per* Laskin J. (as he then was). By enforcing reasonable standards of conduct, so as to prevent the creation of reasonably foreseeable risks of harm, tort law serves as a disincentive to risk-creating behaviour: *Stewart v. Pettie*, [1995] 1 S.C.R. 131, at para. 50, *per* Major J. The major elements of a tort action — duty, breach causing injury and cause — reflect "the principle of moral wrongdoing which is the basis of the negligence law": L. Klar, "Downsizing Torts", in N. J. Mullany and A. M. Linden, eds., *Torts Tomorrow: A Tribute to John Fleming* (1998), 305, at p. 307. [At para. 6.]

6.4 Standard of Care

Many claims against school boards are of the "occupier's liability" or "slip and fall" variety, where a person has slipped on ice or on a wet floor, or has tripped over something. Any occupier of premises or land may face this kind of claim, where the condition of the premises has resulted in a loss or injury. In this chapter, however, we are more concerned with claims that arise from the unique relationship between staff (particularly administrators and teachers) and their students. These claims will typically allege the following kinds of negligence on the part of the board and its staff.

1. lack of adequate supervision by a teacher or other staff member;
2. improper, inadequate or defective equipment;
3. failure to warn pupils of specific dangers in doing an activity;
4. failure to train pupils in the proper use of equipment or in safety procedures;
5. failure to take reasonable precautions against injury or loss;

6. failure to hire competent staff and to provide them with the necessary training;
7. failure to properly treat an injury.

The standard of care owed by teachers toward their pupils has been compared in numerous cases to that of a "careful or prudent parent". In 1893, the standard was established in *Williams v. Eady* (1893), 10 T.L.R. 41 (Eng. C.A.) and it has served as the implicit or explicit starting point for virtually all Canadian school negligence court decisions ever since:

> [T]he schoolmaster was bound to take such care of his boys as a careful father would take of his boys, and there could not be a better definition of the duty of a schoolmaster. Then he was bound to take notice of the ordinary nature of young boys, their tendency to do mischievous acts, and their propensity to meddle with anything that came in their way. (At p. 42.)

The standard of care does not require the presence of a teacher or other responsible person in the classroom or area of activity at all times. For the presence of the teacher to be relevant, it must be shown on the evidence that it might have prevented the accident. The lack of supervision must be causally connected to the events giving rise to the loss or injury.

In *Toronto (City) Board of Education v. Higgs* (1959), 1959 CarswellOnt 91, 22 D.L.R. (2d) 49, [1960] S.C.R. 174 (S.C.C.) at 55 [D.L.R.] Mr. Justice Ritchie of the Supreme Court of Canada stated:

> The duty of supervision which a school authority owes to its pupils while they are at play must of necessity vary from school to school and even from day to day, and it is, therefore, not possible to elicit from the decided cases any guiding principle for the exact measurement of the degree of care to which any particular set of circumstances may give rise. (At p. 55.)

In *Higgs*, the Court also remarked:

> I do not suggest that it is the duty of a school teacher or a supervisor to keep pupils under supervision during every minute while they are in attendance at school. ... He must guard the pupils against danger that could reasonably be foreseen. [1960] S.C.R. 174 at 181

In *Myers v. Peel (County) Board of Education*, 37 N.R. 227, 17 C.C.L.T. 269, 1981 CarswellOnt 612, 123 D.L.R. (3d) 1, [1981] 2 S.C.R. 21, 1981 CarswellOnt 579 (S.C.C.) in response to the argument by the defendant that there was no causal connection between the absence of the teacher and the accident, the Court stated:

> In my opinion, it cannot be said that the presence of a teacher among six to eight students in the exercise room would not have had a restraining effect upon the students which could have influenced the course of events and prevented the accident.

The application of the prudent parent standard of care will vary according to the circumstances. In *Myers v. Peel (County) Board of Education*, the Court stated:

> The standard of care to be exercised by school authorities in providing for the supervision and protection of students for whom they are responsible is that of the careful or prudent parent. ... It is not, however, a standard which can be applied in the same manner and to the same extent in every case. Its application will vary from case to case and will depend upon the number of students being supervised at any given time, the nature of the exercise or activity in progress, the age and the degree of skill and training which the students may have received in connection with such activity,

> the nature and condition of the equipment in use at the time, the competency and capacity of the students involved, and a host of other matters which may be widely varied but which, in a given case, may affect the application of the prudent parent-standard. ...

In *Misir (Litigation Guardian of) v. Children's Rehabilitation Centre of Essex (County)* (September 8, 1989), Doc. Windsor 2624/86, [1989] O.J. No. 1653 (Ont. Dist. Ct.) a teacher was not found to have been negligent when he stepped out of his classroom for three minutes, during which an eight-year-old student injured the 13-year-old plaintiff. In *Little (Litigation Guardian of) v. Chignecto Central Regional School Board*, [2004] N.S.J. No. 386, 720 A.P.R. 103, 227 N.S.R. (2d) 103, 2004 CarswellNS 418, 2004 NSSC 204 (N.S. S.C.); additional reasons at 2004 CarswellNS 526, 2004 NSSC 265, 729 A.P.R. 1, 230 N.S.R. (2d) 1, [2004] N.S.J. No. 494 (N.S. S.C.), the Court carefully considered the statutory duties of boards, principals and support staff to ensure safety under the *Nova Scotia Education Act* and declined to make a finding of liability where the plaintiff was injured during a lunchtime pickup football game at school. The supervisor had turned her back for a minute. The Court placed great emphasis on the fact that the plaintiff knew that tackle football was not permitted. The school board was able to show that it had a disciplinary policy outlining school rules, that it was communicated to students and that it was enforced. However, in *Hentze (Guardian ad litem of) v. Campbell River School District No. 72* (1994), 1994 CarswellBC 1047, [1994] B.C.J. No. 1876, 49 B.C.A.C. 241, 80 W.A.C. 241 (B.C. C.A.), a teacher was found liable for failing to notice roughhousing taking place in the schoolyard during which a seven-year-old student was injured while playing with older students. The teacher had been engaged in a discussion with other pupils at the time of the accident, but the roughhousing had been going on for a few minutes — long enough that it should have been observed by the teacher.

The standard of care imposed upon boards and teachers does not require them to take precautions against accidents that are unforeseeable. "Human prudence would be taxed beyond reason, were it to endeavour to foresee every possibility of human ingenuity, or boyish mischievousness, in its search for opportunities to get into trouble, in even the remotest and most unlikely corners, nooks, or crannies." *Ramsden v. Hamilton Board of Education* (1942), [1942] 1 D.L.R. 770 at 773 (Ont. H.C.). It is also well-established that the mere possibility of an injury resulting from an activity does not mean that it is negligent to permit students to participate in the activity. *Thornton v. Prince George Board of Education*, [1976] 5 W.W.R. 240, 1976 CarswellBC 214, 73 D.L.R. (3d) 35 (B.C. C.A.); varied 3 C.C.L.T. 257, [1978] 2 S.C.R. 267, 1978 CarswellBC 554, 1978 CarswellBC 370, 83 D.L.R. (3d) 480, 19 N.R. 552, [1978] 1 W.W.R. 607 (S.C.C.).

6.5 Causation

There must be a connection between the defendant's conduct and the plaintiff's injury. Courts often use what is known as the "but for" test in determining the issue of causation: would the accident have occurred but for the defendant's negligence? Even if there is a connection, the connection between the defendant's conduct and the loss or injury must not be too remote. Courts have applied a number of different tests to determine the issue of remoteness. Generally speaking, a defendant will not be held liable for an injury or loss which, although it can be traced to the defendant's conduct, was completely unpredictable or which occurred after unforeseeable intervening events or intervening negligence on the part of another person.

In *Hanke v. Resurfice Corp.*, [2007] 1 S.C.R. 333, 357 N.R. 175, [2007] R.R.A. 1, 278 D.L.R. (4th) 643, 45 C.C.L.T. (3d) 1, [2007] 4 W.W.R. 1, 2007 SCC 7, 2007 CarswellAlta 131, 2007 CarswellAlta 130, 394 W.A.C. 333, 404 A.R. 333, 69 Alta. L.R. (4th) 1, [2007] S.C.J. No. 7 (S.C.C.), the Court affirmed that the "but for" test was to be used by courts to determine causation, except where it was not of assistance, in which case a court could use what is referred to as the "material contribution" test:

> 21. First, the basic test for determining causation remains the "but for" test. This applies to multi-cause injuries. The plaintiff bears the burden of showing that "but for" the negligent act or omission of each defendant, the injury would not have occurred. Having done this, contributory negligence may be apportioned, as permitted by statute.
>
> 22. This fundamental rule has never been displaced and remains the primary test for causation in negligence actions. As stated in *Athey v. Leonati*, at para. 14, *per* Major J., "[t]he general, but not conclusive, test for causation is the 'but for' test, which requires the plaintiff to show that the injury would not have occurred but for the negligence of the defendant." Similarly, as I noted in *Blackwater v. Plint*, at para. 78, "[t]he rules of causation consider generally whether 'but for' the defendant's acts, the plaintiff's damages would have been incurred on a balance of probabilities."
>
> 23. The "but for" test recognizes that compensation for negligent conduct should only be made "where a substantial connection between the injury and defendant's conduct" is present. It ensures that a defendant will not be held liable for the plaintiff's injuries where they "may very well be due to factors unconnected to the defendant and not the fault of anyone": *Snell v. Farrell*, at p. 327, *per* Sopinka J.
>
> 24. However, in special circumstances, the law has recognized exceptions to the basic "but for" test, and applied a "material contribution" test. Broadly speaking, the cases in which the "material contribution" test is properly applied involve two requirements.
>
> 25. First, it must be impossible for the plaintiff to prove that the defendant's negligence caused the plaintiff's injury using the "but for" test. The impossibility must be due to factors that are outside of the plaintiff's control; for example, current limits of scientific knowledge. Second, it must be clear that the defendant breached a duty of care owed to the plaintiff, thereby exposing the plaintiff to an unreasonable risk of injury, and the plaintiff must have suffered that form of injury. In other words, the plaintiff's injury must fall within the ambit of the risk created by the defendant's breach. In those exceptional cases where these two requirements are satisfied, liability may be imposed, even though the "but for" test is not satisfied, because it would offend basic notions of fairness and justice to deny liability by applying a "but for" approach.

6.6 Dangerous Activities

The fact that a teacher permits students to participate in a potentially dangerous activity is not, in itself, negligence. However, the care taken must be appropriate to the activity, whether it be sports, outdoor education, laboratory experiments, etc. In each case, the teacher is expected to guard against the reasonably foreseeable dangers of the activity. For example, in *Brost v. Tilley School District*, [1955] 3 D.L.R.

159, 15 W.W.R. 241, 1955 CarswellAlta 31 (Alta. C.A.), the school board and principal were found liable for failing to provide supervision where a six-year-old girl was injured after being pushed too high on a swing set by another student. The Court found that there was a failure "to exercise the degree of care the law required of them to safeguard the small pupils in the use of the swings. ... It was a thing quite foreseeable that this accident or some such accident would happen sooner or later."

6.7 Physical Education

Many school negligence lawsuits arise out of accidents in the gymnasium or on the sports field. An accident may result from faulty or inadequate equipment. In other instances, a pupil may have incurred injuries because he or she was not adequately trained in the activity, or was not properly supervised.

In *Thornton v. Prince George Board of Education*, [1976] 5 W.W.R. 240, 1976 CarswellBC 214, 73 D.L.R. (3d) 35 (B.C. C.A.); varied 3 C.C.L.T. 257, [1978] 2 S.C.R. 267, 1978 CarswellBC 554, 1978 CarswellBC 370, 83 D.L.R. (3d) 480, 19 N.R. 552, [1978] 1 W.W.R. 607 (S.C.C.), the Court dealt with a claim by a 15-year-old pupil who was very seriously injured in gymnastics class. As far as could be determined or inferred from the testimony at trial, the plaintiff jumped off a vaulting box onto a springboard and attempted an aerial somersault. He overshot the landing pit and landed on his head on a thinner mat on the periphery of the pit. The trial judge found the physical education instructor liable, and found the school board vicariously liable for the negligence of the instructor. The British Columbia Court of Appeal provided an important analysis of negligence law as it relates to activities, such as gymnastics, where there is an element of inherent danger:

1. There is an element of risk or danger in gymnastics which was known to the plaintiff and the school authorities.
2. The plaintiff participated in the aerial somersault of his own free will, although this did not mean that he exclusively assumed the risk of the activity.
3. The school authorities had a common law duty to take care of the plaintiff during this activity in the manner of a reasonable and careful parent. This must take into account "the judicial modification of the reasonable-and-careful-parent test to allow for the larger-than-family size of the physical education class and the supraparental expertise commanded of a gymnastics instructor".
4. The school authorities are not "strictly or absolutely liable for any consequential injury however occurring to any pupil in respect of whom the school authorities had accepted the responsibility of care and control". It was not negligent to permit a student to perform an aerial front somersault.
5. Students may be permitted to participate in gymnastic activities provided that the following component criteria of the standard of care are adhered to:
   (a) the activity must be suitable to the pupil's age and mental and physical condition;

(b) the pupil must be progressively trained and coached to do the activity properly and avoid the danger;

(c) the equipment must be adequate and suitably arranged; and

(d) the performance of the activity must be properly supervised.

These criteria are equally applicable to any similar activity by students in which there is an element of inherent danger. The inherent danger enhances the foreseeability that an accident may happen and demands greater caution on the part of school authorities.

6.8 Assumption of Risk in Sports

The written consent of parents should be obtained in order for pupils who are legally minors to participate in any activity which is either unusual or outside the regular classroom routine. A parent expects that his or her child will participate in "gym class". Indeed, unless there are specific medical or other disabilities that cannot be accommodated, a child has a right to attend his or her regular gym class and it is not appropriate to seek parental consent for something the child is entitled to in the first place. Nevertheless, it stands to reason that if the students in the gym class will be engaging in an unusually risky activity that parents would not have expected to be part of the course of study, then parents should have the opportunity to state that their child should not participate. Consent must also be obtained for participation in field trips, intramural or school-league sports, extracurricular clubs, etc. Parental consent should also be obtained if the school wishes a student to help supervise younger children. You do not want a parent saying: "I didn't know you were exposing my child to this danger."

However, the parent must understand what the consent is for. In other words, the proposed activity must be thoroughly outlined in writing in order for the parent to be able to judge whether or not the student should participate. For example, permission to participate in "sports" is inadequate; individual sports must be listed. In the case of sports activities, if the student is sufficiently mature, it is recommended that the student also be asked to sign a form acknowledging that he or she wants to participate despite the potential risk of injury. Legal advice should be obtained when drafting parental and student consent forms. A *waiver* or release of legal rights is distinct from a consent or permission to participate. Generally speaking, a parent may not waive a child's legal right to sue for negligence.

A defendant to a negligence lawsuit may defend it on the basis that the plaintiff voluntarily assumed the risk that he or she would suffer injury or loss. Risk may be voluntarily assumed by the express act of the plaintiff, or may be implied from the plaintiff's actions. Mere knowledge by the plaintiff that an activity is risky is not enough to establish the defence. There must be a voluntary express or implied agreement by the plaintiff to waive the right to claim damages for any injury which might occur as a result of the defendant's breach of the duty of care. *Waldick v. Malcolm* (1991), 1991 CarswellOnt 1020, 125 N.R. 372, 3 O.R. (3d) 471 (note), 1991 CarswellOnt 766, [1991] R.R.A. 560, EYB 1991-67619, [1991] S.C.J. No. 55, [1991] 2 S.C.R. 456, 47 O.A.C. 241, 83 D.L.R. (4th) 114, 8 C.C.L.T. (2d) 1 (S.C.C.).

For boards and teachers, the concept of voluntary assumption of risk is most relevant in the area of sports. Participation in many sports involves an implied consent by the participants to accidental injuries that arise in the normal course of the activity. Players will not be held liable for actions that might constitute negligence outside the sports activity. However, implied consent only extends to normal risk. The courts will draw the line at injuries that result from deliberate attempts to cause severe injury, and they will not imply consent to dangers that are not obvious to the plaintiff or are not a necessary part of the activity.

A person who participates in a game or sport assumes the inherent risks of participation. This assumes that the player is of an age and experience to be aware of the inherent risks. Dangers which are not inherent, or which are unreasonable, are not assumed. A player does not assume the risk of being intentionally injured and does not assume that other players will act with wanton disregard for his or her safety.

In the case of *Thomas v. Hamilton (City) Board of Education* (1994), 20 O.R. (3d) 598, 1994 CarswellOnt 1203, 85 O.A.C. 161 (Ont. C.A.), which involved very serious injuries sustained by a pupil during a school football game, the Ontario Court of Appeal had this to say about pupils consenting to participate in dangerous sports:

> The appellant does not take the position that football is so inherently dangerous a game that high school students should not be permitted to participate in it. Nor does the appellant contend that his high school should not have participated in junior and senior football programs. This latter issue arose because many of Scott Park's players have part-time employment with the result that they are not available for practice on Fridays.
>
> The appellant participated in his high school's junior football program of his own free will. He was aware of the risk of injury, even serious injury, that is inherent to participation in a contact sport such as football. However, he did not, through his consent to participate (and that of his mother), assume all risk of injury to the extent that the school authorities were relieved of the duty of care that they owed to him.
>
> The appellant was not incapacitated, let alone obviously incapacitated, as was the case in *Crocker v. Sundance Northwest Resorts Ltd.*, [1988] 1 S.C.R. 1186, 51 D.L.R. (4th) 321. He had his mother's consent, and his family doctor's certificate stating that he was fit to play football. He knew football was a contact sport which carried with it the risk of serious injury. He wore a "horse collar" because he was aware of the fact that his neck was exposed to injury. He said, as the trial judge noted in his reasons for judgment, that even if he had specifically contemplated the risk of a catastrophic neck injury, he would probably have continued to play.
>
> The appellant was appropriately and progressively coached. He was an excellent athlete who excelled in a number of sports, including football. His equipment was adequate. The injury he sustained occurred during a routine play and, although the consequences of his injury were, and continue to be, devastating, the injury came within the ambit of those risks inherent in a contact sport such as football. He did not, of course, give a consent which would overcome negligent conduct on the part of the Board or his coaches. However, I agree with the trial judge that neither the Board nor the coaches were negligent and that the appellant and his mother "consented to the normal risks of the game". I am not prepared to say that the trial judge was wrong in reaching that conclusion. (20 O.R. (3d) 598, at p. 619.)

6.9 Activities Outside the School Day

The school's duty of care applies in relation to students during school hours and during school-related activities outside normal school hours. These activities include field trips and extracurricular activities. Students participate in these activities as students, not as members of the general public, and the "prudent parent" standard applies.

Issues arise as to the board's legal responsibility when a student is injured on board property before or after school hours while not participating in a school-related activity. The classic example occurs when a child shows up too early for school, or does not leave in a timely fashion after school. When does a person become a "student"? The court must determine what the child was doing on the property outside school hours, and what the expectations of the child, the parents and the school were in relation to the provision of supervision and other safety measures.

If a child is not participating in a school-related activity, and is using the property outside regular school hours, then the child is owed the same duty of care which applies to any young member of the public using the property. This duty arises because the school board is the "occupier" of the property.

It is well-established as a general rule that the board is not responsible for accidents to children that occur on the way to and from school. However, if a board arranges pupil transportation, it could be found liable if pupils are injured while being transported or after being let off a school bus. Depending on the facts and the transportation arrangements, the board, the driver and the bus charter company could be found liable. However, in *Baldwin v. Erin District High School Board*, 1961 CarswellOnt 137, [1961] O.R. 687, 29 D.L.R. (2d) 290 (Ont. C.A.); affirmed 36 D.L.R. (2d) 244, [1962] S.C.R. vii (S.C.C.), a school board was able to defend itself successfully. The Ontario Court of Appeal held that the board was not liable for injuries to students arising from a school bus accident where the bus was operated by an independent contractor and the board had no control, or entitlement to assert control, over the manner of driving the bus or the hiring of the drivers.

School opening and closing times must be clearly communicated to parents and children. There is a strong obligation upon parents to respect the designated school hours and not to presume that schools will automatically provide supervision outside those hours.

There is also a strong obligation upon schools to be consistent in their practices. Otherwise, children, parents and staff will not know when the supervision actually starts and finishes. Legislation in Ontario prescribes the maximum length of the school day and the time at which the school and yard must be open to the pupils. Regulation 298, section 6(7) states:

> Every board shall determine the period of time during each school day when its school buildings and playground shall be open to its pupils, but in every case the buildings and the playgrounds shall be open to pupils during the period beginning fifteen minutes before classes begin for the day and ending fifteen minutes after classes end for the day.

Regulation 298, section 11(3) states that a principal shall,

> provide for the supervision of pupils during the period of time during each school day when the school buildings and playgrounds are open to pupils.

In a civil lawsuit, the actual opening or closing times of the school and yard are more relevant that the regulatory minimums; in other words, have parents been led to believe that their children will be supervised at school at times beyond 15 minutes before and after class?

Another legal obligation is to avoid sending younger pupils into a situation of danger off school property. If a child is stranded at school due to an emergency, or must unexpectedly go home early, it is not sufficient for schools to say that they owe no legal duty to the child after the child leaves the property. Common sense precautions must be taken, even if it means driving the child home or calling a taxi. In addition, keeping pupils after school for detentions may give rise to safety and transportation concerns, depending on their age and the distance they must travel to home.

6.10 Negligence of Children

A student who injures another person may be named as a defendant in a lawsuit. For example, a student who accidentally injures another student with a snowball during recess may be sued by the injured student. (*Mainville v. Ottawa (Board of Education)* (1990), 1990 CarswellOnt 2719, 75 O.R. (2d) 315 (Ont. Prov. Ct.)). The issue arises, therefore, as to what circumstances permit a court to find a young person negligent, or contributorily negligent. Minors of "tender age" cannot be found negligent or contributorily negligent. Although there is no firm rule, "tender age" appears to be under six years.[1]

Minors between tender age and adulthood may be found negligent but the standard of care which is applied depends on a number of variables. The court will ask whether the child "exercised the care to be expected from a child of like age, intelligence and experience."[2] When a child is engaged in an activity which is considered to be an adult activity, such as driving an automobile, the child will generally be held to the same standard of care as would be expected of an adult. One might conclude from this that the practice of placing senior students as volunteer supervisors in charge of younger pupils may result in a senior student being held to the careful parent standard of care if an accident occurs, despite the fact that the student may be lacking the knowledge and experience of an adult supervisor. This could attract personal liability on the part of the student-supervisor. The board could be held liable for using the student as a supervisor, and vicariously liable for the student's actions.

6.11 Custom or Practice

In defending a negligence claim, the defendant may try to show that he or she was following a well-established custom or practice with respect to the alleged negligent act or omission. However, if the practice or custom itself is negligent, it is not a defence to say that something has always been done in a certain way.

---

[1] Allen M. Linden and Bruce Feldthusen, *Canadian Tort Law*, 8th ed., pp. 151–157 (Butterworths, 2006)

[2] *McEllistrum v. Etches*, 6 D.L.R. (2d) 1, 1956 CarswellOnt 79, [1956] S.C.R. 787 (S.C.C.)

6.12 Vicarious Liability and Fiduciary Duty

6.12.1 Vicarious Liability

In many instances, the defendants in a tort action are the teacher involved, the principal (whether directly involved or not) and the school board. The plaintiff's lawyer will issue a statement of claim against everyone who is potentially liable because he or she cannot always predict how a judge or jury will find or apportion liability.

Boards are corporations, and as such they may be sued for their own negligence. Sexual misconduct may, like other forms of unwanted conduct, comprise the intentional tort of either "assault" or "battery", or both. The intentional action of a staff member or student in sexually abusing, attacking or molesting a student is not negligence. However, under some circumstances, teachers, administrators and the board itself may be found liable for negligently permitting such misconduct to occur or continue to occur.

This overriding duty means that, quite apart from their statutory duty to report child abuse, school administrators cannot afford to ignore information which comes to them, from whatever source, in relation to possible abuse of pupils by staff, visitors or fellow pupils. Moreover, comprehensive documentation must be maintained in order to be in a position to prove to a court that oral or written reports of abuse were dealt with quickly and appropriately by those who had the authority to act.

Provided that the elements of negligence are proved by the plaintiff, the board itself may incur liability for negligence where its pupils have been sexually assaulted or abused. In *Lyth v. Dagg* (1988), 1988 CarswellBC 686, [1998] B.C.J. No. 1350, 46 C.C.L.T. 25 (B.C. S.C.), for e.g., the Court held a teacher liable in tort for causing a pupil emotional trauma caused by the teacher's sexual misconduct. Although the board and vice-principal were found to have a duty of care toward the student, on the facts it was found that they had discharged that duty and they were not found liable.

Although a board is not the absolute insurer of the safety of its pupils, it has a clear legal obligation to take reasonable steps to ensure their safety from foreseeable harm. This includes taking appropriate steps to ensure that board employees do not pose a risk to the pupils. This obligation involves proper screening during the hiring process, checking of references, investigating properly whenever suspicions are reported, and ensuring that substantiated incidents are properly dealt with through dismissal or other disciplinary measures.

The board must also take reasonable steps to ensure pupils' safety from the sexual misconduct of other students and of visitors to the school. For instance, if a student is known, from prior incidents, to have a propensity to engage in sexually inappropriate conduct with other students, extra supervision on the part of the school is required, and the school may ultimately need to separate the dangerous pupil from potential victims, or consider expulsion or exclusion of the pupil.

In Ontario, the *Education Act* (s. 170(1)(12.2)) requires a school board that has become aware that a teacher or temporary teacher employed by it has been charged with or convicted of an offence under the *Criminal Code* involving sexual conduct and minors or any other offence that in the opinion of the board indicates that pupils may be at risk, to take prompt steps to ensure that the teacher or temporary teacher performs no duties in the classroom and no duties involving contact with pupils. The *Ontario College of Teachers Act, 1996*, (ss. 43.2 and 43.3) requires an employer of a member of the Ontario College of Teachers to make a report to the College when the employer terminates the member's employment or restricts the member's duties for reasons of professional misconduct, or if the employer intended to terminate the member's employment or restrict the member's duties for reasons of professional misconduct but did not do so because the member resigned. The employer is required to report to the College if the member resigns while the employer is engaged in an investigation into allegations of an act or omission by the member that would, if proven, have caused the employer to terminate the member's employment or to impose restrictions on the member's duties for reasons of professional misconduct. Employers must also report to the College when they become aware that a member who is or has been an employee has been charged with or convicted of an offence under the *Criminal Code* involving sexual conduct and minors or any other offence that in the opinion of the employer indicates that pupils may be at risk of harm or injury, or has engaged in conduct or taken action that, in the opinion of the employer, should be reviewed by a committee of the College. Section 12 of the *Teaching Profession Act* provides that a member of the Ontario Teachers' Federation who makes an adverse report about another member of the Federation respecting suspected sexual abuse of a student by that other member need not advise the other member of the report.

Vicarious liability is different from a board being held liable for its own negligence. Where an employee is found to have been negligent, the school board, even though it may not be at fault itself, may be held vicariously liable for the employee's conduct. The board's fault is not relevant in determining whether it should be vicariously liable.

In recent years, the issue has arisen as to institutional liability for physical and sexual assault committed by staff members upon children in their care. While it is clear that an employer is vicariously liable for an employee's acts *authorized* by the employer, acts such as sexual assault are never authorized by an employer. The "test" for vicarious liability in these circumstances was articulated by the Supreme Court of Canada in *Bazley v. Curry*, 1999 CarswellBC 1264, 1999 CarswellBC 1265, [1999] S.C.J. No. 35, [1999] 2 S.C.R. 534, 62 B.C.L.R. (3d) 173, (sub nom. *P.A.B. v. Children's Foundation)* 124 B.C.A.C. 119, (sub nom. *P.A.B. v. Children's Foundation)* 203 W.A.C. 119, (sub nom. *B. v. Curry)* 99 C.L.L.C. 210-033, 43 C.C.E.L. (2d) 1, (sub nom. *P.A.B. v. Children's Foundation)* 241 N.R. 266, 174 D.L.R. (4th) 45, [1999] 8 W.W.R. 197, 46 C.C.L.T. (2d) 1, [1999] L.V.I. 3046-1 (S.C.C.).

The defendant Curry was employed as a residence counsellor by the Children's Foundation in British Columbia. He was expected and permitted to act very much in the role of a parent toward the young children under his care, and he took advantage of this position of control in order to engage in sexual misconduct.

The Supreme Court of Canada held (at para. 46) that the "... test for vicarious liability for an employee's sexual abuse of a client should focus on whether the employer's enterprise and empowerment of the employee materially increased the risk of the sexual assault and hence the harm. ... This requires trial judges to investigate the employee's specific duties and determine whether they gave rise to special opportunities for wrongdoing. Because of the peculiar exercises of power and trust that pervade cases such as child abuse, special attention should be paid to the existence of a power or dependency relationship, which on its own often creates a considerable risk of wrongdoing."

In *Jacobi v. Griffiths*, 1999 CarswellBC 1262, 1999 CarswellBC 1263, [1999] S.C.J. No. 36, [1999] 2 S.C.R. 570, 124 B.C.A.C. 161, 203 W.A.C. 161, (sub nom. *J. v. Griffiths)* 99 C.L.L.C. 210-034, (sub nom. *G.T.-J. v. Griffiths)* 241 N.R. 201, 174 D.L.R. (4th) 71, 63 B.C.L.R. (3d) 1, [1999] 9 W.W.R. 1, 46 C.C.L.T. (2d) 49, [1999] L.V.I. 3046-2, 44 C.C.E.L. (2d) 169 (S.C.C.), released at the same time as *Curry*, the Supreme Court of Canada found that a Boy's and Girl's Club was not vicariously liable for sexual assault committed by an employee. The employee took advantage of his position with the Club to make friends with children, but whatever power he used to achieve his ends was not conferred by the Club, nor was it characteristic of the type of enterprise that the Club put into the community.

In *G. (E.D.) v. Hammer* (cited below), the trial judge held that a school board was not vicariously liable for the sexual misconduct of a school janitor toward a young female student. This finding was not appealed to the appellate courts in this case because the *Jacobi v. Griffiths* (cited above) made it clear that the appeal would be unsuccessful on this ground. (See also *B. (K.L.) v. British Columbia* (2003), 2004 C.L.L.C. 210-014, [2003] S.C.J. No. 51, 19 C.C.L.T. (3d) 66, [2003] 11 W.W.R. 203, 230 D.L.R. (4th) 513, [2003] R.R.A. 1065, 38 C.P.C. (5th) 199, 307 W.A.C. 42, 187 B.C.A.C. 42, 44 R.F.L. (5th) 245, 18 B.C.L.R. (4th) 1, REJB 2003-48042, [2003] 2 S.C.R. 403, 309 N.R. 306, 2003 SCC 51, 2003 CarswellBC 2406, 2003 CarswellBC 2405 (S.C.C.) in which the Supreme Court of Canada held that the Province was not vicariously liable for sexual abuse committed by foster parents, although it was held directly liable for negligence in the placement and supervision of the children.

6.12.2 Fiduciary Duty

The concept of vicarious liability is different from that of liability for "breach of fiduciary duty". To begin with, as mentioned above, vicarious liability does not require a finding of fault on the part of the employer, whereas "fault" is required to find a breach of fiduciary duty. In *G. (E.D.) v. Hammer* (2003), 2004 C.L.L.C. 210-011, 19 C.C.L.T. (3d) 38, [2003] 11 W.W.R. 244, 230 D.L.R. (4th) 554, [2003] 2 S.C.R. 459, [2003] R.R.A. 1069, 310 N.R. 1, 307 W.A.C. 193, 187 B.C.A.C. 193, 18 B.C.L.R. (4th) 42, REJB 2003-48043, [2003] S.C.J. No. 52, 2003 SCC 52, 2003 CarswellBC 2408, 2003 CarswellBC 2407 (S.C.C.), the Supreme Court of Canada recognized that a school board does have a fiduciary duty toward its pupils, but held that, in the circumstances, it did not breach that duty. The issue in *Hammer* case was the nature and scope of the fiduciary duty. The Court rejected the argument that the board's fiduciary duty meant that it had a duty to act in the "best interests of the child". In drawing a parallel to parental fiduciary duty, the Court noted (at para. 23):

> The maxim that parents should act in their child's best interests may help to justify particular parental fiduciary duties, but it does not constitute a basis for liability. The cases on the parental fiduciary duty focus not on achieving what is in the child's best interest, but on specific conduct that causes harm to children in a manner involving disloyalty, self-interest, or abuse of power — failing to act selflessly in the interests of the child.

Turning to the board's fiduciary duty, the Court stated (at para. 24):

> Fiduciary obligations are not obligations to guarantee a certain outcome for the vulnerable party, regardless of fault. They do not hold the fiduciary to a certain type of outcome, exposing the fiduciary to liability whenever the vulnerable party is harmed by one of the fiduciary's employees.

In the *Hammer* case, the Court found that the only person at fault was the school janitor. There was no act or omission on the part of the board that might amount to breach of its fiduciary duty, and the board had no reason to suspect that the janitor was engaged in any inappropriate behaviour with the children.

6.13 Educational Malpractice

In a lawsuit for "education malpractice" the plaintiff will allege that he or she has suffered damages because the school board did not fulfill its duty to educate the plaintiff. For example, some persons have claimed damages because they graduated from school without the necessary skills to get a job. To date, education malpractice claims have been unsuccessful in Canada and the United States. The courts recognize that a child's failure to achieve age-appropriate learning outcomes is subject to many variables that affect an individual's ability to learn, including his or her innate intelligence, home environment, language barriers, and nutrition. See, for example, *Hicks v. Etobicoke (City) Board of Education* (November 23, 1988), Doc. 306622/87, [1988] O.J. No. 1900 (Ont. Dist. Ct.), where a claim for education malpractice was struck by the Court as disclosing no reasonable cause of action. See also *Haynes (Guardian ad litem of) v. Lleres* (March 10, 1997), Doc. Vancouver 969025, [1997] B.C.J. No. 1202 (B.C. Prov. Ct.), where the Court dismissed a negligence claim alleging inadequate implementation of an education program after finding that it was in effect asserting education malpractice.

In addition to the difficulty of actually proving all of the constituent elements of negligence in court (duty, breach of duty, damages, proximate cause), the plaintiff is faced with the reluctance of judges to second-guess the professional judgment of educators in matters of pedagogy. Some courts in the United States have said that even if negligence were proved, they would reject the claim on the basis that allowing it would be contrary to public policy. However, if a very strong fact situation were to arise in which the plaintiff could prove "gross negligence" by the board or its employees, we may yet see a successful lawsuit based on educational malpractice.

In *Gould v. Regina (East) School Division No. 77* (1996), [1996] S.J. No. 843, 7 C.P.C. (4th) 372, 32 C.C.L.T. (2d) 150, 151 Sask. R. 189, 1996 CarswellSask 762, [1997] 3 W.W.R. 117 (Sask. Q.B.), the Saskatchewan Court of Queen's Bench granted an application to strike a statement of claim as disclosing no reasonable cause of action in a case that involved a lawsuit against a school district and an individual teacher. The parents alleged that the teacher treated their daughter (in Grade One) in a manner that was "unsatisfactory, inappropriate and objectionable" (at para. 8). The teacher was accused of a "complete and total failure in advancing the educational standards and efficiency of the ... school, and her own personal professional competence." (At para. 8.) The claim against the school board was that it failed to exercise general supervision over the school, failed to make recommendations regarding placement and replacement of teachers in appropriate circumstances, failed to investigate issues and disputes involving pupils, parents and teachers, and failed to appoint and employ a duly qualified teacher for their daughter.

The Court affirmed that "Canadian law does not recognize a nominiate tort of breach of statute." In other words, the mere fact that a statute may have been violated by a defendant does not automatically mean that the defendant should be held liable for negligence. The Court held, therefore, that:

> It is therefore quite clear that the failure on the part of the Board to perform its duties and obligations as set out in The *Education Act* cannot, without more, provide the basis for the cause of action by the plaintiffs. ... (At para. 15.)

The Court then examined whether the alleged inappropriate conduct of the teacher could, if assumed to be true, give rise to actionable negligence. In essence, this amounted to a claim for education malpractice, and the Court entered into an exhaustive review of the applicable case law. The Court concluded (at paras. 44–48):

> The claims of the plaintiffs are, quite clearly, of the nature of claims of 'educational malpractice'. Do they reveal a justiciable cause of action in this jurisdiction? The complaints voiced by the plaintiffs are essentially with the manner in which [the teacher] performed her in-class tutorial duties-speaking too loudly; making demeaning comments; subjecting students to ridicule; displaying a bullying and intimidating manner; and failing to fulfil the learning needs of the infant plaintiff. If these actions should constitute a reasonable cause of action, the court will then be asked to censure those activities with an award of damages.
>
> But what standard will the court utilize to judge the appropriateness of the complained of activities? When does speaking in a sufficiently loud enough manner to be heard by all students become unacceptably loud? What one person may perceive as an inappropriately loud and intimidating voice, another person may envision as necessary as an attention getter. And while one student may consider the curriculum as inadequate for his or her needs, the majority of the students may reach an opposite conclusion.
>
> It is surely not the function of the courts to establish standards of conduct for teachers in their classrooms, and to supervise the maintenance of such standards. Only if the conduct is sufficiently egregious and offensive to community standards of acceptable fair play should the courts even consider entertaining any type of claim in the nature of educational malpractice.
>
> The allegations of breaches of The Education Act do not establish a cause of action. Even if the acts of the defendants reveal evidence of negligence, the statement of claim does not reveal that the plaintiffs have suffered any 'damage'.

The *Gould* case confirms, in a way, that parents who are dissatisfied with the performance of their child's teacher must find other ways of resolving the issue, instead of resorting to litigation.

6.14 Risk Management

Risk Management consists of:

- identifying risk
- evaluating risk
- controlling risk
- financing risk.

Once risks are known and evaluated, steps must be taken to either control those risks or to obtain insurance to help contain the exposure.

6.14.1 Outdoor Field Trips and Camping Trips

Critical Information

A teacher or other staff who is responsible for organizing a field trip or out-of-school activity must adhere to the school board field trip/excursion policy. This should include:

- obtain permission of the principal and appropriate supervisory officer to take the students on the trip or excursion
- obtain permission of authorities at the location of the field trip or out-of-school activity and where applicable, inform local police or the Ministry of Natural Resources of the itinerary (e.g. trip in a Provincial Park)
- obtain permission or consent of parent or guardian, in writing, for their child to participate, including the legal consent and release form required by the school board
- inform parents and guardians in writing of all pertinent details relating to the trip or activity, including the locale, facts about transportation arrangements, time of departure and return, supervision arrangements, rules of student conduct, need for funds
- compile a list of phone numbers to contact parents or guardians if the return trip is delayed or if there is a medical emergency
- one or more supervisors should be trained in first aid
- supervisors must be aware of any medical or allergy considerations on file with the school that pertain to students on the trip or activity
- supervisors must be aware of the medical facilities closest to the location of the trip or activity
- consents to treatment must have been obtained in respect of emergency administration of medical services
- comply with the board's policy as to what ratio between supervisors and pupils is required
- discuss rules of conduct and safety with the pupils
- ensure that the facilities, if any, are adequately insured and that the proposed activity is within the board's own insurance coverage
- comply with the board's policy on private transportation of students, where applicable. If a van is being used to transport pupils, the driver must have the appropriate driver's licence classification, depending on the number of pupils being transported
- location of all community emergency personnel — police, hospitals, clinics, health centres, etc.

Swimming Safety

It is the school's responsibility to ensure that the persons in charge are competent to operate a swimming program or activity. The following procedures are a helpful guideline:

- Before beginning a swim period, the safety of the swim area must be established.
- An appropriate ratio of supervisors to swimmers must be provided. A ratio of 1 to 10 is often recommended, but much depends on the age and ability of the swimmers.
- Swimmers must know who the supervisors are, and supervisors should wear appropriate attire identifying themselves as supervisors.
- Rescue and reaching aids must be available at all times.
- A "buddy system" must be used for all swimmers.
- The fitness and swimming ability of all participants must be known to the supervisors.

Responding to an Injury

Steps will vary according to the nature and seriousness of the injury.

- attend to injured persons and administer first aid
- check medical records for allergies or for other medical conditions
- notify the nearest hospital or health centre if the injury is serious
- if possible, avoid moving a seriously injured person until medical help arrives. Exercise extreme caution if it is necessary to move an injured person; leave clothing and equipment in place
- after administering first aid and notifying medical services, call the parent or other emergency contact person and make arrangements to meet them at an appropriate location such as the hospital or clinic.

Medication

- Be familiar with your school board's policy on the administration of medication.
- Do not administer medication to a child unless the parent or guardian has completed a permission form, including a schedule outlining the medication, dosage and times for administration.
- Store all medication in a locked container, except asthma inhalers and epipens.
- Ensure that medication is administered only from the original container as supplied by a pharmacist, or the original package, clearly labelled with the child's name, the name of the drug or medication, the date of purchase, and the instructions for storage and administering the drug. (I recall one instance in which a child was sent to school with medication prescribed to his grandmother. The parent figured it would do. The Board refused to administer the medication.)

- Keep a log of all medication administered to a pupil. Do you have the right child, the right medication, the right dosage and the right time of day? Older children can self-administer medication if the parent and the pupil's doctor consider it appropriate.

Readers might find the following reference to be helpful: Scouts Canada "Standard Operating Procedures Section 10000 — Camping and Outdoor Activities".[3] This contains general recommendations for planning an outdoor or camping trip, in addition to specific recommendations for almost every conceivable outdoor activity such as kayaking, swimming, camping, bicycling, rock climbing, etc. In addition, internet sites belonging to experiential learning organizations offer suggestions on organizing safe outdoor activities for students.

---

[3] "Standard Operating Procedures Section 10000 — Camping and Outdoor Activities" (Scouts Canada: 2006) http://sunshine.scouts.ca/bpp/Section%2010000%2005.pdf.

7

COLLECTIVE BARGAINING

7.1 Introduction

It is beyond the scope of this book to discuss in detail the framework of collective bargaining involving boards and their unionized staff. However, an understanding of publicly-funded education must necessarily take into account how collective bargaining and collective agreements affect the operation of schools and the ability of management to implement policies and procedures. The quality of a child's education is directly affected by what happens within the sphere of labour relations. Collective agreements directly affect a school's cleanliness, level of pupil supervision, opportunities for extracurricular activities, pupil-teacher ratio, staff morale and a long list of other ingredients that make a good school or a poor one.

School administrators often feel left out of the bargaining process and relatively powerless to determine what is agreed by the board at the bargaining table. They are left with collective agreements that predetermine many aspects of school operation that, in other jurisdictions, are management rights. Restrictions on class size and on the ability to ask teachers to do hallway supervision or on-call instruction can severely impede the Principal's ability to deliver what parents may expect. On the other hand, collective agreements ensure that teachers and other staff share relatively uniform and fair working conditions and that they are not assigned duties arbitrarily or unfairly. Moreover, collective agreements must be read within the highly-regulated legal context of school board operations under the *Education Act* and within the regulation of the teaching profession under the *Ontario College of Teachers Act*.

The *School Boards and Teachers Collective Negotiations Act* governed teachers' collective bargaining from 1975 until the end of 1997. During this period, collective bargaining for teachers became increasingly sophisticated and agreements expanded in scope to include not just monetary provisions, but also many clauses pertaining to workload. Interestingly, the statute survived to the very end almost un-amended — successive governments avoided the temptation to tinker with the bargaining framework. However, wholesale change came in 1998 when the *School Boards and Teachers Collective Negotiations Act* was repealed. As a result of the *Education Quality Improvement Act, 1997*, teachers and boards now bargain in accordance with the provisions of the *Labour Relations Act, 1995*. This was achieved by amendments to the *Education Act* which established bargaining units and bargaining agents for teachers and occasional teachers, and continued to protect teachers' bargaining agents from raiding by other unions and from termination of bargaining rights.

The *Labour Relations Act, 1995* has certain features such as "the duty of fair representation" and the right to "expedited arbitration" that were not in the *School Boards and Teachers Collective Negotiations Act*. Certain other employment-related matters were also changed, including the repeal of the requirement to have prescribed contracts for "permanent", "probationary", and "continuing education" teachers. "Boards of Reference" appointed to hear and determine teacher terminations were also eliminated, because the same function was more commonly being performed by arbitrators through the grievance arbitration process.

7.2 Definition of "Teacher"

The *Education Act* contains different definitions of "teacher". One definition, in section 1, applies to the entire statute. A "teacher" is defined as "a member of the Ontario College of Teachers". Under the *Education Act*, principals, academic supervisory officers, guidance counsellors, department heads and classroom teachers, for example, are all "teachers" because they are members of the College. A "temporary teacher" is not a "teacher" because he or she is not a member of the College but is permitted to teach under the authority of a Letter of Permission. (Note that for performance appraisal purposes in Part X.2, a "teacher" is specifically defined to include a "temporary teacher" but not an occasional teacher.)

The definition in section 277.1(1) of the Act limits the meaning of "teacher" in the collective bargaining context. Within Part X.1 of the *Education Act*, for collective bargaining purposes a "teacher" means a teacher who is "employed to teach". The definition includes "occasional teachers" (also defined in the Act) but expressly excludes supervisory officers, principals, vice-principals and instructors at teacher-training institutions. The idea behind "employed to teach" does not require that the person be a classroom teacher. Where it is uncertain as to whether a person is employed to teach, one must consider the person's actual responsibilities in light of the statutory duties of a teacher (as found in section 264 of the *Education Act* and section 20 of Regulation 298), the board's practice, and any relevant court or arbitral jurisprudence.

7.3 Teachers' Bargaining Units and Bargaining Agents

Teachers are members of the Ontario Teachers' Federation (OTF), an entity created by the *Teaching Profession Act*. The OTF has affiliated bodies, and teachers are a member of an affiliated body according to OTF by-laws: the Elementary Teachers' Federation of Ontario (ETFO), the Ontario Secondary School Teachers' Federation (OSSTF), the Ontario English Catholic Teachers' Association (OECTA), or l'Association des enseignantes et des enseignants franco-ontariens (AEFO).

For the purposes of the *Labour Relations Act, 1995*, the Federations or Associations are deemed to be trade unions. Teachers' unions act as their bargaining agent, i.e. their exclusive representative in all things to do with collective negotiations and collective agreements. The *Labour Relations Act* prohibits an employer from dealing directly with an individual unionized employee to attempt to interfere with the union's right of representation:

> 70. No employer or employers' organization and no person acting on behalf of an employer or an employers' organization shall participate in or interfere with the formation, selection or administration of a trade union or the representation of employ-

> ees by a trade union or contribute financial or other support to a trade union, but nothing in this section shall be deemed to deprive an employer of the employer's freedom to express views so long as the employer does not use coercion, intimidation, threats, promises or undue influence.

In contrast to many other labour sectors, teachers have no choice as to which teachers' Federation or Association is authorized to act as their bargaining agent (see s. 277.3(2)). The "bargaining agent" is the provincial teachers' Federation or Association, not the local district. Teachers and their union also have no choice as to the description of their bargaining unit — that is, the description of who is in the unit. ETFO is the bargaining agent for elementary teachers and elementary occasional teachers at an English-language public district school board. OSSTF represents secondary teachers and secondary occasional teachers at an English-language public district board. OECTA represents all teachers at an English-language Catholic district school board. AEFO represents all teachers at a French-language public or Catholic district school board.

Each district school board has a separate bargaining unit for elementary teachers, secondary teachers, elementary occasional teachers and secondary occasional teachers (s. 277.3(1)). An elementary teachers' unit is composed of teachers who are assigned to one or more elementary schools or to perform duties in respect of such schools all or most of the time. A secondary teachers' unit is composed of teachers who are assigned to one or more secondary schools or to perform duties in respect of such schools all or most of the time. (See *O.S.S.T.F., District 14 v. Kawartha Pine Ridge District School Board*, 97 C.L.R.B.R. (2d) 57, 2003 CarswellOnt 5891, [2003] O.L.R.B. Rep. 819 (Ont. L.R.B.) for an interpretation of these provisions by the Ontario Labour Relations Board.)

An occasional teacher is in an elementary bargaining unit if he or she is on the roster of teachers for the elementary panel of the board. An occasional teacher is in a secondary bargaining unit if he or she is on the roster of teachers for the secondary panel of the board. A teacher may be a member of more than one occasional teachers' bargaining unit.

Teachers working for "school authorities", as defined in the Act, have an elementary unit for teachers of French-speaking pupils and an elementary unit for teachers who do not teach French-speaking pupils. There are separate units for occasional teachers (one for those who teach French-speaking pupils and one for those who do not). The James Bay Lowlands Secondary School Board only provides secondary school instruction, and therefore has one secondary teachers' unit and one unit for its secondary occasional teachers. Boards established under section 68 of the Act have a bargaining unit structure similar to district school boards.

In negotiations at one school board, bargaining agents may act jointly as one party, either for one agreement or for separate agreements. The bargaining units remain separate. However, where there are bargaining units at a school board that are represented by the *same* bargaining agent, they may be combined into one bargaining unit with the consent of the school board. This applies to Catholic boards and French-language boards. The Act also permits different boards and bargaining agents to bargain jointly, allowing a form of regional bargaining. (See ss. 277.7 and 277.8 of the Act.)

7.4 Bargaining Scope

Are there any restrictions on what terms the parties can bargain? Not many. At the outset, it should be noted that, in the case of conflict between the *Education Act* or regulations and the provisions of collective agreement for teachers, the Act or regulations will prevail (s. 277.13). In addition, although the *Labour Relations Act* applies to teachers' collective bargaining, section 277.2 provides that it cannot be interpreted so as to adversely affect any right or privilege guaranteed by section 93 of the *Constitution Act, 1867* or section 23 of the *Canadian Charter of Rights and Freedoms*. The *Education Act* provides the government with the authority to make regulations about class size and minimum amounts of teaching time (ss. 170.1 and 170.2) and the Act prescribes a maximum probationary period for teachers of two years (s. 261). It prescribes the minimum duration of collective agreements (s. 277.11). It also prescribes a long list of teachers' duties (s. 264) and has provisions about teacher performance appraisal (Part X.2) and new teacher induction (Part X.0.1).

Regulation 298 prescribes the minimum length of the instruction program for pupils (five hours) and collective agreements often make this the instructional day for teachers, as well. There are, in fact, almost no limits on what can be bargained across the table. A school board's bargaining objective is to preserve as many "management rights" as it can and to provide a degree of flexibility to be able to manage the schools. The unions' more recent bargaining objective appears to be to place more limits on what a teacher may be required to do outside his or her classroom. This limits supervision by teachers of pupils in the hallway or schoolyard. It limits when a teacher can be on-call to fill in for absent teachers. It gives teachers discretion as to how to use their preparation time. It limits what can be discussed at staff meetings. Collective agreements typically contain workload clauses that limit the number of pupils in a teacher's class, the number of courses (credits) that will be taught by a teacher, and the number of pupils that the teacher will be scheduled to see in the course of a day. Teachers have the protection of various surplus, transfer and lay-off provisions.

Most support staff in Ontario, such as caretakers, office assistants, bus drivers, classroom assistants, and psychologists, are represented by a union and bargain under the *Labour Relations Act* for salary, benefits, working conditions, workload, lay-off protection and many other protections typically found in collective agreements. They share the teachers' concerns about how much time they are required to spend on supervision of pupils outside the classroom. Boards typically have "partnerships" with outside agencies who come into the school to work with students (e.g. anti-bullying programs), and this is of some concern to unions who perceive that some of these agencies are doing work that belongs to the bargaining unit.

7.5 Bargaining Process

The trend in collective bargaining is to have collective agreements of longer duration so that the parties are not constantly at the bargaining table. This results in periods of "labour peace", but it also means that the unions have to wait longer between agreements to negotiate improvements for their members and will therefore negotiate harder when given the opportunity.

Under the *Labour Relations Act*, notice to bargain may be given by either party to a collective agreement within the period of 90 days before the collective agreement ceases to operate (*LRA*, s. 59). The parties are required by law to negotiate in good faith. After notice to bargain is given, the Minister of Labour may appoint a conciliation officer at the request of either party. If the conciliation officer is unable to effect an agreement between the parties, he or she will so report to the Minister, who will then decide whether to appoint a mediator or conciliation board or to issue a "no board" report which indicates that the Minister does not intend to make such an appointment. Typically, a "no board" report is issued. This step is pivotal, because a "no board" report starts the timeline toward a lawful strike or lockout. It also starts the timeline to the point at which a party may unilaterally alter the terms and conditions of employment, as permitted only in accordance with section 86 of the *Labour Relations Act*. The Act permits the parties to refer their dispute to voluntary, binding arbitration, commonly referred to as "interest" arbitration.

7.6 Strikes and Lockouts

A strike or lockout is permitted if no collective agreement is in operation and seven days have elapsed after the day the Minister has released or is deemed to have released to the parties the report of a conciliation board or mediator or 14 days have elapsed after the release or deemed release of a "no board" report by the Minister. Subsections 79(1)–(3) of the *Labour Relations Act* state:

> 79. (1) Where a collective agreement is in operation, no employee bound by the agreement shall strike and no employer bound by the agreement shall lock out such an employee.
>
> (2) Where no collective agreement is in operation, no employee shall strike and no employer shall lock out an employee until the Minister has appointed a conciliation officer or a mediator under this Act and,
>
> > (a) seven days have elapsed after the day the Minister has released or is deemed pursuant to subsection 122(2) to have released to the parties the report of a conciliation board or mediator; or
> >
> > (b) 14 days have elapsed after the day the Minister has released or is deemed pursuant to subsection 122 (2) to have released to the parties a notice that he or she does not consider it advisable to appoint a conciliation board.
>
> (3) If a collective agreement is or has been in operation, no employee shall strike unless a strike vote is taken 30 days or less before the collective agreement expires or at any time after the agreement expires and more than 50 per cent of those voting vote in favour of a strike.

The 14-day period referred to above equates to a 17-day period when you add the time for the release or deemed release of the report.

The *Education Act* has two definitions of "strike". In Part X.I, section 277.2, the Act states that the definition of "strike" in the *Labour Relations Act* does not apply. Instead, the Act provides that the term "strike":

> includes any action or activity by teachers in combination or in concert or in accordance with a common understanding that is designed or may reasonably be expected to have the effect of curtailing, restricting, limiting or interfering with,
>
> > (i) the normal activities of a board or its employees,

(ii) the operation or functioning of one or more of a board's schools or of one or more of the programs in one or more schools of a board, including but not limited to programs involving co-instructional activities, or

(iii) the performance of the duties of teachers set out in the Act or the regulations under it,

including any withdrawal of services or work to rule by teachers acting in combination or in concert or in accordance with a common understanding.

The second definition of "strike" arises in the context of *closing* a school during a strike by teachers or lockout of teachers. Section 19(2) of the *Education Act* provides as follows:

19. (2) In case of a strike by members of a teachers' bargaining unit or a lockout of those members, the board may close one or more schools if it is of the opinion that,

(a) the safety of pupils may be endangered during the strike or lockout;

(b) the school building or the equipment or supplies in the building may not be adequately protected during the strike or lockout; or

(c) the strike or lockout will substantially interfere with the operation of the school.

Subsection 19(3) states that a teacher is not entitled to be paid his or her salary for the days on which the school in which he or she is employed is closed under subsection (2).

It is important to note that for the purposes of section 19 of the Act, "strike" has the same meaning as term in the *Labour Relations Act*. The definition of "strike" in section 1(1) of the *Labour Relations Act* states:

1. (1) "strike" includes a cessation of work, a refusal to work or to continue to work by employees in combination or in concert or in accordance with a common understanding, or a slow-down or other concerted activity on the part of the employees designed to restrict or limit output;

This definition does not mirror the definition in section 277 of the *Education Act*, resulting in different definitions of "strike" insofar as teachers are concerned.

The term "strike" is also defined in section 57.2, in which "strike" for employees who are unionized support staff (i.e. *not* Part X.1 teachers) has the same meaning as in section 1 of the *Labour Relations Act* and "strike" for Part X.I teachers has the same meaning as in Part X.1 of the *Education Act*.

7.7 Education Relations Commission

Although the *School Boards and Teachers Collective Negotiations Act* was repealed, section 57.2 of the *Education Act* "continues" the Education Relations Commission (ERC) solely for the purpose of advising the Lieutenant Governor in Council (Ontario Cabinet) when continuation of a strike by board employees or of a lockout of board employees will place in jeopardy the successful completion of courses of study of the affected pupils. A "jeopardy advisement" from the ERC is not a statutory condition precedent to introducing back-to-work legislation, although the Provincial government will usually wait to hear from the ERC before considering such drastic action.

7.8 Duty of Fair Representation

The *Labour Relations Act*, section 74, states:

> 74. A trade union or council of trade unions, so long as it continues to be entitled to represent employees in a bargaining unit, shall not act in a manner that is arbitrary, discriminatory or in bad faith in the representation of any of the employees in the unit, whether or not members of the trade union or of any constituent union of the council of trade unions, as the case may be.

When a member of a bargaining unit believes that he or she has not been fairly represented by his or her union, an application may be brought to the Ontario Labour Relations Board (OLRB) to determine if the union has fulfilled its obligation to represent the member. Section 74 applications are heard by a Vice-Chair of the OLRB usually by way of a "consultation", which is a less formal method of proceeding, often without witnesses. Unions take their duty of fair representation very seriously, because under most union by-laws, the union has carriage of a grievance and decides whether or not the grievance should be withdrawn, settled or litigated before an arbitrator. A union's power to withdraw or settle a grievance has long been recognized by the OLRB, but union officials must make their decisions without acting in bad faith and without being discriminatory or arbitrary. They must investigate the circumstances of the employee's grievance and make an honest, knowledgeable assessment of the reasons for and against proceeding to arbitration. There could be good reasons for not taking the risk of placing a matter before an arbitrator, even if the grievance appears to have merit. For example, the same issues may be at the bargaining table, or the facts may be "bad" ("bad facts make bad precedents"), or reliable witnesses may not be available. It should also be noted that there is no duty to seek judicial review (in court) of an arbitrator's decision.

7.9 Paying Union Dues

Under the *School Boards and Teachers Collective Negotiations Act*, teachers were required to pay, through their school board, fees established by regulation made by the Ontario Teachers' Federation (OTF) under the *Teaching Profession Act*. With the move to the *Labour Relations Act* in 1998, the OTF's statutory power to require payment of fees was repealed and teachers' bargaining agents became the direct recipient of union dues from employer boards under the dues check off provisions in the *Labour Relations Act*.

7.10 Principals and Vice-Principals

One of the most controversial amendments in 1998 led to the removal of principals and vice-principals from membership in any bargaining unit. Since then, principals and vice-principals have had the option of belonging to a provincial association (the Ontario Principals' Council, the Catholic Principals' Council of Ontario or l'Association des directions et directions adjointes des écoles franco-ontariennes) as well as associations at the local school board level. These associations have developed a high degree of competence in representing the interests of their members. At the local level, there is normally an agreement between a board and its school administrators setting out important terms and conditions of employment. This is not a collective agreement. Principals and vice-principals do not have the right to unionize and to bargain collectively under the protection of the *Labour Relations Act*.

8

SPECIAL EDUCATION

Ontario Regulation 181/98 sets out the requirements for special education identification, placement and review committees, appeal boards, Individual Education Plans, parent guides, and other important aspects of special education law in Ontario.

8.1 Identification Placement and Review

(a) What is Special Education?

According to section 1 of the *Education Act*, a "special education program" means an educational program for an exceptional pupil that:

- is based on and modified by the results of continuous assessment and evaluation
- includes a plan with specific objectives and an outline of educational services that meets the needs of the exceptional pupil.

The term "special education services" means:

- facilities
- resources

including support personnel and equipment necessary for developing and implementing a special education program.

A board has a statutory duty to provide special education programs and services for its exceptional pupils, or to enter into an agreement with another board to provide them (s. 170).

(b) Who is an Exceptional Pupil?

According to section 1 of the Act, an "exceptional pupil" means a pupil whose behavioural, communicational, intellectual, physical or multiple exceptionalities are such that he or she is considered to need placement in a special education program by [an Identification, Placement and Review Committee] of the board

(a) of which the pupil is a resident pupil,

(b) that admits or enrols the pupil other than pursuant to an agreement with another board for the provision of education, or

(c) to which the cost of education in respect of the pupil is payable by the Minister.

(c) What is an IPRC?

An IPRC is a "special education *identification*, *placement* and *review* committee". A board must have one or more IPRC committees (O. Reg. 181/98, s. 10).

(d) Who Serves on an IPRC?

Each committee must have three or more persons. One of the members must be:

(a) a principal employed by the board

(b) a supervisory officer employed by the board, or

(c) a supervisory officer whose services are used by the board (i.e. in a sharing arrangement with another board, or through agreement with the Ministry).

A principal or supervisory officer appointed to the committee may designate another principal or supervisory officer to act in his or her place on the committee (see O. Reg. 181/98, s. 11).

(e) How is a Pupil Designated as "Exceptional"?

A pupil becomes "exceptional" when an IPRC identifies the pupil as exceptional.

(f) How is an IPRC Initiated?

An IPRC is initiated by:

(1) the principal of the pupil's school (with written notice to the parent)

or

(2) by the pupil's parent, by written request to the principal.

The parent must receive a copy of the "parent guide" which the board is obliged to produce that explains the special education process set out in the regulation and provides parents with other pertinent information as required by section 13 of Ontario Regulation 181/98.

At least 10 days' written notice of the time and place of the IPRC's meeting must be given to a parent of the pupil, and to the pupil if 16 or more years of age.

Communications required under the regulation must be done through braille, large print or audio-cassette formats upon request.

A board shall also initiate an IPRC for a pupil who is leaving a provincial demonstration school.

A parent of a pupil and a pupil (if 16 years of age or more) are entitled to be *present and participate* in all committee discussions about the pupil and to be *present* when the IPRC's identification and placement decisions are made [s. 5(1), O. Reg. 181/98]. A parent or pupil who has a right to be present at or participate during an IPRC's discussion also has a right to have a representative present at the discussion to speak on the person's behalf or otherwise support the person.

(g) What Does the IPRC Do?

The IPRC decides whether to identify a pupil as exceptional and, if so, what the pupil's placement should be.

The committee:

- must obtain and consider an educational assessment of the pupil
- subject to the *Health Care Consent Act, 1996*, may obtain and consider a health assessment or psychological assessment
- shall consider any information about the pupil submitted by the parent and the pupil (if 16 years of age or older)
- shall consider any information submitted to it that it considers relevant
- may interview a pupil who is under 16 years of age with parental consent.

The IPRC may discuss any proposal for special education services or programs, and shall do so if the parent or pupil (16+) requests. The IPRC may make recommendations regarding special education programs and services but it cannot make decisions about them.

Integration

Before considering placement in a special education class, the IPRC must consider whether placement in a regular class, with appropriate special education services, would meet the pupil's needs and is consistent with parental preferences. If such a placement would meet the pupil's needs and is consistent with parental preferences, the IPRC must decide in favour of a regular class placement.

(h) What Happens Pending a Meeting or Decision of an IPRC?

Pending a meeting or decision, the board is not required to provide a "placement" but it must provide an "education program" for the pupil that is appropriate to the pupil's "apparent strengths and needs". It must consider a regular classroom setting, as above, before considering a special education classroom. "Appropriate education services" must be provided. These "interim" rules also apply pending a meeting of an appeal board or a decision of a school board under Ontario Regulation 181/98. (Unless there already was a placement and the parent is appealing a review decision, in which case the new placement is stayed, irrespective of what type of placement it is.)

(i) How Does a Parent Hear about the IPRC's Decision?

As soon as possible after the decision is made, the chair of the IPRC must send a written statement of the decision to the parent, the pupil (if 16 years of age or older), the principal and the "designated representative" of the board that established the IPRC. The designated representative is the Director of Education (or secretary if there is no Director).

The decision must state whether the committee has identified the pupil as exceptional. If the pupil is identified as exceptional, the statement of decision will include:

- the IPRC's description of the pupil's strengths and needs
- the categories and definitions of any exceptionalities identified
- the IPRC's placement decision
- the IPRC's recommendations, if any, regarding special education programs and services.

If the placement is in a *special education class*, the IPRC must give the reasons for this decision.

(j) How Does a Parent Respond to the Decision?

A parent may request a meeting with the IPRC within 15 days of receiving its decision. This is an opportunity to seek clarification about the decision and the basis on which it was made, and to provide comments on the decision. The request must be in writing to the principal who made the referral (or to the designated representative in the case of a referral from a demonstration school). The principal (or representative) must then arrange a meeting as soon as possible. After the meeting, the IPRC chair must send out a notice indicating if any changes to the IPRC decision were made as a result of the meeting. If so, a revised decision is sent out with the notice. The notice and revised decision, if any, are sent to the persons who received the original decision.

(k) When is a Placement Decision Implemented?

A board must implement an IPRC placement decision as soon as possible after (1) the parent has consented in writing to the placement or (2) after the time for appealing the decision has expired (with notice of implementation to the parent).

(l) How are IPRC Decisions Updated?

There is a procedure for reviewing an identification or placement. The principal may request a review. The parent of the pupil may request a review at any time after the placement has been in effect for three months (and not more often than once in every three-month period).

The designated representative of the board that is providing the program may request a review. This is to ensure that there is a review at least once in each school year, but is unnecessary when the parent has indicated that the annual review can be dispensed with.

The principal has 15 days to inform the parent of the approximate date of the review meeting. The principal decides which of the board's IPRCs shall deal with the review. If it is providing services to the pupil on behalf of another board, the purchasing board must be invited to send a representative to be present at the review committee and participate in its discussions.

The committee may decide that it is satisfied with the current identification and placement, or that the identification or placement should be changed. It will notify the parent, pupil (if 16+), principal, designated representative of the board, and (where applicable) representative of the purchasing board.

If a change is recommended, the statement of decision must state:

- (a) the reasons for the change to the identification and/or placement
- (b) whether the pupil should continue to be identified as exceptional
- (c) if the pupil is to continue to be identified as exceptional,
  - (i) the placement decision
  - (ii) description of pupil's strengths and needs
  - (iii) categories and definitions of the exceptionalities identified

(d) if placement is in a special education class, the reason for this placement decision.

As is the case with the original IPRC decision, the parent has a right to request a meeting to discuss a decision made by an IPRC that has conducted a review. After this meeting, a notice is sent by the chair indicating whether any changes to the decision were made as a result of the meeting. If changes are made, they must be reflected in a revised written statement of decision.

The board must implement any changes to a pupil's placement as soon as possible, after the parent consents to the changed placement or after the time to appeal the decision has expired (with notice to the parent).

8.2 Appeals

(a) How is the Decision of an IPRC Appealed?

If a parent is dissatisfied with the decision of an IPRC or a review IPRC, a parent may file a notice of appeal, requiring a hearing by a "special education appeal board". The appeal board comprises:

- one member selected by the board
- one member selected by the parent
- a chair jointly selected by the other two members (or, if they cannot agree, by the appropriate regional manager of the Ministry of Education).

No member of an Appeal Board may be:

- a trustee of the providing or purchasing board
- an employee of the providing or purchasing board
- an employee of the Ministry of Education
- a person with prior involvement in the matter.

(b) What Can be Appealed?

A parent can appeal an identification or placement decision of an IPRC made under Part IV of the regulation or the identification or placement decision made after a review by an IPRC under Part V of the regulation.

A parent can appeal:

- a decision that a pupil is exceptional
- a decision that a pupil is not exceptional
- a decision on placement.

An appeal is filed with the secretary of the school board.

It must be filed within 30 days of the parent receiving the IPRC's statement of decision. If a meeting was requested after the statement of decision was received, then the appeal period is 15 days after receiving notice of the outcome of the follow-up meeting.

The parent's notice of appeal should indicate which of the decisions is being appealed and must include a statement setting out the nature of the disagreement.

(c) What is the Appeal Procedure?

- The parent and the pupil (if 16+) are "entitled to be present at and participate in all discussions about the pupil at the meeting held by the special education appeal board" (O. Reg. 181/98, s. 5(2)).
- At least 10 days written notice of the time and place of the appeal board's meeting must be given to a parent of the pupil, and to the pupil if 16 or more years of age.
- The chair of the IPRC whose decision is being appealed must provide the appeal board with the statement of decision, and the records, assessments and other documents considered by the IPRC.
- The chair of the appeal board arranges for a meeting of the appeal board to "discuss the matters under appeal".
- Notice of the meeting is given to the parent and pupil (if 16+ years).
- The meeting is to take place at a convenient place, no later than 30 days after the day on which the chair is selected unless the parent and the Director of Education (i.e. designated representative) agree to an extension.
- The meeting is to be conducted in an "informal manner".
- The appeal board may invite any person who in the opinion of the chair, may be able to contribute information.
- The appeal board shall invite a purchasing board to sent a representative to the meeting.
- When the appeal board is satisfied that the "opinions, views and information" that bear on the appeal have been sufficiently presented to it, it shall end the meeting.
- Within three days of ending the meeting, the appeal board shall:
    (a) agree with the IPRC and recommend that its decisions be implemented, or
    (b) disagree with the IPRC and make a recommendation to the school board about the pupil's identification, placement or both.

(d) Who Gets the Statement of Recommendations of the Appeal Board?

The statement of recommendations of the Appeal Board are sent to:

- the parent
- the pupil (if 16+)
- the chair of the IPRC committee
- the principal where the pupil is placed
- the designated representative (director/secretary) of the board
- the designated representative (director/secretary) of the purchasing board if any.

Reasons must accompany the written statement of the recommendations.

(e) What Does the Board Do with the Recommendations?

Within 30 days of receiving the appeal board's written statement, the school board must consider the recommendations. It shall decide what action to take with respect to the pupil and must then inform:

- the parent
- the pupil (if 16+)
- the chair of the IPRC committee
- the principal where the pupil is placed
- the designated representative (director/secretary) of the board
- the designated representative (director/secretary) of the purchasing board if any.

Notice of its decision is given in writing. The school board is not limited to the actions that the appeal board recommended or could have recommended.

The school board's decision is implemented:

- once the parent consents to the decision in writing
- after 30 days have passed since the parent received notice of the decision, if no appeal of the school board's decision to the Special Education Tribunal has been commenced under section 57 of the *Education Act*
- after an appeal under section 57 of the *Education Act* has been either dismissed or abandoned.

(f) Does the Appeal Board Actually Decide Anything?

No. The appeal board makes recommendations, which the school board must then consider in deciding the pupil's identification and/or placement.

(g) Can the School Board's Decision be Appealed?

Yes, a parent may appeal an identification or placement decision of a school board to a **Special Education Tribunal**. One or more special education tribunals may be established by the Lieutenant Governor in Council. Members of the Tribunal are appointed by the Lieutenant Governor in Council.

Education Act, R.S.O. 1990, c. E.2, ss. 57(3)–(5)

> 57. (3) Right of Appeal — Where a parent or guardian of a pupil has exhausted all rights of appeal under the regulations in respect of the identification or placement of the pupil as an exceptional pupil and is dissatisfied with the decision in respect of the identification or placement, the parent or guardian may appeal to a Special Education Tribunal for a hearing in respect of the identification or placement.
>
> (4) Hearing by Special Education Tribunal — The Special Education Tribunal shall hear the appeal and may,
>
> (a) dismiss the appeal; or
>
> (b) grant the appeal and make such order as it considers necessary with respect to the identification or placement.
>
> (5) Decision final — The decision of the Special Education Tribunal is final and binding on the parties to the decision.

8.3 Individual Education Plan

(a) What is an "Individual Education Plan"?

Every exceptional pupil must have an Individual Education Plan (IEP) developed for him or her. The IEP must include:

(a) specific educational expectations for the pupil

(b) an outline of the special education program and services to be received by the pupil

(c) a statement of the methods by which the pupil's progress will be reviewed.

If the pupil is 14 years of age or older, the IEP must include a plan for transition to appropriate post-secondary school activities, such as work, further education and community living. Therefore, when a pupil becomes 14 years of age, his or her IEP will have to be changed to include a transition plan. In developing the transition plan, the principal shall consult with the community agencies and post-secondary institutions that the principal considers appropriate. A pupil identified solely as gifted does not require a transition plan.

The IEP is developed by the principal in consultation with the parent and the pupil if 16 years of age or older. It must take into consideration any recommendations of the IPRC or Special Education Tribunal about special education programs or services. It must be completed within 30 days of the placement. The parent and pupil (16+) are entitled to a copy of the IEP. (The requirement to consult the parent does not give the parent a veto over the IEP.)

After an IPRC review, the board notifies the principal of the need to review the pupil's IEP to determine whether it needs to be updated. The review of the IEP must be completed within 30 days of the principal receiving the notice, and must involve the parent and pupil (16+). It must take into consideration any recommendations of the IPRC or Special Education Tribunal about special education programs or services. If the IEP does not include a transition plan, and the pupil is 14 years old or will become 14 years old during the school year, the principal must ensure that a transition plan is developed and included in the IEP.

The pupil's IEP is kept in the pupil's Ontario Student Record, unless the parent objects in writing.

Malpractice Alert!

Lawsuits based on "education malpractice" have not met with success in Canadian courts or in United States appellate courts. However, school boards in the United States have been succesfully sued where they have failed to fulfil the requirements in a special education pupil's Individual Education Plan written pursuant to the United States legislation.

Ontario Regulation 181/98, section 7, specifies the circumstances in which an IEP must be reviewed:

7. (1) Subsection (2) applies when,

(a) a board implements a change in placement under section 25;

(b) a board implements a change in placement under section 31 following an appeal to a special education appeal board in respect of a committee decision under Part V;

(c) a board implements a change in placement in accordance with a decision of the Special Education Tribunal following an appeal to the Special Education Tribunal in respect of a committee decision under Part V;

(d) an existing placement is confirmed in a statement of decision under Part V and a parent of the pupil consents in writing to the decision or the time period provided in section 31 for filing a notice of appeal from the decision expires without a notice of appeal being filed;

(e) an existing placement is confirmed in a decision under subsection 30 (1) and a parent consents in writing to the decision or the time period provided in section 31 expires without an appeal being commenced;

(f) an existing placement is confirmed in a decision under subsection 30 (1), an appeal from the decision is made under section 57 of the Act to the Special Education Tribunal and the appeal is dismissed or abandoned; or

(g) an existing placement is confirmed in an order of the Special Education Tribunal granting an appeal under section 57 of the Act.

(2) The board shall promptly notify the principal of the school at which the special education program is to be provided of the need to review the pupil's individual education plan to determine whether it needs to be updated.

(3) In reviewing the plan, the principal shall,

(a) consult with the parent and, where the pupil is 16 years of age or older, the pupil; and

(b) take into consideration any recommendations of the committee or the Special Education Tribunal, as the case may be, regarding special education programs or special education services.

(4) Where an individual education plan does not include a plan for transition to appropriate post-secondary school activities and the pupil has attained the age of 14 or will attain the age of 14 within the school year, the principal shall ensure that a transition plan is developed and included in the individual education plan.

(5) Subsection (4) does not apply in respect of a pupil identified as exceptional solely on the basis of giftedness.

(6) In reviewing an individual education plan that includes a transition plan or in developing a transition plan under subsection (4), the principal shall consult with such community agencies and post-secondary educational institutions as he or she considers appropriate.

(7) Within 30 school days of an implementation of a change in placement or, where the placement is confirmed, within 30 schools days of receiving the notice under subsection (1), the principal shall ensure that,

(a) the plan has been reviewed and updated as appropriate;

(b) a transition plan has been added to the individual education plan where required by subsection (4); and

(c) a copy of the individual education plan has been sent to a parent of the pupil and, where the pupil is 16 years of age or older, the pupil.

Section 8 of Ontario Regulation 181/98 states:

> 8. The principal shall ensure that the individual education plan for a pupil is included in the record kept in respect of the pupil under clause 265 (d) of the Act, unless a parent of the pupil has objected in writing.

It is important to note that a pupil's educational needs must be addressed pending any meeting or decision under Ontario Regulation 181/98:

> 9. In accordance with requirements under the *Education Act*, no pupil is to be denied an education program pending a meeting or decision under this Regulation.
>
> (2) Where an education program is provided to a pupil pending a meeting or decision under this Regulation,
>
> (a) the program must be appropriate to the pupil's apparent strengths and needs;
>
> (b) the placement for the program must be consistent with the principles underlying section 17; and
>
> (c) appropriate education services must be provided to meet the pupil's apparent needs.

8.4 Human Rights and the Charter of Rights — *The Eaton v. Brant County Board* Decision

Exceptional pupils are entitled to special education programs and services to which other pupils are not entitled. The law provides them with specific entitlements because treating people the same does not always result in equality. Some pupils must be treated differently in order to have equality:

> The treatment of a person differently from others may or may not amount to discrimination just as treating people equally is not determinative of the issue. If the effect of the treatment has adverse consequences which are incompatible with the objects of the legislation by restricting or excluding a right of full and equal recognition and exercise of those rights it will be discriminatory.[1]

Human rights tribunals have become a forum for disputes about special education. Their mandate is to determine whether or not discrimination on a prohibited ground has occurred in the provision of services which are covered by the pertinent human rights legislation. Although it may be subject to some specific provisions, such as the protection of denominational rights, the provision of publicly-funded education in Ontario is a service covered by the *Human Rights Code*.[2]

---

[1] *Canadian Odeon Theatres Ltd. v. Saskatchewan (Human Rights Commission)*, [1985] S.J. No. 268, 1985 CarswellSask 187, 39 Sask. R. 81, 6 C.H.R.R. D/2682, [1985] 3 W.W.R. 717, 18 D.L.R. (4th) 93 (Sask. C.A.), at 115 [D.L.R.], leave to appeal refused [1985] 1 S.C.R. vi (note), 18 D.L.R. (4th) 93n (S.C.C.).

[2] *Ontario (Human Rights Commission) v. Peel (County) Board of Education* (1990), (sub nom. *Pandori v. Peel Board of Education)* 12 C.H.R.R. D/364 (Ont. Bd. of Inquiry); affirmed (1991), 1991 CarswellOnt 969, [1991] O.J. No. 639, 47 O.A.C. 234, 3 O.R. (3d) 531, 14 C.H.R.R. D/403, (sub nom. *Pandori v. Peel Board of Education)* 80 D.L.R. (4th) 475 (Ont. Div. Ct.); leave to appeal to Ont. C.A. refused (1991), 3 O.R. (3d) 531n (Ont. C.A.).

There is little room for argument that most exceptional pupils (except the gifted) would be considered to be "disabled" under the Ontario *Human Rights Code*, which contains the following definition:

> "disability" means,
>
> (a) any degree of physical disability, infirmity, malformation or disfigurement that is caused by bodily injury, birth defect or illness and, without limiting the generality of the foregoing, including diabetes mellitus, epilepsy, a brain injury, any degree of paralysis, amputation, lack of physical coordination, blindness or visual impediment, deafness or hearing impediment, muteness or speech impediment, or physical reliance on a guide dog or other animal or on a wheelchair or other remedial appliance or device,
>
> (b) a condition of mental impairment or a developmental disability,
>
> (c) a learning disability, or a dysfunction in one or more of the processes involved in understanding or using symbols or spoken language,
>
> (d) a mental disorder, or
>
> (e) an injury or disability for which benefits were claimed or received under the insurance plan established under the *Workplace Safety and Insurance Act, 1997*.

Human rights legislation does not provide the right to attend a regular classroom or to a certain kind of placement, and it does not define the type of educational programs or services to be provided by a school board or province.[3]

A decision of the Ontario Special Education Tribunal in *Eaton v. Brant (County) Board of Education*[4] dealt with the issue of the integration of an exceptional pupil into a regular class of a neighbourhood school. The child's parents appealed an IPRC decision that the child be moved to a special class where the integrated class placement was not seen to be working. The parents requested that the child be placed full time in a regular age-appropriate class, "with full accommodation of her special needs, including provision of a full-time educational assistant, any necessary assistive devices, appropriate education materials and resources, and proper training of all staff."

The Special Education Tribunal decided that the placement in a special class should be upheld. It found that, while the parents were strongly of the view that their daughter should have a regular class placement, they had not observed her in school to see for themselves whether or not she could cope in such an environment. Of the three expert witnesses who gave evidence for the parents, only one had actually observed the child in the classroom (for two and one half hours) and all three stated that they were "committed to a philosophy of full inclusion (integration)."

> All three witness (sic) manifest an entirely subjective view of class placement, and in fact could not reasonably be expected to testify in any other way than strongly supportive of integration. Given the absence of clear research support and clear empirical support for the integration of exceptional children like [E.]; viz., the uncertainty in the area for which they are presented as expert, and given that they did not,

---

[3]*Human Rights Code*, R.S.O. 1990, c. H.19, s. 10(1)

[4](November 19, 1993), Ken Weber (Chair) (Ont. Special Education Trib.)

> except for [H.S.], observe [E.] in a school setting, we do not find their testimony significant in the specific matter of [E.'s] placement [at page 72].

The Tribunal accepted that it was bound by the *Canadian Charter of Rights and Freedoms* and the Ontario *Human Rights Code* and stated that consideration of the *Charter* and the *Code* was within its mandate. The tribunal did not specifically respond to, or analyze, the *Charter* or *Code* arguments made by counsel, finding instead that the case law on this issue presented to it "does not have relevance in the matter of [the child's] placement."

> It is our opinion that where a school board recommends placement of a child with special needs in a special class, contrary to the wishes of the parents, and where the school board has already made extensive and significant effort to accommodate the parents' wishes by attempting to meet that child's needs in a regular class with appropriate modifications and supports, and where empirical, objective evidence demonstrates that the child's needs are not being met in the regular class, that school board is not in violation of *The Charter* or the *[Code]*.

The Tribunal's review of the body of literature on placement found that it is "seriously flawed" by: (1) "poor research methods"; (2) the "polemical stance" of many of the researchers; (3) the "inherent difficulty in controlling variables"; (4) "extrapolating conclusions that fit a hypothesis rather than the other way around"; (5) "the regular use of non-cognate cases and situations to demonstrate outcomes for other cases" and, (6) "the inexplicably wide acceptance ... of what has come to be called 'gee whiz' literature (*e.g.*, descriptive, anecdotal, journalistic, and clearly unscientific reports on individual cases of exceptionality)." [At page 71.]

The Tribunal's closing words serve as a useful reminder to parents, school boards and legal counsel:

> The fact that the disagreement over [E. E.'s] class placement has been allowed to continue to the level of a Special Education Tribunal hearing is a grave disservice to this child. The Tribunal has no doubt that everyone involved with [E.] has her present best interests and future well-being at heart. But we also feel that both are being put at risk by an unnecessarily rigorous adherence to principle and by the tyranny of moral certainty. Having examined the historical development of this disagreement over [E.'s] placement, is it clear to us that [E.], the child, is now at risk of becoming [E.], the symbol. It is also clear to us that engaging legal counsel, turning to judicial and quasi-judicial avenues of redress, in short, taking an adversarial approach, has pushed this disagreement away from compromise and into competition, away from accommodation and into dispute. E.'s present and future well-being will not be served by going farther down this road [at page 74].

The parents brought an application for judicial review of the decision of the Special Education Tribunal. The Ontario Court of Justice (General Division)[5] upheld the decision of the Tribunal. The Divisional Court decision was appealed to the Ontario

[5](1994), [1994] O.J. No. 203, 1994 CarswellOnt 908, 71 O.A.C. 69 (Ont. Div. Ct.); reversed (1995), 1995 CarswellOnt 838, [1995] O.J. No. 315, 22 O.R. (3d) 1, 27 C.R.R. (2d) 53, 123 D.L.R. (4th) 43, 77 O.A.C. 368 (Ont. C.A.); reversed (1996), 1996 CarswellOnt 5035, 1996 CarswellOnt 5036, [1996] S.C.J. No. 98, 31 O.R. (3d) 574 (note), 41 C.R.R. (2d) 240, 142 D.L.R. (4th) 385, 207 N.R. 171, 97 O.A.C. 161, [1997] 1 S.C.R. 241 (S.C.C.).

Court of Appeal.[6] In that Court, Arbour J.A. looked at whether Emily Eaton's placement in a special classroom was discrimination within the meaning of section 15 of the *Charter*. Clearly, Emily was placed in a special class because of her disability; a distinction had been made on a prohibited ground. The next stage of the analysis involved the issue of whether the distinction resulted in the imposition of a burden or disadvantage, by reason of being placed in a segregated education placement. Madam Justice Arbour found:

> When a measure is offered to a disabled person, allegedly in order to provide that person with her true equality entitlement, and that measure is one of exclusion, segregation, and isolation from the mainstream, that measure, in its broad social and historical context, is properly labelled a burden or a disadvantage [at page 16].

In effect, this meant that the *Charter* mandates a presumption in favour of integration. Arbour J.A. went on to find that, because section 8(3) of the *Education Act* does not provide for a presumption in favour of integration, it should be read to include a direction that, unless the parents of a disabled child consent to a segregated placement, the board must provide a placement that is the least exclusionary from the mainstream and still reasonably capable of meeting the child's special educational needs. Many school boards were understandably concerned about the implications of this decision in terms of restricting their ability to provide the best educational placement for their exceptional pupils.

The case was appealed to the Supreme Court of Canada (1996), 1996 CarswellOnt 5035, 1996 CarswellOnt 5036, [1996] S.C.J. No. 98, 31 O.R. (3d) 574 (note), 41 C.R.R. (2d) 240, 142 D.L.R. (4th) 385, 207 N.R. 171, 97 O.A.C. 161, [1997] 1 S.C.R. 241 (S.C.C.) on two grounds:

(1) The Court of Appeal had struck down a section of provincial legislation on constitutional grounds without the appellants having given notice to the Attorney General for Ontario, as required under section 109 of the *Courts of Justice Act*.

(2) The Court of Appeal had erred in finding that the decision of the Special Education Tribunal contravened section 15 of the *Charter*.

The Court found that no notice was given to the Attorney General, either in Divisional Court or the Court of Appeal, and the government had no reason to believe that the *Education Act* was under attack. In fact, the Eatons had stated expressly to the Court that they were not attacking the *Education Act*. The absence of notice and the absence of a record developed in the courts and tribunals below were not merely technical defects and the Attorney General was seriously prejudiced by the absence of notice.

The Court did not have to consider the constitutional validity of section 8(3) of the *Education Act* because it found that the Special Education Tribunal's decision was not contrary to the *Charter*. The decision written by Sopinka J., is briefly summarized below.

---

[6](1995), 1995 CarswellOnt 838, [1995] O.J. No. 315, 22 O.R. (3d) 1, 27 C.R.R. (2d) 53, 123 D.L.R. (4th) 43, 77 O.A.C. 368 (Ont. C.A.); reversed (1996), 1996 CarswellOnt 5035, 1996 CarswellOnt 5036, [1996] S.C.J. No. 98, 31 O.R. (3d) 574 (note), 41 C.R.R. (2d) 240, 142 D.L.R. (4th) 385, 207 N.R. 171, 97 O.A.C. 161, [1997] 1 S.C.R. 241 (S.C.C.).

Before a section 15 infringement can be found, the claimant must establish that the impugned provision creates a distinction on a prohibited or analogous ground, and that it withholds an advantage or benefit from the claimant or imposes a disadvantage or burden on the claimant. The principles that (1) not every distinction on a prohibited ground will constitute discrimination, and (2) in general, distinctions based on presumed rather than actual characteristics, are the hallmarks of discrimination, have particular significance when applied to physical and mental disability. The purpose of section 15(1) of the Charter is not only to prevent discrimination by the attribution of stereotypical characteristics to individuals, but also to ameliorate the position of groups within society who have suffered disadvantage by exclusion from mainstream society. Exclusion from the mainstream of society results from the construction of society based solely on mainstream attributes to which disabled persons will never be able to gain access.

Disability, as a prohibited ground, differs from other enumerated grounds such as race or sex because there is no individual variation with respect to these grounds. However, with respect to disability, this ground means vastly different things depending upon the individual and the context. This produces the "difference dilemma": segregation can be discriminatory depending on the person and the disability.

While integration should be recognized as the norm of general application, a presumption in favour of integrated schooling would work to the disadvantage of pupils who require special education in order to achieve equality. The Special Education Tribunal balanced the various educational interests of Emily Eaton. The findings of the Tribunal made it clear that those needs would be best met in a segregated classroom. A decision reached after such an analysis could not be considered a burden or disadvantage imposed upon a child.

The decision-making body must ensure that its determination of the appropriate accommodation for an exceptional pupil be from a subjective, child-centred perspective that attempts to make equality meaningful from the child's point of view. As a means of achieving this, it must also determine that the form of accommodation is in the child's best interests. Where it is not possible to adapt an integrated setting to the child's special needs, that is, where the aspects of the integrated setting which cannot reasonably be changed interfere with meeting the child's special needs, the principle of accommodation will require a special education placement outside the integrated setting.

For older children and those who are able to communicate their wishes and needs, their views will play an important role in the determination of "best interests". For younger children and those incapable of making a choice or who have very limited means of communicating, the decision-maker must make the determination on the basis of the other evidence before it. The application of a test designed to secure what is in the best interests of a child will best achieve that objective if the test is unencumbered by a presumption.

As a result of the *Eaton* decision, school boards know that they do not have to overcome a legal presumption in favour of integration that would make it very difficult for boards to segregate pupils against the wishes of their parents. Instead, boards can attempt to meet the best interests of the child by assessing his or her educational needs. However, if challenged by a pupil or parent, it must still be able to show evidence that its placement meets the "best interests" test. The board's assessment will not be accepted blindly by a tribunal or court in the absence of pedagogical and other relevant evidence.

Children benefit from the decision because it looks to their best interests as being the benchmark. The decision emphasizes that their views should be sought if at all possible. With sensitivity and insight, it analyzes the nature of discrimination based on disability. It says that, while there is no legal presumption in favour of integration, integrated settings should be the norm and that reasonable efforts must be made to accommodate exceptional pupils in integrated settings.

GLOSSARY
A Quick Reference Guide

Advertisements and Announcements in School

No advertisements or announcements are permitted in a school without the consent of the board, except announcements of school activities (Reg. 298, s. 24). Therefore, strictly speaking, the board itself must approve advertisements and announcements in school. Clearly, the trustees are not going to examine each and every request to make an announcement or post an advertisement. The board should provide guidelines to principals as to what is acceptable or unacceptable. Community groups do not have a *right* to advertise in a school; it's not public property. If a school wishes to have a community bulletin board, all postings on the bulletin board should be subject to the approval of the principal.

Offensive, racist, sexist or unduly provocative announcements or advertisements must obviously be disallowed. What about religion? Public schools are required to be secular. Announcements that proselytize about a particular religion have no place in a public school, according to the approach taken to courts that have pronounced against indoctrinational religion being imposed on public school pupils. However, some schools have religious clubs before or after the school day, and I do not see any legal difficulty allowing such clubs to announce or advertise their meeting schedule in the school.

Similarly, the school principal has the right to approve announcements or advertisements made on the official school website. In my view, principals should be cautious before allowing commercial advertisements or links on the school website, unless the board or its administration has given approval.

Care of the School

A principal has responsibility for the care of all teaching materials and other school property, and must provide for the instruction of pupils in the care of the school premises (*Education Act*, s. 265(1)(j) and Reg. 298, s. 11(3)(k)). I suspect that pupils are more often told *to* care for the school premises, rather than being instructed *how* to care for them.

Pupils have a legal duty to "show respect" for school property (Reg. 298, s. 23(1)(h)).

The principal must inform the board if a parent does not comply with a request to compensate the board for damage, destruction, loss or misappropriation of school property by a pupil (Act, s. 265; Reg. 298, ss. 11 and 23).

Communicable Disease

People cannot be excluded from school merely because they are sick or unhealthy. However, they can be excluded if the principal believes that they infected with or have been exposed to a communicable disease (s. 265(1)(l)). Section 265 states that the principal must report to the board and Medical Officer of Health when he or she has reason to suspect the existence of any communicable disease in the school (s. 265(1)(k)). The same duty is found in the *Health Protection and Promotion Act*, R.S.O. 1990, c. H.7, which states:

> 28. **Duty of school principal to report disease** — The principal of a school who is of the opinion that a pupil in the school has or may have a communicable disease shall, as soon as possible after forming the opinion, report thereon to the medical officer of health of the health unit in which the school is located.

Regulation 569, section 2 states that a report required under section 28 (above) shall, with respect to the pupil to whom the report relates, contain the following information:

1. Name and address in full.
2. Date of birth in full.
3. Sex.
4. Name and address in full of the school that the pupil attends.

Section 1 of the *Health Protection and Promotion Act* states that "communicable disease" means a disease specified as a communicable disease by regulation made by the Minister. Ontario Regulation 558/91 specifies the list of communicable diseases; the list is found at the end of this chapter.

Conflict of Interest

Every school board should have a conflict of interest policy that prohibits employees from engaging in activities that place their personal interest in conflict with the board's interest. The *Education Act* only addresses a particular kind of conflict of interest, one that arises if an employee of a board tries to promote or sell products to any school board or to the Ministry. Section 217 states:

> 217. (1) **Promotion or sale of books, etc., by employees of board or Ministry to board, pupil, etc., prohibited** — No teacher, supervisory officer or other employee of a board or of the Ministry shall, for compensation of any kind other than his or her salary as such employee, promote, offer for sale or sell, directly or indirectly, any book or other teaching or learning materials, equipment, furniture, stationery or other article to any board, provincial school or teachers' college, or to any pupil enrolled therein.
>
> (2) **Exception for authors** — Subsection (I) does not apply to a teacher, supervisory officer or any other employee in respect of a book or other teaching or learning materials of which he or she is an author where the only compensation that he or she receives in respect thereof is a fee or royalty thereon.
>
> (3) **Employment of employee of board or Ministry to promote sale of books, etc, to board, pupil, etc., prohibited** — No person or organization or agent thereof shall employ a teacher, supervisory officer or other employee of a board or of the Ministry to promote, offer for sale or sell, directly or indirectly, any book or other teaching or learning materials, equipment, furniture, stationery or other article to any board, provincial school or teachers' college, or to any pupil enrolled therein, or shall, directly or indirectly, give or pay compensation to any such teacher, supervisory officer or employee for such purpose.
>
> (4) **Penalty** — Every person who contravenes any provision of subsection (I) or (3) is guilty of an offence and on conviction is liable to a fine of not more than $1,000.

The exception in subsection (2) is important, because many educators write books and materials for use in schools. If a teacher or other staff member has written a book, learning materials or software that is purchased by a Board, there is no conflict if the employee is only being paid a fee or royalty. In my view, this implies that sales to the board must be conducted through an arm's length, legitimate sales organization (e.g. software producer) or a publisher. A royalty is usually based on a percentage of sales. A fee is generally a flat amount for producing the book or materials for the company. The spirit and intent of the section would be violated if the board employee were to approach a board or the Ministry to convince them to buy the employee's product, and employees cannot hide behind a corporate veil.

Evaluation of Teachers

The *Education Act* sets out a complex scheme for the induction of new teachers and the performance appraisal of new teachers and other teachers, as contained in Part X.0.1 and Part X.2 of the *Education Act* and Regulation 266/06 (New Teacher Induction) and Regulation 99/02 (Teacher Performance Appraisal).

Regulation 298, section 11(3), requires a principal to conduct performance appraisals of the members of the teaching staff. In view of the statutory provisions noted above, most of the requirements in section 11(3) would appear to be out of date. Paragraphs 11(3) (g) to (j) of Regulation 298 state that a principal shall:

> 11. (3)
>
> (g) where performance appraisals of members of the teaching staff are required under a collective agreement or a policy of the board, despite anything to the contrary in such collective agreement or board policy, conduct performance appraisals of members of the teaching staff;
>
> (h) subject to the provisions of the policy of the board or the provisions of a collective agreement, as the case may be, in respect of reporting requirements for performance appraisals, report thereon in writing to the board or to the supervisory officer on request and give to each teacher so appraised a copy of the performance appraisal of the teacher;
>
> (i) where the performance appraisals of members of the teaching staff are not required by board policy or under a collective agreement, report to the board or to the supervisory officer in writing on request on the effectiveness of members of the teaching staff and give to a teacher referred to in any such report a copy of the portion of the report that refers to the teacher;
>
> (j) make recommendations to the board with respect to,
>
> (i) the appointment and promotion of teachers, and
>
> (ii) the demotion or dismissal of teachers whose work or attitude is unsatisfactory;
>
> [. . .]
>
> (4) A principal shall only make a recommendation to the board under subclause (3)(j)(ii) after warning the teacher in writing, giving the teacher assistance and allowing the teacher a reasonable time to improve.

Note that section 11(10) of Regulation 298 requires a principal to make all reports and recommendations to the Board through the appropriate supervisory officer:

> 11 (10) A principal shall transmit reports and recommendations to the board through the appropriate supervisory officer.

Fire and Emergency Drills

In addition to mandatory fire drills, the principal must hold at least one emergency drill during the school year if the board so decides. This includes night school and summer school. Every person in the school must participate in the drill. Section 6 of Regulation 298 states:

> 6. (1) In addition to the drills established under the fire safety plan required under *Regulation 454* of the *Revised Regulations of Ontario, 1990* (*Fire Code*), every board may provide for the holding of drills in respect of emergencies other than those occasioned by fire.
>
> [Note: the Fire Code is now O. Reg. 213/07 under the *Fire Protection and Prevention Act, 1997.*]
>
> (2) Every principal, including the principal of an evening class or classes or of a class or classes conducted outside the school year, shall hold at least one emergency drill in the period during which the instruction is given.
>
> (3) When a fire or emergency drill is held in a school building, every person in the building shall take part in the fire or emergency drill.

A fire safety plan which is acceptable to the Chief Fire Official must be prepared. Schematic diagrams must be prepared showing the type, location and operation of all fire emergency systems. Staff must be instructed in fire emergency procedures as described in the fire safety plan, which must be distributed to all staff and posted on each floor of the school. Under section 2.8.3.2 of the Fire Code, evacuation fire drills must be conducted three times in each of the fall and spring school terms.

Flying the Flag

Every school must fly both the National Flag of Canada and the Provincial Flag of Ontario on such occasions as the board directs, and every school must display in the school the National Flag and the Provincial Flag (Reg. 298, s. 5).

Health and Immunization

The principal is responsible for the health and comfort of the pupils in the school. The principal must promptly report to the board and Medical Officer of Health the unsanitary condition of the school building or school grounds. A teacher has a duty to ensure that all reasonable safety procedures are carried out in courses and activities for which the teacher is responsible (Act, s. 265; Reg. 298, s. 20).

The Medical Officer of Health may order that a pupil be suspended or excluded from school if the pupil is not immunized as required by the *Immunization of School Pupils Act*. A pupil may obtain a medical exemption from immunization, or may file a statement of conscience or religious belief claiming an exemption.

Home Instruction

The principal may arrange home instruction for a pupil where there is medical evidence that the pupil cannot attend school and the principal is satisfied that home instruction is required. The approval of the appropriate supervisory officer is required (Reg. 298, s. 11(11)). Home instruction is delivered by a school board. It is not "home schooling", where a child is excused from attending school because he or she is receiving satisfactory instruction at home.

Inspections

Principals must inspect the school and grounds "weekly" (Reg 298, s. 11(3)(l)), but common sense calls for a daily walk-around, especially in urban neighbourhoods. It is not uncommon for schools in some neighbourhoods to face a daily collection of used hypodermic needles, litter and other objectionable and potentially dangerous items.

The principal's active interest in the school, as exhibited by showing a very real and physical presence, is a vital ingredient to fostering a positive culture. The principal has responsibility for the condition and appearance of the school building and grounds and must inspect the school premises weekly and report repairs that are required (Act, s. 265; Reg. 298, s. 11). It is always advisable to document the fact that you have reported the need to have repairs done.

The *Education Act* also says that the principal has responsibility for the "cleanliness, temperature and ventilation" of the school (s. 265(1)(j)).

Language of Instruction

A teacher must use the English language in instruction in English-language schools, and in communication with pupils in regard to discipline and the management of the school, except where this is impractical because the pupil does not understand English or when teaching another language. In French-language schools or classes, the French language must be used by teachers, subject to the same exceptions (s. 264(1)(f), Act).

There is an exemption under section 264(1.1) to permit teachers to use American Sign Language or Quebec Sign Language in accordance with the regulations.

Morals

A teacher has a duty to inculcate by precept and example respect for religion and the principles of Judaeo-Christian morality and the highest regard for truth, justice, loyalty, love of country, humanity, benevolence, sobriety, industry, frugality, purity, temperance and all other virtues (Reg. 298, s. 264).

Opening Exercises

Section 304 of the Act provides that every school board shall ensure that opening or closing exercises are held in each school under the board's jurisdiction in accordance with the regulations and that the exercises must include the singing of "O Canada" and may include a recitation of a pledge of citizenship in the form set out in the regulations. A pupil is not required to participate in the opening or closing exercises in such circumstances as are prescribed by regulation.

Ontario Regulation 435/00 on "Opening or Closing Exercises" deals with the Pledge of Citizenship, which the principal may include in accordance with board policy and after consultation with the school council. The regulation allows for pupils to be made exempt from the Pledge.

Regulation 435/00 states:

> 1. The requirements set out in this Regulation apply with respect to the opening and closing exercises referred to in section 304 of the Act.
>
> 2. (1) The principal may decide whether the opening or closing exercises at a school will include the recitation of the pledge of citizenship.
>
> (2) The principal's decision about reciting the pledge of citizenship must be consistent with the policies and guidelines, if any, established by the board.
>
> (3) Before making his or her decision about reciting the pledge of citizenship, the principal shall consult the school council.
>
> (4) The principal shall review his or her decision about reciting the pledge of citizenship at the beginning of each school year and must consult with the school council.
>
> 3. The following is the pledge of citizenship:
>
>> I affirm that I will be faithful and bear true allegiance to Her Majesty Queen Elizabeth the Second, Queen of Canada, and to her heirs and successors, and that I will faithfully observe the laws of Canada and fulfill my duties as a Canadian citizen.
>
> 4. A pupil is not required to sing *O Canada* or recite the pledge of citizenship in the following circumstances:
>
>> 1. In the case of a pupil who is less than 18 years old, if the pupil's parent or guardian applies to the principal to be exempted from doing so.
>>
>> 2. In the case of a pupil who is at least 18 years old, if the pupil applies to the principal to be exempted from doing so.

Regulation 298, section 4, also deals with "opening or closing" exercises. It provides that every *public* (i.e. not Catholic) elementary and public secondary school shall hold opening or closing exercises. These exercises may include "God Save the Queen".

The Lord's Prayer is no longer used as a prayer in public schools, although it can be used as a "reading".

Section 4 of Regulation 298 states:

> 4. (1) This section applies with respect to opening and closing exercises in public elementary schools and in public secondary schools.
>
> (2) The opening or closing exercises may include the singing of *God Save the Queen* and may also include the following types of readings that impart social, moral or spiritual values and that are representative of Ontario's multicultural society:
>
>> 1. Scriptural writings including prayers.
>>
>> 2. Secular writings.
>
> (3) The opening or closing exercises may include a period of silence.

(4) In the following circumstances, a pupil is not required to participate in the opening or closing exercises described in this section:

1. In the case of a pupil who is less than 18 years old, if the pupil's parent or guardian applies to the principal of the school for an exemption from the exercises.

2. In the case of a pupil who is at least 18 years old, if the pupil applies to the principal for an exemption from the exercises.

Principals should also be familiar with Ministry of Education Policy/Program Memorandum 108 which explains the policy of using readings instead of prayers. PPM 108 refers to "Regulation 262" which is simply the previous number assigned to what is now Regulation 298.

Passing Grades

The decision as to whether or not a pupil passes into the next grade is up to the principal, not the parent. The Act provides that a principal has a duty to promote such pupils as he or she considers proper, subject to revision by the appropriate supervisory officer.

Pupils are to receive a statement of their promotion (s. 265).

Probation

The probationary period, if any, for teachers when they first become employed by a board shall not exceed two years (Act, s. 261). Probationary and permanent teachers' individual contracts, the form of which was prescribed by Regulation 310, ceased to have effect on August 31, 1998 (*Education Quality Improvement Act, 1997*).

Registration of Pupils

Does a parent have to produce the information required to register a child? The answer to this question would appear to be rather obvious, but the fact is that some parents expect to be able to register their child without providing basic enrolment information. The *Education Act* states that: "It is the responsibility of the parent or guardian to submit evidence that the child has a right to attend an elementary school, including proof of age." (s. 33(5)). In section 36(8), the Act states: "It is the responsibility of the person or the person's parent or guardian to submit evidence that the person has a right to attend a secondary school."

The OSR Guideline sets out what you need in order to establish an OSR, including proof of age.

The *Immunization of School Pupils Act* requires immunization information from parents.

The regulations governing grants to school boards requires boards to obtain information about a pupil's mother tongue in order for the board to obtain ESL grants.

Section 49 of the *Education Act* requires a board to ask certain questions to find out if tuition fees must be charged (e.g. persons who are temporary residents or who are in possession of a study permit).

There are, of course, exceptional instances in which a parent is unable to produce documentation. Persons from other countries may have escaped their homeland without papers or possessions. Spouses escaping abusive households may be starting from scratch, living at a shelter. Schools must be sensitive to these situations and should consult senior administration or board legal counsel to determine when it is appropriate to admit students without documents under these circumstances.

It is the duty of a principal to collect information for inclusion in a record in respect of each pupil enrolled in the school and establish, maintain, retain, transfer, and dispose of the record (s. 265(1)(d)).

Religious Education in Public Schools

According to the *Education Act*: *Subject to the regulations*, a pupil (in the public school system) shall be allowed to receive such religious instruction as the pupil's parent/guardian desires, or where an adult, as the pupil desires. A pupil in the public school system cannot be required to read or study in or from a religious book, or join in an exercise of devotion or religion if this is objected to by his or her parent or guardian or the (adult) pupil (Act, s. 51).

The regulations prohibit indoctrinational religious instruction in public schools. Ministry policy permits public school boards to provide education *about* religion. A board cannot give primacy to or indoctrination in a particular faith. In public elementary schools, programs of education about religion are limited to 60 minutes per week.

A public board may permit its facilities to be used by external groups *before* or *after* the school day for the purpose of religious exercises or instruction. However, these religious activities are not to be under board auspices (Reg. 298, s. 29 and Ministry Policy Memorandum 112).

A Catholic school board may establish and maintain programs and courses of study in religious education for its pupils in all schools under its jurisdiction (Act, s. 52).

Remembrance Day

Regulation 298 requires that a Remembrance Day service shall be held in every school on the 11th day of November, or when the 11th day of November is a Saturday or Sunday, on the Friday preceding the 11th day of November. A service need not be held where the school participates in a service of remembrance at a cenotaph or other location in the community (Reg. 298, s. 9).

Reports

The principal has a duty to prepare such reports for the board as are required by the board. The principal's reports and recommendations to a board are sent through the appropriate supervisory officer. The principal shall give the Ministry and appropriate supervisory officer information on discipline in the school, the condition of school premises, the progress of pupils and other matters affecting the interests of the school. The principal shall give the Minister or designate, upon request, information concerning the instructional program, operation of the school, and administration of the school. He or she must inform the board of such a request (Act, s. 265; Reg. 298, s. 11).

Sexual Misconduct — Reporting

A school board that terminates the employment of a member of the Ontario College of Teachers or imposes restrictions on the member's duties for reasons of professional misconduct must file with the Registrar of the College, within 30 days, a written report setting out the reasons. If the member resigns his or her employment before his or her employment could be terminated or restrictions imposed, the board must nevertheless file a written report setting out the reasons why it intended to act. Similarly, if a member resigns during the course of an investigation by the board of allegations that, if proven, would have caused the board to terminate employment or impose restrictions, then the board must file a written report with the Registrar setting out the nature of the allegations being investigated. When a report is filed with the Registrar, the Registrar must report back to the board respecting the action, if any, taken in response to the board's report (*Ontario College of Teachers Act*, s. 43.2).

A board must make a written report to the College when a member who is or has been in its employ (1) has been charged with or convicted of an offence under the *Criminal Code* (Canada) involving sexual misconduct and minors or that, in the opinion of the board, indicates that students may be at risk of harm or injury; or (2) when the member has engaged in conduct or taken action that, in the opinion of the board, should be reviewed by a committee of the College. Such a report must be made even if the board becomes aware that the charge was withdrawn, the member was discharged following a preliminary inquiry, the charge was stayed, or the member was acquitted (*Ontario College of Teachers Act*, s. 43.3).

Supervision of Pupils

The principal must make provision for the supervision of pupils while the school buildings and playgrounds are open to the pupils, and for the supervision and conducting of any authorized school activity. A teacher shall carry out the supervisory duties assigned to him or her by the principal (Reg. 298, ss. 11 and 20).

Supplies

The principal shall inform the board if a pupil, or the parent of a pupil who is a minor, fails (after reasonable notice) to provide the supplies required by the pupil for a course of study (Reg. 298, s. 11(9)).

Support Staff (Professional)

Psychiatrists, psychologists, social workers, and other professional support staff employed by the board are subject to the administrative authority of the principal while in the principal's school (Reg. 298, s. 26).

Testing and Assessments

The principal must obtain the written permission of the parent or adult pupil where it is proposed to administer a test of intelligence or personality to a pupil (Reg. 298, s. 11(3)(m)).

Ontario Regulation 181/98, on Special Education, also deals with assessments, of a different type. An IPRC committee must obtain an educational assessment of the pupil referred to the committee. However, medical or psychological assessments require a valid consent under the *Health Care Consent Act*:

> 15. (1) A committee that has received a referral under section 14 shall obtain and consider an educational assessment of the pupil.
>
> (2) Subject to the *Health Care Consent Act, 1996*, the committee shall also obtain and consider a health assessment of the pupil by a qualified medical practitioner if the committee determines that the assessment is required to enable it to make a correct identification or placement decision.
>
> (3) Subject to the *Health Care Consent Act, 1996*, the committee shall also obtain and consider a psychological assessment of the pupil if the committee determines that the assessment is required to enable it to make a correct identification or placement decision.

Textbooks

The principal has a duty to ensure that all textbooks used are approved by the board and, where applicable, the Minister (Act, s. 265(1)(h)). The principal, in consultation with the teachers concerned, must select from the list of the textbooks approved by the Minister the textbooks for the use of pupils in the school, and the selection is subject to the approval of the board. Where no textbook for a course of study is included in the list of textbooks approved by the Minister, the principal must, in consultation with the teachers concerned, where they consider a textbook to be required, select a suitable textbook. Subject to the approval of the board, the selected textbook may be used in the school. In making the selection, the principals and teachers are to give preference to books that have been written by Canadian authors and edited, printed and bound in Canada (Reg. 298, s. 7). Section 7 of Regulation 298 states as follows:

> 7. (1) The principal of a school, in consultation with the teachers concerned, shall select from the list of the textbooks approved by the Minister the textbooks for the use of pupils of the school, and the selection shall be subject to the approval of the board.
>
> (2) Where no textbook for a course of study is included in the list of the textbooks approved by the Minister the principal of a school, in consultation with the teachers concerned, shall, where they consider a textbook to be required, select a suitable textbook and, subject to the approval of the board, such textbook may be introduced for use in the school.
>
> (3) In the selection of textbooks under subsection (2), preference shall be given to books that have been written by Canadian authors and edited, printed and bound in Canada.
>
> (4) Every board shall provide without charge for the use of each pupil enrolled in a day school operated by the board such textbooks selected under subsections (1) and (2) as relate to the courses in which the pupil is enrolled.

Section 170(1)13 of the *Education Act* specifically provides for the use of textbooks without charge:

> 13. subject to paragraph 31.1 of subsection 171(1) provide, without charge, for the use of the pupils attending the school or schools operated by the board, the textbooks that are required by the regulations to be purchased by the board;

Paragraph 31.1 of subsection 171(1) of the Act allows a board to charge a refundable deposit on book in continuing education credit courses:

> 31.1 require a pupil enrolled in a continuing education course or class that is eligible for credit towards a secondary school diploma to pay a nominal deposit for a textbook provided by the board that will be forfeited to the board in whole or in part if the textbook is not returned or is returned in a damaged condition;

A teacher has a duty to use only approved textbooks. The *Education Act*, section 264(1)(k) states that it is a duty of a teacher,

> (k) to use and permit to be used as a textbook in a class that he or she teaches in an elementary or a secondary school,
>
> > (i) in a subject area for which textbooks are approved by the Minister, only textbooks that are approved by the Minister, and
> >
> > (ii) in all subject areas, only textbooks that are approved by the board.

Trans Fat

Regulation 200/08 (Trans Fat Standards) imposes upon boards the duty to limit trans fat content in schools. One of the exemptions outlined in section 2 of the regulation is for food sold on special event days. Principals must solicit the views of school councils about the designation of special event days.

Ontario Regulation 200/08 states as follows:

> 1. **Trans fat prohibition** — (1) A board shall ensure that the trans fat content of a vegetable oil or soft, spreadable margarine offered for sale in a school of the board, or used as an ingredient in the preparation, in a school of the board, of a food or beverage offered for sale in the school, does not exceed 2 per cent of the total fat content.
>
> (2) A board shall ensure that the trans fat content of any food, beverage or ingredient, other than vegetable oil or soft, spreadable margarine, offered for sale in a school of the board, or used as an ingredient in the preparation, in a school of the board, of a food or beverage offered for sale in the school, does not exceed 5 per cent of the total fat content.
>
> 2. **Exemptions from the trans fat requirements** — (1) The requirements regarding trans fat content set out in section 1 do not apply to the board in respect of a food, beverage or ingredient,
>
> > (a) in which the trans fat originates exclusively from ruminant meat or dairy products;
> >
> > (b) offered for sale to a person who is on school premises for a purpose other than a school purpose; or
> >
> > (c) offered for sale at a school on a day that is designated by the principal of the school as a special event day for the school.
>
> (2) The principal of a school shall solicit the views of the school council with respect to the designation of special event days for the school.
>
> (3) The maximum number of days in the school year that may be designated as special event days for a school is the lesser of 10 and the number determined by the board for the purpose, if any.

Specification of Communicable Diseases (O. Reg. 558/91, s. 1)

1. The following diseases are specified as communicable diseases for the purposes of the Act:

Acquired Immunodeficiency Syndrome (AIDS)
Amebiasis
Anthrax
Botulism
Brucellosis
Campylobacter enteritis
Chancroid
Chickenpox (Varicella)
Chlamydia trachomatis infections
Cholera
Clostridium difficile associated disease (CDAD) outbreaks in public hospitals
Cytomegalovirus infection, congenital
Diphtheria
Encephalitis, primary viral
Food poisoning, all causes
Gastroenteritis, institutional outbreaks
Giardiasis
Gonorrhoea
Group A Streptococcal disease, invasive
Haemophilus influenzae b disease, invasive
Hemorrhagic fevers, including,
  i. Ebola virus disease
  ii. Marburg virus disease
  iii. Other viral causes
Hepatitis, viral,
  i. Hepatitis A
  ii. Hepatitis B
  iii. Hepatitis D (Delta hepatitis)
  iv. Hepatitis C
Influenza
Lassa Fever
Legionellosis
Leprosy
Listeriosis
Lyme Disease
Malaria
Measles
Meningitis, acute,
  i. bacterial
  ii. viral
  iii. other
Meningococcal disease, invasive
Mumps
Ophthalmia neonatorum
Paratyphoid Fever
Pertussis (Whooping Cough)
Plague
Pneumococcal disease, invasive
Poliomyelitis, acute

Psittacosis/Ornithosis
Q Fever
Rabies
Respiratory infection outbreaks in institutions
Rubella
Rubella, congenital syndrome
Salmonellosis
Severe Acute Respiratory Syndrome (SARS)
Shigellosis
Smallpox
Syphilis
Transmissible Spongiform Encephalopathy, including,
  i. Creutzfeldt-Jakob Disease, all types
  ii. Gerstmann-Sträussler-Scheinker Syndrome
  iii. Fatal Familial Insomnia
  iv. Kuru
Trichinosis
Tuberculosis
Tularemia
Typhoid Fever
Verotoxin-producing E. coli infections
West Nile Virus Illness
Yellow Fever
Yersiniosis

APPENDICES

Appendix A

Policy/Program Memorandum No. 108*

Ontario — Ministry of Education

Issued under the authority of the Deputy Minister of Education

Date of Issue:	January 12, 1989	**Effective**:	Until revoked or modified
Subject:	**OPENING OR CLOSING EXERCISES IN PUBLIC ELEMENTARY AND SECONDARY SCHOOLS**		
Application:	Chairpersons of Boards of Education Directors of Education of Boards of Education Principals of Public Elementary and Secondary Schools		

I. Background

The decision of the Ontario Court of Appeal, dated September 23, 1988, struck down subsection 28(1) of Regulation 262 concerning religious exercises in public elementary schools. This subsection, and the decision of the Court relating to it, did not apply to schools operated by separate school boards.

The spirit of the decision of the Court of Appeal was essentially that one religion must not be given a position of primacy and that the content of opening or closing exercises must reflect the multicultural realities and traditions of Ontario society.

Subsequent to the Court ruling, an interim policy, dated September 28, 1988, was established, whereby opening or closing exercises were made optional for school boards. In schools where such exercises were to be held, however, "0 Canada" and content that reflected the spirit of the ruling of the Court of Appeal were required.

This interim policy was intended to remain in effect only until policy considerations were finalized and amendments to Regulation 262 were adopted.

II. Amendments to Regulation 262

A copy of the amendments to Regulation 262 relating to opening or closing exercises accompanies this memorandum. The amendments provide for a new section 4. Subsections 28(1),

(2), and (3), and subsections 29(1), (2), and (3), as well as other references to "religious exercises" in sections 28 and 29, are deleted.

The following points summarize the content of the new section 4:

1. All public elementary and secondary schools in Ontario must be opened or closed each day with the national anthem. "God Save the Queen" may be included.
2. The inclusion of any content beyond "0 Canada" in opening or closing exercises is to be optional for public school boards.
3. Where public school boards resolve to include, in the opening or closing exercises in their schools, anything in addition to the content set out in item 1 above, it must be composed of either or both of the following:
   a. one or more readings that impart social, moral, or spiritual values and that are representative of our multicultural society. Readings may be chosen from both scriptural writings, including prayers, and secular writings;
   b. a period of silence.
4. Parents who object to part or all of the exercises may apply to the principal to have their children exempted. Pupils who are adults may also exercise such a right.

III. Implementation

When implementing the amendments listed above, school boards should take particular note of the following:

1. Purposes

   The purposes of opening or closing exercises are patriotic and educational. Such exercises are intended to nurture allegiance to Canada and to contribute to the social, moral, and spiritual development of the pupils.

   Contributing to the social, moral, and spiritual development of pupils includes reinforcing the positive societal values that, in general, Canadians hold and regard as essential to the well-being of our society. These values transcend cultures and faiths, reinforce democratic rights and responsibilities, and are based on a fundamental belief in the worth of all persons.

2. Readings

   Readings selected for opening or closing exercises must fulfil educational purposes.

   Since the social, moral, and spiritual development of Canadians has roots in many religious and philosophical traditions, readings must be drawn from a variety of scriptural and secular sources representative of our multicultural society. Prayers, including the "Lord's Prayer", may be included, but only as readings.

   The collective recitation of a specific reading from a particular religious tradition can no longer be permitted, as such a practice is not in accordance with the *Canadian Charter of Rights and Freedoms.*

3. Period of Silence

   A period of silence is intended to be used for such activities as personal reflection or individual silent prayer.

APPENDIX B

Policy/Program Memorandum No. 112*

Ontario — Ministry of Education

Issued under the authority of the Deputy Minister of Education

Date of Issue:	December 6, 1990	**Effective**:	January 1, 1991
Subject:	**EDUCATION ABOUT RELIGION IN THE PUBLIC ELEMENTARY AND SECONDARY SCHOOLS**		
Application:	Chairpersons of Boards of Education Directors of Education of Boards of Education Principals of Public Elementary and Secondary Schools		

I. Background

On January 30, 1990, the Ontario Court of Appeal unanimously struck down subsection 28(4) of Regulation 262 concerning religious education in the public elementary schools. The court ruled that the subsection infringed on the freedom of conscience and religion guaranteed by section 2(a) of the Canadian Charter of Rights and Freedoms. Neither the subsection nor the court decision applied to schools operated by the Roman Catholic separate school boards.

Section 29 of Regulation 262, regarding provision of religious instruction by clergy or designates in the public secondary schools, was not before the court, and the court's ruling did not apply expressly to that section. However, subsequent advice by legal counsel indicates that the principles outlined in the decision make section 29 equally untenable.

In its decision, the court made it very clear that subsection 28(4) of the regulation was invalid because it permitted the teaching of a single religious tradition as if it were the exclusive means through which to develop moral thinking and behaviour. The court also ruled that education designed to teach about religion and to foster moral values without indoctrination in a particular religious faith would not contravene the charter.

In distinguishing between religious indoctrination and education about religion, the court made the following statement:

---

* *Policy / Program Memorandum No. 112 — Education About Religion in the Public Elementary and Secondary Schools* (issued December 6, 1990) found on the web site of the Ministry of Education at http://www.edu.gov.on.ca/extra/eng/ppm/112.html.

While this is an easy test to state, the line between indoctrination and education, in some instances, can be difficult to draw. With this in mind, it may be of assistance to refer to the following more detailed statement of the distinction:

- The school may sponsor the *study* of religion, but may not sponsor the *practice* of religion.
- The school may *expose* students to all religious views, but may not *impose* any particular view.
- The school's approach to religion is one of *instruction*, not one of *indoctrination*.
- The function of the school is to *educate* about all religions, not to *convert* to any one religion.
- The school's approach is *academic*, not *devotional*.
- The school should *study* what all people believe, but should not *teach* a student what to believe.
- The school should strive for student *awareness* of all religions, but should not press for student *acceptance* of any one religion.
- The school should seek to *inform* the student about various beliefs, but should not seek to *conform* him or her to any one belief.

Subsequent to the court's ruling, an interim policy for public elementary schools, dated February 28, 1990, was established, whereby boards were permitted to provide programs in education about religion in the time previously used during the school day, as long as these programs were in accordance with the court's ruling. Boards of education were also advised that they could continue to provide space outside the school day, as they do for various community-related activities, if parents requested that their children be taught religion by clergy or designates. This interim policy for elementary schools was intended to remain in effect only until policy considerations related to the public elementary and secondary schools were finalized.

II. Permanent Policy

The Ministry of Education will amend sections 28 and 29 of Regulation 262 to reflect the following permanent policy, which will apply to public elementary and secondary schools:

1. Boards of education may provide programs in education about religion in Grades 1 to 8 during the school day for up to 60 minutes per week.
2. Boards of education may continue to provide optional credit courses in World Religions in secondary schools, as specified in the curriculum guideline entitled *History and Contemporary Studies, Part C: Senior Division, Grades 11 and 12, 1987*. The program described in the guideline meets the court's definition of permissible education about religion.
3. Schools and programs, including programs in education about religion, under the jurisdiction of boards of education must meet both of the following conditions:
    a) They must not be indoctrinational.
    b) They must not give primacy to any particular religious faith.
4. Boards of education may continue to provide space before the beginning or after the close of the instructional program of the school day for indoctrinational religious education. Given the provisions for equality of treatment in the Canadian Charter of Rights and Freedoms, boards choosing this option must make space available on an equitable basis to all religious groups.

This policy will come into effect on January 1, 1991.

III. Purpose

The purpose of programs in education about religion is to enable students to acquire knowledge and awareness of a variety of the religious traditions that have shaped and continue to shape our world. The programs enable individuals to understand, appreciate, and respect various types of religious beliefs, attitudes, and behaviour.

The purpose of these programs is *not* to instil the beliefs of any particular religion. It is the prerogative of individual pupils and their families to decide which religious beliefs they should hold. Indoctrinational religious education has no place in the curriculum or programs of public elementary and secondary schools of the province.

IV. Content

Since the world's religions are many and varied, a particular program in education about religion cannot be expected to include every one of them. As a minimum, programs in any grade should include a balanced consideration of world religions that have continuing significance for the world's people.

Both content and method should be appropriate to the ages and levels of maturity of the pupils. In developing programs of education about religion, consideration may be given to various organizational frameworks.

V. Resources

The Ministry of Education will develop a resource document to assist boards of education in developing programs in education about religion for elementary schools.

Programs for the secondary schools will continue to be developed in accordance with *History and Contemporary Studies, Part C: Senior Division, Grades 11 and 12, 1987.*

VI. Context

This permanent policy and the forthcoming amendments to Regulation 262 are to be understood within the context of the long-established vision of the public elementary and secondary schools as places where people of diverse backgrounds can learn and grow together. The public schools are open and accessible to all on an equal basis and founded upon the positive societal values which, in general, Canadians hold and regard as essential to the well-being of our society. These values transcend cultures and faiths, reinforce democratic rights and responsibilities, and are founded on a fundamental belief in the worth of all persons.

APPENDIX C

Policy/Program Memorandum No. 123*

Ontario — Ministry of Education

Issued under the authority of the Deputy Minister of Education

Date of Issue:	February 2, 1999	**Effective**:	Until revoked or modified
Subject:	**SAFE ARRIVALS**		
Application:	Chairs of District School Boards and School Authorities Directors of Education Secretaries of School Authorities Director of Provincial Schools Branch Principals of Schools		

Purpose

A safe-arrival program is a system of procedures which are performed together with daily school attendance taking. Parents and guardians are responsible for their children's safety. Safe-arrival programs are a mechanism that parents and schools can use to account for any pupil's unexplained failure to arrive at school.

While recognizing that many exemplary programs are currently in place, this memorandum seeks to encourage safe-arrival programs in all elementary schools in Ontario. It suggests the exercise of local discretion in the design and implementation of the programs in order to take into account the unique circumstances of every school. Such unique circumstances may include, but are not limited to, the number of staff available to implement policies, the size of the student body, and the age of the pupils, as well as the geographic conditions in the vicinity of the school, the kind of transportation used by pupils to travel to school, and the communication methods available in the area.

This policy/program memorandum is not intended to alter the law as it exists with respect to any duty of care or standard of care of school boards, school authorities, directors of education, principals, teachers, Director of Provincial Schools Branch, or other officials and staff.

Policy and Objectives

In order to promote the safety of our pupils, each district school board, each school authority, and the Provincial Schools Branch are requested to develop a policy statement applying to each elementary school within their jurisdiction for the development and implementation of a safe-arrival program. It is suggested that the policy statement be issued by May 31, 1999, for schools to begin implementation of a program at the start of the 1999-2000 school year with full implementation by the end of October 1999.

This policy is intended to provide that:

- all elementary schools have procedures in place that are conducted in conjunction with daily school attendance-taking procedures and that aim to account for any pupil's unexplained failure to arrive at school through reasonable efforts to make timely contact with parents, guardians, or caregivers;
- safe-arrival programs are developed and implemented by schools with advice from school councils, band councils, parents, volunteers, and other community members;
- the design of specific procedures reflects local needs and the particular circumstances of the school and the community;
- schools, parents, school councils, band councils, and communities work cooperatively for the successful development and implementation of safe-arrival programs;
- safe-arrival programs are designed to be flexible, with a view to achieving overall effectiveness, efficiency, and economy.

Guidance on the Design of Safe-Arrival Programs

It is suggested that safe-arrival programs be designed to reflect the following characteristics with respect to program delivery and information and communications. The following characteristics are intended to provide guidance in the design of any safe-arrival programs that are developed.

Program Delivery

- The program should be delivered in a manner that complements other school and community safety programs and initiatives.
- The roles and responsibilities of parents, pupils, the school, school councils, volunteers, and others should be clearly identified and documented, and broadly communicated to all those who have an interest in safe-arrival programs.
- The roles and responsibilities of parents and guardians, at a minimum, could be defined as involving the following:
  - Parents and guardians are responsible for their children's safety. Safe-arrival programs are a mechanism that parents and schools can use to account for any pupil's unexplained failure to arrive at school;
  - Parents, guardians, and caregivers are responsible for communicating planned pupil absences or lateness to the school on a timely basis. Their reports could be reconciled with information obtained through classroom attendance-taking procedures to identify any unexplained absences that require prompt follow-up contacts;
  - Parents, guardians, and caregivers are responsible for providing the school with complete and current emergency information to enable the school to make any necessary follow-up contacts.

- Programs should take into account both normal, recurring circumstances and unusual events and conditions. For example, regular procedures could be modified on days when pupils are likely to arrive late because of inclement weather or bus cancellations.
- Programs should take into account that a language other than the language of instruction may be used in the absent pupil's home.
- Programs should specify the steps that are to be taken when a follow-up contact cannot reasonably be made.
- Individuals involved in delivering the safe-arrival program should receive appropriate training and supervision.
- Programs should be reviewed periodically to confirm their effectiveness.
- Parents and volunteers can make a tremendous contribution to the delivery of these programs. Efforts should be made to develop this potential and to enlist the aid of parents and volunteers to help reduce demands on the time of school administrative staff.

Information and Communications

- Information about the scope and features of the school's safe-arrival program, and about the roles and responsibilities of all interested parties, should be communicated clearly and effectively by the principal to school staff, parents, guardians, caregivers, pupils, school councils, and all volunteers and others in the community who have an interest in the matter.
- There should be a reliable method for parents, guardians, and caregivers to communicate planned pupil absences or lateness to the school on a timely basis, particularly outside school hours. For example, a voice-messaging system and, if appropriate, a telephone device for the deaf (TTY/TDD) may have to be installed.
- A reliable system of documenting key information could be developed and maintained. Subject to the *Municipal Freedom of Information and Protection of Privacy Act*, key information could include:
    - a log of calls from parents or others who report absences or lateness;
    - names and current telephone numbers, in order of priority, of parents, guardians, caregivers, or other individuals to be notified in case of an unexplained pupil absence;
    - parental consent for school staff and/or volunteers to make these contacts, in accordance with the requirements of the *Municipal Freedom of Information and Protection of Privacy Act*;
    - a log of actions taken by school staff in accordance with the provisions of the safe-arrival program.

APPENDIX D

Policy/Program Memorandum No. 128*

Ontario — Ministry of Education

Date of Issue:	October 4, 2007	**Effective**:	Until revoked or modified

Subject: **THE PROVINCIAL CODE OF CONDUCT AND SCHOOL BOARD CODES OF CONDUCT**

Application:
Directors of Education
Superintendents of School Authorities
Principals of Elementary Schools
Principals of Secondary Schools
Principals of Provincial Schools
Chairs of Special Education Advisory Committees

Reference: This memorandum replaces Policy/Program Memorandum No. 128, November 14, 2000.

Introduction

The provincial Code of Conduct has been revised to reflect changes made in the Education Act that pertain to suspension and expulsion of students. On June 4, 2007, the Education Amendment Act (Progressive Discipline and School Safety), 2007, was passed, amending Part XIII of the Education Act dealing with behaviour, discipline, and safety. These amendments come into force February 1, 2008.

The revised provincial Code of Conduct is communicated in this memorandum.[1]

This memorandum also gives direction to school boards[2] on reviewing their own codes of conduct and the local codes of conduct in their schools. Boards must review their codes of conduct to ensure that they are consistent with the provincial Code of Conduct, and must have necessary revisions in place by February 1, 2008.

 Policy / Program Memorandum No. 128 — The Provincial Code of Conduct and School Board Codes of Conduct (issued October 4, 2007) found on the web site of the Ministry of Education at http://www.edu.gov.on.ca/eng/document/ brochure/conduct/conduct.html; or at http://www.edu.gov.on.ca/extra/eng/ppm/128.html.

[1] *Ontario Schools — Code of Conduct*, a booklet published by the Ministry of Education in 2000, is superseded by the Code of Conduct communicated in this memorandum.

[2] In this memorandum, *school board(s)* and *board(s)* refer to district school boards and school authorities.

Boards should note that subsection 301(2) of Part XIII of the Education Act, which outlines the purposes of the provincial Code of Conduct, remains unchanged. The rest of section 301, which relates to the Minister's powers, and all of section 302, which authorizes school board policies, also remain largely unchanged.

For excerpts from the relevant sections of the legislation, see the Appendix to this memorandum.

A school should be a place that promotes responsibility, respect, civility, and academic excellence in a safe learning and teaching environment. A positive school climate exists when all members of the school community feel safe, comfortable, and accepted.

All students,[3] parents,[4] teachers, and staff members have the right to be safe, and to feel safe, in their school community. With this right comes the responsibility to contribute to a positive school climate. The promotion of strategies and initiatives such as Student Success and character development, along with the employment of prevention and intervention strategies to address inappropriate behaviour, fosters a positive school climate that supports academic achievement for all students. Boards and schools should therefore focus on prevention and early intervention as the key to maintaining a positive school environment in which students can learn and teachers can teach.

Policy/Program Memorandum No. 145, "Progressive Discipline and Promoting Positive Student Behaviour", October 4, 2007, provides an overview of the progressive discipline approach to be used when addressing issues of student conduct. When inappropriate behaviour occurs, Ontario schools will be required to utilize a range of interventions, supports, and consequences that are developmentally appropriate, that include opportunities for students to learn from mistakes, and that focus on improving behaviour. In some circumstances, short-term suspension may be a useful tool. In the case of a serious incident, long-term suspension or expulsion, which is further along the continuum of progressive discipline, may be the response that is required.

The provincial Code of Conduct sets clear provincial standards of behaviour. These standards of behaviour apply not only to students, but also to all individuals involved in the publicly funded school system — parents, volunteers, teachers, and other staff members — whether they are on school property, on school buses, at school-related events or activities, or in other circumstances that could have an impact on the school climate.

Responsible citizenship involves appropriate participation in the civic life of the school community. Active and engaged citizens are aware of their rights, but more importantly, they accept responsibility for protecting their rights and the rights of others.

Requirements for School Boards

Boards are required to:

- revise their board code of conduct and, if applicable, require principals[5] to engage in reviews of school codes of conduct to incorporate changes in the provincial Code of Conduct, as outlined in this memorandum;

---

[3]The term *student*, as used in this memorandum, refers to *pupil*, as used in the Education Act.

[4]In this memorandum, *parent(s)* refers to parent(s) and guardian(s). Parental involvement applies, except in cases where the student is eighteen years of age or over or is sixteen or seventeen years of age and has "withdrawn from parental control".

[5]In this memorandum, *principal* refers to the principal or to a person designated by the principal or by the board.

- inform staff members, students, parents, and the school community of the terms of the revised provincial Code of Conduct and school board codes of conduct.

Revision of School Board Codes of Conduct

The standards of behaviour in school board codes of conduct must be consistent with the requirements set out in this memorandum. In reviewing their codes of conduct, school boards must consult with school councils. They should also consult with a wide variety of stakeholders, including parents, principals, teachers, students, their Parent Involvement Committee, their Special Education Advisory Committee, community partners, community agencies,[6] members of Aboriginal communities (e.g., Elders), and those groups that are traditionally not consulted. School board codes of conduct must:

- include the standards stated in the provincial Code of Conduct;
- set out standards of behaviour for all members of the school community (e.g., parents, students, staff, visitors, volunteers);
- link locally developed standards to the relevant provincial standards (e.g., school board rules for the use of electronic devices such as cellphones could be linked to the provincial standard requiring those at school to "respect the need of others to work in an environment that is conducive to learning and teaching" [see **Respect, Civility, and Responsible Citizenship**]);
- indicate where and/or when these standards will apply (e.g., in school sports activities, on school buses, in off-site school-sponsored activities, or in circumstances where engaging in an activity could have a negative impact on the school climate);
- include procedures and timelines for review (reviews must be conducted at least every three years).

Development or Revision of Local Codes of Conduct in Schools

School boards may continue to require principals to develop additional codes of conduct tailored expressly for their schools. Where local codes have been developed, they must be reviewed to ensure that they are consistent with the provincial Code of Conduct and other requirements in this memorandum. These codes must set out clearly what is acceptable and what is unacceptable behaviour for all members of the elementary or secondary school community (e.g., parents, students, staff, visitors, volunteers), and must also be consistent with the school board's code of conduct.

In developing or reviewing these local standards of behaviour, the principal must take into consideration the views of the school council. In addition, he or she should:

- seek input from students, staff, parents, and members of the school community;
- include procedures and timelines for review, in accordance with school board policy;
- develop a communications plan that outlines how these standards will be made clear to everyone, including parents whose first language is a language other than English or French.

School boards should assist principals in developing or reviewing their local codes of conduct by creating clear guidelines for the development of such codes, in keeping with provincial policy.

---

[6]Community agencies include a range of community service agencies, local organizations, and programs.

These local codes of conduct should also be communicated to all members of the school community.

The Provincial Code of Conduct

Purposes of the Code

Subsection 301(1) of Part XIII of the *Education Act* states that "the Minister may establish a code of conduct governing the behaviour of all persons in schools". Subsection 301(2) sets out the purposes of this provincial code of conduct, as follows:

1. To ensure that all members of the school community, especially people in positions of authority, are treated with respect and dignity.
2. To promote responsible citizenship by encouraging appropriate participation in the civic life of the school community.
3. To maintain an environment where conflict and difference can be addressed in a manner characterized by respect and civility.
4. To encourage the use of non-violent means to resolve conflict.
5. To promote the safety of people in the schools.
6. To discourage the use of alcohol and illegal drugs.

Standards of Behaviour

Respect, Civility, and Responsible Citizenship

All members of the school community must:

- respect and comply with all applicable federal, provincial, and municipal laws;
- demonstrate honesty and integrity;
- respect differences in people, their ideas, and their opinions;
- treat one another with dignity and respect at all times, and especially when there is disagreement;
- respect and treat others fairly, regardless of, for example, race, ancestry, place of origin, colour, ethnic origin, citizenship, religion, gender, sexual orientation, age, or disability;
- respect the rights of others;
- show proper care and regard for school property and the property of others;
- take appropriate measures to help those in need;
- seek assistance from a member of the school staff, if necessary, to resolve conflict peacefully;
- respect all members of the school community, especially persons in positions of authority;
- respect the need of others to work in an environment that is conducive to learning and teaching;
- not swear at a teacher or at another person in a position of authority.

Safety

All members of the school community must not:

- engage in bullying behaviours;
- commit sexual assault;

- traffic weapons or illegal drugs;
- give alcohol to a minor;
- commit robbery;
- be in possession of any weapon, including firearms;
- use any object to threaten or intimidate another person;
- cause injury to any person with an object;
- be in possession of, or be under the influence of, or provide others with alcohol or illegal drugs;
- inflict or encourage others to inflict bodily harm on another person;
- engage in hate propaganda and other forms of behaviour motivated by hate or bias;
- commit an act of vandalism that causes extensive damage to school property or to property located on the premises of the school.

Roles and Responsibilities

School Boards

School boards provide direction to their schools to ensure opportunity, academic excellence, and accountability in the education system. It is the responsibility of school boards to:

- develop policies that set out how their schools will implement and enforce the provincial Code of Conduct and all other rules that they develop that are related to the provincial standards that promote and support respect, civility, responsible citizenship, and safety;
- review these policies regularly with students, staff, parents, volunteers, and the community;
- seek input from school councils, their Parent Involvement Committee, their Special Education Advisory Committee, parents, students, staff members, and the school community;
- establish a process that clearly communicates the provincial Code of Conduct and school board codes of conduct to all parents, students, staff members, and members of the school community in order to obtain their commitment and support;
- develop effective intervention strategies and respond to all infractions related to the standards for respect, civility, responsible citizenship, and safety;
- provide opportunities for all of the staff to acquire the knowledge, skills, and attitudes necessary to develop and maintain academic excellence in a safe learning and teaching environment.

Wherever possible, boards should collaborate to provide coordinated prevention and intervention programs and services, and should endeavour to share effective practices.

Principals

Under the direction of their school boards, principals take a leadership role in the daily operation of a school. They provide this leadership by:

- demonstrating care for the school community and a commitment to academic excellence in a safe teaching and learning environment;
- holding everyone under their authority accountable for his or her behaviour and actions;
- empowering students to be positive leaders in their school and community;

- communicating regularly and meaningfully with all members of their school community.

Teachers and Other School Staff Members

Under the leadership of their principals, teachers and other school staff members maintain order in the school and are expected to hold everyone to the highest standard of respectful and responsible behaviour. As role models, teachers and school staff uphold these high standards when they:

- help students work to their full potential and develop their sense of self-worth;
- empower students to be positive leaders in their classroom, school, and community;
- communicate regularly and meaningfully with parents;
- maintain consistent standards of behaviour for all students;
- demonstrate respect for all students, staff, parents, volunteers, and the members of the school community;
- prepare students for the full responsibilities of citizenship.

Students

Students are to be treated with respect and dignity. In return, they must demonstrate respect for themselves, for others, and for the responsibilities of citizenship through acceptable behaviour. Respect and responsibility are demonstrated when a student:

- comes to school prepared, on time, and ready to learn;
- shows respect for himself or herself, for others, and for those in authority;
- refrains from bringing anything to school that may compromise the safety of others;
- follows the established rules and takes responsibility for his or her own actions.

Parents

Parents play an important role in the education of their children, and can support the efforts of school staff in maintaining a safe and respectful learning environment for all students. Parents fulfil their role when they:

- show an active interest in their child's school work and progress;
- communicate regularly with the school;
- help their child be neat, appropriately dressed, and prepared for school;
- ensure that their child attends school regularly and on time;
- promptly report to the school their child's absence or late arrival;
- show that they are familiar with the provincial Code of Conduct, the board's code of conduct, and school rules;
- encourage and assist their child in following the rules of behaviour;
- assist school staff in dealing with disciplinary issues involving their child.

Community Partners and the Police

Through outreach, partnerships already in place may be enhanced and new partnerships with community agencies and members of the community (e.g., Aboriginal Elders) may also be created. Community agencies are resources that boards can use to deliver prevention or intervention programs. Protocols are effective ways of establishing linkages between boards and community agencies and of formalizing the relationship between them. These partnerships must respect all applicable collective agreements.

The police play an essential role in making our schools and communities safer. The police investigate incidents in accordance with the protocol developed with the local school board. These protocols are based on a provincial model that was developed by the Ministry of the Solicitor General and the Ministry of Education.

[Editor's note: Appendices are not included in this publication.]

APPENDIX E

Policy/Program Memorandum No. 131*

Ontario — Ministry of Education

Date of Issue:	June 17, 2002	**Effective**:	Until revoked or modified
Subject:	**HOME SCHOOLING**		
Application:	Chairs of District School Boards Directors of Education Secretaries of School Authorities Principals of Elementary Schools Principals of Secondary Schools Principal of Independent Learning Centre		

Introduction

This memorandum provides direction to school boards[1] and schools concerning policies related to home schooling and the excusing of children from school who are receiving home schooling. School boards should bring this memorandum to the attention of parents[2] who are providing home schooling.

In addition, this memorandum revokes and replaces the memorandum entitled "Determining Satisfactory Instruction Under Subsection 20(2) of the Education Act", issued in 1981 by K. D. Johnson, the Provincial School Attendance Counsellor.

The sections and subsections of the Education Act that are relevant to this memorandum are listed in appendix A.

Home schooling procedures

Procedures for Parents

Parents who decide to provide home schooling for their child(ren) should notify the school board of their intent in writing. Parents should provide the name, gender, and date of birth of each child who is receiving home schooling, and the telephone number and address of the home. The letter should be signed by the parent(s). Parents may use the sample letter pro-

---

[1] In this document, *school board* and *board* refer to district school boards and school authorities.

[2] In this document, *parent(s)* refers to parent(s) and guardian(s).

vided in appendix B to this memorandum. If the home address changes, parents should notify the school board of the change of address.

If parents decide to continue to provide home schooling in subsequent years, they should give notification each year in writing prior to September 1 to the school board in whose jurisdiction their child last attended school. The letter should contain the same information as that in the initial letter described above.

Procedures for School Boards

When parents give a board written notification of their intent to provide home schooling for their child, the board should consider the child to be excused from attendance at school, in accordance with subsection 21(2), clause (a), of the Education Act. The board should accept the written notification of the parents each year as evidence that the parents are providing satisfactory instruction at home. The board should send a letter each year to the parents, acknowledging the notification; for this purpose, the board may use the sample letter in appendix C.

Normally, the board should not investigate the matter. However, if there are reasonable grounds to suspect that the child is not receiving satisfactory instruction at home, the board should take steps to determine whether the instruction is satisfactory, as outlined in the next section.

Board investigations of home schooling

Reasons for an Investigation

As stated above, it is the responsibility of school boards to excuse children from attendance at school when home schooling is provided, in accordance with subsection 21(2), clause (a), of the Education Act. However, where a board has reasonable grounds to be concerned that the instruction provided in the home may not be satisfactory, the board should investigate the matter.

The following is a list of some of the reasons that may give a board cause to investigate a particular instance of home schooling:

- refusal of a parent to notify the board in writing of the intent to provide home schooling
- a credible report of concern by a third party with respect to the instruction being provided in the home
- evidence that the child was removed from attendance at school because of ongoing conflicts with the school, not for the purpose of home schooling
- a history of absenteeism by the child prior to the parent's notifying the board of the intent to provide home schooling

Guidelines for Conducting an Investigation

In conducting an investigation, the board may have one of its officials meet with the family or it may ask the parent to submit information about the home schooling in writing.

Whether meeting with the family or reviewing information submitted in writing, board officials should recognize that the methodology, materials, schedules, and assessment techniques used by parents who provide home schooling may differ from those used by educators in the school system. For example, the parent may not be following the Ontario curriculum, using standard classroom practices in the home, or teaching within the standard school day or school year. Determining whether instruction is satisfactory should therefore focus on the following:

- a plan for educating the child

- plans to ensure literacy and numeracy at developmentally appropriate levels
- plans for assessing the child's achievement

If the board chooses to have a board official meet with the family, the following questions and requests may be used as a guide for the discussion:

- Do you have an instructional plan, regularly planned instructional time, and a daily work schedule? Please provide details.
- What subjects are you teaching?
- What do you expect to accomplish with your child in English, mathematics, and other subjects this year?
- Is your instructional program based on the Ontario curriculum or on a different curriculum?
- If you follow the Ontario curriculum, which documents do you use?
- If you do not use Ontario curriculum documents, please describe the curriculum documents you do use.
- Please describe the typical kinds of activities that you provide for your child in the subjects you are teaching. Please provide samples of your child's work in each subject area.
- What types of materials do you use to assist you in accomplishing your plans (e.g., encyclopaedias, textbooks, magazines, newspapers, television programs, materials on the Internet, computer programs)?
- Please describe the techniques you use to assess your child's learning.
- Do you use community resources to support your instruction? If so, which ones?
- Do you network with other parents who provide home schooling? How?
- Please feel free to provide any other information that would help the board determine whether instruction is satisfactory.

If the board chooses to request a written submission from the parent, board officials may ask the parent to complete a form such as the sample form in appendix D.

If the board is unable to determine from this investigation whether the child is receiving satisfactory instruction at home, it may take further action, in accordance with subsection 24(2) and/or section 30 of the Education Act (for further information, see appendix A to this memorandum and the section entitled "Inquiries by the Provincial School Attendance Counsellor" on page 6 of this memorandum).

The Role of Home-Schooling Support Associations in an Investigation

When a board official is conducting the investigation, a member of a recognized support group for parents who provide home schooling may be present. These support groups include the Ontario Federation of Teaching Parents, the Ontario Christian Home Educators' Connection, the Home School Legal Defence Association of Canada, and the Catholic Home Schoolers' Association — Ontario.

Access to resources for parents providing home schooling

Parents who have given a school board written notification of their intent to provide home schooling may request access to the resources outlined below.

Assessments and Tests Administered by the Education Quality and Accountability Office

Parents providing home schooling may wish their child(ren) to participate in assessments for students in Grades 3, 6, and 9, and/or the Ontario Secondary School Literacy Test (normally given to students in Grade 10), all of which are administered by the Education Quality and Accountability Office (EQAO). These parents must contact the school board by September 30 (or another date specified by the school board) of the year in which the assessments/tests are being conducted for information about the dates, times, and locations. Parents who wish their children to participate in any of these assessments/tests will not be charged a fee either by the board or by the EQAO.

The board should provide space for these children at a local school at the time and on the dates when assessments/tests are being administered to the board's regular day school students. The school will request sufficient assessment/test materials from the EQAO so that the children who are receiving home schooling can participate. The school will also inform the parent of the date, time, and location of the assessment/test. It is the responsibility of the parent to provide transportation for the child to and from the site.

The EQAO will send the results of children who are receiving home schooling to the school where they participated in the assessment/test. Schools will send these children's results directly to the children's homes. The results of children who are receiving home schooling will not be included in school and board reports generated by the EQAO or by the schools and boards.

Courses Offered Through the Independent Learning Centre

A parent who wishes to enrol a child of compulsory school age in courses offered through the Independent Learning Centre (ILC) may do so, provided that the parent has notified the school board of the intent to provide home schooling. To enrol the child with the ILC, the parent must submit the enrolment form to the ILC, along with a letter from the school board (such as the sample letter in appendix C) indicating that the child is receiving home schooling and is excused from attendance at school.

Students taking courses through the ILC pay an administration fee that applies to every course offered by the ILC, including full-credit, half-credit, and non-credit courses. Parents may obtain information about fees and enrolment forms directly from the ILC.

Ministry of Education Curriculum Material

Parents who are providing home schooling may download curriculum policy documents and curriculum support material produced by the Ministry of Education free of charge from the ministry's website, at www.edu.gov.on.ca. This material may also be obtained through Publications Ontario. Parents may contact Publications Ontario by calling its toll-free telephone number, 1-800-668-9938, or they may visit its website, at www.publications.gov.on.ca, for more information.

Support Services Offered by the Ministry of Health and Long-Term Care

Families in which children are receiving home schooling have access to Ministry of Health and Long-Term Care school health support and personal support services (and equipment) through the local community care access centres (CCACs) of the Ministry of Health and Long-Term Care. Regulation 386/99 under the Long-Term Care Act sets out the eligibility criteria for these services. The first criterion is that "the person must be enrolled as a pupil at a school or be receiving satisfactory instruction at home in accordance with clause 21(2)(a) of the Education Act." For a child who is receiving home schooling to be eligible for these services, the parent must provide the local CCAC with a letter from the school board (such as the sample letter in appendix C) indicating that the child is excused from attendance at school because the child is receiving satisfactory instruction at home.

Clarification of related policy

Prior Learning Assessment and Recognition (PLAR)

Sections 6.6 and 6.7.2 and appendix 8, "Equivalent Diploma Requirements", of *Ontario Secondary Schools, Grades 9 to 12: Program and Diploma Requirements, 1999 (OSS)* will also apply to students enrolled in an Ontario secondary school, other than mature students (as defined in OSS), who are entering secondary school after having received home schooling.

Funding for Part-Time Attendance

The Ministry of Education provides funding to boards for students who attend school on a part-time basis. The per-pupil grants are prorated according to the amount of time the student is in attendance at the school.

Enrolment Registers

A school will not record a child who is receiving home schooling on a full-time basis in the enrolment register for full-time day school students. If, however, a student is receiving some instruction at a school operated by a board, the student's enrolment for this instruction will be recorded in the appropriate register. Refer to the Instructions section of the appropriate register for details.

Inquiries by the provincial school attendance counsellor

When a school board is unable to determine whether a child is receiving satisfactory instruction, it may request that the Provincial School Attendance Counsellor inquire into the case under subsection 24(2) of the Education Act. The Provincial School Attendance Counsellor will appoint an inquiry officer to conduct the inquiry. If the inquiry determines that the child is not receiving satisfactory instruction and the Provincial School Attendance Counsellor orders that the child attend school, the school board must determine the appropriate action to be taken.

Before requesting an inquiry by the Provincial School Attendance Counsellor, the board should ensure that it has:

- taken appropriate steps to determine whether the child is receiving satisfactory instruction;
- retained documentation of its communication with the parents, including copies of written communication, notes on telephone calls and other verbal communication, a record of the types of communication (e.g., telephone call, registered letter), and a record of the number of attempts to communicate;
- retained documentation on the nature of the information and material provided by the parent in response to the board's investigation;
- prepared a factual summary of its investigation, including a conclusion, which will be forwarded to the Provincial School Attendance Counsellor.

[Editor's note: Appendices are not included in this publication.]

APPENDIX F

Policy/Program Memorandum No. 136*

Ontario — Ministry of Education

Date of Issue:	December 3, 2004	**Effective**:	Until revoked or modified
Subject:	**CLARIFICATION OF SECTION 49.1 OF THE *EDUCATION ACT*: EDUCATION OF PERSONS UNLAWFULLY IN CANADA**		
Application:	Directors of Education Secretaries of School Authorities		

Introduction

The purpose of this memorandum is to assist school boards[1] in applying section 49.1 of the *Education Act*, which deals with education of children who are living unlawfully in Canada or whose parents[2] are living unlawfully in Canada.

Section 49.1

Section 49.1 was added to the *Education Act* in 1993 to ensure that minor children are not denied an education because of their immigration status or that of their parents. The section reads as follows:

> A person who is otherwise entitled to be admitted to a school and who is less than eighteen years of age shall not be refused admission because the person or the person's parent or guardian is unlawfully in Canada.

Responsibilities of Boards

The admission criteria that are applied to a child who is, or whose parents are, unlawfully in Canada should be no different from the criteria applied to any other child seeking admission to a school under the jurisdiction of a school board. Where the child is otherwise entitled to be admitted to a school, the fact that the child or the child's parents are unlawfully in Canada should not be a barrier to the child's admission. In other words, no children should be excluded from school merely because they or their parents are unlawfully living in Canada.

When admitting children from other countries, a board may make inquiries to determine whether a child is entitled to be admitted to school with or without the payment of a fee, and

[1]Under the *Education Act*, *board* means a district school board or a school authority.

[2]In this document, *parent(s)* refers to parent(s) and guardian(s).

may require proof of entitlement, provided that the standard of proof is no higher than that applied to other children. Once admitted to school, students to whom section 49.1 applies would, in most cases, be designated "pupils of the board" and would therefore generate provincial grants.

Accordingly, no children should be refused admission to school solely because of their or their parents' inability to produce any of the following:

- proof of immigration status or application for legal immigration status
- a work permit or social insurance number
- health documentation that is different from that required of all other children
- other documentation not required of other children seeking admission to school

Please note, however, that for admission to a school in a French-language school board, proof of Canadian citizenship may be required.

Citizenship and Immigration Canada (CIC) has confirmed that there is no federal legal requirement for boards to refer families without immigration status or documentation to a local CIC office to obtain documents before their child is admitted to school.

The following is an example of a situation that a board might encounter:

A family arrived in Canada as temporary residents in the visitor class, and has stayed in Canada beyond the period allowed on the visitor record or passport (usually six months from the date of arrival in Canada) without renewing the documentation. The family's visitor status has been lost, and under the *Immigration and Refugee Protection Act* (Canada), this family can now be considered to be living unlawfully in Canada. The parents now intend to stay in Canada, have established a residence in the jurisdiction of an Ontario school board, and have approached the board about registering their two children, aged eight and ten, at the local school.

In this example, section 49.1 would apply, and the children, who are of school age and are resident in the board's jurisdiction, should be admitted to a school, provided that there is no valid reason for refusing admittance.

Reasons for Refusal of Admission to School

There are many reasons under the *Education Act* why a child may not qualify to be admitted to school. However, the legislation applies equally to all children regardless of immigration status.

Compliance With Protection of Privacy Legislation

School boards are reminded that, when they collect personal information from an individual, they must give the individual notice of the collection, as required by the *Municipal Freedom of Information and Protection of Privacy Act*. That act sets out specific rules for the collection, use, and disclosure of personal information. In addition, parents should be told about the confidential manner in which the information will be kept. Any information kept in the Ontario Student Record (OSR) is also governed by the *Education Act*, which clearly sets out who may have access to a student's records.

Legal Advice

Boards are encouraged to consult their own legal counsel for advice on the application of section 49.1 in individual situations and for interpretation of other relevant sections of the *Education Act* and of other legislation.

APPENDIX G

Policy/Program Memorandum No. 144*

Ontario — Ministry of Education

Date of Issue:	October 4, 2007	**Effective**:	Until revoked or modified
Subject:	**BULLYING PREVENTION AND INTERVENTION**		
Application:	Directors of Education Superintendents of School Authorities Principals of Elementary Schools Principals of Secondary Schools Principals of Provincial Schools Special Education Advisory Committees		
Reference:	The Education Act, as amended by the Education Amendment Act (Progressive Discipline and School Safety), 2007. Ontario Regulation 472/07, "Suspension and Expulsion of Pupils".		

Introduction

School boards[1] in Ontario are required to develop and implement policies on bullying prevention and intervention, and are required to have their policies in place by February 1, 2008. Boards that already have bullying prevention and intervention policies in place must review their existing policies and any other relevant board policies to ensure that they are consistent with the policies in this memorandum.

The purpose of this memorandum is to provide direction to boards on the development and implementation of their policies on bullying prevention and intervention.

Providing students[2] with an opportunity to learn and develop in a safe and respectful society is a shared responsibility in which school boards and schools play an important role. Schools that have bullying prevention and intervention strategies foster a positive learning and teaching environment that supports academic achievement for all students and that helps students reach their full potential.

---

[1]In this memorandum, *school board(s)* and *board(s)* refer to district school boards and school authorities.

[2]The term *student*, as used in this memorandum, refers to *pupil*, as used in the *Education Act*.

A positive "school climate is a crucial component of prevention; it may be defined as the sum total of all of the personal relationships within a school. When these relationships are founded in mutual acceptance and inclusion, and modelled by all, a culture of respect becomes the norm."[3] A positive school climate exists when all members of the school community feel safe, comfortable, and accepted. To help achieve a positive environment in their schools, boards and schools should actively promote and support positive behaviours that reflect their character development initiatives. They should also endeavour to ensure that parents[4] and members of the broader community are involved in the school community.

Boards should support and maintain a positive school climate in their schools. The following are some characteristics of a positive school climate:[5]

- Students and staff feel safe and are safe.
- Healthy and inclusive relationships are promoted.
- Students are encouraged to be positive leaders in their school community.
- All partners are actively engaged.
- Bullying prevention messages are reinforced through programs addressing discrimination based on such factors as age, race, sexual orientation, gender, faith, disability, ethnicity, and socio-economic disadvantage.
- Improvement of learning outcomes for all students is emphasized.

In recognition of the importance of addressing bullying, which can have a significant impact on student safety, learning, and the school climate, bullying has been added to the list of infractions for which suspension must be considered. With the passage of the Education Amendment Act (Progressive Discipline and School Safety), 2007, this change comes into effect February 1, 2008. For the relevant sections of the Education Act and Ontario Regulation 472/07, see the excerpts provided in the Appendix to this memorandum.

Research

Research and experience show that bullying is a serious issue that has far-reaching consequences for individuals, their families and peers, and the community at large. According to the Centre for Addiction and Mental Health, one-third of students are being bullied at school and almost a third of students report having bullied someone else.[6] Research indicates that a clearly articulated school-wide bullying prevention policy is the foundation of effective bullying prevention programming.

If students who are bullied, who bully others, or who witness bullying receive the necessary support, they can learn effective strategies for interacting positively with others and for promoting positive peer dynamics. Research also shows that administrators and teachers need to be provided with opportunities to acquire the knowledge and skills necessary to address bullying through school-level bullying prevention and intervention strategies.

---

[3]*Safe Schools Policy and Practice: An Agenda for Action*, Report of the Safe Schools Action Team (Toronto: June 2006), p. 8.

[4]In this memorandum, *parent(s)* refers to parent(s) and guardian(s). Parental involvement applies, except in cases where the student is eighteen years of age or over or is sixteen or seventeen years of age and has "withdrawn from parental control".

[5]Based on *Safe Schools Policy and Practice: An Agenda for Action*, Report of the Safe Schools Action Team (Toronto: June 2006), p. 7.

[6]Edward M. Adlaf, Angela Paglia-Boak, Joseph H. Beitchman, and David Wolfe, *The Mental Health and Well-Being of Ontario Students, 1991–2005*. Ontario Student Drug Use Survey, CAMH Research Document Series, No. 18 (Toronto: Centre for Addiction and Mental Health, 2005), p. 89.

Definition of *Bullying*

For the purposes of developing and implementing policies on bullying prevention and intervention, boards will use the following definition of *bullying*:

Bullying is typically a form of repeated, persistent, and aggressive behaviour directed at an individual or individuals that is intended to cause (or should be known to cause) fear and distress and/or harm to another person's body, feelings, self-esteem, or reputation. Bullying occurs in a context where there is a real or perceived power imbalance.

Students may attain or maintain power over others in the school through real or perceived differences. Some areas of difference may be size, strength, age, intelligence, economic status, social status, solidarity of peer group, religion, ethnicity, disability, need for special education, sexual orientation, family circumstances, gender, and race.

Bullying is a dynamic of unhealthy interaction that can take many forms. It can be physical (e.g., hitting, pushing, tripping), verbal (e.g., name calling, mocking, or making sexist, racist, or homophobic comments), or social (e.g., excluding others from a group, spreading gossip or rumours). It may also occur through the use of technology (e.g., spreading rumours, images, or hurtful comments through the use of e-mail, cellphones, text messaging, Internet websites, or other technology).

Children who suffer prolonged victimization through bullying, as well as children who use power and aggression as bullies, may experience a range of psycho-social problems that may extend into adolescence and adulthood.

School Board Policies on Bullying Prevention and Intervention

Policy Development

In developing their policies, boards have the flexibility to take into account local needs and circumstances, such as geographical considerations, demographics, cultural needs, and availability of board and community support and resources.

Boards should draw upon evidence-based practices that promote positive student behaviour. In the development of their policies, boards must consult with school councils. They should also consult with parents, principals,[7] teachers, students, their Parent Involvement Committee, their Special Education Advisory Committee, community partners, social service agencies, members of Aboriginal communities (e.g., Elders), and those groups that are traditionally not consulted.

Boards must take into account the needs of individual students by showing sensitivity to diversity, to cultural needs, and to special education needs in their policies, in keeping with the relevant ministry policies on antiracism and ethnocultural equity and antidiscrimination education and with the principles in the ministry document *Ontario First Nation, Métis, and Inuit Education Policy Framework, 2007.* Where possible, the policies should incorporate other relevant board-wide policies, strategies, and initiatives, such as Student Success and character development.

Boards are required to adhere to the Municipal Freedom of Information and Protection of Privacy Act, the Ontario Human Rights Code, and the Education Act and regulations made under the Act in the development and implementation of their policies. Board policies must respect all applicable collective agreements. Boards should consult with their legal counsel and freedom of information coordinators to ensure that they are fulfilling their legal responsibilities.

---

[7]In this memorandum, *principal* refers to the principal or to a person designated by the principal or by the board.

Policy Components and Implementation Strategies

1. Policy Statement

Board policies must include the following statements:

- Bullying adversely affects students' ability to learn.
- Bullying adversely affects healthy relationships and the school climate.
- Bullying adversely affects a school's ability to educate its students.
- Bullying will not be accepted on school property, at school-related activities, on school buses, or in any other circumstances (e.g., online) where engaging in bullying will have a negative impact on the school climate.

2. The Definition of Bullying

Board policies must include the definition of *bullying* that is contained in this memorandum.

3. Prevention Strategies

Board policies must include a comprehensive prevention strategy that includes expectations for appropriate student behaviour.

Board policies should include teaching strategies that support the school-wide bullying prevention policies. These strategies should focus on developing healthy relationships by including bullying prevention in daily classroom teaching (e.g., by including books that deal with bullying on reading lists).

School boards should provide opportunities for all students to participate in bullying prevention training and leadership initiatives within their own school.

4. Intervention Strategies

Board policies must include a comprehensive intervention strategy to address incidents of bullying, including appropriate and timely responses. Intervention should be done in ways that are consistent with a progressive discipline approach. The strategies could range from early interventions to more intensive interventions in cases of persistent bullying, with possible referral to community or social service agencies. Ongoing interventions may be necessary to sustain and promote positive student behaviour.

Boards must also put in place procedures to allow students to report bullying incidents safely and in a way that will minimize the possibility of reprisal. These procedures should also define the responsibilities and roles of the principal, teachers, parents, and students.

Boards must provide support for students who have been bullied, students who have bullied others, and students who have been affected by observing bullying.

Board policies should include teaching strategies that support a comprehensive intervention strategy. These strategies should focus on developing healthy relationships by including bullying prevention throughout the curriculum in daily classroom teaching.

5. Training Strategies for Members of the School Community

Boards must put in place training strategies for all administrators, teachers, and educational assistants on bullying prevention and intervention, including training on cultural sensitivity and on respect for diversity and special education needs. Boards may also make training available to other adults who have significant contact with students (e.g., other school staff, school bus operators/drivers, volunteers). Boards should also recognize the ongoing need to support training for new teachers and support staff.

6. Communication and Outreach Strategies

Boards must actively communicate their policies and procedures on bullying prevention and intervention, as well as the definition of *bullying*, to students, parents, teachers and other school staff, school councils, volunteers, and school bus operators/drivers.

It is important that the roles and responsibilities of all members of the school community (e.g., principals, teachers, students, parents) be clearly articulated and understood.

Boards should make every effort to share this information with parents whose first language is a language other than English or French.

7. Monitoring and Review

Boards must establish a monitoring and review process to determine the effectiveness of their bullying prevention and intervention policies and procedures. This process should include the following:

- an analysis of the school climate through anonymous surveys of students, staff members, and parents provided by their schools (these surveys should be done on a regular cycle, as determined by the board)
- performance indicators for monitoring, reviewing, and evaluating the effectiveness of the board's bullying prevention and intervention policies

School-Level Plans

School boards must require that all their schools develop and implement school-wide bullying prevention and intervention plans as part of their School Improvement Plan. Components of these plans must include the following:[8]

- the definition of *bullying*
- prevention strategies
- intervention strategies
- training strategies for members of the school community
- communication and outreach strategies
- monitoring and review processes

The school plans must be consistent with the policies in this memorandum and with the policies and procedures of the board.

Safe Schools Teams

Each school must have in place a safe schools team responsible for school safety that is composed of at least one student (where appropriate), one parent, one teacher, one support staff member, one community partner, and the principal. The team must have a staff chair. An existing school committee (e.g., healthy schools committee) can assume this role.

[Editor's note: Appendices are not included in this publication.]

---

[8] *Shaping Safer Schools: A Bullying Prevention Action Plan*, Report of the Safe Schools Action Team (November 2005), pp. 24–27.

APPENDIX H

Policy/Program Memorandum No. 145*

Ontario — Ministry of Education

Date of Issue:	October 4, 2007 **Effective:** Until revoked or modified
Subject:	**PROGRESSIVE DISCIPLINE AND PROMOTING POSITIVE STUDENT BEHAVIOUR**
Application:	Directors of Education Superintendents of School Authorities Principals of Elementary Schools Principals of Secondary Schools Principals of Provincial Schools Special Education Advisory Committees
Reference:	The Education Act, as amended by the Education Amendment Act (Progressive Discipline and School Safety), 2007. Ontario Regulation 472/07, "Suspension and Expulsion of Pupils".

Introduction

The Ministry of Education is committed to building and sustaining a positive school climate for all students[1] in order to support their education so that all students reach their full potential. School boards[2] are required to develop and implement policies on progressive discipline and are required to have their policies in place by February 1, 2008. Boards that already have a progressive discipline policy in place must review their existing policy to ensure that it meets all of the requirements set out in this memorandum.

The purpose of this memorandum is to provide direction to boards on the development and implementation of their policies on progressive discipline.

Background

On June 4, 2007, the Education Amendment Act (Progressive Discipline and School Safety), 2007, was passed, amending Part XIII of the Education Act dealing with behaviour, discipline, and safety. Changes to the safe schools provisions of the Act more effectively combine

 Policy / Program Memorandum No. 145 — Progressive Discipline and Promoting Positive Student Behaviour (issued October 4, 2007) found on the web site of the Ministry of Education at http://www.edu.gov.on.ca/extra/eng/ppm/145.html.

[1]The term *student*, as used in this memorandum, refers to *pupil*, as used in the Education Act.

[2]In this memorandum, *school board(s)* and *board(s)* refer to district school boards and school authorities.

discipline with opportunities for students to continue their education. These amendments come into force on February 1, 2008. For excerpts from the relevant sections of the Education Act and Ontario Regulation 472/07, see the Appendix to this memorandum.

The changes to the safe schools provisions of the Act provide the opportunity for students who have been expelled or those on a long-term suspension to continue their education by requiring school boards to provide programs for these students. The ministry provides direction to boards to support this legislative requirement in Policy/Program Memoranda Nos. 141 and 142.[3]

The Act requires that mitigating and other factors be taken into account when considering whether to suspend or expel a student. These factors are described in Ontario Regulation 472/07, "Suspension and Expulsion of Pupils" (for relevant excerpts, see the Appendix to this memorandum). In the case of suspension pending expulsion, mitigating and other factors are only to be taken into account in determining the duration of the suspension.

As part of the legislative changes, bullying has been added to the list of infractions for which suspension must be considered. The policy memorandum on bullying prevention and intervention[4] requires every school board and school in Ontario to develop and implement a policy on bullying prevention and intervention. The memorandum provides direction to boards on the development and implementation of board policies on bullying prevention and intervention. It emphasizes the importance of addressing bullying, which can have a significant impact on student safety, learning, and school climate.

Amendments to the safe schools provisions of the Act support the ministry's Safe Schools Strategy, which places an emphasis on prevention strategies that promote and support positive student behaviour and early and ongoing intervention.

Promoting and Supporting Positive Student Behaviour

The ministry acknowledges the importance of actively promoting and supporting appropriate and positive student behaviours that contribute to and sustain a safe learning and teaching environment in which every student can reach his or her full potential. Linkages to ministry initiatives such as character development and the Student Success Strategy are key in promoting and supporting appropriate and positive student behaviours.

Prevention

Prevention is the establishment and use of programs such as bullying prevention and citizenship development, as well as other positive activities designed to promote the building of healthy relationships and appropriate behaviours.[5]

Generally, prevention measures and initiatives include the whole school and all aspects of school life. Schools that have prevention and intervention strategies foster a positive school climate that supports academic achievement for all students. Boards and schools should focus on prevention and early intervention as the key to maintaining a positive school environment in which students can learn.

---

[3]Policy/Program Memorandum No. 141, "School Board Programs for Students on Long-Term Suspension", August 23, 2007, and Policy/Program Memorandum No. 142, "School Board Programs for Expelled Students", August 23, 2007.

[4]Policy/Program Memorandum No. 144, "Bullying Prevention and Intervention", October 4, 2007.

[5]*Safe Schools Policy and Practice: An Agenda for Action*, Report of the Safe Schools Action Team (Toronto: June 2006), p. 24.

A positive "school climate is a crucial component of prevention; it may be defined as the sum total of all of the personal relationships within a school. When these relationships are founded in mutual acceptance and inclusion, and modelled by all, a culture of respect becomes the norm."[6] A positive climate exists when all members of the school community feel safe, comfortable, and accepted.

Programs and activities that focus on the building of healthy relationships, character development, and peer relations provide the foundation for an effective continuum of strategies within a school and school-related activities. These supportive strategies and empowerment programs are the basis for creating a positive school climate.

In addition to teachers and administrators, other staff such as educational assistants, Native education counsellors, social workers, child and youth workers, psychologists, and attendance counsellors all play an important role in supporting students and contributing to a positive learning and teaching environment. A positive school climate also includes the participation of the school community, including parents,[7] as well as the broader community, which can have a major impact on the success of all students in the school.

Progressive Discipline

Progressive discipline is a whole-school approach that utilizes a continuum of interventions, supports, and consequences to address inappropriate student behaviour and to build upon strategies that promote positive behaviours described above. When inappropriate behaviour occurs, disciplinary measures should be applied within a framework that shifts the focus from one that is solely punitive to one that is both corrective and supportive. Schools should utilize a range of interventions, supports, and consequences that include learning opportunities for reinforcing positive behaviour while helping students to make good choices.

In some circumstances, short-term suspension may be a useful tool. In the case of a serious incident, long-term suspension or expulsion, which is further along the continuum of progressive discipline, may be the response that is required.

For students with special education needs, interventions, supports, and consequences must be consistent with the student's strengths, needs, goals, and expectations contained in his or her Individual Education Plan (IEP).

Schools are expected to actively engage parents in the progressive discipline approach.

A progressive discipline approach includes the use of early and ongoing intervention strategies and strategies to address inappropriate behaviour, which are described below.

Early and Ongoing Intervention Strategies

Early and ongoing intervention strategies will help prevent unsafe or inappropriate behaviours in a school and in school-related activities. Intervention strategies should provide students with appropriate supports that address inappropriate behaviour and that would result in an improved school climate. For example, early interventions may include, but are not limited to, contact with parents, detentions, verbal reminders, review of expectations, or a written work assignment with a learning component.

---

[6]*Safe Schools Policy and Practice: An Agenda for Action*, Report of the Safe Schools Action Team (Toronto: June 2006), p. 6.

[7]In this memorandum, *parent(s)* refers to parent(s) and guardian(s). Parental involvement applies, except in cases where the student is eighteen years of age or over or is sixteen or seventeen years of age and has "withdrawn from parental control".

Ongoing interventions may be necessary to sustain and promote positive student behaviour and/or address underlying causes of inappropriate behaviour. For example, ongoing interventions may include, but are not limited to, meetings with parents, volunteer service to the school community, conflict mediation, peer mentoring, and/or a referral to counselling.

Strategies for Addressing Inappropriate Behaviour

When inappropriate behaviour occurs, schools should utilize a range of interventions, supports, and consequences that are developmentally appropriate, and should include opportunities for students to focus on improving behaviour. Consequences for inappropriate behaviour may include, but are not limited to, meeting with the parent(s), student, and principal;[8] referral to a community agency[9] for anger management or substance abuse; and detentions or loss of privileges.

In considering the most appropriate response to address inappropriate behaviour, the following should be taken into consideration:

- the particular student and circumstances (e.g., mitigating or other factors)
- the nature and severity of the behaviour
- the impact on the school climate (i.e., the relationships within the school community)

School Board Policies On Progressive Discipline

Policy Development

In developing their policies on progressive discipline, boards have the flexibility to take into account local needs and circumstances, such as geographical considerations, demographics, cultural needs, and availability of board and community supports and resources.

Boards should draw upon evidence-based practices that promote positive student behaviour. In developing their policies, boards must consult with school councils. They should also consult with parents, principals, teachers, students, their Parent Involvement Committee, their Special Education Advisory Committee, community partners, social service agencies, members of Aboriginal communities (e.g., Elders), and those groups that are traditionally not consulted.

Boards must take into account the needs of individual students by showing sensitivity to diversity, to cultural needs, and to special education needs in their policies, in keeping with the relevant ministry policies on antiracism and ethnocultural equity and antidiscrimination education and with the principles in the ministry document *Ontario First Nation, Métis, and Inuit Education Policy Framework, 2007*. Where possible, the policies should incorporate other relevant board-wide policies, strategies, and initiatives, such as those related to Student Success and character development.

Boards are required to adhere to the Municipal Freedom of Information and Protection of Privacy Act, the Ontario Human Rights Code, and the Education Act and regulations made under the Act in the development and implementation of their policies. Board policies must respect all applicable collective agreements. Boards should consult with their legal counsel and freedom of information coordinators to ensure that they are fulfilling their legal responsibilities.

---

[8]In this memorandum, *principal* refers to the principal or to a person designated by the principal or by the board.

[9]Community agencies include a range of community service agencies, local organizations, and programs.

Policy Components and Implementation Strategies

1. Policy Statement

Board policies on progressive discipline must include the following statements:

- The goal of the policy is to support a safe learning and teaching environment in which every student can reach his or her full potential.
- Appropriate action must consistently be taken to address behaviours that are contrary to provincial and board codes of conduct.
- Progressive discipline is an approach that makes use of a continuum of interventions, supports, and consequences, building upon strategies that promote positive behaviours.
- The range of interventions, supports, and consequences used by the board and all schools must be clear and developmentally appropriate, and must include learning opportunities for students in order to reinforce positive behaviours and help students make good choices.
- For students with special education needs, interventions, supports, and consequences must be consistent with the expectations in the student's IEP.
- The board, and school administrators, must consider all mitigating and other factors, as required by the Education Act and as set out in Ontario Regulation 472/07.

2. Progressive Discipline Implementation Strategy

In developing their progressive discipline policies, boards must incorporate the following procedures as part of their implementation strategy. Boards must:

- require schools to develop and implement a school-wide progressive discipline policy that is consistent with the board's policy;
- outline a range of interventions, supports, and consequences, including circumstances in which short-term suspension, long-term suspension, or expulsion may be the response required;
- require schools to use the most appropriate response, as outlined in the board's or school's progressive discipline policy, to respond to a student's behaviour. For students with special education needs, interventions, consequences, and supports must be consistent with the expectations in the student's IEP;
- develop a process for building on existing partnerships and for developing new partnerships with community agencies, including local police services, to support students and their families;
- provide for ongoing dialogue with parents on student achievement and behaviour;
- provide opportunities for students to improve the school climate through assuming leadership roles (e.g., peer mediation, mentorship);
- review the board's code of conduct to ensure that it is aligned with a progressive discipline approach.

3. Building Partnerships

Policies and programs that promote a positive school environment and support the progressive discipline continuum should be developed and established by building positive relationships that engage the whole school community and its partners. Linkages and coordination among boards, local schools, and community agencies should be established. Through outreach, partnerships already in place may be enhanced and new partnerships with community agencies and members of the community (e.g., Aboriginal Elders) may also be created.

Community agencies are resources that boards can use to deliver prevention or intervention programs (e.g., early and ongoing intervention strategies). Protocols between boards and community agencies are effective ways to establish linkages and to formalize the relationship between them. These protocols facilitate the delivery of prevention and intervention programs, the use of referral processes, and the provision of services and support for students and their parents and families. Where such protocols already exist, they should be reviewed, and where they do not, protocols should be developed to increase the board's capacity to respond to the needs of students. These partnerships must respect collective agreements.

Boards should, wherever possible, collaborate to provide coordinated prevention and intervention programs and services and, where possible, share effective practices.

4. Training Strategy for Administrators, Teachers, and Other School Staff

Boards must put in place a training strategy for all administrators and teachers, including educational assistants, on the board's policy on progressive discipline.

A board should make sure that others are aware of the board's policy on progressive discipline — for example, school secretaries and custodians, parents, volunteers, community agencies, and school bus operators/drivers.

The training must address the fact that building a supportive learning environment through appropriate interactions between all members of the school community is the responsibility of all staff.

Boards should support ongoing training for teachers and administrators through such opportunities as new-teacher induction programs and e-learning to create and sustain a safe teaching and learning environment.

5. Communication Strategy

For a progressive discipline approach to be effective, it is important that all members of the school community, including teachers, students, and parents, understand and support the progressive discipline approach. Boards must actively communicate policies and procedures to all students, parents, staff members, and school council members. Boards should share this information, as appropriate, with parents whose first language is a language other than English or French.

6. Monitoring and Review

Boards must establish performance indicators for monitoring, reviewing, and evaluating the effectiveness of board policies and procedures. These indicators should be developed in consultation with teachers, students, parents, school councils, their Special Education Advisory Committee, their Parent Involvement Committee, and service providers in the community. Boards will also conduct a cyclical review of their policies and procedures in a timely manner. This review may include an analysis of school climate by their schools on a regular cycle, as determined by the board.

[Editor's note: Appendices are not included in this publication.]

APPENDIX I

OSR — Ontario Student Record (OSR) Guideline*

Contents

---

* *The Ontario Student Record (OSR) Guideline* (2000), ISBN 0-778-9244-8 found on the web site of the Ministry of Education at http://www.edu.gov.on.ca/eng/document/curricul/osr/osr.pdf. Page numbering in the Contents reflects the page numbers in this publication, not in the Guidelines.

Introduction

The Ontario Student Record (OSR) is the record of a student's educational progress through schools in Ontario. The Education Act requires that the principal of a school collect information "for inclusion in a record in respect of each pupil enrolled in the school and to establish, maintain, retain, transfer and dispose of the record". The act also regulates access to an OSR and states that the OSR is "privileged for the information and use of supervisory officers and the principal and teachers of the school for the improvement of instruction" of the student. Each student and the parent(s)[1] of a student who is not an adult (that is, a student who is under the age of eighteen) must be made aware of the purpose and content of, and have access to, all of the information contained in the OSR.

This guideline sets out the policies of the Ministry of Education with regard to the establishment, maintenance, use, retention, transfer, and disposal of the OSR. It replaces the *Ontario Student Record (OSR): Guideline, 1989.*

This guideline will be revised as needed. Each page of the guideline is dated, and replacement pages will be provided with a revision date.

The contents of this guideline have been reviewed for compliance with the provincial Freedom of Information and Protection of Privacy Act and the Municipal Freedom of Information and Protection of Privacy Act. When implementing the policies contained in this guideline or set by the school board,[2] school staff must take into consideration the requirements of the relevant freedom of information legislation.

The OSR folder, Ontario Student Transcript, documentation file folder, and office index card are available from those vendors that are listed on the ministry's website, at http://www.edu.gov.on.ca. Samples of these OSR components are contained in appendices A, C, D, and E, respectively, to this guideline.

Other forms needed for the OSR are available on the ministry's website. Samples are provided in appendices F, G, H, I, J, and K to this guideline. School boards and schools may wish to download and print these forms themselves, or they may have them printed by vendors of their choice. In either case, no changes of any kind may be made to the forms.

For instructions for obtaining the provincial report cards and for samples, boards and schools should refer to the *Guide to the Provincial Report Card, Grades 1–8* and the *Guide to the Provincial Report Card, Grades 9–12*. The provincial report cards are also available on the ministry's website.

[1] Throughout this document, *parent(s)* is used to refer to both parent(s) and guardian(s).

[2] The terms *school board* and *board* refer to district school boards and school authorities.

1 Establishment of the OSR

An OSR will be established for each student who enrols in a school operated by a school board or the Ministry of Education.[3] Each student and the parent(s) of a student who is not an adult must be informed of the purpose and content of the OSR at the time of enrolment.

The OSR is an ongoing record and will be transferred, under the conditions outlined in section 6 of this guideline, if the student transfers to another school in Ontario.

Any part or parts of the OSR may be microrecorded or recorded and stored electronically in a manner that permits the printing of a clear and legible reproduction. Provision should be made to retain original documents when it is important to keep an original signature or initial on a document. Any microrecording, electronic file, reproduction, or facsimile of an OSR is subject to the security and access requirements applicable to the original OSR.

If an OSR folder is lost or inadvertently destroyed, a new OSR folder will be created. Previous information can be obtained from the current office index card and, if applicable, from the card(s) at the previous school(s). A notation will be made in the margin on the front of the new OSR folder that gives the date on which the new folder was created and the reason.

The following schools in Ontario may choose to establish and maintain an OSR for their students:

- private schools
- schools operated by Indian and Northern Affairs, Canada, in First Nation communities (referred to as *federal schools* in this document)
- First Nation schools operated by Native education authorities

All schools that establish and maintain an OSR for their students must do so in accordance with this guideline.

2 Responsibility for the OSR

School boards are responsible for ensuring compliance with the policies set out in this guideline. Boards will specify those persons responsible for performing clerical functions with respect to the establishment and maintenance of the OSR. Boards will also develop policies for determining:

- the types of information beyond those specified in this guideline that could be considered to be conducive to the improvement of the instruction of the student;
- the uses of the information and materials contained in the OSR beyond those specified in this guideline (see section 3.4);
- the relevance of the materials in the OSR, with a view to removing those no longer considered to be conducive to the improvement of the instruction of the student (see section 9);
- the times other than those specified in this guideline at which it could be considered appropriate to issue report cards (see section 3.2.3.1);
- the types of information beyond those required by this guideline that could be added to the office index card (see section 3.5).

In addition, boards will develop procedures to be followed to ensure:

- the security of the information contained in the OSR, whether it is maintained electronically or in hard copy, during both the period of use and the period of retention and storage;

---

[3] Schools operated by the ministry are Provincial Schools and Demonstration Schools.

- the regular review of the OSR for the removal of any material that is no longer considered to be conducive to the improvement of the instruction of the student;
- the storage of the OSR for the period specified in the retention schedule (see section 8);
- the complete and confidential disposal of material removed from the OSR.

Boards will ensure that all persons that they assign to perform clerical functions with respect to the establishment and maintenance of the OSR are aware of the confidentiality provisions in the *Education Act* and the relevant freedom of information and protection of privacy legislation.

It is the duty of the principal of a school to:

- establish, maintain, retain, transfer, and dispose of a record for each student enrolled in the school in compliance with this guideline and the policies established by the board;
- ensure that the materials in the OSR are collected and stored in accordance with the policies in this guideline and the policies established by the board;
- ensure the security of the OSR;
- ensure that all persons specified by a board to perform clerical functions with respect to the establishment and maintenance of the OSR are aware of the confidentiality provisions in the *Education Act* and the relevant freedom of information and protection of privacy legislation.

3 Components of the OSR

An OSR will consist of the following components:

- an OSR folder in Form 1A or Form 1
- report cards
- an Ontario Student Transcript, where applicable
- a documentation file, where applicable
- an office index card
- additional information identified as being conducive to the improvement of the instruction of the student

3.1 The OSR Folder

Principals must establish an OSR folder, Form 1A (see appendix A), for students enrolling in school for the first time after September 1, 1985. For students attending school who enrolled in school before that date, the OSR folder Form 1 must be adjusted to correspond to Form 1A (see appendix B). The folder will contain the parts set out below in sections 3.1.1 to 3.1.7.

3.1.1 Biographical data: Part A

The following information will be provided:

- the student's full name and date of birth (The principal will indicate the method of verification on the folder — e.g., birth certificate, baptismal certificate, passport — and will initial and date the folder.)
- a student number assigned by the school or the school board, where applicable
- a Ministry Identification Number (MIN) or Ontario Education Number (OEN) assigned by the ministry, where applicable

3.1.2 Schools attended: Part B

The following information will be provided:

- the name of each school that the student has attended
- the name of the board, the name of the Native education authority, or the name of the person who operated the private or federal school
- the date of entry and the date of the last day of attendance in each grade
- the name of a teacher contact

Where the student is transferring to a school from an educational institution that was not required to maintain an OSR, Part B may include any information that will complete the record of schools previously attended.

3.1.3 Retirement from an Ontario school: Part C of Form 1A or Parts J and K of Form 1

The following information will be provided on retirement (see also section 7):

- the date of retirement
- the student's address at retirement
- the student's destination at retirement with respect to further education or employment

3.1.4 Names of parent(s): Part D

The following information will be provided:

- the first name of the student's parent(s) or the first name and surname of the student's parent(s) when the surname of the latter differs from that of the student
- if applicable, the date of death of the parent(s) of a student opposite the name of the deceased

3.1.5 Special health information: Part E

A summary of a student's special health conditions will be included when such conditions are disclosed to the principal. Entries in Part E will be dated and kept current.

3.1.6 Photographs and information on school activities: Parts F and G of Form 1A or Parts F, G, and I of Form 1

This information may be inserted if it satisfies the policies on inclusion set out by the board (see section 2).

3.1.7 Additional information: Part H

The following information will be provided, if applicable:

- the date on which the student enters a Supervised Alternative Learning for Excused Pupils (SALEP) program (Regulation 308), as well as the SALEP committee report, which is to be inserted in the OSR documentation file (see section 3.4)

3.2 Report Cards

3.2.1 The Provincial Report Card, Grades 1–8

3.2.1.1 Use and completion

All school boards will use the Provincial Report Card, Grades 1–8, in all their elementary schools at least three times a year.

A completed Provincial Report Card, Grades 1–8 (all three pages), or an exact copy of it, will be filed in the OSR folder for each student who has been enrolled in the school for more than six weeks from the commencement of the reporting period:

- at the time of his or her transfer to another school; or
- at the time of his or her retirement from school; or
- at the end of each of three reporting periods, the first to occur during the fall.

The Provincial Report Card, Grades 1–8, or an exact copy of it, will be forwarded to the parent(s) of a student who is not an adult or to the student if he or she is an adult.

3.2.1.2 Content

See the *Guide to the Provincial Report Card, Grades 1–8* for available versions and information about the content.

3.2.1.3 Quality of paper

The paper used to produce the report card must be suitable for long-term storage.

3.2.1.4 Electronic format

School boards may use an electronic format of the Provincial Report Card, Grades 1–8, to facilitate completion and use. However, a completed Provincial Report Card, Grades 1–8, or an exact copy of the report card, must be filed in the OSR as a hard copy.

3.2.2 The Provincial Report Card, Grades 9–12

3.2.2.1 Use and completion

Beginning with the 1999-2000 school year, boards will use the Provincial Report Card, Grades 9–12, for students in Grade 9 in all their secondary schools. Boards will use the Provincial Report Card, Grades 9–12, for students in Grades 9 and 10 in the 2000-2001 school year; for students in Grades 9, 10, and 11 in the 2001-2 school year; and for students in Grades 9 to 12 in the 2002-3 school year and thereafter.

A completed Provincial Report Card, Grades 9–12 (all three pages), or an exact copy of it, will be filed in the OSR folder for each student who has been enrolled in the school for more than six weeks from the commencement of the reporting period:

- at the time of his or her transfer to another school; or
- at the time of his or her retirement from school; or
- two times in each semester for semestered schools, the first to occur during the fall; or
- at the end of each of three reporting periods, the first to occur during the fall, for non-semestered schools.

The Provincial Report Card, Grades 9–12, or an exact copy of it, will be forwarded to the parent(s) of a student who is not an adult or to the student if he or she is an adult.

3.2.2.2 Content

See the *Guide to the Provincial Report Card, Grades 9–12* for available versions and information about the content.

3.2.2.3 Quality of paper

See section 3.2.1.3.

3.2.2.4 Electronic format

School boards may use an electronic format of the Provincial Report Card, Grades 9–12, to facilitate completion and use. However, a completed Provincial Report Card, Grades 9–12, or an exact copy of the report card, must be filed in the OSR as a hard copy.

3.2.3 Board report cards

3.2.3.1 Use and completion

Boards may develop and use their own report cards for students in Junior Kindergarten and Kindergarten. They will use their own report cards for students in Grades 10, 11, and 12 until required to use the Provincial Report Card, Grades 9–12, as indicated in section 3.2.2.1. In addition, they may use their own report cards for students with an Individual Education Plan (IEP), as indicated in the *Guide to the Provincial Report Card, Grades 1–8* and the *Guide to the Provincial Report Card, Grades 9–12* under "IEP".

Boards that have more reporting periods than those stipulated in sections 3.2.1.1 and 3.2.2.1 may use board-developed reports at such times.

A report card will be completed and filed in the OSR folder for each student who has been enrolled in the school for more than six weeks from the commencement of the reporting period:

- at the time of his or her transfer to another school; or
- at the time of his or her retirement from school; or
- at the end of the school year; or
- at the end of each semester, if the school is organized on a semester plan; or
- at such other times that the board may stipulate.

The report card or an exact copy of it will be forwarded to the parent(s) of a student who is not an adult or to the student if he or she is an adult.

3.2.3.2 Content

For those grades where there is no provincial report card, and under the conditions indicated in section 3.2.3.1, a school board will approve, for use in its schools, report cards that will include the following:

- the full name of the student, as recorded on the OSR folder
- the name and address of the school and any other particulars that may be required to identify the school
- the name of the principal
- the signature of the teacher
- the signature of the principal
- the record of attendance of the student at school
- the date the report card is issued
- for all courses taken, the student's level of achievement (indicated by an anecdotal description, a percentage grade, or a letter grade) or a statement that there has been insufficient time to assess the achievement of the student
- the grade in which the student is placed or to which he or she is promoted
- for each secondary school course, the title and common course code of the course

- for each secondary school course taken for credit, the value of the credit(s) assigned to the course (expressed as a whole number or a number with up to two decimal places), or for a course for which a credit is not given, the words "non-credit course"
- space for comment by the parent(s) of a student who is not an adult or the student if he or she is an adult
- the following statement to parents and students:

  To Parents and Students

  This copy of the report card should be retained for reference. The original or an exact copy has been placed in the student's Ontario Student Record (OSR) folder and will be retained for five (5) years after the student leaves school.

3.2.3.3 Quality of paper

See section 3.2.1.3.

3.3 The Ontario Student Transcript (OST)

The requirements for the OST are outlined in the *Ontario Student Transcript (OST): Manual, 1999*. Beginning with the 1999-2000 school year, the OST will be a cumulative and continuous record of a student's successful completion of Grade 9 and 10 courses, successful and unsuccessful attempts at completing Grade 11 and 12 courses and Ontario Academic Courses, and completion of other diploma requirements. The OST is part of the OSR. When it is maintained as a hard copy, it should be filed in the OSR folder. When it is maintained electronically, a hard copy must be produced and maintained in accordance with the *Ontario Student Transcript (OST): Manual, 1999*. For a sample of the OST form, see appendix C to this guideline.

3.4 The Documentation File

When a documentation file is required, it will be kept in the OSR folder. A documentation file will be established when the following information is required:

- verification of a custody order
- verification of a change of surname (see section 10)
- a written request to be named by repute (see section 10.1)
- the statement of decision of an Identification, Placement, and Review Committee (IPRC); the recommendation of an appeal board and the decision of the school board regarding identification and/or placement, where applicable; and a tribunal's decision regarding identification and/or placement, where applicable
- an Individual Education Plan (IEP) for a student receiving special education programs and services
- educational, psychological, and health assessments
- an Intensive Support Amount (ISA) status form
- the report of a Supervised Alternative Learning for Excused Pupils (SALEP) committee
- letters of request for a correction to, or a deletion from, the record where the request has not been granted (see section 9)
- other reports and/or information identified in accordance with the policies established by the school board (see section 2)

- a Violent Incident Form (see appendix J)[4].

A sample documentation file folder is provided in appendix D.

When a report is requested from a professional, paraprofessional, or other relevant person, that person should be advised that the report will be filed in the OSR and will be subject to the access provisions governing the OSR.

As with other material included in an OSR, these reports should only be included if, in the principal's opinion, they are conducive to the improvement of the instruction of the student.

3.5 The Office Index Card

The office index card provides the school with immediate access to information about a student. It will remain at the school during the period in which the student is enrolled at the school. The card is not filed in the OSR folder and is not transferred with the OSR when the student transfers from the school. A sample office index card is provided in appendix E.

The office index card will record the following information:

- the full name of the student, as recorded on the OSR folder
- the number assigned to the student by the school or school board, where applicable
- a Ministry Identification Number (MIN) or Ontario Education Number (OEN) assigned by the ministry, where applicable
- the gender of the student
- the student's date of birth (year, month, day)
- the name(s) of the student's parent(s)
- if applicable, the name(s) of the individual(s) who has (have) custody of the student
- the student's current address and home telephone number, as well as an emergency number if one has been provided
- the dates (year, month, day) on which the student enrols in the school, transfers from the school, and/or retires from school
- the name and address of the school to which the student transfers and the date on which the OSR is transferred
- the student's address on the date of transfer or retirement
- the name and address or some other means of identification of the school from which the student is transferring or retiring
- other information that is identified in accordance with the policies established by the school board (see section 2)

When a student transfers to another school, or to a private, federal, or First Nation school, or retires from school, the office index card will be stored at the sending school or at a central record office provided by the board.

3.6 Student Record of Accumulated Instruction in French as a Second Language in Elementary School

An individual record of accumulated instruction in French as a second language will be established and maintained for each student enrolled in an elementary school. The record will

---

[4] See the ministry's publication *Violence-Free Schools Policy, 1994*, Part Two, Section V, "Record Keeping of Violent Incidents Leading to Suspension/Expulsion and of Reports to the Police", pp. 39-40, for details on the keeping of records on violent incidents.

be kept on a card that is identical to the one in appendix F, and will include all of the information required for each entry. An entry will be made on the record:

- at the end of a school year, semester, or summer course; and
- when a student transfers to another school, including a private, federal, or First Nation school; and
- when a student retires from school.

If a student has had previous instruction in French but no record is available, the entries on the card must be started at least from the date of enrolment in an Ontario school. A note will be made on the first lines of the instruction card indicating what is known about a student's previous instruction in French as a second language and in other subjects taught in French. If the number of accumulated hours must be estimated, an annotation must indicate that the figure is approximate.

3.7 Prior Learning Assessment and Recognition (PLAR) Challenge for Credit: Cumulative Tracking Record

If a secondary school student challenges for credit for a Grade 10, 11, or 12 course through the Prior Learning Assessment and Recognition (PLAR) challenge process, a record of all credits earned and attempted will be established and will be maintained in the student's OSR. This record will be kept on the form entitled "PLAR Challenge for Credit: Cumulative Tracking Record" (see appendix K). The student's passing percentage grade, failing percentage grade, or withdrawal from the challenge process must be entered on this form. (If it is necessary to use more than one "Cumulative Tracking Record" form to record a student's attempts to challenge for credit, the additional form(s) should be attached to the original form.)

As stated in Policy/Program Memorandum No. 129, "Prior Learning Assessment and Recognition (PLAR): Implementation in Ontario Secondary Schools", issued July 6, 2001, there are two possible tracking forms — the "Cumulative Tracking Record" and the "Interim Tracking Record". Only the "Cumulative Tracking Record" form will be maintained in the student's OSR. If a student earns a credit through the challenge process in a school *outside* his or her regular school (the regular school is the school that maintains the student's OSR), the principal of the school outside the student's regular school will use the "Interim Tracking Record" form (provided in the memorandum) to communicate the results of the student's challenges for credit to the school that maintains the OSR. The principal of the student's regular school will enter the information onto the "Cumulative Tracking Record" form in the student's OSR.

4 Access to the OSR

Access to an OSR means the right of those persons authorized by the *Education Act* or other legislation to examine the contents of the OSR. In addition, municipal and provincial freedom of information legislation permits persons who have the right to have access to personal information to receive copies of the information. This provision applies during both the period of use of the OSR and the period of retention and storage.

Both the Municipal Freedom of Information and Protection of Privacy Act, which applies to schools operated by school boards, and the Freedom of Information and Protection of Privacy Act, which applies to Provincial and Demonstration Schools, prohibit institutions from releasing personal information in their custody or under their control to anyone other than the person to whom the information relates, except in certain circumstances. These circumstances are defined in the legislation, and it is up to the head of an institution to decide whether or not to grant access to personal information in such circumstances. School boards should therefore consult with their freedom of information coordinators to determine whether they should develop policies on access to OSRs. Any such policies must be developed in accordance with the legislation.

Boards should develop their own consent forms, which they must use where the consent of the parent(s) or adult student is required for the release of information from the OSR. It is not acceptable to use Form 14 for this purpose; Form 14 should only be used for the release of clinical records under the Mental Health Act.

4.1 Students

Every student has the right to have access to his or her OSR.

4.2 Parents

The parents of a student have the right to have access to the student's OSR, until the student becomes an adult (age eighteen). Under both the Children's Law Reform Act and the Divorce Act, 1985, the legal right of a non-custodial parent to have access to a child includes the right to make inquiries and to be given information concerning the child's health, education, and welfare.

4.3 Educational Personnel

Under the Education Act, only supervisory officers and the principal and teachers of the school have access to the OSR for the purpose of improving the instruction of the student. As noted above, additional access may be permitted under municipal and provincial freedom of information legislation, under specified and limited circumstances.

4.4 Ministry and School Boards

The Education Act permits the compiling and delivery of information contained in an OSR if it is required by the Minister of Education or the school board. In instances where ministry staff members are seeking to collect information from OSRs, students who are adults and parents of students who are not adults will be notified.

4.5 Courts and Law Enforcement Agencies

Subsection 266(2) of the Education Act states that the OSR will not be produced in the course of any legal proceedings. There may be occasions, however, when access to the OSR of current students or former students will be sought. In such cases, boards should obtain legal advice from their lawyers in order to deal with such issues as the following:

- whether the Education Act in fact prevents the production of the OSR
- whether the OSR in question is relevant to the proceedings
- if the OSR is relevant to the proceedings, whether a copy, rather than the original, may be submitted to the court

All of these issues are relevant in both civil and criminal cases (see sections 4.5.1 and 4.5.2).

Both the municipal and provincial freedom of information acts permit disclosure of personal information for the purposes of law enforcement. The conditions for disclosure and the definition of "law enforcement" are contained in the legislation. School boards should consult with their freedom of information coordinators and their legal counsel to determine whether they should develop policies on the disclosure of personal information in an OSR to courts and law enforcement agencies.

In court proceedings, subject to an appeal, the judge's order must be followed. If a principal receives a court order requiring the release of an OSR, the principal should contact the board's legal counsel. Although court orders must be followed, the principal should obtain legal advice about the issues listed above.

4.5.1 Civil suits

A principal may be served with a subpoena requiring that he or she appear in court on a particular date and bring part or all of an OSR. If a principal receives a subpoena, he or she must comply with it, but should obtain legal advice from the board's legal counsel about the issues in section 4.5 above.

As a general rule, the principal should go to court with both the original OSR and a complete and exact photocopy of it, and should propose to the judge that the photocopy be submitted instead of the original. The principal should also inform the judge that the subpoena is inconsistent with subsection 266(2) of the Education Act. The principal must, however, relinquish the documents if ordered to do so by the judge.

4.5.2 Cases involving the Criminal Code

The Criminal Code is federal legislation; where there is a conflict between it and provincial legislation, it takes precedence. Therefore, if a principal is served with a search warrant under the Criminal Code requiring the surrender of an OSR to the police, or is served with a subpoena requiring his or her appearance at court with the OSR, he or she is obliged to comply with the search warrant or the subpoena. In both cases, the principal should obtain legal advice from the board's legal counsel about any relevant issues, including those on page 15 in section 4.5. The principal should also inform the relevant authority (i.e., the police or the judge) that the use of any part(s) of the OSR as evidence in court proceedings is inconsistent with subsection 266(2) of the Education Act. The principal should present the police or the judge with both the original OSR and a complete and exact photocopy of it, and should propose that the photocopy be submitted instead of the original.

4.5.3 Provisions under the Child and Family Services Act

Under the Child and Family Services Act, R.S.O. 1990, c. C.11, it is possible for a court to order a principal of a school to produce a student's OSR for inspection and copying. A court may make such an order if it is satisfied that (a) a record contains information that may be relevant to a consideration of whether a child is suffering abuse or likely to suffer abuse, and (b) the person in control of the record has refused to permit a Children's Aid Society director to inspect it. If a principal receives a court order under the Child and Family Services Act, he or she should seek legal advice about how to comply with it.

5 Use and Maintenance of the OSR

Information from an OSR may be used to assist in the preparation of a report required under the Education Act or the regulations made under it. Information from an OSR may also be used in the preparation of a report for an application for further education or an application for employment, if a written request for such a report is made by an adult student, a former student, or the parent(s) of a student.

The freedom of information legislation sets out criteria for the use of personal information. The purposes for which personal information in a student's OSR is being used must be consistent with the policies in this guideline and with school board policies. Students who are adults and parents of students who are not adults should be informed of the uses of personal information at the time that that information is collected for inclusion in an OSR.

The contents of the OSR should be reviewed on a regular basis according to the policies established by the school board to ensure that they remain conducive to the improvement of the instruction of the student. Any such review must comply with the provisions of section 9 of this guideline.

6 Transfer of the OSR

The transfer of the OSR means the transfer of all parts of the OSR other than the office index card (see section 3.5 for information on the index card). Subject to the conditions outlined below, the original OSR is transferable only to schools in Ontario.

When a student transfers to another school in Ontario, the receiving school must be sent written notification of the student's transfer (see form in appendix G) indicating that the student's OSR will be sent upon receipt of an official written request (see form in appendix H or I). When a student transfers to another school outside Ontario, only a copy of the student's OSR may be sent upon receipt of an official written request from the receiving school. See sections 6.1 to 6.3.

If the original OSR is being transferred between schools operated by the same school board, it may be transferred by a delivery service provided by the board.

If the original OSR is being transferred to a school in another board, to a private, federal, or First Nation school, or to a Provincial or Demonstration School, it must be transferred by Priority Post or an equivalent delivery method that is approved by the board and that maintains confidentiality and guarantees prompt delivery.

If some or all of the information in the OSR has been microrecorded or stored electronically and if the receiving school is capable of receiving this information in microrecorded form or electronically in such a way that the OSR can be effectively reproduced or viewed, the information may be transmitted to the receiving school either as a microrecording or by electronic transmission in advance of the paper parts of the OSR.

If a school is transmitting OSR information electronically or by means of facsimile, arrangements must be made to ensure the secure and confidential transfer of the information.

6.1 Transfer to a School in Another Board or to a Provincial or Demonstration School in Ontario

Before a principal transfers an original OSR to a school operated by another school board in Ontario, or to a Provincial or Demonstration School in Ontario, the principal must receive a written request for the information from the principal of the receiving school. A sample form for indicating this official request for information is provided in appendix H.

6.2 Transfer to a Private, Federal, or First Nation School in Ontario

Before a principal transfers an original OSR to an inspected private school, a non-inspected private school, or a federal or First Nation school in Ontario, the principal must have received:

- a written request for the information from the receiving school, in which the school agrees to accept responsibility for the OSR and to maintain, retain, transfer, and dispose of the OSR in accordance with this guideline (see appendix I); and
- a written statement indicating consent to the transfer, which is signed by the parent(s) of the student if he or she is not an adult, or by the student if he or she is an adult.

6.3 Transfer to an Educational Institution Outside Ontario

An original OSR may not be transferred outside Ontario. Only an exact copy of the OSR may be sent to the principal of an educational institution outside Ontario after the principal who is responsible for the OSR has received:

- a written request for the information from the principal of the educational institution outside Ontario; and
- a written statement indicating consent to the transfer, which is signed by the parent(s) of the student if he or she is not an adult, or by the student if he or she is an adult.

7 Retirement of a Student

A student retires from school when he or she ceases to be enrolled in school. A student is not considered to have retired if he or she (a) withdraws for a temporary period with the written consent of the principal, or (b) transfers to another school in Ontario.

When a student retires from the school that maintained an OSR for the student, the principal will give the following to the parent(s) of the student if he or she is not an adult, or to the student if he or she is an adult:

- an up-to-date copy of the student's OST, if applicable
- the information and materials stored in the OSR folder that are not required to be retained under the retention schedule provided in section 8

8 Retention, Storage, and Destruction of Information in the OSR

Regulations under freedom of information legislation require that personal information that has been used by an institution be retained by the institution for at least one year after use, unless the individual to whom the information relates consents in writing to its earlier disposal. Therefore, any personal information placed in an OSR should be retained by the school for at least one year after use, unless the principal receives written consent to its earlier disposal.

The following components of the OSR will be retained for five years after a student retires from school:

- report cards
- the documentation file, where applicable
- additional information that is identified by the school board as appropriate for retention

The following components of the OSR will be retained for fifty-five years after a student retires from school:

- the OSR folder
- the OST
- the office index card

The destruction of all or any part of the OSR when its retention is no longer required under this guideline will be effected under conditions that ensure the complete and confidential disposal of the record.

9 Correction or Removal of Information in the OSR

If certain information or material in an OSR folder is determined, according to the board's policies, to be no longer conducive to the improvement of the instruction of the student, the principal will have the information or material removed from the OSR folder. Such information will be given to the parent(s) of a student who is not an adult or to the student if the student is an adult, or it will be destroyed (see section 8).

If the parent(s) or adult student is (are) of the opinion that the information contained in the student's OSR is inaccurately recorded or that it is not conducive to the improvement of the instruction of the student, the parent(s) or adult student may request in writing that the principal correct the alleged inaccuracy or remove the information from the record. If the principal complies with the request, the material will be corrected or will be removed from the file and destroyed or returned to the parent(s) or the adult student, and no record of the request will be retained in the OSR.

If the principal refuses to comply with the request, the parent(s) or the adult student may request in writing that the principal refer the request to the appropriate supervisory officer. The supervisory officer will either (a) require that the principal comply with the request, or (b) submit the OSR and the request to a person designated by the Minister of Education. If the supervisory officer requires that the principal comply with the request, no record of the request will be retained in the OSR. If the supervisory officer submits the request to a person designated by the Minister, that person will hold a hearing, which the principal and the person(s) who made the request will attend. After the hearing, the person designated by the Minister will make a decision on the matter. This decision will be final and binding. If the person designated by the Minister requires that the principal comply with the request, no record of the request will be retained in the OSR. If the person designated by the Minister denies the request, the original request, including the date on which it was made, and the statement of this final decision will be retained in the documentation file.

Freedom of information legislation also permits persons to request that recorded personal information be corrected.

Every principal will ensure that no OSR discloses (a) the contravention or alleged contravention by a student of any statute or regulation to which the Young Offenders Act or Part V-A of the Provincial Offences Act applies, or (b) the disposition of any proceedings brought under those statutes or regulations. If an entry in an OSR does disclose such information, the principal of the school in which the student is enrolled will ensure that the entry is altered appropriately or deleted from the OSR.

10 Change of Surname

10.1 Change by Repute

When a principal receives a written request from an adult student or the parent(s) of a student who is not an adult that the student be identified by a surname other than the legal surname of the student and when (a) the student is known by a surname other than his or her legal surname, (b) the surname is a name obtained by repute, and (c) the use of the surname is in the student's best interests, the principal will record the requested surname in Part A of the OSR folder in addition to the legal surname of the student, and the requested surname will be used henceforth. In this case, the legal surname will be enclosed in brackets. The written request will be stored in the documentation file (see section 3.4).

10.2 Change by Marriage

When a principal receives a document that establishes that a student for whom the principal maintains an OSR has had his or her surname changed by marriage, the principal will file the document, a copy of the document, or a verification of his or her knowledge of the document in the documentation file, and will change the surname of the student on all current and future components of the OSR.

10.3 Change by Law

When a principal receives a document that establishes that a student for whom the principal maintains an OSR has had his or her surname changed in accordance with the law of the province, state, or country in which the document was made, the principal will file the document, a copy of the document, or a verification of his or her knowledge of the document in the documentation file, and, on request, will change the surname of the student on all components of the OSR so that the record will appear as if originally established in the new surname.

11 Continuing Education Records

For each student enrolled in a school board continuing education course or program for the purpose of achieving an Ontario secondary school credit or credits, the principal of the continuing education course or program will establish an office index card, which will contain the following information:

- the full name of the student
- the number assigned to the student by the school or school board, where applicable
- a Ministry Identification Number (MIN) or Ontario Education Number (OEN) assigned by the ministry, where applicable
- the gender of the student
- the student's date of birth (year, month, day) and the source used to verify the date
- if applicable, the name(s) of the individual(s) who has (have) custody of the student and for whom verification of the custody order is included in the documentation file
- the student's current address and home telephone number, as well as an emergency number if one has been provided
- the dates (year, month, day) on which the student enrols in the program, transfers from the program, and/or retires from the program
- the name and address of the school to which the student transfers and the date
- the student's address on the date of transfer or retirement
- the name and address or some other means of identification of the continuing education program from which the student is transferring or retiring
- other information that is identified in accordance with the policies established by the school board (see section 2)

The OST will be maintained by the principal of the continuing education program. If, however, the student is also enrolled in a day school program, the principal of the continuing education program will forward information on credits earned to the principal of the day school program for inclusion in the student's OST.

Appendices

Samples of folders and forms are provided on the following pages. For information on obtaining these materials, see page 3 of this guideline.

[Editor's note: Appendices are not included in this publication.]

LEGISLATION AND REGULATIONS

REGULATIONS UNDER THE *EDUCATION ACT*

REGULATIONS UNDER THE *ONTARIO COLLEGE OF TEACHERS ACT, 1996*

LEGISLATION

REGULATIONS UNDER THE EDUCATION ACT

ONT. REG. 285 — CONTINUING EDUCATION

made under the *Education Act*

R.R.O. 1990, Reg. 285, as am. O. Reg. 441/92 (Fr.); 96/95; 97/96; 71/03; 192/04; 503/07.

PART I

1. (1) The following classes or courses provided by a board other than as part of the day school program on an instructional day as defined in *Regulation 304* of the *Revised Regulations of Ontario, 1990* (School Year Calendar, Professional Activity Days) are continuing education courses or classes for the purpose of paragraph 31 of subsection 171(1) of the Act and the regulations:

1. A class or course that is designed to develop or to improve the basic literacy and numeracy skills of adults to a level that does not exceed the grade 8 level of competency.

2. A class or course in English or French for adults whose first language learned and still understood is neither English nor French and that is not a class in which a pupil may earn a credit in English or French as a second language.

3. A class or course in citizenship and, where necessary, in language instruction in the English or the French language for persons admitted to Canada as permanent residents under the *Immigration and Refugee Protection Act* (Canada).

4. A class or course in driver education in which a pupil may not earn a credit.

5. A class or course in the primary or junior division or in the first two years of the intermediate division in which a language other than English or French is the subject of instruction.

6. A class or course in which a pupil may earn a credit.

7. A class for the purpose of extending the knowledge of adults, for the purpose of improving the skills of adults, for the specific interest of adults or for the enhancement of the knowledge or skills of elementary or secondary school pupils beyond that expected or required of the pupils as part of the regular program in an elementary or secondary school,

    i. for which the board charges registration fees to persons taking the class and the fees are not calculated in accordance with the regulations, or

    ii. in which the work required for its successful completion is not acceptable to the Minister as partial fulfilment of the requirements for a diploma granted by the Minister.

(1.1) A continuing education course or class referred to in subsection (1) may be provided by a board at any time of the day or evening.

(2) The following classes or courses provided by a board between the hours of 8.00 a.m. and 5.00 p.m. that start after the completion of one school year and that end before the next following school year are continuing education classes or courses for the purposes of paragraph 31 of subsection 171(1) of the Act and the regulations:

1. A class or course for remedial purposes for pupils who are enrolled in an elementary school operated by the board and that is,

    i. a class or course that the board is required or authorized to provide during the school day to pupils enrolled in elementary schools and, in the school year immediately preceding commencement of the class or course, was a class or course that was provided to its elementary school pupils, and

    ii. approved by the Minister.

2. A class or course that is operated by the board for pupils who are identified as having a developmental disability.

3. A class or course in which a pupil may earn a credit.

O. Reg. 97/96, s. 1; 71/03, s. 1; 192/04, s. 1; 503/07, s. 1

2. (1) Subject to subsection (2) and Part II, a board that establishes continuing education courses or classes shall determine the courses to be given in each of its continuing education classes, the number of times that each continuing education course or class is held per week, the length of time per session of each continuing education course or class and the dates and the time of the day or evening upon which each continuing education course or class is given.

(2) An elementary school board may offer continuing education courses and classes only in courses of study that the board is authorized or required to provide in its day school program in the primary and junior divisions and the intermediate division.

(3) An elementary school board may, subject to Part II, offer as a subject a language other than English or French in the primary and junior divisions and in the first two years of the intermediate division in its continuing education courses and classes.

(4) The principal of a school shall be the principal of the continuing education courses and classes in the school unless the board appoints as principal thereof another person who holds the appropriate principal's qualifications set out in section 9 of *Regulation 298* of the *Revised Regulations of Ontario, 1990* (Operation of Schools — General).

(5) A school site that was used for school purposes and a school site that is used as a school during the school year may be used for a continuing education course or class.

(6) Two or more boards may jointly establish continuing education courses and classes in a school or schools operated by one or more of the boards concerned and determine where such courses and classes shall be conducted.

3. (1) A valid certificate of qualification or a letter of standing is required to be held by a person,

(a) who provides the classroom teaching in a continuing education course or class referred to in paragraph 6 of subsection 1(1) or in subsection 1(2); or

(b) who is employed in respect of the development or co-ordination of the program of which a continuing education course or class referred to in clause (a) is a part.

(2) A board may employ a person who is not a teacher to provide instruction in a continuing education course or class, other than a continuing education course or class referred to in paragraph 6 of subsection 1(1) or in subsection 1(2), if the person holds qualifications acceptable to the board for such employment.

PART II

4. In this Part,

"board", other than in section 6, means a board of education, public school board, Roman Catholic separate school board or Protestant separate school board, The Metropolitan Toronto French-Language School Council and the public sector and the Roman Catholic sector of The Ottawa-Carleton French-language School Board;

"commencement date" means the last school day of the month of January or September, as the case requires;

"parent" includes guardian;

"program" means a program of instruction in a continuing education course or class referred to in paragraph 5 of subsection 1(1);

"qualified person", in respect of a board, means a person who is enrolled or is eligible to be enrolled in an elementary school, a kindergarten or a junior kindergarten operated by the board, and who is not enrolled or is not eligible to be enrolled in a secondary school operated by the board, but if the board does not operate a secondary school, does not include a person who is enrolled or is eligible to be enrolled in the last two years of the intermediate division.

5. (1) If a board is not providing a program and receives from parents written requests on behalf of 23 or more qualified persons of the board for the establishment of a program, the board shall establish the program requested.

(2) If a board is providing one or more programs and the board receives from parents written requests on behalf of 23 or more qualified persons of the board for the establishment of a program that the board is not providing, the board shall establish the program requested.

(3) Despite subsections (1) and (2), a board may enter into an agreement with another board for the other board to provide the program requested.

(4) A program established under this section shall start not later than the commencement date that first occurs ninety days or more after the date of the request.

(5) A board that establishes a program under this section shall provide a class or course in the program for all qualified persons of the board who wish to attend if at least ten qualified persons of the board attend the first scheduled class or course of the program.

(6) A program provided by a board shall be provided throughout the school year in which the program was established so long as a person attends the class or course in the program.

(7) If a board, other than a Roman Catholic separate school board or the Roman Catholic sector of The Ottawa-Carleton French-language School Board, establishes a program under this section, it shall admit to a class or course in the program a qualified person in respect of another board that is not a Roman Catholic separate school board or the Roman Catholic sector of The Ottawa-Carleton French-language School Board.

(8) If a Roman Catholic separate school board establishes a program under this section, it shall admit to a class or course in the program a qualified person in respect of another Roman Catholic separate school board or the Roman Catholic sector of The Ottawa-Carleton French-language School Board.

(9) If the Roman Catholic sector of The Ottawa-Carleton French-language School Board establishes a program under this section, it shall admit to a class or course in the program a qualified person in respect of a Roman Catholic separate school board.

(10) A board may admit to a class or course in a program a person who is enrolled or eligible to be enrolled in an elementary school, a kindergarten or a junior kindergarten operated by a board and the person is not enrolled or eligible to be enrolled in a secondary school operated by a board, despite the fact that the board is not required to admit the person under this section.

O. Reg. 503/07, s. 2

6. (1) In this section,

"board" means the Conseil des écoles publiques d'Ottawa-Carleton, the Conseil des écoles catholiques de langue française de la région d'Ottawa-Carleton, the Conseil des écoles séparées catholiques de langue française de Prescott-Russell and The Metropolitan Toronto French-Language School Council;

"French-speaking person" means a child of a person who has the right under subsection 23(1) or (2), without regard to subsection 23(3), of the *Canadian Charter of Rights and Freedoms* to have his or her children receive their primary and secondary school instruction in the French language in Ontario.

(2) Despite section 5, a board shall not admit to a program that it operates or provides for another board a person who is not a French-speaking person.

(3) Subsection (2) does not apply to a person who is enrolled in an elementary school, a kindergarten or a junior kindergarten operated by the board or another board.

O. Reg. 96/95, s. 1

7. (1) Subject to subsections (2) and (3), a qualified person of a board may attend one or more programs provided in one or more languages by one or more boards.

(2) The maximum period in each week during the school year that a qualified person of a board may attend a program in any one language is two and one-half hours.

(3) The maximum period during a day that falls after the completion of one school year and before the commencement of the next following school year that a qualified person of a board may attend a program in any one language is two and one-half hours.

8. A board that provides a program before the end of the instructional program of a school day may do so only in a school site that is used for school purposes by the board during the school day.

9. (1) A board that provides a program following the end of the instructional program of a school day or on a day that is not a school day may provide a class or course in the program in a place that is not a school site.

(2) If a board conducts a class or course in a program in a place that is not used as a school site during the school day, the time that the class begins shall be not earlier than the time at which the instructional program of the board ends.

(3) A board that conducts a class or course in a program in a place that is not used as a school site during the school day shall allow an interval of time between the end of the instructional program and the beginning of the class sufficient to permit pupils enrolled in the instructional program to travel to the place in which the class is being conducted.

10. (1) A board may discontinue a program at the end of the school year if the number of qualified persons of the board enrolled in courses or classes provided under the program is fewer than 23 at the conclusion of the school year in which the program is provided.

(2) A board that proposes to discontinue a program shall advise any person who participated in the program to the end of the school year that the program will be discontinued and that the program may be reestablished in accordance with this Part.

O. Reg. 503/07, s. 3

ONT. REG. 298 — OPERATION OF SCHOOLS — GENERAL

made under the *Education Act*

R.R.O. 1990, Reg. 298, as am. O. Reg. 339/91 (Fr.); 242/92; 95/96; 425/98; 436/00; 613/00; 492/01; 209/03; 191/04; 132/05; 258/07; 29/08, ss. 1–3, 4 (Fr.); 132/08 [ss. 1, 2(1), (3)–(10) to come into force May 31, 2009.]; 297/08.

1. In this Regulation,

"business studies" means the courses prescribed or developed under subsection 8(1) of the Act and described in,

(a) the document entitled "Business Studies — The Ontario Curriculum, Grades 9 and 10 — 1999", available on the Ministry of Education web site at *www.edu.gov.on.ca*, and

(b) the document entitled "Business Studies — The Ontario Curriculum, Grades 11 and 12 — 2000", available on the Ministry of Education web site at *www.edu.gov.on.ca*;

"certificate of qualification" means a certificate of qualification granted under Ontario Regulation 184/97 made under the *Ontario College of Teachers Act, 1996*;

"division" means the primary division, the junior division, the intermediate division or the senior division;

"French as a second language" includes programs for English speaking pupils in which French is the language of instruction;

"general studies" means the courses prescribed or developed for the intermediate and senior divisions under subsection 8(1) of the Act and described in the secondary curriculum documents available on the Ministry of Education web site at *www.edu.gov.on.ca*, excluding the courses described in,

(a) the document entitled "Technological Education — The Ontario Curriculum, Grades 9 and 10 — 1999", other than the sections relating to Computer and Information Science, Grade 10, Open and Computer Engineering Technology, Grade 10, Open, and

(b) the document entitled "Technological Education — The Ontario Curriculum, Grades 11 and 12 — 2000", other than Part B: Computer Studies;

"OSIS" [Revoked O. Reg. 191/04, s. 1(4).]

"parent" includes guardian;

Proposed Addition — 1 "technological education"

"technological education" means the courses prescribed or developed under subsection 8(1) of the Act and described in the documents entitled "The Ontario Curriculum, Grades 9 and 10 — Technological Education (2008)" and "The Ontario Curriculum, Grades 11 and 12 — Technological Education (2008)", available on the Ministry of Education website.

O. Reg. 132/08, s. 1(1) [To come into force May 31, 2009.]

"technological studies" means the courses prescribed or developed under subsection 8(1) of the Act and described in,

(a) the document entitled "Technological Education — The Ontario Curriculum, Grades 9 and 10 — 1999", other than the sections relating to Computer and Information Science, Grade 10, Open and Computer Engineering Technology, Grade 10, Open, available on the Ministry of Education web site at *www.edu.gov.on.ca*, and

(b) the document entitled "Technological Education — The Ontario Curriculum, Grades 11 and 12 — 2000", other than Part B: Computer Studies, available on the Ministry of Education web site at *www.edu.gov.on.ca*.

Proposed Repeal — 1 "technological studies"

"technological studies" [Repealed O. Reg. 132/08, s. 1(2). To come into force May 31, 2009.]

O. Reg. 191/04, s. 1

ACCOMMODATION

2. (1) A board shall file with the Ministry plans for the erection of, addition to, or alteration of a school building together with details of the site thereof.

(2) It is a condition of the payment of a legislative grant in respect of capital cost that the plans and details referred to in subsection (1) be approved by the Minister.

DAILY SESSIONS

3. (1) The length of the instructional program of each school day for pupils of compulsory school age shall be not less than five hours a day excluding recesses or scheduled intervals between classes.

(2) The instructional program on a school day shall begin not earlier than 8 a.m. and end not later than 5 p.m. except with the approval of the Minister.

(3) Despite subsection (1), a board may reduce the length of the instructional program on each school day to less than five hours a day for an exceptional pupil in a special education program.

(4) Every board may establish the length of the instructional program on each school day for pupils in junior kindergarten and kindergarten.

(5) Each pupil and each teacher shall have a scheduled interval for a lunch break.

(5.1) A pupil's interval for a lunch break shall be not less than forty consecutive minutes and need not coincide with the scheduled interval for the lunch break of any other pupil or any teacher.

(5.2) A teacher's interval for a lunch break shall be not less than forty consecutive minutes and need not coincide with the scheduled interval for the lunch break of any other teacher or any pupil.

(6) In the intermediate division and the senior division, a principal may, subject to the approval of the board, provide for recesses or intervals for pupils between periods.

(7) Every board shall determine the period of time during each school day when its school buildings and playgrounds shall be open to its pupils, but in every case the buildings and the playgrounds shall be open to pupils during the period beginning fifteen minutes before classes begin for the day and ending fifteen minutes after classes end for the day.

(8) There shall be a morning recess and an afternoon recess, each of which shall be not less than ten minutes and not more than fifteen minutes in length, for pupils in the primary and junior divisions.

O. Reg. 492/01, s. 1

Opening or Closing Exercises

4. (1) This section applies with respect to opening and closing exercises in public elementary schools and in public secondary schools.

(2) The opening or closing exercises may include the singing of *God Save the Queen* and may also include the following types of readings that impart social, moral or spiritual values and that are representative of Ontario's multicultural society:

1. Scriptural writings including prayers.
2. Secular writings.

(3) The opening or closing exercises may include a period of silence.

(4) In the following circumstances, a pupil is not required to participate in the opening or closing exercises described in this section:

1. In the case of a pupil who is less than 18 years old, if the pupil's parent or guardian applies to the principal of the school for an exemption from the exercises.
2. In the case of a pupil who is at least 18 years old, if the pupil applies to the principal for an exemption from the exercises.

O. Reg. 436/00, s. 1

Flag

5. (1) Every school shall fly both the National Flag of Canada and the Provincial Flag of Ontario on such occasions as the board directs.

(2) Every school shall display in the school the National Flag of Canada and the Provincial Flag of Ontario.

Emergency Procedures

6. (1) In addition to the drills established under the fire safety plan required under *Regulation 454* of the *Revised Regulations of Ontario, 1990* (*Fire Code*), every board may provide for the holding of drills in respect of emergencies other than those occasioned by fire.

(2) Every principal, including the principal of an evening class or classes or of a class or classes conducted outside the school year, shall hold at least one emergency drill in the period during which the instruction is given.

(3) When a fire or emergency drill is held in a school building, every person in the building shall take part in the fire or emergency drill.

TEXTBOOKS

7. (1) The principal of a school, in consultation with the teachers concerned, shall select from the list of the textbooks approved by the Minister the textbooks for the use of pupils of the school, and the selection shall be subject to the approval of the board.

(2) Where no textbook for a course of study is included in the list of the textbooks approved by the Minister the principal of a school, in consultation with the teachers concerned, shall, where they consider a textbook to be required, select a suitable textbook and, subject to the approval of the board, such textbook may be introduced for use in the school.

(3) In the selection of textbooks under subsection (2), preference shall be given to books that have been written by Canadian authors and edited, printed and bound in Canada.

(4) Every board shall provide without charge for the use of each pupil enrolled in a day school operated by the board such textbooks selected under subsections (1) and (2) as relate to the courses in which the pupil is enrolled.

ELEMENTARY SCHOOL BOARDS

8. (1) Where the area of jurisdiction of a district school area board, a Roman Catholic school authority, or a Protestant separate school board is not within a secondary school district, the board shall provide instruction that would enable its resident pupils to obtain sixteen credits towards a secondary school graduation diploma or an Ontario secondary school diploma.

(2) A board referred to in subsection (1) that offers courses of instruction during July or August or both in any year may provide instruction that would enable its resident pupils to obtain two credits in addition to the sixteen credits referred to in subsection (1).

(3) Where a board referred to in subsection (1) provides,

(a) daily transportation for its resident pupils; or

(b) reimbursement for board and lodging and for transportation once a week to and from the places of residence of its resident pupils,

that it considers necessary to enable its resident pupils to attend a school operated by another board, the other board may provide such instruction as would enable such resident pupils to obtain the number of credits referred to in subsections (1) and (2).

(4) A Roman Catholic school authority, or a Protestant separate school board that has jurisdiction in a secondary school district may provide instruction for its resident pupils that would enable the pupils to obtain up to eighteen credits towards a secondary school graduation diploma or an Ontario secondary school diploma.

O. Reg. 191/04, s. 2

QUALIFICATIONS FOR PRINCIPALS AND VICE-PRINCIPALS

9. (1) The principal and vice-principal of a school having an enrolment greater than 125 shall each be a teacher who,

(a) holds or is deemed to hold, under Ontario Regulation 184/97, made under the *Ontario College of Teachers Act, 1996*, principal's qualifications; or

(b) holds a principal's certificate that is a qualification to be principal or vice-principal, as the case may be, in the type of school identified on the certificate, or is deemed under section 50 of Ontario Regulation 184/97, made under the *Ontario College of Teachers Act, 1996* to hold such a certificate,

and, in the case of a school,

(c) in which English is the language of instruction; or

(d) that is established under Part XII of the Act and in which French is the language of instruction,

shall each be a person who is eligible to teach in such school under subsection 19(11), (12) or (13), as the case may be.

(2) Despite subsection (1), where a teacher who does not hold the degree of Bachelor of Arts or Bachelor of Science from an Ontario university or a degree that the Minister considers equivalent thereto was, prior to the 1st day of September, 1961, employed by a board as principal or vice-principal of an elementary school that had an enrolment of 300 or more pupils, the teacher shall be deemed to be qualified as principal or vice-principal, as the case may be, of any elementary school operated by that board or its successor board.

(3) Despite subsection (1), where a teacher who does not hold the qualifications referred to in subsection (1),

(a) was employed by a board prior to the 1st day of September, 1972 as principal of an elementary school that had an enrolment of 300 or more pupils and is employed by such board as principal of an elementary school on the 8th day of September, 1978;

(b) was employed by a board on the 1st day of September, 1978 as vice-principal of an elementary school that had an enrolment on the last school day in April, 1978 of 300 or more pupils; or

(c) was employed by a board on the 1st day of September, 1978 as principal or vice-principal of an elementary school that had an enrolment on the last school day in April, 1978 that was greater than 125 and less than 300,

such teacher shall be deemed to be qualified as principal or vice-principal, as the case may be, of any elementary school operated by that board or its successor board.

(4) A board may appoint a person who holds the qualifications required by subsection (1) as a supervising principal to supervise the administration of two or more elementary schools operated by the board and such person shall be subject to the authority of the appropriate supervisory officer.

(5) A supervising principal may be principal of only one school.

(6) Despite subsection (1), a teacher who, before the 1st day of September, 1970, held the necessary qualifications as principal of a secondary school continues to be qualified as principal or vice-principal of a secondary school.

O. Reg. 191/04, s. 3

10. [Revoked O. Reg. 191/04, s. 4.]

Duties of Principals

11. (1) The principal of a school, subject to the authority of the appropriate supervisory officer, is in charge of,

(a) the instruction and the discipline of pupils in the school; and

(b) the organization and management of the school.

(2) Where two or more schools operated by a board jointly occupy or use in common a school building or school grounds, the board shall designate which principal has authority over those parts of the building or grounds that the schools occupy or use in common.

(3) In addition to the duties under the Act and those assigned by the board, the principal of a school shall, except where the principal has arranged otherwise under subsection 26(3),

(a) supervise the instruction in the school and advise and assist any teacher in co-operation with the teacher in charge of an organizational unit or program;

(b) assign duties to vice-principals and to teachers in charge of organizational units or programs;

(c) retain on file up-to-date copies of outlines of all courses of study that are taught in the school;

(d) upon request, make outlines of courses of study available for examination to a resident pupil of the board and to the parent of the pupil, where the pupil is a minor;

(e) provide for the supervision of pupils during the period of time during each school day when the school buildings and playgrounds are open to pupils;

(f) provide for the supervision of and the conducting of any school activity authorized by the board;

(g) where performance appraisals of members of the teaching staff are required under a collective agreement or a policy of the board, despite anything to the contrary in such collective agreement or board policy, conduct performance appraisals of members of the teaching staff;

(h) subject to the provisions of the policy of the board or the provisions of a collective agreement, as the case may be, in respect of reporting requirements for performance appraisals, report thereon in writing to the board or to the supervisory officer on request and give to each teacher so appraised a copy of the performance appraisal of the teacher;

(i) where the performance appraisals of members of the teaching staff are not required by board policy or under a collective agreement, report to the board or to the supervisory officer in writing on request on the effectiveness of members of the teaching staff and give to a teacher referred to in any such report a copy of the portion of the report that refers to the teacher;

(j) make recommendations to the board with respect to,

(i) the appointment and promotion of teachers, and

(ii) the demotion or dismissal of teachers whose work or attitude is unsatisfactory;

(k) provide for instruction of pupils in the care of the school premises;

(l) inspect the school premises at least weekly and report forthwith to the board,

(i) any repairs to the school that are required, in the opinion of the principal,

(ii) any lack of attention on the part of the building maintenance staff of the school, and

(iii) where a parent of a pupil has been requested to compensate the board for damage to or destruction, loss or misappropriation of school property by the pupil and the parent has not done so, that the parent of the pupil has not compensated the board;

(m) where it is proposed to administer a test of intelligence or personality to a pupil, inform the pupil and the parent of the pupil of the test and obtain the prior written permission for the test from the pupil or from the parent of the pupil, where the pupil is a minor;

(n) report promptly any neglect of duty or infraction of the school rules by a pupil to the parent or guardian of the pupil;

(o) promote and maintain close co-operation with residents, industry, business and other groups and agencies of the community;

(p) provide to the Minister or to a person designated by the Minister any information that may be required concerning the instructional program, operation or administration of the school and inform the appropriate supervisory officer of the request;

(q) assign suitable quarters for pupils to eat lunch.

(4) A principal shall only make a recommendation to the board under subclause (3)(j)(ii) after warning the teacher in writing, giving the teacher assistance and allowing the teacher a reasonable time to improve.

(5) A principal of a school,

(a) in which there is a French-language instructional unit as defined in subsection 1(1) of the Act, who does not hold qualifications to teach in the French language as required by subsection 19(12) or is qualified to teach in such unit only under subsection 19(13); or

(b) in which pupils receive instruction in the English language under subsection 290(5) or 291(4) of the Act, who does not hold qualifications to teach in the English language as required by subsection 19(11) or is qualified to teach in each unit only under subsection 19(13),

shall notify the appropriate supervisory officer in writing of the impracticability of the duty placed on the principal, having regard to the qualifications of the principal, to supervise the instruction, to conduct performance appraisals and to assist and advise the teachers referred to in the notice.

(6) Where arrangements are made under subsection 26(3), the principal is relieved from compliance with clauses (3)(a), (g), (h) and (i) to the extent that such duties are performed by another qualified person or persons.

(7) The other qualified person or persons who perform the duties shall be responsible to the board for the performance of such duties.

(8) The outlines of the courses of study mentioned in clause (3)(c) shall be written and provided,

(a) in the French language in the case of courses of study provided in a French-language instructional unit operated under Part XII of the Act; and

(b) in both the English and French languages in the case of a course of study in a program established in the school under paragraph 25 of subsection 8(1) of the Act.

(9) Where, after reasonable notice by the principal, a pupil who is an adult, or the parent of a pupil who is a minor, fails to provide the supplies required by the pupil for a course of study, the principal shall promptly notify the board.

(10) A principal shall transmit reports and recommendations to the board through the appropriate supervisory officer.

(11) A principal, subject to the approval of the appropriate supervisory officer, may arrange for home instruction to be provided for a pupil where,

(a) medical evidence that the pupil cannot attend school is provided to the principal; and

(b) the principal is satisfied that home instruction is required.

(12) The principal of a school shall provide for the prompt distribution to each member of the school council of any materials received by the principal from the Ministry that are identified by the Ministry as being for distribution to the members of school councils.

(12.1) The principal shall post any materials distributed to members of the school council under subsection (12) in the school in a location that is accessible to parents.

(13) In each school year, the principal of a school shall make the names of the members of the school council known to the parents of the pupils enrolled in the school, by publishing those names in a school newsletter or by such other means as is likely to bring the names to the attention of the parents.

(14) The principal shall meet the requirements of subsection (13) in each school year not later than 30 days following the election of parent members of the school council.

(15) The principal of a school shall promptly provide the names of the members of the school council to a supporter of the board that governs the school or to a parent of a pupil enrolled in the school, on the request of the supporter or the parent.

(16) The principal of a school shall attend every meeting of the school council, unless he or she is unable to do so by reason of illness or other cause beyond his or her control.

(17) The principal of a school shall act as a resource person to the school council and shall assist the council in obtaining information relevant to the functions of the council, including information relating to relevant legislation, regulations and policies.

(18) The principal of a school shall consider each recommendation made to the principal by the school council and shall advise the council of the action taken in response to the recommendation.

(19) In addition to his or her other obligations to solicit the views of the school council under the Act and the regulations, the principal of a school shall solicit the views of the school council with respect to the following matters:

1. The establishment or amendment of school policies and guidelines that relate to pupil achievement or to the accountability of the education system to parents, including,

    i. a local code of conduct established under subsection 303(1) or (2) of the Act governing the behaviour of all persons in the school, and

    ii. school policies or guidelines related to policies and guidelines established by the board under subsection 302(5) of the Act respecting appropriate dress for pupils in schools within the board's jurisdiction.

2. The development of implementation plans for new education initiatives that relate to pupil achievement or to the accountability of the education system to parents, including,

    i. implementation plans for a local code of conduct established under subsection 303(1) or (2) of the Act governing the behaviour of all persons in the school, and

    ii. implementation plans for school policies or guidelines related to policies and guidelines established by the board under subsection 302(5) of the Act respecting appropriate dress for pupils in schools within the board's jurisdiction.

3. School action plans for improvement, based on the Education Quality and Accountability Office's reports on the results of tests of pupils, and the communication of those plans to the public.

(20) Subsection (19) does not limit the matters on which the principal of a school may solicit the views of the school council.

O. Reg. 425/98, s. 1; 613/00, s. 1; 191/04, s. 5

Vice-Principals

12. (1) A board may appoint one or more vice-principals for a school.

(2) A vice-principal shall perform such duties as are assigned to the vice-principal by the principal.

(3) In the absence of the principal of a school, a vice-principal, where a vice-principal has been appointed for the school, shall be in charge of the school and shall perform the duties of the principal.

Principals, Vice-Principals and Teachers in Charge of Schools and Classes Established Under Part XII of the Act

13. (1) Where, under section 290 of the Act, more than two classes where French is the language of instruction are established in an elementary school that is not a French-language elementary school, the board that operates the school shall appoint one of the teachers of such classes or a teacher who holds the qualifications required to teach such classes to be responsible to the principal for the program of education in such classes.

(2) Where the enrolment in classes established under section 291 of the Act in a secondary school that is not a French-language secondary school is more than seventy-five but not more than 200 pupils, the board that operates the school shall appoint one of the teachers of such classes or a teacher who holds the qualifications required to teach such classes to be responsible to the principal for the program of education in such classes.

(3) Where, in a secondary school, the enrolment in the classes referred to in subsection (2) is more than 200 pupils, the board shall appoint for such school a vice-principal who is qualified to teach in such classes and who shall be responsible to the principal for the program of education in such classes.

(4) Despite subsections (1), (2) and (3), where a teacher who does not hold the qualifications referred to in such subsections was, on the 8th day of September, 1978, employed by the board as a teacher or vice-principal, as the case may be, to carry out the responsibility referred to in such subsections, the teacher shall be deemed to be qualified for such position in any elementary or secondary school, as the case may be, operated by that board or its successor board.

(5) Subsections (1) to (4) apply with necessary modifications to schools or classes for English-speaking pupils established under sections 290 and 291 of the Act.

O. Reg. 191/04, s. 6

Teachers in Charge of Organizational Units

14. (1) The organization of a secondary school may be by departments or other organizational units.

(2) The organization of an elementary school may be by divisions or other organizational units.

(3) A board may appoint for each organizational unit of an elementary or secondary school a teacher to direct and supervise, subject to the authority of the principal of the school, such organizational unit.

(4) A teacher appointed under subsection (3) may be appointed to direct and supervise more than one organizational unit.

O. Reg. 95/96, s. 1

15. [Revoked O. Reg. 95/96, s. 1.]

16. [Revoked O. Reg. 95/96, s. 1.]

Subject and Program Supervision and Co-Ordination

17. (1) A board may, in respect of one or more subjects or programs in the schools under its jurisdiction, appoint a teacher to supervise or co-ordinate the subjects or programs or to act as a consultant for the teachers of the subjects or programs.

(2) A teacher appointed under subsection (1) shall hold specialist or honour specialist qualifications, if such are available, in one or more of the subjects or programs in respect of which the teacher is appointed.

(3) Despite subsection (1), a teacher who, on the 8th day of September, 1978, was employed by a board to supervise or co-ordinate a subject or program in its schools or to act as a consultant shall be deemed to be qualified for such position in the schools operated by that board or its successor board.

18. (1) Subject to the authority of the appropriate supervisory officer, a teacher appointed in a subject or program under section 17 shall assist teachers in that subject or program in maintaining proper standards and improving methods of instruction.

(2) A teacher appointed under section 17 in performing duties in a school is subject to the authority of the principal of that school.

Qualifications of Teachers

19. (1) No person shall be a teacher in a school unless he or she,

(a) holds or is deemed to hold a certificate of qualification of any kind or class provided for in Ontario Regulation 184/97 made under the *Ontario College of Teachers Act, 1996*; and

(b) subject to subsections (4), (5), (11) and (12), is assigned or appointed to teach according to a qualification recorded on the certificate of qualification.

(2) [Revoked O. Reg. 132/05, s. 1.]

(3) [Repealed O. Reg. 29/08, s. 1(2).]

(4) Subject to subsections (6), (11), (12), (14) and (15), and with due regard for the safety and welfare of the pupils and the provision of the best possible program, a teacher whose certificate of qualification, indicates qualification in the primary division, the junior division, the intermediate division in general studies or the senior division in general studies may, by mutual agreement of the teacher and the principal of a school and with the approval of the appropriate supervisory officer, be assigned or appointed to teach in a division or a subject in general studies for which no qualification is recorded on the teacher's certificate of qualification.

(5) Subject to subsections (11), (12) and (15), and with due regard for the safety and welfare of the pupils and the provision of the best possible program, a teacher whose certificate of qualification, has entries indicating qualifications in technological studies may by mutual agreement of the teacher and the principal of a school, with the approval of the appropriate supervisory officer, be assigned or appointed to teach a subject in technological studies for which no qualification is recorded on the certificate of qualification.

Proposed Amendment — 19(5)

(5) Subject to subsections (11), (12) and (15), and with due regard for the safety and welfare of the pupils and the provision of the best possible program, a teacher whose certificate of qualification, has entries indicating qualifications in technological education may by mutual agreement of the teacher and the principal of a school, with the approval of the appropriate supervisory officer, be assigned or appointed to teach a subject in technological education for which no qualification is recorded on the certificate of qualification.

O. Reg. 132/08, s. 2(1) [To come into force May 31, 2009.]

(6) Subject to subsections (7), (8), (9) and (10), a teacher who does not hold an acceptable post-secondary degree as defined in subsection 1(3) of Ontario Regulation 184/97 made under the *Ontario College of Teachers Act, 1996* shall not be assigned or appointed to teach general studies in a secondary school, except that where the teacher is qualified to teach in the primary division, the junior division and the intermediate division of an elementary school and,

(a) on the 30th day of June, 1981 was teaching in a secondary school; or

(b) on or before the 2nd day of October, 1981 was assigned or appointed to teach general studies in a secondary school, and on the 30th day of June, 1982 was teaching in a secondary school,

the teacher may be assigned or appointed to teach general studies to pupils enrolled in a modified or basic level course by that board or its successor board.

(7) Despite subsection (1), a teacher who holds,

(a) a commercial-vocational qualification; or

(b) technological studies qualifications in any one or more of clerical practice, merchandising or warehousing,

Proposed Amendment — 19(7)(b)

(b) technological education qualifications in any one or more of clerical practice, merchandising or warehousing,

O. Reg. 132/08, s. 2(3) [To come into force May 31, 2009.]

may be assigned or appointed to teach the courses in business studies equivalent to the courses in business studies shown on the teacher's certificate of qualification.

(8) A teacher who holds qualifications in technological studies in sewing and dressmaking, or textiles and clothing, or home economics may be assigned or appointed to teach in a secondary school the clothing portion of the family studies course.

Proposed Amendment — 19(8)

(8) A teacher who holds qualifications in technological education in sewing and dressmaking, or textiles and clothing, or home economics may be assigned or appointed to teach in a secondary school the clothing portion of the family studies course.
O. Reg. 132/08, s. 2(4) [To come into force May 31, 2009.]

(9) A teacher who holds qualifications in technological studies in food and nutrition or home economics may be assigned or appointed to teach in a secondary school the food and nutrition portion of the family studies course.

Proposed Amendment — 19(9)

(9) A teacher who holds qualifications in technological education in food and nutrition or home economics may be assigned or appointed to teach in a secondary school the food and nutrition portion of the family studies course.
O. Reg. 132/08, s. 2(5) [To come into force May 31, 2009.]

(10) A teacher who holds qualifications in technological studies in vocational art, instrumental music or vocal music may be assigned or appointed to teach art, instrumental music or vocal music, as the case may be, in general studies in a secondary school.

Proposed Amendment — 19(10)

(10) A teacher who holds qualifications in technological education in vocational art, instrumental music or vocal music may be assigned or appointed to teach art, instrumental music or vocal music, as the case may be, in general studies in a secondary school.
O. Reg. 132/08, s. 2(6) [To come into force May 31, 2009.]

(11) A teacher who has not received basic teacher education in the English language or who is not otherwise qualified under the regulations for such assignment or appointment shall not be assigned or appointed to teach in classes where English is the language of instruction.

(12) A teacher who has not received basic teacher education in the French language or who is not otherwise qualified under the regulations for such assignment or appointment shall not be assigned or appointed to teach in schools or classes established under Part XII of the Act where French is the language of instruction.

(13) Despite subsections (11) and (12), a teacher who holds qualifications to teach in the intermediate division and the senior division may be assigned or appointed to teach in either or both of such divisions in classes where English or French is the language of instruction.

(14) No teacher shall,

(a) be assigned, or appointed to teach, in any of grades 9, 10, 11 and 12 in any one school year for more than the time required for two courses that are recognized for credit in art, business studies, guidance including counselling, family studies, instrumental music, vocal music or physical education; or

(b) be placed in charge of,

(i) a school library program,

(ii) a guidance program, or

(iii) special education; or

(c) be assigned or appointed to teach,

(i) French as a second language,

(ii) English as a second language,

(iii) design and technology,

(iv) subject to subsections (5) and (15), technological studies,

Proposed Amendment — 19(14)(c)(iv)

(iv) subject to subsections (5) and (15), technological education,
O. Reg. 132/08, s. 2(7) [To come into force May 31, 2009.]

(v) in a special education class,

(vi) in a class for pupils who are deaf, hard of hearing or blind or who have limited vision, or

(vii) as a resource or withdrawal teacher in special education programs,

unless,

(d) the teacher's certificate of qualification indicates qualifications in the subject or program to which the teacher is to be assigned or appointed or placed in charge; or

(e) the teacher is deemed under subsection (17) to be qualified for such assignment, appointment or placement.

(15) On or after September 1, 1982, no teacher shall be assigned or appointed to teach courses in the senior division in technological studies unless the teacher's certificate of qualification indicates qualifications for Grades 11 and 12 in the area of technological studies to which the teacher is to be assigned or appointed.

Proposed Amendment — 19(15)

(15) On or after September 1, 1982, no teacher shall be assigned or appointed to teach courses in the senior division in technological education unless the teacher's certificate of qualification indicates qualifications for Grades 11 and 12 in the area of technological education to which the teacher is to be assigned or appointed.
O. Reg. 132/08, s. 2(8) [To come into force May 31, 2009.]

(16) [Revoked O. Reg. 191/04, s. 7(9).]

(17) A teacher who, on the 8th day of September, 1978, was employed by a board to teach,

(a) French as a second language or English as a second language in an elementary school or a secondary school; or

(b) industrial arts in an elementary school,

and is not qualified for such position under subsection (14), shall be deemed to be qualified for such position in the elementary schools or the secondary schools, as the case may be, that are operated by that board or its successor board.

(18) Where a teacher's certificate of qualification has entries indicating qualifications both in technological studies and in guidance, the teacher may be assigned or appointed to teach guidance and counselling in general studies in a secondary school.

Proposed Amendment — 19(18)

(18) Where a teacher's certificate of qualification has entries indicating qualifications both in technological education and in guidance, the teacher may be assigned or appointed to teach guidance and counselling in general studies in a secondary school.
O. Reg. 132/08, s. 2(9) [To come into force May 31, 2009.]

(19) The provision of subsection (14) that no teacher shall be assigned or appointed to teach in a special education class or program unless the teacher holds qualifications in special education does not apply to the teaching of classes in general studies or technological studies in what was formerly designated a special vocational or occupational program until the 1st day of September, 1985.

Proposed Amendment — 19(19)

(19) The provision of subsection (14) that no teacher shall be assigned or appointed to teach in a special education class or program unless the teacher holds qualifications in special education does not apply to the teaching of classes in general studies or technological education in what was formerly designated a special vocational or occupational program until the 1st day of September, 1985.

O. Reg. 132/08, s. 2(10) [To come into force May 31, 2009.]

(20) A teacher may be assigned or appointed to teach those courses that are equivalent to those courses that appear on the teacher's certificate of qualification.

O. Reg. 242/92, s. 1; 191/04, s. 7; 132/05, s. 1; 29/08, s. 1; 132/08, s. 2(2)

Duties of Teachers

20. In addition to the duties assigned to the teacher under the Act and by the board, a teacher shall,

(a) be responsible for effective instruction, training and evaluation of the progress of pupils in the subjects assigned to the teacher and for the management of the class or classes, and report to the principal on the progress of pupils on request;

(b) carry out the supervisory duties and instructional program assigned to the teacher by the principal and supply such information related thereto as the principal may require;

(c) where the board has appointed teachers under section 14 or 17, co-operate fully with such teachers and with the principal in all matters related to the instruction of pupils;

(d) unless otherwise assigned by the principal, be present in the classroom or teaching area and ensure that the classroom or teaching area is ready for the reception of pupils at least fifteen minutes before the commencement of classes in the school in the morning and, where applicable, five minutes before the commencement of classes in the school in the afternoon;

(e) assist the principal in maintaining close co-operation with the community;

(f) prepare for use in the teacher's class or classes such teaching plans and outlines as are required by the principal and the appropriate supervisory officer and submit the plans and outlines to the principal or the appropriate supervisory officer, as the case may be, on request;

(g) ensure that all reasonable safety procedures are carried out in courses and activities for which the teacher is responsible;

(h) co-operate with the principal and other teachers to establish and maintain consistent disciplinary practices in the school;

(i) ensure that report cards are fully and properly completed and processed in accordance with the guides known in English as Guide to the Provincial Report Card, Grades 1–8 and Guide to the Provincial Report Card, Grades 9–12, and in French as Guide d'utilisation du bulletin scolaire de l'Ontario de la 1ère à la 8e année and Guide du bulletin scolaire de l'Ontario de la 9e à la 12e année, as the case may be, both available electronically through a link in the document known in English as Ontario School Record (OSR) Guideline, 2000 and in French as Dossier scolaire de l'Ontario: Guide,

2000, online at *www.edu.gov.on.ca/eng/document/curricul/osr/osr.html* or *www.edu.gov.on.ca/fre/document/curricul/osr/osrf.html*;

(j) co-operate and assist in the administration of tests under the *Education Quality and Accountability Office Act, 1996*;

(k) participate in regular meetings with pupils' parents or guardians;

(l) perform duties as assigned by the principal in relation to co-operative placements of pupils; and

(m) perform duties normally associated with the graduation of pupils.

O. Reg. 209/03, s. 1

APPOINTMENT TO TEACH IN THE CASE OF AN EMERGENCY

21. (1) Where no teacher is available, a board may appoint, subject to section 22, a person who is not a teacher or a temporary teacher.

(2) A person appointed under subsection (1) shall be 18 years of age or older and hold an Ontario secondary school diploma, a secondary school graduation diploma or a secondary school honour graduation diploma, or an equivalent to any of them.

(3) An appointment under this section is valid for ten school days commencing with the day on which the person is appointed.

O. Reg. 29/08, s. 2

CANCELLED, REVOKED AND SUSPENDED CERTIFICATES

[Heading amended O. Reg. 29/08, s. 3.]

22. (1) A board shall not appoint a person to teach under section 21 or in accordance with a Letter of Permission if the individual is or has ever been a member of the Ontario College of Teachers.

(2) A board shall not appoint a person to teach under section 21 or in accordance with a Letter of Permission unless the person has provided to the board a written statement that any teaching certificate or licence granted to him or her by another jurisdiction is not cancelled, suspended or revoked for any reason other than for failure to pay fees or levies to the governing body.

(3) A person whose teaching certificate is cancelled, revoked or suspended shall not be appointed as a teacher.

O. Reg. 29/08, s. 3

REQUIREMENTS FOR PUPILS

23. (1) A pupil shall,

(a) be diligent in attempting to master such studies as are part of the program in which the pupil is enrolled;

(b) exercise self-discipline;

(c) accept such discipline as would be exercised by a kind, firm and judicious parent;

(d) attend classes punctually and regularly;

(e) be courteous to fellow pupils and obedient and courteous to teachers;

(f) be clean in person and habits;

(g) take such tests and examinations as are required by or under the Act or as may be directed by the Minister; and

(h) show respect for school property.

(2) When a pupil returns to school after an absence, a parent of the pupil, or the pupil where the pupil is an adult, shall give the reason for the absence orally or in writing as the principal requires.

(3) A pupil may be excused by the principal from attendance at school temporarily at any time at the written request of a parent of the pupil or the pupil where the pupil is an adult.

(4) Every pupil is responsible for his or her conduct to the principal of the school that the pupil attends,

(a) on the school premises;

(b) on out-of-school activities that are part of the school program; and

(c) while travelling on a school bus that is owned by a board or on a bus or school bus that is under contract to a board.

Advertisements and Announcements

24. (1) No advertisement or announcement shall be placed in a school or on school property or distributed or announced to the pupils on school property without the consent of the board that operates the school except announcements of school activities.

(2) Subsection (1) does not apply to anything posted in the school in accordance with the regulations.

O. Reg. 613/00, s. 2

Canvassing and Fund-Raising

25. (1) It is the duty of a pupil to ensure that any canvassing or fund-raising activity on school property by the pupil is carried on only with the consent of the board that operates the school.

(2) No principal, vice-principal or teacher, without the prior approval of the board that operates the school at which they are employed, shall authorize any canvassing or fund-raising activity that involves the participation of one or more pupils attending the school.

Supervision

26. (1) The appropriate supervisory officer, in addition to the duties under the Act, may, during a visit to a school, assume any of the authority and responsibility of the principal of the school.

(2) Psychiatrists, psychologists, social workers and other professional support staff employed by a board shall perform, under the administrative supervision of the appropriate supervisory officer, such duties as are determined by the board and, where such persons are performing their duties in a school, they shall be subject to the administrative authority of the principal of that school.

(3) A supervisory officer who is notified under subsection 11(5) shall forthwith notify the French-language education council or section, English-language education council or section or majority language section of the board, as the case requires, and arrange for,

(a) the provision of supervision of instruction;

(b) assistance and advice to the teachers in respect of whom the supervisory officer was given notice under subsection 11(5); and

(c) the conducting of performance appraisals, where appropriate, of the teachers in respect of whom the supervisory officer was given notice under subsection 11(5),

in the language in which the instruction is provided.

Religion in Schools

27. Sections 28 and 29 do not apply to a Roman Catholic board or to a Protestant separate school board.

O. Reg. 191/04, s. 8

28. (1) A board may provide in grades one to eight and in its secondary schools an optional program of education about religion.

(2) A program of education about religion shall,

(a) promote respect for the freedom of conscience and religion guaranteed by the *Canadian Charter of Rights and Freedoms*; and

(b) provide for the study of different religions and religious beliefs in Canada and the world, without giving primacy to, and without indoctrination in, any particular religion or religious belief.

(3) A program of education about religion shall not exceed sixty minutes of instruction per week in an elementary school.

29. (1) Subject to subsections (2) and (3), a board shall not permit any person to conduct religious exercises or to provide instruction that includes indoctrination in a particular religion or religious belief in a school.

(2) A board may enter into an agreement with a Roman Catholic board that permits the Roman Catholic board to use space and facilities to conduct religious exercises or provide religious instruction for the purposes of the Roman Catholic board.

(3) A board may permit a person to conduct religious exercises or to provide instruction that includes indoctrination in a particular religion or religious belief in a school if,

(a) the exercises are not conducted or the instruction is not provided by or under the auspices of the board;

(b) the exercises are conducted or the instruction is provided on a school day at a time that is before or after the school's instructional program, or on a day that is not a school day;

(c) no person is required by the board to attend the exercises or instruction; and

(d) the board provides space for the exercises or instruction on the same basis as it provides space for other community activities.

(4) A board that permits religious exercises or instruction under subsection (3) shall consider on an equitable basis all requests to conduct religious exercises or to provide instruction under subsection (3).

O. Reg. 191/04, s. 9

Special Education Programs and Services

30. A hearing-handicapped child who has attained the age of two years may be admitted to a special education program for the hearing-handicapped.

31. The maximum enrolment in a special education class shall depend upon the extent of the exceptionalities of the pupils in the class and the special education services that are available to the teacher, but in no case shall the enrolment in a self-contained class exceed,

(a) in a class for pupils who are emotionally disturbed or socially maladjusted, for pupils who have severe learning disabilities, or for pupils who are younger than compulsory school age and have impaired hearing, eight pupils;

(b) in a class for pupils who are blind, for pupils who are deaf, for pupils who have developmental disabilities, or for pupils with speech and language disorders, ten pupils;

(c) in a class for pupils who are hard of hearing, for pupils with limited vision, or for pupils with orthopaedic or other physical handicaps, twelve pupils;

(d) in a class for pupils who have mild intellectual disabilities, twelve pupils in the primary division and sixteen pupils in the junior and intermediate divisions;

(e) in an elementary school class for pupils who are gifted,

(i) twenty pupils, if the class consists only of pupils in the primary division,

(ii) twenty-three pupils, if the class includes at least one pupil in the primary division and at least one pupil in the junior division or intermediate division, and

(iii) twenty-five pupils, if the class consists only of pupils in the junior division or intermediate division;

(f) in a class for aphasic or autistic pupils, or for pupils with multiple handicaps for whom no one handicap is dominant, six pupils; and

(g) on and after the 1st day of September, 1982, in a class for exceptional pupils consisting of pupils with different exceptionalities, sixteen pupils.

O. Reg. 191/04, s. 10; 297/08, s. 1

Sign Language

[Heading added O. Reg. 258/07, s. 1.]

32. Where it is practical to do so and if the pupil understands American Sign Language or Quebec Sign Language, as the case may be, a teacher or temporary teacher may use American Sign Language or Quebec Sign Language,

(a) in the classroom; and

(b) as a language of instruction and in communications in regard to discipline and management of the school.

O. Reg. 258/07, s. 1

ONT. REG. 304 — SCHOOL YEAR CALENDAR, PROFESSIONAL ACTIVITY DAYS

made under the *Education Act*

R.R.O. 1990, Reg. 304, as am. O. Reg. 664/91 (Fr.); 91/98; 360/06; 579/07; 15/09, ss. 1(1) (Fr.), (2), 2, 3 [ss. 1(2), 3 to come into force June 30, 2009.].

[Note: The title of this Regulation was changed from "School Year Calendar" to "School Year Calendar, Professional Activity Days" by O. Reg. 360/06, s. 1. It had previously been changed from "School Year and School Holidays" by O. Reg. 91/98, s. 1.]

1. (1) In this Regulation,

"instructional day" means a school day that is designated as an instructional day on a school calendar and upon which day an instructional program that may include examinations is provided for each pupil whose program is governed by such calendar;

"professional activity" includes evaluation of the progress of pupils, consultation with parents, the counselling of pupils, curriculum and program evaluation and development, professional development of teachers and attendance at educational conferences, but does not include preparation by teachers for classes or instruction;

"professional activity day" means a school day that is designated as a day for professional activities on a school calendar;

"school day" means a day that is within a school year and is not a school holiday;

"school year" means the period prescribed as such by or approved as such under this Regulation.

(2) A board may designate half a school day an instructional program and the remainder of the day for professional activities, but such a day constitutes a half-day in determining the number of instructional days in the school year.

O. Reg. 360/06, s. 2

2. (1) Subject to section 5, the school year shall commence on or after the 1st day of September and end on or before the 30th day of June.

(2) [Revoked O. Reg. 91/98, s. 2(2).]

(3) [Revoked O. Reg. 91/98, s. 2(4).]

(3.1) Subject to sections 5 and 5.1, every school year shall include a minimum of 194 school days designated as follows:

1. Two days shall be designated by the board as professional activity days.

2. In addition to the two days required under paragraph 1, up to four days may be designated by the board as professional activity days.

3. Any school days not designated as professional activity days under paragraphs 1 and 2 shall be instructional days.

(4) Subject to section 5, the following are school holidays:

1. Every Saturday and Sunday.

2. When the school is open during July, Canada Day.

3. Labour Day.

4. A day appointed by the Governor General or the Lieutenant Governor as a public holiday or for Thanksgiving.

5. A Christmas vacation consisting of fourteen consecutive days commencing on the Monday next following the Friday preceding the 21st day of December, but when the 21st day of December is a Thursday or a Friday, commencing on the Monday next following.

5.1 Family Day, being the third Monday in February.

6. Five consecutive days commencing on the Monday next following the Friday preceding the 14th day of March.

7. Good Friday.

8. Easter Monday.

9. Victoria Day.

O. Reg. 91/98, s. 2; 360/06, s. 3; 579/07, ss. 1, 2

3. (1) [Revoked O. Reg. 91/98, s. 3(2).]

(2) [Revoked O. Reg. 91/98, s. 3(4).]

(3) Where a school has a policy of granting exemptions to pupils from the writing of examinations, such exemptions may be granted only from the final examinations in a course and only where at least one other set of examinations has been held.

(3.1) With respect to every school year after the 1997–1998 school year, a board may designate up to ten instructional days as examination days.

(4) The teaching staff shall be in school during regular school hours on examination days and accessible to pupils, unless the board directs otherwise.

O. Reg. 91/98, s. 3

4. (1) In each year every board shall, except in respect of a school or class for which the board has submitted a proposed school calendar under section 5, prepare, adopt and submit to the Minister on or before the 1st day of May in respect of the school year next following, the school calendar or school calendars to be followed in the schools under its jurisdiction, and each such school calendar shall,

(a) state the school or schools in which the calendar is to be followed;

(b) conform to section 2; and

(c) identify each day of the school year as an instructional day, a professional activity day or a school holiday.

(2) In preparing a school calendar under subsection (1), the board shall ensure that the two professional activity days required under paragraph 1 of subsection 2(3.1) satisfy the following criteria:

1. The professional activity days are devoted to the professional development of teachers with respect to,

i. improving student outcomes in literacy and numeracy, and

Proposed Amendment — 4(2), para. 1 i

i. special education, and

O. Reg. 15/09, s. 1(2) [To come into force June 30, 2009.]

ii. improving student success in making the transition from elementary to secondary school, graduating from secondary school and obtaining employment or attending college or university after graduation.

Proposed Amendment — 4(2), para. 1 ii

ii. closing the gaps in student achievement.

O. Reg. 15/09, s. 1(2) [To come into force June 30, 2009.]

2. The professional activities on those days,

i. are designed to improve teachers' skills and knowledge in a range of instructional and assessment strategies, and

ii. relate to one or more topics set out in Schedule 1.

(2.1) If a board designates one or more additional professional activity days under paragraph 2 of subsection 2(3.1), it shall ensure that some of the professional activities relate to curriculum development, implementation and review.

(3) A school calendar submitted under subsection (1) shall be accompanied by a general outline of the activities to be conducted on the professional activity days identified on the calendar.

O. Reg. 360/06, s. 4

4.1 With respect to each professional activity day required under paragraph 1 of subsection 2(3.1), every board shall,

(a) prepare an agenda that identifies,

(i) the date, location and timing,

(ii) the school or schools participating, and

(iii) the program and scheduled professional activities; and

(b) at least 10 school days before the scheduled professional activity day, make available the agenda by,

(i) posting it on the website of the board and of each participating school that has a website,

(ii) posting it in a conspicuous location in the main office of the board and of each participating school,

(iii) distributing it to the chair of the school council of each participating school, and

(iv) posting or distributing it in any other manner that the board considers appropriate.

O. Reg. 360/06, s. 5(1)

4.2 [Repealed O. Reg. 360/06, s. 5(2).]

5. (1) For one or more schools under its jurisdiction a board may designate a school year and school holidays that are different from those prescribed in section 2 and, where a board does so, the board shall submit to the Minister on or before the first day of March a proposed school calendar for the school year next following in respect of such school or schools, identifying thereon each day of the school year as an instructional day, a professional activity day or a school holiday, and the board may, upon approval thereof by the Minister, implement such school calendar.

(2) Where the Minister informs a board that he or she does not approve the school calendar submitted under subsection (1), the board may amend its proposed school calendar and submit to the Minister a revised school calendar and, upon approval thereof by the Minister, the board may implement the revised school calendar.

(3) Where a board has submitted a proposed school calendar under subsection (1) and the Minister has not approved on or before the 15th day of April such calendar or a revision thereof submitted under subsection (2), the board shall, on or before the 1st day of May, prepare, adopt and submit to the Minister a school calendar in accordance with section 4.

5.1 [Repealed O. Reg. 15/09, s. 2.]

6. (1) Where in the opinion of the board it is desirable to alter the date of a professional activity day or an examination day on a school calendar that has been submitted under section 4 or subsection 5(3) or approved and implemented under subsection 5(1) or (2), the board may alter the school calendar.

(2) Where, the board alters a school calendar under subsection (1), the board shall notify the parents concerned and the Minister of the altered date as far in advance as possible.

(3) The prior approval of the Minister is required for changes other than to the date of a professional activity day or an examination day.

(4) Where,

(a) a school or class is closed for a temporary period because of failure of transportation arrangements, inclement weather, fire, flood, a breakdown of the school heating plant or a similar emergency, or a school is closed under the *Health Protection and Promotion Act* or the *Education Act*; and

(b) the school calendar is not altered under subsection (1),

the day on which the school or class is closed remains an instructional day or a professional activity day, as the case may be, as designated on the school calendar applicable to such school or class.

7. (1) Every board shall publish annually its school calendar or school calendars and ensure that copies thereof are available at the beginning of the school year for the information of parents and pupils.

(2) A school calendar or school calendars published under subsection (1) shall, in addition to the information required to be listed under subsection 4(1), indicate in a general manner the activities to be conducted on professional activity days.

8. In each year, every board shall undertake an annual evaluation of the activities of the professional activity days of the previous year and retain such evaluations on file.

9. (1) A Remembrance Day service shall be held in every school on the 11th day of November or, when the 11th day of November is a Saturday or a Sunday, on the Friday preceding the 11th day of November.

(2) Subsection (1) does not apply where the school participates in a service of remembrance at a cenotaph or other location in the community.

SCHEDULE 1 — TOPICS FOR PROFESSIONAL ACTIVITY DAYS REQUIRED UNDER PARAGRAPH 1 OF SUBSECTION 2(3.1)

[Heading added O. Reg. 360/06, s. 6.]

1. The following are the possible topics for professional activities relating to the improvement of student outcomes in literacy and numeracy:

1. Differentiating instructional strategies and resources for diverse learners with respect to literacy or numeracy or both.

2. Developing and using literacy strategies that are responsive to the learning needs of students with regard to race, culture, ancestry, place of origin, colour, ethnic origin, citizenship, creed, sex, sexual orientation, family status or disability.

3. Using effective literacy strategies that are responsive to the learning needs of francophone students or Aboriginal students having regard to cultural identity.

4. Identifying appropriate interventions and using accommodations and modifications to improve student outcomes in literacy or numeracy or both.

5. Using differentiated literacy instruction to meet the needs of one or both of the following:

i. English Language learners.

ii. students in Actualisation linguistique en français (ALF) and Perfectionnement du français (PDF).

6. Gathering and analyzing data to make appropriate instructional decisions with respect to literacy or numeracy or both.

7. Integrating the development of character and citizenship attributes throughout the teaching of the literacy curriculum.

8. Using effective techniques to integrate literacy across the curriculum.

9. Using shared reading and interactive writing in small group instruction in kindergarten.

10. Using effective strategies to develop oral communication skills.

11. Using effective strategies to develop reading comprehension.

12. Using the writing process and specific feedback to improve student writing.

13. Connecting reading, writing, talking, listening and thinking to improve student achievement.

14. Using effective instruction in combined grades with respect to literacy or numeracy or both.

15. Integrating the use of manipulatives and technologies for teaching mathematics.

16. Teaching and learning mathematics through problem-solving.

17. Developing skills for communicating mathematical knowledge.

18. Using effective assessment of students learning mathematics to guide instruction.

19. Using a portfolio to engage students in their literacy learning and to communicate to parents.

20. Using strategies to communicate student achievement and to engage parents in supporting their child's learning with respect to literacy or numeracy or both.

21. Developing skills for teacher inquiry and reflective practice in literacy or numeracy or both.

22. Developing coaching and facilitation skills for literacy leaders or numeracy leaders or both.

O. Reg. 360/06, s. 6

2. The following are the possible topics for professional activities relating to the improvement of student success in making the transition from elementary to secondary school, graduating from secondary school and obtaining employment or attending college or university after graduation:

1. Using differentiated instruction and other teaching strategies to,

    i. make instruction relevant to students by addressing student readiness, interests and program pathways,

    ii. engage students in their learning,

    iii. guide instructional and program planning strategies for all types of learners,

    iv. improve the use of effective instructional strategies for all types of courses,

    v. apply age appropriate interventions,

    vi. integrate essential skills required in the workplace, and

    vii. assess and evaluate student achievement.

2. Using students' assessment and evaluation data to inform teachers' instructional and program planning to support students' transition through school.

3. Using cross-curricular instructional and learning strategies to support students' transition through school.

4. Facilitating transitions from elementary to secondary and from secondary school to postsecondary education.

5. Developing and analyzing class profiles to make instructional decisions to support students' transition through school.

6. Developing students' profiles to plan how to enhance achievement.

7. Creating a positive classroom climate conducive to learning.

8. Developing student engagement, character and citizenship attributes necessary for lifelong learning.

9. Teaching students how to set and revise personal learning objectives using assessment and evaluation data.

10. Teaching students how to use assessment and evaluation data to improve their achievement.

11. Developing an understanding of how to be successful in transitions, Program Pathways, Cooperative Education and other forms of Experiential Learning.

12. Using strategies to communicate student achievement and to engage parents in supporting their child's learning.

O. Reg. 360/06, s. 6

Proposed Amendment — Schedule

SCHEDULE 1 — TOPICS FOR PROFESSIONAL ACTIVITY DAYS

[Heading added O. Reg. 360/06, s. 6. Amended O. Reg. 15/09, s. 3. To come into force June 30, 2009.]

1. The following are the possible topics for professional activities relating to special education:

1. Developing individual education plans.

2. Improving the application of applied behaviour analysis to support students with autism-spectrum disorders.

3. Implementing activities related to assistive technologies, differentiated instruction, universal design and professional learning technologies.

4. Facilitating transitions for students who are entering school, changing grades or schools, or leaving school.

5. Facilitating parental involvement in identification, placement and review committees established under Part II of Ontario Regulation 181/98 (*Identification and Placement of Exceptional Pupils*) made under the Act, and in the development of individual education plans.

O. Reg. 15/09, s. 3 [To come into force June 30, 2009.]

2. The following are the possible topics for professional activities relating to closing the gaps in student achievement:

1. Differentiating instructional strategies and resources that are responsive to students' learning needs and their race, culture, and ethnic origin.

2. Developing and implementing strategies to close the gaps in mathematical literacy.

3. Developing and implementing strategies to close the gaps in literacy.

4. Developing and implementing strategies to improve boys' literacy.

5. Developing and implementing early and on-going instructional interventions.

6. Performing assessments and evaluations.

7. Facilitating parental and community engagement.

8. Using strategies to support English language learners and students in Actualisation linguistique en français and Perfectionnement du français.

9. Using data analysis to inform instruction.

10. Integrating the use of manipulative aids and technology to support a range of learning styles.

11. Developing and implementing board and school improvement plans that focus on equity of outcomes.

12. Creating a positive and inclusive classroom climate conducive to learning.

13. Developing student and classroom learning profiles.

14. Promoting instructional leadership.

15. Developing skills for teacher inquiry and reflective practice.

O. Reg. 15/09, s. 3 [To come into force June 30, 2009.]

Ont. Reg. 309 — Supervisory Officers

made under the *Education Act*

R.R.O. 1990, Reg. 309, as am. O. Reg. 665/92; 162/93; 182/97; 189/04; 375/06 (Fr.); 46/08; 225/08.

Part I — Qualifications of Supervisory Officers

1. (1) In this Part,

"acceptable post-secondary degree" means a degree, including a baccalaureate degree in an applied area of study, for which a person is required to complete at least 90 post-secondary credits or their equivalent and that is,

(a) granted by a post-secondary educational institution authorized to grant the degree under an Act of the Assembly, including a person that is authorized to grant the degree under the *Post-secondary Education Choice and Excellence Act, 2000*,

(b) granted by a post-secondary educational institution in a Canadian province or territory other than Ontario and that is considered by the College to be equivalent to a degree described in clause (a),

(c) granted by a post-secondary educational institution in the United States that is recognized by,

(i) Middle States Association of Colleges and Schools,

(ii) New England Association of Schools and Colleges,

(iii) North Central Association of Colleges and Schools,

(iv) Northwest Commission on Colleges and Universities,

(v) Southern Association of Colleges and Schools, or

(vi) Western Association of Schools and Colleges,

and that is considered by the College to be equivalent to a degree described in clause (a), or

(d) granted by a post-secondary educational institution located in a country other than Canada and the United States and that is considered by the College to be equivalent to a degree described in clause (a);

"acceptable university degree" [Revoked O. Reg. 189/04, s. 1(2).]

"architect" means a person who is an architect within the meaning of the *Architects Act*;

"certified general accountant" means a member of the Certified General Accountants Association of Ontario;

"certified management accountant" means a registered or certified member of The Society of Management Accountants of Ontario;

"chartered accountant" means a member of The Institute of Chartered Accountants of Ontario;

"lawyer" means a person licensed under the *Law Society Act* to practise law in Ontario as a barrister and solicitor;

"post-secondary credit" means the credits a student is awarded on successful completion of a post-secondary course, where six credits are awarded for a one-year post-secondary course and a proportionate number of credits are awarded for a post-secondary course of a different duration;

"Principal's Certificate" means a permanent principal's certificate;

"professional engineer" means a person who is a professional engineer within the meaning of the *Professional Engineers Act*;

"professional planner" means a person who is a member of the Ontario Professional Planners Institute;

"program in school board management" means two compulsory graduate courses approved by the Minister that are offered by an institution that grants acceptable post-secondary degrees, one of which is a course in school board finance and the other in school board administration, and four optional graduate courses approved by the Minister that are offered by an institution that grants acceptable post-secondary degrees in education, public administration or political science;

"university" [Revoked O. Reg. 189/04, s. 1(4).]

(2) A person who holds or who under this Regulation is deemed to hold a Supervisory Officer's Certificate is, subject to subsection 6(1), qualified as a supervisory officer for the purposes of the Act and this Regulation.

(2.1) A person referred to in subsection 2.0.1(1) who is employed by a board is qualified as a supervisory officer for the purposes of the Act and this Regulation for the period during which the person is employed by the board in the position referred to in that subsection.

(3) A person referred to in subsection 3(4) who is employed by a board is qualified as a business supervisory officer for the purposes of the Act and this Regulation for the period during which the person is employed by the board in a position referred to in that subsection.

(4) For the purposes of this Regulation, a person shall be deemed to have completed a program in school board management if,

(a) the person holds a master's degree that is an acceptable post-secondary degree and has successfully completed a graduate course, either as part of or in addition to the courses necessary to obtain the degree, in each of school board finance and school board administration; or

(b) the person has other post-secondary education and experience that the Minister considers relevant to the role of a business supervisory officer and equivalent to the program in school board management.

(5) For the purposes of this Regulation, a person who is the holder of an acceptable post-secondary degree and who is a certified general accountant, a certified management accountant or a chartered accountant shall be deemed to be a person who has completed the four optional graduate courses as part of a program in school board management.

O. Reg. 665/92, s. 1; 189/04, s. 1; 46/08, s. 1; 225/08, s. 1

2. The Minister shall issue a Supervisory Officer's Certificate to a person if the person applies for it and the Ontario College of Teachers certifies that the person meets the qualifications of a Supervisory Officer.

O. Reg. 665/92, s. 2; 182/97, s. 1

2.0.1 (1) A board may appoint a person who does not hold or who under this Regulation is not deemed to hold a Supervisory Officer's Certificate to be a supervisory officer for a term of not more than two years, if the person meets the following qualifications:

1. The person holds a certificate of qualification or an interim certificate of qualification issued under the *Ontario College of Teachers Act, 1996*.

2. The person has at least five school years of successful classroom teaching experience in any jurisdiction in a school providing elementary or secondary education.

3. The person holds an acceptable post-secondary degree.

4. The person holds a master's degree that required the completion of at least 30 graduate post-secondary credits or their equivalent, as described in subsection (3), and the degree was granted by an institution identified in clause (a), (b), (c) or (d) of the definition of "acceptable post-secondary degree" in subsection 1(1).

5. The person meets one or more of the criteria listed in paragraph 6 of section 55 of Ontario Regulation 184/97 (*Teacher Qualifications*) made under the *Ontario College of Teachers Act, 1996*.

6. The person has stated, in a written agreement with the board, that he or she will do everything that is reasonably necessary to meet the qualifications listed in section 55 of Ontario Regulation 184/97 for obtaining an additional qualification as a supervisory officer before the end of his or her term.

(2) Despite subsection (1), a board may employ a person appointed under that subsection for an additional period of not more than two years if the person continues to make progress towards meeting the qualifications listed in section 55 of Ontario Regulation 184/97.

(3) To fulfil the requirement in paragraph 4 of subsection (1) relating to the completion of graduate post-secondary credits or their equivalent, the credits or their equivalent must have been completed by the applicant in addition to any credits that he or she was required to complete to be granted a certificate of qualification or interim certificate of qualification issued under the *Ontario College of Teachers Act, 1996*.

O. Reg. 225/08, s. 2

2.1 (1) On application, the Minister shall issue a Business Supervisory Officer's Certificate to a person who meets the following qualifications:

1. The person has at least seven years of successful experience in business administration, including at least three years in a managerial role relevant to the role of business supervisory officer.

2. The person holds an acceptable post-secondary degree.

3. The person,

   i. holds a master's degree that is an acceptable post-secondary degree, or

   ii. is qualified to practise as an architect, certified general accountant, certified management accountant, chartered accountant, lawyer, professional engineer or professional planner, or is qualified to practise in another professional capacity that, in the opinion of the Minister, provides experience appropriate for the position of business supervisory officer.

4. The person has successfully completed a program in school board management.

5. The person has successfully completed the business supervisory officer's qualifications program described in section 2.2 within five years after starting the program.

(2) A person shall be deemed to meet the qualifications set out in paragraphs 1 to 4 of subsection (1) if, not later than the 31st day of December, 1997, the person obtains the qualifications that were required of a candidate for a Business Supervisory Officer's Certificate under subsection 2(3) of this Regulation as it read immediately before the 6th day of November, 1992.

O. Reg. 665/92, s. 2; 189/04, s. 2; 46/08, s. 2

2.2 The business supervisory officer's qualifications program referred to in section 2.1 shall have the following features:

1. The program shall be provided by an organization or institution that has entered into a contract with the Minister to provide the instruction and arrange for the practical experience referred to in paragraphs 3 and 4.

2. No person shall be admitted to the program unless the person has submitted proof to the organization or institution that provides the program that the person meets the qualifications set out in paragraphs 1 to 4 of subsection 2.1(1).

3. The program shall consist of,

   i. four instructional modules, each consisting of at least fifty hours of instruction, and

   ii. one module consisting of at least fifty hours of practical experience in the workplace.

4. The instructional modules shall provide instruction that, in the opinion of the Minister, is relevant to the position of business supervisory officer in the following subject areas:

   i. Statutes, regulations and government policies affecting education in Ontario.

   ii. Curriculum guidelines and other reference material pertaining to elementary and secondary education in Ontario.

   iii. Theories and practices of supervision, administration and business organization.

O. Reg. 665/92, s. 2; 182/97, s. 2

3. (1) A supervisory officer responsible for the development, implementation, operation and supervision of educational programs in schools shall,

(a) hold a Supervisory Officer's Certificate;

(b) be a person who is deemed to hold a Supervisory Officer's Certificate under section 4; or

(c) be qualified as a supervisory officer under subsection 1(2.1).

(2) A senior business official who,

(a) reports to a director of education;

(b) reports to an assistant director of education or associate director of education; or

(c) is employed by a board that has an enrolment of more than 600 pupils and that does not employ a director of education,

shall, subject to subsections (4) and (5), be a person who holds, or who under this Regulation is deemed to hold, a Business Supervisory Officer's Certificate.

(3) A business official who,

(a) is assigned one or more of the duties of a supervisory officer;

(b) reports to a senior business official referred to in subsection (2); and

(c) has been appointed to a position designated by a board as superintendent, assistant superintendent, comptroller, assistant comptroller, business administrator or assistant business administrator or to a position that the board considers equivalent thereto and that has been approved by the Minister,

shall, subject to subsection (4), be a person who holds, or who under this Regulation is deemed to hold, a Business Supervisory Officer's Certificate.

(4) A board may appoint a person who does not hold or who under this Regulation is not deemed to hold a Business Supervisory Officer's Certificate as a senior business official referred to in subsection (2) or as a business official referred to in subsection (3) for a term of not more than two years if the person,

(a) holds an acceptable post-secondary degree or is qualified to practise as an architect, certified general accountant, certified management accountant, chartered accountant, lawyer, professional engineer or professional planner, or in another professional capacity that, in the opinion of the Minister, provides experience appropriate for the position of business supervisory officer; and

(b) has entered into an agreement in writing with the Board that sets out that the person will endeavour to obtain a Business Supervisory Officer's Certificate within the term of the appointment.

(5) Despite subsection (4), a board may employ a person appointed under that subsection for an additional period of not more than two years if the person continues to make progress towards obtaining a Business Supervisory Officer's Certificate.

(6) A person who was appointed under subsection (4) before the 6th day of November, 1992 may, by agreement with the board, amend the agreement under clause (4)(b) to be consistent with the new requirements of that clause.

O. Reg. 665/92, s. 3; 189/04, s. 3; 46/08, s. 3; 225/08, s. 3

4. A person who, prior to the 1st day of July 1974,

(a) held an Elementary School Inspector's Certificate, a Public School Inspector's Certificate, a Secondary School Principal's Certificate, or a Secondary School Principal's Certificate, Type A; or

(b) served as a provincial inspector of secondary schools or a municipal inspector of secondary schools,

is deemed to hold a Supervisory Officer's Certificate.

5. (1) A person who was in the employ of a board on the 31st day of August, 1975 in a position referred to in subsection 3(2) or (3) is deemed to hold a Supervisor Officer's Certificate.

(2) A person employed in the Ministry on the 31st day of August, 1975 in a position that the Minister considers similar to one of those referred to in subsection 3(2) or (3) is deemed to hold a Supervisory Officer's Certificate.

6. (1) A person who,

(a) holds a Supervisory Officer's Certificate and was not required, at the time the certificate was obtained, to have seven years of successful teaching experience;

(b) is deemed to hold a Supervisory Officer's Certificate under section 5; or

(c) holds a Business Supervisory Officer's Certificate,

is qualified as a supervisory officer under this Regulation for business administration purposes only.

(2) A supervisory officer other than a supervisory officer referred to in subsection (1) who, on the 30th day of September, 1986, was performing the duties,

(a) of a senior business official referred to in clause 3(2)(c) and who reports as referred to in clauses 3(2)(a) and (b); or

(b) of a business official referred to in clause 3(3)(c) who reports to a senior business official referred to in subsection 3(2),

is deemed to hold a Business Supervisory Officer's Certificate.

O. Reg. 665/92, s. 4

PART II — TRANSFER AND DISMISSAL

7. (1) In this section,

"redundant" in respect of the position of a supervisory officer means no longer required to be filled by reason of,

(a) the implementation by a board of a long range organizational plan of operation in respect of schools or of supervisory services that eliminates the position or merges it with another position,

(b) a reduction in the number of classes or in the business functions of the board for which supervision is required, or

(c) a change in duties or requirements placed upon boards by or under any Act that renders a supervisory service unnecessary or reduces the need for such service.

(2) Where a board declares the position of a supervisory officer redundant, the board shall,

(a) give the supervisory officer at least three months notice in writing that the position has been declared redundant;

(b) transfer the supervisory officer to a position for which he or she is qualified, with supervisory and administrative responsibilities as similar as possible to those of his or her previous position; and

(c) pay the supervisory officer for at least one year following the date of the transfer with no reduction in his or her rate of salary.

8. (1) A board shall not suspend or dismiss a supervisory officer without first giving the supervisory officer reasonable information about the reasons for the suspension or dismissal and an opportunity to make submissions to the board.

(2) A supervisory officer who wishes to make submissions to the board may make them orally or in writing.

O. Reg. 162/93, s. 1

9. [Revoked O. Reg. 162/93, s. 1.]

10. [Revoked O. Reg. 162/93, s. 1.]

11. [Revoked O. Reg. 162/93, s. 1.]

12. [Revoked O. Reg. 162/93, s. 1.]

13. [Revoked O. Reg. 162/93, s. 1.]

14. [Revoked O. Reg. 162/93, s. 1.]

15. [Revoked O. Reg. 162/93, s. 1.]

Ont. Reg. 463/97 — Electronic Meetings

made under the *Education Act*

O. Reg. 463/97, as am. O. Reg. 234/04; 268/06.

1. Subject to any conditions or limitations provided for under the Act or under this Regulation, a member of a board who participates in a meeting through electronic means in accordance with this Regulation shall be deemed to be present at the meeting for the purposes of every Act.

O. Reg. 234/04, s. 1

2. (1) Every board shall develop and implement a policy providing for the use of electronic means for the holding of meetings of a board and meetings of a committee of a board, including a committee of the whole board.

(2) The policy shall be in accordance with this Regulation and with any policies established and guidelines issued by the Minister under paragraph 3.6 of subsection 8(1) of the Act.

O. Reg. 234/04, s. 2

3. (1) The policy shall provide for the following:

1. At the request of any board member or student trustee, the board shall provide the member or student trustee with electronic means for participating in one or more meetings of the board or of a committee of the board, including a committee of the whole board.
2. The electronic means required by paragraph 1 shall permit the member or student trustee to hear and be heard by all other participants in the meeting.
3. The electronic means shall be provided in such a way that the rules governing conflict of interest of members are complied with.

(2) The policy shall ensure that student trustees who are participating through electronic means do not participate in any proceedings that are closed to the public under clause 207(2)(b) of the Act.

O. Reg. 268/06, s. 1

4. (1) Subsection (2) applies in respect of meetings of the board or of a committee of the board, including a committee of the whole board, that are open to the public.

(2) Every board shall determine, in accordance with any policies established and guidelines issued under paragraph 3.6 of subsection 8(1) of the Act, whether electronic means should be provided at one or more locations within the area of jurisdiction of the board, to permit participation by members of the public in meetings or classes of meetings.

(3) Where the board determines that electronic means should be provided under this section, the board's policy shall,

(a) provide for the extent and manner of participation by members of the public through electronic means; and

(b) ensure that members of the public who are participating through electronic means do not participate in any proceedings that are closed to the public in accordance with the Act.

5. (1) The policy shall require that, at every meeting of the board or of a committee of the whole board, the following persons be physically present in the meeting room of the board:

1. The chair of the board or his or her designate.
2. At least one additional member of the board.
3. The director of education of the board or his or her designate.

(2) The policy shall require that, at every meeting of a committee of the board, except a committee of the whole board, the following persons be physically present in the meeting room of the committee:

1. The chair of the committee or his or her designate.
2. The director of education of the board or his or her designate.

(3) Despite paragraph 1 of subsection 3(1), the policy shall include provisions permitting the board to refuse to provide a member with electronic means of participation in a meeting of the board, a meeting of a committee of the whole board or a meeting of any other committee of the board, where to do so is necessary to ensure compliance with this section.

6. (1) The meeting room of the board or of a committee of the board, as the case may be, shall be open to permit physical attendance by members of the public at every meeting of the board or of the committee of the board.

(2) For the purposes of subsection (1), the meeting room of a committee of the whole board is the meeting room of the board.

(3) Subsection (1) does not apply where a meeting is closed to the public in accordance with the Act.

ONT. REG. 90/98 — PRINCIPALS AND VICE-PRINCIPALS — REDUNDANCY AND REASSIGNMENT

made under the *Education Act*

O. Reg. 90/98, as am. O. Reg. 90/98, ss. 2(6), 5.

1. (1) This Regulation applies when a board declares the position of a principal or vice-principal to be redundant.

(2) This Regulation applies when any of the following positions is declared to be redundant:

1. Principal or vice-principal of continuing education courses and classes that are offered for credit during the day on instructional days.
2. Principal or vice-principal who administers the board's program of continuing education courses and classes that are offered for credit.

(3) This Regulation does not apply when the position of principal or vice-principal of continuing education courses and classes that is not described in subsection (2) is declared to be redundant.

(4) A position is redundant if the board decides that the position is no longer required because of,

(a) the implementation of a restructuring plan that eliminates the position or merges it with another position;

(b) a reduction in the number of classes or schools of the board; or

(c) a change in the board's duties under any Act.

2. (1) The board shall give the affected principal or vice-principal notice in writing that his or her position is declared to be redundant.

(2) The notice must be given at least 90 days before the date on which the position becomes redundant.

(3) The notice must specify the date on which the position becomes redundant.

(4) The board may rescind the notice at any time.

(5) [Revoked O. Reg. 90/98, s. 2(6).]

(6) Subsection (5) is revoked on September 1, 1998.

O. Reg. 90/98, s. 2(6)

3. (1) The board shall assign the principal or vice-principal to another position for which he or she is qualified.

(2) The principal or vice-principal may be assigned to a position in a teachers' bargaining unit if the position is vacant after the procedures under the applicable collective agreement for filling it have been exhausted.

(3) The assignment takes effect on the date on which the principal's or vice-principal's position becomes redundant, or on such other date as the board and the principal or vice-principal may agree upon.

4. (1) The following rule applies if the principal or vice-principal is assigned to a position other than one described in subsection (2):

1. For one year after he or she begins work in the new position, he or she is entitled to be paid the salary that he or she would have been paid as principal or vice-principal.

(2) Subsection (1) does not apply if the principal or vice-principal is assigned to a position in which he or she is employed, other than as a principal or vice-principal, to teach.

O. Reg. 90/98, s. 5

5. On August 31, 2001, section 4 is revoked and the following substituted:

> 4. (1) The following rule applies if the principal or vice-principal is assigned to a position other than one described in subsection (2):
>
> 1. For one year after he or she begins work in the new position, he or she is entitled to be paid the salary that he or she would have been paid as principal or vice-principal.
>
> (2) Subsection (1) does not apply if the principal or vice-principal is assigned to a position in which he or she is employed, other than as a principal or vice-principal, to teach.

6. This Regulation comes into force on April 1, 1998.

ONT. REG. 181/98 — IDENTIFICATION AND PLACEMENT OF EXCEPTIONAL PUPILS

made under the *Education Act*

O. Reg. 181/98, as am. O. Reg. 137/01; 402/05.

PART I — GENERAL

1. (1) In this Regulation,

"committee" means a special education identification, placement and review committee established under Part II and includes a committee established under Regulation 305 of the Revised Regulations of Ontario, 1990; *("comité")*

"designated representative" means,

(a) in relation to a board that has a director of education, the director of education of the board, and

(b) in relation to a board that does not have a director of education, the secretary or equivalent of the board;

("représentant désigné")

"parent" includes a guardian; *("père ou mère")*

"special education appeal board" means a special education appeal board established under Part VI. *("commission d'appel en matière d'éducation de l'enfance en difficulté")*

(2) In this Regulation, a reference to the category and definition of an exceptionality is a reference to the category and definition of the exceptionality as established under subsection 8(3) of the Act.

2. Where the time limited by this Regulation for doing anything expires or falls on a school holiday within the meaning of Regulation 304 of the Revised Regulations of Ontario, 1990, the time so limited extends to and the thing may be done on the next day following that is not a school holiday.

3. (1) Subject to subsection (2), mail shall be deemed to have been received by the person to whom it was sent on the fifth day after the day on which it was mailed.

(2) If the fifth day is a school holiday within the meaning of Regulation 304 of the Revised Regulations of Ontario, 1990, the mail shall be deemed to have been received by the person to whom it was sent on the first day after the fifth day that is not a school holiday.

4. A person or body required by this Regulation to communicate in writing to a parent or pupil shall, at the request of the parent or pupil, use a braille, large print or audio-cassette format for the communication.

5. (1) A parent of a pupil and, where the pupil is 16 years of age or older, the pupil, are entitled,

(a) to be present at and participate in all committee discussions about the pupil; and

(b) to be present when the committee's identification and placement decisions are made.

(2) A parent of a pupil and, where the pupil is 16 years of age or older, the pupil, are entitled to be present at and participate in all discussions about the pupil at the meeting held by the special education appeal board under section 28.

(3) A person who has a right under subsection (1) or (2) to participate in a discussion also has the right to have a representative present at the discussion, to speak on behalf of the person or otherwise support the person.

(4) A person who has a right under clause (1)(b) to be present also has the right to have a representative present to support the person.

(5) At least 10 days in advance of a meeting of a committee or special education appeal board, the chair of the committee or board shall give written notice of the time and place of the meeting to a parent of the pupil and, where the pupil is 16 years of age or older, the pupil.

6. (1) Subsection (2) applies when,

(a) a board implements a placement decision under section 20;

(b) a board implements a placement decision under section 31 following an appeal to a special education appeal board in respect of a committee decision under Part IV; or

(c) a board implements a placement decision following an appeal to the Special Education Tribunal in respect of a committee decision under Part IV.

(2) The board shall promptly notify the principal of the school at which the special education program is to be provided of the need to develop an individual education plan for the pupil in consultation with the parent and, where the pupil is 16 years of age or older, the pupil.

(3) The individual education plan must include,

(a) specific educational expectations for the pupil;

(b) an outline of the special education program and services to be received by the pupil; and

(c) a statement of the methods by which the pupil's progress will be reviewed.

(4) Where the pupil is 14 years of age or older, the individual education plan must also include a plan for transition to appropriate post-secondary school activities, such as work, further education and community living.

(5) Subsection (4) does not apply in respect of a pupil identified as exceptional solely on the basis of giftedness.

(6) In developing the individual education plan, the principal shall,

(a) consult with the parent and, where the pupil is 16 years of age or older, the pupil; and

(b) take into consideration any recommendations made by the committee or the Special Education Tribunal, as the case may be, regarding special education programs or special education services.

(7) In developing a transition plan under subsection (4), the principal shall consult with such community agencies and post-secondary educational institutions as he or she considers appropriate.

(8) Within 30 school days after placement of the pupil in the program, the principal shall ensure that the plan is completed and a copy of it sent to a parent of the pupil and, where the pupil is 16 years of age or older, the pupil.

O. Reg. 137/01, s. 1

7. (1) Subsection (2) applies when,

(a) a board implements a change in placement under section 25;

(b) a board implements a change in placement under section 31 following an appeal to a special education appeal board in respect of a committee decision under Part V;

(c) a board implements a change in placement in accordance with a decision of the Special Education Tribunal following an appeal to the Special Education Tribunal in respect of a committee decision under Part V;

(d) an existing placement is confirmed in a statement of decision under Part V and a parent of the pupil consents in writing to the decision or the time period provided in section 31 for filing a notice of appeal from the decision expires without a notice of appeal being filed;

(e) an existing placement is confirmed in a decision under subsection 30(1) and a parent consents in writing to the decision or the time period provided in section 31 expires without an appeal being commenced;

(f) an existing placement is confirmed in a decision under subsection 30(1), an appeal from the decision is made under section 57 of the Act to the Special Education Tribunal and the appeal is dismissed or abandoned; or

(g) an existing placement is confirmed in an order of the Special Education Tribunal granting an appeal under section 57 of the Act.

(2) The board shall promptly notify the principal of the school at which the special education program is to be provided of the need to review the pupil's individual education plan to determine whether it needs to be updated.

(3) In reviewing the plan, the principal shall,

(a) consult with the parent and, where the pupil is 16 years of age or older, the pupil; and

(b) take into consideration any recommendations of the committee or the Special Education Tribunal, as the case may be, regarding special education programs or special education services.

(4) Where an individual education plan does not include a plan for transition to appropriate post-secondary school activities and the pupil has attained the age of 14 or will attain the age of 14 within the school year, the principal shall ensure that a transition plan is developed and included in the individual education plan.

(5) Subsection (4) does not apply in respect of a pupil identified as exceptional solely on the basis of giftedness.

(6) In reviewing an individual education plan that includes a transition plan or in developing a transition plan under subsection (4), the principal shall consult with such community agencies and post-secondary educational institutions as he or she considers appropriate.

(7) Within 30 school days of an implementation of a change in placement or, where the placement is confirmed, within 30 schools days of receiving the notice under subsection (1), the principal shall ensure that,

(a) the plan has been reviewed and updated as appropriate;

(b) a transition plan has been added to the individual education plan where required by subsection (4); and

(c) a copy of the individual education plan has been sent to a parent of the pupil and, where the pupil is 16 years of age or older, the pupil.

O. Reg. 137/01, s. 2

8. The principal shall ensure that the individual education plan for a pupil is included in the record kept in respect of the pupil under clause 265(d) of the Act, unless a parent of the pupil has objected in writing.

9. (1) In accordance with requirements under the *Education Act*, no pupil is to be denied an education program pending a meeting or decision under this Regulation.

(2) Where an education program is provided to a pupil pending a meeting or decision under this Regulation,

(a) the program must be appropriate to the pupil's apparent strengths and needs;

(b) the placement for the program must be consistent with the principles underlying section 17; and

(c) appropriate education services must be provided to meet the pupil's apparent needs.

PART II — ESTABLISHMENT OF COMMITTEES AND COMMITTEE PROCEDURES

10. Each board shall, in accordance with section 11, establish one or more committees for the identification and placement of exceptional pupils, determine the jurisdiction of each committee and establish the manner of selecting the chair of each committee.

11. (1) A board shall appoint three or more persons to each committee that it establishes.

(2) The board shall appoint, as one of the members of each committee,

(a) a principal employed by the board;

(b) a supervisory officer employed by the board under Part XI of the Act; or

(c) a supervisory officer whose services are used by the board under Part XI of the Act.

(3) A principal or supervisory officer appointed under subsection (2) may designate a person to act in his or her place as a member of the committee without the approval of the board.

(4) Only a person who is eligible to be appointed to the committee under subsection (2) may be designated to act on the committee under subsection (3).

(5) No member of the board may be appointed to a committee under subsection (2) or designated to act on the committee under subsection (3).

12. (1) A board may establish procedures for committees in addition to those set out in this Regulation.

(2) Committee decisions made under this Regulation must be consistent with the board's special education lan.

Part III — Parents' Guide

13. (1) Each board shall prepare a guide for the use and information of parents and pupils that,

(a) explains the function of a committee on a referral under Part IV and on a review under Part V;

(b) outlines the procedures set out in this Regulation or established under section 12 that a committee must follow in identifying a pupil as exceptional and in deciding the pupil's placement;

(c) explains the committee's duty to describe pupils' strengths and needs and to include, in its statements of decision, the categories and definitions of any exceptionalities it identifies;

(d) explains the function of a special education appeal board under Part VI and the right of parents to appeal committee decisions to it;

(e) lists the parent organizations that are, to the best of the board's knowledge, local associations of the board, within the meaning of Ontario Regulation 464/97;

(f) includes the names, addresses and telephone numbers of the provincial and demonstration schools in Ontario;

(g) indicates the extent to which the board provides special education programs and special education services and the extent to which it purchases those programs and services from another board;

(h) explains that no committee placement decision can be implemented unless,

(i) a parent has consented to the decision, or

(ii) the time limit for filing a notice of appeal in respect of the decision has expired and no such notice has been filed.

(2) The board shall ensure that copies of the guide are available at each school in the board's jurisdiction and at the board's head office and shall provide a copy to the appropriate regional office of the Ministry.

(3) The board shall, at the request of a parent or pupil, provide the parent or pupil with a guide in a braille, large print or audio-cassette format.

O. Reg. 402/05, s. 1

Part IV — Referral of Pupils to Committees

14. (1) The principal of the school at which a pupil is enrolled,

(a) may on written notice to a parent of the pupil; and

(b) shall at the written request of a parent of the pupil,

refer the pupil to a committee established by the board, for a decision as to whether the pupil should be identified as an exceptional pupil and, if so, what the placement of the pupil should be.

(2) Where a decision is made that a pupil is to leave a demonstration school and enter a school of a board, the superintendent of the demonstration school shall so notify the designated representative of the board.

(3) On receiving the notice under subsection (2), the designated representative of the board shall ensure that the pupil is referred to a committee established by the board, for a decision as to what the placement of the pupil should be.

(4) The superintendent of the demonstration school acting under subsection (2) and the designated representative of the board acting under subsection (3) shall use their best efforts to ensure that the committee meets as soon as possible after the decision is made to move the pupil from the demonstration school to the school of the board.

(5) Where more than one committee has been established by the board, the referral under subsection (1) or (3) shall be to the committee that the principal or the designated representative, as the case may be, considers to be the most appropriate for the pupil, having regard to the jurisdiction of the committees.

(6) Within 15 days of giving a notice under clause (1)(a) or receiving a request under clause (1)(b), the principal shall provide the parent with,

(a) a copy of the guide prepared under section 13;

(b) a written statement of approximately when the principal expects that a committee will meet for the first time to discuss the pupil; and

(c) in the case of a request under clause (1)(b), a written acknowledgement of the request.

(7) Within 15 days of receiving a notification under subsection (2), the designated representative shall provide the parent with,

(a) a copy of the notification under subsection (2);

(b) a copy of the guide prepared under section 13; and

(c) a written statement of approximately when the designated representative expects that a committee will meet for the first time to discuss the pupil.

15. (1) A committee that has received a referral under section 14 shall obtain and consider an educational assessment of the pupil.

(2) Subject to the *Health Care Consent Act, 1996*, the committee shall also obtain and consider a health assessment of the pupil by a qualified medical practitioner if the committee determines that the assessment is required to enable it to make a correct identification or placement decision.

(3) Subject to the *Health Care Consent Act, 1996*, the committee shall also obtain and consider a psychological assessment of the pupil if the committee determines that the assessment is required to enable it to make a correct identification or placement decision.

(4) Where the committee determines that it would be useful to do so and the pupil is less than 16 years of age, the committee shall, with the consent of a parent, interview the pupil.

(5) A parent of the pupil has a right to be present at the interview.

(6) The committee shall also consider any information about the pupil submitted to it by a parent of the pupil and, where the pupil is 16 years of age or older, the pupil.

(7) In addition to complying with this section, the committee shall consider any information submitted to it that it considers relevant.

(8) As soon as possible after the chair of the committee obtains any information relating to the pupil, the chair shall provide the information to,

(a) a parent of the pupil; and

(b) the pupil, where the pupil is 16 years of age or older.

(9) Subsection (8) does not apply to oral information submitted at a meeting that the committee holds in respect of the pupil in accordance with this Regulation.

16. (1) The committee may discuss any proposal for special education services or special education programs and shall do so at the request of a parent or a pupil who is 16 years of age or older.

(2) The committee may make recommendations regarding special education programs and special education services.

(3) The committee may recommend that an exceptional pupil who is 21 years of age or older remain in a secondary day school program.

(4) Despite subsections (1) to (3), the committee shall not make decisions about special education services or special education programs.

(5) Despite subsection (4), a recommendation of a committee under subsection (3) is effective for the purposes of subsection 49.2(7) of the Act.

(6) A recommendation under this section is not a decision for the purposes of subsection 26(1).

17. (1) When making a placement decision on a referral under section 14, the committee shall, before considering the option of placement in a special education class, consider whether placement in a regular class, with appropriate special education services,

(a) would meet the pupil's needs; and

(b) is consistent with parental preferences.

(2) If, after considering all of the information obtained by it or submitted to it under section 15 that it considers relevant, the committee is satisfied that placement in a regular class would meet the pupil's needs and is consistent with parental preferences, the committee shall decide in favour of placement in a regular class.

18. (1) As soon as possible after making its decisions on a referral under section 14, the chair of the committee shall send a written statement of decision to,

(a) a parent of the pupil;

(b) the pupil, where the pupil is 16 years of age or older;

(c) the principal who made the referral, where the referral was made by a principal; and

(d) the designated representative of the board that established the committee.

(2) In the case of a referral by a principal under subsection 14(1), the statement of decision shall,

(a) state whether the committee has identified the pupil as an exceptional pupil;

(b) where the committee has identified the pupil as an exceptional pupil, include,

(i) the committee's description of the pupil's strengths and needs,

(ii) the categories and definitions of any exceptionalities identified by the committee,

(iii) the committee's placement decision, and

(iv) the committee's recommendation under subsection 16(2), if any; and

(c) where the committee has decided that the pupil should be placed in a special education class, state the reasons for that decision.

(3) In the case of a referral by a designated representative under subsection 14(3), the statement of decision shall,

(a) include,

(i) the committee's description of the pupil's strengths and needs,

(ii) the categories and definitions of any exceptionalities identified by the committee,

(iii) the committee's placement decision, and

(iv) the committee's recommendation under subsection 16(2), if any; and

(b) where the committee has decided that the pupil should be placed in a special education class, state the reasons for that decision.

19. (1) A parent who receives a statement of decision under section 18 may, by written notice delivered to the person specified in subsection (2) within 15 days of receipt of the statement of decision, request a meeting with the committee.

(2) The notice under subsection (1) shall be delivered to the principal in the case of a referral under subsection 14(1) and to the designated representative in the case of a referral under subsection 14(3).

(3) On receiving the request, the principal or designated representative, as the case may be, shall arrange for the committee to meet as soon as possible with the parent and, where the pupil is 16 years of age or older and wishes to attend, the pupil, to discuss the statement of decision.

(4) As soon as possible following a meeting under this section, the chair of the committee shall send a written notice to each of the persons described in subsection 18(1), stating whether any changes in its decisions were made as a result of the meeting.

(5) If changes in the committee's decisions were made as a result of the meeting, the notice under subsection (4) shall be accompanied by a revised statement of decision, together with written reasons for the changes.

20. (1) A board shall implement a placement decision made by a committee under this Part when one of the following two events occurs:

1. A parent of the pupil consents in writing to the placement.

2. The time period provided in subsection 26(2) for filing a notice of appeal from the decision expires without a notice of appeal being filed.

(2) The board shall implement a placement decision made by a committee under this Part as soon as possible after an event described in paragraph 1 or 2 of subsection (1) occurs.

(3) A board that, without the written consent of a parent of the pupil, implements a placement decision made by a committee under this Part shall give written notice of the implementation to a parent of the pupil.

PART V — COMMITTEE REVIEWS

21. (1) The principal of the school at which a pupil's special education program is being provided,

(a) may on written notice to a parent of the pupil;

(b) shall at the written request of a parent of the pupil; and

(c) shall, at the written request of the designated representative of the board that is providing the special education program to the pupil,

refer the pupil to a committee established by the board that is providing the special education program to the pupil, for a review of the identification or placement of the pupil.

(2) A request by a parent under clause (1)(b) may be made at any time after a placement has been in effect for three months but may not be made more often than once in every three month period.

(3) Subject to subsection (4), the designated representative shall make a request under clause (1)(c) when in his or her opinion it is necessary to do so in order to ensure that a review in respect of the pupil is held under this Part at least once in each school year.

(4) Subsection (3) does not apply where,

(a) a committee proceeding with respect to the pupil was held under Part IV during the school year; or

(b) a parent of the pupil gives a written notice dispensing with the annual review to the principal of the school at which the special education program is being provided.

(5) Within 15 days of giving a notice under clause (1)(a) or receiving a request under clause (1)(b) or (c), the principal shall provide the parent with a written statement of the approximate time when the review meeting will take place.

22. (1) Where more than one committee has been established by a board, the principal of the school at which the special education program is provided shall determine which of the committees is most appropriate for the pupil, having regard to the jurisdiction of the committees.

(2) Where one board purchases a special education program from another board, the board that is providing the special education program to the pupil shall invite the purchasing board to select a representative who may,

(a) be present at and participate in all committee discussions about the pupil; and

(b) be present when the committee's identification and placement decisions are made.

23. (1) Sections 15 and 16 apply with necessary modifications to a committee engaged in a review under this Part.

(2) With the written permission of a parent of the pupil, a committee conducting a review under this Part shall consider the pupil's progress with reference to the pupil's individual education plan.

(3) As soon as possible after a committee engaged in a review under this Part decides that it is satisfied with the identification and placement of a pupil, the chair of the committee shall send a written statement of decision confirming the identification and placement to,

(a) a parent of the pupil;

(b) the pupil, where the pupil is 16 years of age or older;

(c) the principal of the school at which the pupil's special education program is being provided;

(d) the designated representative of the board that is providing the special education program to the pupil; and

(e) in the circumstances described in subsection 22(2), the designated representative of the board that is purchasing the special education program.

(4) As soon as possible after a committee engaged in a review under this Part decides that the identification or placement or both should be changed, the chair of the committee shall send a written statement of decision to the persons described in subsection (3).

(5) A statement of decision under subsection (4) shall state,

(a) the reasons for the committee's decision that the pupil's identification or placement or both should be changed;

(b) whether the committee considers that the pupil should continue to be identified as an exceptional pupil;

(c) where the committee considers that the pupil should continue to be identified as an exceptional pupil,

(i) the committee's placement decision,

(ii) the committee's description of the pupil's strengths and needs, and

(iii) the categories and definitions of any exceptionalities identified by the committee; and

(d) where the committee considers that the pupil should be placed in a special education class, the reasons for that decision.

(6) Section 17 applies with necessary modifications where a committee is considering the option of placing a pupil in a special education class and the pupil is not already in such a placement.

24. (1) A parent who receives a confirmation under subsection 23(3) or a statement of decision under subsection 23(4) may request a meeting with the committee by written notice, delivered within 15 days of receiving the confirmation or statement of decision, to the principal of the school at which the pupil's special education program is being provided.

(2) On receiving the request for a meeting, the principal shall arrange for the committee to meet as soon as possible with the parent and, where the pupil is 16 years of age or older and wishes to attend, the pupil, to discuss the statement of decision.

(3) As soon as possible following a meeting under this section, the chair of the committee shall send a written notice to each of the persons described in subsection 23(3), stating whether any changes in its decisions were made as a result of the meeting.

(4) If changes in the committee's decisions were made as a result of the meeting, the notice under subsection (3) shall be accompanied by a revised statement of decision, together with written reasons for the changes.

25. (1) A board shall implement a change in placement as a result of a decision made by a committee under this Part when one of the following two events occurs:

1. A parent of the pupil consents in writing to the placement.

2. The time period provided in subsection 26(3) for filing a notice of appeal from the decision expires without a notice of appeal being filed.

(2) The board shall implement a change in placement as a result of a decision made by a committee under this Part as soon as possible after an event described in paragraph 1 or 2 of subsection (1) occurs.

(3) A board that, without the written consent of a parent of the pupil, implements a change in placement as a result of a decision made by a committee under this Part shall give written notice of the implementation to a parent of the pupil.

PART VI — APPEALS FROM COMMITTEE DECISIONS

26. (1) A parent of a pupil may, by filing a notice of appeal in accordance with subsection (2) or (3), require a hearing by a special education appeal board in respect of,

(a) a committee decision under Part IV or V that the pupil is an exceptional pupil;

(b) a committee decision under Part IV or V that the pupil is not an exceptional pupil; or

(c) a committee decision under Part IV or V on placement of the pupil.

(2) A notice of appeal in respect of a committee decision under Part IV shall be filed with the secretary of the board,

(a) if no meeting is held under section 19, within 30 days of receipt of the statement of decision under section 18 by the parent who is seeking to appeal; or

(b) if a meeting is held under section 19, within 15 days of receipt of the notice under subsection 19(4) by the parent who is seeking to appeal.

(3) A notice of appeal in respect of a committee decision under Part V shall be filed with the secretary of the board,

(a) if no meeting is held under section 24, within 30 days of receipt of the confirmation under subsection 23(3) or the statement of decision under subsection 23(4) by the parent who is seeking to appeal; or

(b) if a meeting is held under section 24, within 15 days of receipt of the notice under subsection 24(3) by the parent who is seeking to appeal.

(4) A notice of appeal shall indicate which of the decisions referred to in subsection (1) the parent disagrees with and shall include a statement that sets out the nature of the disagreement.

(5) The special education appeal board shall not reject or refuse to deal with an appeal by reason of any actual or alleged deficiency in the statement referred to in subsection (4) or by reason of the failure of the parent, in the opinion of the special education appeal board, to accurately indicate in the notice of appeal the subject of the disagreement.

27. (1) The special education appeal board shall be composed of,

(a) one member selected by the board in which the pupil is placed;

(b) one member selected by a parent of the pupil; and

(c) a chair, selected jointly by the members selected under clauses (a) and (b) or, where those members cannot agree, by the appropriate regional manager of the Ministry.

(2) Selections under clauses (1)(a) and (b) shall be made within 15 days of receipt of the notice of appeal by the secretary of the board.

(3) The selection of a chair under clause (1)(c) shall be made within 15 days of the last selection under clauses (1)(a) and (b).

(4) No member or employee of the board providing or purchasing the special education program and no employee of the Ministry may be selected under subsection (1).

(5) No person who has had any prior involvement with the matter under appeal may be selected under subsection (1).

(6) The chair of the committee the decision of which is being appealed shall provide the special education appeal board with the record of the committee proceeding, including the statement of decision and any reports, assessments or other documents considered by the committee.

(7) The board shall provide the special education appeal board with the secretarial and administrative services it requires and shall, in accordance with the rules and policies that apply to members of the board under section 191.2 of the Act, pay the travelling and other expenses incurred by the members of the special education appeal board while engaged in their duties.

O. Reg. 402/05, s. 2

28. (1) The chair of the special education appeal board shall arrange for a meeting of the members of the special education appeal board to discuss the matters under appeal and shall give notice of the meeting, in accordance with subsection 5(5), to a parent of the pupil and, where the pupil is 16 years of age or older, the pupil.

(2) The meeting shall be arranged to take place at a convenient place and at a time that is no more than 30 days after the day on which the chair is selected and shall be conducted in an informal manner.

(3) Despite subsection (2), with the written consent of the parents of the pupil and the designated representative of the board, the meeting may be scheduled for a time that is more than 30 days after the day on which the chair is selected.

(4) Any person who in the opinion of the chair of the special education appeal board may be able to contribute information with respect to the matters under appeal shall be invited to attend the meeting.

(5) Where the pupil's special education program is being purchased by one board from another board, the chair shall invite the purchasing board to select a representative who may be present at and participate in all discussions about the pupil at the meeting held by the special education appeal board under section 28.

(6) Where the special education appeal board is satisfied that the opinions, views and information that bear on the appeal have been sufficiently presented to it, the special education appeal board shall end the meeting and, within three days of ending the meeting, shall,

(a) agree with the committee and recommend that its decisions be implemented; or

(b) disagree with the committee and make a recommendation to the board about the pupil's identification, placement or both.

29. (1) The special education appeal board shall send a written statement of its recommendations under section 28 to,

(a) a parent of the pupil;

(b) where the pupil is 16 years of age or older, the pupil;

(c) the chair of the committee;

(d) the principal of the school in which the pupil is placed;

(e) the designated representative of the board in which the pupil is placed; and

(f) in the circumstances described in subsection 28(5), the designated representative of the board that is purchasing the special education program.

(2) The written statement shall be accompanied by written reasons for the recommendations.

30. (1) Within 30 days of receiving the special education appeal board's written statement, the board shall consider the special education appeal board's recommendations, shall decide what action to take with respect to the pupil and shall give notice in writing of the decision to each of the persons described in subsection 29(1).

(2) In deciding what action to take with respect to a pupil, the board is not limited to the actions that the special education appeal board recommended or could have recommended.

(3) Notice to a parent under subsection (1) shall include an explanation of the further right of appeal provided by section 57 of the Act.

31. (1) The board shall implement a decision under subsection 30(1) when one of the following events occurs:

1. A parent of the pupil consents in writing to the decision.
2. Thirty days have elapsed from receipt of the notice under subsection 30(1) by a parent of the pupil and no appeal has been commenced in respect of the decision under section 57 of the Act.
3. An appeal under section 57 of the Act from the decision is dismissed or abandoned.

(2) In accordance with an agreement between the board and a parent of the pupil, the board may change a decision made by it under section 30,

(a) while an appeal under section 57 of the Act is pending; or

(b) before the end of the period referred to in paragraph 2 of subsection (1).

(3) Where the board changes a decision under subsection (2), the board shall give notice in writing of the change in decision to each of the persons described in subsection 29(1).

(4) Subsections 30(2) and (3) apply with necessary modifications in respect of a change in decision under subsection (2).

PART VII — TRANSITIONAL PROVISIONS

Interpretation

32. In this Part,

"old regulation" means Regulation 305 of the Revised Regulations of Ontario, 1990.

Committees Established Before September 1, 1998

33. (1) Where a matter was referred to a committee under section 2 of the old Regulation, the matter shall be dealt with on and after September 1, 1998 as if it had been referred to a committee under Part IV of this Regulation and, for the purpose, the provisions of this Regulation apply to the committee proceeding and to all related proceedings, including appeals, with appropriate modifications.

(2) Where a matter was referred to a committee under section 8 of the old Regulation, the matter shall be dealt with on and after September 1, 1998 as if it had been referred to a committee under Part V of this Regulation and, for the purpose, the provisions of this Regulation apply to the committee proceeding and to all related proceedings, including appeals, with appropriate modifications.

(3) The modifications required by subsections (1) and (2) are such modifications as the person or body exercising a power or meeting a requirement under this Regulation considers appropriate having regard to the stage to which the matter has proceeded.

Parents' Guide

34. Until December 31, 1998, a board may meet the requirements of subsection 13(2) and clauses 14(6)(a) and 14(7)(b) using copies of a guide prepared under section 2 of the old regulation.

Individual Education Plans

35. Subsections 7(2) to (7) apply with necessary modifications if, as a result of a decision of a committee, a special education appeal board or the Special Education Tribunal,

(a) an existing placement of an exceptional pupil who does not yet have an individual education plan is confirmed; or

(b) a board implements a change in placement of an exceptional pupil who does not yet have an individual education plan.

Appeals Filed Before September 1, 1998

36. (1) This section applies if a notice of appeal is given under section 4 of the old regulation before September 1, 1998 but the appeal is not finally determined before that date.

(2) If three people are appointed before September 1, 1998 under section 7 of the old regulation to form an appeal board to hear the appeal, the appeal shall be held in accordance with the old regulation as it read immediately before it was revoked.

(3) If three people are not appointed before September 1, 1998 under section 7 of the old regulation to form an appeal board to hear the appeal, the appeal shall be held in accordance with this Regulation.

(4) For the purposes of subsection (3),

(a) the notice given under section 4 of the old regulation shall be deemed to be a notice properly given under section 26 of this Regulation; and

(b) selections under clauses 27(1)(a) and (b) shall be made on or before September 15, 1998 rather than within the times specified in subsections 27(2) and (3).

37. (1) This section applies where an appeal is held in accordance with the old regulation as a result of the application of subsection 36(2) of this Regulation.

(2) If the board receives the report of the appeal decision under subsection 7(10) of the old regulation before September 1, 1998, subsection 7(11) of the old regulation applies as it read immediately before it was revoked.

(3) If the board does not receive the report of the appeal decision under subsection 7(10) of the old regulation before September 1, 1998, sections 30 and 31 of this Regulation apply as if the report of the appeal decision given under subsection 7(10) of the old regulation were a statement given under section 29 of this Regulation.

ONT. REG. 435/00 — OPENING OR CLOSING EXERCISES

made under the *Education Act*

O. Reg. 435/00

APPLICATION

1. The requirements set out in this Regulation apply with respect to the opening and closing exercises referred to in section 304 of the Act.

PLEDGE OF CITIZENSHIP

2. (1) The principal may decide whether the opening or closing exercises at a school will include the recitation of the pledge of citizenship.

(2) The principal's decision about reciting the pledge of citizenship must be consistent with the policies and guidelines, if any, established by the board.

(3) Before making his or her decision about reciting the pledge of citizenship, the principal shall consult the school council.

(4) The principal shall review his or her decision about reciting the pledge of citizenship at the beginning of each school year and must consult with the school council.

3. The following is the pledge of citizenship:

> I affirm that I will be faithful and bear true allegiance to Her Majesty Queen Elizabeth the Second, Queen of Canada, and to her heirs and successors, and that I will faithfully observe the laws of Canada and fulfill my duties as a Canadian citizen.

EXEMPTIONS

4. A pupil is not required to sing *O Canada* or recite the pledge of citizenship in the following circumstances:

1. In the case of a pupil who is less than 18 years old, if the pupil's parent or guardian applies to the principal to be exempted from doing so.
2. In the case of a pupil who is at least 18 years old, if the pupil applies to the principal to be exempted from doing so.

ONT. REG. 612/00 — SCHOOL COUNCILS

made under the *Education Act*

O. Reg. 612/00

INTERPRETATION

1. (1) In this Regulation,

"meeting" does not include a training session or other event where a school council does not discuss or decide matters that it has authority to decide; *("réunion")*

"parent" includes a guardian as defined in section 1 of the Act; *("père ou mère")*

"parent member" means a member of a school council who is elected to the council in accordance with section 4 or who fills a vacancy created when a parent member ceases to hold office. *("père ou mère membre")*

(2) In the case of a school that is established primarily for adults, a reference in this Regulation to a parent or to a parent of a pupil shall be deemed, with necessary modifications, to be a reference to a pupil who is enrolled in the school.

PURPOSE

2. (1) The purpose of school councils is, through the active participation of parents, to improve pupil achievement and to enhance the accountability of the education system to parents.

(2) A school council's primary means of achieving its purpose is by making recommendations in accordance with this Regulation to the principal of the school and the board that established the council.

COMPOSITION

3. (1) A school council for a school shall be composed of the following people:

1. The number of parent members determined under subsection (2).

2. The principal of the school.

3. One teacher who is employed at the school, other than the principal or vice-principal, elected in accordance with section 5.

4. One person who is employed at the school, other than the principal, vice-principal or any other teacher, elected in accordance with section 5.

5. In the case of a school with one or more secondary school grades,

   i. one pupil enrolled in the school who is appointed by the student council, if the school has a student council, or

   ii. one pupil enrolled in the school who is elected in accordance with section 5, if the school does not have a student council.

6. In the case of a school with no secondary school grades, one pupil enrolled in the school who is appointed by the principal of the school, if the principal determines, after consulting the other members of the school council, that the council should include a pupil.

7. Subject to subsection (3), one community representative appointed by the other members of the council.

8. One person appointed by an association that is a member of the Ontario Federation of Home and School Associations, the Ontario Association of Parents in Catholic Education or Parent Partenaires en Education, if the association that is a member of the Ontario Federation of Home and School Associations, the Ontario Association of Parents in Catholic Education or Parent Partenaires en Education is established in respect of the school.

(2) For the purposes of paragraph 1 of subsection (1), the number of parent members shall be determined as follows:

1. If the school council has a by-law that specifies the number of parent members, the number specified in the by-law.

2. If the school council does not have a by-law that specifies the number of parent members, the number specified by the board that established the council.

(3) A school council may specify by by-law that the council shall include two or more community representatives, appointed by the other members of the council.

(4) In specifying numbers under subsections (2) and (3), the board or the school council, as the case may be, shall ensure that parent members constitute a majority of the members of the school council.

(5) A person who is employed by the board that established a school council cannot be appointed as a community representative on the council unless,

(a) he or she is not employed at the school; and

(b) the other members of the school council are informed of the person's employment before the appointment.

(6) A member of a board cannot be a member of a school council established by the board.

(7) Paragraphs 5 and 6 of subsection (1) do not apply in respect of a school that is established primarily for adults.

ELECTION OF PARENT MEMBERS

4. (1) A person is qualified to be a parent member of a school council if he or she is a parent of a pupil who is enrolled in the school.

(2) Despite subsection (1), a person is not qualified to be a parent member of a school council if,

(a) he or she is employed at the school; or

(b) he or she is not employed at the school but is employed elsewhere by the board that established the council, unless he or she takes reasonable steps to inform people qualified to vote in the election of parent members of that employment.

(3) A person is qualified to vote in an election of parent members of a school council if he or she is a parent of a pupil who is enrolled in the school.

(4) An election of parent members of a school council shall be held during the first 30 days of each school year, on a date that is fixed by the chair or co-chairs of the school council after consulting with the principal of the school.

(5) Despite subsection (4), if a new school is established, the first election of parent members to the school council shall be held during the first 30 days of the school year, on a date that is fixed by the board that established the school council.

(6) The principal of a school shall, at least 14 days before the date of the election of parent members, on behalf of the school council, give written notice of the date, time and location of the election to every parent of a pupil who, on the date the notice is given, is enrolled in the school.

(7) The notice required by subsection (6) may be given by,

(a) giving the notice to the parent's child for delivery to his or her parent; and

(b) posting the notice in the school in a location that is accessible to parents.

(8) The election of parent members shall be by secret ballot.

Other Elections

5. (1) The elections of members of school councils referred to in paragraph 3, paragraph 4 and subparagraph 5 ii of subsection 3(1) shall be held during the first 30 days of each school year.

(2) A person is qualified to vote in an election of a member of a school council referred to in paragraph 3 of subsection 3(1) if he or she is a teacher, other than the principal or vice-principal, who is employed at the school.

(3) A person is qualified to vote in an election of a member of a school council referred to in paragraph 4 of subsection 3(1) if he or she is a person, other than the principal, vice-principal or any other teacher, who is employed at the school.

(4) A person is qualified to vote in an election of a member of a school council referred to in subparagraph 5 ii of subsection 3(1) if he or she is a pupil enrolled in the school.

Term of Office

6. (1) A person elected or appointed as a member of a school council holds office from the later of,

(a) the date he or she is elected or appointed; and

(b) the date of the first meeting of the school council after the elections held under sections 4 and 5 in the school year,

until the date of the first meeting of the school council after the elections held under sections 4 and 5 in the next school year.

(2) A member of a school council may be re-elected or reappointed, unless otherwise provided by the by-laws of the council.

Vacancies

7. (1) A vacancy in the membership of a school council shall be filled by election or appointment in accordance with the by-laws of the council.

(2) If an election is held to fill a vacancy in the membership of a school council, section 4 or 5, as the case may be, applies, with necessary modifications, to the election.

(3) A vacancy in the membership of a school council does not prevent the council from exercising its authority.

Officers

8. (1) A school council shall have a chair or, if the by-laws of the council so provide, two co-chairs.

(2) A chair or co-chair of a school council must be a parent member of the council, and shall be elected by the members of the council.

(3) A person who is employed by the board that established the council cannot be the chair or co-chair of the council.

(4) A school council may have such other officers as are provided for in the by-laws of the council.

(5) Subject to subsections (2) and (3), vacancies in the office of chair, co-chair or any other officer of a school council shall be filled in accordance with the by-laws of the council.

Collection of Information

9. (1) The Ministry may, for the purpose of consulting and communicating directly with members of school councils, collect the names, mailing addresses, telephone numbers and e-mail addresses of the chair or co-chairs of a school council and of the other members of the council.

(2) The Ministry may disclose information collected under subsection (1) to the Ontario Parent Council, which may use the information for the purpose of consulting and communicating directly with members of school councils.

Ministry Powers and Duties

10. (1) As part of its accountability to parents, the Ministry shall report annually to members of school councils on education in the province.

(2) The Ministry may,

(a) make other reports to members of school councils; and

(b) provide information to members of school councils respecting the roles and responsibilities of school councils.

Remuneration

11. (1) A person shall not receive any remuneration for serving as a member or officer of a school council.

(2) Every board shall establish policies respecting the reimbursement of members and officers of school councils established by the board.

(3) The board that established a school council shall reimburse members and officers of the council, in accordance with the policies referred to in subsection (2), for expenses they incur as members or officers of the council.

MEETINGS

12. (1) A school council shall meet at least four times during the school year.

(2) A school council shall meet within the first 35 days of the school year, after the elections held under sections 4 and 5, on a date fixed by the principal of the school.

(3) A meeting of a school council cannot be held unless,

(a) a majority of the current members of the council are present at the meeting; and

(b) a majority of the members of the council who are present at the meeting are parent members.

(4) All meetings of a school council shall be open to the public.

(5) A school council is entitled to hold its meetings at the school.

(6) All meetings of a school council shall be held at a location that is accessible to the public.

(7) The principal of a school shall, on behalf of the school council, give written notice of the dates, times and locations of the meetings of the council to every parent of a pupil who, on the date the notice is given, is enrolled in the school.

(8) The notice required by subsection (7) may be given by,

(a) giving the notice to the parent's child for delivery to his or her parent; and

(b) posting the notice in the school in a location that is accessible to parents.

COMMITTEES

13. (1) A school council may, in accordance with its by-laws, establish committees to make recommendations to the council.

(2) Every committee of a school council must include at least one parent member of the council.

(3) A committee of a school council may include persons who are not members of the council.

(4) Subsections 12(4) to (8) apply, with necessary modifications, to committees of school councils.

VOTING

14. (1) Subject to subsection (3), each member of a school council is entitled to one vote in votes taken by the council.

(2) Subject to subsection (3), each member of a committee of a school council is entitled to one vote in votes taken by the committee.

(3) The principal of the school is not entitled to vote in votes taken by the school council or by a committee of the school council.

By-Laws

15. (1) A school council may make by-laws governing the conduct of its affairs.

(2) Every school council shall make the following by-laws:

1. A by-law that governs election procedures and the filling of vacancies in the membership of the school council.

2. A by-law that establishes rules respecting participation in school council proceedings in cases of conflict of interest.

3. A by-law that, in accordance with any applicable policies established by the board that established the council, establishes a conflict resolution process for internal school council disputes.

Minutes and Financial Records

16. (1) A school council shall keep minutes of all of its meetings and records of all of its financial transactions.

(2) The minutes and records shall be available at the school for examination without charge by any person.

(3) Subsections (1) and (2) do not apply to minutes and records that are more than four years old.

Incorporation

17. A school council shall not be incorporated.

Principal

18. (1) The principal of a school may delegate any of his or her powers or duties as a member of the school council, including any powers or duties under this Regulation, to a vice-principal of the school.

(2) In addition to his or her duties under this Regulation, the principal of a school shall perform the duties relating to school councils that are imposed on the principal by *Regulation 298* of the *Revised Regulations of Ontario, 1990* (Operation of Schools — General).

Consultation by Board

19. (1) In addition to its other obligations to solicit the views of school councils under the Act, every board shall solicit the views of the school councils established by the board with respect to the following matters:

1. The establishment or amendment of board policies and guidelines that relate to pupil achievement or to the accountability of the education system to parents, including,

    i. policies and guidelines established under subsection 302(1) of the Act with respect to the conduct of persons in schools within the board's jurisdiction,

    ii. policies and guidelines established under subsection 302(5) of the Act respecting appropriate dress for pupils in schools within the board's jurisdiction,

iii. policies and guidelines respecting the allocation of funding by the board to school councils,

iv. policies and guidelines respecting the fundraising activities of school councils,

v. policies and guidelines respecting conflict resolution processes for internal school council disputes, and

vi. policies and guidelines respecting reimbursement by the board of expenses incurred by members and officers of school councils.

2. The development of implementation plans for new education initiatives that relate to pupil achievement or to the accountability of the education system to parents, including,

i. implementation plans for policies and guidelines established under subsection 302(1) of the Act with respect to the conduct of persons in schools within the board's jurisdiction, and

ii. implementation plans for policies and guidelines established under subsection 302(5) of the Act respecting appropriate dress for pupils in schools within the board's jurisdiction.

3. Board action plans for improvement, based on the Education Quality and Accountability Office's reports on the results of tests of pupils, and the communication of those plans to the public.

4. The process and criteria applicable to the selection and placement of principals and vice-principals.

(2) Subsection (1) does not limit the matters on which a board may solicit the views of school councils.

Advisory Authority of School Councils

20. A school council may make recommendations to the principal of the school or to the board that established the council on any matter.

Duty of Board to Respond

21. The board that established a school council shall consider each recommendation made to the board by the council and shall advise the council of the action taken in response to the recommendation.

Fundraising

22. (1) Subject to subsection (2), a school council may engage in fundraising activities.

(2) A school council shall not engage in fundraising activities unless,

(a) the activities are conducted in accordance with any applicable policies established by the board; and

(b) the activities are to raise funds for a purpose approved by the board or authorized by any applicable polices established by the board.

(3) A school council shall ensure that the funds raised by it are used in accordance with any applicable policies established by the board.

Consultation with Parents

23. A school council shall consult with parents of pupils enrolled in the school about matters under consideration by the council.

Annual Report

24. (1) Every school council shall annually submit a written report on its activities to the principal of the school and to the board that established the council.

(2) If the school council engages in fundraising activities, the annual report shall include a report on those activities.

(3) The principal shall, on behalf of the school council, give a copy of the report to every parent of a pupil who, on the date the copy is given, is enrolled in the school.

(4) Subsection (3) may be complied with by,

(a) giving the report to the parent's child for delivery to his or her parent; and

(b) posting the report in the school in a location that is accessible to parents.

Transition

25. Every school council established by a board before this Regulation comes into force is continued.

26. (1) Sections 3, 4 and 5 do not apply until September 1, 2001.

(2) Until the date of the first meeting of a school council after the first election held under section 4 after September 1, 2001, the references in subsection 8(2), clause 12(3)(b) and subsection 13(2) to a parent member shall be deemed to be references to a member of the school council who is a parent of a pupil enrolled in the school.

ONT. REG. 521/01 — COLLECTION OF PERSONAL INFORMATION

made under the *Education Act*

O. Reg. 521/01, as am. O. Reg. 170/02; 49/03; 322/03.

1. (1) Definitions — In this Regulation,

"criminal background check" means, in respect of a board, a document concerning an individual,

(a) that was prepared by a police force or service from national data on the Canadian Police Information Centre database within six months before the day the board collects the document, and

(b) that contains information concerning the individual's personal criminal history;

("relevé des antécédents criminels")

"offence declaration" means, in respect of a board, a written declaration signed by an individual, listing all of the individual's convictions for offences under the *Criminal Code* (Canada) up to the date of the declaration,

(a) that are not included in a criminal background check collected by the Ontario College of Teachers after December 31, 1998 or in the last criminal background check collected by the board under this Regulation, and

(b) for which a pardon under section 4.1 of the *Criminal Records Act* (Canada) has not been issued or granted;

("déclaration d'infraction")

"personal criminal history" means, in respect of an individual, information on criminal offences of which the individual has been convicted under the *Criminal Code* (Canada) and for which a pardon under section 4.1 of the *Criminal Records Act* (Canada) has not been issued or granted to the individual; *("antécédents criminels")*

"service provider" means an individual who comes into direct contact with pupils on a regular basis,

(a) at a school site of a board in the normal course of,

(i) providing goods or services under contract with the board,

(ii) carrying out his or her employment functions as an employee of a person who provides goods or services under contract with the board, or

(iii) providing services to a person who provides goods or services under contract with the board, or

(b) at a school under the jurisdiction of the Minister in the normal course of,

(i) providing goods or services under contract with the Minister,

(ii) carrying out his or her employment functions as an employee of a person who provides goods or services under contract with the Minister, or

(iii) providing services to a person who provides goods or services under contract with the Minister.

("fournisseur de services")

(2) An individual who would be a service provider under this Regulation only by reason of being a school bus driver, a driving instructor or both is not a service provider for the purposes of this Regulation while he or she satisfies the requirements set out by the Ministry of Transportation applicable to school bus drivers or driving instructors, as the case may be.

O. Reg. 49/03, s. 1

2. Personal information to be collected by the board — **(1)** For the purposes of ensuring the safety of pupils, every board shall collect a personal criminal history of every individual who is,

(a) an employee of the board; or

(b) a service provider at a school site of the board.

(2) The board shall collect a personal criminal history of an individual described in subsection (1) at the following times and in the following manner:

1. If the individual commences employment after March 31, 2002, the board shall collect a criminal background check in respect of the individual before the day the individual commences employment with the board and an offence declaration from the individual by September 1 of each year in which the individual is employed by the board after that day.

2. If the individual first becomes a service provider in respect of the board after December 31, 2003, the board shall collect a criminal background check in respect of the individual before the individual first becomes a service provider at a school site of the board and an offence declaration from the individual by September 1 of each year in which the individual is a service provider at a school site of the board after that day.

3. If the individual became a member of the Ontario College of Teachers after December 31, 1998 and commenced employment with the board before April 1, 2002, the board shall collect an offence declaration from the individual by September 1 of each year in which the individual is employed by the board after that day, commencing in 2002.

4. If the individual commenced employment with the board before April 1, 2002 and is not an individual described in paragraph 3, the board shall collect,

i. a criminal background check in respect of the individual by July 31, 2003 if the individual is employed by the board at any time in 2003 after July 31, and

ii. an offence declaration from the individual by September 1 of each year in which the individual is employed by the board after that day, commencing in 2004.

4.1 If the individual became a service provider in respect of the board before December 31, 2003, the board shall collect,

i. a criminal background check in respect of the individual by December 31, 2003 if the individual is a service provider at a school site of the board after that day, and

ii. an offence declaration from the individual by September 1 of each year in which the individual is a service provider at a school site of the board after that day, commencing in 2004.

5. If an employee transfers to a different school site of the board after March 31, 2002, the board shall collect an offence declaration from the employee before the transfer.

6. If an individual is a service provider in respect of the board at one or more school sites and, after December 31, 2003, becomes a service provider at a different school site of the board, the board shall collect an offence declaration from the individual before the individual becomes a service provider at that school site.

O. Reg. 170/02, s. 1; 322/03, s. 1

3. Personal information to be collected by Minister — For the purposes of subsection 315(1) of the Act, the personal information that may be collected by the Minister to ensure the safety of pupils is the personal criminal history of an individual who is,

(a) an employee of the Ministry who works at a school under the jurisdiction of the Minister; or

(b) a service provider at a school under the jurisdiction of the Minister.

4. Commencement — This Regulation comes into force on the later of January 1, 2002 and the day it is filed.

ONT. REG. 99/02 — TEACHER PERFORMANCE APPRAISAL

made under the *Education Act*

O. Reg. 99/02, as am. O. Reg. 1/03; 264/06; 96/07.

PART I — GENERAL

[Heading added O. Reg. 1/03, s. 1.]

1. Interpretation — **(1)** This Regulation applies to performance appraisals of teachers conducted under Part X.2 of the Act.

(2) References in this Regulation to a principal include references to a person other than a principal who conducts a performance appraisal of a teacher under Part X.2 of the Act.

(3) The interpretations and definitions in Part X.2 of the Act apply for the purposes of this Regulation.

(4) In this Regulation,

"classroom observation" includes the observation of a teacher in his or her ordinary teaching environment if that environment is not a classroom.

O. Reg. 264/06, s. 1

PART II — TEACHERS OTHER THAN NEW TEACHERS

[Heading added O. Reg. 264/06, s. 2.]

2. Application — This Part applies with respect to teachers, other than new teachers, and in this Part every reference to a **"teacher"** means a teacher other than a new teacher.

O. Reg. 264/06, s. 2

3. [Repealed O. Reg. 96/07, s. 1.]

4. Evaluation cycle — **(1)** The evaluation cycle for teachers shall be five consecutive years.

(2) Every board shall schedule evaluation years for teachers in a manner that provides for each teacher to have one evaluation year in each evaluation cycle during which the teacher is employed by the board.

(3) The first year in which a teacher is employed by a board shall be an evaluation year.

(4) Within 20 school days after a teacher commences teaching in a year that is scheduled as an evaluation year for the teacher, the appropriate principal shall notify the teacher that the year is an evaluation year.

(5) The board shall ensure that each teacher receives at least one performance appraisal during each of his or her evaluation years.

(6) Once a teacher employed by a board has an evaluation year, each subsequent evaluation year of the teacher, as long as the teacher continues in the employ of that board, must be preceded by four years that are not evaluation years for the teacher.

O. Reg. 264/06, s. 2; 96/07, s. 2

5. Principal's role — **(1)** The performance appraisals under this Part shall be conducted by the principal assigned to the school to which the teacher is assigned in the evaluation year scheduled for the teacher.

(2) The principal may conduct performance appraisals of a teacher under this Part at such intervals as the principal considers appropriate, subject to any requirements in Part X.2 of the Act or any regulation, guideline, rule or policy under that Part.

(3) The principal shall give the teacher written notice of the rating determined for each performance appraisal conducted under this section.

(4) [Repealed O. Reg. 264/06, s. 2.]

(5) [Repealed O. Reg. 264/06, s. 2.]

(6) [Repealed O. Reg. 264/06, s. 2.]

O. Reg. 264/06, s. 2

6. Additional performance appraisals — **(1)** A principal of a school may conduct performance appraisals of a teacher assigned to the school that are additional to those required by section 4, if the principal considers it advisable to do so in light of circumstances relating to the teacher's performance.

(2) Subject to subsection (3), and except during a teacher's evaluation year, a teacher may request performance appraisals that are additional to those required by section 4 and the principal assigned to the school to which the teacher is assigned shall conduct them.

(3) The principal may refuse to conduct a performance appraisal requested under subsection (2) where he or she is of the opinion that it is unlikely that the performance appraisal will lead to improvement in the teacher's performance.

(4) The principal shall give the teacher written notice of the rating determined for each performance appraisal conducted under this section.

O. Reg. 264/06, s. 2

7. Rating scale — The principal shall assign one of the following overall performance ratings to a teacher, based on the results of the performance appraisal:

1. Satisfactory.
2. Unsatisfactory.
3. [Repealed O. Reg. 96/07, s. 3.]
4. [Repealed O. Reg. 96/07, s. 3.]

O. Reg. 264/06, s. 2; 96/07, s. 3

8. Performance appraisal — **(1)** A performance appraisal of a teacher must satisfy the following requirements:

1. The teacher must be evaluated with respect to the competencies set out in Schedule 1 and such other competencies as may be provided for by the appropriate board under subsection 277.32(1) of the Act.
2. The performance appraisal must include the steps listed in subsection (2).

3. The performance appraisal must be conducted in accordance with such guidelines as the Minister may issue and in accordance with such additional policies, rules, standards, methods, processes, timelines and steps as may be established by the appropriate board.

(2) A performance appraisal must include the following steps:

1. A meeting between the principal and the teacher in preparation for a classroom observation of the teacher and to review the teacher's current learning plan.

2. [Repealed O. Reg. 96/07, s. 4(1).]

3. A classroom observation to evaluate the teacher's competencies, including a determination by the principal of whether the teacher has the knowledge and is employing the practices described in the guidelines issued by the Minister under subsection 277.33(1) of the Act.

4. A meeting between the principal and the teacher after the classroom observation,

i. to review the results of the classroom observation,

ii. to discuss other information relevant to the principal's evaluation of the teacher's competencies, and

iii. [Repealed O. Reg. 96/07, s. 4(2).]

iv. to finalize the teacher's learning plan for the current year.

5. [Repealed O. Reg. 96/07, s. 4(3).]

6. [Repealed O. Reg. 96/07, s. 4(3).]

7. Preparation by the principal of a summative report of the performance appraisal, in a form approved by the Minister, containing,

i. the principal's evaluation of the teacher,

ii. the principal's overall performance rating of the teacher, and

iii. the principal's explanation for the rating.

8. Provision to the teacher of a copy of the summative report, signed by the principal, within 20 school days after the classroom observation.

9. Signature by the teacher of a copy of the summative report, to acknowledge receipt by the teacher of a copy of the report.

10. Provision to the appropriate board of a copy of the summative report, as signed by both the principal and the teacher, and the teacher's learning plan for the year.

(3) At the request of either the teacher or the principal, the teacher and principal shall meet to discuss the performance appraisal after the teacher receives a copy of the summative report.

O. Reg. 264/06, s. 2; 96/07, s. 4

9. Records — Every board shall retain each record made under Part X.2 of the Act for a period of at least six years from the date of the summative report of the performance appraisal to which the record relates.

O. Reg. 264/06, s. 2

Special Rules

[Heading added O. Reg. 1/03, s. 2. Amended O. Reg. 264/06, s. 2.]

10. Performance appraisals if teaching only one semester — If a teacher is teaching in only one semester during a year that is scheduled as an evaluation year, all performance appraisals of the teacher required during that evaluation year must be conducted in that semester.

O. Reg. 1/03, s. 2; 264/06, s. 2

11. Periods of time excluded from evaluation cycle — **(1)** The five-year evaluation cycle mentioned in subsection 4(1) excludes the following periods of time:

1. A period during which the teacher does not teach at any time in a school governed by the board.

2. A period in a year in the five-year cycle that is scheduled as an evaluation year for the teacher if, throughout the period, the teacher is on an extended leave that has been approved by the board.

3. A period when the teacher is on secondment to a non-teaching position.

4. A period when the teacher is on secondment to a teaching position outside the Ontario public education system.

(2) If a teacher is on an extended leave during all or part of a year that is scheduled as an evaluation year, any performance appraisal that would otherwise be carried out during that period must be conducted within 60 school days after the teacher returns from leave.

(3) [Repealed O. Reg. 264/06, s. 2.]

(4) [Repealed O. Reg. 264/06, s. 2.]

(5) [Repealed O. Reg. 264/06, s. 2.]

(6) [Repealed O. Reg. 264/06, s. 2.]

(7) [Repealed O. Reg. 264/06, s. 2.]

(8) [Repealed O. Reg. 264/06, s. 2.]

(9) [Repealed O. Reg. 264/06, s. 2.]

O. Reg. 1/03, s. 2; 264/06, s. 2; 96/07, s. 5

12. Rules, seconded teachers — **(1)** The following rules apply to every teacher who is seconded to a teaching position in the Ontario public education system during a five-year cycle:

1. The year that is scheduled as an evaluation year for the teacher during the cycle does not change.

2. The board from which the teacher is seconded must advise the board to which the teacher is seconded of the teacher's position in the teacher's five-year cycle.

3. The board to which the teacher is seconded shall ensure that all performance appraisals of the teacher that are required during the period the teacher is on secondment to the board are carried out.

(2) If a performance appraisal carried out while a teacher is seconded to another board results in an unsatisfactory overall performance rating, the following rules apply:

1. The secondment agreement terminates.

2. The performance appraisal is deemed not to have been conducted except for the purposes of terminating the secondment agreement.

3. The teacher's five-year cycle recommences on the termination of the secondment agreement and the first year in the cycle is an evaluation year for the teacher.

4. The board to which the teacher returns shall ensure that a performance appraisal of the teacher is conducted within 60 school days after the teacher's return.

O. Reg. 264/06, s. 2; 96/07, s. 6

PART III — NEW TEACHERS

[Heading added O. Reg. 264/06, s. 2.]

13. Application — This Part applies with respect to new teachers and in this Part every reference to a teacher means a **"new teacher"**.

O. Reg. 264/06, s. 2

14. [Repealed O. Reg. 96/07, s. 7.]

15. Rating scale — **(1)** The principal shall assign one of the following performance ratings to a new teacher, based on the results of the first performance appraisal conducted in the first 12-month period following his or her being hired as a teacher:

1. Satisfactory.
2. Development Needed.

(2) In the case of a new teacher who was assigned a rating of Satisfactory in the first appraisal, the principal shall assign one of the following ratings to the teacher in the second appraisal conducted in the first 12-month period:

1. Satisfactory.
2. Development Needed.

(3) In the case of a new teacher who was assigned a rating of Development Needed in the first appraisal, the principal shall assign one of the following ratings to the teacher in the second appraisal conducted in the first 12-month period:

1. Satisfactory.
2. Unsatisfactory.

(4) The principal shall assign one of the following ratings to a new teacher in any subsequent appraisal required under the Act:

1. Satisfactory.
2. Unsatisfactory.

(5) In addition to the rating of unsatisfactory, the rating of Development Needed shall be considered not Satisfactory for the purposes of Part X.2 of the Act.

O. Reg. 264/06, s. 2

16. Performance appraisal — **(1)** A performance appraisal of a new teacher must satisfy the following requirements:

1. The teacher must be evaluated with respect to the competencies set out in Schedule 2 and such other competencies as may be provided for by the appropriate board under subsection 277.32(1) of the Act.

2. The performance appraisal must include a classroom observation to evaluate the teacher's competencies, including a determination by the principal of whether the teacher has the knowledge and is employing the practices described in the guidelines issued by the Minister under subsection 277.33(1) of the Act.

3. The performance appraisal must be conducted in accordance with such guidelines as the Minister may issue and in accordance with such additional policies, rules, standards, methods, processes, timelines and steps as may be established by the appropriate board.

(2) A performance appraisal of a new teacher must include the following steps:

1. A meeting between the principal and the teacher in preparation for a classroom observation of the teacher.

2. A classroom observation to evaluate the teacher's competencies, including a determination by the principal of whether the teacher has the knowledge and is employing the practices described in the guidelines issued by the Minister under subsection 277.33(1) of the Act.

3. A meeting between the principal and the teacher after the classroom observation,

   i. to review the results of the classroom observation, and

   ii. to discuss other information relevant to the principal's evaluation of the teacher's competencies, including the teacher's participation in the new teacher induction program.

4. Preparation by the principal of a summative report of the performance appraisal, in a form approved by the Minister, containing,

   i. the principal's evaluation of the teacher,

   ii. the principal's overall performance rating of the teacher, and

   iii. the principal's explanation for the rating.

5. Provision to the teacher of a copy of the summative report, signed by the principal, within 20 school days after the classroom observation.

6. Signature by the teacher of a copy of the summative report, to acknowledge receipt by the teacher of a copy of the report.

7. Provision to the appropriate board of a copy of the summative report, as signed by both the principal and the teacher.

(3) At the request of either the teacher or the principal, the teacher and principal shall meet to discuss the performance appraisal after the teacher receives a copy of the summative report.

O. Reg. 264/06, s. 2; 96/07, s. 8

17. Records — Every board shall retain each record made under Part X.2 of the Act for a period of at least six years from the date of the summative report of the performance appraisal to which the record relates.

O. Reg. 264/06, s. 2

Special Rules

[Heading added O. Reg. 264/06, s. 2.]

18. Periods of time excluded from new teaching period — **(1)** A teacher's new teaching period excludes the following periods of time:

1. A period during which the teacher does not teach at any time in a school governed by the board.

2. A period during which the teacher is on an extended leave that has been approved by the board.

3. A period when the teacher is on secondment to a non-teaching position.

4. A period when the teacher is on secondment to a teaching position outside the Ontario public education system.

(2) With respect to a period during which a teacher is on an extended leave that has been approved by the board, any performance appraisal that would otherwise be carried out during that period must be conducted within 60 school days after the teacher returns from leave.

O. Reg. 264/06, s. 2

19. Extension of evaluation cycle — **(1)** A board shall extend a teacher's new teaching period if all of the following conditions apply:

1. The teacher had three performance appraisals during the first 18 months of the new teaching period and one appraisal resulted in a Satisfactory rating.
2. After the start of the 19th month but before the expiry of the teacher's new teaching period, the teacher,
   i. begins to teach at a different school governed by the same board, or
   ii. becomes employed as a teacher by a different board.
3. The teacher has submitted a request in writing to the appropriate supervisory officer for the new school or the new board, as the case may be, for an extension of his or her new teaching period.
4. The request for an extension was made after the start of the 19th month but before the expiry of the teacher's new teaching period.
5. The new teaching period has not been previously been extended under this section.

(2) A teacher's new teaching period may be extended under subsection (1) for up to 90 school days.

(3) Within 20 school days of receiving a request under paragraph 3 of subsection (1), the board mentioned under subparagraph 2 i or ii, as the case may be, shall provide notice in writing confirming the length of the extension,

(a) to the teacher, and

(b) to the principal of the school to which the teacher is assigned.

O. Reg. 264/06, s. 2

20. Rules, seconded teachers — **(1)** The following rules apply to every new teacher who is seconded to a teaching position in the Ontario public education system during his or her new teaching period:

1. The secondment does not affect the performance appraisal schedule for new teachers set out in section 277.29 of the Act.
2. The board from which the teacher is seconded must advise the board to which the teacher is seconded of the teacher's position in his or her new teaching period.
3. The board to which the teacher is seconded shall ensure that all performance appraisals of the teacher that are required during the period the teacher is on secondment to the board are carried out.

(2) If a performance appraisal carried out while a teacher is seconded to another board results in an overall performance rating that is not satisfactory, the following rules apply:

1. The secondment agreement terminates.
2. The performance appraisal is deemed not to have been conducted except for the purposes of terminating the secondment agreement.

3. The teacher resumes the position in his or her new teaching period that the teacher was in when he or she began the secondment and the 24-month period commences running from that position on the termination of the secondment agreement.

4. The board to which the teacher returns shall ensure a performance appraisal of the teacher is conducted within 60 school days after the teacher's return.

O. Reg. 264/06, s. 2

PART IV — PROVINCIAL SCHOOLS AND DEMONSTRATION SCHOOLS

[Heading added O. Reg. 264/06, s. 2.]

21. Provincial schools — **(1)** Part X.2 of the Act, Parts I, II and III of this Regulation, the other regulations under Part X.2 of the Act, and the guidelines, rules and policies under Part X.2 of the Act, apply to schools established or continued under subsection 13(1), (2) or (4) of the Act and to schools operated by a ministry under the *Provincial Schools Negotiations Act*, subject to such modifications as the circumstances require, including the modifications set out in this section.

(2) If a teacher employed by a board is seconded to a school referred to in subsection (1), subsection (1) does not apply to the teacher unless Part X.2 of the Act applies to the board.

(3) Despite subsection 277.15(1) of the Act and subsection 1(3) of this Regulation, in Part X.2 of the Act, Parts I, II and III of this Regulation, the other regulations under Part X.2 of the Act, and the guidelines, rules and policies under Part X.2 of the Act, unless the context requires otherwise,

(a) a reference to a board is deemed to be a reference to the Provincial Schools Authority;

(b) a reference to the designated bargaining agent for a teachers' bargaining unit is deemed to be a reference to the bargaining agent referred to in subsection 5(4) of the *Provincial Schools Negotiations Act*;

(c) a reference to a teacher is deemed to be a reference to a teacher as defined in section 1 of the *Provincial Schools Negotiations Act*, other than a continuing education teacher;

(d) a reference to a teachers' bargaining unit is deemed to be a reference to the bargaining unit referred to in subsection 5(2) of the *Provincial Schools Negotiations Act*;

(e) a reference to a director of education for a board is deemed to be a reference to the chair of the Provincial Schools Authority;

(f) a reference to a school council is deemed to be a reference to any body that acts in a capacity similar to a school council; and

(g) a reference to a special education advisory committee is deemed to be a reference to any body that acts in a capacity similar to a special education advisory committee.

(4) Subsections 277.15(2) and (3) and sections 277.24 to 277.27 of the Act have no application to the schools referred to in subsection (1).

(5) [Repealed O. Reg. 96/07, s. 9(1).]

(6) Subsections (3) and (4) apply only for the purposes of subsection (1).

O. Reg. 264/06, s. 2; 96/07, s. 9

22. Demonstration schools — **(1)** Part X.2 of the Act, Parts I, II and III of this Regulation, the other regulations made under Part X.2 of the Act, and the guidelines, rules and policies under Part X.2 of the Act, apply to the demonstration schools established under clause 13(5)(a) of the Act, subject to such modifications as the circumstances require, including the modifications set out in this section.

(2) If a teacher employed by a board is seconded to a school referred to in subsection (1), subsection (1) does not apply to the teacher unless Part X.2 of the Act applies to the board.

(3) Despite subsection 277.15(1) of the Act and subsection 1(3) of this Regulation, in Part X.2 of the Act, Parts I, II and III of this Regulation, the other regulations under Part X.2 of the Act, and the guidelines, rules and policies under Part X.2 of the Act, unless the context requires otherwise,

(a) a reference to a board is deemed to be a reference to the Ministry;

(b) a reference to a teacher employed by a board is deemed to be a reference to a teacher employed by a board and seconded to a school referred to in subsection (1);

(c) a reference to a school council is deemed to be a reference to any body that acts in a capacity similar to a school council; and

(d) a reference to a special education advisory committee is deemed to be a reference to the Learning Disabilities Association of Ontario.

(4) Clauses (3)(a) and (b) do not apply to the following provisions with respect to a teacher that is employed by a board and seconded to a school referred to in subsection (1):

1. Subsections 4(1) and (4) of this Regulation.
2. Section 277.29 of the Act.
3. Sections 277.42, 277.43 and 277.44 of the Act.
4. Section 2 of Ontario Regulation 98/02 (Teacher Learning Plans).

(5) Despite subsections 277.15(5) and (6) of the Act,

(a) nothing in Part X.2 of the Act, or any regulation, guideline, policy or rule under that Part, shall be interpreted to limit rights otherwise available to the Ministry or a board relating to discipline of any teacher, including but not limited to rights relating to reassignment of duties, suspension or termination of the employment of the teacher, whether or not a performance appraisal process relating to the teacher is being conducted under that Part; and

(b) nothing in Part X.2 of the Act, or any regulation, guideline, policy or rule under it, shall be interpreted to limit the Ministry's ability or a board's ability to complete a performance appraisal of a teacher begun before that Part begins to apply to the Ministry, board or teacher, or to follow any process or take any action relating to that performance appraisal that the Ministry or board might have followed or taken but for that Part.

(6) Despite subsection 277.18(3) of the Act, in the circumstances described in clause 277.18(1)(b) of the Act, where no other supervisory officer employed by the Ministry is able to perform the duty and exercise the power in a timely way, because of absence or for some other reason, a supervisory officer employed by a board may, by arrangement between the Ministry and the board, perform the duty and exercise the power.

(7) Despite clauses 277.21(1)(b) and (4)(b) of the Act, the Lieutenant Governor in Council may make regulations in relation to Part X.2 of the Act establishing rules to apply where a board seconds a teacher to the Ministry, and the regulations may assign responsibilities under that Part as between the seconding board and the Ministry.

(8) Sections 277.24 to 277.27 and 277.35 to 277.41 of the Act have no application to the schools referred to in subsection (1).

(9) Subsections (3) to (8) apply only for the purposes of subsection (1).

O. Reg. 264/06, s. 2; 96/07, s. 10

PART V — TRANSITION TO NEW APPRAISAL RULES

[Heading added O. Reg. 96/07, s. 11.]

23. Definitions — In this Part,

"changeover date" means the day on which the new appraisal rules first apply to a board in accordance with this Part; *("date de changement")*

"new appraisal rules" mean this Regulation as it reads on April 1, 2007; *("nouvelles règles d'évaluation")*

"old appraisal rules" mean this Regulation as it reads on March 31, 2007. *("anciennes règles d'évaluation")*

O. Reg. 96/07, s. 11

24. Application — **(1)** Despite the coming into force of the new appraisal rules, the old appraisal rules continue to apply to a board until the day preceding the board's changeover date.

(2) The new appraisal rules apply to every board on and after September 1, 2007.

(3) Despite subsection (2), a board may choose any date from April 1, 2007 to August 31, 2007, to be its changeover date, and the new appraisal rules shall apply to the board on and after that date.

(4) If a board intends to have the new appraisal rules apply to it before September 1, 2007, the board shall give notice, in writing, of its proposed changeover date to,

(a) the Minister; and

(b) every teacher of the board, other than a new teacher, for whom the 2006-2007 school year would, under the old appraisal rules, be an evaluation year.

(5) The board shall include in every notice given under clause (4)(b) information regarding the new appraisal rules and the transition to them.

O. Reg. 96/07, s. 11

25. Transition — **(1)** This section applies with respect to teachers, other than new teachers, and in this section every reference to a **"teacher"** means a teacher other than a new teacher.

(2) If the changeover date is a date from April 1, 2007 to August 31, 2007 and the 2006-2007 school year would, under the old appraisal rules, be an evaluation year for a teacher,

(a) the year continues to be an evaluation year for the teacher for the purposes of the evaluation cycle under the new appraisal rules; and

(b) the rules in subsections (3) and (4), and any other applicable rules in the Act, apply for the evaluation year.

(3) If, on the changeover date, the teacher has not received any performance appraisals during the year, the board shall ensure that the teacher receives at least one performance appraisal during the year.

(4) No further performance appraisals are required for the year if, on the changeover date,

(a) the teacher has received at least one performance appraisal during the year for which the rating was not unsatisfactory; and

(b) the performance appraisal referred to in clause (a) was not followed by a performance appraisal in the year for which the rating was unsatisfactory.

O. Reg. 96/07, s. 11

SCHEDULE 1 — COMPETENCIES FOR TEACHERS OTHER THAN NEW TEACHERS

[Heading amended O. Reg. 264/06, s. 3.]

The number in square brackets has been editorially added by Carswell.

Commitment to pupils and pupil learning

Teachers:

(a) demonstrate commitment to the well-being and development of all pupils,

(b) are dedicated in their efforts to teach and support pupil learning and achievement,

(c) treat all pupils equitably and with respect,

(d) provide an environment for learning that encourages pupils to be problem-solvers, decision-makers, life-long learners and contributing members of a changing society,

Professional knowledge

Teachers:

(e) know their subject matter, the Ontario curriculum and education-related legislation,

(f) know a variety of effective teaching and assessment practices,

(g) know a variety of effective classroom management strategies,

(h) know how pupils learn and factors that influence pupil learning and achievement,

Teaching practice

Teachers:

(i) use their professional knowledge and understanding of pupils, curriculum, legislation, teaching practices and classroom management strategies to promote the learning and achievement of their pupils,

(j) communicate effectively with pupils, parents and colleagues,

(k) conduct ongoing assessment of their pupils' progress, evaluate their achievement and report results to pupils and parents regularly,

(l) adapt and refine their teaching practices through continuous learning and reflection, using a variety of sources and resources,

(m) use appropriate technology in their teaching practices and related professional responsibilities,

Leadership and community

Teachers:

(n) collaborate with other teachers and school colleagues to create and sustain learning communities in their classrooms and in their schools,

(o) work with other professionals, parents and members of the community to enhance pupil learning, pupil achievement and school programs,

Ongoing professional learning

Teachers:

(p) engage in ongoing professional learning and apply it to improve their teaching practices.

O. Reg. 264/06, s. 3

SCHEDULE 2 — COMPETENCIES FOR NEW TEACHERS

[Heading added O. Reg. 264/06, s. 4.]

Commitment to pupils and pupil learning

New teachers:

(a) demonstrate commitment to the well-being and development of all pupils,

(b) are dedicated in their efforts to teach and support pupil learning and achievement,

(c) treat all pupils equitably and with respect,

(d) provide an environment for learning that encourages pupils to be problem-solvers, decision-makers, life-long learners and contributing members of a changing society,

Professional knowledge

New teachers:

(e) know their subject matter, the Ontario curriculum and education-related legislation,

Teaching practice

New teachers:

(f) use their professional knowledge and understanding of pupils, curriculum, legislation, teaching practices and classroom management strategies to promote the learning and achievement of their pupils,

(g) communicate effectively with pupils, parents and colleagues,

(h) conduct ongoing assessment of their pupils' progress, evaluate their achievement and report results to pupils and parents regularly.

O. Reg. 264/06, s. 4

Ont. Reg. 357/06 — Honoraria for Board Members

made under the *Education Act*

O. Reg. 357/06, as am. O. Reg. 163/07.

1. Purpose — This Regulation sets out the method for calculating the limits on honoraria paid under section 191 of the Act and deals with public consultation requirements for district school boards.

District School Boards

2. Components of honorarium — **(1)** For a term of office beginning in 2006 or later, the honorarium for a member of a district school board, in respect of any year of his or her term of office, shall consist of such of the following components as the board determines, subject to section 4:

1. The base amount for the year.
2. The enrolment amount for the year.
3. The attendance amounts payable to the member for the year.
4. The distance amounts payable to the member for the year.

(2) A year of a member's term of office begins on December 1 and ends on the following November 30.

3. Citizens' advisory committee on honoraria — **(1)** Every district school board shall establish a citizens' advisory committee on honoraria.

(2) The committee shall consist of six people selected by the board, of whom,

(a) three shall be parent members within the meaning of subsection 1(1) of Ontario Regulation 612/00 (*School Councils*) made under the Act; and

(b) three shall be community representatives who are members of a school council for a school under subsection 3(1) of Ontario Regulation 612/00 (*School Councils*) made under the Act.

(3) For a term of office beginning in 2006 or later,

(a) the board shall provide to the committee all available information needed to make the calculations set out in sections 5 to 9 for a member for each year of the term of office; and

(b) the committee shall review the information provided by the board and shall recommend to the board,

(i) an amount for the base amount, attendance amount and distance amount for a member for each year of the term of office, and

(ii) a percentage to be applied in calculating the enrolment amount limit for a member for each year of the term of office.

(4) The board shall not establish its policy under subsection 4(1) until the committee makes the recommendation under subsection (3).

(5) For the period described in section 11,

(a) the board shall provide to the committee the information needed to make the calculations set out in that section for a member or former member; and

(b) the committee shall review the information provided by the board and shall recommend to the board an amount for the honorarium for the member or former member.

(6) The board shall not establish its policy under subsection 4(4) until the committee makes the recommendation under subsection (5).

O. Reg. 163/07, s. 1

4. Policy re honorarium components — **(1)** For a term of office beginning in 2006 or later, the board shall establish a policy, on or before October 31 of the calendar year in which the term of office begins, with respect to,

(a) which components listed in paragraphs 1 to 4 of subsection 2(1) it will pay during the term of office;

(b) for the base amount, the attendance amount and the distance amount, if the component will be paid, the amount of the component to be paid to a member for each year of the term of office, determined in accordance with sections 5, 7 and 8; and

(c) for the enrolment amount, if it will be paid, the percentage to be applied in calculating the enrolment amount limit for a member for each year of the term of office.

(2) The board may, at any time, change its policy under subsection (1) such that a component is not paid for a year, the amount of a component to be paid is lowered for a year, or the percentage to be applied in calculating the enrolment amount limit is lowered for a year.

(3) If the board changes its policy for a year under subsection (2), it may restore the original policy made under subsection (1) at any time before the end of the period to which the policy applies.

(4) For the period described in section 11, the board shall establish a policy, on or before October 31, 2006, with respect to the amount of the honorarium to be paid to a member for the period, determined in accordance with that section.

O. Reg. 163/07, s. 2

5. Base amount — **(1)** The base amount for a member for a year of a term of office is an amount that does not exceed the base amount limit determined under subsection (2), (3) or (4), as the case may be.

(2) For a member other than the chair or vice-chair, the base amount limit for the year is determined as follows:

1. For each year of the term of office beginning on December 1, 2006, $5,900.

2. For each year of a term of office beginning on or after December 1, 2010, the amount calculated for a year of the previous term of office, increased by the percentage increase in the Ontario Consumer Price Index as published by Statistics Canada for the period between,

   i. July 1 of the calendar year in which the previous term of office started, and

   ii. June 30 of the calendar year in which the term of office starts.

(3) For the chair, the base amount limit for the year is determined by adding $5,000 to the amount determined under subsection (2).

(4) For the vice-chair, the base amount limit for the year is determined by adding $2,500 to the amount determined under subsection (2).

O. Reg. 163/07, s. 3

6. Enrolment amount — **(1)** The enrolment amount for a member for each year of a term of office is an amount determined for that year that does not exceed the enrolment amount limit.

(1.1) The enrolment amount shall be calculated anew in each year of a member's term of office.

(1.2) The enrolment amount limit is determined by multiplying the percentage determined by the board for the year under clause 4(1)(c) or subsection 4(2) or (3), as the case may be, by the amount determined for the member under subsection (2), (3) or (4), as the case may be.

(2) For a member other than the chair or vice-chair, determine an amount as follows:

1. Multiply the enrolment of the board for the year as determined under section 9, by $1.75.
2. Divide the number determined under paragraph 1 by the number of members determined for the board under subclause 58.1(2)(k)(i) or subsection 58.1(10.1) of the Act, as the case may be.

(3) For the chair, add the amount determined under subsection (2) to the amount determined as follows:

1. Multiply the enrolment of the board for the year as determined under section 9 by 5 cents.
2. Determine the greater of,
   - i. the amount determined under paragraph 1, and
   - ii. $500.
3. Determine the lesser of,
   - i. the amount determined under paragraph 2, and
   - ii. $5,000.

(4) For the vice-chair, add the amount determined under subsection (2) to the amount determined as follows:

1. Multiply the enrolment of the board for the year as determined under section 9 by 2.5 cents.
2. Determine the greater of,
   - i. the amount determined under paragraph 1, and
   - ii. $250.
3. Determine the lesser of,
   - i. the amount determined under paragraph 2, and
   - ii. $2,500.

O. Reg. 163/07, s. 4

7. Attendance amount — **(1)** The attendance amount is an amount that does not exceed the attendance amount limit of $50.

(2) The attendance amount may be paid to a member for attending any meeting of a committee of the board that is required to be established by an Act or a regulation made under an Act.

8. Distance amount — **(1)** The distance amount is an amount that does not exceed the distance amount limit of $50.

(2) For a board member described as follows, the distance amount may be paid to the member for attending any meeting of the board or of a committee of the board that is required to be established by an Act or a regulation made under an Act:

1. The board member is a member of a board that has,

    i. a board area greater than 9,000 square kilometres, as set out in Table 1 of Ontario Regulation 412/00 (*Elections to and Representation on District School Boards*) made under the Act, as that regulation reads on the day that the board makes its determination under section 4, or

    ii. a dispersal factor of greater than 25, as set out in Table 5 of Ontario Regulation 412/00 (*Elections to and Representation on District School Boards*) made under the Act, as that regulation reads on the day that the board makes its determination under section 4.

2. On the day of the meeting, the distance between the member's residence and the place where the meeting is held is more than 200 kilometres.

(3) A board member may receive the distance amount only once in respect of any day.

O. Reg. 163/07, s. 5

9. Enrolment — For the purposes of section 6, the enrolment of the board for a year of a term of office is the estimate of the board's day school average daily enrolment that was,

(a) determined for the purposes of the regulation made under section 234 of the Act in respect of calculating average daily enrolment for the school board fiscal year that ends in the calendar year in which the year of the term of office begins; and

(b) submitted to the Ministry together with the estimates required by clause 231(11)(c) of the Act.

O. Reg. 163/07, s. 6

10. Service for a partial year — **(1)** The honorarium for a board member who serves for a partial year, other than a partial year during the period described in section 11, is determined in accordance with this section.

(2) The base amount is an amount that does not exceed the base amount limit for the partial year, which is determined by prorating, according to the time served, the base amount for a board member who serves for a full year.

(2.1) The enrolment amount is an amount that does not exceed the enrolment amount limit for the partial year, which is determined by prorating, according to the time served, the enrolment amount for a board member who serves for a full year.

(3) The attendance amount and the distance amount are determined in accordance with sections 7 and 8, with necessary modifications.

O. Reg. 163/07, s. 7

11. Period from September 1, 2005 to November 30, 2006 — In respect of the period from September 1, 2005 to November 30, 2006, the board may pay to a member or former member an honorarium that does not exceed an amount determined as follows:

1. Divide the amount set out in Table 1 opposite the name of the board by 12.
2. Multiply the amount determined under paragraph 1 by the number of months for which the member or former member served.
3. Subtract from the amount determined under paragraph 2 any honorarium paid to the member or former member before July 12, 2006 in respect of the period.
4. Add to the amount determined under paragraph 3 any honorarium paid under subsection 191(3) of the Act, as it read immediately before the coming into force of section 16 of the *Education Statute Law Amendment Act (Student Performance), 2006*, to the member or former member in respect of the period.

O. Reg. 163/07, s. 8

SCHOOL AUTHORITIES

12. Honorarium for members of school authorities — **(1)** A school authority may pay to its members an honorarium at the same rate and on the same conditions as the allowance being paid to its members on December 1, 1996.

(2) If a school authority was paying an amount as an additional allowance to its chair or vice-chair on December 1, 1996, the school authority may pay that amount as an additional honorarium to its chair or vice-chair, at the same rate and on the same conditions as applied on December 1, 1996.

TABLE/TABLEAU 1 — HONORARIUM FOR SEPTEMBER 1, 2005 TO NOVEMBER 30, 2006/ALLOCATION VERSÉE DU 1ER SEPTEMBRE 2005 AU 30 NOVEMBRE 2006

Item/Point	Column/Colonne 1	Column/Colonne 2
	Name of Board/Nom du conseil	**Amount/Montant $**
1.	Algoma District School Board	7,869
2.	Algonquin and Lakeshore Catholic District School Board	8,002
3.	Avon Maitland District School Board	9,360
4.	Bluewater District School Board	9,764
5.	Brant Haldimand Norfolk Catholic District School Board	8,987
6.	Bruce-Grey Catholic District School Board	6,934
7.	Conseil de district des écoles publiques de langue française n° 59	7,305
8.	Conseil scolaire de district catholique des Grandes Rivières	7,326
9.	Conseil scolaire de district catholique Centre-Sud	7,517
10.	Conseil scolaire de district catholique de l'est Ontarien	8,374

Item/Point	Column/Colonne 1	Column/Colonne 2
	Name of Board/Nom du conseil	**Amount/Montant $**
11.	Conseil scolaire de district catholique des Aurores boréales	5,994
12.	Conseil scolaire de district catholique du Centre-Est de l'Ontario	8,372
13.	Conseil scolaire de district catholique du Nouvel-Ontario	7,090
14.	Conseil scolaire de district catholique Franco-Nord	6,808
15.	Conseil scolaire de district des écoles catholiques du Sud-Ouest	6,939
16.	Conseil scolaire de district du Centre Sud-Ouest	6,821
17.	Conseil scolaire de district du Grand Nord de l'Ontario	6,237
18.	Conseil scolaire de district du Nord-Est de l'Ontario	6,091
19.	District School Board of Niagara	12,356
20.	District School Board Ontario North East	7,384
21.	Dufferin-Peel Catholic District School Board	19,232
22.	Durham Catholic District School Board	11,266
23.	Durham District School Board	16,436
24.	Eastern Ontario Catholic District School Board	9,414
25.	English Language Separate District School Board No. 38	10,530
26.	Grand Erie District School Board	10,738
27.	Greater Essex County District School Board	12,266
28.	Halton Catholic District School Board	11,694
29.	Halton District School Board	13,153
30.	Hamilton-Wentworth Catholic District School Board	11,336
31.	Hamilton-Wentworth District School Board	14,214
32.	Hastings and Prince Edward District School Board	9,348
33.	Huron-Perth Catholic District School Board	7,591
34.	Huron-Superior Catholic District School Board	7,006
35.	Kawartha Pine Ridge District School Board	12,378
36.	Keewatin-Patricia District School Board	7,020
37.	Kenora Catholic District School Board	6,315
38.	Lakehead District School Board	8,415
39.	Lambton Kent District School Board	10,268

Item/Point	Column/Colonne 1	Column/Colonne 2
	Name of Board/Nom du conseil	**Amount/Montant $**
40.	Limestone District School Board	10,073
41.	Near North District School Board	8,546
42.	Niagara Catholic District School Board	11,022
43.	Nipissing-Parry Sound Catholic District School Board	6,812
44.	Northeastern Catholic District School Board	6,479
45.	Northwest Catholic District School Board	6,213
46.	Ottawa-Carleton Catholic District School Board	12,669
47.	Ottawa-Carleton District School Board	15,790
48.	Peel District School Board	25,526
49.	Peterborough Victoria Northumberland and Clarington Catholic District School Board	9,494
50.	Rainbow District School Board	9,250
51.	Rainy River District School Board	6,671
52.	Renfrew County Catholic District School Board	7,330
53.	Renfrew County District School Board	8,170
54.	Simcoe County District School Board	14,297
55.	Simcoe Muskoka Catholic District School Board	10,534
56.	St. Clair Catholic District School Board	8,536
57.	Sudbury Catholic District School Board	7,799
58.	Superior North Catholic District School Board	6,061
59.	Superior-Greenstone District School Board	6,390
60.	Thames Valley District School Board	16,959
61.	Thunder Bay Catholic District School Board	8,241
62.	Toronto Catholic District School Board	18,678
63.	Toronto District School Board	25,993
64.	Trillium Lakelands District School Board	9,600
65.	Upper Canada District School Board	11,559
66.	Upper Grand District School Board	11,534
67.	Waterloo Catholic District School Board	10,287
68.	Waterloo Region District School Board	14,912
69.	Wellington Catholic District School Board	8,271
70.	Windsor-Essex Catholic District School Board	10,902
71.	York Catholic District School Board	14,675
72.	York Region District School Board	20,671

ONT. REG. 7/07 — STUDENT TRUSTEES

made under the *Education Act*

O. Reg. 7/07

1. Application — This Regulation applies to every district school board and every secondary school board established under section 67 of the Act.

2. Board policy — **(1)** The board shall develop and implement a policy providing for matters relating to student trustees and to the payment of honoraria for student trustees.

(2) The policy shall be in accordance with this Regulation and with any policies and guidelines established by the Minister under paragraph 3.5 of subsection 8(1) of the Act.

3. Number of student trustees — The board shall have at least one but not more than three student trustees.

4. Election procedure and timing — **(1)** Student trustees shall be elected in one of the following ways:

1. Directly, by students of the board.
2. Indirectly, by student representative bodies such as student councils.

(2) An election shall be held not later than April 30 in each year.

5. Qualifications — **(1)** A person is qualified to act as a student trustee if he or she is a full-time pupil of the board in the senior division.

(2) Despite subsection (1), a person is not qualified to be elected or to act as a student trustee if he or she is serving a sentence of imprisonment in a penal or correctional institution.

(3) A person who ceases to be qualified to act as a student trustee shall resign from the position.

(4) In this section,

"full-time pupil" has the same meaning as in the most recent regulations made under section 234 of the Act.

6. Term of office — A student trustee's term of office starts on August 1 of the year in which he or she is elected and ends on July 31 of the following year.

7. Vacancies — If the board determines that a vacancy shall be filled, it shall be filled by a by-election.

8. Reimbursement of expenses — If the board has established a policy under subsection 191.2(3) of the Act, the board shall reimburse student trustees for out-of-pocket expenses as if they were members of the board.

9. Honorarium — The amount of the honorarium referred to in subsection 55(8) of the Act is,

(a) $2,500, if the student trustee holds office for a complete term of office;

(b) $2,500 prorated according to the proportion of a term for which the student trustee holds office, if the student trustee holds office for less than a complete term of office.

10. Board to provide names to Ministry — The board shall provide the Ministry with the names of the student trustees elected, not later than 30 days after the date of the election or by-election.

11. Transition — Despite the revocation of Ontario Regulation 461/97 (*Pupil Representation on Boards*) made under the Act, that regulation continues to apply in respect of a pupil representative who holds office in the 2005-2006 school year.

Ont. Reg. 472/07 — Suspension and Expulsion of Pupils

made under the *Education Act*

O. Reg. 472/07

1. Definition — In this Regulation,

"designated tribunal" means the Child and Family Services Review Board continued under section 207 of the *Child and Family Services Act.*

2. Mitigating factors — For the purposes of subsections 306(2), 306(4), 310(3), 311.1(4) and clauses 311.3(7)(b) and 311.4(2)(b) of the Act, the following mitigating factors shall be taken into account:

1. The pupil does not have the ability to control his or her behaviour.
2. The pupil does not have the ability to understand the foreseeable consequences of his or her behaviour.
3. The pupil's continuing presence in the school does not create an unacceptable risk to the safety of any person.

3. Other factors — For the purposes of subsections 306(2), 306(4), 310(3), 311.1(4) and clauses 311.3(7)(b) and 311.4(2)(b) of the Act, the following other factors shall be taken into account if they would mitigate the seriousness of the activity for which the pupil may be or is being suspended or expelled:

1. The pupil's history.
2. Whether a progressive discipline approach has been used with the pupil.
3. Whether the activity for which the pupil may be or is being suspended or expelled was related to any harassment of the pupil because of his or her race, ethnic origin, religion, disability, gender or sexual orientation or to any other harassment.
4. How the suspension or expulsion would affect the pupil's ongoing education.
5. The age of the pupil.
6. In the case of a pupil for whom an individual education plan has been developed,
   i. whether the behaviour was a manifestation of a disability identified in the pupil's individual education plan,
   ii. whether appropriate individualized accommodation has been provided, and
   iii. whether the suspension or expulsion is likely to result in an aggravation or worsening of the pupil's behaviour or conduct.

4. Child and Family Services Review Board — The Child and Family Services Review Board is designated for the purposes of the definition of "designated tribunal" in subsection 311.7(1) of the Act to hear appeals of board decisions to expel pupils.

5. Notice of appeal — **(1)** To appeal a board's decision to expel a pupil, a person who is entitled, under subsection 311.7(2) of the Act, to appeal the decision shall give the designated tribunal a written notice of appeal within 30 days after the date on which he or she is considered, in accordance with the rules set out in subsection 300(3) of the Act, to have received the notice given under subsection 311.6(1) of the Act.

(2) The designated tribunal may extend the period of time for giving the written notice of appeal, before or after the expiry of the period, if it is satisfied that there are reasonable grounds for the extension.

(3) The notice of appeal shall,

(a) set out the date of the decision that is being appealed;

(b) set out the name of the board that made the decision;

(c) state whether the decision expels the pupil from his or her school only or from all schools of the board; and

(d) be in a form acceptable to the designated tribunal.

(4) The designated tribunal shall not refuse to deal with an appeal on the ground that there is a deficiency in the content or form of the notice of appeal.

6. Hearing of appeal — **(1)** The designated tribunal shall commence a hearing within 30 days after receiving a written notice of appeal.

(2) The designated tribunal may extend the period of time for commencing the hearing, before or after the expiry of the period, at the request of any party to the appeal.

(3) A pupil whose expulsion is being appealed has the right to be present at the hearing and to make a statement on his or her own behalf, whether or not the pupil is a party to the appeal.

(4) After hearing an appeal from a decision of a board, the designated tribunal shall do one of the following:

1. Confirm the board's decision to expel the pupil.
2. If the board's decision was to expel the pupil from his or her school only, quash the expulsion and reinstate the pupil to the school.
3. If the board's decision was to expel the pupil from all schools of the board,
   - i. change the expulsion to an expulsion from the pupil's school only, or
   - ii. quash the expulsion and reinstate the pupil to his or her school.

(5) The designated tribunal shall provide each party, or the party's counsel or agent, with,

(a) its decision on the appeal within 10 days after completing the hearing; and

(b) written reasons for its decision within 30 days after completing the hearing.

(6) If the designated tribunal changes an expulsion from all schools of the board to an expulsion from the pupil's school only or quashes an expulsion and reinstates the pupil to his or her school, it may order that any record of the expulsion of the pupil be expunged or amended if the designated tribunal considers it appropriate in the circumstances.

7. Revocations — Ontario Regulations 37/01 and 106/01 are revoked.

8. Commencement — This Regulation comes into force on February 1, 2008.

REGULATIONS UNDER THE ONTARIO COLLEGE OF TEACHERS ACT

ONT. REG. 72/97 — GENERAL

made under the *Ontario College of Teachers Act, 1996*

O. Reg. 72/97, as am. O. Reg. 392/01; 271/06; 369/07.

EMPLOYERS' OBLIGATION TO SUBMIT FEES

1. In sections 2 to 4,

"due date" means the date on which the annual membership fee is due in any year, as specified in the by-laws;

"private school" has the same meaning as in subsection 1(1) of the *Education Act*.

2. (1) Where, on the due date in any year, a school board employs a member, the school board shall,

(a) deduct the amount of the annual membership fee payable in respect of the year by the member from the member's salary; and

(b) submit the amount of the fee to the College.

(2) Where, on the due date in any year, the Provincial Schools Authority employs a member and the Ministry of Education and Training is responsible for paying the member's salary, the Ministry of Education and Training shall,

(a) deduct the amount of the annual membership fee payable in respect of the year by the member from the member's salary; and

(b) submit the amount of the fee to the College.

(3) Where, on the due date in any year, a private school employs a member who contributes to the Ontario Teachers' Pension Plan, the private school shall,

(a) deduct the amount of the annual membership fee payable in respect of the year by the member from the member's salary; and

(b) submit the amount of the fee to the College.

(4) Subsection (3) applies only if the private school has received notice that the member contributes to the Ontario Teachers' Pension Plan.

(5) The amounts referred to in subsections (1) to (3) shall be submitted no later than 35 days after the due date.

(6) The amount may be submitted by cheque or by any other means approved by the Registrar.

(7) When submitting an amount under this section, the school board, the Ministry of Education and Training or the private school, as the case may be, shall provide the Registrar with sufficient information to identify the member on whose behalf the amount is submitted.

(8) The Registrar may issue directions respecting the content and form of the information to be provided under subsection (7).

3. At the written request, made before the due date, of a school board, the Ministry of Education and Training or a private school, as the case may be, the Registrar may extend the period specified in subsection 2(5), if the Registrar is of the opinion that the extension is warranted because of exceptional circumstances.

4. (1) A school board, the Ministry of Education and Training or a private school, as the case may be, shall pay interest on any amount in arrears, from the day the amount was required to be submitted under section 2 or, where applicable, section 3, to the day before the day on which the payment is made.

(2) The interest shall be calculated at the bank prime rate plus 4 per cent per year.

(3) In subsection (2),

"bank prime rate" means the prime rate quoted by the College's bank of record on the day the payment was due.

Oath or Affirmation

[Heading added O. Reg. 271/06, s. 1.]

4.1 (1) A person elected or appointed to Council shall, before taking office, swear an oath or make an affirmation as follows:

> I will faithfully and impartially, to the best of my knowledge and skill, perform the duties of a member of the Council of the College and any committees of the Council on which I sit.
>
> In so doing, I will ensure that the guiding principle in the performance of my duties is the duty to serve and protect the public interest, which is my duty as a Council member and a duty of the College.
>
> I will perform the duties of my position without favour or ill will to any person or entity.
>
> I will ensure that other memberships, directorships, voluntary or paid positions or affiliations that I may hold will not interfere or conflict with the performance of my duties as a Council member.
>
> So help me God. (Omit this line in an affirmation.)

(2) In swearing the oath or making the affirmation, the person shall use the form provided by the Registrar.

(3) The oath shall be sworn or the affirmation shall be made before a commissioner for taking affidavits.

(4) The person elected or appointed to Council shall swear the oath or make the affirmation, and present the completed form referred to under subsection (2) to the Registrar, by,

(a) the first meeting of Council that the person would otherwise be eligible to attend as a Council member; or

(b) such other date as is determined by the Registrar, but in any event no later than one month after the meeting mentioned in clause (a).

(5) The person elected or appointed to Council may not take office if he or she fails to swear the oath or make the affirmation required under subsection (1).

O. Reg. 271/06, s. 1

Quorum at Council Meetings

5. Nineteen members of the Council, at least five of whom shall be persons appointed to the Council under clause 4(2)(b) of the Act, constitute a quorum of the Council.

O. Reg. 271/06, s. 2

Disqualification of Council Members

6. (1) The Council shall disqualify an elected member of the Council from sitting on the Council if, at any point during the member's term, the member,

(a) is found by the Discipline Committee to be guilty of professional misconduct or to be incompetent;

(b) is found by the Fitness to Practise Committee to be incapacitated;

(c) fails, without cause, to attend three consecutive meetings of the Council;

(d) fails, without cause, to attend half the meetings of the Council in any 12-month period;

(e) fails, without cause, to attend three consecutive meetings of a committee of which he or she is a member;

(f) fails, without cause, to attend a hearing of a panel of a committee for which he or she has been selected;

(g) fails or ceases to meet the criteria set out in Ontario Regulation 293/00 (*Election of Council Members*) made under the Act for eligibility to be nominated for the position for which the member was elected, as that regulation read on the day the member was declared elected;

(h) fails or ceases to meet the criteria set out in Ontario Regulation 293/00 (*Election of Council Members*) made under the Act for eligibility to take the position for which the member was elected, as that regulation read on the day the member was declared elected, or takes a position from which he or she would have been required to resign as a condition of eligibility to take the position for which he or she was elected; or

(i) in the case of a person who was a part-time classroom teacher, as defined in Ontario Regulation 293/00 (*Election of Council Members*) made under the Act, on the day the member was declared elected, provides instructional services, within the meaning of that regulation, on fewer than 10 days during each year of the person's term of office.

(1.1) Despite subsection (1), the chair of Council shall not be disqualified for failing or ceasing to meet the criteria for eligibility to take the position for which he or she was elected if the Council determines that the chair could not otherwise fulfil his or her duties as chair.

(1.2) The Council shall disqualify an elected member of the Council from sitting on the Council or suspend the member from his or her office as member of the Council if, at any point during the member's term,

(a) the Executive Committee requests the Council under clause 31(2)(b) to disqualify or suspend the member and no notice of appeal is submitted under subsection 32(1) within the time specified in that subsection; or

(b) if a notice of appeal is submitted under subsection 32(1), the Council determines, after holding a hearing for the appeal, to disqualify or suspend the member under clause 32(5)(b).

(2) An elected member of the Council who is disqualified from sitting on the Council ceases to be a member of the Council.

(3) An elected member of the Council who is the subject of a proceeding before the Discipline Committee or the Fitness to Practise Committee as a result of a referral under section 26 or 29 of the Act is suspended from his or her office as member of the Council pending the outcome of the proceeding.

(4) A person who is suspended under subsection (3) from his or her office as member of the Council shall not participate in any meeting or other proceeding of the Council.

O. Reg. 271/06, s. 3; 369/07, s. 1

VACANCIES ON COUNCIL

7. (1) For the purposes of this Regulation, the seat of an elected member of the Council becomes vacant if the member dies, resigns or is disqualified from sitting on the Council.

(2) For the purposes of this Regulation, the resignation of an elected member of the Council is effective when received by the Registrar, the chair or the vice-chair.

8. (1) If the seat of an elected member of the Council becomes vacant not more than six months before the expiry of the member's term of office, the Council may leave the seat vacant or may fill the vacated position by appointment.

(2) If the Council chooses to fill the vacated position by appointment, it shall appoint the person who had the most votes of all the unsuccessful candidates for the position in the last Council election, not including those persons who, as of the date of the appointment,

(a) are not willing to fill the vacancy; or

(b) do not meet the criteria set out in the regulations for eligibility to be nominated for the position, as those regulations read on the day the member was declared elected.

(3) If no person can be appointed in accordance with subsection (2), the Council may fill the vacated position by appointing any person who, as of the date of the appointment, is willing to fill the vacancy and meets the criteria set out in the regulations for eligibility to be nominated for the position, as those regulations read on the day the member was declared elected.

(4) The Council shall make its determination under subsection (1) as soon as reasonably possible and, if the Council decides to fill the vacated position, the Council shall do so as soon as reasonably possible.

9. (1) If the seat of an elected member of the Council becomes vacant more than six months before the expiry of the member's term of office, the Council shall fill the vacated position by appointing the person who had the most votes of all the unsuccessful candidates for the position in the last Council election, not including those persons who, as of the date of the appointment,

(a) are not willing to fill the vacancy; or

(b) do not meet the criteria set out in the regulations for eligibility to be nominated for the position, as those regulations read on the day the member was declared elected.

(2) If no person can be appointed in accordance with subsection (1), the Council shall fill the vacated position by appointing any person who, as of the date of the appointment, is willing to fill the vacancy and meets the criteria set out in the regulations for eligibility to be nominated for the position, as those regulations read on the day the member was declared elected.

(3) The Council shall fill the vacated position as soon as reasonably possible.

10. Within 10 days of a vacancy to which section 8 or 9 applies arising, the Registrar shall,

(a) notify the members of the Council that the vacancy has arisen;

(b) provide the members of the Council with the information that they need in order to be able to fill the vacancy; and

(c) draw the attention of the Council to its obligation under section 8 or 9, as the case may be, to act expeditiously.

11. (1) If the seat of one or more elected Council members becomes vacant and no quorum of the Council remains in office, the Registrar shall hold an election for the vacant positions and, for the purpose, shall adapt the provisions of the regulation that governed the last election to the Council, as those provisions read on the last voting day in that election, as he or she considers appropriate.

(2) Where an election is required under this section, the Registrar shall,

(a) within 10 days of the requirement to hold an election arising under subsection (1), set a date or time period during which the voting will occur; and

(b) ensure that the election is held as soon as reasonably possible.

12. A person appointed under section 8 or 9 or elected under section 11 shall hold office until the former Council member's term would have expired.

STATUTORY COMMITTEES

13. In sections 14 to 18,

"statutory committee" means,

(a) the Executive Committee,

(b) the Investigation Committee,

(c) the Discipline Committee,

(d) the Registration Appeals Committee, and

(e) the Fitness to Practise Committee.

14. (1) Subject to subsections 25(1), 27(1) and 28(1) of the Act, the Council shall determine the number of members to be appointed by it to the Investigation Committee, the Discipline Committee and the Fitness to Practise Committee.

(2) The members of a statutory committee to be appointed by the Council shall be appointed as soon as reasonably possible.

(3) A person appointed to a statutory committee shall continue to be a member of the committee until the first meeting of the next Council.

(4) Subject to subsection 20(1), the Council shall appoint a chair for each statutory committee, from among the members appointed to the committee.

(5) Subject to subsection 20(2), a statutory committee shall elect a vice-chair from among its members.

(6) In the absence of the chair of a statutory committee, the vice-chair shall temporarily act as and have all the powers of the chair.

(7) In the absence of the chair and vice-chair of a statutory committee, the committee shall elect a person from among its members to temporarily act as and have all the powers of the chair.

(8) The chair of a statutory committee may vote at meetings of the committee.

15. (1) Subject to subsection (4), a quorum of the Investigation Committee, the Discipline Committee or the Fitness to Practise Committee is a majority of the number of positions on the committee, as determined under subsection 14(1), whether or not one or more of the positions is vacant.

(2) Subject to subsection (4), a quorum of the Registration Appeals Committee is three.

(3) Subject to subsection (4), a quorum of the Executive Committee is four.

(4) A quorum of a statutory committee is not constituted unless at least one of the members of the committee participating in the meeting is a person appointed to the Council under clause 4(2)(b) of the Act.

16. (1) The seat of a member of a statutory committee becomes vacant if the member dies, resigns from the committee, resigns from the Council or is disqualified from sitting on the Council.

(2) For the purposes of this Regulation, the resignation of a member of a statutory committee from the committee is effective when received by the Registrar or the chair of the committee.

(3) If the seat of a member of a statutory committee becomes vacant, the Executive Committee shall, as soon as reasonably possible, appoint a member of the Council to fill the vacancy.

(4) Subsection (3) does not apply to vacancies on the Executive Committee.

(5) If the seat of a member of the Executive Committee becomes vacant, the Council shall, as soon as reasonably possible, appoint one of its members to fill the vacancy.

(6) In filling a vacancy under this section, the Executive Committee or Council, as the case may be, shall ensure that the requirements of subsections 25(2), 27(2) and 28(2) of the Act and of section 19 and subsections 23(2) and (3) of this Regulation are complied with.

(7) Within 10 days of a vacancy to which subsection (3) or (5) applies arising, the Registrar shall,

(a) notify the members of the Executive Committee or the Council, as the case may be, that the vacancy has arisen;

(b) provide the members of the Executive Committee or the Council, as the case may be, with the information that they need in order to be able to fill the vacancy; and

(c) draw the attention of the Executive Committee or the Council, as the case may be, to its obligation under this section to act expeditiously.

(8) A person appointed under this section shall hold office until the former committee member's term would have expired.

(9) A person who is suspended under subsection 6 (3) from his or her office as member of the Council is also suspended from his or her office as member of a statutory committee.

(10) A person who is suspended under subsection (9) from his or her office as member of a committee shall not participate in any meeting or other proceeding of the committee or of a panel of the committee.

17. (1) Each statutory committee shall meet at least once a year.

(2) Each statutory committee shall meet,

(a) when requested by its chair;

(b) when requested in writing signed by a sufficient number of members to constitute a quorum under section 15;

(c) when requested by the Council; or

(d) when requested by the Executive Committee.

18. (1) A meeting of a statutory committee may be held by any means that permits every person participating in the meeting to communicate with each other simultaneously.

(2) The chair of a statutory committee shall ensure that minutes are,

(a) taken at each meeting;

(b) reviewed and approved at the meeting following the one at which they are taken; and

(c) signed by the chair after approval.

(3) Subsections (1) and (2) apply with necessary modifications to a meeting of a panel of a statutory committee.

(4) This section does not apply to a hearing of a statutory committee or of a panel of a statutory committee.

EXECUTIVE COMMITTEE

19. (1) The Council shall appoint the chairs of the following committees as members of the Executive Committee:

1. The Fitness to Practise Committee.
2. The Discipline Committee.
3. The Registration Appeals Committee.
4. The Investigation Committee.
5. The Standards of Practice and Education Committee.
6. The Finance Committee.
7. The Accreditation Committee.

(2) The Council shall also appoint the chair and vice-chair of the Council as members of the Executive Committee, where they are not appointed under subsection (1).

(3) The Council shall appoint additional members to the Executive Committee in accordance with the following rules, where applicable:

1. If all the persons appointed under subsections (1) and (2) are members of the Council elected under clause 4(2)(a) of the Act, the Council shall appoint two additional persons to the Executive Committee, both of whom shall be members of the Council appointed under clause 4(2)(b) of the Act.

2. If only one of the persons appointed under subsections (1) and (2) is a member of the Council appointed under clause 4(2)(b) of the Act, the Council shall appoint one additional person to the Executive Committee, who shall be a member of the Council appointed under clause 4(2)(b) of the Act.

3. If all the persons appointed under subsections (1) and (2) are members of the Council appointed under clause 4(2)(b) of the Act, the Council shall appoint two additional persons to the Executive Committee, both of whom shall be members of the Council elected under clause 4(2)(a) of the Act.

4. If only one of the persons appointed under subsections (1) and (2) is a member of the Council elected under clause 4(2)(a) of the Act, the Council shall appoint one additional person to the Executive Committee, who shall be a member of the Council elected under clause 4(2)(a) of the Act.

20. (1) The chair of the Council shall be the chair of the Executive Committee.

(2) The vice-chair of the Council shall be the vice-chair of the Executive Committee.

ROSTER OF ELIGIBLE PANELISTS

[Heading added O. Reg. 392/01, s. 1.]

20.1 The appointment of a person by the Lieutenant Governor in Council under subsection 17(4) of the Act to a roster of eligible panelists for a Committee mentioned in paragraph 2, 3, 4 or 5 of subsection 15(1) of the Act is for the term specified in the appointment.

O. Reg. 391/01, s. 1

INVESTIGATION COMMITTEE

21. (1) A complaint to be considered and investigated by the Investigation Committee under section 26 of the Act shall be considered and investigated by a panel of the Committee selected for the purpose in accordance with section 17 of the Act by the chair of the Committee.

(2) The chair of the Committee shall appoint as the chair of the panel a member of the panel who is a member of the Committee.

(3) If a panelist's term of appointment to the Committee or to the roster of eligible panelists for the Committee ends before the consideration and investigation of the complaint is completed or the panel's decision is given, the panelist's term is deemed to continue for the purpose of participation in the decision.

(4) A panel may exercise all the powers and carry out all the duties of the Committee with respect to the complaint before the panel.

O. Reg. 392/01, s. 2

DISCIPLINE COMMITTEE

22. (1) A hearing on matters directed or referred to the Discipline Committee under section 26, 29 or 33 of the Act shall be conducted by a panel of the Committee selected for the purpose in accordance with section 17 of the Act by the chair of the Committee.

(2) The chair of the Committee shall appoint as the chair of the panel a member of the panel who is a member of the Committee.

(3) If a panelist's term of appointment to the Committee or to the roster of eligible panelists for the Committee ends before the hearing is completed or the panel's decision is given, the panelist's term is deemed to continue for the purpose of participation in the decision.

(4) A panel may exercise all the powers and carry out all the duties of the Committee with respect to the matter before the panel.

O. Reg. 392/01, s. 3

REGISTRATION APPEALS COMMITTEE

23. (1) The Council shall appoint five of its members to the Registration Appeals Committee.

(2) At least two of the members of the Registration Appeals Committee shall be persons appointed to the Council under clause 4(2)(b) of the Act.

(3) At least two of the members of the Registration Appeals Committee shall be persons elected to the Council under clause 4(2)(a) of the Act.

24. (1) A request for review under section 21 of the Act or an application for variation under section 22 of the Act shall be decided by a panel of the Registration Appeals Committee selected for the purpose in accordance with section 17 of the Act by the chair of the Committee.

(2) The chair of the Committee shall appoint as the chair of the panel a member of the panel who is a member of the Committee.

(3) If a panelist's term of appointment to the Committee or to the roster of eligible panelists for the Committee ends before the proceeding is completed or the panel's decision is given, the panelist's term is deemed to continue for the purpose of participation in the decision.

(4) A panel may exercise all the powers and carry out all the duties of the Committee with respect to the matter before the panel.

O. Reg. 392/01, s. 4

FITNESS TO PRACTISE COMMITTEE

25. (1) A hearing on matters directed or referred to the Fitness to Practise Committee under section 26, 29 or 33 of the Act shall be conducted by a panel of the Committee selected for the purpose in accordance with section 17 of the Act by the chair of the Committee.

(2) The chair of the Committee shall appoint as the chair of the panel a member of the panel who is a member of the Committee.

(3) If a panelist's term of appointment to the Committee or to the roster of eligible panelists for the Committee ends before the hearing is completed or the panel's decision is given, the panelist's term is deemed to continue for the purpose of participation in the decision.

(4) A panel may exercise all the powers and carry out all the duties of the Committee with respect to the matter before the panel.

O. Reg. 392/01, s. 5

PUBLIC INTEREST COMMITTEE

[Heading added O. Reg. 369/07, s. 2.]

25.1 (1) The Public Interest Committee shall meet at least four times a year and at any other time requested by its chair, the Council or the Executive Committee.

(2) The chair of the Public Interest Committee shall schedule the Committee's meetings, taking into account the requirements under section 25.2 relating to the Committee's work plan and the reporting requirements under section 25.4.

(3) The Registrar shall give every member of the Public Interest Committee at least 10 days notice of each meeting, except that,

(a) if the members waive the requirement for notice for a meeting, no notice is required for the meeting; and

(b) the chair shall give a reduced amount of notice for a meeting if the members consent to it.

(4) The notice referred to in subsection (3) shall be in writing and shall specify the time, place and proposed agenda of the meeting.

(5) A meeting of the Public Interest Committee shall be held by any means that permits every person participating in the meeting to communicate with each other simultaneously.

(6) The chair of the Public Interest Committee shall ensure that minutes are,

(a) taken at each meeting;

(b) reviewed and approved at the meeting following the one at which they are taken; and

(c) signed by the chair after approval.

(7) A quorum of the Public Interest Committee is three.

O. Reg. 369/07, s. 2

25.2 (1) The Public Interest Committee shall develop a work plan identifying its priorities and its proposed projects and activities for each period between elections of council members.

(2) Despite subsection (1), the first work plan developed after the day Ontario Regulation 369/07 comes into force shall relate to the period from the day the plan is developed until the day of the next election of council members.

(3) The Public Interest Committee shall include in its work plan a schedule for completing the proposed projects and activities.

(4) Each year after the year in which a work plan and schedule are first developed, the Public Interest Committee shall review them and modify them as necessary.

(5) The development of the work plan under subsection (1) or (2) and its modification, if any, under subsection (4) shall be done in consultation with the Council and shall take into account the budget approved by the Council to support the work of the Committee.

O. Reg. 369/07, s. 2

25.3 (1) The Public Interest Committee may request information from the Council to assist the Committee to,

(a) develop or modify the work plan referred to in section 25.2;

(b) implement the work plan; or

(c) provide advice to the Council.

(2) Requests for information shall be made to the Registrar.

O. Reg. 369/07, s. 2

25.4 (1) Each year before the Council's annual meeting, the Public Interest Committee shall provide a report to the Council on the activities of the Committee during the previous year.

(2) The report shall include a copy of the most recent work plan referred to in section 25.2 and any other reports requested by the Council.

O. Reg. 369/07, s. 2

DESIGNATIONS FOR PURPOSES OF SECTION 47 OF THE ACT

26. The following persons or bodies are designated for the purposes of subsection 47(1) of the Act:

1. A private school, as defined in subsection 1(1) of the *Education Act*, in respect of which a current notice of intention has been filed under section 16 of that Act.
2. A college of applied arts and technology established by regulation under subsection 2(1) of the *Ontario Colleges of Applied Arts and Technology Act, 2002*.
3. An institution specified in the Schedule to the *University Foundations Act, 1992*.
4. The Ontario Teachers' Pension Plan Board.
5. The Ontario Teachers' Federation.
6. L'Association des enseignantes et des enseignants franco-ontariens.
7. The Elementary Teachers' Federation of Ontario.
8. The Ontario English Catholic Teachers' Association.
9. [Revoked O. Reg. 392/01, s. 6(2).]
10. The Ontario Secondary School Teachers' Federation.

O. Reg. 392/01, s. 6; 271/06, s. 4

CONFLICT OF INTEREST

[Heading added O. Reg. 369/07, s. 3.]

27. (1) It is a conflict of interest for a member of the Council, a member of a committee of the Council or a member of the Public Interest Committee to make a decision, participate in making a decision or be present when a decision is made in the execution of his or her office if,

(a) there is an opportunity to directly or indirectly confer a benefit on the member or on any person listed in subsection (2); and

(b) the member knows or reasonably should know about the opportunity referred to in clause (a).

(2) The persons mentioned in clause (1)(a) are,

(a) anyone connected with the member by blood relationship, marriage, common-law or adoption;

(b) a corporation wholly owned or effectively controlled by the member; and

(c) an employer of the member.

(3) Despite subsection (1), it is not a conflict of interest for a member of the Council to approve resolutions relating to,

(a) the remuneration of Council members;

(b) the indemnification of Council members; or

(c) the acquisition of insurance in respect of the indemnification of Council members.

(4) Despite subsection (1), it is not a conflict of interest for a member of a committee of the Council to approve resolutions relating to,

(a) the remuneration of members of the committee of the Council;

(b) the indemnification of members of the committee of the Council; or

(c) the acquisition of insurance in respect of the indemnification of members of the committee of the Council.

(5) A member of the Council, a member of a committee of the Council or a member of the Public Interest Committee who has a conflict of interest in relation to a decision by the Council or committee, as the case may be, or who believes that he or she may have one, shall disclose it immediately upon becoming aware of it, to,

(a) the chair of the Council or committee, as the case may be, if the member is not the chair; or

(b) the vice-chair of the Council or committee, as the case may be, if the member is the chair.

(6) If the member becomes aware of the conflict of interest before or at any meeting at which the decision is discussed, the member,

(a) shall not participate in any discussion of the decision,

(b) shall not vote on the decision; and

(c) shall withdraw from the meeting for the discussion of the decision and for any vote on the decision, if requested to do so by the person to whom the member is required to disclose the conflict of interest.

(7) The Registrar shall keep a record of all disclosures made under subsection (5).

O. Reg. 369/07, s. 3

Complaints Against Members

[Heading added O. Reg. 369/07, s. 3.]

28. (1) Sections 29 to 31 set out the process for making and determining the following complaints:

1. A complaint that a member of the Council, a member of a committee of the Council or a member of the Public Interest Committee had a conflict of interest and failed to disclose it as required under subsection 27(5).

2. A complaint that a member of the Council contravened his or her obligations under the oath or affirmation set out in subsection 4.1(1).

(2) In sections 29 to 31, a reference to a member is a reference to a member of the Council, a member of a committee of the Council, or a member of the Public Interest Committee, as the case may be.

O. Reg. 369/07, s. 3

29. (1) Any person may make a complaint described in subsection 28(1).

(2) The complaint shall be in writing, shall contain information regarding the basis for the complaint and shall be submitted to,

(a) the vice-chair of the Council and the Registrar, if the complaint is against the chair of the Council; or

(b) the chair of the Council and the Registrar, if the complaint is against any other member.

(3) The Registrar shall provide a copy of the complaint to the member against whom the complaint is made.

O. Reg. 369/07, s. 3

30. (1) The Executive Committee shall hold a hearing for every complaint made under section 29.

(2) The hearing and any discussions or deliberations related to it shall be closed to the public.

(3) The person who made the complaint may give evidence and make submissions at the hearing but shall not otherwise be present at the hearing or during any discussions or deliberations related to it.

(4) The member against whom the complaint is made may give evidence and make submissions at the hearing and may be present throughout the hearing but shall not be present during any discussions or deliberations related to it.

O. Reg. 369/07, s. 3

31. (1) After considering any evidence given and submissions made at the hearing, the Executive Committee shall, by a majority vote, determine whether the member had a conflict of interest and failed to disclose it, or contravened the oath or affirmation, as the case may be.

(2) If the Executive Committee determines that a member had a conflict of interest and failed to disclose it, or contravened the oath or affirmation, as the case may be, the Executive Committee may,

(a) request the Council to reprimand the member in writing;

(b) for an elected member of the Council, request the Council to,

(i) suspend the member from the Council for a period of at least 30 days but not more than 90 days, or

(ii) disqualify the member from sitting on the Council;

(c) for a member who was appointed to the Council, request the Council to issue a report to the Minister, for referral to the Lieutenant Governor in Council, setting out details of the determination under subsection (1) and stating that if the member were an elected member of the Council, the Council would,

(i) suspend the member from the Council for a period of at least 30 days but not more than 90 days, or

(ii) disqualify the member from sitting on the Council, and

(d) for a member of the Public Interest Committee, request the Council to issue a report to the Minister setting out the information described in clause (c).

(3) The Registrar shall inform the member of the Executive Committee's determination under subsection (1) and any request under subsection (2) within 10 days of the determination and request, if any.

(4) The Council shall act on the requests, if any, made to it under subsection (2) if the time for submitting a notice of appeal under subsection 32(1) has passed and no notice is submitted.

O. Reg. 369/07, s. 3

32. (1) A member against whom a determination under subsection 31(1) or request under subsection 31(2) is made may, within 10 days after receiving notice of the determination or request, submit a written notice of appeal to the Council.

(2) The Council shall hold a hearing for every appeal submitted to it under subsection (1) within 30 days of receiving the notice.

(3) No member of the Council who participated in the decision made by the Executive Committee under subsection 31(1) or (2) shall participate in or be present for the hearing of the appeal.

(4) Subsections 30(2), (3) and (4) apply to the hearing of the appeal.

(5) After considering any evidence given and submissions made at the hearing before the Executive Committee or at the hearing of the appeal, the findings of the Executive Committee and any other information that the Council finds relevant, the Council shall, by a majority vote,

(a) uphold, vary or rescind the determination under subsection 31(1); and

(b) determine whether to do any thing requested under subsection 31(2).

O. Reg. 369/07, s. 3

ONT. REG. 184/97 — TEACHERS QUALIFICATIONS

made under the *Ontario College of Teachers Act, 1996*

O. Reg. 184/97, as am. O. Reg. 505/00; 373/01; 50/04; 188/04; 130/05; 269/06; 342/07 [s. 12(2) to come into force August 31, 2012.]; 30/08; 135/08 [ss. 1, 2(2)–(5), (8), 6, 7(3), 9(2), 11–13 to come into force May 31, 2009.] [s. 9(2) repealed O. Reg. 374/08, s. 5.]; 374/08 [ss. 1(3), 4 to come into force May 31, 2009.].

DEFINITIONS

1. (1) In this Regulation,

"acceptable post-secondary degree" means a degree, including a baccalaureate degree in an applied area of study, for which a person is required to complete at least 90 post-secondary credits or their equivalent and that is,

(a) granted by a post-secondary educational institution authorized to grant the degree under an Act of the Assembly, including a person that is authorized to grant the degree under the *Post-secondary Education Choice and Excellence Act, 2000*,

(b) granted by a post-secondary educational institution in a Canadian province or territory other than Ontario and that is considered by the College to be equivalent to a degree described in clause (a),

(c) granted by a post-secondary educational institution in the United States that is recognized by,

(i) Middle States Association of Colleges and Schools,

(ii) New England Association of Schools and Colleges,

(iii) North Central Association of Colleges and Schools,

(iv) Northwest Commission on Colleges and Universities,

(v) Southern Association of Colleges and Schools, or

(vi) Western Association of Schools and Colleges,

and that is considered by the College to be equivalent to a degree described in clause (a), or

(d) granted by a post-secondary educational institution located in a country other than Canada and the United States and that is considered by the College to be equivalent to a degree described in clause (a);

"acceptable university degree" [Revoked O. Reg. 188/04, s. 1(1).]

"accredited program" means an accredited program as defined in Ontario Regulation 347/02 made under the Act;

"appropriate supervisory officer" means, in respect of a teacher, the supervisory officer assigned by a board in accordance with the *Education Act* and the regulations under it or by the Minister to provide supervisory services in respect of the performance by the teacher of his or her duties under the *Education Act* and the regulations under it;

"approved program" [Revoked O. Reg. 188/04, s. 1(3).]

"band" and **"council of the band"** have the same meaning as in the *Indian Act* (Canada);

"candidate" means a candidate for any qualification granted in a Certificate of Qualification under this Regulation;

"certificate of qualification" means a certificate of qualification referred to in subsection (2);

"division" means the primary division, junior division, intermediate division or senior division, as defined in the *Education Act*;

"general studies" means the courses prescribed or developed for the intermediate and senior divisions under subsection 8(1) of the *Education Act* and described in the secondary curriculum documents available on the Ministry of Education web site at *www.edu.gov.on.ca*, excluding the courses described in,

(a) the document entitled "Technological Education — The Ontario Curriculum, Grades 9 and 10 — 1999", other than the sections relating to Computer and Information Science, Grade 10, Open and Computer Engineering Technology, Grade 10, Open, and

(b) the document entitled "Technological Education — The Ontario Curriculum, Grades 11 and 12 — 2000", other than Part B: Computer Studies;

Proposed Amendment — 1(1) "general studies"

"general studies" means the courses prescribed or developed for the intermediate and senior divisions under subsection 8(1) of the *Education Act* and described in the secondary curriculum documents available on the Ministry of Education website, excluding the courses described in the documents entitled "The Ontario Curriculum, Grades 9 and 10 — Technological Education (2008)" and "The Ontario Curriculum, Grades 11 and 12 — Technological Education (2008)";

O. Reg. 135/08, s. 2(2) [To come into force May 31, 2009.]

"holds a degree" means, in respect of a candidate, that he or she has completed all the requirements for and has been approved for, the granting of a degree, regardless of whether or not the degree has been conferred;

"OSIS" [Revoked O. Reg. 188/04, s. 1(5).]

"post-secondary course" means a one-year post-secondary course, or the equivalent of a one-year post-secondary course, where the course is part of a program leading to an acceptable post-secondary degree;

"post-secondary credit" means the credits a student is awarded on successful completion of a post-secondary course, where six credits are awarded for a one-year post-secondary course and a proportionate number of credits are awarded for a post-secondary course of a different duration;

"program of professional education" [Revoked O. Reg. 188/04, s. 1(7).]

"school year" means a minimum of 194 school days of which not more than four days are designated as professional activity days and the remaining days are instructional days;

Proposed Addition — 1(1) "technological education"

"technological education" means the courses prescribed or developed under subsection 8(1) of the *Education Act* and described in the documents entitled "The Ontario Curriculum, Grades 9 and 10 — Technological Education (2008)" and "The Ontario Curriculum, Grades 11 and 12 — Technological Education (2008)" available on the Ministry of Education website.

O. Reg. 135/08, s. 2(3) [To come into force May 31, 2009.]

"technological qualifications" means, in respect of a candidate for a certificate of qualification, an interim certificate of qualification or a certificate of qualification (limited, restricted),

(a) the holding of the secondary school graduation diploma or the successful completion of courses that are considered by the College to be the equivalent of such diploma,

(b) proof of his or her competence in the area or areas of technological studies selected as options in the program of professional education, and

(c) one of,

(i) five years of wage-earning, business or industrial experience in the area or areas of technological studies selected as options in the program of professional education,

(ii) a combination of education related to the area or areas of technological studies selected as options in the program of professional education beyond that referred to in clause (a) and business or industrial experience in the area or areas of technological studies selected as options in the program of technological studies that totals five years, including at least two years of wage-earning experience, no less than 16 months of which is continuous employment, or

(iii) at least 3,700 hours of wage-earning experience and successful completion of a post-secondary education program acceptable to the College that includes at least 24 months of academic studies, if the wage-earning experience and the education program are related to the area or areas of technological studies selected as options in the program of professional education;

Proposed Amendment — 1(1) "technological qualifications"

"technological qualifications" means, in respect of a candidate for a certificate of qualification, an interim certificate of qualification, a certificate of qualification (limited) or an interim certificate of qualification (limited), the following:

1. The candidate holds a secondary school graduation diploma or has successfully completed courses that are considered by the College to be the equivalent of holding such a diploma.

2. In the candidate's program of professional education, he or she chose the same area of technological education for his or her optional courses for Grades 9 and 10 and for Grades 11 and 12.

3. The candidate has proof of his or her competence based on an assessment of advanced knowledge and skill in the area of technological education selected by the candidate for his or her optional courses.

4. One of,

i. five years of wage-earning experience, including business or industrial experience, where the candidate used skills and knowledge in the area of technological education selected for his or her optional courses,

ii. at least two years of wage-earning experience and successful completion of a post-secondary education program acceptable to the College that includes at least six semesters of academic studies, where the experience and education used the candidate's skills and knowledge in the area of technological education selected for his or her optional courses, or

iii. a combination of the following that totals five years, including at least two years of experience described in sub-subparagraph B:

A. Education beyond that referred to in paragraph 1 that is related to the area of technological education selected for the candidate's optional courses.

B. Wage-earning experience, including business or industrial experience, no less than four months of which is continuous employment, where the candidate used skills and knowledge in the area of technological education selected for his or her optional courses.

O. Reg. 135/08, s. 2(4) [To come into force May 31, 2009.]

"technological studies" means the courses prescribed or developed under subsection 8(1) of the *Education Act* and described in,

(a) the document entitled "Technological Education — The Ontario Curriculum, Grades 9 and 10 — 1999", other than the sections relating to Computer and Information Science, Grade 10, Open and Computer Engineering Technology, Grade 10, Open, available on the Ministry of Education web site at *www.edu.gov.on.ca*, and

(b) the document entitled "Technological Education — The Ontario Curriculum, Grades 11 and 12 — 2000", other than Part B: Computer Studies, available on the Ministry of Education web site at *www.edu.gov.on.ca*.

Proposed Repeal — 1(1) "technological studies"

"technological studies" [Repealed O. Reg. 135/08, s. 2(5). To come into force May 31, 2009.]

"university course" [Revoked O. Reg. 188/04, s. 1(10).]

"university credit" [Revoked O. Reg. 188/04, s. 1(10).]

(2) The following shall be two classes of certificate of qualification and registration:

1. A certificate of registration, which shall set out the holder's membership relationship with the College.

2. A certificate of qualification, which shall set out the holder's qualifications for teaching.

(3) For the purposes of this Regulation, a program of professional education is an accredited program provided in Ontario that prepares persons to teach in elementary or secondary schools in Ontario and that satisfies the following requirements:

1. The program leads to the granting of a degree by an institution identified in clause (a) of the definition of "acceptable post-secondary degree" in subsection (1) and includes a concentrated study of,

i. the primary and junior divisions, with or without a focus on the teaching of French as a second language,

ii. the junior division and one optional course from Schedule A that is in the intermediate division and a course related to grades 7 and 8 of the intermediate division,

iii. the intermediate and senior divisions, including two optional courses from Schedule A, or

iv. technological studies, including a minimum of two optional courses for Grades 9 and 10 from Schedule B, or one optional course for Grades 9 and 10 from that Schedule and one course for Grades 11 and 12.

Proposed Amendment — 1(3), para. 1 iv

iv. technological education, including one optional course for Grades 9 and 10 from Schedule B and one optional course for Grades 11 and 12 from Schedule B, where both courses are in the same area of technological education.

O. Reg. 135/08, s. 2(8) [To come into force May 31, 2009.]

2. The program includes,

i. studies in education, including learning and development throughout the primary, junior, intermediate and senior division,

ii. teaching methods designed to meet the individual needs of pupils,

iii. the Acts and regulations respecting education,

iv. a review of the curriculum guidelines issued by the Minister relating to all of the divisions and a study of curriculum development, and

v. a minimum of 40 days of practical experience in schools or in other situations approved by the College for observation and practice teaching.

(4) Despite subsection (3), a program that satisfies the requirements of paragraph 2 of subsection (3) but not paragraph 1 of that subsection is a program of professional education for the purposes of this Regulation if,

(a) the program includes a concentrated study of technological studies described in subparagraph 1 iv of subsection (3); and

Proposed Amendment — 1(4)(a)

(a) the program includes a concentrated study of technological education described in subparagraph 1 iv of subsection (3); and

O. Reg. 135/08, s. 1(1), item 1 [To come into force May 31, 2009.]

(b) the program prepares persons to be teachers of technological studies.

Proposed Amendment — 1(4)(b)

(b) the program prepares persons to be teachers of technological education.

O. Reg. 135/08, s. 1(1), item 2 [To come into force May 31, 2009.]

(5) Despite subsection (3), a program that does not lead to an acceptable post-secondary degree but otherwise satisfies the requirements of subsection (3) is a program of professional education for the purposes of this Regulation if the program prepares persons to be,

(a) teachers of a Native language as a second language who are entitled to a certificate under section 23;

(b) teachers of the deaf who are entitled to a certificate under section 19; or

(c) teachers who are entitled to a certificate under section 6.

O. Reg. 188/04, s. 1; 342/07, s. 1; 135/08, s. 2(1), (6), (7)

PART I — BASIC QUALIFICATIONS

2. A candidate for the certificate of qualification shall submit to the dean of a college or faculty of education or the director of a school of education in Ontario,

(a) a certificate of birth or baptism, or other acceptable proof of the date and place of birth;

(b) in the case of a candidate who wishes to have the certificate issued in the candidate's married name, a certificate of marriage or other acceptable proof that the candidate is the person referred to in the document submitted under clause (a);

(c) a certificate of change of name where applicable;

(d) evidence satisfactory to such dean or director of his or her academic or technological qualifications; and

(e) in the case of a person who was not born in Canada, the basis upon which the candidate is present in Canada;

(f) [Revoked O. Reg. 188/04, s. 2(3).]

O. Reg. 188/04, s. 2

2.1 A candidate for a certificate of qualification of any kind or class provided for in this Regulation shall provide the following to the Registrar in such manner as the Registrar directs:

1. An original report,

   i. that contains information on criminal offences of which the candidate has been convicted under the *Criminal Code* (Canada) and for which a pardon under section 4.1 of the *Criminal Records Act* (Canada) has not been granted or issued to the individual, and

   ii. that has been prepared by a police force or service not more than six months before the day on which the report is provided to the Registrar and that includes, at a minimum, national data from the Canadian Police Information Centre database.

2. A criminal record declaration, in a form provided for in the by-laws of the College, that lists,

   i. all of the candidate's convictions for offences under the *Criminal Code* (Canada) up to the date of the declaration for which a pardon under section 4.1 of the *Criminal Records Act* (Canada) has not been issued or granted,

   ii. all of the candidate's convictions for criminal offences under the laws of other jurisdictions.

O. Reg. 188/04, s. 3; 130/05, s. 1

3. Subject to section 3.1, the Registrar may grant a certificate of qualification to a candidate, in the form provided in the by-laws of the College and indicating the areas of concentration the candidate has successfully completed, if the dean of a college or faculty of education or the director of a school of education in Ontario reports to the Registrar that the candidate,

(a) has complied with section 2;

(b) holds an acceptable post-secondary degree or qualifications the College considers equivalent thereto, or technological qualifications; and

(c) has successfully completed a program of professional education.

O. Reg. 50/04, s. 1; 188/04, s. 4; 269/06, s. 1

3.1 The Registrar may refuse to grant a certificate of qualification of any kind or class provided for in this Regulation to a candidate who,

(a) has not fulfilled his or her obligations under section 2.1; or

(b) has made a representation or declaration in connection with the application for a certificate of qualification that was false or misleading in a material respect.

O. Reg. 188/04, s. 5; 130/05, s. 2

3.2 [Repealed O. Reg. 269/06, s. 2.]

3.3 If, immediately before section 3.2 was revoked by Ontario Regulation 269/06, a person held a valid certificate of qualification (provisional) that was granted under subsection 3.2(1) or extended under subsection 3.2(3), the person shall be deemed to hold a certificate of qualification as of the day Ontario Regulation 269/06 comes into force.

O. Reg. 130/05, s. 3; 269/06, s. 3

4. (1) An entry on a certificate of qualification in respect of a program successfully completed in Canada shall indicate by the language in which the entry is recorded whether the program was taken in English or in French.

(2) An entry on a certificate of qualification in respect of a program successfully completed out of Canada shall indicate by the language in which the entry is recorded whether the qualification referred to is for teaching in schools and classes where English is the language of instruction or in French-language schools and classes established under Part XII of the *Education Act*.

(3) Despite section 14, qualifications valid in French-language schools and classes established under Part XII of the *Education Act* are valid in French-language classes where the teacher may otherwise be assigned or appointed to teach according to subsection 19(14) of Regulation 298 of the Revised Regulations of Ontario, 1990.

5. An entry on a certificate of qualification in respect of a program in International Languages shall specify which language was studied in the program.

5.1 An entry on a certificate of qualification in respect of a program in Native Languages shall specify which language was studied in the program.

O. Reg. 342/07, s. 2

6. (1) Where the dean of a college or faculty of education or the director of a school of education in Ontario reports to the Registrar that a candidate,

(a) has complied with section 2;

(b) is of native ancestry;

(c) holds the requirements for a Secondary School Graduation Diploma or standing the College considers equivalent thereto; and

(d) has successfully completed a program of professional education with concentration in the primary division and the junior division,

the Registrar may grant to the candidate a certificate of qualification in the form provided for in the by-laws of the College.

(2) The Registrar may grant to a candidate a certificate of qualification (limited) valid for one year for teaching in the primary division and junior division if the dean of a college or faculty of education or the director of a school of education in Ontario reports to the Registrar that the candidate meets the qualifications of clauses (1)(a) to (c) and has successfully completed the first session of a program of professional education with concentration in the primary division and the junior division.

(3) The certificate of qualification (limited) granted under subsection (2) shall be in the form provided for in the by-laws of the College.

(4) The Registrar may renew a candidate's certificate of qualification (limited) for one year for teaching in the primary division and junior division if the candidate submits to the Registrar evidence that the candidate,

(a) holds a certificate of qualification (limited) granted under subsection (2) that has expired or is about to expire; and

(b) has an offer of a position as a teacher in the primary division or junior division from,

(i) a board,

(ii) a private school,

(iii) the Provincial Schools Authority established under section 2 of the *Provincial Schools Negotiations Act*,

(iv) the Department of Indian Affairs and Northern Development of the Government of Canada, or

(v) a council of a band or an education authority, if the council of the band or the education authority is authorized by the Crown in right of Canada to provide education for Indians.

7. (1) Where the dean of a college or faculty of education or the director of a school of education in Ontario at the time of making a report under section 3, 6, 8 or 11 is of the opinion from the information provided under section 2 by the candidate in respect of whom the report is to be made, that the candidate is not entitled under the laws of Canada to obtain employment as a teacher in Canada, the dean or director at the time of making the report shall so inform the Registrar.

(2) Where the Registrar is informed as set out in subsection (1), the Registrar may refuse to grant the certificate referred to in section 3 or 6 or in subsection 11(2), as the case may be, or may withhold the certificate of qualification (limited) referred to in section 8 or its extension under subsection 11(1), until the candidate provides proof to the Registrar that the candidate is entitled under the laws of Canada to obtain employment as a teacher in Canada.

8. Where the dean of a college or faculty of education or the director of a school of education in Ontario reports to the Registrar that a candidate,

(a) has complied with section 2;

(b) holds an acceptable post-secondary degree or qualifications the College considers equivalent thereto or technological qualifications; and

(c) has successfully completed the first session of a program of professional education,

the Registrar may grant to the candidate a certificate of qualification (limited) in the form provided for in the by-laws of the College.

O. Reg. 188/04, s. 6

9. Where a person who is the holder of a certificate of qualification (limited) granted under section 8 that has expired, or is about to expire, submits to the Registrar evidence that he or she has an offer of a position as a teacher from,

(a) a board;

(b) a private school;

(c) the Provincial Schools Authority established under section 2 of the *Provincial Schools Negotiations Act*;

(d) the Department of Indian Affairs and Northern Development of the Government of Canada; or

(e) a council of a band or an education authority where such council of the band or education authority is authorized by the Crown in right of Canada to provide education for Indians,

the Registrar may renew the certificate of qualification (limited) for a period of one year.

10. For the purposes of section 11, a person who holds a Temporary Elementary School Certificate or a Temporary Secondary School Certificate is deemed to hold a certificate of qualification (limited) granted on the date of his or her Temporary Elementary School Certificate or his or her Temporary Secondary School Certificate.

11. (1) Where the dean of a college or faculty of education or the director of a school of education in Ontario reports to the Registrar that a person who holds a certificate of qualification (limited),

(a) has taught successfully for one school year in Ontario as certified by the appropriate supervisory officer; and

(b) has successfully completed the second session of a program of professional education where such second session is not the final session of the program,

the Registrar may extend the person's certificate of qualification (limited) for one year.

(2) Where the dean of a college or faculty of education or the director of a school of education in Ontario reports to the Registrar that a candidate who holds a certificate of qualification (limited),

(a) has taught successfully in Ontario, as certified by the appropriate supervisory officer, for one school year after the granting of a certificate of qualification (limited) and after its extension where it was extended; and

(b) has successfully completed the final session of a program of professional education,

the Registrar may grant to the candidate a certificate of qualification under section 3.

O. Reg. 130/05, s. 4; 269/06, s. 4

12. (1) An applicant for an interim certificate of qualification who completed a teacher education program outside Ontario shall submit to the Registrar with the application,

(a) the items required to be submitted under section 2;

(b) evidence of his or her academic or technological qualifications;

(c) his or her teaching certificate and a transcript of his or her teacher education program;

(d) a statement from the issuing authority that his or her teaching certificate has not been suspended or cancelled;

(e) where the candidate is not a Canadian citizen or a permanent resident of Canada, evidence that the candidate is entitled under the laws of Canada to obtain employment in Canada as a teacher; and

(f) such evidence as the Registrar may require of successful teaching experience in schools and programs similar to those for which the interim certificate of qualification applied for is valid.

(2) An applicant shall submit with the application evidence that he or she successfully completed an English or French language proficiency test if,

(a) he or she completed a teacher education program that was taught outside Canada or in a province or territory outside Ontario; and

(b) that program was not taught in English or French.

(3) The language proficiency test under subsection (2) shall be a test that,

(a) tests the applicant's ability to comprehend and communicate in English or French, as the case may be;

(b) has both an oral and a written component;

(c) is approved by the College; and

(d) is administered by a person or organization approved by the College.

(4) The Registrar may exempt an applicant from the requirement under subsection (2) if, after taking into account the language of the applicant's elementary, secondary and post-secondary education, the Registrar is satisfied that the applicant is able to comprehend and communicate effectively in English or French, as the case may be.

(5) If the applicant completed his or her teacher education program outside Ontario, he or she shall also submit with the application evidence that he or she has successfully completed an orientation program in English or French, as the case may be, that is approved by the College.

O. Reg. 505/00, s. 1

13. (1) The Registrar may grant an interim certificate of qualification to an applicant under section 12 if the Registrar is satisfied that,

(a) the applicant has complied with section 12;

(b) the applicant has successfully completed a teacher education program acceptable to the College,

(i) in a Canadian province other than Ontario or a Canadian territory, or

(ii) outside Canada; and

(c) the applicant holds the academic or technological qualifications required for a certificate of qualification.

(d) [Repealed O. Reg. 269/06, s. 5(1).]

(2) An interim certificate of qualification granted under this section shall be in the form provided for in the by-laws and shall be valid for six years from the date of issue.

(3) [Repealed O. Reg. 269/06, s. 5(2).]

(4) The following rules apply if an interim certificate of qualification that was originally granted under this section after March 14, 2002 and before March 5, 2004 was deemed to be an interim certificate of qualification (provisional) under subsection (3) as it read before it was revoked by Ontario Regulation 269/06:

1. As of the day Ontario Regulation 269/06 comes into force, the certificate shall be deemed to be an interim certificate of qualification.

2. The certificate shall be deemed to have been granted on the day the interim certificate of qualification was originally granted under this section.

3. The interim certificate of qualification shall be valid for six years from the date described in paragraph 2.

O. Reg. 505/00, s. 2; 50/04, s. 2; 269/06, s. 5

13.1 (1) The Registrar may grant an interim certificate of qualification (limited) to an applicant under section 12 if the Registrar is satisfied that,

(a) the applicant has complied with section 12;

(b) the applicant holds a valid teaching certificate for a Canadian province other than Ontario or for a Canadian territory; and

(c) the applicant does not have the academic or technological qualifications required for a certificate of qualification or has not successfully completed a teacher education program acceptable to the College.

(d) [Repealed O. Reg. 269/06, s. 6(1).]

(2) The Registrar may impose conditions on an interim certificate of qualification (limited) relating to any of the following:

1. Requiring the holder to obtain the academic or technological qualifications required for a certificate of qualification.

2. Requiring the holder to complete successfully a program of professional education, as defined in subsection 1(3).

3. Requiring the holder to obtain, while holding the interim certificate of qualification (limited), at least 10 months of successful teaching experience in Ontario and to have such experience certified by the appropriate supervisory officer.

(3) An interim certificate of qualification (limited) must be in the form provided for in the by-laws and is valid for an initial term of three years from the date it is granted.

(4) The Registrar may extend the period of validity of a person's interim certificate of qualification (limited) granted under subsection (1) for an additional term of three years if,

(a) the person requests the extension before the end of the initial term of the certificate;

(b) the person is a member in good standing of the College; and

(c) the Registrar is satisfied that the person has taken reasonable steps during the initial term of the certificate to meet approximately half of the conditions the Registrar has imposed on the certificate.

(5) If the Registrar has extended the period of validity of a person's interim certificate of qualification (limited) under subsection (4), the Registrar may extend its period of validity again for not more than three additional consecutive terms of one year each, if,

(a) the person requests the extension before the end of the most recent extended term of the certificate;

(b) the person is a member in good standing of the College; and

(c) the Registrar is satisfied that there are exceptional circumstances that have prevented the person from meeting all of the conditions the Registrar has imposed on the certificate.

(6) After the third extension under subsection (5) of the period of validity of an interim certificate of qualification (limited), the Registrar shall not extend its period of validity again.

(7) [Repealed O. Reg. 269/06, s. 6(2).]

(8) The following rules apply if an interim certificate of qualification (limited) that was originally granted under this section after March 14, 2002 and before March 5, 2004 was deemed to be an interim certificate of qualification (limited, provisional) under subsection (7) as it read before it was revoked by Ontario Regulation 269/06:

1. As of the day Ontario Regulation 269/06 comes into force, the certificate shall be deemed to be an interim certificate of qualification (limited).
2. The certificate shall be deemed to have been granted on the day the interim certificate of qualification was originally granted under this section.
3. Subsections (4), (5) and (6) apply with respect to the certificate.

O. Reg. 373/01, s. 1; 50/04, s. 3; 269/06, s. 6; 135/08, s. 3

13.2 [Repealed O. Reg. 269/06, s. 7.]

13.2.1 If, immediately before section 13.2 was revoked by Ontario Regulation 269/06, a person held a valid interim certificate of qualification (provisional) that was granted under that section, on the day Ontario Regulation 269/06 comes into force the following rules apply:

1. The certificate shall be deemed to be an interim certificate of qualification.
2. The interim certificate of qualification referred to in paragraph 1 shall be deemed to have been granted on the day the interim certificate of qualification (provisional) was originally granted.
3. The interim certificate of qualification is valid for six years from the date described in paragraph 2.

O. Reg. 269/06, s. 8

13.3 [Repealed O. Reg. 269/06, s. 9.]

13.3.1 If, immediately before section 13.3 was revoked by Ontario Regulation 269/06, a person held a valid interim certificate of qualification (limited, provisional) that was granted under that section, on the day Ontario Regulation 269/06 comes into force the following rules apply:

1. The certificate shall be deemed to be an interim certificate of qualification (limited).
2. The interim certificate of qualification (limited) shall be deemed to have been granted on the day that interim certificate of qualification (limited, provisional) was originally granted.
3. Subsections 13.1(4), (5) and (6) apply, with necessary modifications, with respect to the certificate.

O. Reg. 269/06, s. 10

14. Sections 12, 13, 14 and 15 of this Regulation, as they read on the day before Ontario Regulation 505/00 is filed, continue to apply with respect to every person to whom a letter of eligibility was issued before that day if it was still in effect under those sections on that day.

O. Reg. 505/00, s. 2

15. [Revoked O. Reg. 505/00, s. 2.]

16. The Registrar may grant an interim certificate of qualification, in the form provided for in the by-laws that is valid for a period of one year from the date of issue to a person who,

(a) was the holder of a letter of standing that was issued under Parts I, II and IV of Ontario Regulation 295/73 and that had the force of an Interim Certificate referred to in subsection 28(1); and

(b) is not the holder of a certificate of qualification or an interim certificate of qualification and who is offered a position as a teacher by,

(i) a board,

(ii) a private school,

(iii) the Provincial Schools Authority established under section 2 of the *Provincial Schools Negotiations Act*,

(iv) the Department of Indian Affairs and Northern Development of the Government of Canada, or

(v) a council of a band or an education authority, where such council of the band or education authority is authorized by the Crown in right of Canada to provide education for Indians.

17. (1) Where a person who holds an interim certificate of qualification granted under section 13 or 16, that is still valid or that has expired, submits to the Registrar evidence that the person had, while the person was the holder of the interim certificate of qualification, at least one year of successful teaching experience in Ontario as certified by the appropriate supervisory officer, the Registrar may grant to the person a certificate of qualification in the form provided for in the by-laws, indicating the areas of concentration successfully completed.

(2) Where an interim certificate of qualification issued under section 13 or 16 expires, the person who is the holder of the interim certificate of qualification is not eligible for another interim certificate of qualification.

O. Reg. 505/00, s. 3; 130/05, s. 7

17.1 The Registrar may grant to a person a certificate of qualification in the form provided for in the by-laws, indicating the areas of concentration successfully completed, if,

(a) the person has been granted an interim certificate of qualification (limited) under section 13.1, regardless of whether the interim certificate of qualification (limited) is still valid or has expired; and

(b) the Registrar is satisfied that, before the expiry of the person's interim certificate of qualification (limited), including any extensions of its period of validity, the person met all of the conditions the Registrar imposed on the interim certificate of qualification (limited).

O. Reg. 373/01, s. 1

18. (1) Where a person who holds an interim certificate of qualification granted under section 13 or 16 that has expired or is about to expire, submits to the Registrar,

(a) evidence that the person had while the person was the holder of the interim certificate of qualification fewer than one year of successful teaching experience in Ontario, as certified by the appropriate supervisory officer; and

(b) evidence that the person has an offer of a position as a teacher from,

(i) a board,

(ii) a private school,

(iii) the Provincial Schools Authority established under section 2 of the *Provincial Schools Negotiations Act*,

(iv) the Department of Indian Affairs and Northern Development of the Government of Canada, or

(v) a council of a band or an incorporated education authority established by two or more bands where such council of the band or education authority is authorized by the Crown in right of Canada to provide education for Indians,

the Registrar may, despite subsection 17(2), extend the period of validity of the interim certificate of qualification that has expired or is about to expire, as the case may be, for one-year periods.

(2) Where the Registrar extends the period of validity of an interim certificate of qualification under subsection (1), the interim certificate of qualification issued to the person shall be altered to indicate the extended period of validity.

O. Reg. 505/00, s. 4; 130/05, s. 8

18.1 [Repealed O. Reg. 130/05, s. 9.]

19. (1) Where the dean of a college or faculty of education or the director of a school of education in Ontario reports to the Registrar that a candidate,

(a) has complied with section 2;

(b) is entitled under the laws of Canada to obtain employment in Canada as a teacher, if the candidate is not a Canadian citizen or a permanent resident of Canada;

(c) is unable to undertake a program leading to the certificate of qualification by reason of impaired hearing;

(d) holds an acceptable post-secondary degree or qualifications the College considers equivalent thereto; and

(e) has successfully completed an accredited program of teacher education for teaching the deaf,

the Registrar may grant to the candidate a certificate of qualification (restricted) that is in the form provided for in the by-laws and valid in Ontario for teaching the deaf.

(2) The Registrar may grant a certificate of qualification (limited, restricted) valid for one year for teaching the deaf to a candidate who has successfully completed a program of teacher education outside Ontario for teaching the deaf that is acceptable to the College, if the candidate submits to the Registrar,

(a) evidence that the candidate has complied with section 2;

(b) evidence that the candidate is deaf or hard of hearing;

(c) evidence that the candidate is a Canadian citizen or a permanent resident of Canada or is entitled under the laws of Canada to obtain employment in Canada as a teacher;

(d) evidence that the candidate holds an acceptable post-secondary degree or qualifications that the College considers equivalent to an acceptable post-secondary degree; and

(e) if the candidate is qualified to teach outside Ontario,

(i) the candidate's teaching certificate and a transcript of the candidate's teacher education program, and

(ii) a statement from the authority that issued the candidate's teaching certificate that the certificate has not been suspended or cancelled.

(3) The certificate of qualification (limited, restricted) granted under subsection (2) shall be in the form provided for in the by-laws.

(4) The Registrar may extend a certificate of qualification (limited, restricted) granted under subsection (2) for one-year periods.

(5) The Registrar may grant a certificate of qualification (restricted) for teaching the deaf to a person who holds a certificate of qualification (limited, restricted) granted under subsection (2) if the person submits to the Registrar evidence of at least one school year of experience successfully teaching the deaf in Ontario since the granting of the certificate of qualification (limited, restricted), as certified by the appropriate supervisory officer.

(6) The certificate of qualification (restricted) granted under subsection (5) shall be in the form provided for in the by-laws.

O. Reg. 188/04, s. 7

19.1 A person who held one of the following certificates on the day Ontario Regulation 188/04 came into force remains qualified to teach in the schools and classes for which the certificate qualified him or her immediately before that day:

1. A certificate of qualification (limited, restricted) under section 20, as that section read on the day before Ontario Regulation 188/04 came into force.
2. A renewed certificate of qualification (limited, restricted) under section 21, as that section read on the day before Ontario Regulation 188/04 came into force.
3. A certificate of qualification (restricted) under section 22, as that section read on the day before Ontario Regulation 188/04 came into force.

O. Reg. 188/04, s. 8

20. [Revoked O. Reg. 188/04, s. 9.]

21. [Revoked O. Reg. 188/04, s. 9.]

22. [Revoked O. Reg. 188/04, s. 9.]

23. (1) The Registrar may grant to a candidate a certificate of qualification (limited, restricted) valid for one year for the teaching of a Native language as a second language if the dean of a college or faculty of education or the director of a school of education in Ontario reports to the Registrar that the candidate,

(a) has demonstrated an acceptable degree of fluency in the Algonquian or Iroquoian language;

(b) has complied with section 2;

(c) has successfully completed the first session of an accredited program for Teacher of a Native Language as a Second Language; and

(d) is entitled under the laws of Canada to obtain employment in Canada as a teacher, if the candidate is not a Canadian citizen or a permanent resident of Canada.

(2) A certificate of qualification (limited, restricted) granted under subsection (1) shall be in the form provided for in the by-laws.

O. Reg. 188/04, s. 10

24. The Registrar may extend a candidate's certificate of qualification (limited, restricted) for one year for the teaching of a Native language as a second language if the dean of a college or faculty of education or the director of a school of education in Ontario reports to the Registrar that the candidate,

(a) holds a certificate of qualification (limited, restricted) granted under section 23;

(b) has submitted evidence of at least one school year of successful teaching experience in a Native language as a second language, as certified by,

(i) the appropriate supervisory officer, where the successful teaching experience was in Ontario and was not in a school operated on an Indian reserve, or

(ii) the appropriate supervisory official, where the successful teaching experience was outside Ontario or in a school operated on an Indian reserve in Ontario; and

(c) has successfully completed the second session of an accredited program for Teacher of a Native Language as a Second Language after completing the experience referred to in clause (b).

O. Reg. 188/04, s. 11

25. (1) The Registrar may grant to a candidate a certificate of qualification (restricted) for the teaching of a Native language as a second language if the dean of a college or faculty of education or the director of a school of education in Ontario reports to the Registrar that the candidate,

(a) holds a certificate of qualification (limited, restricted) extended under section 24;

(b) has submitted evidence of at least one school year of successful teaching experience in a Native language as a second language, following the completion of the teaching experience referred to in section 24, as certified by,

(i) the appropriate supervisory officer, where the successful teaching experience was in Ontario and was not in a school operated on an Indian Reserve, or

(ii) the appropriate supervisory official, where the successful teaching experience was outside Ontario or in a school operated on an Indian Reserve in Ontario; and

(c) has successfully completed the third session of an accredited program for Teacher of a Native Language as a Second Language after completing the successful teaching experience referred to in clause (b).

(2) The certificate of qualification (restricted) granted under subsection (1) shall be in the form provided for in the by-laws.

O. Reg. 188/04, s. 12

26. (1) The Registrar may grant to a candidate a certificate of qualification (limited, restricted) valid for one year for teaching dance if the dean of a college or faculty of education or the director of a school of education in Ontario reports to the Registrar that the candidate,

(a) has complied with section 2;

(b) holds a Secondary School Graduation Diploma or has qualifications that the College considers to be equivalent to a Secondary School Graduation Diploma;

(c) has successfully completed, before August 31, 1995, the first session of the program in Dance referred to in Schedule D;

(d) is competent to perform in the areas of dance taught in elementary and secondary schools; and

(e) is entitled under the laws of Canada to obtain employment in Canada as a teacher, if the candidate is not a Canadian citizen or a permanent resident of Canada.

(2) A certificate of qualification (limited, restricted) granted under subsection (1) shall be in the form provided for in the by-laws.

(3) The Registrar may extend a candidate's certificate of qualification (limited, restricted) for one year for teaching dance if the dean of a college or faculty of education or the director of a school of education in Ontario reports to the Registrar that the candidate,

(a) holds a certificate of qualification (limited, restricted) granted under subsection (1);

(b) has submitted evidence of at least one school year of experience successfully teaching dance in Ontario since the granting of the certificate of qualification (limited, restricted), as certified by the appropriate supervisory officer; and

(c) has successfully completed, before August 31, 1996, the second session of the program in Dance referred to in Schedule D.

(4) The Registrar may grant to a candidate a certificate of qualification (restricted) for teaching dance if the dean of a college or faculty of education or the director of a school of education in Ontario reports to the Registrar that the candidate,

(a) holds a certificate of qualification (limited, restricted) granted under subsection (1);

(b) has submitted evidence of at least one school year of experience successfully teaching dance in Ontario following the experience referred to in clause (3)(b), as certified by the appropriate supervisory officer; and

(c) has successfully completed, before August 31, 1997, the third session of the program in Dance referred to in Schedule D.

(5) The certificate of qualification (restricted) granted under subsection (4) shall be in the form provided for in the by-laws.

O. Reg. 188/04, s. 13

27. The Registrar may grant to a candidate a certificate of qualification in the form provided for in the by-laws if the candidate submits to the Registrar evidence that the candidate,

(a) holds a valid certificate of qualification (restricted);

(b) holds an acceptable post-secondary degree or qualifications that the College considers equivalent to an acceptable post-secondary degree; and

(c) has successfully completed an accredited program leading to additional qualifications in two areas of concentration in the primary division, junior division, intermediate division or senior division.

O. Reg. 188/04, s. 14; 135/08, s. 4

28. (1) A person who holds one of the following certificates and who is,

(a) a Canadian citizen; or

(b) a British subject who was granted the certificate prior to September 1, 1973,

is deemed to hold the certificate of qualification:

1. First Class Certificate valid in Secondary Schools.
2. High School Specialist's Certificate.
3. Interim Elementary School Teacher's Certificate.
4. Interim Elementary School Teacher's Certificate, Standard 1, 2, 3 or 4.
5. Interim Elementary School Teacher's Certificate, Standard 1, 2, 3 or 4 (French only).
6. Interim First Class Certificate.
7. Interim High School Assistant's Certificate.
8. Interim High School Assistant's Certificate, Type A.
9. Interim High School Assistant's Certificate, Type B.

10. Interim Occupational Certificate, Type A (Practical Subjects).
11. Interim Occupational Certificate, Type B (Practical Subjects).
12. Interim Primary School Specialist's Certificate.
13. Interim Second Class Certificate.
14. Interim Vocational Certificate, Type A.
15. Interim Vocational Certificate, Type B.
16. Occupational Specialist's Certificate (Practical Subjects).
17. Permanent Commercial — Vocational Certificate.
18. Permanent Elementary School Teacher's Certificate.
19. Permanent Elementary School Teacher's Certificate, Standard 1, 2, 3 or 4.
20. Permanent Elementary School Teacher's Certificate, Standard 1, 2, 3 or 4 (French only).
21. Permanent First Class Certificate.
22. Permanent High School Assistant's Certificate.
23. Permanent Occupational Certificate (Practical Subjects).
24. Permanent Primary School Specialist's Certificate.
25. Permanent Second Class Certificate.
26. Permanent Vocational Certificate.
27. Vocational Specialist's Certificate.

(2) The Registrar shall grant to a person referred to in subsection (1) a certificate of qualification in the form provided for in the by-laws.

(3) A person who holds an interim certificate referred to in subsection (1) continues to be qualified to teach in accordance with the certificate until the date to which the certificate is valid as shown thereon and the person may upon application be granted by the Registrar a certificate of qualification in the form provided for in the by-laws.

(4) Where a person who held a Letter of Standing granted before July 1, 1978 submits to the Registrar evidence of at least one year of successful teaching experience in Ontario, as certified by the appropriate supervisory officer, in a division or subject for which the Letter of Standing is valid, the Registrar may grant to the person a certificate of qualification in the form provided for in the by-laws.

O. Reg. 130/05, s. 10

29. (1) A person who holds one of the following certificates or Letters of Standing that was valid on July 1, 1978 but who was not qualified for an Ontario Teacher's Certificate under Regulation 297 of the Revised Regulations of Ontario, 1990, as it read on the day before this Regulation comes into force holds a certificate of qualification (restricted) indicating qualifications to teach in the classes, schools and subjects that were indicated on the person's certificate or letter of standing:

1. Elementary Certificate in Teaching Trainable Retarded Children.
2. Elementary Instrumental Music Certificate, Type A.
3. Elementary Instrumental Music Certificate, Type B.
4. Elementary Vocal Music Certificate, Type A.
5. Elementary Vocal Music Certificate, Type B.
6. Interim Second Class Certificate (French only).

7. Interim Specialist Certificate in Instrumental Music.

8. Interim Specialist Certificate in Vocal Music.

9. Intermediate Certificate in Teaching Trainable Retarded Children.

10. Intermediate Industrial Arts Only Certificate.

11. Intermediate Instrumental Music Certificate, Type A.

12. Intermediate Instrumental Music Certificate, Type B.

13. Intermediate Vocal Music Certificate, Type A.

14. Intermediate Vocal Music Certificate, Type B.

15. Letter of Standing (Renewable).

16. Permanent Letter of Standing (Renewable).

17. Permanent Second Class Certificate (French only).

18. Permanent Specialist Certificate in Instrumental Music.

19. Permanent Specialist Certificate in Vocal Music.

20. Specialist Certificate as Teacher of the Blind.

21. Specialist Certificate as Teacher of the Deaf.

22. Supervisor's Certificate in Instrumental Music.

23. Supervisor's Certificate in Vocal Music.

24. Teacher of the Trainable Retarded.

25. Temporary Certificate as Teacher of French to English-speaking Pupils in Elementary Schools.

(2) Where the dean of a college or faculty of education or the director of a school of education in Ontario reports to the Registrar that a candidate,

(a) has complied with section 2;

(b) is entitled under the laws of Canada to obtain employment in Canada as a teacher, if the candidate is not a Canadian citizen or a permanent resident of Canada;

(c) holds or is deemed to hold a certificate of qualification (restricted) referred to in subsection (1);

(d) holds an acceptable post-secondary degree or qualifications the College considers equivalent thereto, or technological qualifications or, in the case of a candidate for a certificate of qualification valid for teaching in French-language schools and classes established under Part XII of the *Education Act*, a Secondary School Honour Graduation Diploma; and

(e) has successfully completed approved programs with concentration in two divisions,

the Registrar may grant to the candidate a certificate of qualification in the form provided for in the by-laws, indicating the areas of concentration successfully completed.

(3) A person who holds a Deferred Elementary School Teacher's Certificate or a Deferred First Class Certificate that was valid on July 1, 1978 remains qualified to teach in the schools and classes for which he or she is qualified by the certificate and, upon submission to the College of evidence of completion of the academic requirements for an Interim Elementary School Teacher's Certificate or an Interim First Class Certificate, as the case may be, in force at the time the deferred certificate was issued, the Registrar may grant to the person a certificate of qualification in the form provided for in the by-laws.

O. Reg. 135/08, s. 5

PART II — ADDITIONAL QUALIFICATIONS FOR TEACHERS

30. A session of a course leading to an additional qualification shall consist of a minimum of 125 hours of work that is approved by the Registrar.

31. Where the dean of a college or faculty of education or the director of a school of education in Ontario reports to the Registrar that a candidate,

(a) holds or has been recommended by the dean or the director for a certificate of qualification, an interim certificate of qualification, a certificate of qualification (restricted) or an interim certificate of qualification (limited);

(b) holds an acceptable post-secondary degree or qualifications the College considers equivalent thereto; and

(c) has successfully completed an accredited program leading to qualifications in an additional area of concentration in the primary division, the junior division, the intermediate division in general studies or the senior division in general studies, or has qualifications that the College considers equivalent to the successful completion of such a program,

the Registrar may have entered on the candidate's certificate of qualification such additional area of concentration.

O. Reg. 188/04, s. 15; 130/05, s. 11; 269/06, s. 11; 30/08, s. 1

32. (1) Subject to subsection (2), where the dean of a college or faculty of education in Ontario reports to the Registrar that a candidate,

(a) holds or has been recommended by the dean or the director for a certificate of qualification, an interim certificate of qualification or an interim certificate of qualification (limited);

(b) has successfully completed an accredited program leading to additional qualifications in a subject listed in Schedule B, or has qualifications that the College considers equivalent to the successful completion of such a program;

(c) in the case of a candidate for a qualification listed in Schedule B for Grades 11 and 12, has produced evidence of,

(i) twelve months of business or industrial experience in the area of the qualification,

(ii) academic experience that the College considers equivalent to 12 months of business or industrial experience in the area of the qualification, or

(iii) a combination of academic, business and industrial experience that the College considers equivalent to 12 months of business or industrial experience in the area of the qualification; and

(d) has demonstrated competence in the area referred to in clause (c),

the Registrar may have entered on the candidate's certificate of qualification the additional qualification in such subject.

(2) An additional qualification may not be entered under subsection (1) on the certificate of qualification in respect of such teacher, of a candidate whose areas of concentration in the program of professional education that qualified him or her for the certificate of qualification were not in technological studies unless the candidate meets the requirements of clause (c) of the definition of **"technological qualifications"** in subsection 1(1).

Proposed Amendment — 32(2)

(2) An additional qualification may not be entered under subsection (1) on the certificate of qualification in respect of such teacher, of a candidate whose areas of concentration in the program of professional education that qualified him or her for the certificate of qualification were not in technological education unless the candidate meets the requirements of clause (c) of the definition of **"technological qualifications"** in subsection 1(1).

O. Reg. 135/08, s. 1(1), item 3 [To come into force May 31, 2009.]

O. Reg. 188/04, s. 16; 130/05, s. 12; 269/06, s. 12; 342/07, s. 3; 30/08, s. 2

One-Session Courses

33. Where the principal of a single-session course leading to a qualification listed in Schedule C or the dean of a college or faculty of education or the director of a school of education in Ontario reports to the Registrar that a candidate,

(a) holds or has been recommended by the dean or the director for a certificate of qualification, an interim certificate of qualification, a certificate of qualification (restricted) or an interim certificate of qualification (limited); and

(b) has successfully completed an accredited program leading to additional qualifications in a subject listed in Schedule C, or has qualifications that the College considers equivalent to the successful completion of such a program,

the Registrar may have entered upon the candidate's certificate of qualification the additional qualification in such subject.

O. Reg. 188/04, s. 17; 130/05, s. 13; 269/06, s. 13; 30/08, s. 3

Three-Session Specialist Courses

34. The Registrar may have entered on a candidate's certificate of qualification the Part I qualification in a subject listed in Schedule D if the principal of the first session of a three-session course leading to a specialist qualification in the subject, the dean of a college or faculty of education or the director of a school of education in Ontario reports to the Registrar that the candidate,

(a) holds a certificate of qualification, an interim certificate of qualification or an interim certificate of qualification (limited);

(b) has successfully completed an accredited program leading to the Part I qualification; and

(c) has an entry on the candidate's certificate of qualification that shows,

(i) qualifications in the primary division, the junior division, the intermediate division in general studies or the senior division in general studies, in the case of Part I qualification other than Primary Education, Junior Education or Intermediate Education,

(ii) an area of concentration for the corresponding division, in the case of a Part I qualification in Primary Education, Junior Education or Intermediate Education, or

(iii) qualification in technological studies, in the case of a Part I qualification in one of the following:

Proposed Amendment — 34(c)(iii) opening words

(iii) qualification in technological education, in the case of a Part I qualification in one of the following:

O. Reg. 135/08, s. 1(1), item 4 [To come into force May 31, 2009.]

1. Actualisation linguistique en français et perfectionnement du français.
2. Co-operative Education.
3. English as a Second Language.
4. Guidance and Career Education.
5. Inclusive Classroom.
6. Integration of Information and Computer Technology in Instruction.
7. Media.
8. Music — Instrumental.
9. Music — Vocal, Intermediate and Senior.
10. Music — Vocal, Primary and Junior.
11. Religious Education.
12. Special Education.
13. Teaching Students Who Are Blind.
14. Teaching Students Who Are Deaf-Blind.
15. Visual Arts.
16. [Repealed O. Reg. 342/07, s. 4(1).]
17. [Repealed O. Reg. 342/07, s. 4(1).]

(d) for the specialist qualifications in American Sign Language or Langue des signes québecoise, or Aural and Oral Communication listed in Schedule D, had an entry on his or her certificate of qualification, at the time the candidate began the specialist course, that showed a qualification in The Deaf listed in Schedule D or in Teaching Students Who Are Deaf or Hard of Hearing.

O. Reg. 188/04, s. 18; 130/05, s. 14; 269/06, s. 14; 342/07, s. 4; 30/08, s. 4

35. Where the principal of the second session of a three-session course or the dean of a college or faculty of education or the director of a school of education in Ontario reports to the Registrar that a candidate,

(a) holds or is deemed to hold a certificate of qualification, an interim certificate of qualification or an interim certificate of qualification (limited);

(b) has successfully completed the first session, or the equivalent thereof, of a course leading to an additional qualification in a subject listed in Schedule D;

(c) has submitted evidence of at least one school year of successful teaching experience in Ontario certified by the appropriate supervisory officer or of at least one school year of successful teaching experience outside Ontario certified by the appropriate supervisory official; and

(d) has successfully completed the accredited program for the second session of the course after completing the experience referred to in clause (c),

the Registrar may have entered upon the candidate's certificate of qualification the Part II qualification in such subject.

O. Reg. 188/04, s. 19; 130/05, s. 15; 269/06, s. 15; 30/08, s. 5

36. Where the principal of the third session of a three-session course or the dean of a college or faculty of education or the director of a school of education in Ontario reports to the Registrar that a candidate,

(a) holds or is deemed to hold a certificate of qualification or an interim certificate of qualification;

(b) has successfully completed the second session, or the equivalent thereof, of a course leading to an additional qualification in a subject listed in Schedule D;

(c) submits evidence of at least two school years of successful teaching experience, including at least one school year of experience in Ontario in the subject referred to in clause (b), certified by the appropriate supervisory officer and, if some of the experience was outside Ontario, by the appropriate supervisory official; and

(d) has successfully completed subsequent to the experience referred to in clause (c) the accredited program for the third session of such course,

the Registrar may have entered upon the candidate's certificate of qualification the specialist qualification in such subject.

O. Reg. 188/04, s. 20; 130/05, s. 16; 269/06, s. 16

37. Where the dean of a college or faculty of education or the director of a school of education in Ontario or the principal of a course reports that a candidate who does not hold a certificate of qualification,

(a) holds a certificate of qualification (restricted) valid in Ontario for teaching the deaf only; and

(b) has otherwise met the requirements of section 33, 34, 35, 36, 40, 46 or 47,

the Registrar may grant to the candidate the appropriate additional qualification.

38. (1) A teacher who holds or is deemed to hold a certificate of qualification and who, prior to October 1, 1978, began a Master of Education program that was approved by the Minister as leading to the Specialist Certificate in Guidance may obtain the specialist qualification in Guidance by completing the requirements for such Certificate as they existed on June 30, 1978, and the Registrar shall, upon submission to the Registrar of evidence satisfactory to the Registrar of the completion of such requirements, have entered on such teacher's certificate of qualification the specialist qualification in Guidance.

(2) A teacher who holds or is deemed to hold a certificate of qualification and who, prior to October 1, 1978, began a Master of Library Science program that was approved by the Minister as leading to the Specialist Certificate in Librarianship may obtain the specialist qualification in Librarianship by completing the requirements for such Certificate as they existed on June 30, 1978, and the Registrar shall, upon submission to the Registrar of evidence satisfactory to the Registrar of the completion of such requirements, have entered on such teacher's certificate of qualification the specialist qualification in Librarianship.

39. A teacher who holds a special certificate in a subject listed in Schedule C, D or E, or a special certificate no longer issued, continues to be qualified in accordance with such certificate, and the Registrar shall have the additional qualification corresponding to such special certificate recorded on the teacher's certificate of qualification where the teacher holds or is granted a certificate of qualification.

One-Session Honour Specialist Course

40. (1) Where the dean of a college or faculty of education in Ontario reports to the Registrar that a candidate for an Honour Specialist qualification in a subject or subjects listed in Schedule E,

(a) holds or is deemed to hold a certificate of qualification or an interim certificate of qualification and the candidate's certificate of qualification has an entry showing qualifications in the primary division, the junior division, the intermediate division in general studies or the senior division in general studies; and

(b) holds,

(i) from an Ontario post-secondary educational institution, a Bachelor of Arts degree, a Bachelor of Science degree or a baccalaureate degree in an applied area of study,

(A) that requires four years of post-secondary study, or the equivalent thereof, to a total of at least 120 post-secondary credits, and

(B) in which the candidate has obtained at least second class or equivalent standing in the subject or subjects in which the candidate seeks an Honour Specialist qualification, including, in the case of two subjects, at least 84 post-secondary credits therein and not fewer than 36 post-secondary credits in each subject or, in the case of one subject, at least 54 post-secondary credits therein, or

(ii) qualifications the College considers equivalent to the qualifications referred to in subclause (i);

(c) submits evidence of at least two school years of successful teaching experience, including at least one school year of experience in Ontario in the subject or one or both of the subjects in which the Honours Specialist qualification is sought, certified by the appropriate supervisory officer and, if some of the experience was outside Ontario, by the appropriate supervisory official; and

(d) has successfully completed subsequent to the experience referred to in clause (c) the accredited program for the Honour Specialist qualification in the subject or subjects referred to in sub-subclause (b)(i)(B),

the Registrar may have entered upon the candidate's certificate of qualification the Honour Specialist qualification in such subject or subjects referred to in sub-subclause (b)(i)(B).

(2) A post-secondary credit that has been used to meet the requirements for an Honour Specialist qualification established by clause (1)(b) shall not be used to meet the requirements for another Honour Specialist qualification.

(3) For the purpose of clause (1)(b), a post-secondary credit in Anthropology, Psychology or Sociology shall be deemed to be a post-secondary credit in Social Sciences.

(4) Where the dean of a college or faculty of education in Ontario reports to the Registrar that a candidate for the Honour Technological Studies Specialist Qualification,

Proposed Amendment — 40(4) opening words

(4) Where the dean of a college or faculty of education in Ontario reports to the Registrar that a candidate for the Honour Technological Education Specialist Qualification,

O. Reg. 135/08, s. 1(2), item 1 [To come into force May 31, 2009.]

(a) holds or is deemed to hold a certificate of qualification or an interim certificate of qualification;

(b) has entries on his or her certificate of qualification indicating qualifications in at least,

(i) three of the subjects listed in Schedule B including at least one for both Grades 9 and 10 and for Grades 11 and 12, or

Proposed Amendment — 40(4)(b)(i)

(i) three of the subjects listed in Schedule B including at least one at both the basic and the advanced level,

O. Reg. 135/08, s. 6 [To come into force May 31, 2009.]

(ii) four of the subjects listed in Schedule B for Grades 9 and 10 and an entry indicating the Specialist qualification in one of the subjects in Schedule D listed in subclause 34(c)(iii);

Proposed Amendment — 40(4)(b)(ii)

(ii) four of the subjects listed in Schedule B at the basic level and an entry indicating the Specialist qualification in one of the subjects in Schedule D listed in subclause 34(c)(iii); or

O. Reg. 135/08, s. 6 [To come into force May 31, 2009.]

Proposed Addition — 40(4)(b)(iii)

(iii) two of the subjects in Schedule B for Grades 9 and 10 and the same two subjects for Grades 11 and 12;

O. Reg. 135/08, s. 6 [To come into force May 31, 2009.]

(c) submits evidence of at least two years of successful teaching experience, including at least one year of experience in Ontario in technological studies, certified by the appropriate supervisory officer and, if some of the experience was outside Ontario, by the appropriate supervisory official;

Proposed Amendment — 40(4)(c)

(c) submits evidence of at least two years of successful teaching experience, including at least one year of experience in Ontario in technological education, certified by the appropriate supervisory officer and, if some of the experience was outside Ontario, by the appropriate supervisory official;

O. Reg. 135/08, s. 1(1), item 5 [To come into force May 31, 2009.]

(d) holds a Secondary School Honour Graduation Diploma or an Ontario Secondary School Diploma or has successfully completed the equivalent of one year's full-time study in a program in respect of which a Secondary School Graduation Diploma or its equivalent was required for admission; and

(e) has successfully completed subsequent to the experience referred to in clause (c) the accredited program for the Honour Technological Studies Specialist qualification,

Proposed Amendment — 40(4)(e)

(e) has successfully completed subsequent to the experience referred to in clause (c) the accredited program for the Honour Technological Education Specialist qualification,

O. Reg. 135/08, s. 1(2), item 2 [To come into force May 31, 2009.]

the Registrar may have entered upon the candidate's certificate of qualification the Honour Technological Studies Specialist qualification.

Proposed Amendment — 40(4) closing words

the Registrar may have entered upon the candidate's certificate of qualification the Honour Technological Education Specialist qualification.

O. Reg. 135/08, s. 1(2), item 3 [To come into force May 31, 2009.]

(5) The entry on a candidate's certificate of qualification indicating that he or she has completed successfully the first session of a three-session course leading to the Specialist qualification in Design and Technology or Computer Studies — Computer Technology is deemed to be equivalent to one entry for Grades 9 and 10 for the purposes of clause (4)(b).

O. Reg. 188/04, s. 21; 130/05, s. 17; 269/06, s. 17; 342/07, s. 5; 30/08, s. 6

41. (1) Where a teacher who completed prior to September 1, 1979 the first session of a two-session course leading to an Interim Vocational Certificate, Type A or an Interim Occupational Certificate, Type A completes the requirements for such certificate as they existed on June 30, 1978, the Registrar may have entered on the teacher's certificate of qualification the appropriate qualification.

(2) Where a teacher who,

(a) held an Interim High School Assistant's Certificate, Type A on July 1, 1978; or

(b) completed at a college or faculty of education in Ontario prior to July 1, 1979 the requirements for such certificate as they existed immediately before July 1, 1978,

completes the requirements for the High School Specialist Certificate as they existed immediately before July 1, 1978, the Registrar may have entered on the teacher's certificate of qualification the appropriate Honours Specialist qualification.

42. A teacher who before May 20, 1997 held an Honour Specialist qualification in Latin or Greek shall be deemed to hold an Honour Specialist qualification in Classical Studies.

O. Reg. 342/07, s. 6

Qualification for Teaching Students Who Are Deaf or Hard of Hearing

[Heading added O. Reg. 342/07, s. 7.]

42.1 A qualification for Teaching Students Who Are Deaf or Hard of Hearing — ASL/LSQ Communication or for Teaching Students Who Are Deaf or Hard of Hearing — Aural and Oral Communication is a specialist qualification.

O. Reg. 342/07, s. 7

42.2 (1) The Registrar may have entered on a person's certificate of qualification or interim certificate of qualification, a qualification for Teaching Students Who Are Deaf or Hard of Hearing — ASL/LSQ Communication (Conditional) or for Teaching Students Who Are Deaf or Hard of Hearing — Aural and Oral Communication (Conditional) if the Registrar is satisfied that,

(a) the person has successfully completed,

(i) an accredited Teaching Students Who Are Deaf or Hard of Hearing program leading to that qualification that meets the requirements of section 42.4, or

(ii) a program outside Ontario for teaching the deaf that is equivalent to such a program;

(b) for a person who successfully completed an accredited Teaching Students Who Are Deaf or Hard of Hearing program described in section 42.4, at the time the person was admitted to the program, he or she held a certificate of qualification or an interim certificate of qualification that was in good standing, and,

(i) had successfully completed at least two courses in American Sign Language or Langue des signes québécoise acceptable to the College, or

(ii) his or her proficiency in American Sign Language or Langue des signes québécoise was at least equivalent to the proficiency that would be achieved by completing two such courses; or

(c) for a person who successfully completed a program outside Ontario for teaching the deaf that is equivalent to an accredited Teaching Students Who Are Deaf or Hard of Hearing program described in section 42.4,

(i) at the time the person was admitted to the program,

(A) he or she had successfully completed at least two courses in American Sign Language or Langue des signes québécoise acceptable to the College, or

(B) his or her proficiency in American Sign Language or Langue des signes québécoise was at least equivalent to the proficiency that would be achieved by completing two such courses, or

(ii) at the time the Registrar enters the qualification on the certificate, the person's proficiency in American Sign Language or Langue des signes québécoise is at least equivalent to the proficiency that would be achieved by completing two such courses.

(2) The qualification mentioned in subsection (1) shall be valid for three years from the date of entry.

(3) The Registrar may extend the period of validity of a person's qualification for Teaching Students Who Are Deaf or Hard of Hearing — ASL/LSQ Communication (Conditional) or for Teaching Students Who Are Deaf or Hard of Hearing — Aural and Oral Communication (Conditional), for one-year periods if,

(a) the person requests the extension before the end of the initial term of the qualification or before the end of the most recent extended term of the qualification, as the case may be;

(b) the person has submitted to the Registrar evidence that he or she has an offer of a position in Ontario requiring the qualification; and

(c) at the time of the request, the person holds a certificate of qualification or interim certificate of qualification that is in good standing.

O. Reg. 342/07, s. 7

42.3 (1) The Registrar may have entered on a person's certificate of qualification or interim certificate of qualification, a qualification for Teaching Students Who Are Deaf or Hard of Hearing — ASL/LSQ Communication or for Teaching Students Who Are Deaf or Hard of Hearing — Aural and Oral Communication if,

(a) the person has an entry on his or her certificate of qualification or interim certificate of qualification indicating, as appropriate, a qualification for Teaching Students Who Are Deaf or Hard of Hearing — ASL/LSQ Communication (Conditional) or for Teaching Students Who Are Deaf or Hard of Hearing — Aural and Oral Communication (Conditional);

(b) for a person who successfully completed an accredited Teaching Students Who Are Deaf or Hard of Hearing program described in section 42.4, the person has submitted to the Registrar evidence of at least one school year of successful teaching experience in Ontario in one or more positions requiring the qualification;

(c) for a person who successfully completed a program outside Ontario for teaching the deaf that is equivalent to an accredited Teaching Students Who Are Deaf or Hard of Hearing program described in section 42.4, the person has submitted to the Registrar evidence of at least one school year of successful teaching experience outside Ontario in one or more positions teaching students who are deaf or hard of hearing;

(d) the evidence referred to in clause (b) or (c), as the case may be, has been certified by,

(i) the appropriate supervisory officer, for a position in Ontario, or

(ii) the appropriate supervisory official, for a position outside Ontario; and

(e) the experience referred to in clause (b) was obtained since the granting of the qualification for Teaching Students Who Are Deaf or Hard of Hearing — ASL/LSQ Communication (Conditional) or for Teaching Students Who Are Deaf or Hard of Hearing — Aural and Oral Communication (Conditional), as the case may be, or if an extension was granted under subsection 42.2(3), since the granting of the extension.

(2) The Registrar may exempt a person from the requirements in clauses (1)(a) and (e) if the Registrar is satisfied that the person meets the requirements in subclause 42.2(1)(a)(ii) and clause 42.2(1)(c).

O. Reg. 342/07, s. 7

42.4 An accredited Teaching Students Who Are Deaf or Hard of Hearing program leading to a qualification for Teaching Students Who Are Deaf or Hard of Hearing — ASL/LSQ Communication or for Teaching Students Who Are Deaf or Hard of Hearing — Aural and Oral Communication shall, in addition to any other requirements for accreditation set out in Ontario Regulation 347/02 (*Accreditation of Teacher Education Programs*) made under the Act,

(a) be two academic semesters in duration;

(b) have the same core curriculum for both qualifications;

(c) have additional course content in,

(i) communication in American Sign Language or Langue des signes québécoise, for a program leading to a qualification for Teaching Students Who Are Deaf or Hard of Hearing — ASL/LSQ Communication, or

(ii) aural and oral communication with deaf or hard of hearing students, for a program leading to a qualification for Teaching Students Who Are Deaf or Hard of Hearing — Aural and Oral Communication; and

(d) include a practicum acceptable to the College in teaching students who are deaf or hard of hearing.

O. Reg. 342/07, s. 7

Principal's Qualifications

43. (1) The Principal's Qualification Program shall consist of two one-session courses.

(2) A teacher holds principal's qualifications if the teacher's certificate of qualification has an entry for Part II of the Principal's Qualification Program.

44. (1) An applicant for admission to the Principal's Qualification Program must,

(a) hold an acceptable post-secondary degree or qualifications the College considers to be equivalent to an acceptable post-secondary degree;

(b) hold a certificate of qualification or interim certificate of qualification;

(c) have an entry on his or her certificate of qualification that shows a qualification in technological studies for Grades 9 and 10 or a concentration in the intermediate division, and that shows any two of,

(i) a concentration in the primary division,

(ii) a concentration in the junior division, and

(iii) either a qualification in technological studies for Grades 11 and 12 or a concentration in the senior division;

Proposed Amendment — 44(c)

(c) have an entry on his or her certificate of qualification that shows a qualification in technological education for Grades 9 and 10 or a concentration in the intermediate division, and that shows any two of,

(i) a concentration in the primary division,

(ii) a concentration in the junior division, and

(iii) either a qualification in technological education for Grades 11 and 12 or a concentration in the senior division;

O. Reg. 135/08, s. 7(3) [To come into force May 31, 2009.]

(d) provide evidence of at least five school years of successful teaching experience in a school providing elementary or secondary education, as certified by the appropriate supervisory officer or, in the case of experience outside Ontario, by the appropriate supervisory official; and

(e) hold or provide evidence of one of the following:

1. A Specialist or Honour Specialist qualification as indicated on the applicant's certificate of qualification and,

i. successful completion of at least one-half the number of graduate post-secondary credits required to qualify for a master's degree granted by an institution identified in clause (a), (b), (c) or (d) of the definition of "acceptable post-secondary degree" in subsection 1(1), or

ii. an additional Specialist or Honour Specialist qualification as indicated on the applicant's certificate of qualification.

2. A master's degree for which the applicant was required to complete at least 30 graduate post-secondary credits or their equivalent, or a doctorate, where the master's degree or doctorate is granted by an institution identified in clause (a), (b), (c) or (d) of the definition of "acceptable post-secondary degree" in subsection 1(1).

3. Successful completion of at least 30 graduate post-secondary credits or their equivalent, completed at an institution identified in clause (a), (b), (c) or (d) of the definition of "acceptable post-secondary degree" in subsection 1(1).

(2) To fulfil a requirement in clause (1)(e) relating to the completion of graduate post-secondary credits or their equivalent, the credits or their equivalent must have been completed by the applicant in addition to any credits that he or she was required to complete to be granted a certificate of qualification or interim certificate of qualification.

O. Reg. 188/04, s. 22; 135/08, s. 7(1), (2), (4)–(6)

45. If the principal of a course leading to qualifications in Part I of the Principal's Qualification Program reports to the Registrar that a candidate has met the admission requirements of section 44 and has successfully completed the course, the Registrar may have the Part I qualification entered on the candidate's certificate of qualification.

46. An applicant for admission to a course leading to qualifications in Part II of the Principal's Qualification Program must have an entry on his or her certificate of qualification showing qualifications in Part I of the program.

47. If the principal of a course leading to qualifications in Part II of the Principal's Qualification Program reports to the Registrar that a candidate has met the admission requirements of section 46 or 51 and has successfully completed the course, the Registrar may have the Part II qualification entered on the candidate's certificate of qualification.

48. Where the principal of a Principal's Development Course reports to the Registrar that a candidate,

(a) holds principal's qualifications;

(b) has two school years of successful experience as a principal or vice-principal as certified by the appropriate supervisory officer; and

(c) has successfully completed the Course,

the Registrar may have entered on the candidate's certificate of qualification the Principal's Development Course qualification.

O. Reg. 188/04, s. 23

49. A teacher who holds a High School Principal's Certificate, an Elementary School Principal's Certificate, a Secondary School Principal's Certificate, Type B, a Secondary School Principal's Certificate, Type A, a Secondary School Principal's Certificate or a Vocational School Principal's Certificate, whether such certificate is an interim certificate or a permanent certificate, remains qualified within the limitations of the certificate except that the interim qualification will not lapse after the five-year period of validity and such qualification shall be shown on his or her certificate of qualification.

50. A teacher who holds an Elementary School Inspector's Certificate shall be deemed to hold an Elementary School Principal's Certificate.

51. Despite section 46, a teacher who holds or who is deemed to hold an interim or permanent Elementary School Principal's Certificate, or who holds an interim or permanent Secondary School Principal's Certificate, Type B, an interim or permanent Vocational School Principal's Certificate, an interim Secondary School Principal's Certificate, or an interim Secondary School Principal's Certificate Type A, may be admitted to the course leading to qualifications in Part II of the Principal's Qualification Program.

52. **(1)** Where a teacher held an interim Elementary School Principal's Certificate, an interim Secondary School Principal's Certificate, Type B, or an interim Secondary School Principal's Certificate, Type A, on July 1, 1978 and completes the requirements for the permanent certificate that corresponds thereto as they existed immediately before July 1, 1978, the Registrar shall have entered on the teacher's certificate of qualification the appropriate qualification.

(2) A teacher who holds a permanent Secondary School Principal's Certificate, Type A or a permanent Secondary School Principal's Certificate is deemed to hold principal's qualifications.

52.1 A candidate who began Part I or Part II of a Principal's Qualification Program before August 31, 2008 may complete the requirements for the qualification set out in this Regulation, as it read on August 30, 2008, and on completion shall have an entry recorded on his or her certificate of qualification indicating Part I or Part II of the qualification, as the case may be.

O. Reg. 135/08, s. 8

PART IV — TEMPORARY LETTERS OF APPROVAL

53. (1) The Registrar may grant to a board a Temporary Letter of Approval for a period specified in the letter if the director of education or secretary of the board submits to the Registrar, in duplicate, an application in the form provided for in the by-laws certifying that,

(a) the board finds it necessary to assign or appoint a teacher to teach a subject or hold a position who does not hold the qualifications required by the regulations made under the *Education Act* for teaching the subject or holding the position; and

(b) the teacher in respect of whom the application is made,

(i) holds a certificate of qualification, an interim certificate of qualification, a certificate of qualification (restricted), a certificate of qualification (limited), or a certificate of qualification (limited, restricted), and

(ii) is considered competent to teach the subject or hold the position.

(2) The period for which a Temporary Letter of Approval is granted,

(a) shall not exceed one year; and

(b) shall not extend beyond the end of a school year unless the period begins after the end of a school year and ends before the beginning of the next school year.

O. Reg. 130/05, s. 18; 269/06, s. 18

PART V — QUALIFICATIONS OF SUPERVISORY OFFICERS

54. In this Part,

"acceptable university degree" [Revoked O. Reg. 188/04, s. 24.]

"Principal's Certificate" means a permanent principal's certificate;

"university" [Revoked O. Reg. 188/04, s. 24.]

O. Reg. 188/04, s. 24

55. (1) A person who meets the following qualifications shall have an entry recorded on his or her certificate of qualification or interim certificate of qualification indicating an additional qualification as a supervisory officer:

1. The person has at least five years of successful classroom teaching experience in a school providing elementary or secondary education.

2. The person holds a certificate of qualification or an interim certificate of qualification.

3. The person has,

i. an entry on his or her certificate of qualification that shows a qualification in technological studies for Grades 9 and 10 or a concentration in the intermediate division, and that shows any two of,

A. a concentration in the primary division,

B. a concentration in the junior division, and

C. either a qualification in technological studies for Grades 11 and 12 or a concentration in the senior division, or

ii. qualifications that the Registrar considers equivalent to the qualifications described in subparagraph i.

iii. [Repealed O. Reg. 374/08, s. 1(2).]

Proposed Amendment — 55, para. 3

3. The person has,

i. an entry on his or her certificate of qualification that shows a qualification in technological education for Grades 9 and 10 or a concentration in the intermediate division, and that shows any two of,

A. a concentration in the primary division,

B. a concentration in the junior division, and

C. either a qualification in technological education for Grades 11 and 12 or a concentration in the senior division, or

ii. qualifications that the Registrar considers equivalent to the qualifications described in subparagraph i.

iii. [Repealed O. Reg. 374/08, s. 1(2).]

O. Reg. 374/08, s. 1(3) [To come into force May 31, 2009.]

4. The person holds an acceptable post-secondary degree or qualifications the College considers to be equivalent to an acceptable post-secondary degree.

5. The person holds a master's degree for which the applicant was required to complete at least 30 graduate post-secondary credits or their equivalent, as described in subsection (2), or a doctorate, where the master's degree or doctorate was granted by an institution identified in clause (a), (b), (c) or (d) of the definition of "acceptable post-secondary degree" in subsection 1(1).

6. The person meets one or more of the following criteria:

i. The person holds,

A. an Elementary School Principal's Certificate,

B. a Secondary School Principal's Certificate, Type A,

C. a Secondary School Principal's Certificate, Type B, or

D. a Secondary School Principal's Certificate.

ii. The person holds a certificate of qualification indicating Part I and Part II Principal's Qualifications.

ii.1 The person holds principal's qualifications from a jurisdiction outside Ontario, as certified by a person acceptable to the Registrar.

ii.2 The person holds or has held a principal's position in a jurisdiction outside Ontario that the Registrar considers equivalent to a position in Ontario for which principal's qualifications are required under the *Education Act*.

iii. The person holds specialist or honours specialist qualifications in one or more subjects and has, in addition to the experience required by paragraph 1, at least two school years of successful experience as a teacher appointed by a board under section 17 of Regulation 298 of the Revised Regulations of Ontario, 1990 to supervise or co-ordinate a subject or program or to act as a consultant for the teachers of a subject or program, as certified by the appropriate supervisory officer.

iii.1 The person,

A. holds specialist or honour specialist qualifications from a jurisdiction outside Ontario, as certified by a person acceptable to the Registrar, and the Registrar considers the qualifications equivalent to the qualifications described in subparagraph iii, and

B. has, in addition to the experience required by paragraph 1, at least two years of successful experience in a position that the Registrar considers equivalent to a position described in subparagraph iii.

iv. The person has, in addition to the experience required by paragraph 1, at least two years of experience,

A. as an education officer employed by the Ministry of Education, as certified by a district manager or branch director of the Ministry, or as an employee outside Ontario in a position that the Registrar considers equivalent,

B. as an employee outside Ontario in a position that the Registrar considers equivalent to the position of supervisory officer of a school board, as certified by a person acceptable to the Registrar, or

C. as a program consultant seconded to the Ministry of Education for French language, English language or Native language programs, as certified by a district manager or branch director of the Ministry, or as an employee outside Ontario in a position that the Registrar considers equivalent.

v. The person has, in addition to the experience required by paragraph 1, at least two years of education-related leadership experience in an educational organization in a position that the Registrar considers comparable to one of the positions described in subparagraph iv.

7. The person meets one or more of the following criteria:

i. He or she successfully completed the supervisory officer's qualifications program described in section 56 within five years after starting the program.

ii. The person has qualifications and experience, including experience gained while employed as a supervisory officer under section 2.0.1 of Regulation 309 of the Revised Regulations of Ontario, 1990 (*Supervisory Officers*), made under the *Education Act*, that the Registrar considers equivalent to the successful completion of all of the modules of the supervisory officer's qualifications program described in section 56.

iii. The person has qualifications and experience, including experience gained while employed as a supervisory officer under section 2.0.1 of Regulation 309 of the Revised Regulations of Ontario, 1990, that the Registrar considers equivalent to the successful completion of some of the modules of the supervisory officer's qualifications program described in section 56, and the person successfully completed the remaining modules of the program, as identified by the Registrar, within five years after starting the program.

(2) To fulfil the requirement in paragraph 5 of subsection (1) relating to the completion of graduate post-secondary credits or their equivalent, the credits or their equivalent must have

been completed by the applicant in addition to any credits that he or she was required to complete to be granted a certificate of qualification or interim certificate of qualification.
O. Reg. 188/04, s. 25; 135/08, s. 9(1), (3)–(5); 374/08, s. 1(1), (2), (4)–(8)

56. The supervisory officer's qualifications program referred to in section 55 shall have the following features:

1. The program shall be provided by an organization or institution that has entered into a contract with the College to provide the instruction and arrange for the practical experience referred to in paragraphs 3 and 4.

2. No person shall be admitted to the program unless the person has submitted proof to the organization or institution that provides the program that the person meets the qualifications set out in paragraphs 1 to 6 of section 55.

2.1 If the Registrar determines under sub-subparagraph 7 iii of subsection 55(1) that a person has qualifications and experience that are equivalent to the successful completion of some of the modules of the supervisory officer's qualifications program, the person shall be admitted to the program and be required to successfully complete only those modules of the program identified by the Registrar as requiring completion.

3. The program shall consist of,

i. four instructional modules, each consisting of at least 50 hours of instruction, and

ii. one module consisting of at least 50 hours of practical experience in the workplace.

4. The instructional modules shall provide instruction that, in the opinion of the Registrar, is relevant to the position of supervisory officer in the following subject areas:

i. Statutes, regulations and government policies affecting education in Ontario.

ii. Curriculum guidelines and other reference material pertaining to elementary and secondary education in Ontario.

iii. Theories and practices of supervision, administration and business organization.

O. Reg. 374/08, s. 2

56.1 A candidate who began a supervisory officer's qualifications program before August 31, 2008 may complete the requirements for the qualifications set out in this Regulation, as it read on August 30, 2008, and on completion shall have an entry recorded on his or her certificate of qualification indicating an additional qualification as a supervisory officer.
O. Reg. 135/08, s. 10

PART VI — REGISTRATION

57. A person may apply for a certificate of qualification and registration by submitting to the Registrar a completed application in the form prescribed by the by-laws together with the fee prescribed by the by-laws.

PART VII — TRANSITIONAL

58. The day prescribed for the purposes of subsection 62(1) of the Act is May 20, 1997.

59. For the purposes of subsection 62(2) of the Act, on and after May 20, 1997 any person holding a qualification referred to in one of the following paragraphs shall be deemed to have been granted by the Registrar and to hold the corresponding certificate of qualification under this Regulation containing the same terms, conditions or limitations:

1. Regulation 297 of the Revised Regulations of Ontario, 1990.
2. Ontario Teacher's Qualifications Record Cards.
3. Any other records of qualification held by the Ministry of Education and Training.

60. Any person who is deemed under subsection 63(1) of the Act to have fulfilled the requirements for the issuance of a particular certificate of qualification shall be issued that certificate containing the same terms, conditions and limitations that would have applied to their qualifications referred to in paragraphs 1, 2 and 3 of section 59 before May 20, 1997.

PART VIII

[Heading repealed O. Reg. 269/06, s. 19.]

61. Any person who, on August 30, 2008, holds a qualification that is listed in a schedule to this Regulation, as the schedule reads on August 30, 2008, and that is set out in Column 2 of the Table to this section, is deemed, on and after August 31, 2008, to hold the qualification set out in the corresponding cell of Column 3 of the Table:

TABLE

Item	Column 1	Column 2	Column 3
	Schedule	**Old qualification name**	**New qualification name**
1.	Schedule A	Business Studies — Information Management	Business Studies — Information and Communication Technology
2.	Schedule A	Computer Science	Computer Studies
3.	Schedule A	Individual and Society	Social Sciences — General
4.	Schedule A	English (First language)	English
5.	Schedule A	English (Second language) — anglais	Anglais
6.	Schedule A	French (Second language)	French as a Second Language
7.	Schedule A	French (First language) — français	Français
8.	Schedule A	Native Language (Second language)	Native Languages
9.	Schedule A	Physical and Health Education	Health and Physical Education
10.	Schedule B	Communications Technology (Basic Level)	Communications Technology, Grades 9 and 10

TABLE

Item	**Column 1**	**Column 2**	**Column 3**
	Schedule	**Old qualification name**	**New qualification name**
11.	Schedule B	Communications Technology (Advanced Level)	Communications Technology, Grades 11 and 12
12.	Schedule B	Construction Technology (Basic Level)	Construction Technology, Grades 9 and 10
13.	Schedule B	Construction Technology (Advanced Level)	Construction Technology, Grades 11 and 12
14.	Schedule B	Hospitality Services (Basic Level)	Hospitality Services, Grades 9 and 10
15.	Schedule B	Hospitality Services (Advanced Level)	Hospitality Services, Grades 11 and 12
16.	Schedule B	Manufacturing Technology (Basic Level)	Manufacturing Technology, Grades 9 and 10
17.	Schedule B	Manufacturing Technology (Advanced Level)	Manufacturing Technology, Grades 11 and 12
18.	Schedule B	Personal Services (Basic Level)	Personal Services, Grades 9 and 10
19.	Schedule B	Personal Services (Advanced Level)	Personal Services, Grades 11 and 12
20.	Schedule B	Technological Design (Basic Level)	Technological Design, Grades 9 and 10
21.	Schedule B	Technological Design (Advanced Level)	Technological Design, Grades 11 and 12
22.	Schedule B	Transportation Technology (Basic Level)	Transportation Technology, Grades 9 and 10
23.	Schedule B	Transportation Technology (Advanced Level)	Transportation Technology, Grades 11 and 12
24.	Schedule C	Childhood Education	Kindergarten
25.	Schedule C	Preschool Deaf Education	Pre-School Education for Children Who Are Deaf or Hard of Hearing
26.	Schedule C	Teacher of Ojibway	Teaching Ojibwe
27.	Schedule D	Business Studies — Entrepreneurship Studies	Business Studies — Entrepreneurship
28.	Schedule D	Business Studies — Information Management	Business Studies — Information and Communication Technology
29.	Schedule D	Computer Studies — Computer Science	Computer Studies

TABLE

Item	Column 1	Column 2	Column 3
	Schedule	**Old qualification name**	**New qualification name**
30.	Schedule D	Computers in the Classroom	Integration of Information and Computer Technology in Instruction
31.	Schedule D	Guidance	Guidance and Career Education
32.	Schedule D	Native Language as a Second Language	Native Languages
33.	Schedule D	Physical and Health Education (Intermediate, Senior)	Health and Physical Education, Intermediate and Senior
34.	Schedule D	Physical and Health Education (Primary, Junior)	Health and Physical Education, Primary and Junior
35.	Schedule D	Science in Primary and Junior Education	Science and Technology, Primary and Junior
36.	Schedule D	The Blind	Teaching Students Who Are Blind
37.	Schedule D	The Deaf/Blind	Teaching Students Who Are Deaf-Blind
38.	Schedule E	Classical Studies (Latin, Greek)	Classical Studies
39.	Schedule E	Computer Science	Computer Studies
40.	Schedule E	Contemporary Studies	Social Sciences
41.	Schedule E	English (First language)	English
42.	Schedule E	English (Second language) — anglais	Anglais
43.	Schedule E	French (Second language)	French as a Second Language
44.	Schedule E	French (First language) — français	Français
45.	Schedule E	Physical and Health Education	Health and Physical Education

O. Reg. 269/06, s. 19; 342/07, s. 8

62. Any person who, on August 30, 2008, holds a qualification identified in the Table to this section continues to hold the qualification after that date despite its revocation from the Schedules.

TABLE

Item	Column 1	Column 2
	Schedule	**Qualification**
1.	Schedule A	Business Studies — Data Processing
2.	Schedule A	Business Studies — Marketing and Merchandising
3.	Schedule A	Design and Technology
4.	Schedule A	Science — Geology
5.	Schedule C	Childhood Education in Great Britain
6.	Schedule C	Community School Development
7.	Schedule C	Driver Education Instructor
8.	Schedule C	Law
9.	Schedule C	Teaching Children with Language Difficulties — Aphasia
10.	Schedule C	Teacher of Native Children
11.	Schedule E	Geology

O. Reg. 342/07, s. 8

Proposed Addition — 62.1

62.1 (1) Any person who, on May 30, 2009, holds a qualification that is listed in Column 2 of the Table to this subsection is deemed, on and after May 31, 2009, to hold the qualification set out in the corresponding cell of Column 3 of the Table:

TABLE

Item	Column 1	Column 2	Column 3
	Schedule	**Old qualification name**	**New qualification name**
1.	Schedule B	Hospitality Services, Grades 9 and 10	Hospitality and Tourism, Grades 9 and 10
2.	Schedule B	Hospitality Services, Grades 11 and 12	Hospitality and Tourism, Grades 11 and 12

(2) Any person who, on May 31, 2009, holds a qualification identified in the Table to this subsection continues to hold the qualification after that date despite its revocation from Schedule B.

TABLE

Item	Column 1	Column 2
	Schedule	**Qualification**
1.	Schedule B	Personal Services, Grades 9 and 10
2.	Schedule B	Personal Services, Grades 11 and 12

Proposed Addition — 62.1(3)

(3) A person who began a program before May 31, 2009 for a qualification identified in the Table to subsection (2) and who completes the requirements for the qualification, as set out in this Regulation as it read on May 30, 2009, shall have an entry indicating the qualification recorded on his or her certificate of qualification and is deemed to continue to hold the qualification on and after the date the qualification is recorded, despite its revocation from Schedule B.

O. Reg. 374/08, s. 4 [To come into force May 31, 2009.]

O. Reg. 135/08, s. 11 [To come into force May 31, 2009. Amended O. Reg. 374/08, s. 3.]

63. Any person who, on August 30, 2012, holds a qualification identified in the Table to this section continues to hold the qualification after that date despite its revocation from the Schedules.

TABLE

Item	Column 1	Column 2
	Schedule	**Qualification**
1.	Schedule D	Business Studies — Data Processing
2.	Schedule D	Business Studies — Marketing and Merchandising
3.	Schedule D	Design and Technology
4.	Schedule D	Multiculturalism in Education
5.	Schedule D	The Deaf

O. Reg. 342/07, s. 8

SCHEDULE A — INTERMEDIATE AND SENIOR DIVISION OPTIONS TAKEN IN ENGLISH OR FRENCH

Anglais
Business Studies — Accounting
Business Studies — Entrepreneurship
Business Studies — General
Business Studies — Information and Communication Technology
Classical Studies — Greek
Classical Studies — Latin
Computer Studies

Dance
Dramatic Arts
Economics
English
Environmental Science
Family Studies
Français
French as a Second Language
Geography
Health and Physical Education
History
International Languages
Law
Mathematics
Music — Instrumental
Music — Vocal
Native Languages
Native Studies
Philosophy
Politics
Religious Education
Science — Biology
Science — Chemistry
Science — General
Science — Physics
Social Sciences — General
Visual Arts

O. Reg. 342/07, s. 9

SCHEDULE B — TECHNOLOGICAL STUDIES OPTIONS TAKEN IN ENGLISH OR FRENCH

Communications Technology, Grades 9 and 10
Communications Technology, Grades 11 and 12
Construction Technology, Grades 9 and 10
Construction Technology, Grades 11 and 12
Hospitality Services, Grades 9 and 10
Hospitality Services, Grades 11 and 12
Manufacturing Technology, Grades 9 and 10
Manufacturing Technology, Grades 11 and 12
Personal Services, Grades 9 and 10
Personal Services, Grades 11 and 12
Technological Design, Grades 9 and 10
Technological Design, Grades 11 and 12
Transportation Technology, Grades 9 and 10
Transportation Technology, Grades 11 and 12

Proposed Amendment — Schedule B

SCHEDULE B — TECHNOLOGICAL EDUCATION OPTIONS TAKEN IN ENGLISH OR FRENCH

[Heading amended O. Reg. 135/08, s. 12. To come into force May 31, 2009.]

Communications Technology, Grades 9 and 10
Communications Technology, Grades 11 and 12
Computer Technology, Grades 9 and 10
Computer Technology, Grades 11 and 12
Construction Technology, Grades 9 and 10
Construction Technology, Grades 11 and 12
Green Industries, Grades 9 and 10
Green Industries, Grades 11 and 12
Hairstyling and Aesthetics, Grades 9 and 10
Hairstyling and Aesthetics, Grades 11 and 12
Health Care, Grades 9 and 10
Health Care, Grades 11 and 12
Hospitality and Tourism, Grades 9 and 10
Hospitality and Tourism, Grades 11 and 12
Manufacturing Technology, Grades 9 and 10
Manufacturing Technology, Grades 11 and 12
Technological Design, Grades 9 and 10
Technological Design, Grades 11 and 12
Transportation Technology, Grades 9 and 10
Transportation Technology, Grades 11 and 12

O. Reg. 135/08, s. 12 [To come into force May 31, 2009.]

O. Reg. 342/07, s. 10

SCHEDULE C — ONE-SESSION QUALIFICATIONS TAKEN IN ENGLISH OR FRENCH

Aboriginal Peoples: Understanding Traditional Teachings, Histories, Current Issues and Cultures
Action Research
Adapting Curriculum for Second-Language Learners
Adapting Curriculum for the Catholic School System
Adult Education
Alternative Education
Arts, Grades 7 and 8
Associate Teaching
Computer Studies — Computer Technology
Education Law
Geography, Grades 7 and 8
Health and Physical Education, Grades 7 and 8
History, Grades 7 and 8
Integrated Arts
Kindergarten
Language Arts, Grades 7 and 8
Leadership en milieu minoritaire

L'enseignement en milieu minoritaire
Mathematics, Grades 7 and 8
Mentoring
Outdoor Experiential Education
Pre-School Education for Children Who Are Deaf or Hard of Hearing
Science and Technology, Grades 7 and 8
Special Education — Behaviour
Special Education — Communication — Autism
Special Education — Communication — Learning Disability
Special Education — Communication — Speech and Language
Special Education — Intellectual — Developmental Disabilities
Special Education — Intellectual — Gifted
Special Education — Multiple Exceptionalities
Special Education — Physical
Special Education for Administrators
Student Assessment and Evaluation
Teaching Aboriginal Children
Teaching and Learning Through e-Learning
Teaching Cayuga
Teaching Combined Grades
Teaching Cree
Teaching Delaware
Teaching Mohawk
Teaching Ojibwe
Teaching Ojicree
Teaching Oneida
Teaching in a French Immersion Setting
Teaching in the Catholic School System
Use and Knowledge of Assistive Technology

Proposed Amendment — Schedule C

SCHEDULE C — ONE-SESSION QUALIFICATIONS TAKEN IN ENGLISH OR FRENCH

Aboriginal Peoples: Understanding Traditional Teachings, Histories, Current Issues and Cultures
Action Research
Adapting Curriculum for Second-Language Learners
Adapting Curriculum for the Catholic School System
Adult Education
Alternative Education
Arts, Grades 7 and 8
Associate Teaching
Education Law
Geography, Grades 7 and 8
Health and Physical Education, Grades 7 and 8
History, Grades 7 and 8
Integrated Arts
Kindergarten
Language Arts, Grades 7 and 8
Leadership en milieu minoritaire

L'enseignement en milieu minoritaire
Mathematics, Grades 7 and 8
Mentoring
Outdoor Experiential Education
Pre-School Education for Children Who Are Deaf or Hard of Hearing
Science and Technology, Grades 7 and 8
Special Education — Behaviour
Special Education — Communication — Autism
Special Education — Communication — Learning Disability
Special Education — Communication — Speech and Language
Special Education — Intellectual — Developmental Disabilities
Special Education — Intellectual — Gifted
Special Education — Multiple Exceptionalities
Special Education — Physical
Special Education for Administrators
Student Assessment and Evaluation
Teaching Aboriginal Children
Teaching and Learning Through e-Learning
Teaching Cayuga
Teaching Combined Grades
Teaching Cree
Teaching Delaware
Teaching Mohawk
Teaching Ojibwe
Teaching Ojicree
Teaching Oneida
Teaching in a French Immersion Setting
Teaching in the Catholic School System
Use and Knowledge of Assistive Technology

O. Reg. 135/08, s. 13 [To come into force May 31, 2009.]

O. Reg. 342/07, s. 11

SCHEDULE D — THREE-SESSION QUALIFICATIONS TAKEN IN ENGLISH OR FRENCH

Actualisation linguistique en français et Perfectionnement du français
American Sign Language or Langue des signes québécoise
Aural and Oral Communication
Business Studies — Accounting
Business Studies — Data Processing
Business Studies — Entrepreneurship
Business Studies — Information and Communication Technology
Business Studies — Marketing and Merchandising
Computer Studies
Co-operative Education
Dance
Design and Technology
Dramatic Arts
English as a Second Language
Environmental Science
Family Studies

French as a Second Language
Guidance and Career Education
Health and Physical Education, Intermediate and Senior
Health and Physical Education, Primary and Junior
Inclusive Classroom
Integration of Information and Computer Technology in Instruction
Intermediate Education
International Languages
Junior Education
Librarianship
Mathematics, Primary and Junior
Media
Multiculturalism in Education
Music — Instrumental
Music — Vocal, Intermediate and Senior
Music — Vocal, Primary and Junior
Native Languages
Native Studies
Primary Education
Reading
Religious Education
Science and Technology, Primary and Junior
Social Studies, Primary and Junior
Special Education
Teaching Students Who Are Blind
Teaching Students Who Are Deaf-Blind
The Deaf
Visual Arts
Writing

Proposed Amendment — Schedule D

SCHEDULE D — THREE-SESSION QUALIFICATIONS TAKEN IN ENGLISH OR FRENCH

Actualisation linguistique en français et Perfectionnement du français
American Sign Language or Langue des signes québécoise
Aural and Oral Communication
Business Studies — Accounting
Business Studies — Entrepreneurship
Business Studies — Information and Communication Technology
Computer Studies
Co-operative Education
Dance
Dramatic Arts
English as a Second Language
Environmental Science
Family Studies
French as a Second Language
Guidance and Career Education
Health and Physical Education, Intermediate and Senior
Health and Physical Education, Primary and Junior

Inclusive Classroom
Integration of Information and Computer Technology in Instruction
Intermediate Education
International Languages
Junior Education
Librarianship
Mathematics, Primary and Junior
Media
Music — Instrumental
Music — Vocal, Intermediate and Senior
Music — Vocal, Primary and Junior
Native Languages
Native Studies
Primary Education
Reading
Religious Education
Science and Technology, Primary and Junior
Social Studies, Primary and Junior
Special Education
Teaching Students Who Are Blind
Teaching Students Who Are Deaf-Blind
Visual Arts
Writing

O. Reg. 342/07, s. 12(2) [To come into force August 31, 2012.]

O. Reg. 342/07, s. 12(1)

SCHEDULE E — HONOUR SPECIALIST QUALIFICATIONS TAKEN IN ENGLISH OR FRENCH

Anglais
Biology
Business Studies
Chemistry
Classical Studies
Computer Studies
Dance
Dramatic Arts
English
Environmental Science
Family Studies
Français
French as a Second Language
Geography
Health and Physical Education
History
International Languages
Mathematics
Music
Native Languages
Native Studies
Physics

Religious Education
Science
Social Sciences
Visual Arts

O. Reg. 342/07, s. 13

ONT. REG. 437/97 — PROFESSIONAL MISCONDUCT

made under the *Ontario College of Teachers Act, 1996*

O. Reg. 437/97, as am. O. Reg. 134/08.

1. The following acts are defined as professional misconduct for the purposes of subsection 30(2) of the Act:

1. Providing false information or documents to the College or any other person with respect to the member's professional qualifications.

2. Inappropriately using a term, title or designation indicating a specialization in the profession which is not specified on the member's certificate of qualification and registration.

3. Permitting, counselling or assisting any person who is not a member to represent himself or herself as a member of the College.

4. Using a name other than the member's name, as set out in the register, in the course of his or her professional duties.

5. Failing to maintain the standards of the profession.

6. Releasing or disclosing information about a student to a person other than the student or, if the student is a minor, the student's parent or guardian. The release or disclosure of information is not an act of professional misconduct if,

i. the student (or if the student is a minor, the student's parent or guardian) consents to the release or disclosure, or

ii. if the release or disclosure is required or allowed by law.

7. Abusing a student verbally.

7.1 Abusing a student physically.

7.2 Abusing a student psychologically or emotionally.

7.3 Abusing a student sexually.

8. Practising or purporting to practise the profession while under the influence of any substance or while adversely affected by any dysfunction,

i. which the member knows or ought to know impairs the member's ability to practise, and

ii. in respect of which treatment has previously been recommended, ordered or prescribed but the member has failed to follow the treatment.

9. Contravening a term, condition or limitation imposed on the member's certificate of qualification and registration.

10. Failing to keep records as required by his or her professional duties.

11. Failing to supervise adequately a person who is under the professional supervision of the member.

12. Signing or issuing, in the member's professional capacity, a document that the member knows or ought to know contains a false, improper or misleading statement.

13. Falsifying a record relating to the member's professional responsibilities.

14. Failing to comply with the Act or the regulations or the by-laws.

15. Failing to comply with the *Education Act* or the regulations made under that Act, if the member is subject to that Act.

16. Contravening a law if the contravention is relevant to the member's suitability to hold a certificate of qualification and registration.

17. Contravening a law if the contravention has caused or may cause a student who is under the member's professional supervision to be put at or to remain at risk.

18. An act or omission that, having regard to all the circumstances, would reasonably be regarded by members as disgraceful, dishonourable or unprofessional.

19. Conduct unbecoming a member.

20. Failing to appear before a panel of the Investigation Committee to be cautioned or admonished, if the Investigation Committee has required the member to appear under clause 26(5)(c) of the Act.

21. Failing to comply with an order of a panel of the Discipline Committee or an order of a panel of the Fitness to Practise Committee.

22. Failing to co-operate in a College investigation.

23. Failing to take reasonable steps to ensure that the requested information is provided in a complete and accurate manner if the member is required to provide information to the College under the Act and the regulations.

24. Failing to abide by a written undertaking given by the member to the College or by an agreement entered into by the member with the College.

25. Failing to respond adequately or within a reasonable time to a written inquiry from the College.

26. Practising the profession while the member is in a conflict of interest.

27. Failing to comply with the member's duties under the *Child and Family Services Act*.

O. Reg. 134/08, s. 1

2. A finding of incompetence, professional misconduct or a similar finding against a member by a governing authority of the teaching profession in a jurisdiction other than Ontario that is based on facts that would, in the opinion of the Discipline Committee, constitute professional misconduct as defined in section 1, is defined as professional misconduct for the purposes of subsection 30(2) of the Act.

LEGISLATION

Constitution Act, 1982

Canada Act 1982 (U.K.), c. 11 R.S.C. 1985, Appendix II, No. 44, as am. Constitution Amendment Proclamation, 1983, SI/84-102, Schedule, SI/93-54.

.....

Part I — Canadian Charter of Rights and Freedoms

Whereas Canada is founded upon principles that recognize the supremacy of God and the rule of law:

Guarantee of Rights and Freedoms

1. **Rights and freedoms in Canada** — The *Canadian Charter of Rights and Freedoms* guarantees the rights and freedoms set out in it subject only to such reasonable limits prescribed by law as can be demonstrably justified in a free and democratic society.

Fundamental Freedoms

2. **Fundamental freedoms** — Everyone has the following fundamental freedoms:

(a) freedom of conscience and religion;

(b) freedom of thought, belief, opinion and expression, including freedom of the press and other media of communication;

(c) freedom of peaceful assembly; and

(d) freedom of association.

Democratic Rights

3. **Democratic rights of citizens** — Every citizen of Canada has the right to vote in an election of members of the House of Commons or of a legislative assembly and to be qualified for membership therein.

4. (1) **Maximum duration of legislative bodies** — No House of Commons and no legislative assembly shall continue for longer than five years from the date fixed for the return of the writs at a general election of its members.

(2) **Continuation in special circumstances** — In time of real or apprehended war, invasion or insurrection, a House of Commons may be continued by Parliament and a legislative assembly may be continued by the legislature beyond five years if such continuation is not opposed by the votes of more than one-third of the members of the House of Commons or the legislative assembly, as the case may be.

5. Annual sitting of legislative bodies — There shall be a sitting of Parliament and of each legislature at least once every twelve months.

Mobility Rights

6. (1) Mobility of citizens — Every citizen of Canada has the right to enter, remain in and leave Canada.

(2) Rights to move and gain livelihood — Every citizen of Canada and every person who has the status of a permanent resident of Canada has the right

(a) to move to and take up residence in any province; and

(b) to pursue the gaining of a livelihood in any province.

(3) Limitation — The rights specified in subsection (2) are subject to

(a) any laws or practices of general application in force in a province other than those that discriminate among persons primarily on the basis of province of present or previous residence; and

(b) any laws providing for reasonable residency requirements as a qualification for the receipt of publicly provided social services.

(4) Affirmative action programs — Subsections (2) and (3) do not preclude any law, program or activity that has as its object the amelioration in a province of conditions of individuals in that province who are socially or economically disadvantaged if the rate of employment in that province is below the rate of employment in Canada.

Legal Rights

7. Life, liberty and security of person — Everyone has the right to life, liberty and security of the person and the right not to be deprived thereof except in accordance with the principles of fundamental justice.

8. Search or seizure — Everyone has the right to be secure against unreasonable search or seizure.

9. Detention or imprisonment — Everyone has the right not to be arbitrarily detained or imprisoned.

10. Arrest or detention — Everyone has the right on arrest or detention

(a) to be informed promptly of the reasons therefor;

(b) to retain and instruct counsel without delay and to be informed of that right; and

(c) to have the validity of the detention determined by way of *habeas corpus* and to be released if the detention is not lawful.

11. Proceedings in criminal and penal matters — Any person charged with an offence has the right

(a) to be informed without unreasonable delay of the specific offence;

(b) to be tried within a reasonable time;

(c) not to be compelled to be a witness in proceedings against that person in respect of the offence;

(d) to be presumed innocent until proven guilty according to law in a fair and public hearing by an independent and impartial tribunal;

(e) not to be denied reasonable bail without just cause;

(f) except in the case of an offence under military law tried before a military tribunal, to the benefit of trial by jury where the maximum punishment for the offence is imprisonment for five years or a more severe punishment;

(g) not to be found guilty on account of any act or omission unless, at the time of the act or omission, it constituted an offence under Canadian or international law or was criminal according to the general principles of law recognized by the community of nations;

(h) if finally acquitted of the offence, not to be tried for it again and, if finally found guilty and punished for the offence, not to be tried or punished for it again; and

(i) if found guilty of the offence and if the punishment for the offence has been varied between the time of commission and the time of sentencing, to the benefit of the lesser punishment.

12. **Treatment or punishment** — Everyone has the right not to be subjected to any cruel and unusual treatment or punishment.

13. **Self-crimination** — A witness who testifies in any proceedings has the right not to have any incriminating evidence so given used to incriminate that witness in any other proceedings, except in a prosecution for perjury or for the giving of contradictory evidence.

14. **Interpreter** — A party or witness in any proceedings who does not understand or speak the language in which the proceedings are conducted or who is deaf has the right to the assistance of an interpreter.

Equality Rights

15. (1) **Equality before and under law and equal protection and benefit of law** — Every individual is equal before and under the law and has the right to the equal protection and equal benefit of the law without discrimination and, in particular, without discrimination based on race, national or ethnic origin, colour, religion, sex, age or mental or physical disability.

(2) **Affirmative action programs** — Subsection (1) does not preclude any law, program or activity that has as its object the amelioration of conditions of disadvantaged individuals or groups including those that are disadvantaged because of race, national or ethnic origin, colour, religion, sex, age or mental or physical disability.

Official Languages of Canada

16. (1) **Official languages of Canada** — English and French are the official languages of Canada and have equality of status and equal rights and privileges as to their use in all institutions of the Parliament and government of Canada.

(2) **Official languages of New Brunswick** — English and French are the official languages of New Brunswick and have equality of status and equal rights and privileges as to their use in all institutions of the legislature and government of New Brunswick.

(3) **Advancement of status and use** — Nothing in this Charter limits the authority of Parliament or a legislature to advance the equality of status or use of English and French.

16.1 (1) **English and French linguistic communities in New Brunswick** — The English linguistic community and the French linguistic community in New Brunswick have equality status and equal rights and privileges, including the right to distinct educational institutions and such distinct cultural institutions as are necessary for the preservation and promotion of those communities.

(2) **Role of the legislature and government of New Brunswick** — The role of the legislature and government of New Brunswick to preserve and promote the status, rights and privileges referred to in subsection (1) is affirmed.

SI/93-54, Sched., s. 1

17. (1) **Proceedings of Parliament** — Everyone has the right to use English or French in any debates and other proceedings of Parliament.

(2) **Proceedings of New Brunswick legislature** — Everyone has the right to use English or French in any debates and other proceedings of the legislature of New Brunswick.

18. (1) **Parliamentary statutes and records** — The statutes, records and journals of Parliament shall be printed and published in English and French and both language versions are equally authoritative.

(2) **New Brunswick statutes and records** — The statutes, records and journals of the legislature of New Brunswick shall be printed and published in English and French and both language versions are equally authoritative.

19. (1) **Proceedings in courts established by Parliament** — Either English or French may be used by any person in, or in any pleading in or process issuing from, any court established by Parliament.

(2) **Proceedings in New Brunswick courts** — Either English or French may be used by any person in, or in any pleading in or process issuing from, any court of New Brunswick.

20. (1) **Communications by public with federal institutions** — Any member of the public in Canada has the right to communicate with, and to receive available services from, any head or central office of an institution of the Parliament or government of Canada in English or French, and has the same right with respect to any other office of any such institution where

(a) there is a significant demand for communications with and services from that office in such language; or

(b) due to the nature of the office, it is reasonable that communications with and services from that office be available in both English and French.

(2) **Communications by public with New Brunswick institutions** — Any member of the public in New Brunswick has the right to communicate with, and to receive available services from, any office of an institution of the legislature or government of New Brunswick in English or French.

21. **Continuation of existing Constitutional provisions** — Nothing in sections 16 to 20 abrogates or derogates from any right, privilege or obligation with respect to the English

and French languages, or either of them, that exists or is continued by virtue of any other provision of the Constitution of Canada.

22. Rights and privileges preserved — Nothing in sections 16 to 20 abrogates or derogates from any legal or customary right or privilege acquired or enjoyed either before or after the coming into force of this Charter with respect to any language that is not English or French.

Minority Language Educational Rights

23. (1) Language of instruction — Citizens of Canada

(a) whose first language learned and still understood is that of the English or French linguistic minority population of the province in which they reside, or

(b) who have received their primary school instruction in Canada in English or French and reside in a province where the language in which they received that instruction is the language of the English or French linguistic minority population of the province,

have the right to have their children receive primary and secondary school instruction in that language in that province.

(2) Continuity of language instruction — Citizens of Canada of whom any child has received or is receiving primary or secondary school instruction in English or French in Canada, have the right to have all their children receive primary and secondary school instruction in the same language.

(3) Application where numbers warrant — The right of citizens of Canada under subsections (1) and (2) to have their children receive primary and secondary school instruction in the language of the English or French linguistic minority population of a province

(a) applies wherever in the province the number of children of citizens who have such a right is sufficient to warrant the provision to them out of public funds of minority language instruction; and

(b) includes, where the number of those children so warrants, the right to have them receive that instruction in minority language educational facilities provided out of public funds.

Enforcement

24. (1) Enforcement of guaranteed rights and freedoms — Anyone whose rights or freedoms, as guaranteed by this Charter, have been infringed or denied may apply to a court of competent jurisdiction to obtain such remedy as the court considers appropriate and just in the circumstances.

(2) Exclusion of evidence bringing administration of justice into disrepute — Where, in proceedings under subsection (1), a court concludes that evidence was obtained in a manner that infringed or denied any rights or freedoms guaranteed by this Charter, the evidence shall be excluded if it is established that, having regard to all the circumstances, the admission of it in the proceedings would bring the administration of justice into disrepute.

25. Aboriginal rights and freedoms not affected by Charter — The guarantee in this Charter of certain rights and freedoms shall not be construed so as to abrogate or derogate from any aboriginal treaty or other rights or freedoms that pertain to the aboriginal peoples of Canada including

(a) any rights or freedoms that have been recognized by the Royal Proclamation of October 7, 1763; and

(b) any rights or freedoms that now exist by way of land claims agreements or may be so acquired.

26. Other rights and freedoms not affected by Charter — The guarantee in this Charter of certain rights and freedoms shall not be construed as denying the existence of any other rights or freedoms that exist in Canada.

27. Multicultural heritage — This Charter shall be interpreted in a manner consistent with the preservation and enhancement of the multicultural heritage of Canadians.

28. Rights guaranteed equally to both sexes — Notwithstanding anything in this Charter, the rights and freedoms referred to in it are guaranteed equally to male and female persons.

29. Rights respecting certain schools preserved — Nothing in this Charter abrogates or derogates from any rights or privileges guaranteed by or under the Constitution of Canada in respect of denominational, separate or dissentient schools.

30. Application to Territories and territorial authorities — A reference in this Charter to a province or to the legislative assembly or legislature of a province shall be deemed to include a reference to the Yukon Territory and the Northwest Territories, or to the appropriate legislative authority thereof, as the case may be.

31. Legislative powers not extended — Nothing in this Charter extends the legislative powers of any body or authority.

Application of Charter

32. (1) Application of Charter — This Charter applies

(a) to the Parliament and government of Canada in respect of all matters within the authority of Parliament including all matters relating to the Yukon Territory and Northwest Territories; and

(b) to the legislature and government of each province in respect of all matters within the authority of the legislature of each province.

(2) Exception — Notwithstanding subsection (1), section 15 shall not have effect until three years after this section comes into force.

33. (1) Exception where express declaration — Parliament or the legislature of a province may expressly declare in an Act of Parliament or of the legislature, as the case may be, that the Act or a provision thereof shall operate notwithstanding a provision included in section 2 or sections 7 to 15 of this Charter.

(2) Operation of exception — An Act or a provision of an Act in respect of which a declaration made under this section is in effect shall have such operation as it would have but for the provision of this Charter referred to in the declaration.

(3) Five year limitation — A declaration made under subsection (1) shall cease to have effect five years after it comes into force or on such earlier date as may be specified in the declaration.

(4) Re-enactment — Parliament or a legislature of a province may re-enact a declaration made under subsection (1).

(5) Five year limitation — Subsection (3) applies in respect of a re-enactment made under subsection (4).

Citation

34. Citation — This Part may be cited as the *Canadian Charter of Rights and Freedoms*.

EDUCATION ACT

R.S.O. 1990, c. E.2, as am. R.S.O. 1990, c. E.2, s. 277.6(1), (2); S.O. 1991, c. 10; 1991, c. 15, s. 36; 1992, c. 15, ss. 85–89; 1992, c. 16; 1992, c. 17, ss. 1–3; 1992, c. 27, s. 59; 1992, c. 32, s. 9; 1993, c. 11, ss. 8–43; 1993, c. 23, s. 67; 1993, c. 26, ss. 44, 45; 1993, c. 27, Sched.; 1993, c. 41; 1994, c. 1, s. 22; 1994, c. 17, s. 48; 1994, c. 23, s. 65 [Not in force at date of publication. Repealed 2002, c. 17, Sched. F, s. 1.]; 1994, c. 27, ss. 45, 108; 1995, c. 4, s. 2; 1996, c. 2, s. 65; 1996, c. 11, s. 29; 1996, c. 12, s. 64; 1996, c. 13; 1996, c. 32, s. 70; 1997, c. 3, ss. 2–10; 1997, c. 16, s. 5; 1997, c. 19, s. 33; 1997, c. 22, s. 1; 1997, c. 27, s. 71 [Not in force at date of publication; obsolete.]; 1997, c. 31, ss. 1–142 [s. 101(4) not in force at date of publication.]; 1997, c. 32, s. 10; 1997, c. 43, Sched. G, s. 20; 1998, c. 3, s. 34; 1998, c. 14, s. 1; 1998, c. 33, ss. 39–46; 1999, c. 6, s. 20(1) (Fr.), (2)–(6); 1999, c. 9, ss. 98–100; 2000, c. 5, s. 11; 2000, c. 11, ss. 1–4, 5(1), (2) (Fr.), (3)–(7), 6–25 [ss. 2(1), 3(1), (3)–(5), 17–19, 22(1) not in force at date of publication; ss. 3(3)–(5), 17, 18 obsolete.] [s. 19 repealed 2006, c. 10, s. 63.]; 2000, c. 12, ss. 1–3; 2000, c. 25, s. 45; 2000, c. 26, Sched. C, s. 1; 2001, c. 8, s. 204; 2001, c. 13, s. 16 (Fr.); 2001, c. 14, Sched. A, ss. 1–12; 2001, c. 17, s. 1; 2001, c. 23, s. 65; 2001, c. 24, ss. 1–5 [s. 5 not in force at date of publication.]; 2002, c. 7, s. 1; 2002, c. 8, Sched. A, Sched. I, s. 8; 2002, c. 17, Sched. C, ss. 7–9, Sched. D, ss. 36, 37, Sched. F, s. 1; 2002, c. 18, Sched. G, ss. 1, 2, 3 (Fr.), 4 (Fr.), 5–12; 2002, c. 22, ss. 57–60; 2003, c. 2, s. 20; 2004, c. 8, s. 46; 2004, c. 31, Sched. 10; 2005, c. 4; 2005, c. 5, s. 21; 2005, c. 21; 2006, c. 2, s. 47; 2006, c. 5, s. 52; 2006, c. 9, Sched. H, s. 6; 2006, c. 10, ss. 1–4, 5 (Fr.), 6–8, 9 (Fr.), 10–46, 47 (Fr.), 48, 49 (Fr.), 50, 67; 2006, c. 17, s. 251; 2006, c. 21, Sched. F, ss. 107, 136(1), Table 1 [s. 107(2) conditions not yet satisfied.]; 2006, c. 28, ss. 1–13 [ss. 2, 3, 7(2), (4), (5), 11, 12(1), 13 not in force at date of publication; s. 12(2) conditions not yet satisfied.]; 2006, c. 32, Sched. C, s. 15; 2006, c. 33, Sched. Z.3, s. 8; 2006, c. 34, s. 31; 2006, c. 35, Sched. C, s. 28; 2007, c. 7, Sched. 9; 2007, c. 14; 2008, c. 2; 2008, c. 7, Sched. F; 2008, c. 14, s. 52 [Not in force at date of publication.]; 2008, Sched. D. c. 19.

(EXCERPTS)

. . . . .

Duties

264. (1) Duties of teacher — It is the duty of a teacher and a temporary teacher,

(a) **teach** — to teach diligently and faithfully the classes or subjects assigned to the teacher by the principal;

(b) **learning** — to encourage the pupils in the pursuit of learning;

(c) **religion and morals** — to inculcate by precept and example respect for religion and the principles of Judaeo-Christian morality and the highest regard for truth, justice, loyalty, love of country, humanity, benevolence, sobriety, industry, frugality, purity, temperance and all other virtues;

(d) **co-operation** — to assist in developing co-operation and co-ordination of effort among the members of the staff of the school;

(e) **discipline** — to maintain, under the direction of the principal, proper order and discipline in the teacher's classroom and while on duty in the school and on the school ground;

(f) **language of instruction** — in instruction and in all communications with the pupils in regard to discipline and the management of the school,

(i) to use the English language, except where it is impractical to do so by reason of the pupil not understanding English, and except in respect of instruction in a language other than English when such other language is being taught as one of the subjects in the course of study, or

(ii) to use the French language in schools or classes in which French is the language of instruction except where it is impractical to do so by reason of the pupil not understanding French, and except in respect of instruction in a language other than French when such other language is being taught as one of the subjects in the course of study;

(g) **timetable** — to conduct the teacher's class in accordance with a timetable which shall be accessible to pupils and to the principal and supervisory officers;

(h) **professional activity days** — to participate in professional activity days as designated by the board under the regulations;

(i) **absence from school** — to notify such person as is designated by the board if the teacher is to be absent from school and the reason therefor;

(j) **school property** — to deliver the register, the school key and other school property in the teacher's possession to the board on demand, or when the teacher's agreement with the board has expired, or when for any reason the teacher's employment has ceased; and

(k) **textbooks** — to use and permit to be used as a textbook in a class that he or she teaches in an elementary or a secondary school,

(i) in a subject area for which textbooks are approved by the Minister, only textbooks that are approved by the Minister, and

(ii) in all subject areas, only textbooks that are approved by the board.

(l) **duties assigned** — to perform all duties assigned in accordance with this Act and the regulations.

(1.1) Sign language — Despite clause (1)(f), a teacher or temporary teacher may use American Sign Language or Quebec Sign Language in accordance with the regulations.

(1.2) [Repealed 2001, c. 14, Sched. A, s. 7.]

(1.3) [Repealed 2001, c. 14, Sched. A, s. 7.]

(2) Refusal to give up school property — A teacher who refuses, on demand or order of the board that operates the school concerned, to deliver to the board any school property in the teacher's possession forfeits any claim that the teacher may have against the board.

(3) Teachers, conferences — Teachers may organize themselves for the purpose of conducting professional development conferences and seminars.

1993, c. 11, s. 36; 2000, c. 11, s. 17; 2001, c. 14, Sched. A, s. 7; 2003, c. 2, s. 20(1)

265. (1) Duties of principal — It is the duty of a principal of a school, in addition to the principal's duties as a teacher,

(a) **discipline** — to maintain proper order and discipline in the school;

(b) **co-operation** — to develop co-operation and co-ordination of effort among the members of the staff of the school;

(c) **register pupils and record attendance** — to register the pupils and to ensure that the attendance of pupils for every school day is recorded either in the register supplied by the Minister in accordance with the instructions contained therein or in such other manner as is approved by the Minister;

(d) **pupil records** — in accordance with this Act, the regulations and the guidelines issued by the Minister, to collect information for inclusion in a record in respect of each pupil enrolled in the school and to establish, maintain, retain, transfer and dispose of the record;

(e) **timetable** — to prepare a timetable to conduct the school according to such timetable and the school year calendar or calendars applicable thereto, to make the calendar or calendars and the timetable accessible to the pupils, teachers and supervisory officers and to assign classes and subjects to the teachers;

(f) **examinations and reports** — to hold, subject to the approval of the appropriate supervisory officer, such examinations as the principal considers necessary for the promotion of pupils or for any other purpose and report as required by the board the progress of the pupil to his or her parent or guardian where the pupil is a minor and otherwise to the pupil;

(g) **promote pupils** — subject to revision by the appropriate supervisory officer, to promote such pupils as the principal considers proper and to issue to each such pupil a statement thereof;

(h) **textbooks** — to ensure that all textbooks used by pupils are those approved by the board and, in the case of subject areas for which the Minister approves textbooks, those approved by the Minister;

(i) **reports** — to furnish to the Ministry and to the appropriate supervisory officer any information that it may be in the principal's power to give respecting the condition of the school premises, the discipline of the school, the progress of the pupils and any other matter affecting the interests of the school, and to prepare such reports for the board as are required by the board;

(j) **care of pupils and property** — to give assiduous attention to the health and comfort of the pupils, to the cleanliness, temperature and ventilation of the school, to the care of all teaching materials and other school property, and to the condition and appearance of the school buildings and grounds;

(k) **report to M.O.H.** — to report promptly to the board and to the medical officer of health when the principal has reason to suspect the existence of any communicable disease in the school, and of the unsanitary condition of any part of the school building or the school grounds;

(l) **persons with communicable diseases** — to refuse admission to the school of any person who the principal believes is infected with or exposed to communicable diseases requiring an order under section 22 of the *Health Protection and Promotion Act* until furnished with a certificate of a medical officer of health or of a legally qualified medical practitioner approved by the medical officer of health that all danger from exposure to contact with such person has passed;

(m) **access to school or class** — subject to an appeal to the board, to refuse to admit to the school or classroom a person whose presence in the school or classroom would in the principal's judgment be detrimental to the physical or mental well-being of the pupils; and

(n) **visitor's book** — to maintain a visitor's book in the school when so determined by the board.

(2) **Co-instructional activities** — In addition, it is the duty of a principal in accordance with the board plan to provide for co-instructional activities under subsection 170(1), to develop and implement a school plan providing for co-instructional activities.

(3) **School council** — The principal shall consult the school council at least once in each school year respecting the school plan providing for co-instructional activities.

(4) [Repealed 2001, c. 14, Sched. A, s. 8.]

1991, c. 10, s. 6; 2000, c. 11, s. 18; 2001, c. 14, Sched. A, s. 8

. . . . .

286. (1) **Duties of supervisory officers** — Subject to the policies and guidelines established under paragraph 3.4 of subsection 8(1) and subject to the regulations, a board or the Minister shall assign the following duties to its or the Minister's supervisory officer or officers,

(a) **assist teachers** — to bring about improvement in the quality of education by assisting teachers in their practice;

(b) **co-operate with boards** — to assist and co-operate with boards to the end that the schools may best serve the needs of the pupils;

(c) **visit schools** — to visit schools and classrooms as the Minister may direct and, where the supervisory officer has been appointed by a board, as the board may direct;

(d) **prepare reports** — to prepare a report of a visit to a school or classroom when required by the Minister and, where the supervisory officer has been appointed by a board, when required by the board and to give to a teacher referred to in any such report a copy of the portion of the report that refers to the teacher;

(e) **Acts and regulations** — to ensure that the schools under his or her jurisdiction are conducted in accordance with this Act and the regulations;

(f) **annual report to Minister** — to make a general annual report as to the performance of his or her duties and the condition of the schools in his or her area of jurisdiction when required by the Minister and, where the supervisory officer has been appointed by a board, when required by the board;

(g) **report to M.O.H.** — to report to the appropriate medical officer of health any case in which the school buildings or premises are found to be in an unsanitary condition;

(h) **report to the Minister** — to furnish the Minister with information respecting any school in his or her area of jurisdiction whenever required to do so;

(i) **supervise business** — to supervise the business functions of the board;

(j) **supervise buildings and property** — to supervise the use and maintenance of the buildings and property of the board; and

(k) **others** — to exercise such other powers and perform such other duties as may be prescribed by a regulation made, or a policy established, under Part XIII (Behaviour, Discipline and Safety).

(2) **Responsibility to Minister** — Every supervisory officer appointed by the Minister is responsible to the Minister for the performance of his or her duties.

(3) **Responsibility to board** — Every supervisory officer appointed by a board is responsible to the board through the chief executive officer for the performance of the duties assigned to the supervisory officer by the board.

(4) Full-time position — Except as otherwise provided by this Act or the regulations, a supervisory officer shall not, without the approval of the Minister, hold any other office, have any other employment or follow any other profession or calling, during his or her tenure as a supervisory officer.

(5) Access to books and records, etc. — A provincial supervisory officer or a person designated by the Minister shall have access, as required by the Minister, to any school and to the books and records of a board or a school.

1997, c. 31, s. 126; 2000, c. 12, s. 2

. . . . .

300. (1) Definition — In this Part,

"school premises" means, with respect to a school, the school buildings and premises.

(2) Interpretation — In this Part, where reference is made to a regulation or to a matter prescribed by regulation, it means a regulation to be made by the Minister under this Part.

(3) Receipt of notice — Where notice is given to a person under this Part, it shall be considered to have been received by the person in accordance with the following rules:

1. If the notice is sent by mail or another method in which an original document is sent, the notice shall be considered to have been received by the person to whom it was sent on the fifth school day after the day on which it was sent.

2. If the notice is sent by fax or another method of electronic transmission, the notice shall be considered to have been received by the person to whom it was sent on the first school day after the day on which it was sent.

2000, c. 12, s. 3; 2007, c. 14, s. 1

301. (1) Provincial code of conduct — The Minister may establish a code of conduct governing the behaviour of all persons in schools.

(2) Purposes — The following are the purposes of the code of conduct:

1. To ensure that all members of the school community, especially people in positions of authority, are treated with respect and dignity.

2. To promote responsible citizenship by encouraging appropriate participation in the civic life of the school community.

3. To maintain an environment where conflict and difference can be addressed in a manner characterized by respect and civility.

4. To encourage the use of non-violent means to resolve conflict.

5. To promote the safety of people in the schools.

6. To discourage the use of alcohol and illegal drugs.

(3) Notice — Every board shall take such steps as the Minister directs to bring the code of conduct to the attention of pupils, parents and guardians of pupils and others who may be present in schools under the jurisdiction of the board.

(4) Code is policy — The code of conduct is a policy of the Minister.

(5) Policies and guidelines governing conduct — The Minister may establish additional policies and guidelines with respect to the conduct of persons in schools.

(6) Same, governing discipline — The Minister may establish policies and guidelines with respect to disciplining pupils, specifying, for example, the circumstances in which a pupil is subject to discipline and the forms and the extent of discipline that may be imposed in particular circumstances.

(6.1) **Same, procedural matters** — The Minister may establish policies and guidelines with respect to,

(a) appeals of a decision to suspend a pupil;

(b) principals' investigations to determine whether to recommend that a pupil be expelled; and

(c) expulsion hearings.

(7) **Same, promoting safety** — The Minister may establish policies and guidelines to promote the safety of pupils.

(8) **Different policies, etc.** — The Minister may establish different policies and guidelines under this section for different circumstances, for different locations and for different classes of persons.

(9) **Duty of boards** — The Minister may require boards to comply with policies and guidelines established under this section.

(10) **Not regulations** — Policies and guidelines established under this section are not regulations within the meaning of Part III (Regulations) of the *Legislation Act, 2006*.

2000, c. 12, s. 3; 2006, c. 21, Sched. F, s. 136(1), Table 1; 2007, c. 14, s. 2

302. (1) **Boards' policies and guidelines governing conduct** — Every board shall establish policies and guidelines with respect to the conduct of persons in schools within the board's jurisdiction and the policies and guidelines must address such matters and include such requirements as the Minister may specify.

(2) **Same, governing discipline** — A board may establish policies and guidelines with respect to disciplining pupils, and the policies and guidelines must be consistent with this Part and with the policies and guidelines established by the Minister under section 301, and must address such matters and include such requirements as the Minister may specify.

(3) **Same, promoting safety** — If required to do so by the Minister, a board shall establish policies and guidelines to promote the safety of pupils, and the policies and guidelines must be consistent with those established by the Minister under section 301 and must address such matters and include such requirements as the Minister may specify.

(4) **Same, governing access to school premises** — A board may establish policies and guidelines governing access to school premises, and the policies and guidelines must be consistent with the regulations made under section 305 and must address such matters and include such requirements as the Minister may specify.

(5) **Same, governing appropriate dress** — If required to do so by the Minister, a board shall establish policies and guidelines respecting appropriate dress for pupils in schools within the board's jurisdiction, and the policies and guidelines must address such matters and include such requirements as the Minister may specify.

(6) **Same, procedural matters** — A board shall establish policies and guidelines governing,

(a) appeals of a decision to suspend a pupil;

(b) principals' investigations to determine whether to recommend that a pupil be expelled; and

(c) expulsion hearings.

(6.1) Same — If the Minister has established policies and guidelines under subsection 301(6.1), a board's policies and guidelines under subsection (6) must address such matters and include such requirements as specified by the Minister.

(7) Different policies, etc. — A board may establish different policies and guidelines under this section for different circumstances, for different locations and for different classes of persons.

(8) Role of school councils — When establishing policies and guidelines under this section, a board shall consider the views of school councils with respect to the contents of the policies and guidelines.

(9) Periodic review — The board shall periodically review its policies and guidelines established under this section and shall solicit the views of pupils, teachers, staff, volunteers working in the schools, parents and guardians, school councils and the public.

(9.1) Communication of policies — A board shall ensure that a copy of the policies and guidelines it establishes under subsections (1) and (2) are available to the public.

(10) Not regulations — Policies and guidelines established under this section are not regulations within the meaning of Part III (Regulations) of the *Legislation Act, 2006.*

2000, c. 12, s. 3; 2006, c. 21, Sched. F, s. 136(1), Table 1; 2007, c. 14, s. 3

303. (1) Local codes of conduct — A board may direct the principal of a school to establish a local code of conduct governing the behaviour of all persons in the school, and the local code must be consistent with the provincial code established under subsection 301(1) and must address such matters and include such requirements as the board may specify.

(2) Same, mandatory — A board shall direct a principal to establish a local code of conduct if the board is required to do so by the Minister, and the local code must address such matters and include such requirements as the Minister may specify.

(3) Role of school council — When establishing or reviewing a local code of conduct, the principal shall consider the views of the school council with respect to its contents.

(4) Not regulation — A local code of conduct is not a regulation within the meaning of Part III (Regulations) of the *Legislation Act, 2006.*

2000, c. 12, s. 3; 2006, c. 21, Sched. F, s. 136(1), Table 1

304. (1) Opening and closing exercises at schools — Every board shall ensure that opening or closing exercises are held in each school under the board's jurisdiction, in accordance with the requirements set out in the regulations.

(2) Same — The opening or closing exercises must include the singing of *O Canada* and may include the recitation of a pledge of citizenship in the form set out in the regulations.

(3) Exceptions — A pupil is not required to participate in the opening or closing exercises in such circumstances as are prescribed by regulation.

2000, c. 12, s. 3

305. (1) Access to school premises — The Minister may make regulations governing access to school premises, specifying classes of persons who are permitted to be on school premises and specifying the days and times at which different classes of persons are prohibited from being on school premises.

(2) Prohibition — No person shall enter or remain on school premises unless he or she is authorized by regulation to be there on that day or at that time.

(3) **Same, board policy** — A person shall not enter or remain on school premises if he or she is prohibited under a board policy from being there on that day or at that time.

(4) **Direction to leave** — The principal of a school may direct a person to leave the school premises if the principal believes that the person is prohibited by regulation or under a board policy from being there.

(5) **Offence** — Every person who contravenes subsection (2) is guilty of an offence.

2000, c. 12, s. 3

Suspension

[Heading added 2007, c. 14, s. 4.]

306. (1) **Activities leading to possible suspension** — A principal shall consider whether to suspend a pupil if he or she believes that the pupil has engaged in any of the following activities while at school, at a school-related activity or in other circumstances where engaging in the activity will have an impact on the school climate:

1. Uttering a threat to inflict serious bodily harm on another person.
2. Possessing alcohol or illegal drugs.
3. Being under the influence of alcohol.
4. Swearing at a teacher or at another person in a position of authority.
5. Committing an act of vandalism that causes extensive damage to school property at the pupil's school or to property located on the premises of the pupil's school.
6. Bullying.
7. Any other activity that is an activity for which a principal may suspend a pupil under a policy of the board.

(2) **Factors principal must consider** — In considering whether to suspend a pupil for engaging in an activity described in subsection (1), a principal shall take into account any mitigating or other factors prescribed by the regulations.

(3) **Suspension** — If a principal decides to suspend a pupil for engaging in an activity described in subsection (1), the principal shall suspend the pupil from his or her school and from engaging in all school-related activities.

(4) **Duration of suspension** — A suspension under this section shall be for no less than one school day and no more than 20 school days and, in considering how long the suspension should be, a principal shall take into account any mitigating or other factors prescribed by the regulations.

(5) **Assignment to program, etc.** — When a principal suspends a pupil under this section, he or she shall assign the pupil to a program for suspended pupils in accordance with any policies or guidelines issued by the Minister.

(6) **Policies and guidelines** — The Minister may issue policies and guidelines to boards to assist principals in interpreting and administering this section.

(7) **School-related activities** — A pupil who is suspended is not considered to be engaged in school-related activities by virtue of participating in a program for suspended pupils.

(8) [Repealed 2007, c. 14, s. 4.]

(9) [Repealed 2007, c. 14, s. 4.]

(10) [Repealed 2007, c. 14, s. 4.]

(11) [Repealed 2007, c. 14, s. 4.]

(12) [Repealed 2007, c. 14, s. 4.]

(13) [Repealed 2007, c. 14, s. 4.]

(14) [Repealed 2007, c. 14, s. 4.]

2000, c. 12, s. 3; 2007, c. 14, s. 4

307. Only one suspension per occurrence — A principal may not suspend a pupil under section 306 more than once for the same occurrence.

2000, c. 12, s. 3; 2007, c. 14, s. 4

308. (1) Notice of suspension — A principal who suspends a pupil under section 306 shall,

(a) inform the pupil's teacher of the suspension; and

(b) make all reasonable efforts to inform the pupil's parent or guardian of the suspension within 24 hours of the suspension being imposed, unless,

(i) the pupil is at least 18 years old, or

(ii) the pupil is 16 or 17 years old and has withdrawn from parental control.

(2) Same — A principal who suspends a pupil under section 306 shall ensure that written notice of the suspension is given promptly to the following persons:

1. The pupil.
2. The pupil's parent or guardian, unless,

   i. the pupil is at least 18 years old, or

   ii. the pupil is 16 or 17 years old and has withdrawn from parental control.
3. Such other persons as may be specified by board policy.

(3) Contents of notice — The notice under subsection (2) must include the following:

1. The reason for the suspension.
2. The duration of the suspension.
3. Information about any program for suspended pupils to which the pupil is assigned.
4. Information about the right to appeal the suspension under section 309, including,

   i. a copy of the board policies and guidelines governing the appeal established by the board under subsection 302(6), and

   ii. the name and contact information of the supervisory officer to whom notice of the appeal must be given under subsection 309(2).

(4) [Repealed 2007, c. 14, s. 4.]

(5) [Repealed 2007, c. 14, s. 4.]

(6) [Repealed 2007, c. 14, s. 4.]

(7) [Repealed 2007, c. 14, s. 4.]

(8) [Repealed 2007, c. 14, s. 4.]

2000, c. 12, s. 3; 2007, c. 14, s. 4

309. (1) Appeal of suspension — The following persons may appeal, to the board, a principal's decision to suspend a pupil under section 306:

1. The pupil's parent or guardian, unless,
   i. the pupil is at least 18 years old, or
   ii. the pupil is 16 or 17 years old and has withdrawn from parental control.
2. The pupil, if,
   i. the pupil is at least 18 years old, or
   ii. the pupil is 16 or 17 years old and has withdrawn from parental control.
3. Such other persons as may be specified by board policy.

(2) Board designate — Every board shall designate a supervisory officer for the purposes of receiving notices of intention to appeal a suspension.

(3) Notice of appeal — A person who is entitled to appeal a suspension under subsection (1) must give written notice of his or her intention to appeal to the supervisory officer designated by the board within 10 school days of the commencement of the suspension.

(4) Board to inform all parties — After receiving a notice of intention to appeal under subsection (3), the board shall promptly contact every person entitled to appeal the suspension under subsection (1) and inform him or her that it has received the notice of intention to appeal.

(5) Party may contact supervisory officer — A person who has given notice of intention to appeal under subsection (3) may contact the supervisory officer designated under subsection (2) to discuss any matter respecting the appeal of the suspension and, for the purposes of this section, the supervisory officer has the powers and duties set out in board policy.

(6) Hearing of appeal — The board shall hear and determine the appeal within 15 school days of receiving notice under subsection (3), unless the parties agree on a later deadline, and shall not refuse to deal with the appeal on the ground that there is a deficiency in the notice of appeal.

(7) Appeal process — Subject to this section, an appeal shall be conducted in accordance with the requirements established by board policy.

(8) Parties to appeal — The parties to the appeal are:

1. The principal who suspended the pupil.
2. The pupil, if,
   i. the pupil is at least 18 years old, or
   ii. the pupil is 16 or 17 years old and has withdrawn from parental control.
3. The pupil's parent or guardian, if the pupil's parent or guardian appealed the decision to suspend the pupil.
4. The person who appealed the decision to suspend the pupil, if the decision was appealed by a person other than the pupil or the pupil's parent or guardian.
5. Such other persons as may be specified by board policy.

(9) Pupil may attend — A pupil who is not a party to the appeal under subsection (8) has the right to be present at the appeal and to make a statement on his or her own behalf.

(10) Powers on appeal — The board shall,

(a) confirm the suspension and the duration of the suspension;

(b) confirm the suspension, but shorten its duration, even if the suspension that is under appeal has already been served, and order that the record of the suspension be amended accordingly; or

(c) quash the suspension and order that the record of the suspension be expunged, even if the suspension that is under appeal has already been served.

(11) Decision final — The decision of the board on an appeal under this section is final.

(12) Committee — The board may authorize a committee of at least three members of the board to exercise and perform powers and duties on behalf of the board under this section, and may impose conditions and restrictions on the committee.

(13) [Repealed 2007, c. 14, s. 4.]

(14) [Repealed 2007, c. 14, s. 4.]

(15) [Repealed 2007, c. 14, s. 4.]

(16) [Repealed 2007, c. 14, s. 4.]

(17) [Repealed 2007, c. 14, s. 4.]

(18) [Repealed 2007, c. 14, s. 4.]

(19) [Repealed 2007, c. 14, s. 4.]

(20) [Repealed 2007, c. 14, s. 4.]

(21) [Repealed 2007, c. 14, s. 4.]

(22) [Repealed 2007, c. 14, s. 4.]

(23) [Repealed 2007, c. 14, s. 4.]

2000, c. 12, s. 3; 2007, c. 14, s. 4

Suspension, Investigation and Possible Expulsion

[Heading added 2007, c. 14, s. 4.]

310. (1) Activities leading to suspension — A principal shall suspend a pupil if he or she believes that the pupil has engaged in any of the following activities while at school, at a school-related activity or in other circumstances where engaging in the activity will have an impact on the school climate:

1. Possessing a weapon, including possessing a firearm.
2. Using a weapon to cause or to threaten bodily harm to another person.
3. Committing physical assault on another person that causes bodily harm requiring treatment by a medical practitioner.
4. Committing sexual assault.
5. Trafficking in weapons or in illegal drugs.
6. Committing robbery.
7. Giving alcohol to a minor.
8. Any other activity that, under a policy of a board, is an activity for which a principal must suspend a pupil and, therefore in accordance with this Part, conduct an investigation to determine whether to recommend to the board that the pupil be expelled.

(2) **Same** — A pupil who is suspended under this section is suspended from his or her school and from engaging in all school-related activities.

(3) **Duration of suspension** — A principal may suspend a pupil under this section for up to 20 school days and, in considering how long the suspension should be, the principal shall take into account any mitigating or other factors prescribed by the regulations.

(4) **Assignment to program, etc.** — When a principal suspends a pupil under this section, he or she shall assign the pupil to a program for suspended pupils in accordance with any policies or guidelines issued by the Minister.

2000, c. 12, s. 3; 2007, c. 14, s. 4

311. (1) **Notice of suspension** — A principal who suspends a pupil under section 310 shall,

(a) inform the pupil's teacher of the suspension; and

(b) make all reasonable efforts to inform the pupil's parent or guardian of the suspension within 24 hours of the suspension being imposed, unless,

(i) the pupil is at least 18 years old, or

(ii) the pupil is 16 or 17 years old and has withdrawn from parental control.

(2) **Same** — A principal who suspends a pupil under section 310 shall ensure that written notice of the suspension is given promptly to the following persons:

1. The pupil.
2. The pupil's parent or guardian, unless,

   i. the pupil is at least 18 years old, or

   ii. the pupil is 16 or 17 years old and has withdrawn from parental control.
3. Such other persons as may be specified by board policy.

(3) **Contents of notice** — The notice under subsection (2) must include the following:

1. The reason for the suspension.
2. The duration of the suspension.
3. Information about any program for suspended pupils to which the pupil is assigned.
4. Information about the investigation the principal will conduct under section 311.1 to determine whether to recommend that the pupil be expelled.
5. A statement indicating that,

   i. there is no immediate right to appeal the suspension,

   ii. if the principal does not recommend to the board that the pupil be expelled following the investigation under section 311.1, the suspension will become subject to appeal under section 311.2, and

   iii. if there is an expulsion hearing because the principal recommends to the board that the pupil be expelled, the suspension may be addressed by parties at the hearing.

(4) [Repealed 2007, c. 14, s. 4.]

(5) [Repealed 2007, c. 14, s. 4.]

(6) [Repealed 2007, c. 14, s. 4.]

(7) [Repealed 2007, c. 14, s. 4.]

2000, c. 12, s. 3; 2007, c. 14, s. 4

311.1 (1) Investigation following suspension — When a pupil is suspended under section 310, the principal shall conduct an investigation to determine whether to recommend to the board that the pupil be expelled.

(2) Conduct of investigation — The principal's investigation shall begin promptly following the suspension and shall be conducted in accordance with the requirements established by board policy and, for the purpose of the investigation, the principal has the powers and duties set out in the policy.

(3) Same — As part of the investigation, the principal shall make all reasonable efforts to speak with the following persons:

1. The pupil.
2. The pupil's parent or guardian, unless,
   i. the pupil is at least 18 years old, or
   ii. the pupil is 16 or 17 years old and has withdrawn from parental control.
3. Any other person whom the principal has reason to believe may have relevant information.

(4) Factors principal must consider — In considering whether to recommend to the board that the pupil be expelled, a principal shall take into account any mitigating or other factors prescribed by the regulations.

(5) If expulsion not recommended — If, on concluding the investigation, the principal decides not to recommend to the board that the pupil be expelled, the principal shall,

(a) confirm the suspension and the duration of the suspension;

(b) confirm the suspension but shorten its duration, even if the suspension has already been served, and amend the record of the suspension accordingly; or

(c) withdraw the suspension and expunge the record of the suspension, even if the suspension has already been served.

(6) Same: notice — If the principal does not recommend to the board that the pupil be expelled, the principal shall ensure that written notice containing the following information is given promptly to every person to whom he or she was required to give notice of the suspension under section 311:

1. A statement that the pupil will not be subject to an expulsion hearing for the activity that resulted in the suspension.
2. A statement indicating whether the principal has, under subsection (5), confirmed the suspension and its duration, confirmed the suspension but reduced its duration or withdrawn the suspension.
3. Unless the suspension was withdrawn, information about the right to appeal the suspension under section 311.2, including,
   i. a copy of the board policies and guidelines governing the appeal established by the board under subsection 302(6), and
   ii. the name and contact information of the supervisory officer to whom notice of the appeal must be given under section 311.2.

(7) If expulsion recommended: report — If, on concluding the investigation, the principal decides to recommend to the board that the pupil be expelled, he or she shall prepare a report that contains the following:

1. A summary of the principal's findings.

2. The principal's recommendation as to whether the pupil should be expelled from his or her school only or from all schools of the board.

3. The principal's recommendation as to,

i. the type of school that might benefit the pupil, if the pupil is expelled from his or her school only, or

ii. the type of program for expelled pupils that might benefit the pupil, if the pupil is expelled from all schools of the board.

(8) Same — The principal shall promptly provide a copy of the report to the board and to every person whom the principal was required to give notice of the suspension under section 311.

(9) Written notice — The principal shall ensure that written notice containing the following is given to every person to whom the principal was required to give notice of the suspension under section 311 at the same time as the principal's report is provided to that person:

1. A statement that the pupil will be subject to an expulsion hearing for the activity that resulted in the suspension.

2. A copy of the board policies and guidelines governing the expulsion hearing established by the board under subsection 302(6).

3. A statement that the person has the right to respond, in writing, to the principal's report provided under this section.

4. Detailed information about the procedures and possible outcomes of the expulsion hearing, including, but not limited to, information explaining that,

i. if the board does not expel the pupil, it will, with respect to the suspension imposed under section 310, confirm the suspension, shorten its duration or withdraw it,

ii. the parties will have the right to make submissions during the expulsion hearing as to whether, if the pupil is not expelled, the suspension imposed under section 310 should be confirmed, reduced or withdrawn,

iii. any decision of the board with respect to the suspension imposed under section 310 made at the expulsion hearing is final and not subject to appeal,

iv. if the board expels the pupil from his or her school only, the board will assign the pupil to another school, and

v. if the board expels the pupil from all schools of the board, the board will assign the pupil to a program for expelled pupils.

5. The name and contact information of a supervisory officer whom the person may contact to discuss any matter respecting the expulsion hearing.

(10) Party may respond — A person who is entitled to receive the principal's report under subsection (8) and written notice under subsection (9) may respond, in writing, to the principal and the board.

2007, c. 14, s. 4

311.2 Appeal of suspension — If the principal does not recommend to the board that the pupil be expelled and does not withdraw the suspension, the suspension may be appealed and section 309 applies for that purpose, with necessary modifications, subject to the following:

1. A person who is entitled to appeal must give written notice of his or her intention to appeal within five school days of the date on which he or she is considered, in accor-

dance with the rules set out in subsection 300(3), to have received the notice given under subsection 311.1(9).

2. If the principal confirmed the suspension but reduced its duration under subsection 311.1(8), the appeal is from the reduced suspension and not the original suspension.

2007, c. 14, s. 4

311.3 (1) Expulsion hearing by board — If a principal recommends to the board that a pupil be expelled, the board shall hold an expulsion hearing and, for that purpose, the board has the powers and duties specified by board policy.

(2) Conduct of hearing — Subject to the requirements set out in this section, the expulsion hearing shall be conducted in accordance with the requirements established by board policy.

(3) Parties — The parties to the expulsion hearing are:

1. The principal.
2. The pupil, if,
   i. the pupil is at least 18 years old, or
   ii. the pupil is 16 or 17 years old and has withdrawn from parental control.
3. The pupil's parent or guardian, unless,
   i. the pupil is at least 18 years old, or
   ii. the pupil is 16 or 17 years old and has withdrawn from parental control.
4. Such other persons as may be specified by board policy.

(4) Pupil may attend — A pupil who is not a party to the expulsion hearing under subsection (3) has the right to be present at the hearing and to make a statement on his or her own behalf.

(5) Submissions and views of parties — At the hearing, the board shall,

(a) consider the submissions of each party in whatever form the party chooses to deliver his or her submissions, whether orally, in writing or both;

(b) solicit the views of all the parties as to whether the pupil, if he or she is expelled, should be expelled from his or her school only or from all schools of the board; and

(c) solicit the views of all the parties as to whether, if the pupil is not expelled, the board should confirm the suspension originally imposed under section 310, confirm the suspension but reduce its duration or withdraw the suspension.

(6) Decision — After completing the hearing, the board shall decide,

(a) whether to expel the pupil; and

(b) if the pupil is to be expelled, whether the pupil is expelled from his or her school only or from all schools of the board.

(7) Factors board must consider — In making the decisions required under subsection (6), the board shall take into account,

(a) all submissions and views of the parties, including their views as to whether the pupil, if expelled, should be expelled from his or her school only or from all schools of the board;

(b) any mitigating or other factors prescribed by the regulations; and

(c) any written response to the principal's report recommending expulsion that a person gave to the board under subsection 311.1(7) before the completion of the hearing.

(8) **Restriction on expulsion** — The board shall not expel a pupil if more than 20 school days have expired since the pupil was suspended under section 310, unless the parties to the expulsion hearing agree on a later deadline.

(9) **Committee** — The board may authorize a committee of at least three members of the board to exercise and perform powers and duties on behalf of the board under this section, and may impose conditions and restrictions on the committee.

2007, c. 14, s. 4

311.4 (1) **If pupil not expelled** — If a board does not expel a pupil, the board shall, with respect to the suspension originally imposed under section 310,

(a) confirm the suspension and the duration of the suspension;

(b) confirm the suspension, but shorten its duration, even if the suspension that is under appeal has already been served, and order that the record of the suspension be amended accordingly; or

(c) quash the suspension and order that the record of the suspension be expunged, even if the suspension that is under appeal has already been served.

(2) **Factors board must consider** — In determining which action to take under subsection (1), the board shall take into account,

(a) any submissions made by the parties as to whether the suspension and its duration should be confirmed, the suspension should be confirmed but its duration reduced or the suspension should be withdrawn;

(b) any mitigating or other factors prescribed by the regulations.

(3) **Notice that pupil not expelled** — After determining which action to take under subsection (1), the board shall give written notice containing the following to every person who was entitled to be a party to the expulsion hearing under subsection 311.3(3):

1. A statement indicating that the pupil is not expelled.

2. A statement indicating whether the board has, under subsection (1), confirmed the suspension and its duration, confirmed the suspension but reduced its duration or withdrawn the suspension.

(4) **Decision final** — The decision of the board under subsection (1) is final.

2007, c. 14, s. 4

311.5 **If pupil expelled** — If a board expels a pupil, the board shall assign the pupil to,

(a) in the case of a pupil expelled from his or her school only, another school of the board; and

(b) in the case of a pupil expelled from all schools of the board, a program for expelled pupils.

2007, c. 14, s. 4

311.6 (1) **Notice of expulsion** — A board that expels a pupil shall ensure that written notice of the expulsion is given promptly to,

(a) all the parties to the expulsion hearing; and

(b) the pupil, if the pupil was not a party to the expulsion hearing.

(2) **Contents of notice** — The notice under subsection (1) must include the following:

1. The reason for the expulsion.

2. A statement indicating whether the pupil is expelled from his or her school only or from all schools of the board.

3. Information about the school or program for expelled pupils to which the pupil is assigned.

4. Information about the right to appeal under section 311.7, including the steps that must be taken to appeal.

2007, c. 14, s. 4

311.7 (1) Appeal of expulsion — In this section,

"designated tribunal" means a tribunal designated under the regulations to hear appeals of board decisions to expel pupils.

(2) Certain persons may appeal — The following persons may appeal a board's decision to expel a pupil, whether the pupil is expelled from his or her school only or from all schools of the board, to the designated tribunal:

1. The pupil's parent or guardian, unless,
   i. the pupil is at least 18 years old, or
   ii. the pupil is 16 or 17 years old and has withdrawn from parental control.
2. The pupil, if,
   i. the pupil is at least 18 years old, or
   ii. the pupil is 16 or 17 years old and has withdrawn from parental control.
3. Such other persons as may be specified by the designated tribunal.

(3) Hearing — The designated tribunal shall hear and determine an appeal under this section, and, for that purpose, it has the powers and duties set out in the regulations.

(4) Parties to appeal — The parties to the appeal are:

1. The board.
2. The pupil, if,
   i. the pupil is at least 18 years old, or
   ii. the pupil is 16 or 17 years old and has withdrawn from parental control.
3. The pupil's parent or guardian, if the parent or guardian appealed the decision.
4. The person who appealed the decision to expel the pupil, if the decision was appealed by a person other than the pupil or the pupil's parent or guardian.

(5) Decision final — The decision of the designated tribunal on an appeal under this section is final.

(6) Regulations — The Minister may make regulations,

(a) designating a tribunal to hear appeals of board decisions to expel pupils;

(b) prescribing the procedures to be followed on an appeal under this section;

(c) prescribing the powers and duties of a designated tribunal under this section.

2007, c. 14, s. 4

312. (1) Programs for suspended, expelled pupils — Every board shall provide, in accordance with policies and guidelines issued by the Minister, if any,

(a) at least one program for suspended pupils; and

(b) at least one program for expelled pupils.

(2) **Policies and guidelines** — The Minister may establish policies and guidelines with respect to programs for suspended and expelled pupils and may,

(a) impose different requirements on the provision of the programs for different circumstances, different locations or different classes of pupils;

(b) set criteria respecting pupils' eligibility to participate in the programs and respecting the criteria to be met for successful completion of the programs;

(c) require boards to offer plans to assist pupils who have successfully completed a program for expelled pupils with their transition back to school and to set criteria respecting those plans; and

(d) authorize boards, subject to such conditions and restrictions as the Minister imposes, to enter into agreements with other boards for the provision of the programs.

(3) [Repealed 2007, c. 14, s. 5(1).]

(4) **Programs for expelled pupils** — The Minister may establish one or more programs for expelled pupils to prepare the pupils to return to school and may require boards to give specified information about the programs to expelled pupils.

(5) **Same** — The Minister may establish policies and guidelines respecting pupils' eligibility to participate in a program established by the Minister under subsection (4) and respecting the criteria to be met for successful completion of the program.

2000, c. 12, s. 3; 2007, c. 14, s. 5

313. (1) **Status of expelled pupil** — An expelled pupil continues to be a pupil of the board that expelled him or her if the pupil attends a program for expelled pupils,

(a) offered by that board; or

(b) offered by another board under an agreement between that board and the board that expelled the pupil.

(2) **Same** — An expelled pupil ceases to be a pupil of the board that expelled him or her if,

(a) the pupil is assigned by that board to a program for expelled pupils and does not attend the program; or

(b) the pupil registers as a pupil of another board.

2007, c. 14, s. 6

314. (1) **Powers of other board** — If a pupil who has been expelled from one board registers as a pupil of another board, the other board may,

(a) assign the pupil to a school of that board; or

(b) assign the pupil to a program for expelled pupils, unless the pupil satisfies the requirements of clause 314.1(1)(a) or (b) as determined by a person who provides a program for expelled pupils.

(2) **Clarification** — If the other board assigns the expelled pupil to a school without knowing that he or she has been expelled by another board, the board may subsequently remove the pupil from the school and assign him or her to a program for expelled pupils, subject to the following conditions:

1. The board must assign the pupil to a program for expelled pupils promptly on learning that he or she has been expelled from another board.

2. The board shall not assign the pupil to a program for expelled pupils if the pupil satisfies the requirements of clause 314.1(1)(a) or (b) as determined by a person who provides a program for expelled pupils.

2007, c. 14, s. 6

314.1 (1) Return to school after expulsion — A pupil who has been expelled from all schools of a board is entitled to be readmitted to a school of the board if the pupil has, since being expelled,

(a) successfully completed a program for expelled pupils; or

(b) satisfied the objectives required for the successful completion of a program for expelled pupils.

(2) Determination — The determination of whether an expelled pupil satisfies the requirements of clause (1)(a) or (b) is to be made by a person who provides a program for expelled pupils.

(3) Board must readmit pupil — An expelled pupil may apply in writing to a person designated by the board that expelled him or her to be readmitted to a school of that board and, if the pupil satisfies the requirements of clause (1)(a) or (b) as determined by a person who provides a program for expelled pupils, the board shall,

(a) readmit the expelled pupil to a school of the board; and

(b) promptly inform the pupil in writing of his or her readmittance.

2007, c. 14, s. 6

314.2 Clarification: successful completion of program — A pupil who has successfully completed a program for expelled pupils provided by any board or person under this Part has satisfied the requirements of clause 314.1(1)(a), and no board shall,

(a) require the pupil to attend a program for expelled pupils provided by that board before being admitted to a school of the board; or

(b) refuse to admit the pupil on the basis that the pupil completed a program for expelled pupils provided by another board or person.

2007, c. 14, s. 6

314.3 Return to original school after expulsion — A pupil who has been expelled from one school of a board but not from all schools of the board may apply in writing to a person designated by the board to be re-assigned to the school from which he or she was expelled.

2007, c. 14, s. 6

314.4 Clarification: resident pupils — For greater certainty, nothing in this Part requires a board to admit or readmit a pupil who is not otherwise qualified to be a resident pupil of the board.

2007, c. 14, s. 6

314.5 Transitional provisions — In this section and in sections 314.6 to 314.10,

"coming into force date" means the day on which the *Education Amendment Act (Progressive Discipline and School Safety), 2007* comes into force;

"new Part XIII" means Part XIII as it reads on the coming into force date;

"old Part XIII" means Part XIII as it read immediately before the coming into force date.

2007, c. 14, s. 6

314.6 (1) Old Part XIII applies — Old Part XIII continues to apply with respect to,

(a) suspensions imposed before the coming into force date; and

(b) limited and full expulsions imposed under old Part XIII before the coming into force date, subject to the exceptions set out in sections 314.8 and 314.9.

(2) Same — reviews and appeals — For greater certainty, old Part XIII continues to apply with respect to the review or appeal of a suspension described in clause (1)(a) and with respect to the appeal of an expulsion described in clause (1)(b) and, without limiting the generality of the foregoing,

(a) in the case of a review or appeal of a suspension,

(i) Ontario Regulation 106/01 (*Suspension of a Pupil*), as it read immediately before the coming into force date, continues to apply with respect to the review or appeal, and

(ii) if the review or appeal was required to be conducted in accordance with the requirements established by board policy, the board policy that was in place under old Part XIII continues to apply with respect to the review or appeal; and

(b) in the case of an appeal of a board decision to expel a pupil under old Part XIII, Ontario Regulation 37/01 (*Expulsion of a Pupil*), as it read immediately before the coming into force date, continues to apply with respect to the appeal.

(3) New Part XIII applies — If a pupil engaged in an activity before the coming into force date that was an infraction for which a suspension or expulsion could be imposed or was required to be imposed under old Part XIII but no action had been commenced in respect of the activity before the coming into force date, the pupil is subject to new Part XIII in respect of the activity.

2007, c. 14, s. 6

314.7 Expulsions under old Part XIII — On the coming into force date, every pupil who is still subject to a limited or full expulsion imposed under old Part XIII is deemed to be a pupil of the board from which he or she was expelled.

2007, c. 14, s. 6

314.8 (1) Pupil subject to limited expulsion — With respect to any pupil of a board who is still subject to a limited expulsion imposed under old Part XIII on the coming into force date, the board shall,

(a) assign the pupil to a school of the board and offer a plan to assist the pupil with his or her transition back to school; or

(b) assign the pupil to a program for expelled pupils provided by the board under subsection 312(1).

(2) Return to school — If a pupil is assigned to a program for expelled pupils under subsection (1), the pupil is not entitled to attend school until the date on which he or she would have been entitled to return to school under subsection 309(14) of old Part XIII, as it read immediately before the coming into force date.

2007, c. 14, s. 6

314.9 (1) Pupil subject to full expulsion — With respect to a pupil of a board who is still subject to a full expulsion imposed under old Part XIII on the coming into force date, the board shall, on that date, reassign the pupil to a program for expelled pupils provided by the board under subsection 312(1).

(2) Return to school — Every pupil subject to a full expulsion under old Part XIII may return to school in accordance with new Part XIII and, for the purpose, sections 314.1 and 314.2 of new Part XIII apply with necessary modifications.

2007, c. 14, s. 6

314.10 (1) Regulations — transitional — The Lieutenant Governor in Council may make regulations providing for any transitional matters that the Lieutenant Governor in Council considers necessary or advisable,

(a) for the effective implementation of new Part XIII or regulations made under it;

(b) to facilitate the transition from old Part XIII or regulations made under it to new Part XIII or regulations made under it.

(2) Scope — A regulation under this section may be general or particular in its application.

2007, c. 14, s. 6

315. (1) Collection of personal information — The Minister may collect and may by regulation require boards to collect such personal information as is specified by regulation from, or about, the classes of persons specified by regulation for the following purposes, and the Minister may specify or restrict the manner in which the information is to be collected:

1. To ensure the safety of pupils.

2. To administer programs, courses and services to pupils who are suspended or expelled and to determine whether an expelled pupil has successfully completed a program, course or service and as a result is eligible to return to school.

(2) Disclosure — A board or other person is authorized to disclose the personal information collected under subsection (1) to the Minister for the purposes described in that subsection, and the Minister may disclose it to such persons or entities as may be prescribed by regulation for those purposes.

(3) Definition — In this section,

"personal information" has the same meaning as in section 38 of the *Freedom of Information and Protection of Privacy Act* and section 28 of the *Municipal Freedom of Information and Protection of Privacy Act*.

2000, c. 12, s. 3

316. (1) Regulations — The Minister may make regulations,

(a) prescribing such matters as are required, or permitted, under this Part to be prescribed or to be done by regulation;

(b) specifying when, during a school day, a suspension of a pupil is permitted to begin and to end.

(2) Classes — A regulation under subsection (1) may impose different requirements on different classes of person, place or thing or in different circumstances.

(3) Exceptions — A regulation under subsection (1) may provide that one or more provisions of this Part or of the regulation does not apply to specified persons or in specified circumstances.

2000, c. 12, s. 3

. . . . .

TEACHING PROFESSION ACT

R.S.O. 1990, c. T.2, as am. S.O. 1991, c. 52, s. 9; 1996, c. 12, s. 67; 1997, c. 31, s. 180; 2000, c. 12, ss. 4–8; 2002, c. 7, s. 7; 2006, c. 21, Sched. F, s. 133.

1. Definitions — In this Act,

"Board of Governors" means the Board of Governors of the Federation;

"board of trustees" [Repealed 1997, c. 31, s. 180(1).]

"executive" means the executive of the Federation;

"Federation" means The Ontario Teachers' Federation;

"member" means a member of the Federation;

"Minister" means the Minister of Education;

"Ministry" means the Ministry of Education;

"regulations" means the regulations made under this Act;

"teacher" means a person who is a member of the Ontario College of Teachers and is employed by a board as a teacher but does not include a supervisory officer, a principal, a vice-principal or an instructor in a teacher-training institution.

1996, c. 12, s. 67; 1997, c. 31, s. 180(1), (2)

2. Body corporate — The federation of teachers known as The Ontario Teachers' Federation is continued as a body corporate, under the name The Ontario Teachers' Federation in English and Fédération des enseignantes et enseignants de l'Ontario in French.

3. Objects — The objects of the Federation are,

(a) to promote and advance the cause of education;

(b) to raise the status of the teaching profession;

(c) to promote and advance the interests of teachers and to secure conditions that will make possible the best professional service;

(d) to arouse and increase public interest in educational affairs;

(e) to co-operate with other teachers' organizations throughout the world having the same or like objects; and

(f) to represent all members of the pension plan established under the *Teachers' Pension Act* in the administration of the plan and the management of the pension fund.

4. (1) Membership in Federation — Every teacher is a member of the Federation.

(2) Associate members — The following students are associate members of the Federation:

1. Every student in a college for the professional education of teachers established under clause 14(1)(a) of the *Education Act*.

2. Every student in a school or faculty of education that provides for the professional education of teachers pursuant to an agreement under clause 14(1)(b) of the *Education Act*.

(3) **Persons receiving pension** — Every person who was a member of the Federation upon retirement and who is receiving a pension or an allowance under the *Teachers' Pension Act* or a predecessor to that Act may, on request, be an associate member of the Federation.

(4) **Restrictions** — A person described in paragraph 1 or 2 of subsection (2) or in subsection (3) is not eligible to vote in respect of any Federation matter and cannot be required to pay a fee to the Federation.

2000, c. 12, s. 4

5. (1) **Board of Governors** — There shall be a Board of Governors of The Ontario Teachers' Federation, to be composed of 40 members as follows:

1. The immediate past president, the president, the first vice-president, the second vice-president and the secretary-treasurer of each of The Ontario Secondary School Teachers' Federation, the Elementary Teachers' Federation of Ontario, the Association des enseignantes et des enseignants franco-ontariens and The Ontario English Catholic Teachers' Association.

2. Five representatives of each of The Ontario Secondary School Teachers' Federation, the Elementary Teachers' Federation of Ontario, the Association des enseignantes et des enseignants franco-ontariens and The Ontario English Catholic Teachers' Association, to be elected annually at the annual meeting of the federation or association from among its members.

(2) **Term of office** — The members of the Board of Governors shall take office at the conclusion of the annual meeting of the Federation and shall hold office until their successors take office.

(3) **Vacancies** — If a vacancy occurs on the Board of Governors, it shall be filled by the executive of the affiliated body that the person who vacated the office represented and the person so named to fill the vacancy shall hold office for the remainder of the term of the person who vacated the office.

2000, c. 12, s. 5

6. (1) **Executive** — There shall be an executive of The Ontario Teachers' Federation, to be composed of 13 members as follows,

1. The immediate past president, the president, the first vice-president, the second vice-president and the secretary-treasurer of The Ontario Teachers' Federation.

2. The president and the secretary-treasurer of each of The Ontario Secondary School Teachers' Federation, the Elementary Teachers' Federation of Ontario, the Association des enseignantes et des enseignants franco-ontariens and The Ontario English Catholic Teachers' Association.

(2) **Term of office** — The members of the executive shall take office at the conclusion of the annual meeting of the Federation and shall hold office until their successors take office.

(3) **Vacancies** — If a vacancy occurs on the executive, it may be filled by the Board of Governors from among its members who represent the affiliated body that the person who vacated the office represented, and the person so named shall hold office for the remainder of the term of the person who vacated the office.

2000, c. 12, s. 6

7. President and vice-presidents — There shall be a president, a first vice-president and a second vice-president of the Federation to be elected annually at the annual meeting of the Board of Governors from among its members in such a manner that the offices of immediate past president, president, first vice-president and second vice-president represent each of the affiliated bodies.

2000, c. 12, s. 7

8. Secretary-treasurer — There shall be a secretary-treasurer of the Federation appointed by the Board of Governors who may be a member of the Board of Governors and who shall receive such remuneration as may be fixed by the Board of Governors.

9. Functions of executive — The executive is responsible for carrying on the business of the Federation and may,

(a) subject to the approval of the Minister, acquire and hold in the name of the Federation such real and personal property as may be necessary for the purposes of the Federation and may alienate, mortgage, lease or otherwise dispose of such property as occasion may require;

(b) invest the funds of the Federation in any securities in which a trustee is authorized to invest money under the *Trustee Act*;

(c) make such grants as it considers advisable to organizations having the same or like objects as the Federation;

(d) act as the representative of the members of the pension plan established under the *Teachers' Pension Act* including carrying out the following functions:

1. Appointing persons to be members of the Ontario Teachers' Pension Plan Board created under that Act.

2. Entering into agreements as described in that Act.

3. Negotiating, agreeing to or directing amendments to the plan as permitted under that Act or an agreement entered into under that Act.

4. Entering into an agreement on behalf of the Federation to indemnify a member of the Ontario Teachers' Pension Plan Board or a member of a committee of the Board against any costs sustained with respect to legal proceedings arising out of an act or omission done in the execution of his or her duties as a member of the Board or committee.

1991, c. 52, s. 9

10. Conferences — In the interests of the advancement of education and the improvement of teaching conditions in Ontario, the Board of Governors shall meet annually and confer with the Minister and the senior officials of the Ministry on matters touching and concerning the objects of the Federation, and the Board of Governors shall at such meeting and may at any other time make such representations and recommendations either of a general nature or which relate to any particular school, teacher or matter as it considers advisable and as are in keeping with the objects of the Federation.

11. [Repealed 1997, c. 31, s. 180(3).]

12. (1) Regulations — Subject to the approval of the Lieutenant Governor in Council, the Board of Governors may make regulations,

(a) prescribing a code of ethics for teachers;

(b) [Repealed 1997, c. 31, s. 180(4).]

(c) providing for voluntary membership in the Federation of persons who are not members thereof and prescribing the duties, responsibilities and privileges of voluntary members;

(d) prescribing the duties, responsibilities and privileges of associate members;

(e) providing for the suspension and expulsion of members from the Federation and other disciplinary measures;

(f) [Repealed 2000, c. 12, s. 8.]

(g) providing for the holding of meetings of the Board of Governors and of the executive and prescribing the manner of calling and the notice to be given in respect of such meetings;

(h) prescribing the procedure to be followed at meetings of the Board of Governors and of the executive;

(i) providing for the payment of necessary expenses to the members of the Board of Governors and the executive;

(j) conferring powers upon or extending or restricting the powers of and prescribing the duties of the Board of Governors and of the executive;

(k) providing for the appointment of standing and special committees;

(l) providing for the establishment of branches of the Federation or of the recognition by the Federation of local bodies, groups or associations of teachers which shall be affiliated with the Federation.

(2) Reporting sexual abuse — Despite any regulation made under subsection (1), a member who makes an adverse report about another member respecting suspected sexual abuse of a student by that other member need not provide him or her with a copy of the report or with any information about the report.

(3) Definition — In subsection (2),

"sexual abuse" of a student by a member means,

(a) sexual intercourse or other forms of physical sexual relations between the member and the student,

(b) touching, of a sexual nature, of the student by the member, or

(c) behaviour or remarks of a sexual nature by the member towards the student.

(4) Legislation Act, 2006 — Part III (Regulations) of the *Legislation Act, 2006* does not apply to a regulation made under subsection (1).

1997, c. 31, s. 180(4); 2000, c. 12, s. 8; 2002, c. 7, s. 7; 2006, c. 21, Sched. F, s. 133(1)

13. (1) Restriction re by-laws — A by-law governing the membership of teachers in an affiliated body of the Federation shall not authorize a teacher to be a member of an affiliated body that is not his or her designated bargaining agent, if any, under Part X.1 of the *Education Act*.

(2) Changes to regulations, by-laws — The Minister may request the Board of Governors to make, amend or revoke a regulation or by-law if the Minister considers it appropriate to do so.

(3) Same — If the Board of Governors fails to comply with the Minister's request within 60 days after receiving it, the Lieutenant Governor in Council may, by regulation, make, amend or revoke the regulation or by-law.

(4) Legislation Act, 2006 — Part III (Regulations) of the *Legislation Act, 2006* does not apply to a regulation made under subsection (3).

1997, c. 31, s. 180(5); 2006, c. 21, Sched. F, s. 133(2)

Transitional Provision

— 2000, c. 12, s. 9:

9. Despite the amendments made to the *Teaching Profession Act* by sections 4 to 8 of this Act and subject to subsections 5 (3) and 6 (3) of that Act,

(a) the persons who were members of the Board of Governors of The Ontario Teachers' Federation immediately before this Act received Royal Assent continue to be the members of the Board of Governors until the conclusion of the first annual meeting of the Federation that takes place after this Act receives Royal Assent;

(b) the persons who were members of the executive of The Ontario Teachers' Federation immediately before this Act received Royal Assent continue to be the members of the executive until the conclusion of the first annual meeting of the Federation that takes place after this Act receives Royal Assent; and

(c) the persons who were the immediate past president, president, first vice-president, second vice-president and third vice-president of The Ontario Teachers' Federation immediately before this Act received Royal Assent continue to be the immediate past president, president, first vice-president, second vice-president and third vice-president of the Federation until the conclusion of the first annual meeting of the Federation that takes place after this Act receives Royal Assent.

REGULATION MADE UNDER THE TEACHING PROFESSION ACT[1]

** Editor's Note: Section 1 of the Regulations Act, R.S.O. 1990, c. R.21 expressly excludes regulations made pursuant to the Teaching Profession Act from the application of the Regulations Act, R.S.O. 1990, c. R.21, and as such, they are not required to be published in the Ontario Gazette. Accordingly, the Regulation made under the Teaching Profession Act does not have a conventional "R.S.O. 1990, Reg. ***" or an "O. Reg. ***/9*" citation.*

Section 12 of the Teaching Profession Act gives the Board of Governors of that organization the authority to pass regulations pursuant to that Act.

1. Affiliated Bodies — The Ontario Secondary School Teachers' Federation, the Federation of Women Teachers' Associations of Ontario[2], the Ontario Public School Teachers' Federation[3], l'Association des enseignantes et des enseignants franco-ontariens and the Ontario English Catholic Teachers' Association shall be affiliated with the Federation and known as "affiliated bodies."

2. Voluntary Membership — **(1)** The Board of Governors shall grant voluntary membership in the Federation to a person who,

(a) is not a member thereof;

(b) holds a Certificate of Qualification;

(c) is engaged in an educational capacity;

(d) is a member of an affiliated body; and

(e) makes application to the Board of Governors for voluntary membership in the Federation.

(2) The Board of Governors shall grant voluntary membership in the Federation to a person who is not a member thereof and who is from outside Ontario and is on an assignment of two years or less as a teacher in Ontario under a teacher exchange program.

(3) The duties of a voluntary member shall be the same as those of a member under Sections 13 to 18.

(4) A voluntary member shall have such privileges as are common to all members of the Federation. (AB73)

---

[1]The Regulation has not been updated to reflect the changes in the Teaching Profession Act in 1997 or the changes in 2000. In such a case, the Act takes precedence.

[2]As of July 1, 1998, these two organizations have come together to form the Elementary Teachers' Federation of Ontario (ETFO).

[3]As of July 1, 1998, these two organizations have come together to form the Elementary Teachers' Federation of Ontario (ETFO).

3. Application for Membership by a Former Member — **(1)** A teacher who has withdrawn from membership under subsection (1) or (2) of Section 4 of the *Teaching Profession Act*, 1944, may make application to the Board of Governors for reinstatement as a member.

(2) The Board of Governors shall refer the application to the proper affiliated body for its opinion of the application.

(3) Where the Board of Governors, after considering the opinion of the affiliated body, accepts the application, the secretary-treasurer of the Federation shall notify the Minister and the applicant forthwith.

4. Fees — **(1)** Subject to subsections 2 and 4, a member shall pay the Federation an annual membership fee as follows:[4]

1. A secondary school teacher, 1.18 per cent of total annual salary. (SB90)
2. A statutory member of the Ontario Public School Teachers' Federation $150.00 plus 1.35 per cent of the total annual salary of the member. (AB97)
3. A female public school teacher,
   - (i) working more than half-time, $650.00,
   - (ii) working half-time or less, $325.00.[5] (AB92)
4. A separate school teacher,
   - (i) working more than half-time, $710.00,
   - (ii) working half-time or less, an amount which bears the same relation to $710.00 as does the teacher's total annual salary the teacher would earn if full-time.[6] (SB96)
5. A teacher in a French-language school or class who is a member of L'Association des enseignantes et des enseignants franco-ontariens, 1.5% of the teacher's total annual salary; where "total annual salary" means salary in accordance with the terms and conditions under which the member is employed, and includes a cost of living or other similar bonus.

(2) A member who is employed by a board exclusively in respect of the continuing education classes provided by the board shall pay the Federation an annual membership fee as follows: (AB87)

1. A secondary school teacher, 1.18 per cent of the salary attributable to such teaching. (SB90)
2. A statutory member of the Ontario Public School Teachers' Federation, 1.2 per cent of the salary attributable to such teaching. (AB89)
3. A female public school teacher $0.20 in respect of each day on which the teacher performs teaching duties to a maximum amount of $4.00 for each month in which the teacher performs such teaching duties.
4. A separate school teacher, 1.25 per cent of the salary attributable to such teaching duties. (SB88)

---

[4]Until other changes proposed by OTF are legislated, the *Teaching Profession Act* remains as is.

[5]Subject to Cabinet approval

[6]Subject to Cabinet approval

5. A teacher of a French-language school or class who is a member of L'Association des enseignantes et des enseignants franco-ontariens, 1.5 per cent of the salary attributable to such teaching duties.

(3) A member to whom subsection (1) applies who is also employed for the purpose of a class referred to in subsection (2) shall pay an annual membership fee that is the sum of the annual membership fee applicable to the member under subsection (1) and the annual membership fee that would be applicable to the member under subsection (2), if the member were a person employed exclusively for the purpose of a class referred to in subsection (2).

(4) Where a fee, or a portion thereof, that is payable under subsection (1) is not based upon salary, such fee or portion thereof shall be reduced, in the case of a teacher who is not employed for the full school year, by multiplying such fee or portion thereof by the ratio of the number of full and part months that the teacher was employed in the school year to 10.

(5) A board of trustees, in respect of a teacher employed by the board, shall,

(a) where a single deduction is made, remit to the secretary-treasurer of the Federation the full annual fee,

(i) by the 30th day of November, or

(ii) in the case of a teacher whose employment commences after the first school day in November, by the last day of the first full month that the teacher is employed by the board; and

(b) where deductions are made in instalments, place the instalment fee on deposit with the Federation on or before the 15th day of the month immediately following the month of deduction.

5. Meetings of the Board of Governors — **(1)** The annual meeting of the Board of Governors shall be held in each year on the days during the three weeks next preceding Labour Day that are, and at a time and place that is, determined by the president.

(2) Subject to subsection (5), there shall be a special meeting of the Board of Governors on the days during or within two weeks following each of the Christmas vacation and the Easter vacation that are, and at a time and place that are, determined by the president.

(3) The Board of Governors shall meet at such other dates and times as the executive may by resolution determine.

(4) A member of the Board of Governors shall be allowed a leave of absence not exceeding four days a year to attend meetings of the Board of Governors referred to in subsections (2) and (3).

(5) Upon the recommendation of the executive and with the approval of at least 32 members of the Board of Governors, the Board of Governors may, by resolution, waive the holding of one of the meetings under subsection (2). (AB72)

(6) The secretary-treasurer of the Federation shall send to members of the Board of Governors a written notice of the date, time and place of a meeting of the Board of Governors,

(a) at least 14 days before the date of a meeting under subsection (1) or (2); and

(b) at least three days before the date of a meeting under subsection (3).

(7) A quorum at a meeting of the Board of Governors shall be 32 members thereof. (AB72)

6. Meetings of Executive — **(1)** The executive shall meet immediately before and immediately after a meeting of the Board of Governors.

(2) The secretary-treasurer of the Federation shall send to members of the executive at least seven days in advance of a meeting of the executive written notice of date, time and place of the meeting under subsection (1).

(3) The president of the Federation may at any time call a special meeting of the executive.

(4) A quorum at any meeting of the executive shall be six members thereof.

7. Nominating Committee — **(1)** At the meeting of the executive immediately before the annual meeting of the Board of Governors, the executive shall appoint a nominating committee and include thereon a representative of each of the affiliated bodies.

(2) The nominating committee shall meet on the first day of the annual meeting of the Board of Governors to prepare nominations for the executive for the year next following.

(3) The nominating committee shall present the report of its nominations to the Board of Governors and, upon these and other nominations which may be submitted from the floor by any member of the Board of Governors, a secret ballot shall be taken.

8. Relations and Discipline Committee — There shall be a Relations and Discipline Committee appointed by the Board of Governors.

9. Standing Committees — **(1)** There shall be standing committees as follows:

1. Educational Finance (AB72)
2. Educational Studies (AB72)
3. Legislation (AB72)
4. Pension (AB90)
5. Teacher Education

(2) A committee under subsection (1) shall,

(a) be composed of the chairman or a member of the corresponding committee of each affiliated body, together with the president and secretary-treasurer of the Federation; and

(b) be convened by a member designated by the executive, following the annual meeting of the Board of Governors.

(3) The Board of Governors may, by by-law, establish such standing committees, in addition to those set out in subsection (1), as it considers expedient, and terminate any standing committee so established.

(4) A by-law passed under subsection (3) establishing a standing committee shall make provision for the composition of the committee.

(5) Clause (b) of subsection (2) applies to a standing committee established under subsection (3).

10. Special Committees — The Board of Governors or the executive may, by resolution, appoint such special committees as it considers necessary from time to time.

11. Procedure at Annual Meeting of Board of Governors — **(1)** The order of procedure at the annual meeting of the Board of Governors shall be as follows:

1. Call to order.
2. Appointment of committees.

3. Reading and confirming the minutes of the next preceding meeting.
4. Business arising from the minutes.
5. Reading of correspondence and action thereon.
6. Reports of officers.
7. Reception of delegations.
8. Reports from affiliated bodies.
9. Reports of standing and special committees.
10. General business.
11. Elections.
12. Installation of officers.
13. Adjournment.

(2) The Board of Governors may omit one or more items of the order of procedure from the agenda of the annual meeting.

12. Expenses — The Federation shall pay such necessary expenses as members of the Board of Governors and of the executive incur in carrying out their duties under the Act and this Regulation.

13. General Duties of Members — A member shall strive at all times to achieve and maintain the highest degree of professional competence and to uphold the honour, dignity, and ethical standards of the teaching profession.

14. Duties of a Member to His or Her Pupils — A member shall,

(a) regard as his first duty the effective education of his pupils and the maintenance of a high degree of professional competence in his teaching;

(b) endeavour to develop in his pupils an appreciation of standards of excellence;

(c) endeavour to inculcate in his pupils an appreciation of the principles of democracy;

(d) show consistent justice and consideration in all his relations with pupils;

(e) refuse to divulge beyond his proper duty confidential information about a pupil; and

(f) concern himself with the welfare of his pupils while they are under his care.

15. Duties of a Member to Educational Authorities — **(1)** A member shall,

(a) comply with the Acts and regulations administered by the Minister;

(b) co-operate with his educational authorities to improve public education;

(c) respect the legal authority of the board of trustees in the management of the school and in the employment of teachers;

(d) make in the proper manner such reports concerning teachers under his authority as may be required by the board of trustees; and

(e) present in the proper manner to the proper authorities the consequences to be expected from policies or practices which in his professional opinion are seriously detrimental to the interests of pupils.

(2) A member shall not,

(a) break a contract of employment with a board of trustees;

(b) violate a written or oral agreement to enter into a contract of employment with a board of trustees; or

(c) while holding a contract of employment with a board of trustees, make application for another position the acceptance of which would necessitate his seeking the termination of his contract by mutual consent of the teacher and the board of trustees, unless and until he has arranged with his board of trustees for such termination of contract if he obtains the other position.

16. **Duties of a Member to the Public** — A member shall,

(a) endeavour at all times to extend the public knowledge of his profession and discourage untrue, unfair or exaggerated statements with respect to teaching; and

(b) recognize a responsibility to promote respect for human rights.

17. **Duties of a Member to the Federation** — A member shall co-operate with the Federation to promote the welfare of the profession.

18. **Duties of a Member to Fellow Members** — **(1)** A member shall,

(a) avoid interfering in an unwarranted manner between other teachers and pupils;

(b) on making an adverse report on another member, furnish him with a written statement of the report at the earliest possible time and not later than three days after making the report;

(c) notwithstanding section 18 (1) (b), a member who makes an adverse report about another member respecting suspected sexual abuse of a student by that other member need not provide him or her with a copy of the report or with any information about the report. (WB02)

(d) refuse to accept employment with a board of trustees whose relations with the Federation are unsatisfactory; and

(e) where he is in an administrative or supervisory position, make an honest and determined effort to help and counsel a teacher before subscribing to the dismissal of that teacher.

(2) Under clause (c) of subsection (1), the onus shall be on the member to ascertain personally from the Federation whether an unsatisfactory relationship exists.

(3) A member shall not attempt to gain an advantage over other members by knowingly underbidding another member, or knowingly applying for a position not properly declared vacant, or by negotiating for salary independently of his local group of fellow-members.

19. **Relations and Discipline Procedure** — **(1)** In this section and Sections 20 to 28

(a) "Committee" means the Relations and Discipline Committee of the Ontario Teachers' Federation;

(b) "teaching certificate" means an Ontario Teacher's Certificate or other qualification to teach prescribed under Regulation 269 as amended and revised from time to time.

(2) The Committee shall be composed of 10 members who are teachers, appointed by the Board of Governors, two of whom shall be from each affiliated body.

(3) A person is not eligible for appointment to the Committee who,

(a) holds office on a disciplinary body of an affiliated body;

(b) holds office on the executive of an affiliated body; or

(c) is employed by either an affiliated body or the Federation.

(4) The Committee shall appoint one of the members of the Committee to be chairman.

(5) The chairman of the Committee may assign a panel of five members of the Committee to hold a hearing.

(6) Three members of the panel assigned under subsection (5) constitute a quorum for a hearing and all disciplinary decisions require the vote of a majority of members of the Committee present at the hearing.

(7) The secretary-treasurer of the Federation shall act as secretary to the Committee but shall not participate in any decision of the Committee.

20. (1) The Committee shall,

(a) consider complaints regarding professional misconduct or unethical conduct of a member;

(b) consider applications for reinstatement of the teaching certificate of a former member or the lifting of a suspension thereof.

(2) A hearing of the Committee shall be held in camera unless the member requests otherwise by notice delivered to the Committee not later than the day before the day fixed for the hearing, in which case the Committee shall conduct the hearing in public except when,

(i) matters involving public security may be disclosed; or

(ii) the possible disclosure of intimate financial or personal matters outweighs the desirability of holding the hearing in public.

(3) No hearing in respect of alleged professional misconduct or unethical conduct shall be conducted by the Committee unless,

(a) a written signed complaint has been filed in the office of the secretary-treasurer of the Federation;

(b) a copy thereof has been served on the member whose conduct is being investigated; and

(c) the member whose conduct is being investigated has been served with notice of the time, place and purpose of the hearing.

(4) The secretary-treasurer of the Federation shall,

(a) prepare and complete or cause to be completed a written complaint and file it in the office of the secretary-treasurer of the Federation;

(b) serve upon the member whose conduct is being investigated,

(i) a copy of the complaint; and

(ii) a notice of the hearing which shall include,

A. statement of the time, place and purpose of the hearing;

B. a reference to the statutory authority under which the hearing will be held;

C. a statement that if the party notified does not attend at the hearing the Committee may proceed in his absence and he will not be entitled to any further notice of the proceedings; and

D. a statement that the member may,

1. be represented by counsel or an agent;

2. call and examine witnesses;

3. present arguments and submissions; and

4. conduct cross-examination of witnesses as reasonably required for full and fair disclosure of the facts in relation to which they have given evidence; and

(c) make all necessary arrangements for the conduct of the hearing including,

(i) the appointment of counsel for the Federation;

(ii) the arrangement for oral evidence to be recorded; and

(iii) the notification to all members of the Co mittee of the time and place of the hearing.

21. In proceedings before the Committee, the Federation and the member whose professional misconduct or unethical conduct, or reinstatement is being investigated shall be parties to the proceedings.

22. (1) A member whose professional misconduct or unethical conduct or reinstatement is being investigated shall be afforded an opportunity to examine, before the hearing, any written or documentary evidence that will be produced or any report, the contents of which will be given in evidence at the hearing.

(2) Members of the Committee conducting the hearing shall not,

(a) have taken part before the hearing in the investigation of the subject matter of the complaint;

(b) have taken part in any previous hearing involving the member whose professional misconduct, unethical conduct or reinstatement is being investigated; or

(c) communicate directly or indirectly in relation to the subject matter of the hearing with any person or with any party or representative of a party, except upon notice to and opportunity for all parties to participate.

23. (1) The evidence before the Committee shall be recorded by a person appointed by the chairman of the Committee.

(2) Nothing is admissible in evidence before the Committee that would be inadmissible in a civil case and the findings of the Committee shall be based exclusively on evidence before it.

(3) No member of the Committee shall participate in the decision of the Committee unless he has been present throughout the hearing.

24. At a hearing before the Committee, a party to the proceedings may,

(a) be represented by counsel or an agent;

(b) call and examine witnesses;

(c) present arguments and submissions; and

(d) conduct cross-examination of witnesses as reasonably required for full and fair disclosure of the facts in relation to which they have given evidence.

25. (1) A member may be found guilty by the Committee of a professional misconduct or unethical conduct if in the opinion of the Committee he has contravened any of the provisions of Sections 13 to 18.

(2) In the case of hearings into complaints of professional misconduct and unethical conduct, the Committee shall,

(a) consider the allegations, hear the evidence and ascertain the facts of the case;

(b) determine whether upon the evidence and the facts so ascertained the allegations have been proved;

(c) determine whether in respect of the allegations so proved, the member is guilty of professional misconduct or unethical conduct; and

(d) determine the penalty to be imposed, as hereinafter provided, in cases in which it finds a member guilty of professional misconduct or unethical conduct.

(3) Where the Committee finds a member guilty of professional misconduct or unethical conduct, it shall,

(a) recommend to the Minister the cancellation of the teaching certificate of the member;

(b) recommend to the Minister the suspension for a stated fixed period of the teaching certificate of the member; or

(c) reprimand the member, or proceed with any combination of the foregoing.

26. (1) Where the Federation receives a request for a recommendation in respect of the reinstatement of a teaching certificate of a former member or the lifting of the suspension thereof, the secretary-treasurer shall refer the matter to the Committee for a hearing.

(2) Following a hearing under subsection (1), the Committee shall recommend to the Minister that the teaching certificate be reinstated or the suspension lifted, or that the teaching certificate remain cancelled or the suspension not be lifted, as the case may be.

27. (1) The Committee shall give its decision and recommendation, if any, under subsections 25.(3) or 26.(2) in writing and shall give reasons in writing, therefor, if requested by a party.

(2) The decision of the Committee shall be served upon the parties.

28. Any notice or other document required to be served by this regulation may be served by pre-paid first class mail addressed to the person to whom notice is to be given at his last known address and where notice is served by mail, the service shall be deemed to have been made on the fifth day after the day of mailing unless the person to whom the notice is given establishes that he, acting in good faith, due to absence, accident, illness or other cause beyond his control, did not receive the notice or did not receive the notice until a later date.

29. Evidencing Regulations and Resolutions — Regulations made by and resolutions passed by the Board of Governors may be evidenced by the signatures of the president and the secretary-treasurer of the Federation.

30. (1) This Regulation comes into force on the 1st day of January 1986, and applies in respect of any complaint of professional misconduct or unethical conduct filed in the office of the secretary-treasurer of the Federation on or after that date, and in respect of a request referred to in Section 26 received by the Federation on or after that date.

(2) The provisions of the Regulation made under the *Teaching Profession Act* that are revoked by this Regulation shall continue to apply to any matter or proceeding brought thereunder and not disposed of prior to the 1st day of January 1986 notwithstanding the coming into force of this Regulation.

The language in this section is quoted directly from the Regulation made under the Teaching Profession Act. The non-inclusive language is within the purview of the Legislature.

TRESPASS TO PROPERTY ACT

R.S.O. 1990, c. T.21, as am. S.O. 2000, c. 30, s. 11.

1. (1) Definitions — In this Act,

"occupier" includes,

(a) a person who is in physical possession of premises, or

(b) a person who has responsibility for and control over the condition of premises or the activities there carried on, or control over persons allowed to enter the premises,

even if there is more than one occupier of the same premises; ("occupant")

"premises" means lands and structures, or either of them, and includes,

(a) water,

(b) ships and vessels,

(c) trailers and portable structures designed or used for residence, business or shelter,

(d) trains, railway cars, vehicles and aircraft, except while in operation. ("lieux")

(2) School boards — A school board has all the rights and duties of an occupier in respect of its school sites as defined in the *Education Act*.

2. (1) Trespass an offence — Every person who is not acting under a right or authority conferred by law and who,

(a) without the express permission of the occupier, the proof of which rests on the defendant,

(i) enters on premises when entry is prohibited under this Act, or

(ii) engages in an activity on premises when the activity is prohibited under this Act; or

(b) does not leave the premises immediately after he or she is directed to do so by the occupier of the premises or a person authorized by the occupier,

is guilty of an offence and on conviction is liable to a fine of not more than $2,000.

(2) Colour of right as a defence — It is a defence to a charge under subsection (1) in respect of premises that is land that the person charged reasonably believed that he or she had title to or an interest in the land that entitled him or her to do the act complained of.

3. (1) Prohibition of entry — Entry on premises may be prohibited by notice to that effect and entry is prohibited without any notice on premises.

(a) that is a garden, field or other land that is under cultivation, including a lawn, orchard, vineyard and premises on which trees have been planted and have not attained an average height of more than two metres and woodlots on land used primarily for agricultural purposes; or

(b) that is enclosed in a manner that indicates the occupier's intention to keep persons off the premises or to keep animals on the premises.

(2) **Implied permission to use approach to door** — There is a presumption that access for lawful purposes to the door of a building on premises by a means apparently provided and used for the purpose of access is not prohibited.

4. (1) **Limited permission** — Where notice is given that one or more particular activities are permitted, all other activities and entry for the purpose are prohibited and any additional notice that entry is prohibited or a particular activity is prohibited on the same premises shall be construed to be for greater certainty only.

(2) **Limited prohibition** — Where entry on premises is not prohibited under section 3 or by notice that one or more particular activities are permitted under subsection (1), and notice is given that a particular activity is prohibited, that activity and entry for the purpose is prohibited and all other activities and entry for the purpose are not prohibited.

5. (1) **Method of giving notice** — A notice under this Act may be given,

(a) orally or in writing;

(b) by means of signs posted so that a sign is clearly visible in daylight under normal conditions from the approach to each ordinary point of access to the premises to which it applies; or

(c) by means of the marking system set out in section 7.

(2) **Substantial compliance** — Substantial compliance with clause (1)(b) or (c) is sufficient notice.

6. (1) **Form of sign** — A sign naming an activity or showing a graphic representation of an activity is sufficient for the purpose of giving notice that the activity is permitted.

(2) **Idem** — A sign naming an activity with an oblique line drawn through the name or showing a graphic representation of an activity with an oblique line drawn through the representation is sufficient for the purpose of giving notice that the activity is prohibited.

7. (1) **Red markings** — Red markings made and posted in accordance with subsections (3) and (4) are sufficient for the purpose of giving notice that entry on the premises is prohibited.

(2) **Yellow markings** — Yellow markings made and posted in accordance with subsections (3) and (4) are sufficient for the purpose of giving notice that entry is prohibited except for the purpose of certain activities and shall be deemed to be notice of the activities permitted.

(3) **Size** — A marking under this section shall be of such a size that a circle ten centimetres in diameter can be contained wholly within it.

(4) **Posting** — Markings under this section shall be so placed that a marking is clearly visible in daylight under normal conditions from the approach to each ordinary point of access to the premises to which it applies.

8. **Notice applicable to part of premises** — A notice or permission under this Act may be given in respect of any part of the premises of an occupier.

9. (1) **Arrest without warrant on premises** — A police officer, or the occupier of premises, or a person authorized by the occupier may arrest without warrant any person he or she believes on reasonable and probable grounds to be on the premises in contravention of section 2.

(2) **Delivery to police officer** — Where the person who makes an arrest under subsection (1) is not a police officer, he or she shall promptly call for the assistance of a police officer and give the person arrested into the custody of the police officer.

(3) **Deemed arrest** — A police officer to whom the custody of a person is given under subsection (2) shall be deemed to have arrested the person for the purposes of the provisions of the *Provincial Offences Act* applying to his or her release or continued detention and bail.

10. **Arrest without warrant off premises** — Where a police officer believes on reasonable and probable grounds that a person has been in contravention of section 2 and has made fresh departure from the premises, and the person refuses to give his or her name and address, or there are reasonable and probable grounds to believe that the name or address given is false, the police officer may arrest the person without warrant.

11. **Motor vehicles and motorized snow vehicles** — Where an offence under this Act is committed by means of a motor vehicle, as defined in the *Highway Traffic Act*, or by means of a motorized snow vehicle, as defined in the *Motorized Snow Vehicles Act*, the driver of the motor vehicle or motorized snow vehicle is liable to the fine provided under this Act and, where the driver is not the owner, the owner of the motor vehicle or motorized snow vehicle is liable to the fine provided under this Act unless the driver is convicted of the offence or, at the time the offence was committed, the motor vehicle or motorized snow vehicle was in the possession of a person other than the owner without the owner's consent.
2000, c. 30, s. 11

12. (1) **Damage award** — Where a person is convicted of an offence under section 2, and a person has suffered damage caused by the person convicted during the commission of the offence, the court shall, on the request of the prosecutor and with the consent of the person who suffered the damage, determine the damages and shall make a judgment for damages against the person convicted in favour of the person who suffered the damage, but no judgment shall be for an amount in excess of $1,000.

(2) **Costs of prosecution** — Where a prosecution under section 2 is conducted by a private prosecutor, and the defendant is convicted, unless the court is of the opinion that the prosecution was not necessary for the protection of the occupier or the occupier's interests, the court shall determine the actual costs reasonably incurred in conducting the prosecution and, despite section 60 of the *Provincial Offences Act*, shall order those costs to be paid by the defendant to the prosecutor.

(3) **Damages and costs in addition to fine** — A judgment for damages under subsection (1), or an award of costs under subsection (2), shall be in addition to any fine that is imposed under this Act.

(4) **Civil action** — A judgment for damages under subsection (1) extinguishes the right of the person in whose favour the judgment is made to bring a civil action for damages against the person convicted arising out of the same facts.

(5) **Idem** — The failure to request or refusal to grant a judgment for damages under subsection (1) does not affect a right to bring a civil action for damages arising out of the same facts.

(6) **Enforcement** — The judgment for damages under subsection (1), and the award for costs under subsection (2), may be filed in the Small Claims Court and shall be deemed to be a judgment or order of that court for the purposes of enforcement.

INDEX